Report of the Committee of Inquiry into the Personality Disorder Unit, Ashworth Special Hospital

VOLUME I

His Honour Peter Fallon QC
Professor Robert Bluglass CBE
Professor Brian Edwards CBE
Mr Granville Daniels

Presented to Parliament by the
Secretary of State for Health
by Command of Her Majesty, January 1999

Cm 4194-II

£36

First published 1999

ISBN 010 1419430

Letter to the Secretary of State

The Rt Hon Frank Dobson MP
Secretary of State for Health
Richmond House
79 Whitehall
London SW1A 2NS

6 January 1999

Dear Secretary of State,

We were appointed by your predecessor in February 1997 to investigate the functioning of the Personality Disorder Unit (PDU) at Ashworth Special Hospital, following allegations made by a former patient, Mr Steven Daggett, about the misuse of drugs and alcohol, financial irregularities, possible paedophile activity and the availability of pornographic material on the Unit. We were also asked to review in the light of our investigations the policies, clinical care and procedures on the Unit; its security arrangements; the management arrangements for assuring effective clinical care and appropriate security for patients; and the arrangements for visiting on the PDU.

We enclose our report, which has been agreed and signed by all four of us. We would call attention to the following points.

- We found Mr Daggett's description of the environment on Lawrence Ward to be largely accurate. Pornography was widely available on the ward; patients were running their own businesses; Hospital policies were ignored; and security was grossly inadequate.
- The child at the centre of the paedophile allegations was, in our view, being groomed for paedophile purposes. She was permitted, often unsupervised, to associate with men with appalling criminal records. One of them visited the child at her home when on escorted leave. That this was allowed to happen is disgraceful in what was supposed to be a hospital, and a high security hospital at that. Perhaps worst of all, the clinical staff did nothing about it, and some of them even judged it to be in the interests of the patient.
- The PDU was a deeply flawed creation. A number of highly serious reports have demonstrated Ashworth Hospital's failure to care for and manage a large group of severely personality disordered patients.
- The management culture of the Hospital was dysfunctional. Senior managers were secretive, out of touch and totally unable to control this large institution.

- Four critical internal reports were suppressed. Ministers were misled on two occasions about events at Ashworth.
- We have no confidence in the ability of Ashworth Hospital to flourish under any management. It should close.
- More positively, we offer our view for how high security services could develop within regional forensic networks involving both the NHS and the Prison Service.
- We suggest changes to the law to introduce reviewable sentences for severely personality disordered offenders.
- Last, but not least, we believe the current accountability arrangements within the NHS are unclear and unsatisfactory and recommend changes. We make judgements about the conduct and performance of those most directly involved in these events.

We have found conducting this Inquiry a challenging, often depressing, but also fascinating task. Whilst there is much we have found to criticize, both at Ashworth and in the wider context within which it operates, we are convinced that now is the time to grasp the nettle and replace the system we have found to be so fundamentally flawed with one which will serve patients, staff and the public far better.

Yours sincerely, Peter Fallon

His Honour Peter Fallon QC
Bristol

Membership of the Inquiry Panel

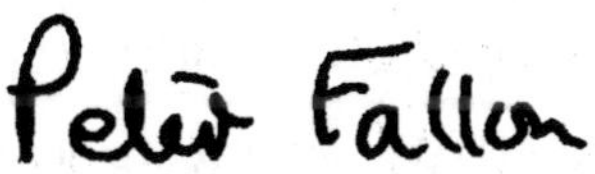

His Honour Peter Fallon QC (Chairman)
Former Senior Circuit Judge and Recorder of Bristol.

Professor Robert Bluglass CBE, MD, FRCP, FRCPsych, DPM
Emeritus Professor of Psychiatry, University of Birmingham; previously Clinical Director of the Reaside Clinic, Birmingham, and Medical Director, South Birmingham Mental Health Trust.

Professor Brian Edwards CBE, FHSM, CBIM, Hon FRC Path
Professor of Health Care Development, University of Sheffield; formerly Regional General Manager, Trent Regional Health Authority and Regional Director (West Midlands).

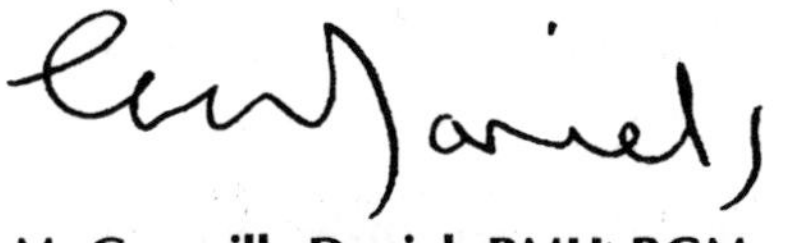

Mr Granville Daniels RMH, RGM
General Manager of the Millbrook Mental Health Unit, Central Nottinghamshire NHS Trust.

Acknowledgements

When the Committee was set up Dr Tim Baxter was appointed its Secretary. He was assisted throughout by Mrs Judith Peachey. After some months during which a vast quantity of documents had been assembled, all of which had to be efficiently organized, Judith was joined by Mrs Bukky Aina. Even so, it is incredible how such a small Secretariat has so ably and efficiently provided such sterling service. Looking back over many months it is extraordinary to find that nothing went wrong. The growth of the paper mountain never stopped, and a large part of it had to be distributed to interested parties; a number of different venues for our sittings had to be organized and accommodation for the Committee arranged. The administration and organization has been second to none.

In the months following February 1997 when our Chairman and Tim were gathering material and planning the ultimate shape of the Inquiry, Tim's intelligent advice and knowledgeable approach to the subject was invaluable, so too was his guidance throughout the Inquiry. It has taken five and a half months to write this Report. During that time Tim and our Chairman have been in close contact sifting the evidence and assembling the bulk of the Report in the hope of producing it before Christmas. Without Tim's invaluable contribution it would have been impossible to let the Secretary of State have our final draft, as we did on 16 December.

We have been well served by our legal team. Of course, our contact was much closer with counsel Mr John Royce QC, and Mr Peter Blair, than with our solicitor Mr Huw James. Our Chairman, in particular, spent much time in conclave with John and Peter discussing and shaping procedure and the management of the hearing sessions. The fact that our hearings did not over run, by even one day, is testimony of the efficiency and skill of Counsel to our Inquiry. Both during the course of hearing of evidence, and while writing the Report they have provided valuable and well considered guidance. From time to time they were able to clarify issues for a puzzled Committee. We are most grateful to them.

In the text of the Report we have tried to acknowledge the help and assistance we have had from many sources, but we do not mention there the Department of Health and Home Office Working Group on Personality Disorder which was set up shortly after our Committee was appointed. During the past 18 months we met the group twice. There was obviously much sense in sharing our thinking as it developed. We are grateful for their help.

Contents

Timetable of Key Events

1911	Building commenced on a large hospital on the Moss Side site.
1914	Moss Side site sold to Lunacy Board of Control. After the outbreak of war the hospital was used to treat soldiers suffering from nervous disorders.
1920	The Hospital was requisitioned by Ministry of Pensions and soldiers returned.
1933	The Hospital became the Moss Side State Institution, run by the Board of Control.
1948	Moss Side became part of the new NHS, although still under the management of the Board of Control.
1959	The Mental Health Act 1959 transferred ownership of Moss Side and its sister hospitals to the Ministry of Health.
1974	Park Lane Advance Unit opened.
1984	Park Lane Hospital opened.
1 July 1989	Special Hospitals Service Authority (SHSA) established to run the Special Hospitals.
19 February 1990	Ashworth Hospital came into existence. The old Moss Side site became Ashworth South and East, Park Lane became Ashworth North.
8 March 1990	Stephen Mallalieu killed in his bedroom on Owen Ward.
19 November 1990	Derek Williams killed by another patient on Forster Ward.
4 March 1991	*Cutting Edge* television documentary alleged ill-treatment of patients by staff at Ashworth.
25 April 1991	Secretary of State for Health William Waldegrave announced an inquiry into the complaints of ill-treatment of patients, to be chaired by Sir Louis Blom-Cooper QC.
1 April 1992	Bradford Social Services wrote to Dr Sylvester, the Director of Medical Services at Ashworth Hospital, requesting information about the father of Child A. They never received a reply.
5 August 1992	The Blom-Cooper Inquiry was published.
3 November 1992	Task Force set up under Chairmanship of Mr Peter Green, Acting General Manager.
December 1992 – February 1993	Task Force Reports to SHSA
July 1993	Mrs Janice Miles took over as Unit General Manager.
September 1993	SHSA approved new Management Structure of the Hospital.
September 1993	Lawrence Ward PCT consented to several patients (including Mr Daggett) conducting their own financial affairs.
December 1993	Dr Ian Strickland appointed as Clinical Manager of the Personality Disorder Unit (PDU).
1 April 1994	PDU formally came into existence.
20 April 1994	Dr Crispin wrote to Dr Strickland re her concerns about drugs and alcohol on Owen Ward.
18 May 1994	Patient Mr O'Neill absconded on a home visit.
19 May 1994	Mr O'Neill involved in fights with other patients.

20 May 1994	Arson attack on Mr O'Neill's bedroom.
1 June 1994	Mr Brennan, Ward Manager of Owen Ward, sent a memorandum to Dr Strickland re the situation on the ward.
8 June 1994	Owen Ward incident.
15 July 1994	Mr Green and his team completed their investigation of the hostage-taking.
8 August 1994	Mr Tarbuck took over as Clinical Manager of the PDU.
September 1994	Mrs Miles presented the 19-page Owen Ward report to the SHSA; a 9-page version was later circulated to staff.
6 March 1995	Security Department issued a message to wards banning patients from handling cash and credit cards, birth certificates, passports, driving licences and Premium Bonds.
23 March 1995	Mrs Miles issued a directive banning patients from engaging in commercial activities.
1 April 1995	Ashworth Hospital Board (a sub-committee of the SHSA) established.
	HMG split into strategic HEG and operational HMT.
June 1995	Department of Health published *High Security Psychiatric Services: Changing in Funding and Organisation.*
10 July 1995	HEG reaffirmed ban on cash cards; HMT noted the decision the next day.
4 August 1995	Mr Arnold wrote to Mrs Miles with draft policy for cash cards.
October 1995	Dr Strickland wrote to Mrs Miles setting out the patients' views.
1 November 1995	Parcel to Mr Braund containing embossing machine intercepted.
1 April 1996	SHSA dissolved. The High Security Psychiatric Services Commissioning Board established as a non-statutory body advising Ministers through the Chief Executive of the NHS Executive on the commissioning of high security services. The three hospitals became Special Health Authorities: Ashworth Hospital Authority came into existence.
2 April 1996	Mr Tarbuck wrote to Ms Young saying "definitely no" to cash cards.
14 May 1996	Mr Murphy briefed Hospital Policy Board on his concerns about the PDU.
30 May 1996	Mr Murphy attended Lawrence Ward and insisted cards were destroyed.
June 1996	Lawrence Ward shop closed.
7 June 1996	Patient Stephen Finney took an overdose. His room was searched. Following his return he attacked a nurse on Shelley Ward with a knife. A further search revealed a number of sensitive documents.
25 September 1996	Steven Daggett absconded.
28 September 1996	Search of Lawrence Ward bootroom revealed 41 pornographic videos.
8 October 1996	Steven Daggett returned to Ashworth.
29 October	Steven Daggett discussed the contents of *My Concerns* with Mr Gardner, Mr Murphy and Ms Bamber.
30 October 1996	Steven Daggett transferred to Rampton.
14 November 1996	Nurse James Corrigan, Mr Daggett's escort on 25 September, sacked for gross misconduct.
25 November 1996	Mrs Miles received a copy of *My Concerns*. Bradford Social Services contacted.
29 November 1996	Visits to the PDU wards by children under 14 stopped.
17h December 1996	Steven Daggett raised his concerns about Ashworth with a Mental Health Act Commissioner at Rampton.
17 January 1997	Lawrence Ward searched.
22 January 1997	Story about the search in the *Daily Express*.

28 January 1997	Merseyside Police informed about suspicions of possible paedophile activity on Lawrence Ward.
29 January 1997	Mrs Miles briefed Mr Tinston, Regional Director of the North West Regional Office of the NHS Executive.
30 January 1997	Dr Jones of the HSPSCT received a copy of *My Concerns*. Mr Murphy contacted Mr Rowden.
31 January 1997	Case Conference re Child A in Bradford.
	Police raided the home of Child A and her father, removing videos and other items.
3 February 1997	Mrs Miles briefed Mr Rowden and Mr Tinston.
	Mr Rowden travelled to Merseyside to meet Mr Murphy, who expressed concern about the senior management of Ashworth Hospital. Mr Murphy confirmed that 90 per cent of the Daggett allegations were true.
6 February 1997	Officials met Mr Dorrell, the then Secretary of State, to discuss the allegations. Mrs Miles suspended.
7 February 1997	Inquiry established.

Abbreviations and Glossary

Absconsion	Technically, an **absconsion** is an unauthorized absence from a Leave of Absence trip, i.e., the patient escapes whilst on an arranged visit outside the walls of the hospital. An escape, by contrast, refers to a patient escaping from within the secure perimeter of the hospital.
Butler	The Report of the Committee on Mentally Disordered Offenders, established in 1972 under the chairmanship of Lord Butler of Saffron Walden KG, which reported in 1975 and made many recommendations on the treatment and management of mentally abnormal offenders.
CAS	**Continuous Assessment Scheme**, the special scheme within the Prison Service for monitoring the most disruptive prisoners.
Code of Practice	Under section 118 of the Mental Health Act 1983 the Secretary of State is required to produce detailed guidance on how the provisions of the Mental Health Act should operate. The Code is currently published as *Code of Practice: Mental Health Act 1983*. A revised edition is currently under consideration and will published early in 1999, subject to Parliamentary approval.
CPA	**Care Programme Approach**. The CPA, described in Health Circular HC(90)23 and Local Authority Letter LASSL(90)11, is designed to ensure that patients receive well-planned and coordinated care.
CSC	**Close Supervision Centre**, part of the new approach within the Prison Service towards managing highly disruptive prisoners.
DSMIV	***Diagnostic and Statistical Manual of Mental Disorders***, fourth edition (1994). Published by the American Psychiatric Association.
Forensic Psychiatry	The branch of psychiatry which deals principally with mentally disordered individuals who offend or otherwise come into contact with the Criminal Justice System.
HAS	**The NHS Health Advisory Service**. The Health Advisory Service (formally Hospital Advisory Service) was established in 1969 to encourage and disseminate good practice and to advise the relevant Secretaries of State on standards of care and management practices in hospitals for elderly and mentally ill people in England and Wales. The existing HAS was wound up in March 1997.
Health Care Service for Prisoners	Formerly the **Prison Medical Service**. This part of the Prison Service is responsible for the delivery of health care to prisoners.
HEG	**Hospital Executive Group (Ashworth Hospital)**
HMG	**Hospital Management Group (Ashworth Hospital)**
HMT	**Hospital Management Team (Ashworth Hospital)**
Hospital Direction	A new order known as a **Hospital Direction** has been created by section 46 of the Crime

(Sentences) Act 1997. This allows a judge in the Crown Court to pass a sentence and order the detention of an offender in a hospital, as if a hospital order had been made. A restriction direction would be passed at the same time. At present this power only applies to those classified as suffering from psychopathic disorder.

Hospital Order — A **hospital order** under section 37 of the Mental Health Act is an alternative to a sentence. The convicted individual is detained in hospital for treatment. Generally the hospital order will be subject to a **restriction direction** under section 41, giving the Home Secretary powers over various aspects of the convicted person's management.

HSPSCB — **High Security Psychiatric Services Commissioning Board**, the non-statutory body set up to advise Ministers on the funding and commissioning of high security psychiatric services, and on a future strategy for secure psychiatric services.

HSPSCT — **High Security Psychiatric Services Commissioning Team**, the group of civil servants who are responsible for the day to day commissioning and monitoring of high security psychiatric services.

ICD10 — ***International Classification of Diseases***, 10th Revision (1992). Published by the World Health Organization.

LOA — **Leave of Absence**. The term used for a trip outside the hospital grounds.

Mental Disorder — A legal term. Section 1(2) of the Mental Health Act defines mental disorder as "mental illness, arrested or incomplete development of mind, psychopathic disorder and any other disorder or disability of mind".

MHAC — **Mental Health Act Commission**. The statutory body charged with visiting detained patients and safeguarding their rights.

MHRT — **Mental Health Review Tribunal**. Tribunals are independent quasi-judicial bodies charged with reviewing the compulsory detention of patients in psychiatric hospitals.

MHU — The **Mental Health Unit** of the Home Office, the Unit which supports the Home Secretary in exercising his statutory duties with regard to restricted patients.

Moss Side — **Moss Side** was the original psychiatric hospital at Ashworth, comprising what is now Ashworth South (which was closed in 1995) and Ashworth East.

MSU (RSU) — **Medium Secure Unit (Regional Secure Unit)**. Secure psychiatric hospitals for patients who do not need the level of security found in the High Security Hospitals. There are now approximately 1,700 medium security beds in the NHS and private hospitals.

NHS — **National Health Service**.

NWRO — **North West Regional Office**, one of the Regional Offices of the NHS Executive, itself part of the Department of Health. The NWRO oversees the performance of the NHS in the North West of England.

Park Lane — **Park Lane** was built to relieve overcrowding at Broadmoor. It opened in stages between 1974 and 1984. It is now known as Ashworth North.

PCL-R — ***Psychopathy Checklist – Revised***, devised by Professor Hare. This checklist comprises 20 items, in which each item is scored 0, 1 or 2. At a score of 30 or more an individual is designated as a "psychopath" for research purposes.

PCT — **Patient Care Team.** The multi-disciplinary team on a given ward which discusses and makes decisions on the care and treatment of patients on that ward.

PDU — **Personality Disorder Unit (Ashworth Hospital)**

Personality Disorder(s)	Abnormality or abnormalities of personality which are long-standing (usually beginning in childhood) and persistent, and which constitute a basic feature of a person's functioning.
POA	**Prison Officers' Association**, one of the three main unions at Ashworth. The others are the **RCN (Royal College of Nursing)** and **UNISON**.
Psychopathic Disorder	Psychopathic Disorder is defined in the Mental Health Act as "a persistent disorder or disability of mind (whether or not including significant impairment of intelligence) which results in abnormally aggressive or seriously irresponsible conduct on the part of the person concerned".
Reed Review	**The Department of Health/Home Office Review of Services for Mentally Disordered Offenders and Others Requiring Similar Services** (1992). This review was chaired by Dr John Reed CB and made a number of recommendations for improving services for mentally disordered offenders.
RMO	**Responsible Medical Officer**, defined in law as "the medical practitioner in charge of the treatment of the patient". The RMO exercises various powers, including the power to discharge, renew detention and grant leave of absence. These powers are circumscribed somewhat in the case of restricted patients by the powers of the Home Secretary.
SHA	**Special Health Authority**. Ashworth, Broadmoor and Rampton are all Special Health Authorities.
SHSA	**Special Hospitals Service Authority**, the Special Health Authority which ran the Special Hospitals between 1989 and 1996.
Special Hospitals	The traditional term for the three **High Security Hospitals** in England. The other two are Broadmoor and Rampton. The State Hospital at Carstairs in Scotland is the High and Medium Security facility for Scotland and Northern Ireland.
SSI	**Social Services Inspectorate**. The SSI is part of the Department of Health. One of its key functions is carry out a programme of independent inspections of personal social services.
TBS	**Terbeschikkingstelling** – roughly equivalent to a hospital order in the Dutch system. *See* Appendix 8.
Transfer Direction	A **transfer direction** is an order for a convicted prisoner to be transferred to an NHS hospital under section 47 of the Mental Health Act. Usually restrictions are attached under section 49. A move in the opposite direction is known as remitting back to prison.
Treatability	Before an individual classified as suffering from psychopathic disorder (and mental impairment) can be detained in hospital for treatment the treatability test must be satisfied, i.e., that the treatment "is likely to alleviate or prevent a deterioration of his condition" (*see* sections 3, 37).
UGM	**Unit General Manager**

PART 1 Background to the Inquiry

1.1.0 The Establishment of the Inquiry

1.1.1 On 7 February 1997 the Right Honourable Stephen Dorrell MP, then Secretary of State for Health, established a statutory inquiry under section 84 of the National Health Service Act 1977 to investigate serious allegations made by Mr Steven Daggett, a former patient of the Personality Disorder Unit (PDU) at Ashworth High Security Hospital. The allegations concerned possible paedophile activity on one of the wards of the PDU, the availability of pornography, drugs and alcohol, and financial irregularities. At the same time, the then Chief Executive, Mrs Janice Miles, was suspended and Mr Erville Millar was appointed as Acting Chief Executive.

1.1.2 Dr Hilary Hodge was appointed as substantive Chief Executive in October 1997. Her appointment was not a success and she left the Hospital in June 1998, with Mr Peter Clarke, Chief Executive of Mental Health Services of Salford NHS Trust, taking over as Acting Chief Executive.

1.1.3 We deal with the events leading up to the establishment of this Inquiry in greater detail below.

1.2.0 Composition of the Committee and Terms of Reference

1.2.1 The Chairman was appointed on 7 February 1997 and the other members of the Committee of Inquiry shortly thereafter. Our membership reflects a broad range of experience and expertise in the law, forensic psychiatric services and health service management.

1.2.2 We were asked to work to the following terms of reference:

(i) to investigate the functioning of the Personality Disorder Unit at Ashworth Hospital following allegations about misuse of drugs and alcohol, financial irregularities, possible paedophile activity and the availability of pornographic material within the Personality Disorder Unit;

(ii) to review, in the light of these investigations:

(a) the policies, clinical care and procedures of the Personality Disorder Unit;

(b) the security arrangements for the Personality Disorder Unit;

(c) the management arrangements at the Hospital for assuring effective clinical care, appropriate security for patients and arrangements for visiting on the Personality Disorder Unit;

(iii) to submit a full report to the Secretary of State for Health and to make recommendations for action.

1.2.3 In his statement to the House of Commons (*see* Appendix 1), The Rt Hon Stephen Dorrell MP, made clear that the inquiry should focus on the policies, clinical care and management of the PDU, as this was where problems had emerged. But he noted that the inquiry would wish to follow up any wider questions necessary to a proper consideration of the issues. Mr Dorrell's successor, the Rt Hon Frank Dobson MP, also encouraged us to look more widely than our relatively narrow brief to focus on matters of broad policy interest.

1.2.4 We have indeed used that freedom where we thought it necessary. Thus we have not limited ourselves to a narrow focus on the events alleged and, in many cases, proved to have taken place on Lawrence Ward in and around 1995 and 1996. To do so would have ignored the context within which those events took place. First, Lawrence Ward was not the only ward within the PDU to have suffered very major problems since the Unit's inception (we are thinking here in particular of the Owen Ward hostage-taking in June 1994, of which much more below). Second, we could not discuss the various security weaknesses of Lawrence Ward without examining the overall security failures of the Hospital. Third, this Inquiry follows the earlier Blom-Cooper Inquiry of 1991/2, which quite rightly launched a radical change in the nature of the Hospital. But the implementation of its recommendations was fatally flawed as far as the Hospital's personality disordered patients were concerned. To understand the troubled history of the PDU one needs to understand the aftermath of the Blom-Cooper Inquiry.

1.2.5 At the same time we were aware that we needed to give our work clear chronological limits. We decided it would be sensible to go back in time as far as 1989, the year management transferred from the Department of Health to the new Special Hospitals Service Authority and to continue up to October 1996, when Mr Daggett returned from his absconsion. For obvious reasons we have concentrated in particular on the years 1993–1996, but there was an inevitable drift into 1997.

1.2.6 We have also taken the view that to tackle the second part of our remit sensibly we had to examine in detail the controversies surrounding the diagnosis, treatment and treatability of personality disorder and the right services for individuals with personality disorder. In this we concentrated our attention on the severe end of the spectrum of personality disorders, on the sorts of offender who have found themselves in Ashworth Hospital's PDU. We therefore devoted some two weeks of hearings to evidence from some of the acknowledged experts in personality disorder. We have published their expert submissions as a separate volume. We are very grateful to the experts who generously gave their time. We have been much helped by their thoughts.

1.2.7 Furthermore, although the holding of seminars by public committees of inquiry has not always proved worthwhile, we decided to hold three - one on the management of this difficult group of patients, the second on matters of accountability within the National Health Service and the third on legal issues which appeared to require to be considered. We held all the seminars after we had heard all the evidence with the object of testing preliminary views which we had formed. Because we were testing preliminary views we decided not to hold the seminars in public, and we invited prominent experts to assist us in these sounding board exercises. This enabled us to hear from a wider range of people with appropriate expertise than we could possibly have invited to give evidence.

1.2.8 The seminar which looked at the management of severely personality disordered individuals was attended by some 50 clinicians, managers and others. The third, which focused on the legal issues raised by severely personality disordered offenders, was attended by a small group of judges, academic lawyers, forensic psychiatrists, civil servants and others. The second which we organized concerned accountability. Any inquiry such as ours focuses on serious problems and inevitably judgements have to be made about where responsibility for any errors lies and who should be accountable to the outside world for the effective running of a service. It is also important to judge individuals in the context of the system in place during their time. A defective system within which individuals have to work can contribute substantially to personal failure. To help us refine our views on what principles of accountability are appropriate for a service such as the NHS we invited a small group of interested parties to discuss a number of the relevant issues.

1.2.9 We are extremely grateful to all those who attended these sessions. We found them extremely helpful in challenging and refining our thinking.

1.2.10 We turn now to the nuts and bolts of the inquiry process.

1.3.0 Gathering Material

1.3.1 For some months after the Inquiry was established a steady stream of papers emerged, largely, but not wholly, from the Hospital. Initially, in order to decide the main routes to be explored, the Chairman, Secretary and Solicitor to the Inquiry in various combinations met a number of people with in-depth knowledge of Ashworth Hospital and indeed of the High Security Hospitals in general. We received much helpful information and assistance, for which we are most grateful.

1.3.2 In the meantime the Hospital set up a small team led by Mr Peter Green who rendered us much assistance in identifying relevant material. Having been at Ashworth for some years he was well placed to coordinate the production of potentially relevant documents. We are grateful to Mr Green and his team, who at all times have responded to our requests to the very best of their ability. As will be seen, he and his team did not enjoy the same level of cooperation from within the Hospital and in particular the PDU.

1.3.3 By the time we started to hear evidence in November 1997 we had amassed a formidable quantity of documents, with many thousands of pages being disclosed to parties to the Inquiry, although we had sifted out many more. We were confident we had received more or less all of the potentially relevant material. However, during the first session of hearings it emerged that this was not the case. At a very late stage large quantities of documents were served relating to serious incidents. One particular set of documents related to very serious allegations made by a personality disordered patient who later died. This late service of documents greatly inconvenienced us and other parties to the Inquiry. Mr Green gave evidence on a number of different days, but just before his final appearance, for some reason he had been relieved of his duties at Ashworth Hospital. We lost a valuable assistant at a critical time.

1.3.4 Mr Green's last appearance came about because we recalled him to explain these problems. He told us that the vast amount of information that was sent to the Inquiry did not emanate from the PDU, which had been obstructive from the beginning of the Inquiry. It got to the stage where he had written to the Acting Chief Executive expressing his frustration at the PDU's lack of support. Things did not improve greatly thereafter. From time to time we felt that the flow of documents later disclosed, and which could have been disclosed much earlier, was being controlled so as to inhibit their thorough digestion.

1.3.5 We are quite satisfied that Mr Green and his team fulfilled their duties diligently and honestly. Unfortunately some members of the PDU appear to have been less than cooperative, for whatever reason.

1.3.6 This episode also reflects the lack of a central information system within the Hospital itself, which would have given the Inquiry ready access to much of the information which emerged so late. There was no reason why any of the material we were given late in November 1997 could not have been in our hands in March or April.

1.4.0 The Nature of an Inquiry

1.4.1 Unlike Sir Louis Blom-Cooper's Inquiry into Ashworth Hospital in 1991–2,[1] this Inquiry was given statutory powers from the outset. The effect of section 84 of the National Health Service Act 1977 is to give an inquiry powers to compel persons to give evidence or to produce papers; and to take evidence on oath or affirmation.

1.4.2 A public Inquiry such as this is not like a civil or criminal trial which are adversarial in nature. A public inquiry which is inquisitorial, is aimed primarily at establishing the truth rather than proving guilt or innocence. In Paragraph 28 of the Royal Commission on Tribunals of Inquiry, Cmnd 3121 (1966) (chaired by the Rt Hon Lord Justice Salmon) Lord Justice Salmon points out that it is the Committee's responsibility, as an inquisitorial tribunal:

> "to make and direct all necessary searching investigations and to produce the witnesses in order to arrive at the truth".

The Inquiry has the freedom to conduct its operations as it sees fit; to decide what documents it needs to see; whom to call as witnesses; and how to proceed, in order to discharge its responsibility to the public to arrive at the truth. There is some guidance available, particularly in the six principles set out in Lord Salmon's Report. These are:

> "1. Before any person becomes involved in an inquiry, the Tribunal must be satisfied that there are circumstances which affect him and which the Tribunal proposes to investigate.
>
> 2. Before any person who is involved in an inquiry is called as a witness he should be informed of any allegations which are made against him and the substance of the evidence in support of them.
>
> 3.(a) He should be given an adequate opportunity of preparing his case and of being assisted by legal advisers.
>
> (b) His legal expenses should normally be met out of public funds.
>
> 4. He should have the opportunity of being examined by his own solicitor or counsel and of stating his case in public at the inquiry.
>
> 5. Any material witness he wishes called at the inquiry should, if reasonably practicable, be heard.
>
> 6. He should have the opportunity of testing by cross-examination conducted by his own solicitor or counsel any evidence which may affect him." [Paragraph 32.]

The thread that runs through those principles is that an Inquiry should be both **fair** and **thorough**. However, a limited adoption of some adversarial practices can assist in the process.

1.4.3 Committees of Inquiry have considerable freedom to pursue their enquiries as they see fit. It is a freedom with a mixed blessing. Unlike a judge in a civil or criminal trial, the panel does not receive papers which have already been prepared by lawyers. In paragraph 30 of the 1966 Royal Commission it is said:

> "There are important distinctions between inquisitorial procedure and the procedure in an ordinary civil or criminal case. It is inherent in the inquisitorial procedure that there is no *lis*. The Tribunal directs the inquiry and the witnesses are necessarily the Tribunal's witnesses. There is no plaintiff or defendant, no prosecutor or accused; there are no pleadings defining issues to be tried, no charges, no

---

1 Sir Louis Blom-Cooper QC, Martin Brown, Dr Robert Dolan and Professor Elaine Murphy, *Report of the Committee of Inquiry into Complaints about Ashworth Hospital* (London: HMSO, 1992), Cmnd 2028.

indictments or depositions. The inquiry may take a fresh turn at any moment. It is therefore difficult for persons involved to know in advance of the hearing what allegations may be made against them".

1.4.4 Preparation is therefore a Committee of Inquiry's first task, and we touched on that in **1.3.1–5** above. Members of the public may be surprised when a committee set up as a matter of urgency does not immediately begin to hear evidence. It cannot do so. The oral and documentary evidence is "out there somewhere", but it has to be found, considered and sifted for relevance. Additionally an appropriate scheme for dealing with relevant evidence at hearings has to be devised.

1.4.5 Each judicial inquiry is different, and has its own particular issues of process to address. We discuss below the major procedural issues facing us and how we have addressed them, and outline other important aspects of our approach to our remit. At Appendix 2 are copies of Press Notices we issued on 28 July 1997 and 17 October 1997.

1.5.0 The Criminal Investigations

1.5.1 Firstly, we have always had to bear in mind that ours was not the only investigation into aspects of these allegations. Merseyside Police have investigated very thoroughly the suggestions that a child visitor may have been abused within Lawrence Ward and we have been careful throughout not to interfere with the progress of their investigations. For their part, Merseyside Police have been extremely helpful to us and we are grateful to them.

1.5.2 The existence of these investigations, and the possibility of criminal charges, have had serious implications for how we tackled our remit. Early on it became clear that the best way to avoid any interference with the criminal investigations was to reverse the order in which we handled its two main parts, tackling the more general part of our remit first. We anxiously considered whether such a decision would "put the cart before the horse". Part One of our remit involves a fact-finding exercise concerning what happened on Lawrence Ward. Part Two involves considering how things happened, why they could have been allowed to happen and what needs to change. Part Two also involves the wider consideration of the policies, clinical care and procedures of the Personality Disorder Unit and its security arrangements. Additionally we were charged with considering the management arrangements for securing effective clinical care and appropriate security needs of patients.

1.5.3 The two parts are not separated by water-tight bulkheads, but there was no disadvantage in tackling Part Two first. On the contrary there was a positive value to be gained. The more we learned about the management, care and treatment of personality disordered patients, the better able we were to appraise the management, clinical care, security and other arrangements prevalent at the time with which Part One of our remit is concerned.

1.5.4 From another point of view the decision to deal with Part Two first was fortuitous. The investigation by Merseyside Police took some months longer than expected. As a result the Crown Prosecution Service did not receive papers until September 1997. Had we opted to deal with Part One first we may have had to delay the November hearings. In the event the Crown Prosecution Service did not decide whether any prosecutions should be brought until about four weeks after our hearings had commenced.

1.6.0 Taking of Evidence on Oath

1.6.1 A second issue was whether or not to take evidence on oath or affirmation. There are arguments on both sides. Asking each witness to swear an oath or to affirm may give the inquiry more of an adversarial court-room air than is desired and affords no protection against a witness determined to mislead. Yet by taking evidence on oath one can give witnesses who have unpalatable evidence some measure of protection, by in effect forcing them to reveal the truth on pain of perjury. Also if one feels that would be helpful in some cases, it would be best to apply it in all, so that all witnesses are subject to the same process. We decided to ask all witnesses to give evidence on oath or affirmation.

1.7.0 Salmon Letters[2]

1.7.1 A third thorny problem was that of the issue of these documents, so-called "Salmon letters". The Royal Commission had recommended their issue as a result of their historical review of inquisitorial processes. From the middle of the seventeenth century until 1921 the investigation of events giving rise to public concern had been by Select Parliamentary Committee or Commission of Inquiry. By 1921 this type of inquiry was entirely discredited and the Tribunals of Inquiry (Evidence) Act 1921 was passed. The 1921 Act had its defects and the Royal Commission was set up to examine whether it should be abolished or kept in its then, or amended, form. It was concluded that certain matters which gave rise to public concern could not be dealt with by ordinary civil or criminal proceedings. Although the inquisitorial procedure was "alien to the concept of justice generally accepted in the United Kingdom", it must be used "to preserve the purity and integrity of our public life without which a successful democracy is impossible".

1.7.2 Having recognized defects in the 1921 Act Lord Salmon recommended six cardinal principles to remove the difficulties and injustices with which people involved in an inquiry may be faced. These are quoted in paragraph **1.4.2** above. The issue of Salmon letters was recommended to implement the second of those cardinal principles.

1.7.3 Lord Salmon recognized that the form of the document disclosing to the witness the substance of the case against him must be left in each case to the discretion of the tribunal. The point is this: the six cardinal principles introduce into the inquisitorial process limited elements of the adversarial system so that the Tribunal is as fair as possible to the witnesses it calls. What has to be remembered is that the inquisitorial process has none of the formality of the adversarial process, as Lord Salmon recognized (Paragraph 30).

1.7.4 In their Report into Complaints at Ashworth Hospital Sir Louis Blom-Cooper and his team warn against the tendency to interpret the Salmon letter process too rigidly. We agree. There is a lack of precision in the machinery of an inquisitorial inquiry. If this were not so the *raison d'être* for its use would be defeated.

1.7.5 We would also note in passing that all of the six Salmon principles are recommendations, rather than rules. As Sir Richard Scott, Vice Chancellor, said in the context of his own Inquiry:

> " . . . there has been a tendency for the media and some commentators to regard the six cardinal principles in the Salmon Report not as recommendations but as rules. I regard this as an unhelpful approach. The Salmon recommendations are rightly recognized as providing important guidelines to inquiries about how injustice and unfairness to witnesses can be avoided. But . . . every inquiry must adapt its procedures to meet its own circumstances." [3]

Our general procedure, however, was different from that adopted by Sir Richard Scott.

---

2 In paragraph 50 of Lord Salmon's Report it is said:

> "As soon as possible after he [a witness from whom a statement has been taken] has given his statement, and certainly well in advance, usually not less than seven days before he gives evidence, he should be supplied with a document setting out the allegations against him and the substance of the evidence in support of those allegations".

Such documents became known as Salmon letters.

3 Scott, Sir Richard, (1996) *Report of the Inquiry into the Export of Defence Equipment and Dual-Use Goods to Iraq and related Prosecutions.* Paragraph B2.31, volume 1, p.39. London: The Stationery Office.

1.7.6 In this spirit it must be understood that a Salmon letter is not a precise document. It is intended to help a witness who may be criticized to understand what he may have to address when he gives evidence. It does not however circumscribe permitted questioning of a witness, and any attempt by legal representatives to seek to treat it as a quasi-pleading must be resisted.

1.7.7 In this Inquiry we were conscious that a large number of individuals could potentially be subject to Salmon letters in relation to relatively minor criticisms. It seemed more appropriate to restrict the use of Salmon letters to more central figures.

1.7.8 We adopted a policy of sending those individuals who were judged to be at risk of serious criticism a letter setting out the main areas where the Committee requested their assistance. These letters made clear that further issues might arise during the course of the Inquiry to which individuals would have to respond. We tried to draw these letters as a series of issues or questions. (An example is found in Appendix 2.)

1.8.0 Representation of Parties

1.8.1 One of the issues that arise in an inquiry such as ours is the representation of parties, and in particular, who should be represented at public expense. With regard to the latter point there is a well-known rule of thumb to the effect that the public purse will meet the reasonable costs of any necessary party to an inquiry or tribunal who would be prejudiced in seeking representation were he or she in any doubt about funding. However, the costs of substantial bodies are generally not met from public funds unless there are special circumstances.

1.8.2 We granted representation at public expense to the patients within the PDU and a number of individuals connected with the events in the PDU. Apart from the patients on the PDU, we sought to restrict representation strictly to those parts of the hearings which touched upon an individual's own interest.

1.8.3 With regard to the patients within the PDU we followed the eminently sensible precedent of Sir Louis Blom-Cooper's Inquiry by selecting a single firm to represent all patients, thereby avoiding a multiplicity of representation. Pannone and Partners was selected after a tendering exercise. We did grant separate representation for the Liverpool hearings to Mr Steven Daggett, whose original dossier of complaints made allegations against a number of patients. It was felt that any one firm would face a conflict of interests in representing both Mr Daggett and the other patients within the PDU.

1.8.4 Appendix 3 lists the parties represented at the Inquiry.

1.9.0 Handling of Statements

1.9.1 We took the view that witness statements should be kept confidential and not circulated to parties until decisions had been taken on which witnesses to call and until we could judge with reasonable accuracy the extent to which particular parties needed access to the statements of particular witnesses.

1.9.2 This is another area where the distinction between inquisitorial and an adversarial proceedings becomes apparent. It is the Committee which is inquiring. Other witnesses are only "cross-examined" by parties with the permission of the Committee, and not as of right. As a matter of fairness, if a witness testifies adversely to a party, then it is right that such a party should be enabled to challenge such a witness, but when the witness' evidence in no way affects another party there is no need for that party to have the witness statement or to cross-examine.

1.9.3 Lord Salmon, suggested that even those to whom Salmon letters are sent need only be given the substance of the evidence against them. Thus in making witness statements available at a reasonable time before the hearing we took the view that we were being as fair as possible.

1.10.0 Hearings

1.10.1 We were determined to hold as many of the hearings as possible in public, whilst recognising that some evidence might need to be heard in camera. On several occasions we had discussions over whether or not to allow names to come into the public domain. For the most part we took the view that names should be revealed. On some occasions we deemed it right to use a coded procedure.

1.10.2 We held two preliminary hearings, on Thursday 7 August and Friday 10 October 1997. These hearings provided an opportunity to establish clearly the procedures of the Inquiry and to clarify any questions, as well as to identify the parties to the Inquiry.

1.10.3 The main hearings began on Monday 3 November 1997 at the Great Western Royal Hotel London and continued, sitting Monday to Thursday, until Thursday 11 December. The hearings resumed on Monday 2 February 1998 in Ashworth Hospital itself, where we took evidence from a number of patient witnesses. On Thursday 5 February we held a special session at Maghull Town Hall, to give local councillors the opportunity to put their views directly to the Committee of Inquiry. The hearings continued in London from 10 February until 19 March, first at the Great Western Royal Hotel, and latterly at the New Connaught Rooms, Holborn.

1.10.4 The final set of hearings started on Monday 27 April 1998 at Knutsford Crown Court, where we sat to facilitate the hearing of more patient witnesses. After two weeks in Knutsford we moved to the Adelphi Hotel in Liverpool for the final two weeks, where we finished hearing evidence on Thursday 21 May. A final hearing took place in London on 6th July to hear final submissions from the parties. In all we sat on 69 days.

1.10.5 A word should be said about the location of the hearings. We decided that the hearings concerned with the second part of our remit, namely the general policies of the PDU as opposed to the specific allegations about events on Lawrence Ward, should be heard in London rather than Liverpool. The reason for this was the convenience of potential witnesses. We had decided that in order to tackle this part of our remit appropriately we would have to consider very general issues concerning personality disorder. We therefore intended to invite a large number of people to give evidence from different parts of the country and duly picked London as the most convenient point to meet. But when the focus of attention was firmly on the PDU, and in particular on Lawrence Ward, we heard evidence in the North West.

1.11.0 Cross-Examination

1.11.1 We were concerned to ensure that legal representatives kept their cross-examination relevant and reasonably brief. In the event we found that in order to keep to our timetable we had to guillotine cross-examination time. This was with hindsight a very important step. It forced representatives to focus on their key points in cross-examination and enabled us to get through a very large amount of evidence. From time to time within his discretion, the Chairman allowed counsel a little more than their allotted time. Having allocated time on a guillotine basis it was important that parties were allowed their full allotment if they needed it. To ensure this a chess match dual clock was acquired. One clock was marked panel and the other marked party. When members of the panel asked questions counsel's clock was stopped and only re-started when counsel recommenced questioning. We are very grateful to all parties for their cooperation.

1.12.0 Credibility of Witnesses

1.12.1 As far as the credibility of witnesses is concerned Sir Louis Blom-Cooper's Report contains an interesting and instructive chapter. Sir Louis and his team state:

> "We have started from the proposition that it cannot, and must not be assumed that persons who are diagnosed as 'personality disordered' or 'psychopathic' are invariably likely to be lying or giving unreliable testimony about specific events or issues in question. One looks at the quality of evidence being supplied by the individual witness. Preconceptions and prejudices about who is giving the evidence should not influence the assessment of reliability of testimony. They can, and do give reliable and complete accounts of events, as do mentally normal persons."

1.12.2 We agree that personality disordered patients can give reliable evidence. However, the more manipulative they are, and many of the patients we were concerned with were not only manipulative but also intelligent, the greater is the need for care in evaluating their evidence. If, for example, they can spend years creating an aura of respectability and trustworthiness so as to gain privileged status, so they can be selective with the truth. We took the view that our hearings should not be delayed by wrangles over the credibility of individual patient witnesses. Of greater importance in judging the credibility of the patient witnesses is that we had an abundance of other evidence.

1.13.0 Use of LiveNote

1.13.1 We made the decision early on to use the LiveNote Computer-aided transcription system which the Chairman had used extensively in court. This system, which gives users a highly accurate, virtually "real time" running transcript, is widely used in courts both in the UK and overseas, and has been tried and tested in a number of public inquiries. It was used by Sir Richard Scott VC in his Inquiry and by the Terminal 5 Inquiry at Heathrow. The Chairman's experience had been that the system saved considerable amounts of time in court (approximately 20 per cent of the usual time) and afterwards in analysing material and producing judgements. As a Panel we would concur. We found the system extremely helpful and are very grateful to our highly efficient stenographers.

1.13.2 We also took the decision to scan disclosed documents and statements on to CD-ROM, both in "read-only" and searchable form. This meant that we could display relevant documents during the hearings, both for our benefit and that of witnesses, which reduced lengthy and tedious delays spent searching for hard copies to a minimum.

1.13.3 The searchable text of the documents has been invaluable during writing this report.

1.13.4 Copies of "read-only" CD-ROMs were made available free of charge to parties.

1.14.0 Disclosure of Documents

1.14.1 A large number of documents were disclosed to parties to the Inquiry, a number of them highly sensitive documents containing patient confidential information. In deciding to disclose these documents we were conscious that disclosure might conceivably result in such confidential information reaching unsuitable hands. At the same time, we were determined that all parties should have the opportunity to see relevant documentation and were unconvinced that editing documents would have been a satisfactory alternative. We took the precaution of insisting that all parties sign written undertakings not to use the documents for other purposes and to return the documents at the close of the Inquiry. Parties were also bound to seek our permission before copying the documents to any third party, eg for an expert opinion. We insisted that any such third party should likewise sign the written undertaking (*see* Appendix 2).

1.14.2 We are aware of no instance when our trust has been abused and we are very grateful to all parties for their cooperation in this matter.

1.15.0 Assessment of the Personality Disorder Unit

1.15.1 Part of our remit was to review the clinical care provided by the PDU. In order to help us carry this out we commissioned an assessment of the PDU as it now appeared from a small expert team, comprising Dr Adrian Grounds, from the Institute of Criminology at Cambridge University; Mr Tony Hillis, Director of Nursing at the Reaside Clinic, Birmingham; and Ms Lyn Suddards of the Henderson Hospital in Surrey.

1.15.2 The remit of the team was to spend several days within the Unit, observing practice, studying clinical notes and talking to staff, before reporting their findings. We particularly asked the team to examine the care plans and cross-check them against what was actually happening to patients during the time of the visit; to examine records of serious incidents; to review the medication regimes of patients; to find out the views of staff on the leadership of the PDU and its philosophy of care; and to examine staffing levels and skill mix and the training available.

1.15.3 We heard evidence from Dr Grounds and Ms Suddards and have incorporated their findings into our report. We are most grateful to them for their hard work.

1.16.0 Visits to Other Services

1.16.1 We are very conscious that we have been asked to investigate only one part of one of the three Special Hospitals. But we did not believe we could do our job properly without at least some familiarity with the other British High Security Hospitals, and indeed other services which have to manage severely personality disordered individuals.

1.16.2 We have therefore visited a number of services at home and in Europe over the course of the Inquiry, either as a Panel or in smaller groups, including the other Special Hospitals and the State Hospital at Carstairs; prisons, including Grendon, the Max Glatt Centre at Wormwood Scrubs and the Close Supervision Centre at Woodhill; medium secure units; and facilities in Holland, Germany and Switzerland. A full list is included at Appendix 8. We are most grateful for the hospitality of staff at all these institutions, who gave freely of their time and offered stimulating but occasionally depressing advice.

1.17.0 Terminology

1.17.1 It is important to be clear about terminology. Where we talk about psychopathic disorder this refers to the legal classification under the Mental Health Act 1983. It is not in itself a clinical diagnosis. We discuss at length below some of the difficulties surrounding clinical diagnosis, definition and terminology in this area. The reader should be aware that we use the term "severe personality disorder" to refer to a relatively small group comprising individuals who both suffer from a personality disorder or disorders, one of which will generally be anti-social personality disorder, and who pose a risk of causing serious harm to others. Most, if not all, of the men housed within the PDU at Ashworth can be described as suffering from severe personality disorder.

1.17.2 The term "Special Hospital" has not yet been universally replaced by "High Security Hospital". We use both interchangeably through this report.

1.17.3 We turn now to the history of the Special Hospitals.

1.18.0 The Special Hospitals: a Short History

1.18.1 Section 4 of the National Health Service Act 1977 imposes a duty on the Secretary of State to

> "provide and maintain establishments (in this Act referred to as 'special hospitals') for persons subject to detention under the Mental Health Act [1983] who in his

> opinion require treatment under conditions of special security on account of their dangerous, violent or criminal propensities."

There are three such Special (High Security) Hospitals in England, Broadmoor at Crowthorne in Berkshire, Rampton near Retford in Nottinghamshire and Ashworth on Merseyside.

1.18.2 The Department of Health has always had a close and special interest and involvement in these hospitals. For much of their history they were accountable directly to the Department and were outside the regional framework of the National Health Service. There is, in the NHS, a necessary tension between delegating authority as far as possible to local management and clinicians to do the most effective job possible and maintaining central oversight and control over what is a national, publicly-funded service. The balance between delegation and central direction has shifted at various points over the last half-century and will continue to do so.

1.18.3 The Special Hospitals are perhaps an extreme example of how this tension operates in practice. There was, and is, a very strong and legitimate central interest in the detailed operation of these hospitals, given the nature of the patient population. Most of them are subject to some form of restriction order, giving the Home Office a veto on various aspects of their care; a small number are very high profile indeed, attracting a considerable amount of media attention. The importance of ensuring the safety of the public means that the centre of government has, and will continue to have, an abiding interest in the detailed management of these institutions.

1.18.4 Government's interest in this area is longstanding. The first institution in England specifically built for the "criminally insane" was Broadmoor, which opened in 1863. Previous to that the most dangerous criminal lunatics were housed in Bethlem, although the majority were in ordinary county asylums. There were several calls for a separate asylum or asylums for the criminally lunatic during the first half of the nineteenth century, but it was not until the Tenth Report of the Commissioners in Lunacy, 1856, that such calls were heeded. This report pointed to the apparent success in aiding recovery of the Central Criminal Asylum in Dundrum near Dublin, opened in 1852, and condemned the state of wards for male criminal lunatics at Bethlem. The Act for the Better Provision for the Custody and Care of the Criminal Lunatics 1860 gave authority for the construction of Broadmoor, which was built to house 400 men and 100 women. By the end of the 1860s more than two-thirds of the country's criminal lunatics were said to be in Broadmoor.

1.18.5 From 1863 until 1948 Broadmoor was managed by a Council of Supervision, appointed by the Home Secretary. It was perennially overcrowded, and had to expand its capacity on a number of occasions. By 1903 it was housing 750 patients. Rampton was built to relieve this overcrowding and opened in 1912.

1.18.6 The Mental Deficiency Act 1913 established the Board of Control and required it to provide and maintain provisions for mental defectives who were violent and dangerous. The Moss Side site in Maghull (later Ashworth South) was purchased by the Board for use as an asylum, but was not actually used as such until 1933. Until 1960 patients could only be admitted to Moss Side and Rampton under the Mental Deficiency Acts of 1913 and 1938, and most were transferred from other hospitals for mental defectives, whether or not they had faced previous criminal charges. Since 1960 both hospitals have accepted patients under all the categories specified in the Mental Health Act 1959 and re-enacted in the 1983 Act.

1.18.7 The National Health Service Act 1946 transferred ownership of Rampton and Moss Side to the Ministry of Health, but they continued to be managed by the Board of Control. The Criminal Justice Act 1948 passed responsibility for managing Broadmoor to the Board of Control and ownership to the Ministry of Health. The Home Secretary retained responsibility for admissions and discharges. The Board of Control was dissolved in 1959 and the Ministry of Health took over responsibility for the three Special Hospitals.

1.18.8 The perennial problem of overcrowding at Broadmoor led to the building of a fourth hospital, Park Lane, adjacent to Moss Side. Park Lane opened in stages between 1974 and 1984.

1.18.9 By the late 1980s the hospitals had for many years been centrally managed by a division of the Department of Health in its various manifestations. The officials directly responsible for this management function combined to form the Special Hospitals Service Board, chaired by an Under-Secretary, which made major policy decisions concerning the hospitals, controlled financial and manpower allocations and played a part in senior appointments. The day to day management of the hospitals was entrusted to local hospital management teams, consisting of a medical director, chief nurse and hospital administrator.

1.18.10 This situation combined notional central control with actual neglect. Local managers did not have the authority to run the hospitals effectively; the central Board was a clumsy and ineffective way of managing large hospitals. The end result was a management vacuum at the local level, a vacuum which the Prison Officers' Association in particular was happy to fill.

1.18.11 Dissatisfaction with this situation led to the establishment of the Special Hospitals Service Authority in 1989. In the "Operational Brief", a document setting out for the new Authority its key aims and objectives, the Government gave the SHSA six main aims:

(i) ensure the continuing safety of the public;

(ii) ensure the provision of appropriate treatment for patients;

(iii) ensure a good quality of life for both patients and staff;

(iv) develop the hospitals as centres of excellence for the training of staff in all disciplines in forensic and other branches of psychiatry, psychiatric care and treatment;

(v) develop closer working relationships with local and regional NHS psychiatric services;

(vi) promote research into fields related to forensic psychiatry.

1.18.12 Two policies underpinned the establishment of the SHSA. First, to integrate the special hospitals fully into the NHS. Second, to strengthen leadership and accountability through the appointment of general managers within each hospital directly accountable to the Chief Executive of the SHSA. Mr Charles Kaye was appointed the Chief Executive of the SHSA. New Unit General Managers were appointed to each of the three hospitals.

1.18.13 The SHSA was designed to introduce a different form of management to the Special Hospitals. The Operational Brief made this very clear:

> ". . . the SHSA should be constituted as a small organization, operating flexibly and maximizing delegation of operational responsibility to hospital level, rather than acting as a centralized interventionist body".

1.18.14 Despite this injunction, there was, at the same time, a formidable management agenda which the SHSA was charged with driving forward. This agenda could perhaps be summed up as being to bring the ethos of modern forensic psychiatric care into the Special Hospitals. This involved, for example, recruiting high quality staff; stamping out unacceptable practices such as those later identified by the Blom-Cooper Inquiry Report; redeveloping the hospital estate; and making the hospitals more manageable in size.

1.18.15 In the early 1990s the NHS saw further radical change with the introduction of the purchaser-provider split and the internal market. One of the SHSA's original main aims had been to bring the hospitals closer to the rest of the NHS; by the later years of the SHSA's life this translated into preparing the hospitals for trust status, whilst taking part in developing new purchasing arrangements, which eventually emerged in April 1996.

1.18.16 Throughout the lifetime of the SHSA there was regular liaison between the Department of Health's mental health policy division and the Authority. There was a review meeting once a year which constituted the formal accountability mechanism. The review meeting would discuss the Authority's performance against agreed targets over the previous year and Ministerial priorities for the coming year. Beyond this there were occasional informal meetings between members of the SHSA and Ministers and their officials. A branch within the Department had the day to day responsibility for liaising with and overseeing the work of the SHSA, and for advising and briefing Ministers.

1.18.17 These arrangements were not of course perfect; the tension between central "control" and local freedom was played out between the Department and the SHSA. We will discuss below occasions when the system of alerting Ministers appears to have broken down. As will be seen later when we deal with the Owen Ward Report the liaison relationship proved to be too dependent on the goodwill of the Chief Executive of the SHSA to keep the civil servants with whom he liaised properly informed. At that stage liaison broke down.

1.18.18 In 1996 the purchaser-provider split was introduced into the Special Hospitals. The SHSA was disbanded; in its place appeared three Special Hospital Authorities and their purchaser, the High Security Psychiatric Services Commissioning Board (HSPSCB). The Board was charged with commissioning high security psychiatric care; developing a coordinated strategy for secure psychiatric services; advising on the development of services for patients currently in the Special Hospitals and elsewhere who required longer-term secure care at levels below high security; and advising Ministers through the Chief Executive of the NHS Executive. The following paragraphs are based on the statement of Sir Alan Langlands, Chief Executive of the NHS Executive, who set out the arrangements introduced in 1996 and further recent changes as a result of the allegations made by Mr Daggett.

The Special Health Authorities

1.18.19 The original goal of trust status for the hospitals was not realized, as this would not have been consistent with the Secretary of State's responsibilities for carrying out the functions of "managers" in respect of patients detained in the special hospitals under the Mental Health Act 1983 (see Section 145(1)). But the three SHAs, Ashworth, Broadmoor and Rampton Hospital Authorities, are responsible for managing the special hospitals as separate provider units in much the same way as other NHS hospitals managed by NHS trusts.

1.18.20 The three SHAs are each required to have a non-executive chairman and eight or ten members, half of whom must be non executives (either four non executives and four executives, or five and five). The chairman and non-executive members are appointed by the Secretary of State. The executive members must include a chief executive, director of finance, a registered nurse and a registered medical practitioner. The Chief Executive and Director of Finance are appointed by the non-executive members; the other executive members are appointed by the non-executive members and chief executive. Each authority is required to hold at least one public meeting a year and to present its audited accounts and annual report at such a meeting.

1.18.21 The SHAs are funded through a top-sliced allocation from within the Department of Health/Hospital and Community Health Services budget (Vote 1). The allocation is managed by the NHS Executive through the HSPSCB. Thus the Special Hospitals still, in effect, appear a "free good" to local purchasers.

1.18.22 The SHAs are accountable to Ministers through the NHS Executive. The accountability arrangements introduced in 1996 were as follows:

(i) for patient services – accountability was to be discharged through the High Security Psychiatric Services Commissioning Team (HSPSCT) (see below);

(ii) on matters relating to the management of the hospitals, including employment of staff, management of the estate, security, financial control and other operational issues – accountability was to be exercised through the Directors of the three NHS Executive Regional Offices covering the areas where the hospitals are located. That is Anglia and Oxford (Broadmoor); North West (Ashworth); and Trent (Rampton). The Regional Directors were and remain accountable to the Chief Executive of the NHS Executive.

The Chairmen of the SHAs also have direct links with the relevant Regional Chairmen and meet the Minister at least once a year on an informal basis.

The High Security Psychiatric Services Commissioning Board (HSPSCB)

1.18.23 The HSPSCB is a non-statutory committee which advises Ministers through the NHS Executive. The Board's terms of reference are to provide advice on:

(i) funding and commissioning of high security psychiatric services – having regard to numbers and categories of patients (including special needs groups), cost, quality assurance and strategic developments;

(ii) developing professional training, research within the special hospitals and other NHS secure psychiatric services;

(iii) developing a coordinated strategy for commissioning high and long-term secure psychiatric services within the NHS;

(iv) developing services for patients currently in the special hospitals and elsewhere who need longer term secure care at levels below high security;

(v) developing a strategy for child and adolescent forensic mental health services.

1.18.24 The HSPSCB has a non-executive chairman, Mrs Anne-Marie Nelson CBE (immediate past chairman of the SHSA); the Director of North Thames Regional Office is the Vice Chairman. Other members include representatives of NHS commissioners in England and Wales, the Home Office, Prison Service, Probation Service, Social Services and Mental Health Act Commission. The HSPSCB meets at least six times a year and provides an annual report to the Chief Executive of the NHS Executive.

1.18.25 The Secretary of State's responsibilities for commissioning high security psychiatric services are discharged through the NHS Executive. Services provided by the three SHAs are commissioned and monitored through a contract process which is similar to that which operates between Health Authorities and NHS Trusts. North Thames Regional Office is the centre of responsibility for commissioning high security psychiatric services and for ensuring consistency with Ministers' overall direction on mental health policy. This accountability is by way of the Regional Director to the Chief Executive of the NHS Executive. The Regional Director is supported by the officials of the High Security Psychiatric Services Commissioning Team (HSPSCT).

1.18.26 In determining the strategy for commissioning, the Director of the Commissioning Team works closely with the High Security Psychiatric Services Commissioning Board (HSPSCB). The Chairman and individual members of the Board work closely with HSPSCT. The Chairman of the Board also has occasional informal meetings with Ministers.

1.18.27 One might be forgiven, from a perusal of the above for asking what went wrong at Ashworth in February 1997. Clearly those events leading up to the establishment of this Inquiry highlighted problems in the operation of the arrangements instituted in April 1996. Sir Alan Langlands commissioned work to examine the working arrangements and to advise on changes that might be required.

1.18.28 That review identified a lack of clarity about the relationship of each of the three SHAs to the relevant Regional Office. As a result, the North West Regional Office had been less engaged with Ashworth Hospital than is likely to have been the case had it been an NHS trust. It was felt also there had been an over-reliance on the HSPSCT to monitor operational issues within the special hospitals, and to coordinate any briefing required. These problems, it was found, had both been compounded by, and resulted in, communication problems and difficulties in achieving effective working relationships between organizations and individuals.

1.18.29 A number of measures were taken to clarify the situation. North Thames Regional Office was reaffirmed as the centre of responsibility for the commissioning of high secure psychiatric services, whilst the three relevant Regional Offices (Anglia and Oxford (Broadmoor); North West (Ashworth), Trent (Rampton)) were given full provider monitoring responsibilities, including responsibility for tracking the implementation of Government policy and performance; for providing management support to the Special Hospital Authorities; and for undertaking an annual performance review. The Department's Mental Health Branch (HSD4) maintained overall responsibility for mental health policy.

1.18.30 Briefing for Ministers is provided by officials in the relevant part of the NHS Executive – regional offices, HSPSCT or HSD4 depending on whether the issue in question relates to operational matters at one of the hospitals, policy on commissioning services, or broader mental health policy respectively – following consultation as necessary with staff in the hospitals, colleagues in other branches and the Home Office.

1.18.31 The four Regional Directors concerned now meet with the Deputy Director of the Health Services Directorate on a regular basis to review progress on strategy, policy and operational matters relating to high security psychiatric services.

1.18.32 It remains to be seen of course whether the amended arrangements will stand the test of time. We go into more detail below on the problems and lack of clarity in the arrangements in place in 1996/7. What is clear is that the tension between central control and oversight and local freedom and autonomy will remain under the current arrangements.

1.19.0 The Problems of the Special Hospitals

1.19.1 All three Special Hospitals have been the subject of damning outside inquiries over the last 20 years. In 1980 Sir John Boynton chaired an Inquiry into Rampton,[4] prompted by a critical television programme. Sir John and his team pointed to a number of serious problems, for example: the isolation, geographically, professionally and culturally, of the Special Hospitals; a general lack of medical and nursing professional leadership, a vacuum which, in the case of nursing staff, was filled by the Prison Officers' Association; recruitment difficulties, notably of clinical psychologists; a focus on containment rather than therapy; a poor complaints procedure (of 178 complaints made between January 1974 and December 1978 not one was substantiated); and poor facilities for visitors, particularly relatives.

1.19.2 In 1988 the Health Advisory Service (HAS) visited Broadmoor.[5] Their report makes

4 *Report of the Review of Rampton Hospital* (Chairman Sir John Boynton) (1980) London: HMSO, Cmnd 8073.

5 NHS Health Advisory Service/DHSS Social Services Inspectorate (1998), *Report on the Services Provided by Broadmoor Hospital*, London: DHSS, July, HAS/SSI(88)SH 1.

similar criticisms. The prevailing culture appeared to be non-therapeutic; multi-disciplinary working was under-developed; only five consultants were in post, with some having over 100 patients in their care; and the management structure was unwieldy.

1.19.3 In 1991–2 Sir Louis Blom-Cooper and his team examined Ashworth and recommended a thorough-going change in the culture of the Hospital. Sir Louis and his colleagues went so far as to "question the need for the Special Hospitals within contemporary forensic psychiatric services" (see below). [6]

1.19.4 In the wake of the publication of Sir Louis' report in August 1992 one of our number, Professor Bluglass, argued strongly for the closure of the Special Hospitals. He commented:

> "The three special hospitals have not been able to rid themselves of an institutionalised culture of geographical, therapeutic, and professional isolation, which can be traced back to their origins within the penal system until 1946 . . . Nursing staff have continued to join the Prison Officers' Association, and, although there have been many notable advances, the continuation of these large and unwieldy institutions into the 1990s, when most large mental hospitals have closed, perpetuates anachronistic attitudes and makes the altruistic aim of transforming them into 'centres of excellence' difficult, if not impossible."

Professor Bluglass[7] recommended replacing the hospitals with new, smaller local high security units, linked to local regional secure units.

1.19.5 Reducing the size of the Special Hospitals and linking them more closely with regional services was also the key recommendation of the Working Group on High Security and Related Psychiatric Provision set up in the wake of the Blom-Cooper Report. In the covering letter to his team's report Sir Louis Blom-Cooper QC, had said the following:

> " . . . a review of the size and location of the Special Hospitals . . . seems to us to be a matter of some urgency, and should form a vital part of any wider review of the Special Hospital System. Indeed, we would even question the need for the Special Hospitals within contemporary forensic psychiatric services."

The then Government duly responded to these remarks by setting up the above Working Group in October 1992, under the chairmanship of Dr John Reed. Professor Bluglass was a member of the Group. The Group finished its work in April 1993, but their report was not published until 1994. They recommended that high security services should become more dispersed, with units catering for no more than 200 patients each. The number of units required would be determined in the light of needs assessment. The Group also recommended that NHS purchasing contracts should aim to meet the needs of those patients requiring long-term medium security.

1.19.6 More recently Professor Elaine Murphy, a member of Sir Louis' Inquiry team, has argued that the overly-custodial and anti-therapeutic ethos of the hospitals would not change until the POA was ousted from the hospitals.[8]

1.19.7 These reports and articles paint a picture of insular, closed institutions whose predominantly custodial and therapeutically pessimistic culture had isolated them from the mainstream of forensic psychiatry. Recruitment of adequate numbers of high quality managerial and clinical staff had therefore proved almost impossible. Patients had little or no say in their own lives. But as we set out later, the implementation of the Blom-Cooper Report throughout the Hospital was flawed and provided no effective solution.

---

6 *Op.cit.*, p.iv.

7 Bluglass R. (1992) 'The special hospitals should be closed', *British Medical Journal* 305, pp.323–4.

8 Murphy E. (1997) 'The future of Britain's high security hospitals', *British Medical Journal* 314, pp.1292–3.

1.19.8 The SHSA's six objectives quoted above reflect a determination to address the problems of isolation, inadequate care and therapeutic pessimism. It is generally agreed that life within the hospitals has improved. The philosophy of the Patient's Charter has been extended to the high security sector, but ineptly. Ashworth has had its own Patients' Advocacy Service for several years (as recommended in the Blom-Cooper report). Patients' Councils are in place in each hospital and millions have been spent in upgrading the estate. The balance has shifted away from an overtly custodial ethos to one which professes to be therapeutic. Links have been forged with outside academic institutions, albeit not always successfully. And the creation of a purchaser-provider split has brought the hospitals greater freedom to run their own affairs, but whether they were ready for that is doubtful.

1.19.9 However, has the pendulum swung too far the other way, creating institutions which, although more like hospitals and less like prisons, now sit uneasily in the middle, unable to balance security and therapy appropriately? Our Inquiry prompts that question. So too does the review of Broadmoor, which took place shortly after our Inquiry was established.

1.20.0 The Broadmoor External Management Review

1.20.1 During February 1997 the then Secretary of State for Health, The Rt Hon Stephen. Dorrell MP was alerted to concerns expressed by staff associations about the security of Broadmoor Hospital, the alleged undue influence of the Patients' Council and the quality of patient care. There were allegations of drugs finds and a possible child pornography ring. Mr Dorrell ordered an External Management Review of the Hospital to investigate the truth or otherwise of the allegations. The Review, led by a senior official from the Anglia and Oxford Regional Office of the NHS Executive, took place in March 1997.

1.20.2 The Review team demonstrated that most of the allegations made so vociferously in the media were unfounded. They reported that substantial improvements had been made at Broadmoor since the damning 1988 HAS Report. They rejected the charge that the Patients' Council "ran the hospital". And they found that security was given a high profile at Broadmoor.

1.20.3 This Review also made a number of comments and recommendations pertinent to our own Inquiry. Thus the team pointed out that whilst all visitors were required to pass through an anti-metal detector, official visitors, such as solicitors and visiting health professionals, were not, nor were staff. There were no rub-down searches at all. The team recommended random rub-down searches of all staff and visitors. They also recommended introducing an X-ray machine to scan all bags and packages being brought into the hospital.

1.20.4 As will be seen these are recommendations we also make concerning Ashworth.

1.20.5 The team noted that the security manual was not comprehensive and required updating, a task which they regarded as a high priority. They were concerned that the Director of Security post was advisory only and lacked the requisite authority; they recommended that the Director of Security become a non-voting associate director of the Hospital Board.

1.20.6 We are also of the view that the Director of Security should be on the main Hospital Board.

1.20.7 The team found inconsistent practices as far as searching was concerned and heard that staff were afraid sometimes to search for fear of complaints from patients. Many patients had more than the Hospital limit of personal belongings in their rooms, making searching very difficult. The team recommended that it be made clear to staff that patient areas could and should be searched. The policy on personal belongings should be reinforced.

1.20.8 It will be seen hereafter that in our view security policies need to be enforced rather than reinforced.

1.20.9 The team pointed out that introducing a new therapeutic culture to the Hospital was heavily dependent upon the skills of Ward Managers. In some places clinical practice had moved forward, and in other places it had not.

1.20.10 Although the Patient's Charter had been introduced into the Hospital some years earlier, the team felt that senior managers had not given enough thought to how such a charter should be applied in a secure setting. This had led to the promotion of patients' rights at the expense of maintaining a safe and secure environment. They recommended redrafting the Charter to take into account the unique nature of Broadmoor.

1.20.11 The appropriateness of the contents of the Patient's Charter should also be reviewed for the whole high security sector.

1.20.12 There was a widespread perception amongst staff that patients used the complaints system to try to undermine staff. Some nurses told the team that they were reluctant to undertake basic security tasks for fear of a complaint. This perception was not well-grounded in fact, but it was a common feeling nevertheless.

1.20.13 It is also a common feeling at Ashworth.

1.20.14 The team examined the workings of the Patients' Council. Whilst rejecting the media allegations, the team pointed out that the Council was not representative of the general patient population, since most of the representatives suffered from personality disorder. They recommended that the working of the Council be reviewed to make it more representative of the patient population. See paragraph **2.29.7**. below regarding the recommendation we make concerning Ashworth Hospital.

1.20.15 This problem is by no means unique to Broadmoor.

1.20.16 The team noted that personality disordered patients were generally treated on the same wards as mentally ill patients, although there were several wards specializing in the treatment of personality disorder. Staff told the team that where more relaxed regimes were introduced on mixed wards psychotic patients appreciated the improvements, whereas personality disordered patients took advantage of them.

1.20.17 It will be seen that, in our judgement, patients with a sole or primary diagnosis of personality disorder should be managed in a separate high security facility.

1.20.18 The team reviewed internal and external communications within Broadmoor. Whilst praising the latter, the team saw internal communications as being rather more complex:

> "Broadmoor may be one hospital, but in practice it can be described as '23 federal institutions', each relating to wards in the hospital which seem to harbour a wide variety of practices in their interpretation and implementation of hospital policy."

1.20.19 The team concluded:

> "There seems to be a clear need to identify the policy and procedures which are non-negotiable across the whole hospital. For those policies and procedures which can be flexible to meet differing patient needs the extent of the latitude in interpretation should be clearly stated."

1.20.20 We find this to be not only essential but elementary.

1.20.21 The issues raised above are all germane to our own Inquiry. This Review demonstrates that the task of managing a large high security psychiatric hospital is a huge one, made more difficult in some respects by recent policy changes. Has the move towards creating a therapeutic environment gone too far? The existence of our Inquiry and the Broadmoor Management Review are vivid reminders of the need continually to pay attention to the first of the SHSA's six objectives, **ensuring the continuing safety of the public**.

1.20.22 We turn our attention now to Ashworth Hospital.

1.21.0 The History of Ashworth Hospital

1.21.1 Ashworth High Security Hospital is situated in Maghull, some ten miles north of Liverpool city centre. There has been a hospital on the site for over 100 years. Originally the estate was owned by a prominent local merchant, Thomas Harrison. In 1878 it was sold to the Liverpool Select Vestry, overseers of the Liverpool Workhouse, who used the large house as a convalescent home for children from Liverpool workhouses. Eventually a new hospital was planned as an epileptic colony and construction began in 1911. In 1914 the Lunacy Board of Control bought the whole estate, including a large unfinished hospital. Before it could be pressed into use as a State Institution, however, the Hospital was taken over for the treatment of shell-shocked soldiers from the Great War. In 1920 the Ministry of Pensions took the Hospital over and it was not until 1933 that the Hospital became a State Institution. In 1948 the Hospital became part of the new National Health Service and in 1959 the Ministry of Health took over responsibility for running the Special Hospitals.

1.21.2 The Hospital was enlarged from the 1920s by building on what is now Ashworth East. Further enlargement came in the 1970s when the decision was taken to build a fourth Special Hospital to relieve overcrowding at Broadmoor. There was still land available from the original estate in Maghull and 50 acres of land were made available for the new Park Lane Hospital. Park Lane opened in stages between 1974 and 1984. Unlike Moss Side, it was surrounded by a high security wall, completely separating it from the rest of the site. Moss Side and Park Lane shared some facilities but operated as independent hospitals.

1.21.3 One of the first acts of the new Special Hospitals Service Authority (SHSA) was to merge the two hospitals. On 19 February 1990 the new hospital, Ashworth, was born. The old Moss Side Hospital became known as Ashworth South and East, and Park Lane was renamed Ashworth North. Ashworth South, the original Moss Side Hospital, closed in 1995. There are now plans to build a prison on that site.

1.21.4 In March 1991, the Hospital was severely criticized in a *Cutting Edge* television programme alleging widespread abuse of mentally ill patients by staff at Ashworth. This led to a wide-ranging public inquiry, chaired by Sir Louis Blom-Cooper QC, which put forward 90 recommendations which amounted to no less than a clarion call for wholesale culture change at Ashworth. This led to a further reorganization of the Hospital and much work to try to change the culture of the institution.

1.21.5 In April 1996 the Hospital became a Special Hospital Authority when the High Security Psychiatric Services Commissioning Board succeeded the SHSA.

1.22.0 Ashworth Hospital Today

1.22.1 The total capacity of 520 beds was gradually reduced. As one of the three Special High Security Hospitals, Ashworth receives patients from the North of England, Wales, the West Midlands and North West London. Approximately 80 per cent of patients have been convicted of a criminal offence, most of whom are subject to restriction orders. The average length of stay is eight years, but a small number of patients will never be regarded as ready to leave and will spend the rest of their lives at Ashworth.

1.22.2 Ashworth Hospital today consists of two sites, Ashworth East and Ashworth North. Ashworth East consists of six refurbished wards, two newly built wards and the Wordsworth Ward, a new 16-bedded "ward" consisting of four separate four-bedded flats. It has a total capacity of approximately 150 patients. All of Ashworth's female patients are located on the East Site, as well as a large number of mentally ill men. Physical security is provided by a high wire wall.

1.22.3 Ashworth North has 17 wards with a total capacity of approximately 370 patients. The Personality Disorder Unit and most of the male mental illness wards are located on the North Site, which also contains extensive recreational, rehabilitative and educational facilities. It is surrounded by a high concrete wall providing very considerable physical security.

1.22.4 The total capacity of 520 beds was gradually reduced. As of 12 February 1997 there were 478 patients within the Hospital as a whole, 427 men and 51 women. 79 (16.5%) had come from Medium Secure Units, 158 (33.1%) from the prison system and 105 (21.9%) from the Crown Court. A further 80 (16.7%) had come from other Special Hospitals. The largest single legal classification was mental illness (284, 59.4%), followed by psychopathic disorder (136, 28.6%). 20 patients (4.2%) had a legal classification of mental impairment and five (1%) one of severe mental impairment. A number of other patients had dual classifications, the most significant being mental illness with a secondary classification of psychopathic disorder (24 patients, 5% of the hospital). 77% of patients were subject to restriction orders.

1.22.5 The Hospital employs approximately 1,500 staff, the majority (more than 900) being nurses. Over 60 per cent of the nurses are qualified .

1.23.0 The Personality Disorder Unit

1.23.1 The Personality Disorder Unit (PDU) came into its present form in April 1994, bringing together male patients diagnosed as suffering from a personality disorder onto six Wards, namely Lawrence, Macaulay, Newman, Owen, Ruskin and Shelley. Lawrence and Owen had already cared for personality disordered patients since the 1980s, Owen (previously Forster) Ward caring for younger PD patients and Lawrence older men.

1.23.2 The decision to create a PDU was taken in the wake of the Blom-Cooper Inquiry. A Task Force was set up to oversee implementation of the Report, in particular, the creation of a new, more therapeutic ethos. As we shall see, the Task Force pointed to problems of outdated attitudes, anti-therapeutic care, professional isolation and resulting recruitment difficulties and bureaucratic and over-interfering management. They argued for the creation of a new, more patient-centred culture, with effective multi-disciplinary working and greater delegation. The Task Force recommended restructuring the Hospital into generalist mental illness units relating to specific geographical areas, and specialist units. One of the specialist units proposed was a unit for men classified as suffering from psychopathic disorder.

1.23.3 Even at the time this was recognized to be a bold, perhaps foolhardy step. Those classified as "psychopathically disordered" (in legal terms) or "personality disordered" (in clinical terms) have an unenviable reputation for being difficult and resistant to treatment. As we describe in detail in Part Six, personality disorder is little understood; there is little consensus as to the nature of the disorder, its management and treatment and, indeed, its treatability. Furthermore, the men in the PDU at Ashworth are at the severest end of the spectrum of personality disorder. Most, if not all, have extremely disordered personalities and many have a history of very serious violent and sexual offending. They tend to test boundaries between staff and patients to destruction and undermine, sometimes even corrupt their carers and therapists. Very few services within the NHS have any kind of specialist expertise in the care and management of personality disordered patients, let

alone severely personality disordered patients. Thus putting together over 100 highly disordered men in just six wards was not something to be done lightly.

1.23.4 That said, the patients in the PDU are not a homogeneous group. They have various offending histories (indeed not every PDU patient has a criminal conviction, as we shall see below); their clinical diagnoses differ, as do the sections of the Mental Health Act under which they are detained; the management problems they present vary and they have very different prognoses. Not all by any means are detained under the "Psychopathic Disorder" label.

1.23.5 We feel it is important to understand a little more about the nature of the patient group on the PDU. In what follows we first give a statistical snapshot of the Unit on 12 February 1997, less than a week after the establishment of our Inquiry. We then summarize the evidence of a number of patients from the PDU about their treatment, and about life on the Unit.

1.23.6 We do not accept these patients' evidence uncritically. A patient's views on his or her treatment needs and suitability for discharge must be treated with extreme caution. That said, the views expressed to us were not all negative by any means. We do believe their testimony offers a very useful overview of the PDU from the patients' perspective.

1.24.0 A Snapshot of the PDU, 12 February 1997

1.24.1 On that day 112 patients were on the Unit, on six wards. This was slightly under a quarter of the whole hospital population of 478. Lawrence Ward, described in security terms as coping with High Security and Long Term Medium Security patients, had 18 patients on the day in question (all wards have a maximum occupancy of 25). Macaulay, described as caring for Long Term Medium Security patients, had 22 of its 25 beds occupied. Newman, housing patients with a mixture of High Secure and Low Dependency High Security needs, had 17 patients. Owen, Ruskin and Shelley were all described as High Security Wards; Owen had 21 patients, Ruskin 20 patients and Shelley 14. Shelley Ward was to close during the course of our hearings.

1.24.2 Of the 112 patients, 41 (37%) had come from the prison system and 31 (28%) direct from the courts. 21 (19%) had come for another Special Hospital. Only ten had come from Medium Secure Units (compared to 79 of the patients in the Hospital as a whole). There were also some civilly-committed patients.

1.24.3 86 patients had a pure psychopathic disorder classification, but 25 did not have a primary classification of psychopathic disorder. 13 had a mental illness legal classification. Outside the PDU there were 54 patients, 28 men and 26 women, with a psychopathic disorder component to their legal classification.

1.24.4 77 of the PDU's patient population were on section 37/41 orders, 19 on section 47/49 orders and one was on a section 46 order. 97 (87%) were therefore subject to restriction orders, or were treated as if restricted. This compared to a Hospital-wide rate of 77%. 106 of the 112 patients were white.

1.24.5 The average age on admission to the PDU was 30, a year younger than in Ashworth as a whole. The average length of stay was, however, a year longer (nine rather than eight years). Comparison of the average age of admission, current age and length of stay demonstrated that the patient population in the PDU was for the most part static, apart from Newman Ward.

1.24.6 Of the 22 patients across the Hospital who had been assessed by external units for transfer at that point, 15 had been referred back as unsuitable. None of the five personality disordered patients referred to NHS facilities had been accepted. Whilst a similar percentage of personality disordered patients and patients as a whole were in the transfer process (approximately 30%) many of the personality disordered patients remained in the early stages, with care teams finding it difficult to identify units prepared to accept such patients.

1.24.7 During the period 1 April 1996 to 12 February 1997 only ten patients were discharged from the PDU (8% of the 122 patients within the Unit during the year) compared to 81 across the Hospital (14.5% of the 559 patients within the Hospital over this time). Four of the ten went to a Medium Secure Unit, compared to 39 across the Hospital.

1.24.8 One can conclude from this that the PDU draws its patients largely from the courts and prisons and has a relatively dangerous population (using the proportion of restricted patients as an indicator of dangerousness). Perhaps as a result the Hospital has found it difficult to transfer patients to other NHS facilities, with the result that the PDU has a relatively static population, with a longer average length of stay compared to the rest of the Hospital. There were very few patients in the PDU from the ethnic minority population.

1.24.9 It is well known that people of black and other ethnic minority origins are represented in prison and psychiatric hospitals in a higher proportion than their representation in the population. We have noted the studies summarised in the Reed Review[9] which have established that black people are more likely than white people to be:

(i) apprehended by the police on suspicion of committing a crime;

(ii) charged with a criminal offence rather than be cautioned;

(iii) less likely to receive bail; and

(iv) more likely to receive a custodial sentence.

Studies over the past 25 years also show that black people who come to the attention of psychiatric services are more likely than white people to be:

(i) removed by the police to a place of safety under section 136 of the Mental Health Act 1983;

(ii) detained in a hospital under sections 2,3, and 4 of the 1983 Act;

(iii) be detained in locked wards of psychiatric hospitals;

(iv) receive higher doses of medication.

They are less likely to:

(i) receive appropriate and acceptable diagnoses or treatment for possible mental illness at an early stage;

(ii) receive treatments such as psychotherapy or counselling.

It is surprising to find these groups are under-represented in the PDU. The Reed Review in a discussion paper said that "a number of studies have shown that patients from minority ethnic communities receive an inferior or discriminatory service and stereotyping is common." Professor Bluglass questioned most of our expert witnesses about this but none could provide an explanation.

Recommendation 1 **1.24.10 We recommend that the service needs of individuals from minority ethnic groups who suffer from severe personality disorder should be the subject of further study.**

9 *Review of health and social services for mentally disordered offenders and others requiring similar services* (1992) (Chairman Dr John Reed CB), *Services for People from Black and Ethnic Minority Groups: Issues of Race and Culture: A discussion paper.* London: Department of Health and Home Office.

1.25.0 The Patients' Evidence

1.25.1 We asked nine patients in all to give evidence to us, representing a sample of the patients on the PDU. This sample group was selected by the patients' legal representatives and we are grateful to them for their work in this matter.

Patient A

1.25.2 This patient was 29 years old. He had a history of manic depression and had tried to harm himself, but had never been convicted of a criminal offence. After attempting to set fire to his parents' house he had been admitted to hospital, absconded, then was detained under section 2 of the Act. He was assessed by a team from his local MSU and transferred there. After the 28 days assessment period allowed under section 2 expired he was detained under section 3 and was diagnosed as suffering from psychopathic disorder. After four months at the MSU, during which time he was disruptive, he was transferred to Ashworth Hospital in May 1994.

1.25.3 Patient A was thoroughly disenchanted with the Hospital and made a number of criticisms. He complained about the mix of patients on the wards: new patients were mixed with men who had been in the Hospital 20 years or more, were fiercely critical of the system and who thereby undermined the treatment prospects of newly admitted patients. Treatment was minimal: the main therapy he received was from his primary nurse, with occasional sessions from a psychologist. The only time other PCT members took an interest was when a Tribunal, care programming meeting or deadline for re-sectioning approached. Yet the primary nurse, who had spent most time with a patient, would have very little say at such meetings. When a psychologist had written a report saying that the treatment he needed was not available at Ashworth at present it was, as far as he could see, ignored. Despite the views of some members of the PCT that he did not need high security, the RMOs were able to keep him in regardless.

1.25.4 The power held by doctors was made worse in his case by the turnover of RMOs, which disrupted progress. He had had a total of six RMOs in under five years, including several locums, who were reluctant to make any positive decisions about discharge or LOA trips. His current RMO had forgotten that his section was up for renewal and a locum RMO had had to do the necessary paperwork, despite the fact she did not work on his ward.

1.25.5 Patient A's view of his continuing detention was that it was based not on actual behaviour but on comments he had made during therapy sessions. This left him in what he described as a "no-win situation":

> "Basically what ends up happening is the more you tell them, the more sort of ammunition, if you like, they have got to use against you at the Tribunal. At first I was open and honest and told them all the things I thought were relevant. Then once I was transferred here it became apparent that talking was actually a bad thing and basically it has got to the stage now where I tell them absolutely nothing. In fact I do not cooperate with treatment now."

The nature of his section meant, in his view, that there was a constant need to search for new reasons for continuing his detention. Hence his reluctance to give the Hospital "ammunition". He did not see either the MHAC or the Hospital Mental Health Act Managers as potential sources of help, as neither could challenge the RMO's clinical decisions.

1.25.6 In his statement to us Patient A challenged the label "psychopathic disorder", which was in his view very unclear. He was being detained in hospital for treatment, but there was great uncertainty as to whether he was in fact "treatable"; this uncertainty was only resolved it seems at the time of Tribunal hearings. The well-known reluctance of MSUs to take personality disordered patients meant that a move on to medium security was very difficult to arrange, leaving him with no idea of when he might leave the Hospital. This contrasted with the position for most prisoners. Lastly, he criticized the Hospital for not being more open and honest with him and his family about the reasons why he was being detained and what they were trying to do for him.

Patient B

1.25.7 Patient B was 38 years of age, a former soldier who had been discharged following psychiatric problems and had subsequently committed manslaughter of a member of his family and arson. He was charged with murder, but accepted the offer to plead guilty to manslaughter by way of diminished responsibility, with a place at a secure hospital. He was initially admitted to Broadmoor in 1986 on a section 37/41 hospital order with restrictions under a mental illness classification. In 1987 he was transferred to Ashworth with a number of other Broadmoor patients. Since then he had been on a number of wards in what is now the PDU, treated in effect as a personality disordered patient, but his legal classification remained unchanged, as he was regarded as being vulnerable to psychosis in certain conditions.

1.25.8 Patient B was broadly speaking positive about what the Hospital had done for him. He had recognized he had problems and had embraced whatever treatment was available to him, with the result that he had been recommended for a transfer to a medium secure unit in 1990. In the event this transfer took five years to arrange. There were no beds available, then one became available, but the Home Office insisted on a further assessment. By the time this was done the bed had disappeared and the wait began again.

1.25.9 When the transfer finally came in 1995 it was not successful. Part of the problem was that the MSU had relatively few personality disordered patients, staff were not so used to them and there were fewer facilities available. He returned to Ashworth at his own request. A further transfer to another MSU had now been arranged, but was still awaiting Home Office approval at the time we heard evidence from Patient B, some six months after the request had been made.

1.25.10 Patient B told us that he had not had a problem in accessing the treatment he felt he needed, although he had reservations about some of the group work offered. For example, an anger management group he attended was led by a psychologist who was known to have had a fight with another psychologist in the hospital car park. This rather undermined the therapeutic value of the group. He was also concerned about the caseload RMOs were carrying, reducing the time they could realistically spend with patients. He saw nurses as more security guards than therapists. And he was critical of the lack of power held by MHRTs, which in his case had repeatedly recommended transfers to a MSU, with little success.

1.25.11 Patient B made the point to us that isolating personality disordered patients in a large group had its problems. One was the problem of moving on, discussed above, when the mix of patients in the average MSU was very different from the PDU at Ashworth. He was aware of a number of other patients who had had similar difficulty in adapting to a MSU regime. Secondly, putting personality disordered patients together also in one sense created a "better psychopath". In order to survive amongst manipulative, clever personality disordered patients one learnt the "tricks of the trade". Finally, mixing relatively new and enthusiastic patients with men who did not accept they had problems and who were not willing to engage in therapy damaged the treatment opportunities of others who did wish to engage. Those patients who were resistant to treatment would be better off in prison.

1.25.12 We asked Patient B about the recent security clamp-down. He felt this had succeeded in getting rid of the gang culture, in almost eradicating pornography and in reducing drug use, although he did not think the latter could be eradicated completely. He was critical of the blanket restriction that had been imposed because of the behaviour of a few.

Patient C

1.25.13 Patient C was 47 years of age. He had been convicted of rape and burglary and sent to Rampton in 1970, where the regime was, in his words, brutal. In 1981 he was conditionally discharged to a low security unit. In October 1981 he absconded whilst on unescorted parole and re-offended in a similar fashion to his original offence. He was sentenced to 14 years imprisonment but not released from his previous hospital order with restrictions, although he was given a conditional discharge from the hospital order in 1985. Patient C's earliest date of release (EDR) was in February 1991; some two years before that he was seen by a various psychiatrists, including Dr Strickland, with a view to a recall to hospital. Dr Strickland advised against admitting Patient C to Ashworth, as in his view he was not treatable, although he did regard him as a danger to women. Any return to Special Hospital would therefore amount to preventive detention. But on the actual day of his EDR Patient C was transferred to Ashworth.

1.25.14 Patient C was understandably very angry about this decision. The opportunity had been there to recall him to hospital back in 1981; it had not been taken. No psychiatrist appears to have been confident about his "treatability". No one had told him that he could have applied to a Mental Health Review Tribunal whilst in prison to have his hospital order removed. Once in Ashworth Dr Strickland had told him that the Hospital had been forced to accept him by the Home Office. Despite this his RMO had opposed a conditional discharge at his most recent MHRT in 1995. His treatment had been limited whilst in Ashworth to a number of hours of psychology work, although he had been offered, and rejected, a place on a sex offenders group. He regarded his detention in Ashworth as purely preventive detention.

1.25.15 Patient C thought that roughly half of the patients on his ward wanted treatment and half did not, but the lack of treatment options left people deteriorating. He thought that most personality disordered offenders should be in prison.

Patient D

1.25.16 Patient D was almost 55 years old. He had been sent to Broadmoor in 1963 after committing two murders; had he been a little older at the time he would probably have been hanged. He was in Broadmoor for some 18 years until July 1981 when he was transferred to Ashworth, where he had remained ever since. A few months after he arrived at Ashworth he saw Dr McCulloch, who told him that he would have to start from scratch as far as treatment was concerned, to which he responded by saying he would not comply with any treatment. Since then he had never had in his view any active treatment whatsoever. He occupied his weekdays in the print shop. The greatest benefit he had received had been from discussing matters with fellow patients.

1.25.17 Patient D firmly believed he would die in Ashworth. He saw prison as a far better alternative than hospital for people like him, given that he would never have served 34 years in prison. He told us that he never discouraged younger patients from giving treatment a try, as he felt he had done at Broadmoor, although he warned them about the long waits to gain a transfer to a medium secure unit.

Patient E

1.25.18 Patient E was almost 44 when he gave evidence. He had a series of offences against women, which had led to a four year sentence from 1975 to 1979. In 1986 he had re-offended, attacking a teenage girl. He was given a life sentence, despite expert psychiatric opinion that he should be given a hospital order with restrictions. Having appealed successfully against the sentence he came to Ashworth on a hospital order in November 1987. At that time he had denied that he had problems, although he eventually realized this was not the case.

1.25.19 He was generally positive about the treatment Ashworth had offered him, although he was very critical of one psychologist who had consistently cancelled appointments. He had attended a number of groups, including anger management and a sex offenders group; the latter in particular was helpful in forcing him to confront what he had done in a way he would never have done in prison, where sex offenders were regarded with great loathing. He himself had never regarded himself before as a sex offender. Prison had not worked in his case as he had simply re-offended when released. Nothing had been done to try to address the causes of his offending. Ashworth had been very different. He believed this kind of group could only really work well within a hospital, where there was much less stigma attached to particular offences.

1.25.20 Patient E agreed with the suggestion that it was up to the patient to want to participate in treatment. But he did not see the mix of patients between those who wanted treatment and those who did not as a particular problem.

1.25.21 Despite his general enthusiasm, Patient E did have a number of criticisms of the Ashworth regime. He disliked for example the blanket ban on various activities following the absconsion by Mr Daggett. He criticized the way in which ward policies varied for no good reason, for example with regard to limits on possessions. And he criticized the lack of imaginative treatments which gave patients experiences which helped them move forward. He quoted the example of a fellow patient who was terrified of the idea of climbing stairs, because in all his years at Ashworth he had never climbed stairs, Ashworth being almost entirely on one level. He also told us that he had had little contact with his RMOs over the years, even before Tribunal hearings.

1.25.22 Patient E was broadly supportive of 24-hour opening. He occasionally had nightmares and welcomed the opportunity to make himself a cup of tea, or have a cigarette and talk to nursing staff.

Patient F

1.25.23 Patient F was almost 50 years old. He had been sent to Broadmoor on a hospital order with restrictions in 1972 after being convicted of the manslaughter of his sister, an offence involving firearms. He stayed at Broadmoor for 21 years before receiving a conditional discharge in 1993 to a medium secure unit. He was broadly complimentary of the treatment he had received in Broadmoor, but found the MSU a great change, not least because it was far more restrictive than Broadmoor had been. In 1995 he moved into a hostel, but complained about the lack of support from the MSU and hostel staff. That same year Patient F acquired, quite legally, some deactivated firearms. The police investigated and concluded no offence had been committed, but Patient F was told he had breached the conditions of his discharge and was recalled to Ashworth in October 1995.

1.25.24 Patient F applied for a Tribunal hearing and was given an independent psychiatric assessment. That doctor concluded that he should be given a conditional discharge back to the MSU. However, this report was disregarded. This made him feel very bitter. Since arriving in Ashworth Patient F told us that he had been recommended for a full psychological assessment on several occasions. As far as he was aware this had not been done. Recommendations to maintain links with the MSU had also been ignored, as far as he could see. He had seen his first RMO, Dr Strickland, three times in two years and not seen his new RMO in five months for a one-to-one conversation, despite a request under the Patient's

Charter (we should point out this was contested by the Counsel for the Hospital). Although there was in theory an opportunity to see Dr Strickland before PCT meetings, in practice he never allowed time for this to happen. Patient F told us that most patients complained they were never able to see their RMO.

1.25.25 At the time he gave evidence Patient F told us he was not attending any groups nor was he receiving any psychology input. He thought the treatment he had received in Broadmoor had been far better than that in Ashworth and was critical of the PDU, preferring the mix of patients in Broadmoor. He took the view that personality disordered patients tended to help those who were mentally ill.

1.25.26 Despite having spent almost 25 years in the High Security Hospitals Patient F was in favour of the hospital system in the right circumstances. He felt his treatment at Broadmoor had helped him change and develop as a person, whereas in prison he would have just developed a criminal mentality. Hospitals could be therapeutic communities in a way in which prisons never could be; after some therapy sessions it was essential to talk and have support, rather than be locked up in a cell.

Patient G

1.25.27 Patient G was 22 years of age when he gave evidence. He had a history of trouble with the police and had come to Ashworth for an assessment under section 38 of the Act in June 1996. He was formally admitted under a section 37/41 hospital order in November of that year. Although during assessment he was seen by numerous people, since admission he had received little active treatment, save for a session with a psychologist once every week or so, and psychosexual treatment. In August 1997 he had had his first CPA Review, which recommended a neuropsychological assessment, cognitive skills work and further psychological interventions. He had been told there was a two-year waiting list for neuropsychological assessments, and neither the cognitive skills work or other psychological interventions had commenced. He found it very surprising that a so-called specialist hospital could identify treatment needs but not provide them. (It was pointed out to us by Counsel for the Hospital that other items of the treatment plan could precede the neuropsychological assessment.)

1.25.28 Patient G told us that he passed the time sleeping on the ward if he was not working. He told us he was ready to participate in groups; it was up to the doctors to sort them out. He had now accepted he needed help for his behavioural difficulties. He was not impressed by the treatment at Ashworth but felt that he saw his RMO reasonably frequently.

Patient H

1.25.29 Patient H was 37 years of age when he gave evidence. He had been convicted of manslaughter and came to Ashworth on a hospital order with restrictions in 1989. He told us that he had benefited from a number of therapeutic groups which, although not suitable for everyone, nevertheless could be good with the right people leading them and patients who wished to participate. He had also received high quality individual psychotherapy. That said, he was angry that it had taken several years before a psychologist's view that he did not require high security was supported. He was at present hoping to move to a MSU.

1.25.30 Patient H described the despair he and others felt at times by not knowing when one might get out of hospital:

> "That is the worst part of being a special hospital patient. You are sentenced to natural life imprisonment in a mental institution and from there . . . it is down to a lottery whether you ever get out: whether your doctor is competent, whether the RSU doctor likes you and is competent, whether the RSU wants you considering the

pressures on RSU beds now, and, again, going back to treatment, a lot of people just do not receive the appropriate treatment.

"And security is overtaking treatment. Indeed, on the PDU now treatment is being abandoned for the sake of security, simply because there is another Inquiry going on. So there are so many problems, so many frustrations and you watch year after year of your life going down the toilet and, no, you do not see an end to this . . ."

It was no wonder, Patient H concluded, that some patients turned to alcohol and drugs, just as people did anywhere. He knew of people whose health declined whilst waiting. It was a situation he feared being in himself.

1.25.31 Patient H was very critical of management as a whole and called for Ashworth to become a genuine hospital. He was extremely critical of Dr Strickland, whom he blamed for ignoring warnings about the patient who killed Mr Williams and for allowing Owen Ward to get out of control. He made a plea for patients to be treated as individuals rather than being lumped together as "mental illness patients" or "personality disordered patients". While the concept of a specialist unit to treat patients with a whole multitude of problems had merit, the personality disorder label itself was meaningless and should be dropped.

Patients' Council

1.25.32 We also received a submission from the Patients' Council and heard evidence from its Chairman, Patient M. The Patients' Council criticized our terms of reference for being restricted to the working of the PDU, arguing that the overall level of care and treatment for all patients within the Hospital was no better than that prevailing at the time of the Blom-Cooper Inquiry, and that patients throughout the Hospital experienced great difficulties in accessing the treatments which had been recommended for them. In particular, mentally ill patients suffered just as much as personality disordered patients from a lack of access to non-pharmacological treatments such as psychological treatments. The Council criticized the quality of medical reports which, in their view, merely rehashed old reports. They alleged that the Home Office was only interested in their cases when a patient was seriously considered for transfer or discharge. They accused other services of creating a number of obstacles to Special Hospital patients moving on to lower security establishments. But if the Hospital were to start consistently offering patients well-planned and coordinated multi-disciplinary care of the kind they had been prescribed then patients would respond.

1.25.33 When he gave evidence Patient M told us that misuse of drugs and alcohol, financial irregularities and the availability of pornographic material had always been a feature of the Hospital, although he did note that the recent tightening-up of security had had a marked effect, judging by the very high asking price of pornography. The information he had was that pornography had all but been eradicated as a result of the more intensive searching regime.

1.25.34 The evidence of these patients raises important issues, such as access to treatment, patient mix, inadequate services, the relative merits of hospital and prison and the current legal framework. Overall they gave a sense of time passing with precious little progress. Such an atmosphere of inertia creates the kind of situation in which poor practice, apathy and corruption can flourish.

1.26.0 The Local Community

1.26.1 Ashworth Hospital is located within Maghull, about ten miles outside the centre of Liverpool. We were invited by Maghull Town Council to visit them to hear their views on the Hospital, which we did on Thursday 5 February 1998. Two councillors, Councillor Bamber and Councillor Robertson, gave evidence. The views they expressed were not dissimilar to the evidence of many other witnesses during the course of the Inquiry.

1.26.2 Both councillors pressed upon us the importance of the Hospital to the local communities. But they also stressed the concerns, particularly about security, which local residents expressed to them, and the need for residents to feel confident in the management of the Hospital. The spate of absconsions in the latter part of 1996, that by Mr Daggett being just one, had fuelled their fears. The Council had also picked up suggestions that staff were afraid to speak out and that there was a confrontational relationship between management and staff associations. Mr Robertson suggested that the pace of change since the previous inquiry had possibly proved too great to handle.

1.27.0 The Mental Health Act Commission

1.27.1 The Mental Health Act Commission has a statutory remit to visit detained patients and Mental Health Review Tribunals are independent quasi-judicial bodies charged with reviewing the continued justification for the detention of detained patients. We discuss both below. We include for convenience in this part of our Report the Social Services Inspectorate of the Department of Health, which has an independent inspectorial function. The SSI carried out reviews of the social work services at the three hospitals in 1993.

1.27.2 The origins of the Mental Health Act Commission (MHAC) go back to the Commissioners in Lunacy, first appointed in 1774, and the Board of Control, which lasted from 1913 until the 1959 Mental Health Act. Between 1959 and 1983, when the Commission was established as a Special Health Authority, there was no organization charged with visiting psychiatric hospitals and safeguarding the rights of detained patients. The periodic scandals in psychiatric hospitals in the 1960s and 1970s increased pressure for an independent body to promote the rights of detained patients and to promote high standards of care (the creation of the HAS in 1969 was an early response to this pressure); eventually the MHAC came into being in September 1983. In what follows we draw heavily upon the Commission's written evidence.

1.27.3 The MHAC's statutory and other responsibilities can be summarised as follows:

(i) to keep under review the operation of the Mental Health Act 1983 in respect of patients liable to be detained under the Act;

(ii) to visit and interview, in private, patients detained under the Act in hospitals and mental nursing homes;

(iii) to investigate complaints which fall within the Commission's remit;

(iv) to review decisions to withhold the mail of patients detained in the Special Hospitals;

(v) to appoint medical practitioners and others to give second opinions in cases where this is required by the Act;

(vi) to publish a report every two years;

(vii) to monitor the implementation of the Code of Practice and propose amendments to Ministers; and

(viii) to offer advice to Ministers on matters falling within the Commission's remit.

1.27.4 Until 1995, the Commission was comprised of approximately 90 part-time Commissioners (appointed by the Secretary of State for Health or the Secretary of State for Wales) drawn from the clinical professions, social work, lay people and the law. From 1 November 1995 Commission membership increased to approximately 190 members and visiting members. On average, Commissioners contribute three days per month to Commission activities. The Commission Secretariat is located in Nottingham and its 35 staff work under the direction of the Chief Executive.

1.27.5 The Commission undertakes its responsibilities on behalf of the Secretary of State and occasionally exercises its right to draw matters of serious concern to the formal and direct attention of the Secretary of State. The Commission meets Ministers once a year to discuss its work and liaises on a regular basis with officials of the Department of Health, principally about matters relating to finance, personnel and the appointment of members to the Commission.

1.27.6 Two of the Commission's statutory responsibilities are of particular relevance to the matters being considered by our Inquiry – visiting and complaints.

Visiting

1.27.7 The Commission's statutory responsibility to review the operation of the Mental Health Act 1983 and visit and interview in private detained patients can be found at section 120(l) of the Act:

> "The Secretary of State will keep under review the exercise of the power and discharge of the duties conferred or imposed by this Act so far as relating to the detention of patients or to patients liable to be detained under this Act and shall make arrangements for persons authorised by him in that behalf
>
> > a. To visit and interview in private patients detained under this Act in hospitals and mental nursing homes . . ."

1.27.8 For each High Security Hospital the Commission has a panel of Commissioners responsible for undertaking the Commission's statutory duties to visit and also to review the withholding of patients' mail. The Commission panel is led by a Convenor (a member of the Commission) and, until 1 November 1995, one member of the panel also took responsibility for the undertaking of the Commission's statutory responsibilities to investigate complaints. Thereafter, overall responsibility for the investigation of complaints was transferred to a member of the Commission based in Nottingham who maintains close liaison with the panel about complaints from Ashworth patients.

1.27.9 The Commission's role is visitorial rather than inspectorial. It is primarily concerned with the operation of the Act and the treatment of detained patients. This limits the extent to which the Commission can become involved in organizational and managerial issues. Such matters are relevant to the work of the Commission only to the extent that they are directly connected with either or both of the Commission's primary concerns. It is this that most clearly distinguishes the visitorial from the inspectorial approach. The Commission's right of access to documents is defined (and limited) by the terms of DHSS Circular HC(83)19, which empowers any person authorized by the Mental Health Act Commission for the purpose of carrying out any review mentioned in Section 120(l) of the Mental Health Act 1983 to:

> " . . . require the production of and inspect any records *relating to the detention or treatment* of any person who is or has been detained in a hospital for which the Authority is responsible." (Italics added.)

1.27.10 The right of access is therefore strictly speaking limited to documents relating to patients' detention and treatment. In practice the hospitals also provide the Commission with copies of various internal policy and procedure documents as a matter of courtesy and in recognition of the collaborative nature of the relationship with the visiting Commissioners, but they reserve the right to withhold documents they do not wish the Commission to see. The Commission's limited right of access to documents is another illustration of the difference between the Commission's current role and that of an inspectorate.

1.27.11 The visiting process has been significantly refined since the reorganization of the Commission in 1995. Each of the High Security Hospitals has been allocated a panel of

Commissioners whose primary responsibility is to visit the designated hospital on a more regular and frequent basis than was formerly the case. This arrangement has enabled the visiting Commissioners to become more familiar with the Hospital, more recognisable to the staff and more accessible and better known to the patients. Since the Commission's reorganization the Ashworth panel of Commissioners has been divided into four visiting teams. Teams 1 and 2 visit the 12 wards of the Mental Health Directorate, Team 3 visits the six wards of the Personality Disorder Unit (PDU) and Team 4 visits the other seven wards in the Special Needs Directorate. Ms Breach, the current convenor of the PDU visiting team, told us that the changes had led to a more consistent pattern of visiting, which had led to increased respect from patients and staff.

1.27.12 The purpose of visiting High Security Hospitals is to meet detained patients, either individually or in groups; to observe the conditions in which they are detained; to examine the patients' statutory documentation; to monitor and advise on the application of the Act and the Code of Practice; and to review decisions to withhold a postal packet addressed to a patient. Although the Commission's aim is for each patient in the High Security Hospitals to be contacted and given the opportunity to meet a member of the Commission at least once a year, many patients are seen much more frequently. Meetings with patients can be very time consuming and on many visits there is little time for the examination of documents and for discussions with the manager and staff of the wards. The latter however are very useful in helping to keep Commissioners abreast of changes to the ward regime. They also give an opportunity to clarify and, sometimes, to resolve issues raised by patients in the course of their meetings with Commissioners.

1.27.13 The teams visit each ward at least once every two months (in comparison Medium Secure Units are routinely visited twice a year and other units holding detained patients are normally visited only three times in a two year period). A letter is subsequently sent to the ward manager if any matters have arisen during the course of the visit which require his attention. Most visits are undertaken in accordance with a previously notified programme and take place between 9 am and 5 pm, but arrangements are also made for wards and other facilities to be visited in the evenings and at weekends. The Commission requires that at least 20 per cent of all visits to High Security Hospitals are unannounced.

1.27.14 The visiting teams have a formal meeting with the relevant Clinical Director, together with representatives of the clinical team of each of the wards they visit, at least twice a year. A written report of the visiting teams' activities and their findings is also sent to each Clinical Director every six months. The Convenor and the visiting team leaders meet the Hospital Executive Group twice a year and there is an annual meeting of the Commission and the Hospital Authority, which is attended by the Chairman of both organizations. The Commission was lukewarm in its written evidence about the degree of cooperation it had received in its dealings with the Hospital Executive Group, noting that whilst requests for information had been well received, the information itself had often not followed. Ms Breach, said that the meetings had not been very productive in the past, although this situation had improved under Mr Millar.

1.27.15 Given the pressure of time and other resources the visiting Commissioners' activities are usually, but not exclusively, reactive in nature and the issues raised by the patients largely determine priorities. The Commission allocates additional resources to enable thematic reviews and other projects to be undertaken. The issues examined by the Ashworth Panel of Commissioners within the last two years include the misuse of drugs, the quality of seclusion facilities and the related documentation, and the techniques used to control and restrain violent patients. In relation to the Owen Ward Inquiry, Mr Paterson told us that the MHAC had told the Security Department of their concerns over illicit substances coming into the

Hospital. There had been several meetings with them on the subject at which different strategies to tackle the problem were discussed.

1.27.16 The Commission stressed to us in their written evidence that despite a significant increase in the consistency of attendance, and in the frequency and regularity of visits to the High Security Hospitals, the limitations imposed by the statutory remit determine the extent to which the Commission can adopt a more proactive operating procedure.

Complaints

1.27.17 The Commission's remit to investigate complaints is set out at section 120(l)(b)(i) and (ii) of the Act:

> "... to investigate –
>
> (i) any complaint made by a person in respect of a matter that occurred while he was detained under this Act in a hospital or mental nursing home and which he considers has not been satisfactorily dealt with by the managers of that hospital or mental nursing home; and
>
> (ii) any other complaint as to the exercise of the powers or the discharge of the duties conferred or imposed by this Act in respect of a person who is or has been so detained."

1.27.18 The Commission's current Complaints Policy and Procedure was adopted in September 1996 and the Complaints Coordinator, who is a member of the Commission based in the Nottingham office, takes overall responsibility for the Commission's pursuit of its complaints remit. He is assisted by a small team of Commissioners who undertake any investigations that may be required. Since the introduction by the SHSA of a common complaints policy for all three hospitals in 1992 fewer complaints by patients at Ashworth have had to be investigated by the Commission. A number of other grievances which have been drawn to the Commission's attention have subsequently been referred for processing through the Hospital Complaints Procedure.

1.27.19 Prior to April 1996, the operation of the Hospital Complaints Procedure was monitored by the Convenor of each High Security Hospital's visiting panel. The monitoring function is now undertaken by a specially appointed Commissioner who visits each of the High Security Hospitals at least once a quarter, reviews the procedures and scrutinizes a random selection of individual complaints files. A written report of his findings is sent to the Hospital's Complaints Manager and copies are sent to the Complaints Coordinator, the Convenor of the appropriate visiting panel and to the High Security Psychiatric Services Commissioning Board.

1.28.0 The Commission and the Impact of the Blom-Cooper Inquiry

1.28.1 The Commission told us that following the publication of the Ashworth Hospital Inquiry Report in 1992, visiting Commissioners became aware that many members of the staff had recognized the need to exercise control in a less authoritarian and autocratic manner. However, it soon became clear that a significant minority were adopting a more passive approach to exercising their authority, despite the risk of control problems, using the pretext that they might again be accused of using oppressive measures to control patients. The Commission interpreted this as a device to demonstrate the need for staff to reassert their authority and thus discredit some of the criticisms contained in the Blom-Cooper Report. This unreasonably defensive attitude gradually diminished with time, but visiting Commissioners believed that it had contributed to the tendency for patients to resist engaging in therapy, for example by staying in bed in the mornings and remaining on the wards rather than attending workshops.

1.28.2 The Commission told us that in their experience most members of staff did believe there had been a significant change in the ethos of the Hospital since the publication of the Blom-Cooper Inquiry Report, and that many would acknowledge that the change had been for the better. However, the Commission did note that the Hospital appeared to have been in a state of almost permanent organizational flux.

1.29.0 The Commission and the Personality Disorder Unit

1.29.1 The initial response of the Ashworth Panel was that the PDU seemed an appropriate development, bearing in mind the previous difficulties experienced in dealing with this particular group of patients. It was thought likely to benefit many mentally ill patients who often found it difficult to cope with the behaviour of some psychopathic disorder patients.

1.29.2 In its Sixth Biennial Report (1993–1995) the Commission reported that:

> "difficulties are emerging in relation to the personality disorder unit where there are clearly more patients than beds currently available (resulting in some patients being accommodated elsewhere) and Commission members get the impression that nurses do not feel adequately trained to 'manage' the often challenging behaviour of these patients".

On their visits to the wards in the unit in 1996, Commissioners did not receive information from either staff or patients or observe any activity that indicated any significant problems of control or security.

1.29.3 The Commission was made aware however of concerns over the shortage of psychologists at Ashworth Hospital and towards the end of 1996 the Commission became seriously concerned about the situation, not least in the PDU. A number of patients told Commissioners that they had not been given the psychological treatment and support they needed and had expected to receive; this picture was supported by ward staff. The Ashworth panel of Commissioners concluded that unless there was a significant increase in the number of psychologists employed, the situation would not improve. Whilst this development in part reflects a national shortage of psychologists, the Commission told us they believed the shortage at Ashworth Hospital may have been exacerbated by the abolition of the Psychology Department as part of the reorganization that followed the Ashworth Hospital Inquiry. This was certainly the view of psychologists at the Hospital.

1.29.4 The Commission has a remit to vindicate the rights of detained patients and drew attention to what it saw as the disproportionate influence of the Security Department on management decisions. Interestingly the Commission also criticized the Hospital for lax security procedures which made it easier for drugs and other illicit material to enter the Hospital. Visiting Commissioners had pointed out to the Hospital the consequences of failing to search patients on leaving and re-entering the Hospital, the need to exercise greater supervision of visitors and the desirability of introducing random searching of staff and visitors, including visiting Commissioners.

1.30.0 The Commission: Conclusions

1.30.1 We have dwelt at length on the Commission because here, one might think, was the body that could and should have had its finger on the pulse of things at Ashworth. Clearly visiting Commissioners had seen some of the security weaknesses evident in the Hospital, but not the kind of insidious problems on Lawrence Ward.

1.30.2 Mr Bingley reflected on the limits of his organization's remit:

> " . . . the remit of the Commission is to monitor the operation of the 1983 Mental Health Act and it is asked to do that in a number of ways, the primary one of which is

to visit and interview patients in private. So the Commission I think has always interpreted its role, from its establishment . . . as primarily a visitorial organization, and it seems to me that one of the things that thought will have to be given to is, whether it is a commission or some other organization, it needs to have a broader remit which makes it clear, for example, that it can go and inspect the security arrangements off its own bat, or to look at other aspects of the service.

"The fact was that Commissioners going into Lawrence Ward in particular were not being told anything. In that sense I think it is quite difficult to know precisely what further the Commission could do."

1.30.3 If the remit were to change that would in turn require, he thought, a different sort of organization with more permanent commissioners, equipped with different skills, and undertaking more intensive and longer visits. This would require an increase in resources.

1.30.4 Mr Bingley also thought it would be sensible if the Commission was given access to management documents as of right. He pointed out to us that it was no good allowing inspectorates to become a substitute to good management, and becoming confused with the management of the Hospital. There was also a danger of information overload if part-time commissioners were sent too much information.

1.30.5 Clearly there are difficult issues of balancing the need to allow managers to manage hospitals with the requirements of external security. We make recommendations for a new regime of monitoring and inspection in Part Two, paragraphs **2.39.11-12**.

1.31.0 Mental Health Review Tribunals

1.31.1 Mental Health Review Tribunals (MHRTs) were established under the Mental Health Act 1959 to provide an independent means to review the compulsory detention of patients in psychiatric hospitals. A Mental Health Review Tribunal is made up of three people, one of whom is legally qualified and who presides over the hearing, a consultant psychiatrist who must examine the patient, and a lay member.

1.31.2 Tribunals have a general discretion to discharge unrestricted patients, and are required to discharge such patients if any of certain criteria is met, principally, that the patient is not suffering from a mental disorder of a nature or degree requiring detention in hospital; or that detention is not necessary for the patient's health or safety, or the safety of others (section 72). In the case of a restricted patient, Tribunals must direct an absolute discharge if he or she is not suffering from a mental disorder of a nature or degree requiring detention in hospital; or if detention is not necessary for his or her health or safety, or the safety of others; and if it is not appropriate for him or her to remain liable to be recalled for further treatment. If the Tribunal considers it appropriate for the patient to remain liable to recall it must conditionally discharge him or her.

1.31.3 Since the 1983 Act MHRTs have been able to discharge restricted patients. This followed a ruling of the European Court of Human Rights in **X v The United Kingdom** [1981] 4 E.H.R.R. 181. Patients can be represented, with the costs met by legal aid. In the cases of restricted patients the Tribunal will seek the views of the Home Secretary. Patients who are detained under sections 37/41 are able to apply for a Tribunal on an annual basis; when they do not exercise this right the Home Secretary or the Hospital Managers refers their cases to a Tribunal on a three yearly basis.

1.31.4 Restricted patients who have been transferred to hospital under sections 47 and 49 may still apply to a Tribunal. The Tribunal in this case makes recommendations to the Home Secretary on whether or not the individual need remain in hospital. The Tribunal advises on whether or not the patient would have been entitled to an absolute or conditional discharge, had she or he been subject to a restriction order. The Home Secretary can then release the individual on parole (if he or she is eligible); remit him or her to prison; or take no action. The Tribunal can make a recommendation that he or she remain in hospital rather than being remitted to prison.

1.31.5 The Tribunal takes evidence from the patient's doctor, social worker, nearest relative (if they choose to attend the Tribunal) and other interested parties. Patients do usually exercise their right to be legally represented and often their legal representatives will submit independent reports to the Tribunal and call independent witnesses. Patients generally see documentation submitted by the detaining authority and are given the reasons for the Tribunal's decision.

1.31.6 Whilst offering an important counter-balance to the powers of the executive to detain restricted patients in hospital, MHRTs are not a soft option. Although the referral may be automatic or as a result of the patient's application, the onus of proof is on him, for he must demonstrate to the satisfaction of the Tribunal that he does not continue to suffer from mental disorder or is not otherwise continuing to fulfil the requirements for detention. These criteria are, more or less, the mirror image of the criteria which have to be satisfied for admission or continued detention (sections 3 and 20). Once the patient has 'passed' the statutory hurdles for admission it becomes in practice very difficult to demonstrate that the previously diagnosed disorder is no longer present to a degree warranting detention. RMOs will not always oppose change. Sometimes they will welcome the independent support of the Tribunal taking responsibility for the patient's discharge or recommendations to the Home Secretary.

1.32.0 Social Services Inspectorate

1.32.1 Given that personal social services are provided by local authority social services departments and by private and voluntary agencies, the Secretary of State for Health does not have the same direct responsibilities and the same measure of political accountability as he does within the NHS sphere. He does have statutory powers of guidance, direction, inspection and inquiry, and duties to register and approve accommodation for children.

1.32.2 The Secretary of State is supported in this work by the Social Care Group of the Department of Health, of which the Social Services Inspectorate (SSI) is a part. The SSI, headed by the Chief Inspector, reports independently and directly to the Secretary of State on the quality of social services and publishes an annual report. One of the Inspectorate's main functions is to carry out a national programme of inspection of personal social services provided by local authority social services departments and voluntary and private agencies.

1.32.3 Social workers within the Special Hospitals have always been employed by the hospitals, rather than by a local authority social services department. By contrast, social workers working within trusts are usually (though not always) employed by a local social services department, giving them access to the extended networks and line management arrangements to be found in a typical social services department. The lack of these networks has left social workers within the Special Hospitals at particular risk of professional isolation. Yet they had and have a key role in helping prepare patients for moving on and eventual rehabilitation into the community.

1.32.4 Historically following the creation of the NHS responsibility for the three Special hospitals passed from the Home Office to the Department of Health.

1.32.5 In 1989 direct management responsibility, including the management of the social work service, transferred to the SHSA. At the time the SHSA was set up, some concern was expressed that there was no social work representative on the SHSA to whom the social work service could relate. During the course of a review of the SHSA in June 1990 Ministers requested the Social Services Inspectorate to carry out an inspection of social work services in the three hospitals. This was undertaken in 1993. At Ashworth at least it was the first-ever such inspection.

1.32.6 In the meantime the Blom-Cooper Inquiry had reported. It recommended, *inter alia*, that "specific performance targets should be set for the Social Work Service at Ashworth and for individual members of staff in the Social Work Department" (recommendation 46, p.160).

1.32.7 The SSI inspection of Ashworth Hospital took place in August and September 1993. The Report made a number of strong criticisms. The key message was that, despite recommendation 46 of Blom-Cooper, the Social Work Department had not articulated a clear view of what the social work function within a Special Hospital was. None of the social workers in Ashworth was aware of the SHSA approved policy statement on social work and work on their own policy documents was at an early stage.

1.32.8 The lack of a clear statement of objectives and service standards had a number of unfortunate consequences. Given that there were no clear service standards, there was no operational guidance to help staff meet those standards and no monitoring. Similarly, there was no formal induction, training strategy or system of professional supervision. Social workers typically described themselves as autonomous; this in part reflected the desire to be self-motivated and exercise substantial degrees of judgement, but in part stemmed from the lack of clear objectives and standards and a corporate sense of identity. As a result they determined their own priorities, which meant that the social work role within PCTs, and the level of service to patients and their families, varied considerably. In some cases clinical colleagues felt that social workers concentrated too much on therapeutic activities to the exclusion of working with families and community agencies. The lack of clear service standards was also reflected in the poor quality of many case files.

1.32.9 The Report stressed the importance of social workers in preparing patients for transfer out of the Hospital but noted that social workers in Medium Secure Units (MSUs) had expressed dissatisfaction on the whole with their links with social workers in the Special Hospitals. It was clear that social workers in both the Special Hospitals and MSUs had little common understanding of what each side could offer. A similar picture emerged with regard to local authority social services departments.

1.32.10 Other problems were identified, including continuing recruitment difficulties (the post of Director of Social Work had at that point been vacant for some time) and a lack of influence on senior management (the Director of Social Work was not a member of the Hospital Management Team).

1.32.11 Following that inspection the SHSA and SSI agreed that a member of the Inspectorate would undertake to attend meetings of the Social Work Policy and Development Group four times a year. (This group was made up of the Directors of Social Work in the three hospitals and reported directly to Mr Kaye.) It was also agreed that this inspector would make himself available to be consulted by the three Directors. His role was always one of professional support and advice only, with the knowledge and assent of the three Chief Executives of the hospitals. We gather that since the 1994 SSI Reports much has been done to tackle the shortcomings identified in the three hospitals.

1.32.12 The above arrangement has more or less remained intact following the setting up of the HSPSCB. More recently, civil servants from the Department's child care section and regional SSI inspectors have begun to work with the three hospitals to address child welfare and protection issues, with a view to drawing up guidance on child visiting for the three hospitals.

1.32.13 We will see below the professional isolation of the Social Work Department vividly demonstrated in the Hospital's approach to child protection, which appeared to reflect almost complete ignorance of the Children Act 1989 and its guiding principles. We shall see an example of the lack of clarity over the social work role when it came to vetting visitors. We shall also see the problems caused by a particular autonomous professional who neglected core social work duties for therapy; whose record-keeping was poor; and whose general approach to his social work duties demonstrated poor standards and reflected poor supervision.

1.32.14 As far as we are aware the SSI has no plans to repeat its inspection of the social work departments at the three Special Hospitals.

1.33.0 Ashworth Hospital and the Criminal Justice System

1.33.1 As at 11 November 1997 the majority (405) of Ashworth's patient population had been convicted of a criminal offence. Of the total population the majority were subject to a restriction order or restriction direction giving the Home Secretary various powers to ensure public safety (*see* paragraph **1.36.0** *et seq.* below). Whilst a number were admitted under a hospital order, many had come from prison under section 47 (or 48) of the Mental Health Act 1983. In so far as personality disordered patients are concerned, over the preceding ten years, this had become the more usual route for them to arrive at a special hospital.

1.33.2 There were some 1,335 individuals detained in the three Special Hospitals. Of that total 344 were detained under the legal category of psychopathic disorder, 48 were detained under that category with a predominant diagnosis of personality disorder and 100 with a secondary diagnosis of personality disorder. We discuss in Part Six the current best estimates for the number of personality disordered individuals in prison and high security hospitals. (*See* Part Six, paragraphs **6.7.0** *et seq.*)

1.33.3 We make reference in this report at various points to what we call the "lottery": the game of chance which determines whether or not an offender who is suffering from a severe personality disorder ends up in prison (the vast majority) or hospital.

1.33.4 There are various elements to the lottery. First, whether an individual gets assessed at all. Second, if he is assessed, is he assessed by someone who is, crudely, "pro-treatment", or by someone who is more sceptical. Third, if he is regarded as "treatable", is there a bed available. Fourth, if there is a bed available, does the judge accept such a recommendation. Fifth, if one does get into hospital, particularly on a hospital order with restrictions without limit of time has that man won or lost? An individual diagnosed as suffering from psychopathic disorder and committed to a hospital on a section 37/41 hospital order does not know when he will ever be regarded as safe to come out of hospital.

1.33.5 Our proposals in Part Seven are aimed at improving the current lottery arrangements. Below we discuss the existing arrangements and some of the problems they raise.

1.34.0 Personality Disordered Prisoners within the Prison System

1.34.1 It is generally agreed that the vast majority of offenders with personality disorders go to prison. However, as Dr Michael Longfield, the Director of Health Care for the Prison Service, admitted in his evidence to us, the Prison Service cannot say how many personality disordered individuals there are amongst its population at any one time, for a number of reasons. The medical assessments carried out when inmates arrive at a prison are perfunctory at best; not all prisoners are referred to a psychiatrist at any particular point of their prison careers; any assessment is usually concerned with whether an individual fits the category of psychopathic disorder in the Mental Health Act, rather than any particular diagnostic category of personality disorder; and there are different diagnostic systems, not always rigorously applied. The difficulty in reaching any informed view was illustrated by our discussions with Dr Longfield, when we spent much time trying to clarify the best available evidence that suggests the size of the problem.

1.34.2 We have had the benefit of seeing the most recent of several studies of the prevalence of psychiatric disorder within prisons, a study of the Prevalence of Mental Disorder amongst the Prison Population of England and Wales commissioned by the Department of Health from the Office of National Statistics. We discuss our estimate of the number of severely personality disordered prisoners within the Prison System in Part Six.

1.35.0 The Services

1.35.1 At present the services within the Prison Service for individuals with personality disorder are very limited and in no way meet the existing potential demand. The most well-known facility is Grendon, which offers a therapeutic community for around 225 prisoners. Recent research has indicated that Grendon not only benefits inmates themselves by reducing distress, and the Prison Service through improving the behaviour of disruptive prisoners within the system, but also has a positive effect on re-offending.[10] We also heard that, although Grendon is more expensive than the average prison (£26,000 per prisoner per year compared to £23,000) it is cheaper than the average cost of the seven High Security Prisons which provide more than half of its population (£30,600). Given the disruptive nature of this population it offers a very cost-effective regime. A second "Grendon" is being developed at Marchington in Staffordshire.

1.35.2 One of our number, Mr Daniels, visited Grendon on an open day and commented favourably on the regime and the staff's commitment and self-confidence. Grendon's 'therapeutic community' regime is now well-established in the Prison Service and there is a considerable amount of literature available on both the style of working and the outcome for prisoners who have been through the service. Two important factors must be borne in mind. First, the referred prisoners are long-term sentenced inmates who have made a commitment to change. Second, non-compliance or infringement of rules leads to transfer back to mainstream prisons.

1.35.3 It should be noted however that in his recent review of Grendon[11] Sir David Ramsbotham, HM Chief Inspector of Prisons, whilst supporting strongly the work done by Grendon, criticized the Prison Service for failing to give Grendon proper support, leadership and direction. Sir David's report recommended that the Prison Service create a high level group within the Prison Service Headquarters to oversee and champion the work of Grendon and the other therapeutic communities within the Service.

1.35.4 There are also therapeutic community facilities at Gartree (some 20 or so life sentence prisoners), the Max Glatt Centre at Wormwood Scrubs (which caters for 35 men, focusing particularly on drug abuse and sexual offending), and facilities for young offenders at Feltham and Aylesbury Young Offender Institutions. A well-established small therapeutic community unit at Glen Parva Young Offender Institution recently closed, although it is intended to re-open the service in the future.

1.35.5 We visited the Max Glatt Centre and were very impressed by the evident

10 Marshall P. (1997) *A reconviction study of HMP Grendon therapeutic community*, Home Office Research and Statistics Directorate Research Findings No.53, London: Home Office.

11 HM Chief Inspector of Prisons for England and Wales (1997) *HM Prisons Grendon and Springhill; Report of a Full Inspection 1–12 September*, London: Home Office.

enthusiasm and commitment of the staff, but dismayed by the lack of support in terms of training they received. The Unit suffered by being insufficiently autonomous: prison officers could be taken away at short notice to deal with problems elsewhere. This seems to us to be similar to the strategic problem identified by Sir David, that the therapeutic centres within the Prison System have insufficient status and autonomy to do their job properly.

1.35.6 The vast majority of personality disordered prisoners are dealt with on general location, with no specific provision to meet their needs, although some participate in the Sex Offender Treatment Programme which, whilst not specifically set up for prisoners with personality disorders, does cater for some who fall into that category. This programme does however exclude those deemed to be suffering from severe disorder. The rationale for this is that such individuals' problems are thought to be rooted in a much more general disorder of personality which requires tackling if sustained change is to be achieved.

1.35.7 Our expert witnesses acknowledged that the Prison Service often did good work with personality disordered offenders, particularly at Grendon, but there was general agreement that prison units could not be truly therapeutic. That was not their function. In a prison, any treatment was likely to be a once-weekly group session, after which the prisoner returned to normal location. In hospital, staff would be seeking to reinforce the group work throughout the week. Hospitals were also resourced to carry out individual therapy with patients, whereas the Prison Service was simply not resourced to carry out such work.

1.35.8 There is a very small number of sentenced prisoners within the prison system who are highly disruptive. A number of these men do suffer from severe personality disorders and some have been in Special Hospitals in the past. The Prison Service has over the years had to devise a variety of strategies for this small group, for example by using Special Units such as the old "C" Wing at Parkhurst. In their evidence to us the Prison Service said that in the past the most disruptive men, a group numbering no more than 40, had been transferred from segregation unit to segregation unit, often every six weeks. There they would receive no more than one hour's exercise a day and little or nothing in the way of constructive activity or opportunity to address their behaviour. This system has now been reviewed. A new policy of creating a small number of special units has been adopted.

1.35.9 A new approach was launched in February 1998, based on a system of five Close Supervision Centres (CSCs), each holding a small number of prisoners, with varying regimes ranging from highly restricted to more open regimes. A total of 60 places is planned. The centres are intended to operate as part of a national management strategy that aims to secure the return of problematic or disruptive prisoners to a settled and acceptable pattern of behaviour. Prisoners have the opportunity for graduated progression through the system and back into the mainstream prison estate through sustained good behaviour. The intention is that they will be able to contribute to individual activity programmes and to attend weekly meetings to discuss their progress. Prison staff in CSCs are to attend a centrally approved training course to equip them to achieve the aims of the centre and to meet the needs of individual prisoners.

1.35.10 The CSC estate is based at Woodhill Prison in Milton Keynes (which operates three of the five centres), Hull and Durham. Prisoners entering the system go to the Structured Regime Centre at Woodhill for assessment; prisoners who continue to be disruptive or dangerous move to the Restricted Regime Centre at Woodhill with a strict, no association regime. Compliance earns a move to the Intervention Centre at Woodhill offering structured therapy and full association. There is a further Intervention Centre at Hull, offering an activity-based regime preparing prisoners who have progressed from Woodhill for a return to mainstream prison life and an Intervention Centre at Durham, offering psychiatric assessment and specialist input to the practical management of prisoners with personality disorders. Recently there has been some indication that the CSC system at these centres is to be reviewed.

1.35.11 The Durham CSC aims to manage prisoners who have a history of highly disturbed behaviour in a therapeutic small unit environment (with psychological and psychiatric input) and to monitor, assess and review individual prisoners' cases so as to prepare them for a return to normal location, progress to an alternative CSC or transfer to a psychiatric hospital as appropriate. It has nine places. It is expected that a significant proportion of the prisoners who pass through the Durham CSC will have personality disorders which have been assessed as untreatable in terms of the Mental Health Act 1983. They, therefore, have to be managed within a prison setting, using appropriate psychiatric and psychological interventions. A full psychiatric assessment will be carried out on any prisoner recommended for the Durham CSC.

1.35.12 In his oral evidence Dr Longfield told us that many of the group going into the CSC system would be suffering from anti-social personality disorder, and a number would have been in the Special Hospital system in the past. They were, however, highly disruptive and generally unmotivated for treatment. By a letter dated 13 October1998 we were informed that 12 of the prisoners who were on the Continuous Assessment Scheme (CAS) in March 1998 had been admitted to Special Hospitals at some time during their sentences. However, there was no diagnostic information about them or the other 28 prisoners who were on the scheme.

1.35.13 We visited Woodhill CSC. We were very impressed by the security and believe that the Centre will offer a very useful safety valve for the Prison System by taking the most disruptive prisoners out of circulation. It is too early to comment on how effective the therapeutic side of the equation will be.

1.35.14 In his submission to us Dr Longfield stated that the Prison Service considers the management of individuals with severe personality disorder to be more appropriately undertaken in a therapeutic rather than a custodial setting, not least because of the inadequate funding for therapy available to the Prison Service. He expanded upon this in oral evidence:

> "The Prison Service is clear that there are benefits to providing therapeutic community regimes for prisoners and also in terms of protecting the public because of the impact on reducing recidivism rates that latest research from Grendon now suggests is there.
>
> "The difficulty for us in expanding the availability of therapeutic community settings for prisoners, although we are addressing this with the new prison at Marchington for instance, has been the tactical management of the ever-increasing prison population which has tended to cause difficulty in earmarking significant numbers of places for dedicated facilities because of the need to move prisoners around the system and the difficulty in ring-fencing prison places for special regimes such as therapeutic communities, but as we expand the availability of prison places we are trying to take the opportunity to expand the therapeutic community places availability."

1.35.15 When pressed by counsel for Ashworth Hospital Dr Longfield admitted that the Prison Service could build more therapeutic facilities, as indeed was planned, but he believed that a non-penal environment was likely to be more conducive to the therapeutic goals of such a service.

1.35.16 We visited La Pâquerette Sociotherapeutic Centre at Champ-Dollon Prison near Geneva, a small unit for 11 severely personality disordered men. It is within a remand

prison, but autonomous. It is an impressive unit, which shows that, given the right leadership and staff skills, there is no reason why therapeutic units within prisons cannot flourish.

1.35.17 There are many personality disordered individuals within the prison system who could benefit from therapeutic regimes but who do not necessarily need to enter a hospital setting. Could not the Prison Service attract more therapists of whatever discipline to work within the penal system? The answer unfortunately is probably no. Throughout its history the Prison Medical Service has struggled, without much success, to attract high quality medical, nursing and other clinical staff.[12] It remains a service separate from the NHS. Recent experiments with contracting in services from NHS trusts have increased calls for the NHS to take over responsibility for medical services within prisons lock, stock and barrel. Dr Longfield would not be drawn on whether he recommended that particular solution, but stressed that close collaborative arrangements between prison and the NHS were key, whatever the organizational structure.

1.36.0 The Role of the Home Office Mental Health Unit

1.36.1 The Home Office's involvement in the management of mentally disordered offenders goes back to 1800 when James Hadfield was found not guilty by reason of insanity of an attempt to kill King George III. The court, recognizing that Hadfield needed treatment not punishment, ordered the Home Secretary to detain him under humane conditions. An Act of that year put the court's decision on a statutory footing and it became the Home Secretary's practice to order detention in Bethlem Hospital. The Criminal Lunatic Asylums Act in 1860 led to the founding of Broadmoor in 1863.

1.36.2 The Home Secretary is responsible only for mentally disordered offenders subject to restriction orders, restriction directions or hospital directions under the Mental Health Act 1983 or the Criminal Procedure (Insanity and Unfitness to Plead) Acts 1991. A restricted patient may be detained under:

(i) section 37/41 of the 1983 Act (hospital order with restrictions);

(ii) section 47/49 of the 1983 Act (sentenced prisoners transferred to hospitals);

(iii) section 48/49 of the 1983 Act (remand and unsentenced prisoners and immigration and civil detainees transferred to hospital);

(iv) section 45A of the 1983 Act (hospital direction patients);

(v) paragraph 2 of the Schedule to the 1991 Act (not guilty by reason of insanity, or unfit to plead).

1.36.3 In exercising these powers the Home Secretary is responsible for protecting the public from undue risk; he seeks, therefore, in his decisions to give priority to public safety whilst still supporting the objective of rehabilitation. While responsibility for treatment rests with the RMO and clinical team, the Home Secretary needs to be aware of the treatment programme and a patient's progress in order to fulfil his statutory duties.

1.36.4 In 1996 the Home Secretary transferred 265 prisoners to hospital under section 47 and 481 prisoners under section 48. Of the 265, 18 were suffering from psychopathic disorder and two from mental impairment and psychopathic disorder.

1.36.5 We were told that currently around 15 per cent of the restricted patient population had a primary diagnosis of psychopathic disorder.

1.36.6 With respect to all restricted patients the Home Secretary's consent is required for:

---

12 Bluglass R. (1988) 'Mentally disordered prisoners: reports but no improvements', *British Medical Journal* 296, p.1757.

(i) the grant of leave of absence;

(ii) transfer between hospitals;

(iii) discharge into the community (both conditionally and absolutely);

(iv) he also has power to recall a conditionally discharged patient.

The powers of discharge operate in parallel with those of Mental Health Review Tribunals. Authority to authorize leave and transfer rests with the Home Secretary alone.

1.36.7 In addition with respect to sentenced prisoners the Home Secretary can authorize their transfer to hospital for treatment and order transferred prisoners and hospital direction patients to be remitted to prison. In the case of remand prisoners, only prisoners legally classified as suffering from mental illness and severe mental impairment who are in urgent need of treatment may be transferred to hospital. The hospital direction applies at present only to those legally classified as suffering from psychopathic disorder, but the legislation allows for this to be extended to other forms of disorder.

1.36.8 The Mental Health Unit within the Home Office (previously C3 Division) is responsible for the casework on restricted patients. The Head of the Unit is a member *(ex officio)* of the HSPSCB and he and colleagues from the Unit meet the Chief Executives and Medical Directors of the three Special Hospitals twice a year to discuss matters of common interest.

1.36.9 We were shown a copy of the checklist of points used in considering particular requests concerning the management of restricted patients. The general areas which the RMO and multi-disciplinary team would need to consider cover issues such as whether a patient needs continuing detention; if so, the level of security required; the multi-disciplinary team's current understanding of the factors underpinning the index offence and previous dangerous behaviour; any change that has taken place so as to lower the perceived level of dangerousness; potential risk factors in the future; the patient's current attitudes to the index offence, other dangerous behaviour and any previous victims; any outward evidence of change; the role of drugs and/or alcohol in the patient's behaviour; any issues which still need to be addressed, and the short and longterm treatment plans; and any information on the circumstances of the victim or victim's family.

1.36.10 Particular points mentioned in regard to psychopathic patients are the individual characteristics of the personality disorder; the treatment approaches to specific problem areas; evidence as to whether the patient is now more mature, predictable and concerned about others; and evidence as to whether the patient now takes into account his or her actions and learns from experience.

1.36.11 In carrying out their functions we were told that members of the Mental Health Unit do not try to second-guess clinical teams, but they do look for evidence of thorough assessment and management of "risk" of danger, the aim being to ensure that any risk of danger to the public has been properly identified and evaluated and that sound measures have been taken to guard against any risk.

1.36.12 We heard evidence from Mr Mike Boyle, Head of the Unit. He told us that to try to second-guess clinical judgements would be dangerous:

> "We, I think, feel that it would be a very dangerous and slippery slope if we were to get into that kind of area. There would be no logical stopping point short of, in effect, equipping ourselves with a whole range of clinical specialists and I think there would be a source of a whole range of confusion.
>
> "One benefit I think from the present system is that there is a clear separation of roles

and that our role is clearly confined to one of a non-clinical risk assessment on the basis purely of a criterion of public safety."

1.36.13 That said, Mr Boyle did stress that his Unit took very seriously the need to be in close touch with clinicians, to attend case conferences and to visit hospitals and units. He agreed that it was difficult to draw a line between second-guessing clinical judgements and reviewing an RMO's assessment of risk to the public, but it was an important distinction to seek to uphold.

1.36.14 We and counsel for the parties raised a number of policy issues with Mr Boyle, which he helpfully debated. We discuss these below. In Part Seven we outline our recommendations for a system which, we believe, would provide better outcomes for patients/prisoners, staff and the public.

1.37.0 The Use of Hospitals as "Quasi-Prisons"

1.37.1 There has been considerable anxiety in the past over the transfer of prisoners to Special Hospitals just before their Earliest Date of Release (EDR). This practice can be argued to be a form of preventive detention, protecting society but at the cost of leaving the Hospital with a disgruntled patient, who is unlikely to be inclined to therapy. As any restriction order lapses once the EDR is passed, the responsibility for deciding the time of release and therefore of safeguarding the safety of the public is passed from the Home Secretary to the RMO and/or MHRT who have to say when they think the patient is fit to be let out of hospital.

1.37.2 It is fair to say that our Forensic Psychiatrist witnesses, whilst deprecating the practice of transferring prisoners to hospital just before their EDR, also said it was not now a particular problem.

1.37.3 Mr Boyle argued that the problem of such late transfers had been exaggerated. He pointed out that it might be years before prisoners on general location were properly assessed. Clinicians might be reluctant to take people until they neared their EDR because of the pressure of more urgent referrals. He also noted that such transfers required the clinical evidence of two doctors before they could take place, so it was not based on a crude measure of public risk, although risk to the public was a key part of the assessment.

1.37.4 A similar issue is raised by the refusal to accept remissions back to prison. Mr Boyle did tell us that the Home Office would occasionally resist attempts to remit an individual back to prison if it was deemed not to be in the individual's interest to return to prison, perhaps because he had spent many years in hospital and could not survive on general location in a prison. Generally the Mental Health Unit tried to have good working relationships with Special Hospitals. Nonetheless a more sinister motive might, it is argued, be at play: if a patient deemed untreatable but dangerous is remitted to prison on the completion of sentence, that individual would be liable to be released, however dangerous he was, on completion of that sentence. Mr Boyle thought that more positive elements would generally be involved, such as the prevention of any deterioration in the individual's condition.

1.37.5 Mr Boyle did not disagree with Professor Bluglass' suggestion that the Home Office occasionally turned down recommendations from RMOs that a patient should be let out as not requiring or responding to further treatment on the grounds of risk and danger to the public, rather than on a health care basis.

1.38.0 Directing Prisoners to Unwilling Hospitals

1.38.1 If attempts to find a bed fail the Home Secretary can direct the admission of a prisoner to a Special Hospital. Eight prisoners were admitted in this way to Ashworth between April 1994 and the end of 1997; in each case the prisoner was classified as suffering from mental illness. This of course presents RMOs with a very difficult situation, where they have to take responsibility for someone for whom they truly believe they can do nothing positive.

1.38.2 This is the extreme end of a spectrum of pressure put on Special Hospitals to take particular patients. Dr Shetty, until recently Medical Director of Ashworth Hospital, told us that on occasions pressure came from various sources to accept individuals whose treatability and security needs were questionable, including the courts, prison doctors, medium secure units, the Mental Health Unit at the Home Office, and sometimes on the basis of reports by "freelance psychiatrists", doctors with no admission facilities of their own but who write reports for courts. The problem was that over a number of years the Hospital could acquire a ward full of such people for whom nothing positive could be done.

1.38.3 Dr Coorey, of Ashworth Hospital, discussed how pressure was put on the Hospital to take patients, particularly where there was concern about a man's dangerousness:

> "Sometimes the problem arises where the judge cannot give anything more than a four to five year sentence, and everyone recognizes that the man is dangerous, so the Hospital is the only option where he will be detained indefinitely."

Of course such a result would only follow if there was appropriate evidence from two doctors. If by contrast, a person who is dangerous receives a relatively short prison sentence, he could be made the subject of a transfer order from prison to hospital if he qualifies for transfer.

1.38.4 Mr Boyle stressed to us that directing patients to hospitals was done as a last resort; usually it was because of a difference of view as to the level of security required, and very rarely over treatability (to his recollection the direction power had not been used with respect to treatability for over two years). In an ideal world the Home Office would want the receiving doctor to be willing to receive the patient, but for the sake of public safety that reserve power was needed.

1.39.0 Recall to Hospital

1.39.1 The Home Secretary can also recall to hospital a patient conditionally discharged from a section 37/41 court order. There is no requirement for the Home Secretary to consult an RMO about a patient's recall. We heard evidence from an individual at Ashworth who, having offended at an RSU and received a lengthy prison term, was recalled on the day of his EDR. Mr Boyle assured us that the Home Office was cautious about using the power of recall save when the RMO was in agreement. That said:

> "The Government's concern, and certainly the Home Secretary's primary concern, is not to put the public at risk in any situation of that kind . . . if his assessment is that recall is necessary in the interests of public safety and it is in accordance with the terms in the Act then we regard it as part of our duty to advise him to use those powers."

1.40.0 Detention versus Rehabilitation

1.40.1 A further issue is how to cope with prisoners transferred to hospital who still have some years to run before their EDR. It is a long-standing principle that such patients, being still subject to a term of imprisonment, should not serve less time in detention than if they were still in prison. This means that embarking upon rehabilitation programmes aimed at preparing an individual for freedom is problematic to say the least if he has many years yet to serve and will quite possibly (if on a transfer direction) be transferred back to prison to serve out his sentence. This creates problems for the Special Hospitals of coping with patients who know they have little incentive to work at therapy for some time, creating the potential for some of the problems we have encountered at Ashworth. Dr Robertson, who gave evidence, commented on this feature, saying that a tariff element entered the equation: even if a patient was "cured" he knew he would not be let out until he had served an appropriate length of time, and did not expect to be released early. It was only when patients had served what they regarded as their time for the offence that they became frustrated at the lack of movement.

1.41.0 Leave of Absence

1.41.1 The Home Office we were told supports the objective of rehabilitation but considers requests for allowing leave of absence visits (LOAs) on the degree of risk involved, the contribution of the planned activity to the treatment programme and to future assessments of behaviour, and likely public concerns, particularly on the part of victims.

1.41.2 Permission for LOA visits can be assumed in some cases, for example, for certain group outings, to prevent institutionalization in some cases and for compassionate reasons.

1.41.3 Mr Boyle told us that his Unit would look particularly closely at sensitive requests, for example if a convicted sex offender was to be taken to a pleasure park where he would be exposed to children. But his Unit did not get involved in hospitals' decisions on the sorts of places patients went on leave until a request arrived. We noticed that Ashworth and Rampton have rather different policies on LOA trips, Rampton's policy being very (and rightly in our view) restrictive, Ashworth's quite the opposite. Yet the Home Office does not seem to take any overall view on the suitability or otherwise of overall policies on LOA visits, regarding this presumably as beyond its remit.

1.41.4 Mr Boyle did admit that although his Unit did not keep "league tables" of the outcome of particular clinicians' decisions, he thought it might be helpful to have information on outcomes to feed back to RMOs to improve future decision-making.

1.42.0 Interim Transfer Directions

1.42.1 A point which counsel for Ashworth Hospital made consistently through the hearings was that although section 38 of the Mental Health Act 1983 gave courts the power to make interim hospital orders for a period up to six months (since increased to 12 months under section 49(1) of the Crime (Sentences) Act 1997), there is no equivalent of section 38 for transferred prisoners. Dr Coorey told us how he and his colleagues would occasionally stretch a point and give a prisoner some form of Mental Health Act diagnosis so that he could be brought into hospital for "treatment", even if they were unsure whether or not he would respond.

1.42.2 Dr Keitch of Rampton Hospital did not see the absence of such a power as a particular problem; if he felt that before a patient came in they were not going to benefit he would not recommend admission. Dr Snowden of Prestwich Hospital thought that the important issue in any future legislative change was to ensure that there were mechanisms for moving people between prison and hospital, depending upon their needs. Mr Boyle agreed that the section 38 power was very valuable, but his Unit only came into the picture at a later point, after an assessment had been carried out.

1.43.0 The Hospital Direction

1.43.1 Section 46 of the Crime (Sentences) Act 1997 amended the Mental Health Act 1983, giving the Crown Court the power when passing sentence on an offender convicted of an offence, other than one for which the sentence is fixed by law, to give a direction for immediate admission to, and detention in, a specified hospital ("hospital direction"), together with a direction that the offender be subject to the special restraints in section 41 of the 1983 Act ("limitation direction"). At present this provision only applies to offenders suffering from psychopathic disorder under the Act, although the Crime (Sentences) Act 1997 does give the

Home Secretary power to extend it to other categories of mental disorder. **We have not heard of a case in which such a direction has been made.**

1.43.2 This power means that an offender could serve his entire sentence in hospital, if treatment were deemed to be working. Alternatively, he could be remitted back to prison if in the opinion of doctors he no longer required, or was not responding to, treatment.

1.43.3 The Home Office stated in its submission to the Inquiry that it was not possible to predict with certainty how the courts would use the power in practice. The Home Office considered that its phased introduction, with initial availability only for those with a diagnosis of psychopathic disorder, combined with the safeguard that courts must first consider the use of a section 37 hospital order, meant that hospital directions were likely to be used only for a very small number of cases. Mr Boyle in his oral evidence to us suggested at most a dozen or so cases a year, where the appropriateness of a hospital order was most difficult to assess at the time of sentence.

1.43.4 The Home Office argued that the hospital direction was most likely to be applied in connection with the automatic life sentence made under section 2 of the Crime (Sentences) Act 1997. A section 37 hospital order is not available as an alternative to the mandatory life sentence. Consequently, when the offender sentenced under section 2 was psychopathically disordered, the hospital direction represented the only route whereby the court could order hospital treatment when a mandatory life sentence was imposed.

1.43.5 The Mental Health Unit's view was that the hospital direction would be more likely to replace a hospital order, by virtue of the effects of section 2 of the 1997 Act, than it was to replace a simple prison sentence. Accordingly, there was unlikely to be any significant increase in the number of serious offenders admitted to hospital. Where a hospital direction was made, psychiatrists would be able to recommend the offender's transfer to prison under section 50 of the 1983 Act if he refused to cooperate with treatment or when all effective treatment had been given, whereas with a restricted hospital order, there might be a need to detain the offender in hospital in those circumstances, because of the danger he would pose to others if discharged. The power should, in the Home Office's view, therefore, ease the pressure on the High Security Hospitals of having to detain long term personality disordered offenders who are arguably untreatable, but who would pose a potential danger to others if discharged. When combined with the extension from six to twelve months of the maximum duration of the interim hospital order, the Home Office anticipated that the power would represent an overall saving for the Health Service in terms of long term detention of personality disordered offenders.

1.43.6 The power has only been available since October 1997. It is too early to say what effect it will have, if any, on sentencing practice. **However, since the option has not been used, it does not appear to be an attractive option.**

1.43.7 Mr Boyle, with practised Civil Service dexterity, avoided admitting too much, but we feel the conclusion is inevitable: the functions of hospitals and prisons as far as personality disordered offenders are concerned are dreadfully confused and need to be disentangled. Hospitals are being used as surrogate prisons because we lack the means to detain a category of dangerous offender indefinitely. In Part Seven we outline a radical approach to improving the legal framework for dealing with personality disordered offenders.

1.44.0 The Advisory Board on Restricted Patients

1.44.1 It is important also to mention the Advisory Board on Restricted Patients. In cases where the prediction of future re-offending is particularly difficult the Home Secretary can take the advice of the Advisory Board on Restricted Patients. The Board is a non-statutory body which was set up in 1973 in accordance with the recommendations of the Aarvold Committee following public concern about the conviction of Graham Young, a mass poisoner who re-offended after discharge from Broadmoor.

1.44.2 The Board consists of eight members. The Chairman is a Circuit Judge, there is a second legally-qualified member, two consultant forensic psychiatrists, a Chief Probation Officer, a Director of Social Services and two other members selected for their wider knowledge of the criminal justice system. Members are appointed for a three-year term and may be re-appointed. The Board meets about once a month. One member is asked to visit the Hospital where a given patient is detained and will interview the patient, the RMO and other members of staff as appropriate. A copy of the visit report and a note of the Board's discussion is forwarded to the Minister.

1.44.3 Decisions on whether to refer cases to the Board are taken within the Mental Health Unit or by a junior Home Office Minister. The cases of individuals classified as suffering from psychopathic disorder are routinely considered for reference to the Board. Individuals who have committed very serious offences or high profile patients are more likely to have their cases referred to the Board.

1.44.4 Dr Snowden told us a little about the practical working of the Board. The Board's headline function is to give the Home Secretary independent advice on the risk to the public of transferring or releasing a particular individual, although the Board does often get involved with difficult cases before they even reach the stage of a submission for transfer or discharge. The sort of case the Board reviews concern the most worrying patients, who would typically have a personality disorder or some form of dual diagnosis. A lesser number are mentally ill.

1.44.5 Dr Snowden explained that the individual in question will not always be seen by a doctor member of the Board. This is because the purpose of the Board is not to second-guess the clinical team as far as diagnosis and treatment are concerned, but rather to focus attention on the offending behaviour and risk to the public. Dr Snowden told us he approached his work for the Board as an educated person with knowledge of the system, rather than as a psychiatrist; in his view it was sometimes very helpful not to have a doctor interviewing the patient so as to gain an alternative perspective on risk. He praised his fellow-members of the Board as highly-experienced individuals. He added that the Board had a good record in decision-making.

1.45.0 The Parole Board

1.45.1 A formal system of parole was introduced to the British penal system for the first time by the Criminal Justice Act 1967. The philosophy underpinning this was that early release into the community under a degree of supervision could help rehabilitation and so lessen the risk of re-offending in the future. However, in deciding whether or not to release prisoners early the primary consideration was, and continues to be, the risk to the public of a further offence being committed at a time when the prisoner would otherwise be in prison.

1.45.2 The Criminal Justice Act 1991 introduced major changes concerning parole. In particular, it established that all prisoners must spend at least half of their sentence in prison. Those serving less than four years are now released automatically at the half-way point. Those serving determinate sentences of four years or more become eligible to be considered for parole at the half-way stage. Those who are not released on parole are automatically released at the two-thirds point of the sentence.

1.45.3 The Parole Board carries out risk assessments to assist in the making of decisions about the early release of determinate sentence prisoners (four years or more) and life sentenced prisoners. The Board has the power to make final decisions in cases involving (i) determinate sentence prisoners serving sentences between four and seven years, and (ii) discretionary lifers. In other cases, the Board makes a recommendation to the Secretary of State. The Board also plays a key role in the recall of offenders to prison.

1.45.4 Applications for early release are dealt with by three-member Parole Board panels. Decisions are made on the basis of documentary evidence (and, in the case of discretionary lifers, oral evidence). All Lifer Panels include a consultant psychiatrist member. Some of the panels dealing with determinate sentence prisoners are specially designated as 'psychiatric panels', and are responsible for considering cases where it is believed that the input of a psychiatrist would assist in the decision-making (for example, in dealing with offenders with a history of psychiatric treatment, and sex offenders).

1.45.5 Research is currently underway into parole decision-making, looking at (amongst other issues) the importance of parole decisions being informed by the specialist knowledge of psychiatrists and others.

1.45.6 Life sentence prisoners transferred to hospital under the Mental Health Act 1983 remain prisoners while they are in hospital. However, in **R v Secretary of State for Home Department Ex. P. Hickey** [1994] 3 W.L.R. 1110, the Court of Appeal held that for such prisoners the provisions of the 1983 Act take precedence over the Criminal Justice Act 1991. The effect of this judgment is that prisoners transferred under the Mental Health Act do not have the same access to the Parole Board as if they had remained in prison. However, a transferred lifer is eligible for a Parole Board review in hospital where:

> (i) the Home Secretary is satisfied on the advice of a doctor that the prisoner no longer requires treatment in hospital, but would be likely to become ill if returned to prison; or
>
> (ii) the MHRT recommends that the prisoner is ready for discharge, but should not be returned to prison.

Any prisoner subject to a sentence of more than 12 months remains on licence until three quarters of his full term has elapsed. If he reoffends during that licence period he may be ordered to return to prison for a period equivalent to the remainder of his original sentence outstanding at the date of his new offence. This can be ordered concurrently with, or be served before, any sentence for the new offence.

1.46.0 The Probation Service

1.46.1 The Probation Service is responsible for supervising many personality disordered offenders when they are eventually released, either absolutely or on licence. They are a vital part of the overall Criminal Justice response to personality disordered offenders, although their role is somewhat beyond our remit. In the opinion of Dr Keitch of Rampton Hospital the Probation Service has a lot of experience and skill in handling this group. For what follows we are grateful to Mr John Harding, the Chief Probation Officer of the Inner London Probation Service.

1.46.2 The origins of the Probation Service can be traced back to the late Victorian era and the First Offenders Act 1887 which introduced so-called police court missionaries who supervised offenders on conditional release from the courts. The service grew slowly, only to mushroom in the 1970s and 1980s as several major Acts widened the scope of the Service, including the Criminal Justice Act 1967, which introduced parole and voluntary prison aftercare for offenders; the Powers of the Criminal Court Act 1973 which introduced community service by offenders, day training centres and extended the scope of probation and bail hostels for offenders over the age of 17; and the Criminal Justice Act 1982, which, *inter alia*, widened the range of community service for juveniles over the age of 16.

1.46.3 The Probation Service in England and Wales is currently made up of 54 probation Areas. Its primary responsibilities are to protect the public through reducing offending behaviour. The service in 1997 prepared over 225,000 pre-sentence reports for Crown Courts, Magistrates' Courts and Youth Courts. It also supervised 32,000 Community Service Orders, 20,000 Combination Orders (probation and community service combined), 50,000 Probation Orders and over 66,000 prisoners were under probation officer supervision before and after release. The forms of after-care supervision are variously described as parole, life licence, automatic conditional release and, in a small minority of cases, social supervision from special prison hospitals.

1.46.4 Since the beginning of this decade three significant Acts of Parliament have extended the scale of the statutory responsibilities of the Service. The first, the Criminal Justice Act 1991 introduced Combination orders, changed the scope of parole for those offenders serving over four year terms of imprisonment and led to limited periods of supervision under automatic conditional release for those serving sentences of between one and four years imprisonment. The second, the Sex Offenders Act 1997, introduced a number of measures relating to sex offenders involving the police and probation service. The third, the Crime and Disorder Act 1998, with its phased implementation over a period of two years, extends the post-release supervision periods for sex offenders released from prison for up to ten years; for violent offenders for up to five years. The Act also introduced mandatory testing and treatment orders for drug misusing offenders and Home Office Detention Curfews with electronic monitoring for low risk prisoners released for up to two months earlier than their normal prison expiry date.

1.46.5 Under the Victim's Charter, the service provides information to the victims and families of violent crime immediately after an offender is sentenced. When the Parole Board is reviewing a prisoner's application for release, the Service contacts the victim and his/her family to inform them of the prisoner's application and ascertains whether the victim wishes to include any restraining clause in the parole requirements.

1.46.6 Apart from supervising offenders, probation officers spend most of their time preparing pre-sentence reports for the courts on those offenders who are at risk of custody or being placed under some form of statutory supervision. Such reports address the offender's offending behaviour, response to victims, and chronicle the offender's personal and social circumstances. They also include a risk assessment of the likelihood of further offending and possible harm to the public. Finally they refer to the options open to the Court and weigh up the offender's likely response to a non-custodial sentence.

1.46.7 The Service has developed a range of programmes to address specific offending behaviour. They are evidence based, relying on evaluation and structured disciplined forms of intervention whether using a one to one approach or group work. Most probation areas run programmes for sex offenders, drink drivers, domestic violence offenders, disqualified drivers, alcohol and drug misusing offenders. There are also courses relating to offending behaviour and anger management. In addition there are also courses for women offenders and young offenders.

1.46.8 A variety of conditions may be attached to probation orders by the courts, and the Service offers intensive, focused work in probation and bail hostels and day centres.

1.46.9 In relation to sex offenders, partly arising out of the Sex Offenders Act 1997, with regard to serious and potentially dangerous offenders, probation areas take part in risk assessment management conferences on a regular basis with the Police, Social Services and Health Trusts. Most areas have also developed information exchange protocols with local police forces so that risks posed by serious offenders released from prison or subject to supervision under a community penalty are known and shared.

1.46.10 In so far as mentally disordered offenders are concerned the Service liaises closely with court-based psychiatric assessment staff, community health teams, and psychiatric in-patient and out-patient services as well as children and adolescent mental health services. A small minority of probation orders contain conditions whereby probationers who do not require hospital treatment can be seen on an out-patient basis by a forensic or community psychiatrist.

1.46.11 The cost of community penalties managed by the Probation Service are considerably less than the cost of prison in all its manifestations. Community service costs approximately £30 a week, a probation order £35 a week. Probation with a day centre condition costs £100 a week; a combination order costs £80 a week and a probation/bail hostel order £150 a week. By contrast, prison costs vary, from £400 per week for a local prison to £800 a week for a maximum security prison. Local Authority secure accommodation for a juvenile offender costs £2,000 a week.

1.47.0 Care Programme Approach and Post-Discharge Arrangements

1.47.1 Conditional discharge of restricted patients allows the Home Secretary to recall to hospital a patient if he or she fails to comply with the agreed conditions of discharge. Section 117 of the Mental Health Act 1983 requires Health Services and Social Services to provide aftercare for patients who have been detained in hospital. This is now coordinated by an agreed package of care and treatment which is described as the Care Programme Approach (CPA). The CPA was implemented by Health Circular and Social Services Letter (HC(90)23/LASSL(90)11) in 1991 and requires Health Authorities to undertake a systematic assessment of health and social care needs, in consultation with the patient and his and her carers, and to produce a written care plan coordinated by a named key worker.

1.47.2 In April 1994 a further initiative was implemented with the introduction of the Supervision Register. This required NHS Provider Units to maintain a register of mentally disordered patients who were regarded as posing a significant risk of suicide, severe self-neglect or serious violence to others. Such patients' care would again be coordinated through the CPA and receive the highest priority for aftercare and follow-up, with regular review by the multi-disciplinary team.

1.47.3 Supervised Discharge was implemented as an amendment to the Mental Health Act 1983. This allows for recall to hospital for treatment if the mental state of a discharged detained patient deteriorates to the point at which he is again detainable. This power is particularly related to non-compliance with medication and/or other treatment. Again this is underpinned by the patient's CPA plan.

1.47.4 We have described the background to this Inquiry and the context within which the Hospital has to operate. We now examine the more recent history of Ashworth Hospital, focusing in particular on a number of serious incident reports.

PART 2 The Long Road to Lawrence Ward 1989–96

2.0.0 Introduction

> " . . . Insofar as conviction rates are appropriate measures of institutional effectiveness, follow-up studies consistently show that if the special hospitals confined themselves to the admission and treatment of the mentally ill they could bask in the glow of success, but both the mentally subnormal/impaired and those with psychopathic disorder damage apparent success by the frequency of their re-convictions . . . further, those with a legal classification of psychopathic disorder are almost entirely responsible for the major scandals . . . In an important sense our status would be much improved in the absence of association with those detained under the Mental Health Act 1983 category of psychopathic disorder."[1]

2.0.1 The events on Lawrence Ward which we were asked to investigate were scandalous. But, as the quotation above implies, scandal and personality (psychopathic) disorder are frequent bed-fellows. In this section of our Report we trace the recent history of Ashworth, starting more or less when the Special Hospitals Service Authority (SHSA) took over the running of the high security psychiatric service from the Department of Health. This actually occurred in October 1989, although the SHSA had been in place for some months prior to that time.

2.0.2 We consider below the management changes occurring at both national and hospital levels which were intended to improve high security psychiatric services, the systems in place to identify problems, the many attempts to create a robust system for the care of personality disordered patients in a high security hospital. We demonstrate how these changes fell short of their ambitious goals, at least as far as the personality disordered population at Ashworth was concerned, a failure reflected in the various Reports which appeared in those years, beginning with the Mallalieu and Rowe Reports of 1990 and 1991. We trace the various chains of accountability and attempt to identify who should shoulder the blame for the failures we have examined. We have been careful, however, not to pin blame on individuals where we believe the system was at fault because the job staff were being asked to do was impossible.

2.0.3 Given that the High Security Hospitals had been a backwater where relatively little had changed over many years, certainly before the advent of the SHSA, change was imperative. In common with the rest of the NHS, Ashworth Hospital has undergone considerable change in recent years; some witnesses complained about too much change, too quickly imposed. In his evidence Mr Kaye said he would have preferred five years to effect the changes at Ashworth.

2.0.4 No one should underestimate the challenge of caring for and managing the particular group of patients found on the PDU at Ashworth. We also recognize the difficulty facing staff

1 Taylor P. (1992 'Introductory note to the 1991 SHSA seminar on psychopathic disorder'. *Criminal Behaviour and Mental Health*, vol 2, No. 2.

in trying to move forward after the trauma of the Blom-Cooper Inquiry. Was the task then too difficult for staff at the ward level? Alternatively were the problems on Lawrence Ward a mere aberration caused by errors of the PCT and nurses on the ward? Or were there weaknesses in the management systems put in place to help the Hospital improve its clinical care whilst maintaining security for patients, staff and public, to integrate it more firmly within the NHS family? Were there flaws in the systems for developing, implementing and monitoring robust policies and procedures? Our task has been to consider whether the changes introduced have been flawed, either in conception or implementation. In short, whether the system itself was the greatest villain of the piece.

We think it was.

2.0.5 We would not argue against the proposition that much had been achieved in the Special Hospitals, Ashworth included, between 1989 and 1996. The Special Hospitals are now much improved compared to ten years ago. Ashworth Hospital was the first hospital to end the degrading practice of "slopping out". Another change, "24-hour opening" which became fully operational later in this seven year period has proved to be an expensive investment producing mixed benefits. Although the Special Hospital system has had considerable difficulty in recruiting professional staff with the requisite ability to revitalise a system which evolved from the past, there remains within it much expertise and dedication directed to the complex task it undertakes.

2.0.6 However, we argue below that, notwithstanding some serious failings by individuals the job staff were being asked to do in the Personality Disorder Unit was fundamentally ill-conceived. Sadly, nobody was able to dissipate the treacle in which, historically, the system has wallowed. Poorly thought-out policies and changes have been thrust upon staff without adequate thought as to how those changes could be wrought. Of course, some people have been proved inadequate to the tasks, others have given up hope, but there can be no doubt that the lion's share of fault lies with the system. There are a number of reasons for this which we set out. In Part Seven of our Report we outline a system which, we believe, has a better chance of success.

The Patient Mix

2.0.7 As Professor Taylor points out in the passage we have quoted above, personality disordered patients are, generally speaking, the patient group most likely to cause management problems. This is not a particularly original point. The different problems presented by mentally ill and personality disordered patients are well known. For many years there has been a difference of opinion amongst consultant forensic psychiatrists as to whether or not offenders with psychopathic disorder are treatable. There is probably less difference of opinion as to whether the most severe cases are curable. The general opinion is that they are not. However, there is common ground concerning the problems that people at the very severe end of the personality disorder spectrum create. They are highly manipulative of other patients and staff. They can be compliant when it suits them, even for years, in order to earn privileges which they can then exploit. They require very well trained staff to maintain necessary distance, but still to retain effective relationships. By contrast the mentally ill, who can be just as dangerous, are, in general, more susceptible to treatment. Not all serious personality disordered offender patients require the highest security, but all of them require a sufficient level of security to ensure the protection of the public, other patients and staff.

2.0.8 Therefore if such individuals are to be cared for in a hospital due recognition has to be paid to their particular needs, and the particular security issues they present. Yet the SHSA consistently failed, in our view, to distinguish between the discrete needs of the different groups of patients. Having said this, it seems to us that for some of the severe personality disordered offenders who are currently in hospital the preferred option should be prison.

2.0.9 The SHSA was given broad guidance on its objectives by the Department of Health in the form of the so-called "Operational Brief". However, this document states a confusion of objectives which it says "are prescriptive on the SHSA and must inform all its activities". The Special Hospital service is said to cope with patients whose "underlying clinical condition is susceptible to treatment and rehabilitation in the same degree as that of patients with similar conditions cared for within the NHS". This statement is then qualified by saying the special hospital patients exhibit an additional dimension, having all been assessed as displaying "dangerous, violent or criminal propensities" to an extent which would represent a risk to public safety if they were not managed in facilities of security which the rest of NHS does not provide. Such patients are admitted against a criterion of "presenting grave and immediate danger" so their care and treatment "has to be carried through in conditions of security much more stringent than needs exist in the NHS".

2.0.10 So far so good, but confusion of thought now takes over. No distinction is made between the different types of mentally disordered offenders the service has to deal with or their various responses to different forms of treatment. They are treated as a homogeneous group. It is asserted that modern psychiatric therapies for the care and treatment of patients call for "supportive socially-orientated and rehabilitative regimes", but the inescapable security requirements dictated by the need to protect the public, staff and other patients, have, in the past, inhibited the application of such regimes.

2.0.11 By 1989 developments in pharmacological, psychological and social treatments of the mentally ill had advanced and have continued to advance. Such advances play a much less significant part in the treatment of personality disorder uncomplicated by any other problems. Its treatability is still unresolved. Research commissioned by the Reed Working Group's Report on Psychopathic Disorder and carried out by Drs Dolan and Coid in 1993[2] resulted in the conclusion that there was no convincing evidence whether people with psychopathic disorder could or could not be successfully treated. In evidence Mr Kaye referred to personality disordered offender patients as presenting "one of the greatest challenges"; their particular psychopathology which often included considerable ability to plan and challenge boundaries, when combined with their potential for dangerousness, made ward management particularly difficult. He added that if patient-mix was not carefully planned their influence on other patients was often disruptive and disturbing. He continued: "those with personality disorder are amongst the patients most capable of organising adverse situations and careful high security planning is essential". All of this was known in 1989, just as it had been known in 1975 (*see* the Butler Report).

2.0.12 The controversy over treatability results in the so-called lottery over who gets sent to hospital and who ends up in prison. A number of severely personality disordered individuals who commit serious offences are seen by psychiatrists who favour treatment and are admitted to hospital. The same person, had they been seen by another psychiatrist could have been judged untreatable and sent to prison. In both cases the individual is potentially dangerous and disruptive and needs to be cared for or imprisoned in a very secure environment. The prisoner may need some specialist health care but will rarely receive it. The patient finds himself in an environment where security is a significant restraint on therapeutic options.

2.0.13 Those health professions who work in the secure environment have to accept the discipline that this imposes and shape and sometimes limit their clinical practice accordingly. They do not see themselves as jailors. However, for long-term patients who are either resistant to treatment or judged, over time, to be untreatable, hospital does indeed become a prison, sometimes for life.

---

2 Dolan B. and Coid J. (1993) *Psychopathc and anti-social personality disorders: Treatment and Research Issues.* London: Gaskell Press.

2.0.14 Since 1989 the more usual route of admission into the Special Hospitals for individuals judged to have a severe personality disorder has been by way of transfer order under section 47 of the Mental Health Act 1983 with a restriction under section 49. Many psychiatrists are unwilling to recommend other routes which might have the practical consequence of commitment to hospital for a wholly indefinite period even when treatment is not possible.

2.0.15 The mentally ill also end up in both the hospital world and prisons but this is not usually the consequence of differential diagnosis by psychiatrists. For the mentally ill the diagnostic framework has a high degree of professional consensus. The individuals do of course change over time. Prisoners develop problems with their mental health and patients, once their mental health has been stabilized, could return to custody. In both cases the individual may still be judged potentially dangerous and need care or custody in a secure environment.

2.0.16 Consider now that approximately 150 of the most dangerous and disruptive personality disordered patients were put together in a single unit of six wards at Ashworth, on the same campus as mentally ill patients, with few effective restrictions on interaction between the two groups. Most had been in the Special Hospital system for some years. When the Hospital began to become more liberal, post-Blom-Cooper, the fruits of this liberalization were applied to all. No account was taken of the special needs of personality disordered patients; as indeed, if anything, this group benefited most in terms of reduced security and personal freedom. **That these freedoms would be abused by some of this group should have been anticipated. Because it was not, the lives of many staff and patients have been blighted.**

The Conflict between Security and Therapy

2.0.17 The SHSA's first stated objective was "to balance the provision of appropriate care and clinical treatment with the safety of the public, the staff and the patients themselves". Balancing the need for security with the requirements of therapy, was thought to be the way to pull the Special Hospitals out of the treacle in which they were bogged down, but, as an objective, it is far easier to state than achieve. From what we have seen, while there may have been odd pockets of success, the general picture, as far as the personality disordered population at Ashworth is concerned, is of failure to achieve this goal and this is a major reason, and probably the principal reason, why Ashworth has made limited progress in these years. This is also why, after Mr Daggett's absconsion and whistle blowing activity towards the end of 1996, the continuance of pre-existing problems could be brought to light.

2.0.18 We trace below two conflicting trends, one towards greater liberalization, an understandable reaction to the abuses of former years so graphically demonstrated by the Blom-Cooper Report. The other is a rearguard action by those charged with security within the hospitals and those called upon to investigate successive incidents, who argued with little success that liberalization could only take root if it was underpinned by sound security principles.

2.0.19 Thus on the one hand in came the devolution of responsibility for care and security down to ward level recommended by the Task Force set up to implement the recommendations of the Blom-Cooper Report; 24-hour care; patient empowerment in the form of Patients' Councils; new complaints procedures; the requirements laid down by the 1993 revision of the Mental Health Act Code of Practice and the SHSA's Patient's Charter; and the implicit downgrading of the Security Department to the status of unwanted advisers. On the other hand we see the highly critical security audit of the Hospital in 1992 carried out by Miss Joy Kinsley, the SHSA's Director of Security; the continuing security problems being raised year after year by Security Managers; and a long stream of serious incident Reports raising similar issues.

2.0.20 Much of what the SHSA was doing made good sense. But it could only work for personality disordered patients in particular if the demands of security were firmly grounded in the running of the Hospital. Yet with the publication of the Blom-Cooper Report on Ashworth Hospital in 1992, which had largely been concerned with the ill-treatment of mentally ill and mentally impaired patients, the SHSA had to set about implementing the majority of its 90 recommendations throughout the Ashworth campus irrespective of patients' different security requirements. It did this by way of the Task Force referred to above. As we shall show, the Task Force's objectives were quite different from those of Miss Joy Kinsley carrying out her security audits. The radical changes brought about following the Task Force's Reports of December 1992 and February 1993 were fatally flawed because they did not recognize the differential needs of the personality disordered patients. Those who did see the problems were often regarded, we were told, as "dinosaurs". Those changes gave rise to the justifiable comment noted in the Owen Ward Report that "security was sacrificed in the headlong rush to therapy". No wonder staff felt confused.

2.0.21 Generally speaking a satisfactory balance between security and therapy was never achieved in the PDU at Ashworth during the lifetime of the SHSA. This is seen through the various inquiry Reports we have examined and which we discuss below. The same problems stemming from inadequate security provisions appear time and again. Similar recommendations to remedy them are made; resolutions are made to implement the recommendations; frequently efforts are made to implement those recommendations although they often prove to be ineffectual; management structures are changed in efforts to improve control sometimes before previous changes have even taken root. Significantly Mr Kaye said that searching never appeared in the Special Hospitals' contracts until the end of the life of the SHSA.

2.0.22 The task in hand was complicated by further factors. First, the sheer size of Ashworth (and indeed of Broadmoor and Rampton). The Hospital had some 480 beds at a time when in the NHS the old long-stay psychiatric hospitals were dramatically reducing in size or closing as alternative community services emerged. The PDU was too big in a hospital that was too big. Managers simply could not keep track of what was happening.

2.0.23 Second, one must remember the legacy of the past: poor industrial relations, a lack of trust between managers and staff which led to secrecy on the one hand and (it is alleged) disclosure of sensitive information to the press on the other. The failure to circulate informative versions of key Reports such as the Owen Ward Hostage-Taking Report (which we discuss in para **2.14.0** *et seq.*) reflects in part the secrecy of the management culture. Additionally the quality of professional staff was variable and professional isolation did not help. Nor did fragile relations with the rest of the NHS.

Lack of Success with the PDU

2.0.24 The SHSA's success was limited in so far as personality disordered patients are concerned. Until we analysed the evidence concerning these years, it seems to us that the success of the SHSA was more limited than it wanted to believe itself or wanted others to believe. The Owen Ward Report, one of the most important, if not the most important, in the life of Ashworth Hospital, was concealed; it was reduced from a 59-page version, with 385 pages of appendices, to a 19-page version with no appendices. Finally it was reduced to its circulated version of nine pages which was a travesty of the original. The Swan Report into women's services at Ashworth was not disclosed, essentially because it recommended removing that service from Ashworth. As will be seen, in our judgment, these two Reports were concealed because the SHSA wanted to keep alive the notion that changes introduced were working when they were not. Furthermore, through the quarterly quality Reports as well as Inquiry Reports, and the minutes of the meetings of the Security Managers of the three special hospitals, the SHSA knew they were not working.

2.0.25 In 1994 the SHSA wished to review the progress made following the implementation of the Blom-Cooper Report's recommendations and invited the Health Advisory Service (HAS) to do this for them to present a picture of independence and impartiality. We believe that Dr Williams' HAS team was to some extent deceived. At the very least they were induced into complacency. They were deprived of the sight of the Swan Report and the Owen Ward Report in their Inquiry which led to the publication of their own Report, *With Care In Mind Secure*. In his evidence to this Inquiry, Mr Kaye relied on that Report, not as demonstrating achievement of all that the SHSA set out to do, but as significant evidence that much had been achieved. In our judgment, the background events leading to the publication of *With Care In Mind Secure* undermine the reliability of that claim.

2.0.26 At this time the Special Hospitals were moving towards greater autonomy and finally became independent authorities in 1996. This process itself was very consuming of senior management's time and energy. In the meantime, two other Inquiries reported, one into the affairs of Stephen Braund and the other into the possessions of Stephen Finney, which disclose similar and serious problems. The sorry tale we recount in this part of our Report takes us up to the absconsion of Mr Daggett in September 1996 and our account of that event and the Reports which followed. The whole story is one of years of failure to learn lessons from mistakes and bitter experience. Inquiry after inquiry produced fine words, but little action. This was particularly true when the lessons were about tightening security rather than relaxing it in pursuit of the admirable but misguided goal of therapy for all. All too often the Hospital's preoccupation with secrecy blocked the learning process. **Yesterday's mistakes should be today's agenda for change.**

2.0.27 It is now time to tell this sorry story. We start in 1989 with the creation of a new national body to take the Special Hospital Services forward, namely the Special Hospital Service Authority (SHSA).

2.1.0 The Establishment of the Special Hospital Service Authority

2.1.1 Under section 4 of the National Health Service Act 1977 the Secretary of State for Health is charged with the duty:

> " . . . to provide and maintain establishments (in the Act referred to as 'special hospitals') for persons subject to detention under the Mental Health Act 1959 [subsequently the Mental Health Act 1983] who, in his opinion, require treatment under conditions of special security on account of their dangerous, violent or criminal propensities".

This ultimate accountability cannot be delegated. In the final analysis the Secretary of State is accountable for what happens within the High Security Hospitals (just as he is accountable for other hospitals and services within the NHS). He has a duty to ensure that the High Security Hospitals are properly run; this can perhaps be summarized as ensuring that adequate resources are obtained to run the hospitals; that the hospitals are given a strategic direction to follow; and that arrangements are in place to ensure that the operational management of the hospitals is delivering appropriate care to patients and ensuring the security of the public.

2.1.2 Whether Secretaries of State are *responsible* for everything that happens inside the Special Hospitals is another matter. One view is that much of the organizational changes of the last decade or so in public services, not just the NHS, is a process of careful distancing of Ministers from the consequences of their strategic decisions. Another view is that it is a nonsense to saddle Ministers with detailed operational problems. There has to be a separation of high policy from detailed operations. We know of no Minister who has resigned in recent times for an operational failure in a public service. If that were the tradition it would be difficult to find a more extreme example than the events at Ashworth Hospital. However, Ministers cannot escape final responsibility for the system if the system is so fundamentally defective that the Special Hospitals cannot operate effectively. Ministers, advised by their officials, are responsible for tackling the problems.

2.1.3 In practice of course the Secretary of State delegates his functions. Before 1989 these functions were executed by a Special Hospitals Service Board based within the Department of Health in its various guises.The four Special Hospitals were managed by three Hospital Boards (Moss Side and Park Lane were managed by one Board) and were answerable to this Board; all Special Hospital staff were Department of Health civil servants, and a central admissions panel decided upon admissions to the hospitals.

2.1.4 By the late 1980s, when the rest of the NHS had embraced general management, this arrangement was looking increasingly untenable. Running three large, geographically disparate hospitals from Alexander Fleming House in the Elephant and Castle in South London was a nonsense.

2.1.5 The then government decided to create a new Special Health Authority, namely the SHSA, with a Chief Executive at the centre and general managers at the three (Moss Side and Park Lane becoming Ashworth) hospitals. As we have seen, the new body was given six basic objectives which were to inform all of its work:

(i) ensure the continuing safety of the public;

(ii) ensure the provision of appropriate treatment for patients;

(iii) ensure a good quality of life for patients and staff;

(iv) develop the hospitals as centres of excellence for the training of staff in all disciplines in forensic and other branches of psychiatry and psychiatric care and treatment;

(v) develop closer working relationships with NHS local and regional psychiatric services;

(vi) promote research in fields related to forensic psychiatry.

2.1.6 We mentioned in Part One that the SHSA was given an Operational Brief, dated May 1989, which outlined the rationale for the change of management arrangements and set out the ground rules for the operation of the new body. It is worth examining in some detail.

2.1.7 The SHSA's first, and obviously very important objective, was set out in paragraph 1.2, "to balance the provision of appropriate care and clinical treatment with the safety of the public, the staff and the patients themselves". That task is easy to state but very difficult to execute, particularly regarding serious personality disordered offenders. Failure to solve this difficult conundrum is a major cause of the systemic malaise which has afflicted Ashworth Hospital, as we shall see.

2.1.8 Paragraph 1.5 of the Operational Brief explains that from July 1989 the SHSA, would run the Special Hospitals, exercising its management responsibilities "through General Managers at Hospital level, and accountable to the Secretary of State represented by appropriate machinery within the Department of Health working closely with the Home Office." The arrangements would be reviewed after three to five years.

2.1.9 Chapter 3 of the Operational Brief sets out the factors which are said to influence "the whole of the conduct of the Special Hospital service". Those factors are set out in the next three sub-paragraphs of the section. The first is said to be to care for about 1,400 men and just over 300 women about 75 per cent of whom are either mentally ill or mentally impaired and 25 per cent of whom are psychopathic. It is said **"their underlying clinical condition is susceptible to treatment and rehabilitation to the same degree as that of patients with similar conditions cared for within the NHS"**. As we have said above there are important features distinguishing this group of patients from those in the rest of the NHS. The most important of these features is that they have all been assessed as displaying "dangerous, violent or criminal propensities" to an extent which would represent a risk to public safety if they were not cared for and treated in facilities of security which the NHS does not provide. The Department of Health "Admission Panel" decided admissions to the Special Hospitals against a criterion of "presenting grave and immediate danger" so their care and treatment

> "has to be carried through in conditions of security much more stringent than needs to exist in the NHS . . . This emphasis on security – the need to protect the public – is an essential characteristic of the Service: over 80 per cent of the patients have been convicted of actual criminal offences, and about 60 per cent of patients are 'restricted' . . . Security is the dominant theme in public, media and political perception of the service . . ."

2.1.10 Paragraph 3.2.4 says that the preceding matters create the central challenge to the Service. On the one hand modern psychiatric therapies for the care and treatment of patients' clinical conditions call for "supportive socially-oriented and rehabilitative regimes", whether group or individual, but "the inescapable security requirements dictated by the need to protect the public, staff and other patients has in the past inhibited the application of such regimes. Moreover, a consequence of this situation is that the majority of patients remain under the care of the Service for long periods – the average stay is seven to eight years – so the custodial requirements also diminishes the effectiveness of the indicated therapeutic regime."

2.1.11 What is set out above has to be linked with paragraph 3.3 of the Operational Brief: "Until recently the custodial aspect has tended to dominate operational activity. Increasingly, however, and in keeping with modern concepts of psychiatric care and treatment, the service has sought ways of enabling appropriate therapies to be made available to patients to the maximum extent possible within the dictates of security.To this end, the Government has set six basic objectives to be sought in the evolution of policy and the conduct of operations by the service. These objectives are **prescriptive on the SHSA and must inform all its activities**." (*See* paragraphs **1.18.11** and **2.1.5** above).

2.1.12 In our view, in relation to personality disordered offenders, the strategy set out in the Operational Brief involved considerable risk, particularly since it was "prescriptive on the SHSA and must inform all its activities". This was a factor we bore in mind in concluding that the SHSA was at fault, despite political pressure, in failing, in its lifetime, to make it clear that the same mix of therapy and security for mentally ill offenders and personality disordered offenders was inappropriate.

2.1.13 In his evidence, Mr Kaye, the Chief Executive of the SHSA throughout its life, showed a clear understanding of this problem. He also shows the same understanding in *Service Strategies for Secure Care* (1995), which was apparently published to pass on to the High Security Psychiatric Services Commissioning Board the experience of the SHSA. In his Introduction, Mr Kaye writes: In a clinical context terms such as 'Special Hospital patient' or worse 'Special Hospital patients' are largely meaningless. What is required is an approach that groups patients clinically and coherently and which paves the way for clear, common statements of treatment, management and outcome for each group."

Of personality disordered offenders he writes: "From the mental health service planning perspective, the diagnostic group providing one of the greatest challenges is that with personality disorder. Recent Reports have identified a number of the unresolved issues where research and clinical practice have yet to provide answers to inform the best way forward. These include problems regarding treatability, the characteristics of the disorder, and which treatment interventions are most effective. The issue is often compounded by the particular psychopathology of this group of patients which often includes considerable ability to plan and challenge boundaries. When combined with their potential for dangerousness, this group can be particularly problematic to manage." He recognises a number of matters which we also recognise and accept.

Assessment of the needs of the personality disordered is complex both pre-admission and in the period immediately following admission. Time is required; multi-disciplinary assessment is required and assessment teams should use standardised assessment protocols and procedures. "If patient-mix is not carefully planned their influence on other patients is often disruptive/disturbing making ward management particularly difficult." Later on he says "Patient-mix requires careful thought and planning to avoid potentially explosive situations. Many patients with personality disorder have a great capacity to plan because their psychopathology is such that they are much more able to influence other patients, staff and the hospital system. Adverse events have occurred in high security settings when particular individuals with personality disorder have collaborated. Those with personality disorder are amongst the patients most capable of organising adverse situations and careful high security planning is essential." He refers to other problems as being:

> "Lack of clarity about which interventions are most effective;
>
> Lack of well developed outcome methods;
>
> Assessment of risk: those with personality disorder in Special Hospitals have the highest rate of re-offending post discharge;
>
> Where specific interventions are thought to be useful for particular sub-groups it is based on anecdote rather than clear research evidence – the interventions have not been matched to such groupings in a consistent way;
>
> There is evidence to suggest that in the therapeutic setting the behaviour of the patient will change but following discharge or release there is negligible evidence to show that any improvement is maintained other than in the short term."

2.1.14 By contrast he says the needs of the mentally ill patients who form about two thirds of the special hospital population are different. They present different management and treatment problems. Many respond to modern drug treatment.

2.1.15 Mr Kaye's words contrast sharply with the Operational Brief, which implies that there is one problem which covers all types of patient: too much security is impeding modern therapy which is available to all. Therefore, security must take second place although it must still be there.

2.1.16 Early on in his evidence, Mr Kaye was asked about paragraph 3.2.4 of the Operational Brief, referred to in paragraph **2.1.10** above. He said: "I think this states one of the key dilemmas, tensions and challenges that the SHSA looked at. Certainly in the time leading up to my appointment it was quite clear to me that one of the essentials that the Department of Health wanted to see was the introduction into the Special Hospitals of the hospital ethos of the concept of mental health in its contemporary forms. The balance which is a continual thing between therapy and security, is stated there and runs as a consistent vein throughout the whole life of the SHSA."

2.1.17 In our view in laying down this prescriptive practice, the Operational Brief failed to recognize the distinction made in it between patients in Special Hospitals and NHS units.

Thereafter, throughout its lifetime, as stated above, the SHSA failed to focus on this vital difference. Mr Kaye's counsel appeared to recognize this, because shortly afterwards he asked Mr Kaye, "Did you yourself, when you came to take up your position as Chief Executive, see there as being an inevitable tension between the requirements of therapy and security?" Mr Kaye replied, "Obviously it is quite clear, really from your first visit to a special hospital which is an experience that stays with you, that the twin factors that control the hospital require a great deal of careful approach to ensure that they are complementary and that neither one dominates the other to the inevitable bad outcome of the Hospital's task overall."

2.1.18 This was neither the first nor last time that both question and answer failed to take account of the difference between the patient-mix of the Special Hospitals, but concentrated on the difference between patients in special hospitals and patients in other NHS units. There seems to have been a total failure to recognize the fact, that to bring the twin factors into equilibrium, the type of special hospital patient must be balanced against the security requirements of that type of patient. The security needs of the various types of patient in the special hospitals vary as much as do their therapeutic needs.

2.1.19 Mr Kaye went on to say that his 30 years' experience as a professional manager in the Health Service, including working in the mental health field and in the management of large psychiatric hospitals, had not prepared him for the dimensions of the special hospital world. He wanted "to stress very strongly that it was a different world". He explained this in the following way:

> "– every patient who enters a special hospital is adjudged to be dangerous clinically, physically dangerous;
>
> – every patient who enters a special hospital is very ill, with a severe mental illness or a personality disorder of an extreme nature, or a combination of illnesses;
>
> – every patient who enters a special hospital has exhausted every other type of care. These individuals have been through the whole gamut of health services, social services, the criminal justice system, the whole gamut of what is on offer, and none of that has had a significant effect on their condition;
>
> – these hospitals are the end of the line for these individuals;
>
> – I stress these factors and I stress them very strongly because that trio of values I have just outlined sets the special hospitals apart from any other sort of health care institution . . . and for Professor Edwards to compare [meaning contrast] Rampton, Ashworth and Broadmoor to St Thomas's Hospital neatly puts the point. They [patients] are forced to be there, they are forced to have treatment, and most of them do not want treatment. The whole milieu, the whole ethos, is radically different from anything you are going to see in the Health Service. Until you accept that and take that as your base line for looking at special hospitals, what they do, what problems arise, you will not understand at all what is going on within those institutions."

2.1.20 In saying that, and in what he wrote in *Service Strategies for Secure Care,* there is no doubt that Mr Kaye was aware that the dilemma posed by paragraph 3.2.4 of the Operational Brief, the challenge of providing therapy within a high security institution, has proved impossible to resolve. It could not be resolved. No one hearing the evidence we have heard, or reading the documents we have read, can do other than conclude that there is a great deal of truth in an observation made during the 1994 Owen Ward Inquiry that "security was sacrificed in the headlong rush to therapy". That observation was made in an Inquiry into the taking hostage of a clinical psychologist and a patient by another patient who was on a long-stay ward while undergoing assessment. It was a situation not only involving the usual wrong patient mix; it involved a much more dangerous type of wrong patient mix. The patient who took two hostages was still an unknown quantity; his treatment had not been determined; he had no care plan yet he was admitted unassessed on a ward providing for long term patients. These other patients were needlessly exposed to risk of danger.

2.1.21 No one can criticize the concept that where therapy is appropriate it should be available; nor that patients should not be kept in conditions of security greater than is necessary for their management provided the necessary security structure is in place to ensure the safety of other patients, staff and the public. However, the way Ashworth was organized resulted in scant attention being paid to the balance between the therapy and security needs of patients.

2.1.22 We have no doubt that the application of the recommendations of the Blom-Cooper Report across the whole campus of Ashworth Hospital, without regard to the different regimes needed by the different sub-groups of patients, was a fundamental error which created complex managerial problems rather than an enlightened solution.

2.1.23 The Operational Brief goes on to discuss the new Authority's relationships with other bodies. The Brief notes that:

> 4.3 ". . . the primary objective in creating the SHA is to remove from the Department its present task of operational management, and to place it in the hands of appropriately qualified and experienced managers and practitioners. In short, the intention is that the SHA should stand in the same relationship to the Department on the one hand and the individual hospitals on the other hand, as Health Authorities stand within the NHS framework. *However, the purity of this principle has in practice to be modified to reflect other overriding considerations, including, for example, the responsibilities of the Home Secretary and, at a different level, the nature of public and political perception of the Special Hospitals Service.*" [Our emphasis.]

> 4.4 "The basic functions of the Department and the SHA can be described thus simply: the Department prescribes national strategic guidelines, provides resources, monitors performance and holds the SHA formally to account in these respects; and the SHA, working through the individual hospitals, implements those policies and deploys those resources so as to deliver service to the public at a level acceptable to the Secretary of State."

2.1.24 The Operational Brief noted that, ideally, monitoring by the Department should be minimal. But:

> 4.6 "Even so, the SHA will be accountable, formally and directly to the Secretary of State for Health: the management of the individual hospitals will be directly accountable to the SHA; and these relationships will be reflected in appropriately promulgated powers of direction and usurpation."

It concluded that:

> 4.8 "The intention is that in carrying out the role described above, the SHA should be constituted as a small organisation, operating flexibly and maximising delegation of operational responsibility to Hospital level rather than acting as a centralised interventionist body."

2.1.25 The SHSA was set up with a non-executive Chairman, four executive directors, namely the Chief Executive, and three directors responsible for clinical policy, nursing and finance respectively; and four non-executive directors. As a statutory authority the Chief Executive was accountable to his Board and to the Chairman of his Board, who was appointed by, and accountable to, the Secretary of State. As we noted above, Mr Kaye was appointed

Chief Executive, a position he was to hold throughout the SHSA's life. He commented in his statement as follows:

> "Undoubtedly the key emphasis from the Department of Health was to bring the Special Hospitals from their isolated and vulnerable position halfway between prisons and hospitals towards a status and a recognition of their function as therapeutic centres. Thus the direction was towards integration within the Health Service whilst still maintaining those aspects of security and containment which were essential for the safe and proper functioning of hospitals."

2.1.26 He stressed that there was no intention of replacing one centralized bureaucracy in the Department of Health with another at the SHSA. It was "farcical" to think one could control what was happening on 72 wards on three different sites far away from London:

> "So one of the key activities was to identify, to attract, recruit people, managers and clinicians, of the best quality obtainable, who could take that responsibility at local level and who could enact the decisions and policies of the Authority within their particular patch, so that, as we defined it within the SHSA, the operational responsibility had to rest with the Chief Executive and the General Manager and his or her staff. There is a key relationship between the Chief Executive and the General Manager in analysing and pursuing that, but in no real sense could a Chief Executive sitting in London be in charge of what is happening in wards in Rampton Hospital, Ashworth Hospital, or Broadmoor Hospital."

2.1.27 The division of responsibility for operational issues between Mr Kaye and his General Managers, principally in this case Mrs Miles, is a key issue in this Inquiry. The distinction between aspects of operations and policy has been much discussed in recent years, notoriously in the case of the Prison Service. The dividing line cannot be drawn too firmly, but we would stress that, whilst day to day management must rest with the General Manager of the Hospital, the Chief Executive of the SHSA was the chief accountable officer of the body set up to manage the system. If something was consistently going wrong he had the responsibility to do something.

2.1.28 The role of the Medical Director needs to be understood. Dr Pamela Taylor's principal role was to act as advisor to the Board. She had no line of management relationship with the General Managers of the Hospitals or the consultant doctors. We shall return to this later.

2.1.29 Such was the Operational Brief, one replete with tensions and ambiguities. But the SHSA also had other problems. In Mr Kaye's words, the SHSA was in charge of three hospitals deficient in high quality clinical input, appropriate management systems and management talent, yet they were having to tackle decades of isolation and a prevailing custodial culture which was at best paternal, at worst punitive. The management arrangements still meant that all key decisions were made in London. Inhibition of local management remained a problem.

2.1.30 Mrs Nelson, who became Chairman of the SHSA in 1993, confirmed the picture of the Hospitals as unduly custodial, isolated, clinical backwaters, where sound managerial capacity across all disciplines was lacking. However, whether Ashworth Hospital was "unduly custodial" by that time is questionable. If "unduly custodial" is meant to be equated with "too much security", then Miss Kinsley's 1992 Security Audits of each of the Special Hospitals tell a different story – one of inadequate security policies and practices.

2.1.31 In calling for devolution of management as far as possible to the local level the Operational Brief created a significant dilemma for the SHSA Headquarters team. They were required to retain accountability of the Services but to devolve day to day responsibility to the general managers of each of the Special Hospitals. In the case of Ashworth this balancing act failed. Without being more interventionist the task of the SHSA was virtually an impossible one. The end result was a rather large gap between rhetoric and reality.

2.1.32 The SHSA's First Development Plan for the five years from April 1991, devised by the SHSA to implement its responsibilities under the Operational Brief, illustrates the point.

2.1.33 Section 7 of the Development Plan concerns "**A better balance between quality and security of care**". It begins as follows, "There is an unavoidable tension in providing treatment and care within a secure environment as, to some extent, security considerations will always represent an intrusion into quality of life. This places a double obligation upon the SHSA. First, while acknowledging the fundamental importance of maintaining security in our hospitals we need to remain constantly open to the possibility that the balance between security and treatment can be improved through changes in one regime or the other. In that respect we have identified opportunities to improve quality of care (different approaches to delivery of treatment and care, improvements in environmental standards, less restrictive practices and so on) which do not prejudice security considerations. In pursuing these we intend to be innovatory ourselves and to take full account of developments elsewhere in methods of treatment and care and to respond to changes of thinking with regard to their delivery to particular categories of patient. The second obligation is to do all that we can to ensure that the patients in our hospitals are those who need to be there and to minimise the number of potential patients of ours placed inappropriately elsewhere."

2.1.34 What in fact happened, as we shall see below, is that far from creating a "better balance", in 1992/1993 two competing projects were put in hand: the security audits of Miss Kinsley focused on security and the work of the Task Force just a few months later which focused on the "liberalization" agenda post-Blom-Cooper. These two pieces of work clashed and began to create tensions at the Hospital.

2.1.35 Over decades security has always been within the province of the therapeutic staff and there has been a traditional resistence to placing it in the hands of specialist security staff. **In Part Three we recommend changes in certain matters of security.**

2.1.36 Section 8 of the Development Plan concerns "Openness to other views and influences". This section of our Report is concerned, among other matters with "years of concealment of information". Witness after witness has given evidence critical of the failure to share full Reports and their recommendations, particularly from the point of view that it is the best way to explain what has gone wrong and why changes have to be made. In the evidence gathering months of the life of this Inquiry, when the Chairman and Secretary were asking for copies of Reports and other documents, the first Owen Ward Report they received was the 19-page Report with no appendices. Eventually they received the so called "Interim Report" (which is in fact the full Report) and the appendices. The first time the Committee saw the Report actually circulated to staff at Ashworth (the so-called nine page Report) was when we received and read the submission of UNISON to which it was attached as an appendix. The management culture was as secretive and inward looking as the Hospital itself. **Censorship and secrecy do not provide openness to other views and influences.**

2.1.37 The last section of the Development Plan, section 10, concerns "Managing the Business". It begins: "We have placed this item at the end of our programme of action, but we are in no doubt about its importance. If we do not achieve the objectives described in this section, we will also fail in our other, more higher profile aims, because good management underpins and drives all our action programmes." Another bulleted intention under the programme theme "Managing the Business" was: "We register our intention to introduce ward management in all our hospitals. This will devolve management further down the organisation, draw in a new generation of managers and be a key factor in changing the existing culture." As we know effective control of security went to ward level. Miss Kinsley told us that if she had known that security was to be devolved to ward teams she would have regarded that as "totally unacceptable". **So it was.**

2.1.38 In respect of the above the performance of the SHSA did not meet with its fine rhetoric. The words did, but the results were poor.

The SHSA and the Department

2.1.39 To return to 1989, the intended direction of travel was clear: the dead hand of Whitehall was to be lifted and a new, more streamlined organization was to take its place. Central government would no longer try to second-guess managers on the ground. Increased delegation to the hospitals would help them to develop in line with the rest of the NHS.

2.1.40 The central government involvement was largely limited to a policy branch within the Department of Health, headed by Mr Ian Jewesbury, which liaised with the SHSA. Mr Jewesbury's branch advised Ministers on setting the SHSA's annual action plan and on achievement against that plan, and briefed them on any issues such as serious incidents.

2.1.41 Although delegation was the order of the day, there were powerful forces which meant that the centre of government would continue to maintain a careful watch over the activities of the SHSA and the hospitals. Not only the statutory duties of the Home Secretary, but also the high profile of many of the patients concerned meant that Ministers were bound to want to know about the high security hospitals and have the capacity to take firm decisive action if needed. It is instructive to note that one of the issues that the Operational Brief lists as requiring early attention was, "clarification of how much discretion the SHA will have to develop and implement policies for Special Hospitals, subject to reporting arrangements to the Minister akin to those for Regional Health Authorities."

2.1.42 The Department set the SHSA an action plan every year and every year the responsible Minister met members of the SHSA in a formal review meeting to discuss progress. This annual plan would be divided into a series of tasks, each with its target date. Thus, for example, the Ministerial Review action plan for 1995/6 included the following tasks:

(i) to incorporate the recommendations of the HAS Review into Ashworth into the business plan and to Report on progress by October 1995;

(ii) to develop a set of quality standards with reference to security and to report on progress by October 1995;

(iii) to produce policies for future provision for various patient groups, including personality disordered patients, by September 1995;

(iv) to audit multi-disciplinary working; and

(v) to complete the introduction of 24-hour therapeutic care on to all wards in each hospital by April 1996.

Thus, Mr Jewesbury told us, the Department of Health delegated responsibility for operational matters and avoided getting involved in the detail of issues such as supervision of visits and searching. But the Department did give a broad detailed strategic steer to the SHSA and it was well understood, we were told, that Ministers still needed to know when things went wrong.

2.1.43 The liaison between the Department and the SHSA was as follows. Mr Jewesbury told us that he and colleagues met Mr Kaye and other officers of the SHSA monthly. They would discuss the Action Plan tasks and other matters of concern. Outside those meetings there was considerable *ad hoc* contact, in particular to discuss serious incidents. The Department received papers and minutes of Authority meetings, although some papers were circulated to Authority members only.

2.1.44 The SHSA was the main point of contact for the Department, given that that was the body set up to oversee the Hospitals; rarely did Mr Jewesbury or his colleagues contact the Hospitals directly. In the case of serious incidents his branch's role was to ensure that the matter had been properly investigated and any necessary action taken by the SHSA, although the Department was much more heavily involved in the implementation of the Blom-Cooper Report.

2.1.45 Both Mr Kaye and Mr Jewesbury argued that the system generally worked well. Mr Kaye noted the inherent tension between keeping the Department of Health and the Home Office aware of what was going on without compromising the independence of the Authority. There were disputes and arguments, but these were overcome. He argued that he was open in communicating serious incidents, although he admitted the Department was not always shown Reports of serious incidents, such as the Owen Ward Report. That Report, which we discuss below, is an example of how the liaison links broke down, leaving the Department and Ministers badly ill-informed.

2.1.46 The relationship was not one of equals. When we pressed Mr Jewesbury on the extent of his powers to force the SHSA to release Reports he was clear that he could have demanded that the SHSA gave the HAS a Report. The Department's reserve powers were always in place.

2.1.47 The Department of Health had delegated operational management to the SHSA. To paraphrase the Rt Hon Aneurin Bevan MP, bedpans in the Special Hospitals were now Mr Kaye's business. But individual failures of care and management were still likely to rouse public anger and concern, and thus involve Ministers. We have speculated that if the Owen Ward Report had reached Ministers, a public inquiry such as ours might have been established in 1994. The very fact of our Inquiry demonstrates the (entirely legitimate) continuing close interest in, and need for oversight of, these Hospitals by the centre of government.

2.2.0 The Creation of Ashworth

2.2.1 We have seen that one of the first tasks for the SHSA was to merge Moss Side and Park Lane Hospitals into a single entity. Before 1989 Moss Side and Park Lane were managed by a single Hospital Board with a single administrator in charge, but there were two hospital management teams. In practice they were run virtually as two completely separate institutions. They had different security systems, so that staff and patients could not easily move from one to the other and patients from Moss Side had grave difficulty in accessing the superior facilities in Park Lane (now Ashworth North). The staff at Park Lane would have nothing to do with those at Moss Side and vice versa.

2.2.2 Moss Side, which occupied what is now Ashworth South (which has since been sold to the Prison Service) and Ashworth East, was an old-fashioned hospital for patients suffering from learning disabilities or mental illness. Park Lane was a new hospital which had taken much of the Broadmoor overspill, including many patients classified as psychopaths. It had a high, very secure wall and saw itself as a modern and therapeutic institution. We were told the two hospitals had very different cultures; the fact that the Blom-Cooper Inquiry into complaints at Ashworth largely focused on the ill-treatment of mentally ill patients on the South Site bears this out. Mr Peter Green, the Director of Business Development, told us that since that Report criticized the Hospital a lot of the staff within the North Site were very angry at being tarred with the same brush. Others made similar comments.

2.2.3 The new Hospital came into being in February 1990. No witness we heard regarded this as a positive change. Mr Ryan, the Assistant Secretary of the UNISON branch at Ashworth, said that he and colleagues in Park Lane had thought it a mistake creating a larger hospital in this way. Others including the Chief Executive and senior members of the SHSA were unenthusiastic about the merger.

Thus Professor Taylor told us that the Department of Health had taken the decision that they were to combine the two hospitals under one management "regardless". She remarked:

> "I have to say I do not think it was a good idea at the time and nothing that has happened subsequently has encouraged me to change that view."

Miss Kinsley did not think that the SHSA would have chosen to amalgamate the two hospitals. She is probably right, but merging the two hospitals was the first task assigned to the SHSA. That said, we have seen no evidence that anyone in the SHSA sought to persuade the Department of Health that the decision to merge the two Hospitals was ill-conceived. In the same way despite strongly held contrary views, eloquently expressed by Mr Kaye, as will be seen, the SHSA did not impress upon Ministers that the needs of the different groups required a more sophisticated approach than blanket implementation (if indeed they had formed this view at the time).

2.2.4 Dr Strickland in his statement noted that the doctors in both Park Lane and Moss Side had been resistant to the merger due to the different cultures and the retrograde step of creating a larger hospital with more remote management. We asked a number of witnesses how things had been run in the pre-merger days. Mr Preece had the following comments on policies:

> "Certainly prior to 1990 our experience was that there were very few procedures, but that they were standardised throughout the whole hospital [sc. Park Lane]. The room for interpretation on those procedures was minimal, if you like . . .
>
> . . . I think we have to understand that as Ashworth North was opening up very rapidly in the early 1980s, mid-1980s, the amalgamation of the two sites in 1990, the reorganization and restructuring of the Hospital into Ashworth, policies and procedures were secondary to just managing the system as it was developing. I do not think there was any ward on Ashworth at that time that had a complete set of policies or procedures, or would know where to find them."

2.2.5 Mr Ryan told us that when he had started at Park Lane in the early 1980s communication between the rehabilitation unit, where he worked, and the wards had been very good. There was a three shift system with a charge nurse in charge of each. The charge nurse had been able to sort out problems on the ward quickly. A long handover allowed good communication between shifts. **The three shift system, however, had its own problems (*see* the Mallalieu Report in paragraph 2.4.0 *et seq.* below).**

2.2.6 Mr Maxwell told us that rigorous searching was carried out at Park Lane and the amount of possessions in patients' rooms was reasonably well controlled, although he did note that security in those days was a bit oppressive.

2.2.7 One can well imagine that these witnesses are looking back with rose-tinted spectacles. But it is certainly arguable that Park Lane before the merger had been functioning effectively. Moss Side clearly had very major problems, as Blom-Cooper demonstrated, but it helped no one for the whole of the new hospital to be tarred with the same brush. The very right and proper reforms recommended by Sir Louis and his team were primarily aimed at ensuring that vulnerable mentally disordered people were given the care they needed and protection from abuse. The problems arising from the application of those reforms across the board to all patients, including those suffering from severe personality disorder, are a leitmotiv of our Report.

2.2.8 We have the benefit of hindsight, but merging the two Hospitals with profoundly

different cultures was to present enormously difficult problems. This imposed merger no doubt saved management costs and improved efficiency but did little to improve the overall quality of the clinical environment for what were, by any standards, very difficult patients.

2.3.0 The New Hospital's Structure

2.3.1 In 1989 Unit General Managers (UGMs) were appointed at each of the three Special Hospitals. Mr Brian Johnson was appointed UGM at Ashworth. He was responsible to Mr Kaye who, we were told, kept in close touch with what was happening in the Hospital, visiting regularly and meeting staff and patients.

2.3.2 The overall hospital management was the responsibility of a Hospital Management Group (HMG). The Management Group consisted of a number of functional heads, responsible for individual clinical groups, etc, although the creation of a Director of Rehabilitation did reflect the development of a more multi-disciplinary approach. The security function was vested in the Director of Nursing. We discuss the importance of having a dedicated security presence on the Board below.

2.3.3 In early 1992 Ward Managers were introduced to bring a greater cohesion to the work of the three nursing shifts (inconsistency between shifts had been a criticism of the Mallalieu and Rowe Reports, as discussed below) and to the management of wards in general. The nurse management structure was restructured to flatten the hierarchy leaving only one tier between the Director of Nursing Services and the Ward Managers. We discuss the Ward Manager system in Part Four below.

2.4.0 The Report into the Deaths of Patient Stephen Mallalieu

2.4.1 The Mallalieu Report resulted from an external Inquiry into the death of Stephen Mallalieu in his bedroom on the evening of 8 March 1990. He was strangled in his bedroom on Owen Ward by a fellow ward patient, Gary Murphy, who was later convicted of his murder. The Inquiry team comprised Dr J. Higgins (a member of the SHSA), Chairman, Mr D. Atha (retired administrator of Rampton), and Mr A. Backer-Holst (Nursing Officer, Department of Health).

2.4.2 At the time the Ward which housed 24 patients was full. It had been opened in 1987 and was the latest ward to be opened on the Ashworth North site. It was intended to be run in a highly structured way to deal with difficult patients from medium and low dependency wards, and patients in transition from high dependency wards. However, it was described to the Inquiry Team as a "dumping ground". Indeed the three nursing shifts operated manifestly different regimes. In 1988 a new RMO took over and sought to introduce a coherent ward policy; this was met with resistance by many of the nursing staff.

2.4.3 The proposed changes in how the Ward was to be run, what types of patients were to be accepted and how many staff were required came to be crystallized in the differing nursing attitudes towards the dormitory areas, where the patients were to have access and how this access was to be supervised by staff based at the night station. Easy agreement was not possible and the senior nurse manager had to insist that the Ward be seen and manned as a medium dependency ward, not as a medium/high dependency ward and the patients allowed access to the dormitory areas in accordance with the existing policy. Nevertheless the function of the Ward remained unclear and not fully agreed, for all the staff still saw Owen Ward as being the ward next in dependency in level to the highest dependency wards.

2.4.4 On duty at the time of the killing were a charge nurse, two staff nurses and two enrolled nurses. At 4.30 pm the patients returned from work areas of the Hospital. The dormitory area, where the bedrooms were, was unlocked for a short time to allow patients to deposit their working clothes, then the patients received medication and their tea after the dormitory area had again been locked. At 5.30 pm the dormitory area was unlocked to allow patients access to washing facilities and their clothes and then remained open. At 6.15 pm the patients were asked if they were going to evening social activities. Seven elected to do so and were escorted to them by one of the staff nurses, who remained with them. Whilst carrying out a patient count the remaining staff nurse checked with the patients what periodicals they wanted to order, and reported the patients' orders to the Charge Nurse, who was in his office. The Charge Nurse asked for Mr Murphy to be sent to his office where, it is said, he remained until 7.30 pm discussing with the Charge Nurse the wisdom of his order, because the Charge Nurse considered he had ordered "nasties",which he would not have allowed his children to buy. It is not suggested that he had ordered pornographic periodicals. Mr Murphy then returned to the dormitory area, and in particular to the corridor in which both he and Mr Mallalieu had bedrooms (called side rooms at Ashworth). The staff nurse and an enrolled nurse had by this time returned to the night station from which the corridors could be observed. The staff nurse and the Charge Nurse then did a corridor patrol and Mr Mallalieu was seen to be alive and well. The Charge Nurse returned to his office and the staff nurse returned to the night station. At about 7.40 pm he went to the toilet leaving the enrolled nurse in the night station. The enrolled nurse then commenced another patrol leaving the night station unmanned. The second enrolled nurse was making drinks for the staff. At about 7.40 pm the Charge Nurse called for help and the others appeared to see him putting Murphy into a Ward side room. He recounted what Murphy had told him and they went to Mr Mallalieu's room. Help was called and he was pronounced dead at 8.10 pm.

2.4.5 Paragraph 4.7 of the Report concludes that between 7.30 pm and 7.40 pm the night station was unmanned. No one saw Murphy leave his room, visit Mr Mallalieu and then return to his room. Thereafter no one saw him leave his room again, re-visit Mr Mallalieu's room and then pass through the night station to go to the charge nurse's room where he told his story.

2.4.6 On further investigation the Team found that the practice of management of the night station varied from shift to shift. An analysis of the practice of the material shift demonstrated that from time to time the night station was not manned. The only policy document there was gave instructions of what had to be done but not how it had to be done.

The Report notes that the day to day management of the Ward was at the direction of the Charge Nurse who based the general activities of the patients on a general policy applicable to all wards in the Hospital drawn up in August 1988. That comprised guidelines, the interpretation of which was at the discretion of the charge nurse.

2.4.7 The disagreements amongst the staff, referred to in paragraph **2.4.2** above, had still not been resolved, and in paragraph 6.4 of the Report it is said the difficulties and uncertainties "are reflected in the different practices of the different nursing teams. The autonomy of the Charge Nurse on each shift was felt to be sacrosanct. There was not felt to be a pressing need for a unified set of policies to provide guidelines within which each team could perform in an individual way and in response to day to day variation of patient needs."

There was an Operational Policy Document for the ward, drawn up in 1988, which described the regime of Owen Ward, general management, the expected behaviour of patients, the philosophy of care and the timetables of patients' activities. Again, how this policy was implemented was at the discretion of the Charge Nurse.

2.4.8 In commenting on the Owen Ward Policy Document, the Report argued that:

> " – The role of the Charge Nurses in policy matters was unclear; whether they were to implement policy made by the entire clinical team and agreed with management on a day to day basis and in the light of the needs of patients, or whether they,

together with the Senior Nurse manager, decided the policy of the ward.

– The section on general philosophy contained ambiguities about the types of patients to be admitted and whether dependence on security was the principle criterion for admissions.

– It was far too vague and contained unresolved ambiguities which allowed too much scope for varying interpretation of day to day management by the three nursing teams."

The Inquiry team thought "the adverse characteristics" of the document were,

"probably a reflection of the history of Owen Ward, the lack of clarity about its purpose, the need to provide a compromise between differing views of the Charge Nurses, the lack of multi-disciplinary input when the document was drawn up, the lack of proper mechanism for producing policy, reviewing it and monitoring its implementation, and an inadequate understanding of the proper role of different individuals in this process."

2.4.9 In Chapter 8 the Report concluded:

"– Owen Ward lacked a proper operational policy.

– Although Mr Murphy apparently showed no obvious management problem, only two weeks before at a PCT meeting he had been described as probably dangerous as he had talked about killing people in the past and had expressed a number of previously violent fantasies. So it was concluded that he had been given an insufficient level of supervision when he was in his side room.

– Management at Ashworth had not appreciated the deficiencies in the operational policies of Owen Ward and had not provided a proper mechanism for the production, monitoring and review of them.

– The term dependency was not understood. It covered both the level of dangerousness and the level of clinical nursing required by a patient, but they were two distinct and separate issues.

– It was unacceptable that the general management of the ward should vary from shift to shift according to the wishes or beliefs of the charge nurse."

2.4.10 Attached to the Report is the response of the Ashworth Hospital Management. As so often with regard to reports the management accepted the Report and set out its intentions:

"– The Owen Ward operational policy was inadequate,

– Multi-disciplinary agreed operational policies for every ward in the Hospital were being formulated;

– House rules would be developed for each ward to give patients and staff better understanding;

– Significant difference of application of agreed operational policies by different shifts was unacceptable;

– The way forward was to appoint ward managers and work on that was underway with the Special Hospital Service;

– Work would be undertaken to clarify 'dependency'.

2.4.11 If, during the years under consideration, Ashworth Hospital had been willing and able to bring good intentions to fruition the story we have to tell would have been different.

2.4.12 Some attempt to follow-up this Report was made. Mr Green told us that Mr Johnson the then Unit General Manager demanded in the wake of the Mallalieu Report that each ward submit two policies, one on access to bedrooms, the other on the general policy of the ward. The Hospital Management Team reviewed the documents and made comments. Mr Green thought that wards did produce policies on access to bedrooms; not all managed to produce a document on the general policy and function of the wards. **This is a recurring theme of recommendations accepted but only part-implemented at best**.

2.5.0 The Rowe Report (Report of the Independent Inquiry into the death of Derek Anthony Williams, who died on 19 November 1990 in Forster Ward, Ashworth Hospital (North).)

2.5.1 Mr Williams was allegedly killed by another patient, 'A'. who had a personality disorder and had been on the ward for the previous ten weeks in order to be assessed under section 38 of the Mental Health Act 1983. At the time of the Inquiry 'A' had not been tried but he was later tried and acquitted of murder.

2.5.2 It seems that Mr Williams was homosexual and 'A' was his regular partner at the time, but the day before his death, Mr Williams and another patient had discussed the possibility of having a more permanent relationship.

2.5.3 At the Inquiry, the nurse members of the POA refused to give evidence on the basis that the Committee refused to adjourn to allow inspection of documents believed by the POA to exist and which the solicitor for the POA had previously asked to see. In paragraph 14 of the Report it is said the nursing staff could have made an enormous contribution to the Inquiry. In the event the Committee heard no evidence from nurses, saw no post mortem Reports, and saw no statements made to the police save for that of an acting charge nurse. So it was impossible to draw any conclusions as to the circumstances of the death, how or why Mr Williams died or the identity of the killer.

2.5.4 We find it disquieting, to say the least that an investigation into the death of a patient should have proved so difficult. In a proper, effective and caring clinical environment, the search for the truth would have been second nature and urgent. Today a failure to respond in such a manner would rightly be regarded as wholly unprofessional and unacceptable.

2.5.5 However, the Committee of Mr John Rowe QC (Chairman) and the other two members, Dr D. Chiswick (a consultant forensic psychiatrist) and Mr W. Jones (Chief Administrative nursing officer, Clwyd Health Authority) were able to consider and comment on the management, structure, and policies which applied to Forster Ward. Their Report was circulated in full, although, due to the criminal trial, some time after the event. However, the Hospital's response to the Report was rolled up in the response to the Blom-Cooper Report.

2.5.6 Forster Ward was a medium dependency ward for about 25 personality disordered patients. Prior to its creation by a former senior consultant personality disordered patients were treated on the same wards as mentally ill patients. Its concept was that the patients should live in a therapeutic community in which there was no compulsion to work, be educated or take recreation.

2.5.7 The only written provisions as to the strategy for Forster Ward were contained in two documents exhibited with the Report as appendices A and B. "A" dated 12 December 1988 is described as a "Policy Document", but it was considered to be an introduction to the ward, and was a collection of statements and directions from different disciplines. It was not, according to the Committee, "a statement of operational policy, with instructions for practices and procedures, stating the aims of the ward, and setting out, by encouragement and direction and instruction, the precise steps which are needed to achieve those aims". Its directions "are vague, and it is difficult to discern what practices and procedures are intended for whom."

2.5.8 The Committee, in commenting on the Mallalieu Report, which they saw, and which had been produced in August 1990, said, "it is interesting to note that the first conclusion of their Report was that Owen Ward lacked a proper operational policy."

2.5.9 Appendix "B" was compiled on 10 October 1990. It authors knew of Mallalieu's death but they did not have knowledge of the contents of the Report which had not been published. The Committee considered appendix "B" to be "defensive and resistant to change". It is a document entitled "Supervision of patients' bedrooms and access by patients". It is signed by Mr Fenwick, the then Senior Clinical Nursing manager, and counter-signed by the members of the PCT including two RMOs, one of whom was Dr Strickland. Towards the end of the first part (Preamble and Ward Philosophy), the following statement appears:

> "The Patient Care Team discussed the possibility of restrictions following the death of a patient on Owen Ward earlier this year, but unanimously agreed that any major change in the current regime would be disastrous."

The Rowe Inquiry team considered that this betrayed the fact that minds were closed to change.

2.5.10 The Report continues, "Our view is that appendices A and B provided no strategy or philosophy; the head of medical services told us that she regretted that these appendices had not been drafted under medical direction, and she acknowledged that there was no real medical or psychological policy provided for Forster Ward."

We note, however, that by counter-signing the document, two RMO consultant forensic psychiatrists clearly approved of appendix B. In later reports this situation is repeated, and PCTs and RMOs continue to challenge policies which are not ward-devised.

2.5.11 The Report also mentions the attitude of other professionals. "The clinical psychologist on the ward described the intention of it as being liberal, where there was peer group pressure, so that, in the course of daily living, relationships were formed in the ward and patients advised and assisted each other. His views are that the patients should take responsibility, and there should be a minimum amount of security, with a relaxed atmosphere; he said the patients 'should have space'." Later in paragraphs 8.9 and 8.10 the Report continues, "The clinical psychologist on the ward told us that within reason the patients should be allowed to express their sexuality. His view was that in the ordinary community outside the Hospital, persons would be free to pursue their sexual proclivities and that to restrict them within the Hospital would be to follow double standards. He regarded himself has having acquired expertise in sexual counselling and therapy, and he thinks it appropriate to have a number of homosexuals in the community on Forster Ward . . . The clinical psychologist was an influential figure on the ward, and his authority was accepted. He adopted a permissive, even liberal attitude towards the homosexual behaviour . . . But this activity distorted both the population of the ward and its atmosphere. Tensions were produced; and furthermore, there was unfairness, in that one group was allowed to indulge their sexuality, whereas another, the heterosexuals, could not."

2.5.12 The Committee found a good deal of evidence to show "that homosexual conduct took place in bedrooms on Forster Ward, either during the afternoon or in the evening; senior social workers accepted that it took place and said the nursing staff turned a blind eye to its activity; and the patients gave us very clear accounts of the way in which sexual activity could take place, during the afternoons or in the evenings, without any danger of being disturbed, and that such sexual activity took place either as predatory chance encounters, or in pursuance of committed sexual association. One patient described how the homosexuals flaunted their sexuality, and openly referred to their practice of it and enjoyment of it, to the annoyance and irritation of the patents who were not homosexual; he said he had warned the nursing staff because tension was growing, but there was no response. The evidence of nursing management was that a member of staff who was passing a bedroom and suspected some sexual activity would cough or rattle his keys."

2.5.13 The Committee found evidence of a sexual association between Mr Williams and patient A and some indication of a possible break in that association which might have displeased A. They considered the sexual behaviour on Forster Ward needed to be addressed. "As a witness has said, the ethos of Forster Ward was to live in this small society with rules; yet there were no rules for patients' sexual conduct . . . The blind eye which the staff were turning to homosexual behaviou . . . is the clearest possible indication that there were no rules governing sexual behaviour at all."

2.5.14 At paragraph 8.12 the Report concludes that there was no strategy and no medical or psychological policy for Forster Ward, and, at paragraph 8.13, that, "there was too great a latitude both as to the criteria for the admission to Forster Ward and as to its way of life. No one stated what was the purpose of the Ward. No one stated how patients should be assessed as to their suitability for admission to Forster Ward . . . These failures became all the more critical when the tensions and problems created by homosexual behaviour had their effect."

2.5.15 So, within the same year (1990), the PCTs on two separate wards were seriously criticised for lacking clear operational policies of strategy and searching as well as poor admission criteria.

2.5.16 The Report commended the suggestion of the Head of Medical Services that there should be a two level structure of the ward, or two linked wards – one for assessment and the other residential. They noted that A was on the ward and still being assessed, and that in the short time he had been there he had shown some resentment and obduracy. Apart from the individual considerations relating to A, they said:

> "we think that the concept of collecting a number of young psychopaths on one ward in a Special Hospital for the purpose of living in a therapeutic community calls for the utmost care in the assessment and preparation of those patients. The assessment and preparation should be undertaken at the first stage, or in one of the two wards, to which we have referred in the idea above".

2.5.17 This was also suggested in the later Owen Ward Report in 1994, and the creation of the PDU served only to exacerbate the problem of inadequate patient mix referred to in the Rowe Report.

2.5.18 In the setting of Ashworth Hospital the hope expressed in the Report at paragraph 8.16, was as vain a hope, as many expressed before and later. "We hope our conclusion is clear. In all the circumstances to which we have referred there was a foreseeable risk of violence, and it could and should have been reduced. Urgently, a conclusion must be reached as to what is the purpose of Forster Ward, and what is its strategy and philosophy, with particular reference to sexual behaviour, and that conclusion must be committed to writing, and published to every person concerned in the work on the ward."

2.5.19 The Report then turns its attention to management. It considers that while a rigid, hierarchical model is inappropriate, and non-therapeutic, there must be clinical leadership which is recognised by and acceptable to all members of the ward team. That leadership can only be vested in the RMOs under whose care the patients are admitted and treated. "Within Forster Ward there seems to have been a reluctance to recognise any leadership, and our impression is that cultural leadership seems to have devolved into the hands of the clinical psychologist. This is not appropriate, because the clinical psychologists do not have to carry the same obligations as the Responsible Medical Officer. They do not have the responsibility imposed by section 34."

Even this is not the panacea some might believe. We have commented, in paragraph 2.5.9 (above), that two RMOs counter-signed appendix B, described in the Report as "defensive and resistant to change". The Report, itself, stresses this at paragraph 9.6, "But there seems to be a reluctance on the part of the staff to consider change"; that is evident in appendix B, and in the passage cited above in paragraph 8.4, from appendix B, where it is said that "any major change in the current regime would be disastrous."

2.5.20 In the absence of clear leadership the Committee said that the ward policy of Forster Ward had been allowed to drift, and a lack of structure had developed. The patient care team had no fixed chairman or leader, and the Charge Nurse of the day simply took notes, and conducted proceedings. This was unsatisfactory and it should be put and run on a properly established basis.

2.5.21 In dealing with "nursing", the gist of the criticism of the Report was that to run a therapeutic community required a high quality of nursing. On Forster Ward there was insufficient nurse/patient contact to provide real therapy. Nursing staff, including primary nurses, were often away on escort duties. They provided no therapy to those they were escorting and provided no therapy for those they left behind. Often there were three nurses to look after 15 to 29 patients which was quite inadequate for therapeutic purposes. The Report recommended that health care assistants should be used to provide pure security as escorts and managing the night station.

2.5.22 In paragraph 10.6 the Report identified four important features which undermined therapy on Forster ward:

1. POA insistence on minimum staffing levels for internal escorting duties. They insisted on escorting patients to physical education where they just waited around or used the appliances themselves.
2. Bitter inter-departmental rivalry which has existed for a long time before 1990 between nursing staff and physical education staff. It disrupted the physical education programme. The nursing staff were dictating the running of the Hospital.
3. The attitude of some of the nursing staff. One member of staff apparently described himself to patients as a "lunatic attendant". Some apparently swore at patients with obscenities and exchanged oaths with them.
4. The industrial action by the POA adversely affected therapy on the ward.

2.5.23 In the section of appendix B dealing with "Nursing Procedure for the Observation of Patients Sleeping area", item 7 states, "Patients based on the ward may visit one another in their bedrooms but will be responsible for avoiding antagonism . . . " However, in paragraph 11.1 the Report says, "But the general opinion was that the occupier alone should have access to his bedroom, and that non-occupiers should not be permitted such access or visits". At paragraph 11.2, the Report concludes that this should be the rule. "The ward does indeed provide opportunity, quite apart from the bedrooms, to develop relationships between patients."

2.5.24 The lack of clear operational policies, the failure to confront patients' behaviour in a misjudged attempt to create a therapeutic community and the lack of medical leadership will become all too familiar themes.

2.6.0 Miss Kinsley's Security Audits

2.6.1 Miss Joy Kinsley was the first full time employee of the SHSA. She had been a prison governor, and after being the Head of Personnel, she became the Director of Security in 1991. In 1992 she carried out security audits at each of the three High Security Hospitals. Her Audit of Ashworth Hospital was produced in July 1992 shortly before the publication of the Blom-Cooper Inquiry Report.

2.6.2 We quote some extracts from her Report:

"4.3 There was no evidence of an adequate policy on searching, or indeed on physical security checks. Practice varied, not only in line with the level of security or dependency but also with the judgment or whim of the charge nurse. We suspected considerable differences in practice between the shifts and this was confirmed by one ward manager who claimed to have found that 90% of security checks were carried out by one shift. We were able to meet some of the new ward managers who again seemed to have varying attitudes and perceptions of security needs. Two were of the view that searching was not an appropriate nursing task and one of those actually thought it conflicted with the UKCC Code of Practice. This was disturbing, particularly combined with an apparent lack of willingness to accept advice. Unfortunately the attitudes that produce these situations can lead to a general disregard for security matters.

4.4 There should be clear policies, and specific operational instructions setting out the frequency and method of physical security (fabric) and room searches. Staff should be left in no doubt about this important task and management should set parameters so that there are constant checks as to the efficiency and appropriateness of the procedures.

4.5 There was the related problem of how much property it was reasonable for patients to have in their rooms. This problem is common to all three special hospitals and there is a need for guidelines which will both allow the patients to develop their own individuality and the staff to be able to search without serious difficulty. In some places there was a lack of commonsense with curtains presenting a fire risk in rooms where patients were able to smoke. There was a general shortage of storage facilities, which also helped to make matters worse. It really is no more than a good housekeeping matter and should be seen as such.

5.9 . . . The staff seen on Lawrence considered that searching was not so important because of the type of patient on the ward, whereas their colleagues on Macaulay appreciated that it was important because parole patients have so much more opportunity to acquire items they should not have. The relaxed atmosphere on both wards was appropriate to low dependency patients, but nevertheless basic principles of security need to be adhered to.

17.1 . . . The Security Manager and his staff are based in offices in the central nursing office in Parkbourn. There can be no doubt that the amalgamation of the two hospitals with their totally different traditions and attitudes to security has brought very considerable problems to this vital department. Internal staffing problems, the removal of the escorts, the rapid changes being brought about by the inception of ward management, the sheer weight of work caused by the 1990 industrial action and the Ashworth Inquiry, to name only a few factors, have been responsible for the tremendous pressure on security personnel. My anxiety is that despite the valiant efforts of the Acting Security Manager (and that position ought to be clarified as soon as possible) there is a creeping marginalisation of security matters which will be harmful. It is perhaps part of an understandable reaction to the philosophy of those who caused the strike, but the Authority has now produced its own Principles of Security which need to be absorbed by the staff. Fresh thought should be given to the structure and position of the Security Department and the way that it operates within the organisation. Certainly, clear standards have to be established and made clear to staff.

17.4 The Security Department essentially does nothing to ensure that searching and security checks generally are carried out. In the past this was considered to be the responsibility of the ward Senior Clinical Nurse Manager and now the Ward Manager. The Department has a two hour slot on Control and Restraint refresher courses when it addresses the need for effective searching (rooms and patients) to be carried. The Department also conducts induction training which covers such matters as control of keys and radios. The Security Department, judging by its proposed induction training brief, views the Ward Managers as a 'focus for devolved security'. This can be dangerous in that it can further isolate security staff if Ward Managers do not accept security constraints. Already there had been instances where Ward Managers were taking the attitude that their ward was self-contained and they managed their own needs. The 'Security staff were only advisers' was their response. The Department needs to develop a more positive role to ensure that Ward Managers maintain an effective stance on security and ensure that checking is carried out regularly in accordance with hospital policy – modified as necessary as a result of this Audit. At present the style of security management is insufficiently prescriptive.

19.1 The challenges of a modern and secure forensic psychiatric unit need to be recognised and confronted. This means accepting that security is a basic fact of life from which the therapeutic approach and all that goes with it should grow and prosper."

2.6.3 Among Miss Kinsley's recommendations the following appear:

"20.3 There should be a comprehensive policy on the searching of patients.

20.4 There should be clear policies and specific operational instructions regarding the frequency and method of physical security checks and room searches.

20.5 There needs to be a clear policy on the amount of possessions patients are allowed in their rooms.

20.8 The storage space on Ashworth North wards should be reassessed and increased where possible.

20.15 Further consideration needs to be given to the supervision of patients during visiting in the recreation hall and clear instructions given.

20.27 The structure of the Security Department and the way that it operates in the Hospital's organisation should be reviewed in order to develop a more positive role in ensuring that an effective stance on security issues is maintained."

2.6.4 In her evidence she expanded on her Report and her role as Director of Security of the SHSA. Her concern about the non-searching of parole patients in Lawrence Ward was that:

> "patients who have so-called parole within the grounds are often those who attempt to escape, and they are often those who are trusted and not seen as needing to be searched particularly frequently and do acquire the items that make it possible for them to do those things . . ."

2.6.5 In dealing with paragraphs 20.4 and 20.5, of her recommendations she said she had been at pains to point out to people that what staff needed were not "thick policies", but operational instructions of what to do. Staff did not have time to read "great thick policies", or to translate them into instructions. It was much more difficult to take disciplinary action against someone if he had not carried out a policy. It was much easier if he had not carried out an instruction.

2.6.6 Her position as Director of Security was advisory, but she did, so she said, receive the backing of Charles Kaye, the Chief Executive. They got feedback that searching was happening in quality assurance terms, but quite plainly it was patchy, did not always happen or continue. Although structures were put in place, on the ground it was difficult to make things happen. Miss Kinsley saw the creeping marginalization of security matters as something that could be harmful. She added that in the final analysis she was proved right. In her view the devolution of responsibility for security to clinical teams (ward teams) was totally unacceptable. She had felt like a voice crying in the wilderness in all the Special Hospitals, but at Ashworth it was just like wading through treacle.

2.6.7 The Security Audits of the three Special Hospitals went to Mr Kaye and the General Managers of the Hospitals, and then to the SHSA. Miss Kinsley said the reaction from the Authority was "Get on and do it, but it did not work out that way." In a noble effort to foster the Security Departments within the Hospitals she set up bi-monthly meetings with the Security Managers, which she continued to chair, at Mr Kaye's invitation, until 1995, although she was very much part-time after September 1992. No one had replaced her as Director of Security because the Hospitals were about to go independent as they did in 1996.

2.6.8 Miss Kinsley retired from full-time employment with the SHSA at a time when the Special Hospitals sensed they were going to be made independent units. There had always been tension between the Hospitals and the centre. She said "they did not really want to be controlled by or managed by the SHSA; they really thought they were big enough boys to go it alone". She added that once they got the scent of independence:

> "it became extremely difficult to manage them. I do not know whether I should give this as a personal opinion or not, but I personally think it was a mistake to abolish the SHSA at that time because there was not sufficient depth of management in the hospitals to really see through yet another change, and we had not finished."

2.6.9 We examine in detail the minutes of the Security Managers' meetings at paragraph **2.20.0** *et seq.* below. This is one part of the equation: the attempt to ensure that security was given its due weight within the Hospital. As we shall see, Miss Kinsley was a veritable Cassandra: she spoke the truth about the need for greater security but no one (or at least far too few people) believed her.

2.7.0 The Blom-Cooper Report

2.7.1 The publication of the Blom-Cooper team's Report took place in August 1992, with an accompanying statement by the Secretary of State for Health. The UGM was forced to step down, as was the Director of Medical Services. The Director of Nursing Services had already been moved to other duties by the SHSA.

2.7.2 The Report made 90 recommendations, of which perhaps the most important tackled the "culture of denigration and devaluing of patients" at Ashworth (recommendation 35), medical leadership (44), multi-disciplinary working (45 and 47), complaints (3, 14, 16, 18, 19, 20, 21,22, 23 and 86); Patients' Advocacy (25 and 26); the facilitation of visiting and families' involvement in patients' treatment (75, 77 and 78); greater patient access to telephones (76); and slopping-out (32).

2.7.3 The Blom-Cooper Report uncovered appalling abuses of patients. Quite rightly Sir Louis and his team were shocked at what they had found and made it very clear that the standards that had prevailed in parts of the Hospital were unacceptable. The Inquiry team was very critical of a reliance on security for security's sake at the expense of therapy. They, however, were concerned with ill-treatment of the mentally ill. Their Report understandably barely mentions psychopathically disordered patients. Our committee has no quarrel with a more humane and liberal regime for many mentally ill patients, although by definition, every

High Security Hospital must be made and kept secure. They are meant to have the level of security found in category B prisons. What our Committee is concerned about is that across campus liberalization is inappropriate in a high security hospital which houses both mentally ill and personality disordered offender patients, particularly severely personality disordered offender patients, without complete segregation, and different levels of security. The fact that liberalization was applied across the whole campus of Ashworth was, apparently, a decision taken by the Department of Health. No one appears to have thought about the possible ramifications for security from this policy.

2.8.0 The Task Force

2.8.1 Following the publication of the Blom-Cooper Inquiry Report a small Task Force was created to oversee and advise on the process of implementing the Inquiry's recommendations. The Task Force was chaired by the newly appointed Acting General Manager, Mr Peter Green, with a membership comprising four prominent professionals from outside the Hospital: Dr James Higgins a non-executive director of the SHSA and consultant forensic psychiatrist at the Scott Clinic; Mr Malcolm Rae, a Director of Nursing from Salford; Ms Lindsay Dyer, representing the patients' interests; and Mr Rodney Hurford, an expert on industrial relations.

2.8.2 In December 1992 the Task Force presented a Report to the SHSA and a second Report in February 1993. The February Report recommends a new management structure for the Hospital but the December Report essentially concerns the Task Force's view of the Hospital. At paragraph 1.6 of this Report it is said:

> "The Task Force considers, as the inquiry Team did [the Blom-Cooper team] that Ashworth Hospital has many of the adverse characteristics of a 'total institution' (Goffman), it is an expensive, closed, inward looking hospital, highly resistant to change. It is out of step with many of the attitudes and practices of psychiatry elsewhere. It has an intolerable intrusive management structure intent on conformity and sameness. The preoccupation with security, although appropriate, is all pervasive, often unnecessary and seems designed as justification for rigid, institutionalised attitudes of some staff and as a bar to the appropriate progress of patients. It is perhaps not too great an exaggeration to suggest that the Hospital functions more in the interests of staff than patients and that, were there a ready alternative, current calls for speedy closure might well be heeded."

2.8.3 Part 2 of the Report was concerned with lack of autonomy and influence of patients mirrored by a similar lack of autonomy and influence by staff. At paragraph 2.3 it is said:

> "Each Patient Care team has to seek approval on security matters from bodies which are not involved in immediate patient care. Procedures for determining parole and leave of absence are bureaucratic, restrictive and inflexible. Parole, even within the very secure perimeter of Ashworth North, is a gift to be granted to the very deserving, not a right which may only be denied with good cause. It cannot readily be titrated in duration, location and level of supervision to fluctuating clinical condition. The entirely ward-based security of Ashworth South prevents the development of an effective flexible system of security."

2.8.4 These two extracts are difficult to understand following so closely on Miss Kinsley's audit which must have been available to the Task Force. Readers of both the Task Force Report and her Report might think they referred to different hospitals. It is one thing to say that relational security, founded upon an intimate knowledge of the changing characteristics of individual patients, is a central feature of good security in the forensic field and can only be determined by those working with patients at the ward level. It is another to treat other aspects of security in the same fashion. For relational security to be effective it needs to operate within a clear framework of standards and rules that everybody understands. This framework needs to distinguish between those rules that are mandatory in all circumstances, and those which may be tempered by a professional judgment about the needs of an individual patient.

Such a framework was missing at Ashworth and produced a dangerous and risky security situation. Some PCTs did their own thing in a total disregard of the impact on the rest of the Hospital. There was no reporting system that informed senior managers that this was happening.

In his evidence Mr Kaye drew a distinction between patients in a NHS psychiatric unit and a high security unit. Those in the latter were dangerous clinically and physically; these Hospitals were the end of the line for such patients who had exhausted every other type of care; such matters set these hospitals apart form any other sort of health care institution; patients in them are forced to be there and to have treatment and most of them do not want any treatment; **"the whole milieu, the whole ethos is radically different from anything else you are going to see in the Health Service. Until you accept that and take that as your base line for looking at special hospitals you will not understand at all what is going on within those three institutions."** We agree, and are concerned that this radical difference was not kept in mind. And not just by those more remote, by varying degrees, from immediate patient care, but also by those actually involved in immediate patient care. This includes the very experienced members of the Task Force. Is it really unreasonable to circumscribe what may be seen as rights for patients in such radically different institutions? Later investigations demonstrate the absurdity of not recognizing the need for security, particularly in relation to personality disordered patients. The difference between special and other hospitals was also referred to in the Judicial Review of the Broadmoor Security Policy (*see* paragraph **2.12.14** *et seq.* below).

2.8.5 The minutes of the Task Force meetings indicate the different approach of the Task Force concerning security matters from that of Miss Kinsley. Difference in approach to security policies can only add confusion. The minutes of the Task Force meetings illustrate this.

Meeting 10 December 1992

> 92/102 'Patients Mail'
>
> "Discussion took place on issues arising out of the opening of patients' correspondence. It was agreed that mail should best be dealt with at ward level, and be received unopened by patients unless otherwise decided by the PCT. The PCST [Patient Care Support Team] would be asked to draw up suitable operational policies."

Meeting 11 February 1993

> 93/49 'Review of Regulations relating to personal and security items'
>
> "The Task Force received the 2nd draft of the above document from Dr J. B. Ashcroft, Chair of the Risk Management Team, which sought to incorporate the points made at a previous meeting. The Task Force welcomed the Report, although it expressed its disappointment at the poor response from Ward PCTs, and the continued use of terms such as 'rules' rather than procedures."
>
> **This was the converse of Miss Kinsley's concern: "I was at some pains to point out to people what staff needed were not thick policies, but operational instructions of what to do, and I think it did get through to some extent, but staff have not enough time to read great thick policies."**
>
> "It was agreed that Mr A. Menkin, chair of the PCST, be asked to ensure that PCTs

take the issue forward and that he consult with interested parties. Mr Menkin was also asked to report back to the Task Force within two weeks on patients' mail."

Meeting 18 February 1993

> 93/49 'Review of Regulations relating to personal and security items.'
> "The acting unit general manager indicated that over-prescriptive security had been highlighted during his tour of the female wards and he would be asking the Security Department for their Report on the use of a fenced area by patients."

Mr Peter Green, the Acting General Manager, was to take a more robust view of security when he chaired the Owen Ward Inquiry Team.

Meeting 18 March 1993

> 93.51 'Women's Services'
> "The Acting General Manager reported that the SHSA was extremely concerned about Women's services and had decided to form a team of outside professionals to examine and report on them. Mr Rae was asked to assist in the preparation of terms of reference."

This, no doubt, was the origin of the Swan Report.

2.8.6 The Task Force Report to the SHSA dated 16 February 1993 which concerned the future management of the Hospital gives a similar impression. As far as recommendation 35, to change the culture of Ashworth Hospital, was concerned the Task Force's December Report had outlined a proposed "Way Forward" containing interlinked proposals to reorganize the delivery of direct patient care and to revise the management structure. Having considered it the SHSA thought the proposals for patient care should only take place after the new management structure had been developed and asked the Task Force to produce a management structure to a tight deadline. The Task Force duly produced this Report in February 1993.

2.8.7 This Report sets out a proposed structure based on seven principles:

> "1. There is a need to develop effective multi-disciplinary working governed by a comprehensive set of operational policies which have been agreed by all members of individual PCTs, unit management groups and by the Hospital as a whole . . .
>
> 2. As far as possible all management decisions concerning patient care should be devolved to the lowest level practicable . . .
>
> 3. There must be clear delineation of the clinical, managerial and professional roles of all members of staff in order to increase awareness of and understanding of roles, to improve communications and to clarify responsibility and accountability.
>
> 4. As far as is possible patients should have a say in the clinical management of their cases and in the managements [sic] of the units in which they are treated.
>
> 5. Each devolved Unit of Management must be able to make an effective contribution not only to support and encourage high quality patient care, but to the achievement of the strategic objectives of the SHSA and Ashworth Hospital.
>
> 6. The new management structure must be able to forge more effective links with all those agencies who refer patients to the Hospital and who receive patients from it. It must also be flexible and innovative enough to respond to changing patterns of healthcare management and delivery in the wider NHS.
>
> 7. It must be able to ensure that appropriate levels of security are maintained at all times."

2.8.8 These objectives contain the usual lack of realism seen in many such documents. In the event the stress was put on devolution and not on the comprehensive set of operational policies. A fundamental problem at Ashworth has been the inability to get PCTs to agree anything, and having regard to the policy to devolve management to the PCTs, this was doomed at the outset very much as Miss Kinsley thought it would be. In the circumstances such a policy was an incentive for PCTs to do their own thing rather than to agree to work within comprehensive operational policies or, as Miss Kinsley would have preferred, "operational instructions". Ill-defined lines of accountability have been a constant feature at Ashworth. Patients, said by Mr Kaye to be distinguished by their dangerousness, serious mental illness or serious personality disorder can only effectively contribute to the management of the Unit if their impact is strictly limited. Many PD patients are interested in mismanagement rather than management of their unit. If hospital general policies, particularly those relating to security, can be changed by PCTs without reference to higher authority, the prospect of maintaining appropriate levels of security is remote.

This seemed to be well understood in the TBS Units in Holland (*see* Appendix 8). When asked about the part, if any, played by patients in management relating to security matters, we were told that patients could discuss and argue, but they could not change policy. Although the first principle states that operational policies should be agreed by PCTs, Units and the Hospital as a whole, in the event, as we shall see, Lawrence Ward PCT at least did not feel the need to refer its policies to the Hospital Management. As the Mallalieu Report (above) shows, nursing shifts could be particularly obdurate.

2.8.9 The current management, the Task Force Report remarks, does not meet these criteria, being "too hierarchical, too distant from patient care delivery, too unresponsive to patient need, too conservative, bureaucratic and outmoded. It is also highly inefficient."

We have no doubt that devolution of management to ward level made matters rather worse in the absence of clearly established and generally applied basic principles of security.

2.8.10 The Report proposes a new model whereby immediate patient care was to be devised and provided by multi-disciplinary Patient Care Teams. A number of Patient Care Teams dealing with particular patient groups would be aggregated to form a series of Unit Management Groups. An Executive Forum consisting of representatives from each Unit Management Group and senior representatives of the various Corporate Service Departments and Senior Representatives of Professional Advisory Groups would both advise and act as an executive body to an Ashworth Hospital Board with the responsibility to determine the strategic policy of the Hospital, within the framework of SHSA policy. At 2.4 a very simplistic flowchart of this concept is set out and the rest of the document deals with the components of the structure.

At this stage it is sufficient to say, that in the course of evidence, a bewildering number of much more complex structures was described, and some were put in place before preceding structures had been allowed to take root. We saw no structure this simple, and none so simple was ever put in place.

2.8.11 The Report goes on to deal with the Patient Care Teams. They were to:

> "1. . . . be multi-disciplinary consisting of an RMO (plus supporting medical staff), nursing staff led by a ward manager, clinical psychologist, social worker and other disciplines as necessary.
>
> "2. . . . perform to an agreed set of operational policies appropriate to the patients being cared for.
>
> "3. . . . meet at suitably regular intervals to draw up, implement and review a Care Plan for each patient covering all aspects of his or her treatment, habilitation,

rehabilitation and security needs, utilising the full range of facilities of the Hospital.

"4. The RMO, with his statutory responsibilities, will chair multi-disciplinary meetings, the Ward Manager will coordinate the patients' Care Plans but the proper areas of expertise and responsibilities of members of all disciplines must be acknowledged.

"5. There must be a clear understanding of how various aspects of the clinical work with each patient is to be allocated, recorded, reported and monitored and how the individual professional responsibility of all members of the team is to be integrated."

In the event this proved to be a vain hope.

"6. There must also be an explicit mechanism, 'Peer Review', to deal with differences of professional opinion which cannot be resolved in discussion at Patient Care Team meetings, either by reference for an opinion to another Patient Care Team in that Unit Management Group or from another Unit Management Group or by the involvement of senior professional representatives for advice."

In the PDU were peer groups going to interfere? They were not cohesive, but had common interests. Other management groups were not concerned with psychopathic patients, so how could they help? The system did not allow senior professionals to intervene if the PCTs were to be the devolved level of management, so how would their views carry any weight? There is no evidence anyway that these proposals ever became effective.

"7. Patient Care Teams will receive requests for assessment and admission, will consider these urgently as a multi-disciplinary group, will decide what further information is required, will determine when and how to conduct an assessment, will decide whether admission should be offered for assessment or for treatment, and will speedily convey its opinion to the referring agent. If there is uncertainty, dispute or other difficulties the 'Peer Review' mechanism should be utilized."

Again this never happened so far as we can see.

"8. Decisions on the movement of patients within the Unit Management Group, between Units, inside or outside the Hospital, must be decided upon by the multi-disciplinary team.

"9. To ensure that each patient remains in hospital for the minimum appropriate length of time, a high priority must be given to ensuring the continuing and active involvement of health and social agencies who have a responsibility for each patient."

This is a correct objective, but totally unachievable unless there are long term medium secure facilities available in the NHS. No mention is made of this in the Plan.

2.8.12 The Report next deals with the proposed new Unit Management Groups. A number of PCTs dealing with patients with broadly similar needs would be managed by a Unit Management Group, with the number of such groups to be determined. To provide gradations of security and a breadth of care and treatment options, all Unit Management Groups would consist of facilities in all parts of the Hospital. Two broad specialist units were proposed, a personality disorders unit and a behavioural treatment unit. The personality disorders unit would provide treatment on the basis of a predominantly psychotherapeutic approach for a range of patients.

2.8.13 The PDU would be quite large (about 150). There would be sub-specialization to produce a range of facilities for assessment, intensive care, on-going treatment and pre-discharge groupings of patients. Such a large unit would permit the recruitment of substantial numbers of staff with an interest and skills in the treatment of personality disorder.

In the light of the long established difficulty in attracting professional staff to these large units, this was just pie in the sky.

2.8.14 The Behavioural Unit would be smaller (about 70) and would in theory decrease in size as patients were discharged. It was probable, the Report argued, that the remaining patients would be a small number requiring high perimeter security, and a few patients with quite specific disabilities, for example patients with brain damage and females with intractable mental illness.

2.8.15 The leader of each Unit Management Group would be a Unit Manager, preferably one with a professional management background. He would hold the Unit budget and agree job plans for all the professionals working there. Once the business planning process was implemented, the Unit Management Group would need a business manager. The Unit Manager would coordinate and monitor the activities of professionals in the Unit. He or she would determine non-performance of duties to an agreed specification, referring apparent poor professional performance to senior professional advisers for advice and, if necessary, a course of appropriate remedial action.

2.8.16 A Unit Management Group would determine the overall strategic framework of the Unit policies and meet regularly. It would consist of the Unit Manager, Business manager, Senior Nurse, Ward manager, RMOS, psychologists, social workers, patients representative(s). Other professionals might be co-opted as necessary. The Senior Nurse would manage and lead the nursing staff; the Security Adviser, presumably from the nursing discipline, would advise on security policies within the unit and between units and within the Hospital as a whole. Staff of all Unit Management Groups would be sited as close as possible to the wards of their patients.

2.8.17 Much of what is said above was impossible to achieve in reality. When across-hospital security is the order of the day, as it was, differential levels, which should exist cannot be put in place. With a small number of large wards, inevitably many patients in the same wards, would, if treated individually from the security point of view, create a number of levels of security in the same ward. This is a recipe for disaster. It did not work to have different rules for the mentally ill and the personality disorder wards on the same campus. By way of example, on one mentally ill ward (Elms), patients were allowed to carry cash. Was it not to be expected that the personality disorder patients would raise a grievance on the basis that if psychotic patients could carry cash, why could personality disorder patients, who were not psychotic, not do the same? See the observations of Potts J. in the Judicial Review brought by Broadmoor patients concerning its Security Policy (S 1) in paragraph 2.12.14 *et seq.* below.

2.8.18 Four departments would provide corporate services of one sort or another, namely the Finance Department, the Personnel Department, a Clinical Support Department managing rehabilitation and other patient care services available to the PCTS and Unit Management Groups and a general support services department, responsible for providing hotel and other administration services.

2.8.19 The proposed new management structure attempted to separate as far as possible the clinical, managerial and professional roles of all disciplines. Clinical responsibility was to be exercised at the multi-disciplinary level of the PCT, management responsibility at the level of the Unit Management Group. Maintenance of professional standards would be achieved by constant review and improvement by audit and education; smaller disciplines, such as psychology, psychiatry and social work, would meet as a discipline on a regular basis to discuss relevant professional and education issues. The senior nurse at the Unit level would promote professional standards in the unit; the Senior Chief Nurse with his senior professional and educational colleagues would set standards throughout the Hospital.

2.8.20 The Report proposed that senior representatives from all areas of the Hospital would meet in an Executive Forum to discuss issues of common concern, to develop proposals for strategic policy for consideration by the Board, and ensure its efficient implementation. It would be chaired by the Operations Director and comprise the finance director, personnel director, all unit managers, clinical support manager, general support services manager, and senior professional advisors from nursing, psychology, psychiatry, and social work. When appropriate a representative from the patients' council would be invited.

2.8.21 The Report noted that it was generally agreed that the Hospital Board would include the Hospital General Manager, Finance Director, Personnel Director and Operations Director as essential members. It pointed to disagreements as to the level at which professional advice should influence strategy and operations policy. One view was that this should take place at the level of the Executive Forum; another was that medical and nursing representation should be at Board level; a third view was that if medical and nursing representation should be at board level then psychology and social work should also be represented at Board level.

2.8.22 The development of these extremely complex managerial and professional mechanisms is typical of organizations that are inward looking and introspective. When parts of the mechanism failed to work, they invented even more complex solutions. Clearly focused professional and managerial leadership was submerged in the treacle.

2.9.0 The New Structure

2.9.1 After the Task Force produced the draft management structure in February 1993, the SHSA consulted upon a new structure based on this draft in April 1993. Following the consultation period a further Report was published in June 1993. Whilst there were several amendments as a result of consultation the key elements were endorsed.

2.9.2 The key changes to the structure were:

(i) the creation of discrete patient care units with a regional and specialist focus;

(ii) decision-making was to be devolved to multi-disciplinary teams responsible for the quality of patient care, staff development and communication;

(iii) the clinical, managerial and professional roles of all staff were to be clearly delineated, with responsibilities towards Clinical Managers and Heads of Practice set out;

(iv) Clinical Manager posts were to be established to lead the new units, responsible to the General Manager.

2.9.3 The responsibility for implementation of the proposals was undertaken by the new General Manager Mrs Janice Miles, who took up post in July 1993. She had been employed within the NHS since 1966, originally as a medical secretary, and subsequently in various management positions. Her most recent post had been Chief Executive of the Aylesbury Vale Community Healthcare NHS Trust. This experience stood her in good stead when she applied for the post of UGM at Ashworth, as the Hospital was at that stage looking forward to Trust status.

Mrs Miles stressed the size of the task facing the Hospital and her in July 1993. This included: developing 24-hour care; addressing a large overspend; progressing the major changes demanded in the wake of the Blom-Cooper Report; and developing closer links with the NHS. She stressed that her number one objective on taking up her new post was implementing the Blom-Cooper Report recommendations. She described the scale of the task facing her and her management team as "massive, absolutely massive", and admitted that she had not appreciated the scale of the task until she was in post. Just the creation of the Units was an enormous task, necessitating moving around half of the patients in the Hospital.

2.9.4 She noted that when she arrived the management structure was based on functional hierarchies. This tended to lead to day to day decisions about the operational management of the Hospital being sucked-up to the highest level, involving senior managers in clinical decisions about patient care. Mr Green, in evidence to us, confirmed that in the past he and a senior colleague Mr Dale had often had to make essentially clinical decisions about, for example, moves of patients because clinicians could not agree. Mrs Miles was determined that in future the senior management team would stay out of day to day clinical decisions.

2.9.5 Mrs. Miles made some refinements to the senior management structure, including the creation of a new post of Director of Business Development. The post-holder was to co-ordinate the Hospital's business planning process and the management of the contracting process which was to be introduced in April 1994 when the SHSA adopted a quasi-purchasing role and established a service level agreement with the Hospital. The post-holder was also to look outside the organization as Ashworth prepared for Trust status. The Head of Nursing post disappeared, to be replaced by the Director of Professional Development, responsible for nursing, psychology, social work and other professions allied to medicine. Research was also absorbed into this Director's responsibilities. Security remained part of his responsibilities.

2.9.6 Four clinical units emerged: Mental Illness (North), Mental Illness (South), Special Services (i.e., women, learning disabled patients and patients with brain injury and challenging behaviour); and the Personality Disorder Unit. In the new structure Ward Managers became accountable to the Clinical Managers, as did individual social workers, psychologists and administrators. As Mr Green put it, the basic principle was to move as close as possible to the patients all those involved in their care, both geographically and functionally. Doctors still reported to the General Manager (on non-clinical matters). Dr Ian Strickland was appointed Clinical Manager of the PDU, supported by a Business Manager, Mr Martin Royal.

2.9.7 As Mrs Miles said in her statement, the development of a specialist PDU was supported by the SHSA, HAS and later the HSPSCB. She told us that some people thought the Hospital was being brave, even foolhardy, but the predominant feeling back in 1993 was that this was the right way to go. We discuss the creation of the PDU in detail below.

2.9.8 A feature of the reorganization that struck us was that the Heads of Psychology and Social Work were left high and dry, not managing anyone, whilst social workers and psychologists moved into the Clinical Units. When Mr Backhouse, the Head of Social Work Practice, gave evidence, the sense of his isolation from the work of the wards was palpable. Whilst all social workers within the Hospital were professionally accountable to him for their practice, they were managerially responsible (since April 1994) to the Clinical Managers of the Clinical Units and, since April 1996, to the Clinical Directors of the Clinical Directorates. There was, Mr Backhouse told us, considerable debate about the existence and position of the interface between professional and operational accountability.

2.9.9 The psychologists felt the same. When Professor Blackburn gave evidence to us he said that the Head of Professional Practice for Psychology had an almost meaningless position. Making psychologists responsible to the Director of Nursing downgraded the discipline; they should have reported to the General Manager or another senior manager who was not limited to a particular discipline. He told us that many psychologists subsequently voted with their feet and left the Hospital.

2.9.10 Mr Paul Lever, Chairman of the Ashworth Hospital Authority Board, agreed that the structure was flawed. He considered that the devolution of power down to clinical unit and ward level only went half-way, as it left hanging the Heads of Psychology and Social Work with no responsibility for the function they nominally "managed".

2.9.11 The General Manager, five directors and four clinical managers and rehabilitation manager met in a forum which continued to be known as the Hospital Management Group. Mr Green commented that many people would argue this structure was a good one. Certainly the Mental Illness Units were in his view well-run. He noted that he had continuing doubts about the wisdom of not having a Director of Operations to tie together the work of the four Clinical Directors. Such a post had been proposed in the original Task Force suggested structure. Mr Dale in his evidence to us strongly supported this point. We return to this point below.

2.10.0 The Implementation of the Blom-Cooper Recommendations: A Political Imperative

2.10.1 This is a convenient point at which to discuss in more detail the implementation of the Blom-Cooper Report's recommendations. A number of witnesses, including Mr Kaye himself and Mr Jewesbury, testified to the strong political pressure on the Hospital to implement the recommendations. Mrs Miles confirmed this, adding that no one was saying at the time that implementing these recommendations Hospital-wide was inadvisable. Mr Dale, told us that the then Secretary of State, the Rt Hon Virginia Bottomley MP, gave the Hospital six weeks to respond to 90 recommendations.

2.10.2 We heard much criticism of the way in which that Report's recommendations were implemented (or, more exactly, the way in which the Task Force's proposals, which were based on the Blom-Cooper Report's vision, were implemented). Thus Mr Lever argued persuasively in evidence that the implementation of the Blom-Cooper recommendations was rushed and ill-thought through, in particular the blanket application of the reforms to all parts of the Hospital. Although he was very critical of the "command and control" policies of pre-1989, he pointed out that the new organization at Ashworth had had little time to absorb new thinking about management before the Blom-Cooper Report-inspired reforms were upon them.

2.10.3 Mr Roger Kendrick gave his perspective of the management of the Hospital as someone who came in as a Non-Executive Director in April 1996 and later became an Executive Director. He was conscious early on in his time at Ashworth of a gap between clear policies and strategies and poor monitoring and follow-up. He noted that in devolving things down to ward level following the implementation of the Blom-Cooper Report's recommendations some valuable things had been lost, for example the Central Nursing Office, which was a central intelligence source for the Hospital. Staff began to lose sight of the dynamics of a secure institution; they separated out the security side from "dynamic security" and treatment, whereas these elements need to be constantly brought together.

2.10.4 Professor Sines, Professor of Community Nursing and head of the School of Health Services (University of Ulster), who carried out an audit of nursing standards at Ashworth on behalf of Sir Louis and his team, returned to carry out a similar audit of the PDU Wards some six or so years later. He commented:

> "I do believe staff were very poorly prepared for the abundance of change that Blom-Cooper's recommendations actually required. I still believe it was never Blom-Cooper's intention that those 90 changes should have been implemented so rapidly, and certainly not to each of the wards in Ashworth in the way they were."

2.10.5 When Mr Lever gave evidence to us for a second time he reflected on the rush to devolve management downwards and made the following comments:

> "I think the decision to devolve at that point in Ashworth's history was a wrong one. It was not a sufficiently mature organization in terms of management understanding and controls to do that . . . . You have got to be as certain as you can be that the management are up to it and have the track record and that you have the right controls to be able to measure."

Mr Lever felt that the more recent changes to centralize management was right in the context of an organization in crisis.

2.10.6 Mr Dale admitted that in implementing the Blom-Cooper recommendations more sophisticated measures were required to cope with the machinations of the PD patients. Very quickly good intentions could be undermined, for example, by abuse of the new ward telephones.

2.10.7 Mr Erville Millar, Acting Chief Executive from February to October 1997, told us that the general feeling amongst staff at Ashworth was that the implementation of the Blom-Cooper Report's recommendations was right, but went "too far". By this people seemed to mean the pace of implementation and the failure to reflect the differing demands of the different patient groups. Mr Millar put it graphically:

> "Indeed it was one of the personality disordered patients who shared with me and others the view that the implementation of these recommendations were to that group of patients like giving some children the keys of the sweet shop; what do you expect, that people would gorge themselves until they were sick."

2.10.8 Mr Millar thought that the broad rump of staff did not welcome the work of the Task Force and that the changes had been introduced without staff ownership (although this was a common problem elsewhere, when management changed). Staff did not feel confident themselves in the environment which complicated the delivery of such a large change agenda.

2.10.9 This view was reinforced by the evidence of Mr Ryan of UNISON, who told us of the bitterness many staff in Park Lane felt about the Blom-Cooper Report, which described a hospital they did not recognize. He was critical of the speed of implementation of the recommendations and also of some of the changes it brought.

2.10.10 Mr Kaye was asked whether the Blom-Cooper Report was implemented too quickly and without adequate thought of the implications for the care and management of personality disordered patients. He said, "There was enormous political pressure and the Secretary of State gave personal instructions to me and to my Chairman, which did not happen every day of the week, and the whole pursuit of the Blom-Cooper agenda became a key issue in reviews between us and the Department." He added that those instructions were given personally and were not minuted.

A little earlier he had been asked to comment on the view of various witnesses that matters had gone wrong with the implementation of the Blom-Cooper recommendations because of "the dash for therapy" at the expense of security. He was asked whether he accepted that the recommendations of Blom-Cooper had been implemented much too quickly. He replied:

> "First of all, the Secretary of State made it clear to me personally and to my Chairman, that Blom-Cooper had to be pursued with all vigour. She said to us, 'These are a serious set of recommendations and I want to see them brought into place without delay in that hospital.' There was no question. We discussed some of the problems attendant upon that, but she said: 'That is your remit, get on with it.'
>
> "Secondly, as I have already said, a number of them [sc. the recommendations] echoed themes that we had already identified, and we were happy to get hold of them and work with them. Thirdly, within the Hospital there was significant opposition to a lot of the recommendations of Blom-Cooper."

He added:

> "So we knew we had a big agenda, we knew we had problems as usual with resources and the right skills to bring that agenda into fruition, and we knew that

> there was opposition within the Hospital. So the picture there is again of a difficult task on a wide front which has to be pursued with vigour because that is the will, not only of ourselves but also of our political masters."

He continued:

> "In an ideal world, yes, I would have liked to have had five years and a lot more resources and a lot more skilled people to be able to take the programme through at Ashworth, but management is not an ideal world."

2.10.11 We asked Mr Kaye about the decision to implement the recommendations across the Hospital. Mr Kaye replied that as far as the Blom-Cooper Report dealt with human rights, those rights had to be extended to all patients. The important qualification was that the patient care team should interpret those broad rights when dealing with a particular patient. However this is easy to say but rather harder to achieve in practice in a hospital with large wards, where personality disordered and mentally ill patients are cared for on the same campus. It is all too easy for security to gravitate to suit the patients who require less security, rather than those who require the most. His point requires further explanation.

Rights and Privileges

2.10.12 We have already commented on the difference between patients in other psychiatric hospitals and those in the Special Hospitals, a difference well understood and recognized by Mr Kaye. If that difference is not recognized and made clear as a matter of hospital policy it can only lead, as it did to confusion, and as Miss Kinsley predicted it would. Mr Kaye's evidence to us demonstrates the point. We cite two passages in his evidence:

> Q: (Dealing with recommendations 75 and 76) A review of visiting procedures, (75 and 76) relates to a review of the use of telephones within Ashworth. Again, so far as the authority was concerned, was this in any sense seen as an expectation to relax security?
> A: No, the same answer as before. It obviously had security implications, but it was not a challenge to the need to maintain basic security.
>
> Q: How can that be with recommendation 76, which recommends a personal telephone system like those available in general hospitals and NHS psychiatric hospitals? Surely that was a further profound change to the setting in which these patients were being looked after, was it not?
> A: It was a change in as much as it gave them a right and an access which they had not previously had. It was capable of abuse, as was fully realised, in terms of abuse of that access, but at the same time, there would be a need to plan the introduction in such a way so that abuse did not take place.
>
> Q: Was there any consideration at any point about operating this recommendation differentially across the grounds of Ashworth Hospital, so that personal telephones might be appropriate on some wards for some patients, but not appropriate on other wards for other patients?
> A: No. That was not considered.
>
> Q: It was seen as the whole hospital policy?
> A: Yes.
> Q: Is that right?
> A: Yes.
>
> Q: So you wanted everybody to be treated in the same way?
> A: I wanted them to have the same opportunities and to be subject to the same restrictions according to the judgment of the clinical teams.
>
> Q: Does that mean you were expecting some form of differential to be brought

because of the more difficult problem apprehended with the psychopathic patient as opposed to the mentally ill patient?
A: No, this is an individual differentiation, not a diagnostic one.

Q: Was the expectation that decisions would be made at local level about it, ward level?
A: There should be a policy which would then be the responsibility of the ward to implement.

Q: Can we just pursue that a little further. Let us assume the policy is that patients should have access to a personal telephone system. That was the big policy level. Could an individual team say, but not for our patients, they cannot have it?
A: They could say that if they could justify it in the case of each individual patient, yes. This is not an absolute right so that a patient can pick up a phone whenever he or she wants; this is a right which has to be mediated through the judgment of the clinical team. In the very unlikely event this is a clinical team [which] looked at all its patients and decided that was not an appropriate right, then yes, they had that ability. But obviously, if that had happened, I think one would have been rather sceptical about it.

Q: Could they make the decision, or did they have to go to and ask somebody, if they could break the rules?
A: No they could make the decision.

Q: So they had a discretion to modify Hospital-wide policy?
A: Yes, very much so. The clinical team within the ward has the responsibility for the control, treatment and pathway of each patient, so they very much have those decisions.

Q: What is behind this question, you see, is that one of the problems we have been looking at is the difficulty created by patient-mix, the different types of patient in the same ward. If you have a policy which is essentially linked to individual needs as opposed to the needs of a selected group, you can create, for a particular ward, a difficult management situation. One of the answers we have had frequently from a number of people from Ashworth is that it is the patient-mix that has caused a great deal of their difficulties, irrespective of what policies they have tried to implement. Do you follow? Do you think that causes a difficulty for the Hospital?
A: If by "patient-mix" you mean having together on the same ward personality disordered patients and mentally ill patients, that is seen as presenting problems, just as having a concentration of personality disordered patients in one ward is also seen as presenting problems.

Q: If they are of different types of personality disorder?
A: Both situations have their difficulties. I do not think either, as such, are a reason for a clinical team to say that they do not know what to do.

Q: Just pursuing that a little further, the ability of the Patient Care Team to interpret the Hospital rules when making decisions about individual patients, are there no limits? Can they do almost anything as long as they judge it to be in the interests of the patients. Could they breach almost all the rules of the Hospital?
A: By definition, if they are operating within a set of policies and rules, no, they cannot breach those rules. What we are talking about is the interpretation and the application of rules, not the abandonment of the rules.

Q: That seems to have been a problem on some of the wards where the boundaries were not very clear, at least to people on the Patient Care Teams making the decisions?

A: I think the boundaries were quite clear. I think the problems that some of the clinical teams had was in actually enforcing the boundaries and using policies and guidance that was available to them. I do not think there is any confusion about what was expected. The difficult task, and it really is a difficult task, was for staff on the ward to apply the guidance and regulations that existed.

Q: Can we take it through an example? There came a point of time at Ashworth, for instance, when it was discovered that cash cards had been issued to at least four patients on Lawrence Ward. A debate seems to have ensued in documents, ending up with more or less a disagreement, as a result of which the general manager, Mrs Miles, issued an edict, in effect saying that there will be no cash cards on the wards. When you get that type of situation, what did you expect to happen? Did you expect those in charge of the running of the wards to bow to the rule of the general manager, or to ignore it?
A: If that had been – I am not familiar with that, but if an issue had been taken up from a clinical team or clinical teams having difficulties saying we are not sure, we do not know how things apply and that passed through the hierarchy and a decision was made about it, then yes, that decision becomes part of the policy of the Hospital.

Q: And should be followed?
A: And should be followed.

Q: You would expect that Hospital-wide policies, which have been decided at senior level, would be well known to everyone working at ward level, and they would be expected to be familiar with the policies?
A: They must be, yes. They would have to be promulgated properly, and then it would be the duty of staff to be aware of what those policies were.

The second passage comes later in his evidence:

Q: Did you know that the reduction in the levels of security, with which some of your correspondence was concerned, was apparently being applied across the whole of the Hospital?
A: I do not know that I ever thought it was being applied across the whole of the Hospital. No. I thought there were areas, particularly wards where they were failing to be as tight as I felt they should be. There were one or two issues that were whole Hospital issues, like the question of visitors, and those addressed on a whole Hospital basis, but I do not think I ever realized if that was the case that in the whole of any of the Hospitals, a specific standard had been let drop.

Q: You see, one of the pictures which has come through is of the – it comes very close to the absurdity actually as being a not inappropriate word, of applying the relaxations which, whilst they could be appropriately applied to the mentally ill, were totally inappropriately applied to the PD type of patient, and to apply the same relaxation comes through as being an absurd thing to have done. What was your sort of knowledge of that at the time?
A: I think we discussed this in December, and I said then that I felt that, in so far as Blom-Cooper dealt with patients' rights, obviously those rights were shared by all patients. The question of diagnosis does not directly rob you of particular rights. What did seem to me important and what we stressed, was that the clinical team had to assess how far a particular right or a particular freedom could be applied in an individual case. So if you were looking, for instance at the use of telephones, that is something that the team needed to assess in relation to that patient. How far could that patient be trusted with that privilege? So that there were broad policies, there were broad rights, and the interpretation of those as it applied to the individual patient had to be done through the team. A lot of my correspondence with the

General Managers was saying : "Look, you must fix the boundaries with the PD patients. If you do not maintain firm boundaries with PD patients you are lost. Once they erode the basics, then their manipulative skills will carry you into dangerous territory."

Q: Is it fair to say then that you appreciated, and if you did not say so, that the effect of the task force's work, I am not saying it was a recommendation because I do not think it was specific on the point to my recollection, but one of its effects was that insofar as a general hospital policy on security that apparently no longer applied?
A: No, I do not think I ever had that impression. That is not in my mind.

Q: On the other hand, what you are just saying about it going down to the teams rather gives the impression that you were anticipating there could be modifications of significance at that level?
A: But not in terms of dispensing with basic procedures. I do not think a team could say: "That is a basic policy in the Hospital but we can disregard that." Everybody's room had to be searched and everybody's room should be in a state where it could be searched. No team could say "We can disregard that." What a team could say is, "Well, a privilege, an access to telephones, that is more appropriate for patient X than patient Y because of his clinical condition."

Q: So, insofar as that may have occurred, that over-relaxation, that was not an intended relaxation?
A: No, and, in fact, as I say, a lot of my correspondence was saying to the General Managers: "This is wrong. You are allowing things to slip where they should not slip and we know the dangers with PD patients because they are well documented."

Q: Did it strike you to set in train a form of inspection to see whether or not those policies which you were suggesting on paper were ultimately carried out?
A: It did, and we tried to do that in two ways: one through Miss Kinsley and her reviews of the sites –

Q: That was not a happy result. She was quite critical?
A: She was, yes, you are quite right.

Q: But you still had a problem?
A: So that reinforced it and then secondly, we actually built in some of those standards into the contract so that they were the subject of monitoring and reporting by the Hospitals to us.

Q: One thing we did discuss before Christmas was that the quarterly review team reports again left a good deal to be desired?
A: I am afraid they did and we were commenting both to them and to the Authority on the inadequacies of some of the procedures that were there. Again, as I said, this is a problem; all three Hospitals found some of these procedures and some of these boundaries very difficult. They really had a lot of trouble with them. Looking back, what does occur to me about the reformation of Ashworth after the Task Force's Report was that creating the PD Unit in the form that we did, we knew it was high risk. I think it was higher risk than we realized at the time.

Q: You did point out the risk to Mrs Miles in a letter, that is true?
A: Yes.

Q: What you are saying is you, yourself, the Board itself, may have underestimated the actual risk of it?
A: Certainly, I think, in retrospect, we probably did given the problem that we had with trying to attract the right staff who could manage the system that we put together.

2.10.13 We have cited these passages in Mr Kaye's evidence, because they demonstrate in an acute way the flaws in the way in which the Blom-Cooper recommendations were implemented. Those flaws remained in place throughout the life of the SHSA. In order to understand people's **rights**, and **privileges**, it is necessary to bear in mind their jurisprudential meanings.

There is a distinction first of all between fundamental human rights and other rights people enjoy as members of particular nations or groups within them. The main difference is that fundamental human rights should be considered immutable. Social rights are not immutable and they are closely associated with duties. For example, people living in a country have a duty to comply with the laws of that country, and if they breach those laws they can be punished and also lose rights.

A sentence of imprisonment involves the loss of the right to freedom for the duration of the sentence. People in closed societies such as institutions should abide by fundamental rules necessary for the well being and interests of the others with whom they live and are in close contact. Units housing different diagnostic groups may require different fundamental rules.

It is clear that the personality disordered group require fundamental rules different from those needed by the mentally ill. If the fundamental rules are not put in place, or having been in place are eroded, then manipulative skills of the personality disordered group become very difficult, if not impossible, to control.

What was wrong was to call "privileges" "rights" and to do so throughout the Hospital. Thus everyone became entitled to privileges "as of right". There is an essential difference between being allowed access to a telephone because you are considered trustworthy and being allowed access to one because it is said to be everyone's right.

This important consideration was missing in the thinking behind Ashworth's reconstruction. Security policies remained in place on paper and continued to go through various reincarnations but they were not applied properly. Staff were confused and it is not surprising that they were. It is difficult to say "no" when to do so is said to deprive a patient of a "right" as opposed to a "privilege".

No doubt Mr Kaye thought that patients' rooms should be searched and in a state in which they could be searched, but others – patients and staff – were undoubtedly of the view that searching interfered with a patient's "right" to treat his room as his private domain. This was a recipe for confusion. When the PDU was first created, its essential need for different rules should have been recognized.

The **rights** were to be given across the Hospital irrespective of diagnosis said Mr Kaye who also said he was not aware that relaxation of security took place across the Hospital. Unless he had his head in the sand he must have known this was inevitable.

In the extracts quoted above he refers to some basic policies [meaning rules] that should apply throughout the Hospital and which should not be capable of change at ward level. At one stage he placed the horse in its right place in front of the cart. He said: "What a team could say is, 'Well, **a privilege**, an access to telephones, that is more appropriate for patient X than for patient Y, because of his clinical condition.' That is, of course, how it should have been, but access to telephones was said to be a **right** not a privilege! The clinical team could not say what he suggests. It had to say, 'Well, access to telephones is a right and we cannot deprive a patient of his right without being able to fully justify it.'

2.10.14 The problems this caused can be demonstrated from Mrs Miles' evidence. She similarly thought it would not have been possible to implement the Blom-Cooper Report's recommendations selectively, given the position in 1993, when personality disordered patients were mixed up on wards with mentally ill patients. She admitted that by 1996 it had been recognized that policies and procedures for personality disordered patients had to be stricter, although this then created problems in terms of taking away perceived entitlements.

Twenty-Four Hour Care

2.10.15 Mr Millar told us of his conversations with staff which revealed the powerful legacy of the implementation of the Blom-Cooper Report's recommendations. Thus staff would tell him how powerless they felt with regard to challenging the behaviour of patients who, for example, did not engage in therapy, but stayed up all night and slept all day. Ideally that is something that should have been addressed by the PCT. Some PCTs did do this. All too frequently though, it was regarded as a nursing problem, and nurses were very reluctant, with the memory of the Blom-Cooper Report still fresh, to take action which might appear oppressive.

This is not the picture painted in SHSA publications. In the SHSA Review 1995 the Round the Clock Hospital is referred to. Prior to the general implementation of "24-hour therapeutic care", a pilot study had been conducted at Rampton Hospital and Mr Temple, Support Nurse to the Director of Patient Services at Rampton is quoted as saying: "The biggest change is that staff and patients can now talk to each other at night. Before, if a patient had a physical or therapeutic problem at night, he or she could only communicate with staff by shouting through a locked door. The problems that were anticipated in 1991 have not happened. There were concens at first about patients staying up all night. Now the patients and staff on each ward agree their own house rules about bedtimes."

We question whether this represented the true position at Rampton itself, and certainly at the other two Special Hospitals. The problems which had been envisaged in 1991 had, in fact, arisen and were commented upon in the minutes of the Security Managers meetings.

Thus Item 10.1 of the minutes of the meeting of 26 April 1994 states:

> "The Security managers referred to the increasing number of difficulties caused by patient Councils and the Advocacy Service in their challenges to such matters as searching and the new 24-hour opening arrangements. There was a perception that WMs [Ward Managers] were losing control of their wards and patients having too great a say in what they could do. Again there was reference to the failure of care plans in that some patients were being allowed to stay in their rooms all day and only get up for meals. Others stayed up late and remained in bed until lunch time. This was a feature at all three hospitals and critical comment by the Security Departments on these practices, simply increased the resistance to the Department's advice and recommendations."

Item 7.4 of the minutes of the meeting of 13 September show that the meeting discussed the problems that were arising following the introduction of 24-hour care. Some patients wanted to play cards or watch television all night, then sleep during the day and refuse to join in activities on and off ward. The result was that the structure was breaking down because of the alienation caused by staff's reduced contact with patients. The comment was made that although patients were no longer locked into their rooms, they were being locked into themselves.

The SHSA Review of 1995 does not give a date of publication, and the change at Rampton only took place in 1995. In the minutes of the Security Managers' meeting of 8 August 1995, item 6.2 reads, "Rampton's wards had introduced a nursing policy to dissuade patients from remaining up, and after midnight all were in their rooms. This had been fully accepted and had overcome the problems that had been experienced over the disturbance to sleeping patterns and activities. These remained problems at Ashworth and Broadmoor."

2.10.16 The 24-hour Care Policy was the flag ship to liberalising the Hospital. It was given top priority by the then Secretary of State who pushed for its early introduction. It cost a fortune in additional staffing costs and created a new range of security problems. In our view the underlying philosophy is right for a hospital. We see no reason, however, why there should not be an expectation that patients should stay in their rooms at key times such as shift handover. At night security concerns are paramount and we are not persuaded by those who argue that much therapy could also be done. Having a large number of skilled nursing staff on duty at night strikes us as inappropriate. Their skills could be better deployed during the day. We discuss this further in Part Seven.

Patient Power

2.10.17 Staff felt the implementation of the Blom-Cooper recommendations had gone too far, not least in tipping the balance against staff trying to do their jobs. Mr Ryan of UNISON summed up the general picture. He said that prior to the implementation of the Blom-Cooper recommendations patients had to earn things and staff were able to say "no". Then these things began to be seen as rights of patients and staff were expected to say "yes". "Yes" is an easier word to say than "no".

2.10.18 Mr Ryan also argued that there was a certain climate of fear after the Blom-Cooper Report as staff were increasingly reluctant to express concerns for fear of being labelled a "dinosaur".

The elaborate new complaints system was mistrusted. Staff felt concerned about the way in which even malicious complaints went through a labourious system, creating uncertainty for the staff concerned. Staff did not feel confident that senior mangers would support them at times of difficulty. We discuss this further below.

2.10.19 This is a matter of leadership at the PCT level. It is also a matter of Hospital-wide leadership, communicating to staff the message that proper professional behaviour would be supported by managers. Senior managers at Ashworth need to reiterate this message clearly and often.

The Downgrading of Security

2.10.20 Mr Day, Security Liaison Officer for the PDU from January 1995 until March 1996, told us that security had been reduced after the implementation of the Blom-Cooper Report's recommendations:

> "When I first started there, which was Park Lane, it was quite secure and everybody knew the policies and adhered to the policies. After the Blom-Cooper Report things just got lax and the policies seemed to go out the window, and if a patient wanted a certain thing they seemed to get it."

When asked by Professor Edwards whether the change to a more "liberal" environment had been planned and considered or was mere anarchy and confusion, Mr Day told us that policies in many cases remained the same, they were merely ignored as far as the PDU was concerned. But on the Mental Illness side of the Hospital core policies were better observed.

2.10.21 Dr Williams remarked that when the HAS team visited Ashworth in November 1994 the impact of the Blom-Cooper Inquiry was immediately apparent. People tended to start sentences with "After the Inquiry . . ."; staff did not seem to be confident in their roles and were confused about the relationship between security and therapy, believing any increase in security automatically meant a decreased emphasis on therapy.

Conclusions

2.10.22 No one appears to have made any warning noises, either at the time of the

conception of the Task Force's plan for Ashworth or later, despite the risks involved in attempting rapidly to change the culture of a very old-fashioned institution; to create a clinical experiment with some of the most difficult patients in the system; to apply across the whole hospital reforms which were primarily geared to the undoubted needs of mentally ill and learning disability patients; and despite the growing knowledge that the system was still very defective. The SHSA was at fault in failing, at least, to recommend an effective change of course. But the Department of Health and Ministers made a mistake in driving forward this programme of change without due recognition of the problems involved.

2.10.23 It is impossible to escape the conclusion that the implementation of the Blom-Cooper recommendations was ill-considered:

(i) it was driven too fast;

(ii) the SHSA should have realized that the PDU and the personality disordered patients within it required a different level of security from that provided for the mentally ill; and

(iii) staff were inadequately prepared for a very sophisticated and complex programme of change.

2.11.0 The Swan Report: *A Review of The Services for Women at Ashworth Hospital* (July 1993)

2.11.1 This Report was compiled by an external team consisting of Dr Marion Swan, a consultant forensic psychiatrist, a Director of Nursing, Ms Tricia Ball and a psychologist, Maggie Hilton. The team was asked to review the services in the light of the relevant three recommendations of the Blom-Cooper Report:

"**Women in Ashworth**

72. We recommend that management should review the training needs of staff working on opposite sex wards.

73. We recommend that management action be taken to ensure that all disciplines work together to develop a common philosophy and purpose for the regime of women.

74. We recommend that Ashworth develops specialist services to meet the needs of women with severe emotional and behavioural disorders."

2.11.2 At the time there were 59 women patients at Ashworth Hospital housed in three wards on the South site (Herons, Laurels and Eiders), and two wards on the East site (Acacias and Elms).

2.11.3 We did not examine this Report in detail because women's services were not within our terms of reference. Our main interest in the Report was that it had not been disclosed to the HAS team led by Dr Williams which produced the review of Ashworth's services entitled *With Care in Mind Secure.* But many of the problems identified are very similar to those identified in other inquiries.

2.11.4 The Review is highly critical of the services provided for women at Ashworth Hospital. Although the team was considering the recommendations of the Blom-Cooper Report, it is said there was little evidence that anything had been done. The Review is dismissive of the reasons given by Ashworth staff for the women having accommodation considerably inferior to the accommodation for men. A considerable proportion of the nursing staff working on the women's wards were trained in mental handicap nursing only and not in mental illness nursing. Male nurses going onto the women's wards did not have any training for dealing with female patients. The nursing staff were generally unaware of the key documents normally and necessarily found in the ward office. Trust between psychologists and nurses had clearly been compromised by the Blom-Cooper Inquiry leading to mutual anxieties. There appeared to be three sets of notes relating to each patient on the wards: medical, psychology and nursing notes whereas it was crucial that all notes should be filed within the ward notes.

2.11.5 The catalogue of problems continues. There was no option for women to see a female psychiatrist. The three female consultant psychiatrists employed at Ashworth at the time the team visited were exclusively employed with male patients, and one had since left. Serious concerns were expressed about over-medication. The Review records:

> "We were told that medication was often given on demand, sometimes as a result of threats of physical violence to doctors, rather than from genuine need . . . Doctors apparently felt that heavy sedation in order to help patients cope with an impoverished environment was appropriate . . . The use of medication to resolve the quality of the environment or threatening, demanding acting-out behaviour is inappropriate".

2.11.6 The Review says, "We were told that patients were moved from one ward to another, on occasions, against nursing advice, and that some patients who were seen as 'problems' were moved frequently. These moves mostly took place between Herons, Elms and Laurels wards rather than involving Eiders or Acacias. **They did not have clear ward policies or integrated cohesive ideas about working together to achieve the best care for each patient and decisions to move patients were often taken urgently by the consultants rather than planned by the team. Patients as a result were not always placed on the most suitable ward for their needs**."

This problem is seen in the Mallalieu and Rowe Reports. It appears again in later Reports, and has never been effectively resolved.

2.11.7 Multi-disciplinary working was poor; the team were aware of intense professional and interpersonal rivalries, and very little mutual trust.

2.11.8 The team reflected on the recent troubled history of the Hospital and its effects on staff:

> "It is important . . . to acknowledge that change requires time. However, possibly as a result of generally low morale in the Hospital following the Inquiry we were at times confronted with staff who were unclear about their roles and felt frustrated by their inability to effect change as rapidly as they would like. There was a sense that management favoured some services/wards than others. It was felt better services were provided for the men and their wards had been up-graded."

2.11.9 The team's conclusions was damning:

> "We have been so disturbed by our findings that we have felt it necessary to consider whether the women's service at Ashworth should continue. We have concluded that it should not. This decision was made only after the most serious evaluation of various other options but it was not felt that any of these would meet the long term needs of the women and we could not be satisfied that they would be implementable or effect the changes required . . . ."

The team set out a number of factors influencing their decision, including the inadequate physical environment; the anti-therapeutic attitudes amongst some staff; dangerous prescribing practices; chaotic multi-disciplinary working, caused by personal, political and professional rivalries; the failure by management to recognize women's needs; and the fact that most, if not all, of the women in Ashworth did not need high security care.

2.11.10 The Review recommended that no more women should be admitted to Ashworth.

We have no doubt that Mr Kaye did not want the HAS team led by Dr Williams to see this Review but we will refer to that point in more detail in considering *With Care In Mind Secure.*

2.12.0 The Code of Practice (August 1993)

2.12.1 The Code of Practice is issued under section 118 of the Mental Health Act 1983 by the Secretary of State, for guidance in relation to the admission and treatment of patients suffering from mental disorder. In its preparation the Secretary of State is enjoined to consult such bodies as appear to him to be concerned. One such body is, of course, the Mental Health Act Commission which is entrusted with monitoring the operation of the Act. There is no legal duty to comply with the Code but failure to follow the Code may be referred to in evidence in legal proceedings.

2.12.2 Parts of the Code are cited by patients, the Patients' Advocacy Service, patients' lawyers and the Mental Health Act Commission cite parts of the Code in argument to support alleged breaches of patient rights. In addition there have been many instances of staff failing to apply security procedures or misinterpreting them because of apparent conflict with the Code, or fear of complaints being made against them, and in fear of receiving threatening letters from patients' solicitors.

2.12.3 We refer below to the areas of the Code of Practice which give rise to difficulty in the Special Hospitals. We suggest the Code be re-written to reflect the special circumstances of any high security setting.

Assessment

2.12.4 Paragraph 1.3 provides that people being assessed for possible admission should "be delivered any necessary treatment or care in the least controlled and segregated facilities practicable". Paragraph 1.4 states that "when treatment and care is provided in conditions of security, patients should be subject only to the level of security appropriate to their individual needs and only for so long as it is required."

2.12.5 This provision is worded in a way which encourages assessing patients in less than suitably secure facilities. A number of serious incidents, the death of Mallalieu, for example, was caused by a patient placed on a long-stay ward for assessment purposes.

Personal Searches

2.12.6 Paragraph 25 is concerned with personal searches.

2.12.7 25.1 provides "Authorities should ensure that there is an operational policy on the searching of patients and their belongings. Such a policy should be checked with the health authority's legal advisers."

25.2 provides "It should not be the part of such a policy routinely to carry out searches of patients and their personal belongings. If, however, there are lawful grounds for carrying out a search, the patient's consent should be sought. In undertaking such a search staff should have due regard for the dignity of the person concerned and the need to carry out the search in such a way as to ensure the maximum privacy."

25.3 provides "If the patient does not consent to the search, staff should consult with the unit general manager (or such other delegated senior staff, e.g. senior nurse manager, when he is not available) before undertaking any lawful search. The same principles relating to the patient's dignity and the need for maximum privacy apply. Any such search should be carried out with the minimum force necessary and in the case of a search of a patient's person, unless urgent necessity dictates otherwise, such a search should be carried out by a staff member of the same sex."

2.12.8 Paragraph 25.2. is a prime example of how not to draft paragraphs of a Code. What does it mean? Routine personal or property searches should not be carried out, but searches can be carried out if there are lawful grounds. What are lawful grounds? Why should routine or random searches (which are not mentioned) not be carried out? High Security Hospitals, to quote Mr Kaye again, "are radically different from NHS hospitals" and "until you accept that . . . you will not understand at all what is going on within them . . . " They contain patients who present dangers to themselves, other patients, staff and the general public. They are there pursuant to the Secretary of State's duty under section 4 of the National Health Service Act 1977 because they require treatment under conditions of special security on account of their dangerous, violent or criminal propensities.

2.12.9 Not surprisingly, perhaps to be expected, various interested parties have sought to interpret a high secure hospital's powers to search differently. Patients have claimed searching is illegal, so have their lawyers. More particularly the Mental Health Act Commission has also done so, giving weight to the arguments of patients and their lawyers, and adding to the confusion among hospital staff. The general confusion over searching, in the face of written policies at all three Hospitals has undoubtedly been a cause, if not the cause, of patients having too much property in their rooms which made searching of many rooms too time consuming to be practical.

The Security Managers at each Hospital were very concerned and enlisted Mr Kaye's help to fight their corner with the MHAC. On the 31 January 1995 he wrote to Mr William Bingley the Chief Executive of the MHAC in the following terms:

> "Patients' Property And Searching Of Rooms
>
> Over the past few months, each of the special hospitals has encountered some difficulties with regard to the above policies and I know that the subject has been discussed with your visiting Commissioners. I thought it might be helpful if I made clear the SHSA's views in both respects. While in the normal course of events we would encourage each patient to have personal property in his or her room, we must and will restrict this to what we consider to be a reasonable level. This level will be dictated by the need to be able to search quickly and efficiently any patient's room at short notice. We cannot be in a position where the sheer volume of patient's property stored in a room makes it impossible to carry out an effective search. While we again would encourage the patients to see their room on the ward as their base and somewhere where they can have their property, we will, as we think appropriate, institute searches. These searches will be carried out according to a proper protocol and patients involved would normally be given the opportunity to witness the search."

2.12.10 The SHSA was committed to applying the Code of Practice, yet at no stage was any effort made to clarify the undoubted confusion which the terminology of paragraph 25 created. In his evidence, Mr Kaye said he had had a lot of anxieties about searching. "The twin problems that I saw, which was the stockpiling of possessions within rooms, whereby then it becomes physically difficult to search a room, and then the reluctance of staff to undertake regular searches as required to check what was happening in individual rooms." He went on to say that on a number of occasions he wrote to the general managers pointing out the essential importance of searching. "We all knew the problems the staff had at ward level in enforcing these disciplines."

2.12.11 Despite the seriousness of this well known problem, and despite the confusion surrounding the practice of searching, nothing was done to clarify the situation until towards the end of the lifetime of the SHSA. Mr Kaye said "the searching criteria in the contract did not appear until towards the end of the SHSA's lifetime." This was the reason he gave why no criticism was made about searching in any of the Quarterly Quality Reviews of Ashworth and the other two Hospitals. "So," he added, "I doubt actually within the SHSA's life if they were taken as specific standards by any visiting group."

2.12.12 We are in no doubt that because this was a chronic problem in all three Hospitals, the SHSA should not have left individual general managers to go on hitting their heads against the security wall for so long. We criticize the SHSA and Mr Kaye for failing to resolve the conflict between paragraph 25 of the Code of Practice which the SHSA espoused, and the obvious need to carry out searches in a High Security Hospital.

Recommendation 2 **2.12.13 We recommend that paragraph 25 of the Code of Practice be rewritten to reflect the special circumstances of any high security setting.**

The Broadmoor Judgment

2.12.14 At the end of the day it was left to five patients, "S","H" and "D" and two others to challenge the undoubted need of these three Hospitals to conduct random and routine searches on patients detained under the Mental Health Act 1983. They sought **Judicial Review** of the Security Policy (S 1) which was to be implemented by Broadmoor Special Hospital Authority as from 1 July 1997 (14 years after the Act came into force).[3] That Security Policy was published on 13 May 1997. Prior to its issue, as Potts J. said in his judgment, there had been no policy of random searches at Broadmoor. Some random searching without cause had been taking place at Ashworth, Rampton and Carstairs, but certainly at Ashworth when it was done it was done with little confidence and usually in a cursory fashion. No doubt the policy that searching should only be for cause stemmed from what was a timid but safe interpretation of paragraph 25 of the Code of Practice.

The background to the introduction of Broadmoor's policy was as follows. On the 18 August 1996 a patient attacked a visiting priest with a drinking mug in Broadmoor Chapel. The attack could have proved fatal. The patient who carried out the attack was not regarded by staff as at particular risk of behaving violently. As a result of the attack, on 19 August 1996 a policy of random rub-down searches of patients was instituted. It was withdrawn three days later pending the recommendations of an Internal Inquiry Report. The Report drew attention to the defects in the existing system of searching only "for cause" and recommended consideration of a system of random and routine searches of all patients. Eventually that policy was produced as Security Policy (S 1).

2.12.15 Affidavit evidence placed before Mr Justice Potts summarises the opposing views which existed, and exist at all three Special Hospitals.

2.12.16 The case for random searching was as follows. Patients are received either directly from the courts or upon transfer from the prison service, and the majority bring with them an element of drug abuse. Without random searching it is not possible to prevent illicit substances reaching the Hospital or being circulated within the Hospital. Illicit substances arrive at the Hospital by way of patients returning from leave of absence, visitors coming to the Hospital, and potentially by being brought in by staff or being sent through the post. At the Hospital circulation of such substances can take place at social events. In parole wards the opportunity for trafficking drugs is very much greater given the much greater freedom that such patients have by access round the site but within the secure perimeter. Ms Boswell, the Director of Patient Care Services, knew that vulnerable patients had been coerced into not only carrying drugs for other patients but trading in them as well. Patients taking psychotropic

3 R v Broadmoor Hospital Authority and Others, *ex parte* S and Others (CO/2284/97).

medication can have their mental state seriously and adversely affected by the use of illegal drugs. Patients conceal dangerous items and if random searching is not allowed dangerous materials and weapons can be carried and circulated within the Hospital.

2.12.17 The other view is expressed in the affidavit evidence of Dr Chandra Ghosh, a consultant psychiatrist and RMO of a medium dependency ward and a pre-discharge ward at Broadmoor. If the therapeutic alliance between staff and patients is not to be lost, intrusive security searches of patients, without consent, should only be carried out if there is overriding clinical necessity, as perceived by members of the clinical team. The Security Policy did not allow clinical teams to make decisions based on individual patients' needs and required members of the clinical team to carry out intrusive searches without giving them any responsibility in deciding whether or not the searches should be carried out. Dr Ghosh, who at the time was the RMO to more patients at the Hospital than any other consultant, said advice from the British Medical Association was that it was the Doctor's personal responsibility to balance the requirements of security with the dignity of the patients, and that that responsibility could not be delegated to the Management.

The doctor's affidavit continued "In my view rub-down searches would be as obtrusive to some of my abused and personality disordered patients as an intimate search and I would, therefore, feel obliged to follow the BMA Resolution and would not be willing to authorise rub-down searches except in accordance with the guidelines." In another affidavit Dr James MacKeith a former consultant psychiatrist at Broadmoor and now of the Denis Hill medium secure unit, said, "The maintenance of a hospital culture requires that the management of patients and the constraints applied to them must be used electively, in accordance with the clinical judgment of the multi-disciplinary team. Unlike a prison, the unselective application of intrusive security measures must be avoided. Unless these principles are maintained, a hospital culture will disappear and be replaced by that of a prison. The price of compromising these principles is the loss of an environment in which effective treatment can take place. It is unlikely that skilled, professional staff would be willing to work in such an environment."

2.12.18 In the course of his Judgment Mr Justice Potts referred to relevant general observations. Even searching for reasonable cause could conflict with the treatment power of the clinician if the clinician concluded that such a search would be detrimental to the medical treatment of his patient. In the absence of a consistent policy of minimum requirements throughout Broadmoor every RMO in the Hospital would be free to exempt their patients and adopt their own policy. This would jeopardize security and create a sense of grievance in those patients on the wards subject to the more onerous search policies.

2.12.19 Mr Justice Potts concluded that since "detain" means "keep in confinement" a general power to search patients in order to prevent escape from detention must be implicit. A general power to search patients must necessarily be implied as part of the duty to create and maintain a safe therapeutic environment. In order to exercise that power the decision of the Hospital Authority must necessarily prevail over an objection by an RMO on behalf of a patient on medical grounds. Once that general power was established, the sole remaining issue was whether the power was lawful on the basis of Wednesbury reasonableness (Associated Provincial Picture Houses v Wednesbury Corp. [1948] 1 K.B. 223). On that basis the question was whether such a power to search may be rationally exercised on a routine and random basis in the conditions prevailing at Broadmoor. He concluded that the Wednesbury reasonableness of the policy could not be doubted bearing in mind the very serious risks to be prevented or reduced, the practice and experience of the other Special Hospitals, and the limitations of the pre-existing

search policy based upon reasonable cause or suspicion identified in the evidence. It followed, of course, as the learned Judge said, that what may be reasonable for a Special Hospital would not necessarily be reasonable for other institutions containing less dangerous patients.

2.12.20 Towards the end of his Judgment, Mr Justice Potts referred to paragraph 25 of the Code of Practice and, in particular to sub-paragraph 2. In his judgment the Code was no more than the Secretary of State's view as to the best practice to be followed in hospitals *in general.* It failed to draw any distinction between the different types of detaining hospitals covered by the 1983 Act by reference to the level of security required. To that extent he said the terms of the paragraph may be thought to require reconsideration.

2.12.21 In paragraph 2.12.13 above we have recommended that paragraph 25 of the Code of Practice should be rewritten.

2.12.22 The five patients appealed Mr Justice Potts' decision and Auld and Judge L.J., both gave Judgments with which Nourse L.J. concurred. The appeal was dismissed on 5 February 1998[4].

2.12.23 Between the first instance Judgment and the date of the appeal the Broadmoor Hospital Authority amended the policy by introducing a new right of appeal to the Medical Director in cases where an RMO was unhappy for a search to take place:

> "If the RMO (Responsible Medical Officer) advises that subjecting the patient to search would have adverse consequences for the mental health of the patient, the nurse in charge must refer the matter to the Medical Director who will decide, after taking into account the advice of the RMO and the interests of security and safety of the individual and the Hospital, whether the search should proceed."

2.12.24 In the course of his Judgment Auld L. J., said of the first instance judgment, "In my view, his general reasoning was sound, though I have some doubt whether he was right to go as far as to hold lawful his characterisation of the original policy that, in the exercise of the power, Broadmoor's decision 'must necessarily prevail over an objection by an RMO on behalf of a patient on medical grounds'. After all . . . assessment of risk is a function of treatment. However, I do not consider that paragraph 5.2 of the policy in its original form is to be construed as going that far. It provided, where a patient objected to a search, for reference to his or her responsible medical officer before taking the matter further . . . However, the new paragraph 5.3 puts beyond doubt that the responsible medical officer is required to consider whether the proposed search would harm the patient's mental health and, if that is his view, to refer it to the Medical Director for decision, who should take into account that view and the interests of security and safety of the individual and the Hospital. The policy thus provides for a balancing of the two main and important factors. The fact that it permits those of safety and security to prevail over treatment requirements of an individual patient where considered appropriate cannot, in my view, take it outside the implied power of search . . . . Such a power, necessary as it is for the maintenance of a safe therapeutic environment for all patients and for the safety of staff and visitors, must include the ability, where circumstances require it, of overriding the individual therapeutic requirements of an individual patient. As Mr Parker observed, that is not because security objectives 'trump' treatment objectives, but because security is a necessary part of the background to treatment."

2.12.25 Later in his Judgment Auld L.J., said:

> "I am satisfied that the Judge correctly concluded that there is a general power of search and, as part of it, of search without cause capable of overriding medical opinion against its exercise."

4 QB. COF97/1614/4.

2.12.26 In the course of his Judgment, Judge L.J., who agreed with the judgment of Auld L.J., observed:

> "The problem . . . is that the patient is to be cared for and protected from self-inflicted harm at all times, including occasions when the responsible medical officer is not available to supervise him, and simultaneously, while he is detained securely for the protection of the public outside Broadmoor, the risk which he represents to other patients, staff and visitors within Broadmoor must be minimised."

2.12.27 Later in his Judgment, having dealt with the position of patients admitted under section 3 he said:

> "The offender represents a serious danger from which it is necessary to protect the public. This risk does not evaporate on admission . . . The responsibility for the safe detention of each individual and the collective security of the Hospital itself is a problem for the management rather than any individual medical officer. These considerations fall within the concept of 'control and discipline' identified by Lord Edmund Davies in **Pountney v Griffiths** [1976] A.C. 314, which, in my judgment, remain undiminished by the amendments to the Mental Health Act 1959 enacted by the 1983 Act, and lead me to the conclusion that random searches without the consent of the patient are permissible as part and parcel of necessary internal control and discipline. To restrict such searches to the occasions postulated by Mr Gordon [counsel] is, without disrespect, simply inadequate. Disaster will strike when no-one has any reasonable grounds to anticipate or suspect it, save in the general sense that most of the patients, including these five appellants personally, represent an ongoing danger."

2.12.28 It may well be that some RMOs will argue that the Medical Director has no line management control over individual RMOs in so far as clinical matters are concerned, but we have no doubt that this Judicial Review was rightly rejected.

In the Special Hospitals there are fundamental requirements of security that must prevail and be seen to prevail. For far too long there has been uncertainty in this important area. We welcome the clarification provided by this Judgment.

Visiting

2.12.29 Paragraph 26 of the Code of Practice is concerned with "Visiting patients detained in hospital or registered nursing homes."

2.12.30 In this paragraph, 26.1 states "All detained patients are entitled to maintain contact with and be visited by whomsoever they wish, subject to some carefully limited exceptions." 26.2 is concerned with the grounds for excluding a visitor.

There are two principal grounds which may justify the exclusion of a visitor :

> a. Restriction on clinical grounds:
> This is concerned with situations in which a patient's relationship with a relative or friend is considered to be anti-therapeutic.
>
> b. Restriction on security grounds:
> "The behaviour or propensities of a particular visitor may be, or have been in the past, disruptive or subversive to a degree that exclusion from the hospital or mental nursing home is necessary as a last resort. Examples of such behaviour or propensities are incitement to abscond, smuggling of illicit drugs/alcohol into the hospital, mental nursing home or unit, transfer of potential weapons, or unacceptable aggression or unauthorised media access."

2.12.31 On the evidence we have heard, visitors are a potential source of entry of such matters as are mentioned. **We take the view, as with searching referred to in paragraph 25, that paragraph 26 must be applied according to the nature of the hospital concerned. There is a vast difference between Special Hospitals and nursing homes for the mentally ill. It must be necessary to have the ability to search visitors and without cause. The only distinction we would make is that visitors do not inhabit the Hospital and there should be no need to search if the visitor refuses to be searched, but it should be clearly understood that the Special Hospitals have a right to refuse entry to the Hospital to a visitor who refuses to be searched.**

Recommendation 3

2.12.32 We recommend that Ashworth Hospital introduces searches of visitors and that Paragraph 26 of the Code of Practice be amended to make it crystal clear that in a high security setting visitors who refuse to be searched will not be admitted.

2.12.33 Paragraph 26.3 of the Code of Practice concerns "facilitation of visiting". One matter it states is that "ordinarily, inadequate staff numbers should not be a deterrent to regular visiting".

In the Special Hospitals it is essential to have the power to insist on visits being properly supervised. We have heard a considerable amount of evidence concerning the supervision of visits, whether ward-based or centrally-based. The need for that power is for purposes identical to the need for the power to search. There is inevitably a limitation on the number of staff available to supervise visits. In the Special Hospitals this is usually controlled by ensuring that visits are pre-arranged so that the number of visits occurring at any one time does not result in inadequate staff availability, but we are of the view that, if at any time, there is an inadequate number of staff available properly to supervise visits, there should be a power to refuse a visitor entry to the Hospital. However, this should not normally occur in the case of pre-arranged visits.

Telephone and Mail

2.12.34 Paragraph 26.4 of the Code concerns "other forms of communication". It states:

> "Every effort should be made to assist patients, where appropriate to make contact with relatives, friends and supporters. In particular patients should have readily accessible and appropriate daytime telephone facilities and no restrictions should be placed upon dispatch and receipt of their mail over and above those referred to in section 134 of the Act."

2.12.35 Recommendation 76 of the Blom-Cooper Inquiry recommended "that patients at Ashworth should have a readily accessible personal telephone system like those available in general hospitals and NHS psychiatric hospitals." Yet misuse of telephones by patients has featured in a number of internal inquiries.

2.12.36 It is clear from the evidence before us that the wide interpretation of that recommendation throughout the Hospital led to abuse, significantly affected the security of the Hospital and, in particular, the Personality Disorder Unit.

Recommendation 4

2.12.37 We recommend that it is essential to control and monitor the use of ward-based telephones carefully in order to prevent abuse, control fraud and prevent the introduction into the Hospital of prohibited substances and articles.

2.12.38 Relaxation of the inspection and opening of mail and parcels following the work of the Task Force has undoubtedly led to breaches of security and the introduction into the Hospital of prohibited substances and articles. The minutes of the meetings of the Security

Managers, to which reference has already been made, illustrate the different approaches that came into being concerning the inspection of mail and packages as well as problems connected with the use of telephones.

Recommendation 5 **2.12.39 We recommend that policies which allow staff effectively to control and monitor patients' mail are agreed and consistently implemented.**

2.12.40 We have also examined the use of computers and computer related equipment which has developed in recent years and made recommendations relating to their possession and use by patients. (*See* paragraph **3.39.0** *et seq.*)

2.13.0 The Creation of the PDU

The Rationale

2.13.1 We turn now to the PDU itself. Dr Higgins, the medical member of the Task Force set up after the Blom-Cooper Report, described the rationale for creating the PDU. He and Mr Rae, the nurse member of the Task Force, had focused their attention on developing multi-disciplinary working within the Hospital. He remarked that there were some areas of the Hospital where effective multi-disciplinary working was in place, others where it was not. At the time some staff were unused and even resistant to the concept of multi-disciplinary working. Professional rivalry was also very evident. And the management structures and policies of the Hospital were not conducive to consistent multi-disciplinary working.

2.13.2 Dr Higgins, in his statement, outlined a number of weaknesses which he and Mr Rae had identified:

(i) there was no protocol for dealing with referrals, with a haphazard allocation to consultants of referred patients. Some consultants saw more referrals than others and consultants did not limit themselves to assessing the types of patients they claimed a special expertise with, or whom they might look after if admitted;

(ii) there was an Admission Ward shared by all the consultants on the North site. Some patients were not seen regularly by some consultants during their period of assessment. There were delays in moving patients on to other wards after assessment;

(iii) wards in the Hospital contained mixtures of personality disordered patients and mentally ill patients determined by security and dependency criteria, though the understanding of the difference between these concepts was sometimes muddled;

(iv) except in the few specialised wards the treatment programme was much the same for everyone;

(v) the wards rarely had a set of effective operational policies;

(vi) rather than working together each clinical discipline pursued its own agenda. Nurses were the principle arbiters on security and levels of dependency and could effectively facilitate or obstruct treatment and rehabilitation plans. The medical staff, particularly consultants, were much burdened by administration. The wide catchment area of their patients limited opportunities for forging links with regional services. Waiting lists for individual therapies were considerable. Social workers took little part in case management or ward management except as discharge neared. They were employed by the Hospital rather than a local Social Services Department and seemed isolated from the ethos of social work outside. In addition to all of this there was a varying degree of enthusiasm, clinical expertise and managerial skills in members of all of the disciplines.

2.13.3 The Task Force decided that changes had to be made to improve the poor co-operation between disciplines and the inadequate development of care programmes defined by patient need. Dr Higgins told us that he and his Task Force colleagues did try to engage the different staff groups in developing ideas about the future, but with limited success. The eventual analysis of the problems was largely the Task Force's own.

2.13.4 We have discussed the Task Force's proposed changes in **2.8.0** *et seq.* above. The Task Force produced an initial Report to the SHSA in December 1992 making its observations on the working of the Hospital. The SHSA considered this and commissioned the Task Force to suggest a detailed reorganization of patient groupings to improve the focus of their care and to produce a revised management structure which would better service the changed hospital.

2.13.5 In their original Report to the SHSA the Task Force outlined a number of considerations to be borne in mind when planning the reorganization of patient services. They argued that there was a clear distinction between the treatment needs of different groups of patients: adult men with mental illness; adult men and some young men with pure or predominant personality disorder; men with learning disabilities; women with mental illness, personality disorder and learning disabilities; and other small specialist groups. The largest group was men with a mental illness; this group would almost inevitably leave the Hospital *via* the psychiatric services in their home locality, usually via their local secure unit. It might therefore be wise to manage together such patients from the same region or adjacent regions in a regime where they were not on the same ward as personality disordered patients with whom they were traditionally mixed. Liaison with smaller numbers of receiving and referring units would therefore be made much easier.

2.13.6 The case for a specialist unit for personality disordered patients was, in short, that by developing a specialist unit some of the well-recognized shortcomings in care and treatment of this group might be tackled. At that time there was no guarantee that a patient suffering from personality disorder referred for assessment would be assessed by a consultant working with personality disordered patients. A specialist unit could ensure that consultants who would potentially be working with a patient actually did the assessment. Such a unit could facilitate the development of recognized forms of assessment, treatment, and outcome measures for personality disorder; it might attract staff of all disciplines interested in this form of work; help facilitate the development of audit and research; and enable clearer distinctions to be drawn between those admitted for assessment, those undergoing treatment and those for whom treatment had failed and who required long-term humane containment on grounds of enduring risk. Furthermore, security considerations would presumably be much higher on the agenda than they would be for the patients elsewhere given that experience had shown that it was predominantly the personality disordered patient who presented the most major difficulties within the Hospital.

We applaud these principles, but sadly they were not implemented.

2.13.7 Dr Higgins noted that there were some concerns about the establishment of the personality disorders unit, but these concerns were not raised very vigorously. They included clinical issues about patients who might require mental illness and personality disorder facilities at different times or who, despite the diagnosis, might be better placed for rehabilitative and transfer purposes in a unit not specifically designated to their diagnosis. There were comments about the difficulty of attracting the required numbers of interested and suitably qualified staff, but this was not felt to be insurmountable if the unit truly developed as a dynamic successful entity. Some doubted whether agglomerating the most potentially difficult patients would be manageable. Experience with the two existing longstanding personality disorder wards had shown that problems of control and security might occur.

These problems might be far greater in a personality disordered unit. However, these objections were not decisive.

2.13.8 After extensive consultation at Ashworth Hospital and on the SHSA Board it was felt that the balance favoured the formation of a discrete personality disorder unit. If it was properly managed; if realistic operational policies were produced; if effective multi-disciplinary working emerged; if greater expertise developed; and if security was always seen as a matter continually under review, then Ashworth Hospital could safety and securely not only manage its personality disordered patients well, but also contribute to the continuing debate about the treatability of those with a severe personality disorder in a secure hospital setting. Dr Higgins in his evidence admitted that there were a large number of "ifs", but argued that nevertheless the proposal was better than leaving matters as they were.

2.13.9 To allow such a clinical reorganization of the Hospital, the Task Force recommended a parallel reorganization of the management structure, with greater autonomy for the new units and a multi-disciplinary management structure. The professional fiefdoms needed to be removed and strong general management introduced, not least to produce a range of operational policies for each unit and to develop multi-disciplinary working. High calibre managers were seen as a crucial feature of the reorganization process.

2.13.10 We have described above the subsequent Task Force Report to the SHSA in February 1993 which outlined a proposed ward reconfiguration and new management structure in considerable detail. This was broadly accepted and then remitted to Ashworth Hospital for further consideration. The Task Force was wound-up shortly afterwards. Mrs Janice Miles, the new General Manager of Ashworth Hospital, attended the SHSA Board Meeting on 16 September 1993, and presented a paper describing the restructuring proposals for her Hospital, proposals which had emerged after further internal discussions at the Hospital and which were slight modifications of the proposals of the Task Force. Her proposals were accepted.

2.13.11 The PDU became functional in December 1993 and formally came into being in April 1994. It consisted of six wards. Two of the six, Lawrence and Owen, changed little as they had both housed a population of largely personality disordered patients for some years, although the population of Owen had to move from Forster Ward. By contrast, Macaulay, Ruskin and Shelley were significantly involved in the clinical restructuring. Firs Ward (later Newman Ward) was on the East Site.

2.13.12 Dr Ian Strickland was the first Clinical Manager; because he still carried a clinical caseload he was supported by a Business Manager, Mr Martin Royal. The six Ward Managers reported to a Clinical Area Nurse Manager, who in turn reported to Dr Strickland. This structure then changed and the Ward Managers reported directly to Dr Strickland, with a Clinical Nurse Manager introduced in an advisory capacity.

Was the PDU Ever Viable?

2.13.13 It is appropriate to consider at this point in the history of the PDU whether bringing together more than 100 personality disordered patients into a single unit was a sensible option. The Mental Illness Units/Directorate have been relatively successful, but the PDU has never lived up to the hopes of the Task Force. Was this foreseeable?

2.13.14 At the theoretical level the argument for a discrete specialist unit is sound. We ourselves are convinced of the need to have specialist units. But were the practical issues thought through? Was the Task Force naive?

2.13.15 We heard considerable evidence to the effect that the PDU, in its early days, was in a parlous state. Dr Strickland noted in his statement that after his appointment in December

1993 he was given the task of bringing together all the personality disordered patients onto six wards, in just two or three months. The intention was that Lawrence and Macaulay Wards would be low dependency; Owen Ward medium dependency, Ruskin Ward medium to high dependency, Shelley Ward high dependency and admissions, and Newman Ward a ward for younger patients. But, in practice, patients moved to where there was a bed available. Sometimes patients separated previously for security reasons were brought back together again thanks to the small number of available wards. In evidence Dr Strickland said he had argued for a smaller PDU, with just three wards.

2.13.16 Dr Strickland also argued that 25-bedded wards were too large for this group, preferring 8-bedded wards instead, with a proper assessment process. He told us that the doctors working on the Unit had had no say in its creation. (Dr Sylvester, the former Director of Medical Services and Lead Consultant on the PDU agreed on this point.) Dr Strickland admitted that there was no real treatment model at the start; the priority had been to manage a large group of heterogeneous patients.

It is disingenuous of Dr Strickland to say that doctors had no say at all; we accept Dr Higgins' evidence that, despite trying to involve staff in developing the Task Force's proposals, he and his colleagues received little help from the generality of staff. That said, the establishing of the Unit was highly flawed.

We agree with Dr Strickland that both the Unit and the Wards were too big, and that there should have been a proper assessment process.

2.13.17 Dr Strickland's successor as Clinical Manager, Mr Tarbuck, confirmed the overall picture presented by Dr Strickland. He described the PDU when he took it over in the summer of 1994 in the wake of the Owen Ward incident thus:

> "The PDU Unit was dreadful when I first took over. There had been a serious lapse of control; in addition there appeared to be no clear vision for the Unit, no objectives, no direction . . . I thought at the time the staffing levels were too low, both in terms of the clinical establishments and in terms of vacancies. It was almost impossible to recruit to the PDU when I took over. It was, in effect, a ghetto."

2.13.18 Many of the staff in post did not want to be there. They were generally ill-equipped to deal with these patients all grouped together: "There were lots of good staff there, but quite a sizeable minority were not able to cope with the work they were being able to do." Mr Melia, now a Senior Clinical Nurse within the PDU, confirmed this picture. He told us that when he became Ward Manager of Macaulay Ward in August 1994, 18 patient moves had taken place over the previous nine months as the mentally ill population of the Ward was replaced by personality disordered patients. The staff were totally ill-equipped to deal with the change of patients, lacking as they did knowledge of the nature and treatment of personality disorder.

2.13.19 In evidence Mr Tarbuck elaborated further on the state of the Unit in mid-1994. The management and staff were not really in control of the Unit; patients had got used to crossing boundaries and staff felt demotivated and disempowered. The Unit was under-established as far as nursing staff were concerned; around one in six staff was on sick leave. He approached Mrs Miles and senior colleagues on a number of occasions and made a detailed case for more resources in a paper entitled *Benchmarks for Practice* in June 1995. His request was turned down.

2.13.20 Like Dr Strickland, Mr Tarbuck thought that the rationale of the Unit and the therapies it was to offer had not been thought through. He and his colleagues spent much time trying to articulate what might or might not work. He noted that, at the start of his tenure, most of the PCTs lacked psychology input and some lacked social work input; in some instances there was no trust and little respect between members; and minutes were sometimes of variable quality. Mr Tarbuck noted tensions in PCT practice in 1994, with people arriving excessively late; reading notes when being spoken to; leaving meetings to answer telephone calls and so forth.

Mr Tarbuck felt that he was "firefighting" until mid-1995, coping with crisis after crisis. Staff had allowed patients inappropriately to cross boundaries; certain patients were colluding and needed to be split up. But Lawrence Ward was not seen to be one of the problematic wards:

> "I would say post-June 1994 Owen was doing very well. The rest were struggling for a considerable period. Lawrence Ward was an exception in that it had a very mature group of people who had been together a long time, saw themselves to be something different, and attempted to protect that. So that was a slightly less problematic area.
>
> I regarded Lawrence Ward as well-managed."

2.13.21 Mr Tarbuck's successor, Mr James Murphy, thought the Unit had been created too quickly, with inadequate preparation of staff and too little thought given to the nature of the problems created by putting this group of patients together. Some "untreatable" patients were accommodated with patients just coming into the system, undermining the treatment of the latter. Some staff could not cope.

2.13.22 Mrs Miles confirmed the general picture. She admitted that a number of factors militated against the Unit's success, including the questionable competence of some of the consultants. She agreed that the clinical mix was not ideal; that the wards were larger than she and the SHSA would have liked; and that the creation of the Clinical Units made moving patients more difficult, as there was very little spare capacity within the PDU itself. Nevertheless she defended the decision to create the PDU, even with hindsight; it was necessary she argued, to create the other Clinical Units.

2.13.23 What had happened? A radical new change had been made too fast, with inadequate preparation. Many of the Unit's problems should have been foreseen. To take one example: Dr Higgins made it clear that a high quality manager was key to the success of the PDU. Yet Dr Strickland was appointed as the first Clinical Manager, someone who by his own admission lacked management experience and was not up to the job. There were apparently no external candidates for the job.

2.13.24 Such an innovative venture as this required an in-depth consideration of the implications of putting 150 personality disordered patients together. Once this particular decision was made the die was cast and the Hospital had to live with the consequences.

2.13.25 The SHSA was responsible for agreeing the new structure. They should have been aware of the risks and invested heavily in time and effort to ensure that the right quality of managerial and clinical staff were appointed to the Unit. Mr Kaye admitted that the SHSA had not foreseen the potential problems adequately:

> **"... creating the PD Unit in the form we did, we knew it was high risk, I think it was higher risk than we realized at the time".**

2.13.26 Nobody emerges from this with any credit. The risks involved in creating such a large PDU were recognised from the start, but were sharply increased by poor leadership and implementation. As the Chief Executive of the SHSA Mr Kaye must carry the ultimate responsibility, but many others are also blameworthy. This was not just a reasonable risk that went wrong despite the best efforts of all those involved. It was a high risk that was sharply increased by incompetence.

2.14.0 The Owen Ward Report: Report of the Investigation into the Events leading up to the Hostage-Taking Incident on Owen Ward on 8 June 1994 and related matters.

We discuss this Report at considerable length, for which we make no apology. The Report formed a vital part of our investigations and its contents were never published. We have speculated that had this Report been published in 1994, the necessary in-depth examination of the PDU at Ashworth Hospital would have taken place some years earlier than our Inquiry.

The Reports

2.14.1 We have already referred to this internal Report as being one of the most serious if not the most serious Report in the history of Ashworth Hospital. It is dated 18 July 1994. The Chairman of the Inquiry was Mr Green (then Director of Business Development), and the other members were Dr P. Coorey (a consultant forensic psychiatrist), Mr Ian Paterson (the Security Resources Manager), and Mr George Alan (the Nursing Informatics Manager). The original Report is 59 pages long and, more importantly, attached to it are 385 pages of appendices. The Report itself presents an appalling picture but with the appendices we can only describe it as horrendous. During the course of our Inquiry we felt it right to congratulate Mr Green and his team for presenting a fearlessly thorough Report which makes a significant number of findings concerning the Hospital's failure to create a safe and secure therapeutic environment on Owen Ward.

2.14.2 The first version of the Report we received came from London. It was 19 pages long and without appendices. The first three pages comprise the title page, and a letter from the then General Manager Mrs Miles. The last three pages are a summary by Mrs Miles of the findings of an external advisor she had appointed to look at the work of the Inquiry and to comment on it. She had appointed Mr J. Parry, the Senior Nurse Manager of the Merseyside Regional Forensic Psychiatry Service, because it was being said that the internal Report would be a whitewash. The original Report was certainly not a whitewash, and Mr Parry's Report was not based on any shorter version. He saw the whole Report and the appendices. Despite being a significant abridgement of the original, the 19-page Report made disquieting reading even though, within it, most of the original recommendations had either been omitted or truncated, and criticisms of policies and practices in place or management's failure to formulate or introduce them had been removed. It omits the whole of the 27-page narrative of the original which is based on the appendices and deals with the terms of reference. It reduces the original 20 pages of recommendations to eight pages. From a reading of the 19-page version, it soon became apparent that a fuller Report existed as well as appendices, and those we eventually obtained from Ashworth Hospital. For many months we were under the impression that at least the 19-page version had been circulated, because in a letter attached to it Mrs Miles writes:

> **"Because this Report is to be widely circulated, it omits names and details of the interviews conducted to underpin the findings and recommendations. Hopefully the Report will provide all with the information necessary whilst protecting patient and staff confidentiality."**

We were to discover this was not the case. It was not until we received the statement of Mr Harry Ryan of UNISON that we discovered, appended to that statement, a yet shorter version of the Owen Ward Report. This is the only version which was ever circulated. It is not surprising that its circulation gave rise to serious indignation. Appended to Mr Ryan's submission is a press release condemnatory of the handling of the Owen Ward Report:

> "Management at the Hospital set up its own investigation team conducted by managers for managers to be vetted by management before publication . . . The publication caused immediate outrage amongst staff, as its total eight page contents contained:

Front cover	one page.
Introduction	three pages.
Findings	there was a total of six findings, one page.
Recommendations	there was a total of eight, one page.
Appendix	References, one page.
Appendix	Circulation list, one page.

This publication could have been written about emptying waste paper bins . . . The hospital is now a pit of rumours and suspicion, without any form of coherent leadership or purpose, and the staff and patients are left to work one day at a time."

2.14.3 On the 31st day of our hearings we received a copy of this third version in a short bundle. The first page is a letter from Mrs Miles addressed to "Dear Colleague" which describes the Report as the "final Report into the investigation following events on Owen Ward", and indicates that "it is not a public document and is not being circulated outside the Hospital".

2.14.4 We deal later with why, in our judgment, this Report and also the Swan Report were concealed.

Owen Ward in 1994

2.14.5 Owen Ward has had a chequered history. The killing of Stephen Mallalieu took place on Owen Ward in 1990, that of Derek Williams on Forster Ward the same year. The patient population of Forster Ward later moved to Owen Ward. By 1994 the Ward was in a parlous state. A general description of the Ward is given in paragraph 2 of the full Report:

> "Forster Ward, and from early January 1994, Owen Ward, had been established under the aegis of a therapeutic community since 1982 and was conceived by Dr Chris Hunter and Dr Malcolm MacCulloch. Its history has been eventful, and would have been expected to have been so, but it has never reached the level of disruption experienced immediately prior to the events in early June 1994. The young patient population within Owen Ward ideally 'graduate' to Lawrence Ward when they have responded and matured in their treatment programme and demonstrate appropriate behavioural responses."

We discuss the problems of the "post-graduate" Lawrence Ward in Part Three below.

The condition of the ward was clear from the Report into a very serious incident on Owen Ward just a month before the hostage-taking, when the bedroom of Mr J. O'Neill had been set on fire, and that incident has been described as an attempted murder. It was, however, not investigated until the full Owen Ward Report had been received, and Mrs Miles ordered an investigation in a letter to Mr Tarbuck dated 4 October 1994. That Report demonstrates that for some months Owen Ward was in a parlous state and out of control. Both patients and staff were fearful for their lives.

We must stress at this point that Owen and Lawrence Wards were not the only wards with problems. There were also serious problems in 1995 and 1996 on other wards in the PDU. We deal below with the investigation into the activities of Stephen Braund on Ruskin Ward, formerly Macaulay Ward, and the investigation of the possessions of Stephen Finney (whose death, after being taken to hospital gave rise to some suspicion as to its cause) found in his room on Shelly Ward in June 1996.

These events point inexorably to the conclusion that the conception of the PDU was wrong. Incident followed incident, without effective policies and structures being established and put in place. The simple fact is that it is impossible effectively to manage many patients in this group in the absence of a basic immutable security structure. For them a structured

environment providing an appropriate degree of control and security is essential. This was never achieved.

2.14.6 In Appendix 8 of the Owen Ward Report an index offence profile of the 20 patients on the ward at the time of the Report is given:

No.	Section	Index Offence
1	37/41	Arson, burglary
2	37/41	Attempted murder x 2, Firearms, Criminal damage
3	37	Rape
4	37/41	Attempted murder, Wounding with intent
5	37/41	Indecent assault
6	37/41	Abduction, Attempted rape, Indecent assault, Attempt to choke
7	47/49	Murder
8	47/49	Murder
9	47/49	Manslaughter (diminished responsibility), Theft
10	47/49	Robbery, Escape, Burglary, Taking conveyance without authority
11	47/49	Rape, Wounding
12	37/41	Wounding with intent
13	37/41	Grievous Bodily Harm (GBH) with intent, False imprisonment
14	47/49	Rape x 2, Theft, Deception, Taking conveyance without authority
15	37/41	Arson with intent, Burglary
16	37/41	Manslaughter (diminished responsibility) x 2, Actual Bodily Harm (ABH), GBH
17	37/41	ABH
18	37/41	Wounding, Indecent assault
19	37/41	Indecent assault, Assault with intent to rob
20	7/41	Manslaughter, Unlawful possession of firearm and ammunition, Indecent assault (on male)

2.14.7 So there were 14 patients in the Ward under hospital orders pursuant to section 37 and 13 of them were also under restriction orders pursuant to section 41 of the Mental Health Act 1983. The other six had been transferred from prison under transfer directions pursuant to section 47 with restriction directions pursuant to section 49. In all 19 of the patients were restricted patients.

The Fire in Mr O'Neill's Bedroom

2.14.8 The Report of the investigation into the fire in patient J. O'Neill's bedroom on Owen Ward, demonstrates the tensions affecting Owen Ward in the early Summer months of 1994. The Investigation Team comprised Mrs Julie Owen, a Senior Clinical Nurse on the PDU, and Mr Paterson, who was also a member of the Owen Ward inquiry team. They found that on the 18 May 1994 Mr O'Neill went on a home visit to see his mother in London with two nurse escorts Messrs Kelly and Jones. He absconded but turned up at the Hospital that night in a very disturbed state, threatening to smash and set fire to his room. He threatened a nurse with a piece of timber. The absconsion was the subject of a separate inquiry.

On the 19 May Mr O'Neill made allegations about ward staff and patients concerning his possessions and the availability of drugs and alcohol on Owen Ward. It seems that these allegations promoted the searching of Owen Ward which was going on when the hostage-taking incident occurred in June.

2.14.9 Mr Kelly was suspended following the trip to London. Mr O'Neill told the investigating team, "Some of the lads put it down to me he got suspended." Another witness said, in his interview, "On the day they were taunting him, there were problems with the Paul Kelly suspension."

A number of patients and staff were interviewed and described increasing unrest within the ward community. Although accounts differed, it appears that there was a violent altercation between Mr O'Neill and several other patients. Mr O'Neill was clearly worried and was found in the evening armed with a snooker cue; staff managed to persuade him to relinquish this. Sometime during the afternoon of 19 May "grass" and "scab" were written on Mr O'Neill's bedroom door. The Inquiry Team were told , by Mr Swinnerton and Mr Gardner, that it was after those words were written on the door staff nurse Kelly was suspended.

The next day the safety of Mr O'Neill continued to be a source of concern for the staff. Dr Strickland and Mr Brennan, the Ward Manager, saw him, and at 3.55 pm he was placed in seclusion in his own room until things calmed down or he could be moved to another ward. He was observed according to the seclusion procedure.

2.14.10 On the evening of 20 May at 7 pm Mr O'Neill's Arsenal football pennant which was hanging on the outside of his door was set alight and pushed under his door. This was not reported to the staff. Mr O'Neill first reported it when he was interviewed later at Wakefield Prison. From recognizing the footsteps he said it was done by another patient.

Sometime between tea time and 9.05 pm (the time of the fire) the keyhole of Mr O'Neill's door was stuffed with boot polish and paper. It was thought that the last time his door had been opened was at 8 pm. At 9.05 pm Mr O'Neill pressed his nurse call button and claimed his room was on fire. The lock key hole was found to be blocked. His side window was opened and the fire was put out. He was distressed and taken to Shelley Ward on Dr Strickland's instructions.

Patient J.I. said later that when he left his room, several patients were outside Mr O'Neill's room trying to open his toilet window. It was opened and one patient lit "bog paper" or a towel and threw it in. The patients concerned, of course, denied involvement. Later six toilet rolls were found in various stages of combustion, and a further five toilet rolls were found in a bin in the toilet area.

2.14.11 The inquiry concluded that Mr O'Neill had not started the fire, and that a group of patients had sought revenge following the suspension of staff nurse Kelly. In the team's view control was being exercised on Owen Ward by some patients concerned with supplying alcohol and drugs. A gang-type structure existed and it had been decided to exact revenge on someone who had "grassed".

Nine pm had probably been chosen because that was the shift hand-over time resulting in minimal staff presence in the corridor. It should be noted that the fire in Mr O'Neill's bedroom was set at the same sort of time as the Mallalieu and Williams deaths, when staff were occupied elsewhere and observation was relatively poor. As Mr Green observed to us, if patients are going to do anything, this is the time they will do it.

2.14.12 The Investigation Team noted that:

> ". . . it is important to recognise that a gang structure existed on the ward, and to put the act down to a single individual's action would underestimate the dangerous situation which was present on the ward. This, as subsequent events saw, led to a total disintegration of control on Owen Ward."

They also said:

> "General lack of observation by the staff was partly explained by the level of fear and intimidation staff described in the wider Owen Report."

Further Warnings

2.14.13 That serious problems existed at the time is confirmed by two documents. One is a letter dated 20 April 1994 from Dr Zona Crispin, one of the RMOs of Owen Ward, to her RMO colleague Dr Strickland, but written to him in his capacity as Clinical Manager of the PDU.

The other is a memorandum written by Mr Brennan, the Ward Manager, to Dr Strickland dated 1 June 1994. Dr Crispin's letter reads as follows:

"Dear Ian,

Re: Substance Abuse on Owen Ward

I am writing to express my continued concerns regarding the abuse of alcohol and drugs by patients on Owen Ward. In the last two weeks, two of my patients have been found in a drunken state and one of these required transfer to a general hospital. Despite a recommendation being made at last week's PCTM (12 April 1994) that all patients who are suspected of abusing alcohol and drugs should be requested to provide a sample of urine or blood for analysis, this was not done and the nursing staff at PCTM on 19 April 1994 did not appear to be aware of this recommendation. Communication between members of nursing staff on Owen Ward needs to be improved generally, and particularly in this area, as I feel that it is essential to carry out drug and alcohol screening on patients suspected of abuse. I think we also need to consider random testing of all the ward community given the widespread nature of the problem.

I was surprised to hear at the PCTM on 19 April 1994 that nursing staff appeared to consider that the problem was restricted to one or two individuals, when I know of several incidents myself and have been informed by other patients that drinking and drug abuse goes on frequently amongst several members of the ward community. I find it difficult to believe that nursing staff are unable to recognise either the smell of alcohol brewing and drugs being smoked, or the symptoms and signs of intoxication in patients. Further, I would have thought that the alcohol being brewed on the ward would be detectable but nursing staff informed me that room searches do not occur on Owen Ward! In my opinion, frequent random room searches are required at the present time in order to reduce the incidence of such abuse. I also believe that a breathalyser should be obtained, as previously recommended.

I am still gravely concerned at the suggestion by several patients that staff are involved in this, either by "turning a blind eye" to it, or actively bringing in substances for the patients. I have discussed this issue with the Ward Manager already but feel that, at present, little is being done to investigate the matter which could have serious consequences, particularly in patients who are taking prescribed medication and large quantities of alcohol. I should be grateful for your thoughts on the matter."

Mr Brennan's memorandum is reproduced in section 10 of the Report. It reads as follows:

"Ian, after long discussion with Derek Sharples and Steve Pearshouse, it is apparent we have a serious problem involving drugs, alcohol and possibly the buying and selling of stolen property. As well as two main groups of patients who seem to be vying for the chance to dominate a market for selling, I also believe that there are nursing staff from Owen Ward embroiled in this.

The proposal I am making at this moment, is to co-ordinate some room searches, with back up staff, even C&R staff, available on standby, while the rooms are searched.

My view is that we need to move the main group of patients from Owen Ward around the Hospital, certainly to other wards. I also believe that some staff need to be moved from the ward.

I have advised staff to increase the number of corridor patrols, to every ten minutes, with the proviso, that should the tension remain and the likelihood of any problem occur, then we revert back to manning the night station.

> The view of the staff and the patients is that we could have the makings of another Derek Williams incident unless we act. I would welcome your views on this matter."

The Williams' incident was the subject of the Rowe Report.

We find it extraordinary that this letter and memorandum met with no effective response.

The Hostage-Taking

2.14.14 The actual events have to be distilled from a number of the Report's appendices. On the night of 6 June 1994, at about 9.05 pm Mr Thorpe, the Care and Restraint Coordinator/ Manager, was informed that a number of patients on Owen Ward were causing trouble. He arrived at 9.20 pm and spoke to Mr Newton and Mr Gardner. There was concern that some patients were refusing to go to bed; it had been reported that weapons had been made and it seemed that some patients were suffering from the effects of alcohol or drugs. Most of the patients went to their rooms, but two, who were particularly difficult, did not, and they were removed from the Ward. Some patients who had gone to their rooms then became troublesome. Some were threatening and some were suspected of having weapons. By midnight the rooms of two patients had been entered and they had been taken to other wards. That is how matters stood until the next morning, Tuesday, 7 June. At about 7.30 am searching began of the rooms from which patients had been removed the night before. The other patients were not moved from the Ward and at that stage remained in their rooms. There was a great deal of tension and patients began to smash windows and destroy property. Some tried to kick their room doors down; threats and abuse were directed towards the Response Team. One patient shouted, "We will kill you bastards, there are 18 of us"; another smashed the observation window of his door with a large metal bar. It was decided that some other patients had to be removed and two were removed with some difficulty. Searching resumed and the Ward seemed settled. Although it caused concern, some patients were allowed out of their rooms. Items found included lighters, broken bottle glass, a metal weapon with a protrusion attached to pass between the fingers (a knuckle duster); keys which fitted the internal ducts; bottles thought to contain alcohol; and a listening device. Items which had been reported as missing, knives, forks and a snooker ball were also found. On the following morning, Wednesday 8 June, searching recommenced. Early on Byron Tomlinson, the eventual hostage-taker, was disruptive but calmed down and went to the day area while his room was being searched.

The issue that precipitated the hostage-taking was the cancellation of Mr Tomlinson's "visit" that afternoon. There had been concerns over Mr Tomlinson's intended visitor and the previous evening it had, apparently, been decided to ban her. This information was not passed on to Mr Tomlinson, despite the fact it was known he became very volatile when receiving news he could not cope with. Mr Green and his colleagues were of the view that on the balance of probabilities Dr Strickland knew of the ban, yet he told patients at lunchtime on the day of the hostage-taking, that visiting would take place in the Central Assembly Hall. As a result Mr Tomlinson took a shower and changed his clothes in preparation for his visit.

He was told later that his visit had been cancelled. He burst into the Ward office and shouted at a nurse, Mr Len Jones, "Why has my visit been cancelled? the RMO [Dr Strickland] has agreed that it could take place." He was calmed to some extent and he was allowed to telephone the girl who had been intending to visit. He could not speak to her because she had already left home. Apparently Mr Jones could not understand why Mr Tomlinson had been told the visit could take place because he thought her visits had been stopped two weeks previously on security grounds. Mr Thorpe left the office to go to a corridor where searching was taking place. Suddenly an alarm bell rang and he went back to the office to see Mr Tomlinson waving a long carving knife around and shouting that he wanted to kill a member of staff. Protecting his way by slashing around with the knife Mr Tomlinson went to the library where Ms El-Jazairi, a psychologist, was holding a prearranged meeting with her patient Roger Packham.

2.14.15 Ms El-Jazairi had heard that there had been trouble on Owen Ward, and at 1.30 pm she rang the duty nurse to ask if it was advisable to keep her 2 pm appointment with Roger Packham. The duty nurse had consulted the ward manager and he told her it was perfectly safe to see her patient in the library. Both she and the patient were taken hostage at knife point and they suffered a terrible and terrifying ordeal. The police arrived and after some considerable time Mr Tomlinson was "talked down" and surrendered his knife. Ms El-Jazairi's statement gives a vivid account of the horrifying event. Sadly she has been unable to return to work.

2.14.16 During the course of the search many other items were found including a hacksaw and blades, keys of the ward stationery cupboard, a large quantity of ward stationery, numerous lighters, alcohol, and broken snooker-cue ends. Garden equipment consisting of two spades, two forks, a pick-axe, a hedge cutter, two hoes, two garden rakes and a lawn rake were found in the ward. Telephone cards including two which had been tampered with, three metal rods with knobs at one end, pieces of electrical wire, nails and screws, a computer modem connector and various metal bars and tubes were found. 257 video tapes were removed from the ward, and by 11 July, of those that had been examined, ten were found to contain hardcore pornographic material. One depicted bestiality and another torture and rape.

The Inquiry team concluded that the hostage-taking was avoidable. Numerous pieces of evidence point to the fact that all was not well on Owen Ward. **We agree.**

Executive Summary of the Report

2.14.17 The Executive Summary at the beginning of the Report is worth citing at length:

> "1. The patient care team which was the same senior professional team operating at the time of the death of Derek Williams on 19 November 1990, had not addressed the findings of the Rowe Report in any systematic or considered way. The aftermath of the murder of a patient in their care had not spurred them to actively address the resulting Rowe Report recommendations."
>
> "2. We found the work of the Patient Care Team was inconsistent, vague, fragmented, un-coordinated, poorly recorded and marginalised the nursing staff from the other professionals within the team. There was no clear criteria for admission to the ward and the patient group previously within the Forster Ward community had changed significantly with a different intake of patients. Dr Crispin was beginning to develop a lone voice in trying to improve consistency in communication and underpin the relentless and difficult task of ensuring ward security and patient care were met. Her memo to the Clinical Manager dated 20 April 1990 is significant and spurred the Ward Manager to some action . . . "
>
> "3. Effective searching of patients' bedrooms had not taken place for a period of 15 plus months. They were recommended, albeit cursory in nature, following Dr Crispin's memo. One nursing team was not happy with the previous unrecorded arrangement not to search rooms, which is believed to have been sanctioned by a Patient Care Team Meeting, and attempted some room searches. These were recorded at the back of the search register, as if it was a secretive activity for which they would be criticised if caught doing it."
>
> "4. The ward policy is poorly constructed, not contained in one cohesive document, undated, and those policies which were in place were not enforced, or were

unenforceable because of the lack of staff. They also failed because of ineffective support and monitoring by the Patient Care team. To date there has been no discussion of the work of the group considering Recommendation 45 of the Ashworth Inquiry (multi-disciplinary working). There were clear tensions between the Ward manager and the Clinical manager which were demonstrably witnessed by the Investigating Team when we visited the ward on 24 June 1994. Tension, rivalry, undermining and lack of communication between the three nursing shifts was also apparent."

"5. The nursing complement was considered in detail and a picture of dilution of staff qualification, rapid turnover of staff (with some qualified staff leaving because of their fear of working on the ward) and the recruitment of inexperienced staff who were inadequately prepared, as were all staff, for the task before them. The nursing staff were demoralised because their role was not clearly defined, particularly in relation to sanctions and keeping good ward order. If they made any attempt to enforce ward rules they were gratuitously complained about by patients to the PCT."

"We were constantly told not to look for nursing care plans or coherent multi-disciplinary treatment plans. Simple record keeping with allocation of tasks, outcomes, and who is responsible did not exist. Clinical supervision was not apparent. There are significant implications for the opening of Owen Ward on a 24-hour basis, and throughout the Personality Disorder Unit as a whole, which require serious re-consideration."

"6. The commencement of rigorous room searching on the evening of Monday, 6 June 1994 to locate missing knives, a fork, and a snooker ball, and to allay patient fears that some other patients were arming themselves with weapons created probably one of the most serious incidents in Ashworth Hospital's history. Mr Thorpe the C&R Coordinator of the response teams gave a frightening account of the events from the Monday evening up to the post-hostage-taking period into the afternoon of Wednesday 8 June 1994. The level of anger, aggression, and threat made collectively and individually by patients was unprecedented on such a scale. If patients had not initially been locked behind their doors in their rooms, with the exception of two patients who refused to go to bed, the situation could have been riotous. Mr Thorpe and his teams require praise for their sensitive, fair, safe and firm handling of the situation."

"7. We strongly feel that the ward should have been 'closed' to all external personnel not associated with the on-going searching process. Patients should have been kept in their rooms, being allowed up for showers and the occasional break etc., until all the ward and rooms had been searched. This would have taken most of the week from the Monday evening because of the amount of personal possessions patients had. When the patients were allowed up, while searching continued, some of them were less than helpful and the atmosphere quickly became tense. If the ward had been closed and activities such as visiting cancelled then the hostage-taking incident would not have occurred. The closing of the ward is what should have happened."

"8. The setting fire to the bedroom of a patient John O'Neill on the evening of 20 May 1994 when he was in it was a clear attempt to murder him by a patient or patients. His door locks had been blocked up with shoe polish and wet paper. The 'pill box' window from the corridor to his room was opened (by a Chubb-type key or a Phillip's screw driver) and a burning towel and lighted toilet rolls thrown in. The words 'grass' and 'scab' on his door reminded him that he had made allegations against a member of staff which would not help those patients, who had a 'special' relationship with that staff member, to exploit it further. (Messrs Swinnerton and

Gardner are investigating this member of staff's activities.) Previously John O'Neill had been assaulted by a group of patients with a snooker cue."

"9. Catalogue fraud, 'liberalisation' of mail, and ward-based telephones have all contributed to the loss of control of patients' activities. Catalogue fraud has helped underpin patients' corrupting activity and has resulted in some patients amassing money, status, practising extortion and blackmail. Staff involvement in this activity is being investigated. It is highly likely that money is sent in or out of the Hospital through the mail system with ease. Not once has the Patient Care Team exercised its right to withhold a patient's mail, open it, or return it if incorrectly addressed. The telephone for patients was unmonitored and abused by them."

"10. The vetting, monitoring and supervising of visits to Owen Ward has broken down . . . the Personagram [a system for recognizing authorized visitors] is in a state of disrepair and breaks down easily, and visitors' bags are not searched. No different arrangements for problem visitors are made. The banning of visitors is poorly handled. Mr Swinnerton confirmed that it is alleged that on Owen Ward two patients separately had intercourse with a prostitute in the patient's bedroom area."

"11. Alcohol and drugs were freely available over a period of time and concern was expressed and recorded in the PCTM book, again over a period of time. Little or no action was taken to attack the root cause. Simply to address the alcohol problem the PCT decided to buy a breathalyser . . ."

"12. Incident recording and reporting was poor and in many cases non-existent and therefore gave a misleading view that all was well on the ward. The marginalisation of the staff from the security department was apparent and the Hospital wide security policies enshrined in the 'Red Book' were ignored. Some members of the Patient Care Team did not know of the security manual's existence. Random and routine searching of the ward did not take place."

"13 There is a significant conflict between the roles of one person being a Responsible Medical Officer and a Clinical Manager which requires further consideration."

The Patients' Views

2.14.18 Appendix 34 is based on the interviews with patients who had been on the Ward prior to the disturbances. The comments of the patients were generally acute and supported the picture outlined above. They took the view that the causes of the build up of the problem were inappropriate patient-mix, lack of direction by the PCT and ward management, and staff morale and complicity. In summary:

Inappropriate mix of patients
This was the catalyst of the incidents prior to the hostage-taking. Most said tensions were considerably heightened by the arrival of two patients. One, referred to as 24, was paranoid and used ethnic origins to get his own way. He was probably involved in drug dealing in direct opposition to another group which included the other referred to as 15. The arrival of 15 on the Ward coincided with an increase in the level of alcohol consumption on the Ward. Many were of the view that putting all personality disordered patients together might be a mistake, and were critical of the process of allocating patients to wards.

Lack of direction by PCT and Ward Management
There was universal condemnation of the PCT and Ward Management. Both were said to be totally ineffective. Most said they would have felt safer in an environment in which rules were laid down and then enforced by staff and respected by patients.

Owen Ward was little more than a free for all where everything goes. Neither managers nor the PCT were strong enough to set down ward protocols or, where there were any, to enforce them. The result was that staff on the Ward felt disempowered, and some patients felt they could do as they liked without sanction. The PCT knew what was going on, but so long as there were no repercussions, were prepared to turn a blind eye.

Within the PCT the RMOs were singled out for particular criticism. Dr Crispin was felt to be overly influenced by Patient 24 and Dr Strickland was hampered by the tension between his duties as RMO and Clinical Manager. The most damning criticism was of the Ward Manager, described as distant, unable to cope, and never there.

Staff Morale and Complicity

Morale deteriorated as the staff became more compliant with patient demands. Patients traced this to the Ashworth [Blom-Cooper] Report after which the emphasis changed from custody to therapy leaving staff fearful that any stand against a patient would leave them vulnerable to complaints from patients or the disciplinary process and hence loss of employment. The result was that staff either turned a blind eye or participated with patients and, in effect, "crossed the line".

Staff must have been aware of alcohol consumption. One patient had been taken to hospital following taking drink; on occasions others had taken so much they could hardly walk. Home brew kits were widely used on the Ward although they were difficult to disguise. Many patients regularly smoked cannabis and had abandoned attempts to hide the smell by using air fresheners. Yet no action was taken. A small number of staff were said to be providing drugs and alcohol, and a few were alleged to be involved in trading goods with patients.

The Working of the Owen Ward Patient Care Team

2.14.19 In dealing with its first term of reference concerning the management, treatment and care circumstances leading up to the hostage-taking, the Report makes a number of pertinent observations on the working of the PCT and ward-based staff. We select a number of pertinent extracts below.

The team note that:

a. "There is a balance to be kept between treatment and security and the aim must be to ensure that a patient gets the treatment he needs and is subject to that degree of supervision and restraint which his condition, character and abilities need. Dr Strickland when seen by the Investigation Team stated the PCT had 'concentrated on the therapeutic bit' and had failed to observe the behaviour of patients and how it affected the ward as a whole and agreed with us that the PCT were acting as individuals and this is when the problems start".

The Rowe Report is referred to in paragraph 4 of the Report where it is said:

"The sections describing and commenting on management, nursing and access to bedrooms appear prophetic. The conclusions and recommendations and text of the Report attached at appendix 9, pages 88 to 90 were not discussed. This was confirmed by the two RMOs, Ward Manager, Team Leaders, Social Workers, Psychologist and Nurses. The nurses made a written attempt to respond to the Report." This is attached at appendix 10 pages 91 to 102.

"Ms Swindells told us the Report was not discussed because the PCT did not have time to discuss the relevant points. It seems the death of one of their patients didn't warrant further discussion or review of practice."

In dealing with the ward "Conversation Books" (in which nurses of the three shifts made notes for information purposes) the following observations are made:

> "Of note there were no 'conversations' recorded in this book about the death of Derek Williams, the murderous attempt on the life of John O'Neill, or the hostage-taking incident."
>
> "On 5 November 1992 S Braund received an electric fan heater, contrary to the standing instruction regarding electrical appliances. He should not have been allowed it. Messrs Tanner and Fox acquired imitation firearms, and ward tools were in such proportion as to probably be difficult to control. Non-parole patients had access to each other on the ward. Despite the new search register for 'days out and rooms' arriving on the ward on 31 March 1994, room searches were only started on 21 April 1994 after Dr Crispin's memo raising her alarm at the problems on the ward. One staff member may or may not have bought S Tanner's Atari computer and the patients purchased a fridge from one of the Patients' Education Lecturers."
>
> "On 21 May 1994 the Night Station was to be manned by staff once again. This clearly implies that it had not been the case as per the access to bedrooms policy and Mr Scully's clear message of 21 July 1992 that this should continue." [nearly two years previously].
>
> "There is no trend analysis of the activity contained within these books, despite important information being contained within them. The Ward Manager, Clinical Nursing Manager and Clinical Nursing Manager thought it inappropriate to view these records."

The team comment:

> "We heard from nursing staff, individually and collectively, that the leader of the PCT did not listen to them and paid little regard to the experience of the staff and their desire to be consulted about the treatment of patients . . ."
>
> "The investigation team concluded that symbolically the 'towel had been thrown into the ring' by this demoralised staff group. They had been failed by their managers following the Ashworth Inquiry . . ."
>
> "The PCT should have been aware of these difficulties, but individually many of them were struggling with the same problem. They felt disempowered."
>
> "There is evidence from Mr Swinnerton that some staff have actively undermined the upholding of security and have crossed the boundary between the professional staff/patient relationship."

Paragraph 6 of the Report deals with "policy". The team note:

> "The establishment of operational policy and the rigorous pursuit of its observation would have derived strength for the PCT and nursing staff who were the front line defenders of its structure. Security policies affecting the Ward would benefit by distinction being made between general precepts of security, which are to be applied in a flexible way, and Standing instructions /Rules to be strictly followed."

Having reviewed a number of policy statements the team concluded:

> "They are weak, first attempts at policy. They were not acted upon in the main. It is of interest to note that Firs Ward has a clear policy, 16 patients and staff make the policy work. They are part of the Personality Disorder Unit but located on the East site. They do not wish to move to the North with their patients."

In paragraph 7 the Report considers Nursing Staff:

> "Of the four Units the Personality Disorder Unit had the lowest level of qualified staff (55.16%) and the highest level of non-qualified staff (44.84%). By contrast, 'Mental Illness (Northern)' had a staff complement of 72.62% qualified and 27.38% non-qualified."
>
> "Coupled with the haemorrhaging of staff over the past year from the ward we can only pose the question, how any continuity to patient care and treatment can be given. How can nursing staff be motivated by these circumstances, and can 24-hour opening be a safe and achievable reality?"
>
> "The Clinical Nursing manager had said a woman staff nurse had left after many years at the Hospital because she now feared for her own safety. At weekends staffing levels had fallen on occasions to a staff nurse and four nursing assistants. The problem of insecurity expressed by staff must be tackled urgently if there is to be any real prospect of delivering patient care and ensuring safety for all."
>
> "We were told by the ward manager, team leaders, and nurses not to look for any thorough and active nursing care plans. Mr Allan did not find any when he looked and only located treatment plans for patients allocated to Dr Crispin."

"Care Circumstances" are dealt with in paragraph 8.

> **"Owen Ward bedrooms had been established as veritable 'Aladdin's Caves' of possessions. The patients were less disruptive than most patients caught up in the Hospital's restructuring as the whole ward moved leaving behind on Forster Ward some rooms which were virtually uninhabitable by the patients moving from Owen Ward to take up residence. Furniture had been taken out previously, new beds and furniture had been constructed. Within days of moving on to Owen Ward some patients had broken up and taken out fixed furniture, banged nails into walls and door frames. Their rooms with the totality of possessions were impossible to search.**
>
> "Patient day time activity off the ward was limited by the patient's own choice and one patient, Roger Packham, was allowed to obtain a personal tool box and made furniture in the ward's boot room when less then 200 yards away there is a 'state of art' workshop. Some patients would stay awake all night, sleep through the day and contributed nothing to the ward's activity. When they asked for a day out they would get it. There is little intelligent application of persuasive skills or sanctions to modify aberrant behaviour."
>
> "The ward rules . . . agreed by staff and patients were inoperable in the period during and post the Ashworth Inquiry. The introduction of ward-based visiting had been seriously abused. Drugs, alcohol and, it is alleged, a prostitute has been introduced to the ward by visitors."

Members of the Patient Care Team

2.14.20 In paragraph 11, the Report goes on to draw conclusions following interviews with the multi-disciplinary staff and staff associations. We quote from the team's comments:

Wally Brennan – Ward Manager

He was described as a "man of good intentions, [who] clearly did not grasp the management of this ward."

Dr Strickland

The team noted that Dr Strickland had been involved with Forster/Owen Ward since 1987. He said what was discussed at PTCMs was not necessarily followed up. He claimed that he had been told both that alcohol abuse was not a problem and that patient use of telephones was observed. The team commented:

> "The responses to our questions were lacking in substance, in depth knowledge, and showed little understanding of the staff of whom he was the leader".

Mr Michael Potts – Team leader

Mr Potts had recently been recruited from High Royds Hospital. He felt "criticism of a liberal regime may not be appreciated" and that, "patients were allowed every liberty with no clear limits", which resulted in no safety net being there when the situation did not work.

He commented that monitoring of patients' use of telephones was unworkable and that the issue of wards dealing with patients' mail had increased confrontation on the ward. He was frank in his criticism of a PCT which still did not know what it was doing, and of the creation of a special personality disorder unit, which in his view was a disaster: "what happened on Owen Ward will happen on others". He noted that the nursing team found it "difficult to keep the compassion of nursing to the fore with this patient group".

Mr Michael Berry

Mr Berry was the only member of the staff who managed to upset some of the investigating team:

> "His language is ill chosen and inappropriate for a senior member of the Patient Care team."

Mr Derek Sharples – Acting Team Leader

The team noted that:

> "He told us how patients unsuitable for the ward were referred with the threat that if that particular patient was not taken then another would have to be. Patients were allowed by the Patient Care Team to deal on credit and he saw no checking of a patient's financial situation, even when one wished to purchase a £1,700 electric piano without the appropriate resources."

Mr Mark Stowell-Smith – Senior Social Worker

The team comment:

> "He confirmed that he knew 18 months ago that rooms were not being searched, and stated that the Security Department was derided by some members of the team, who did not see it as a positive entity, and that indeed there was an expressed view there was no place for the Security Department in their work."

The team note that Dr Stowell-Smith had been working on Forster/Owen Ward for seven years and "viewed the ward as never being a true therapeutic community and that this ambiguity had developed as an empty concept for staff."

The team made a number of comments on the Patient Care Team interviews.

> "There was very little evidence that this group of professional individuals work as a team. There is obvious friction between the Senior RMO, who is also the Unit's clinical manager, and the Psychologist, who were both required to review their style following the Rowe Report. The Social workers see themselves as therapists first and social workers second. All four have little regard for helping to monitor and set the security implications for the care of patients on Owen Ward on a consistent basis. On the one hand they wish to have a say about rules and activity which impinged on security but on the other did little to ensure that security was maintained. Their

decision-making appears questionable, inconsistent, autocratic, erratic and complacent. Dr Crispin is an exception to this picture . . ."

"The Ward Manager struggled to bring consistency to the management of the three nursing shifts, did not seem capable of undertaking the task, was not a leader of the nursing profession and did not insist on ward security following agreed procedures. He appeared subjugated by the RMO."

We would note that several of the PCT on Owen Ward in 1994 were also members of the Lawrence Ward PCT.

Security

2.14.21 At paragraph 12 the Report turns to "Security". The inquiry did not believe the PCT could identify "unacceptable risk" or had the will to take remedial action. The Ashworth Security Manual (the Red Book) was issued in May 1992. **But the Owen Ward psychologist, social workers and consultants were not aware of its existence. Ms El-Jazairi had never seen it.**

The Report deals with searching and makes a number of trenchant comments:

"Room searches were in essence non-existent and all rub-down searches were for leave of absence purposes. None took place following a visit. Searching of patients' rooms was a mere glance. The amount of possessions within patients' rooms in some cases is enormous: computers, videos, TVs, fish tanks, animals, birds, carpets, smoke glass coffee tables, wall hangings, posters; the list is endless.

"Lighters were common place and the videos removed from the ward are being systematically searched through. To date, having viewed only a small number, some ten tapes have been identified as containing hardcore pornography, one with bestiality and one of torture and rape. Of considerable concern must be two brass keys found in S Tanner's fish tank gravel. These keys fit the internal ducting entrances, where a bottle containing home made alcohol and a bottle of gin were found. There can only be two explanations for him obtaining these keys. Either a member of staff gave them to him having had them cut, or a member of staff gave them to a visitor to have them cut. They are part of the ward security keys. The implications are considerable."

Paragraph 21 of the Report deals with "Mail and Catalogue Fraud". The team note that handling of mail had recently been devolved to ward level and as a task it had not been well received by the nursing staff. It is said:

"The PCT have exercised no control over any mail following this devolution, the nurses are confused by their responsibilities and altercations between staff and patients have ensued. The system does not appear to be working."

Catalogue fraud had been dealt with by HMG in March 1990 and all PCTs had been written to on 8 March 1990, by Mr Johnson (the then General Manager) whose letter set out the Hospital policy on credit transactions and procedures for handling parcels received from mail order companies.

The effect of policy was:

(i) patients would not be allowed to trade on credit;

(ii) Mail Order parcels would be sent by the mail room to wards in the usual way;

(iii) the Charge nurse would only allow patients to have parcels if they could show payment had already been made, or signed immediately a payment authorisation for the full amount;

(iv) any correspondence or parcel wrongly addressed to patient to be returned to sender;

(v) payments on existing agreements should continue.

The team note that:

> "Catalogue fraud has been a corrupting force on Owen Ward and must be stopped."

Paragraph 22 of the Report deals with "Telephone calls on the patients' pay phone". The Ward Manager indicated that the telephone procedure devised by the PCT had not been adhered to and that patients were trusted not to abuse the telephone facility. There was no book to record approved numbers; staff did not monitor patients' calls; and there was evidence of tampering with telephone cards to make "free" calls. The team note:

> "There is evidence of calls being made to sex contact lines and voice box numbers, where people requiring 'contacts' leave personally recorded messages. There was evidence of a high number of calls to one particular number. This may have been due to one of the patients actually having a 'Box Number' for people to leave messages."

Paragraph 24 concerns "Processing Visitors". The team comment that the Security Department had had enormous problems verifying visitor status. Searching of bags was not undertaken; there were no separate arrangements to enable problem visits to take place. Patients' visitors arriving on Owen Ward were inadequately supervised, if supervised at all.

The interface between Patient Care Teams and the Security Department is considered in section 27. The team note:

> "There has been considerable documentation produced on security needs within the Hospital over the past two years which has been significantly marginalised, in what is being described by some as the 'dash for therapy'."
>
> "Simply there is a need for a special security manager with the authority vested from the General Manager to be responsible for the monitoring and setting of procedures specific to the needs of the patients in the personality disorder unit. They will require the right to inspect records, have unrestricted access to wards and PCTs and would be responsible for the development of the Security Information System pertinent to the clinical unit. Ideally each Clinical Unit should have its own Security Manager. We would strongly recommend the restructuring proposals for the security department are concluded urgently, and consideration is given within that structure to the appointment of a security training officer."
>
> "We have considered the issue of the overall responsibility at ward level for security. We have tried to 'pin the tail to the donkey', this time without the blindfold, and would strongly suggest that this overall responsibility is vested in the Ward Manager. The responsible Medical Officer and the core PCT membership should be responsible for helping to determine individual patients security needs. How they are dovetailed into the wider ward community will be for the Ward Manager to determine. We feel this will help clarify the confusion that currently exists."

Recommendations

2.14.22 Finally the Report makes Recommendations. We set them out in full; they represent nothing less than a challenge to rethink fundamentally the operation of Owen Ward, the PDU and indeed the Hospital.

a) UNIT/WARD PHILOSOPHY AND PRACTICE

1. An overall policy needs to be formulated with the role of each ward in the Unit

clearly defined and circulated to other Clinical Units and Departments.

2. The role of Owen Ward within the PD Unit as well as its relationship to the other Units within the Hospital needs to be clarified. Its decision making processes need describing.

3. The "therapeutic community" approach, though feasible in a security setting, must be re-examined. (There seems to be a misapprehension that such a community approach revolves around permissiveness only, without considering the other relevant principles, the most important of which is reality confrontation).

4. Clear criteria for admission/departure from Owen Ward needs to be formulated with goals and expectations of treatment made explicit. 'Contracts' are required of patients. (Should admission be devolved to the PD Unit, in time, then an independent clinician should chair the panel considering admission).

5. No patient should be admitted directly, or within 12 months, from an admission ward.

6. House rules in Owen Ward will need to be re-defined with the PCT, as soon as possible, and discussed with patients and made available for all to see. These should be attached to the contract made with the patients. There needs to be practical utility with agreed sanctions for non-compliance.

7. The rules will need to be reviewed formally with patients and staff at least annually. The ward policy needs to be comprehensive and contained within one document.

8. A range of policy needs to be determined within the PD Unit (We recommend the commendable start made on Firs Ward which helps set the base line.)

9. Research and outcome studies of the patients who move through Owen Ward and the PD Unit is essential.

10. Clinical Audit Quality Assurance should monitor that policy/procedures are adhered to and standards maintained. This work must be completed with the Clinical Nursing Manager. Published comparisons on wards within the PD Unit may be a helpful way in raising standards.

11. Patients' treatment programmes must encourage patients to attend appropriate off ward activities. This would promote an organised and purposeful experience for patients. Rewards for such activity can be determined. Patients who are not involved in meaningful day time activity should not be considered for external rehabilitation.

12. The admission of black patients with personality disorder must be addressed by this Unit.

b) MULTI-DISCIPLINARY WORKING – THE PATIENT CARE TEAM

1. Patient Care Teams must take precedence over all activity of disciplines. (The two Social Workers on Owen Ward must attend.) The Ward Manager's attendance is crucial. The business section of the PCT agenda must be chaired by the Ward Manager. The clinical and business part of the meeting must be comprehensively minuted. Minutes and future agendas must include matters arising to deal with follow-up issues. Tasks must be allocated and responsibilities determined.

2. The Ward Manager must act as the co-ordinator between the three nursing teams and ensure continuity of care and security for the ward.

3. Psychology and Social Worker staff must not act as the arbiters of core security issues affecting ward security. They must remain aware of the security policy affecting their work with patients. They should support the RMO in determining the individual patient's security needs.

4. Recommendation 45 must be discussed by Owen Ward immediately and the outcome reported to the General Manager.

5. Treatment determination is the domain of the RMO and the PCT; security need for the individual patient must be determined by the PCT; implementation of the overall security needs of the ward is the Ward Manager's responsibility.

6. The Ward Manager must ensure "community meetings" are held with a pre-determined agenda. These must occur at least monthly and be recorded with action again allocated to individuals. The PCT must attend.

7. External rehabilitation should be closely linked to patient's treatment programmes and dependent on co-operation with the patient's treatment plan and day to day behaviour. Patients must have an active treatment plan.

8. Monthly information requirements for the PTC and Clinical Manager (including information relevant to the Service Level Agreement with the SHSA) must be determined. Examples are, patient day time activity, external rehabilitation, incidents, complaints, searches, inter-ward transfers etc. A six monthly Report should be provided to the Clinical Manager by each ward, and an annual Unit Report to the General Manager.

9. The Ward Manager must read the conversation book which should be renamed a Communication Book.

10. Security notices must be kept in the central security manual – not stapled to the "Communication Book".

c) NURSING

1. Staff selected to work on the PD Unit's wards should be selected on the basis of their ability to relate to patients with challenging personalities and be sufficiently experienced to be able to cope with and manage the manipulative behaviour they will encounter. We recommend this type of ward is not suitable for newly appointed unqualified staff.

2. The implementation of 24 Hour Care in the PD Unit should stop and be reviewed against adequate staffing being consistently available and delivered by experienced staff in suitable numbers. (There are significant difficulties caring for this patient group for 14 hours a day and we have been told that many patients would prefer the resources to be invested in the waking day, treatment and care. Their views should be sought.)

3. A nursing recruitment strategy and manpower evaluation is required to determine the safe balance between qualified and unqualified staff. The role of nurses within the PD Unit needs to be described.

4. Exit interviews by the Clinical Nursing Manager should take place and trends identified.

5. The policy banning staff from trading with patients should be strictly enforced through the disciplinary procedures, and should be highlighted in the induction process. Staff should be constantly reminded of this.

6. The role and responsibilities of the Clinical Nursing Manager in relation to the Ward Manager and Team Leaders needs clarifying.

7. The Director of Professional Development and Ward Manager must give a high degree of priority to planning staff development (care planning, which is part of PREP training provided, has not been attended by Owen Ward nurses).

8. The provision of clinical supervision, and a model for its implementation needs to be achieved and a contract established between the Clinical Tutors and Practitioners

and the PD Unit. The Clinical Nursing Manager must monitor this contract.

9. There is need for professionally delivered confidential staff support outside that of the Line Management structure, and should be provided. (This service is urgently required for all staff and women in particular).

10. Clear guidance should be issued to staff emphasising the need to be vigilant in the area of personal relationships with patients.

11. No unqualified nurse should be allocated on a temporary contract to the PD Unit and bank staff should be specifically chosen and trained to work on this Unit.

12. The induction of new staff must be thorough and adequate.

d) CARE CIRCUMSTANCES

1. The fixed furniture of patients must remain in a fixed position and be maintained as designated. No patient must be allowed to re-arrange the fixed furniture or fittings in his room.

2. Observation hatches should be not be screened or blocked under any circumstances. All wards and patients should be immediately notified of this.

3. Possessions should be equitable to the patient's mental state, needs and behaviour, and at a level which provides for safety and security measures (e.g. video tapes are a fire hazard and we recommend a maximum of ten tapes per patient's room).

Instead of limiting the number of tapes, quite properly, on security grounds, the staff at Ashworth chose instead to use what they regarded as the less controversial ground of the Health and Safety legislation. As will be seen later from the evidence of Professor Sammes in Part Three it can take up to half an hour to check a computer floppy disk. Checking a video cassette involves checking all its contents. This also takes time. An equally valid reason for limiting the number of video cassette tapes as well as computer floppy disks, is to ensure that pornographic material is not being kept in bedrooms. Neither can be checked adequately unless their numbers are strictly limited.

4. Patients' significant property should be recorded and agreed with them. Any trading amongst patients should be energetically discouraged and, if any takes place, then the Hospital can take no responsibility.

5. A limit should be placed on the quantity of electrical items in bedrooms.

6. No alcohol should be allowed in the ward areas (except for the usual quota during the Christmas/New Year period) – it is imperative that staff must not consume alcohol when accompanying patients on day trips and that the patient's consumption should be restricted to only the quantity specified on the gate pass. Consumption of alcohol by patients on trips should be the exception rather than the rule.

7. Patients' behavioural problems should be dealt with on the wards they are allocated to. Moving them in an arbitrary way should be discouraged. The patient's RMO (or his 'partner' RMO) must have the final say.

8. Non-parole patients must not be allowed to undertake inter-ward visits. Exceptional circumstances must be agreed by the Clinical Manager.

9. We would repeat the Rowe Report recommendation that patients should not have access to each other's bedrooms.

10. No patient should be allowed to keep tools in their rooms – they should be stored as security items.

11. A firm policy regarding substance abuse (alcohol and drugs) needs to be produced. Notices should be displayed prominently at reception that visitors

discovered attempting to smuggle such items, or other security items may be prosecuted.

12. The issue of patients having lighters requires detailed consideration and a policy should be determined which is workable and considered jointly with the Staff Associations.

13. The Patients' Reward system should be reviewed and reconsidered and consideration given to re-introduction.

e) SECURITY

1. A Security Manager for the Personality Disorder Unit should be appointed as soon as is practical. Appointments should also be considered for other clinical units.

2. There is a need urgently to establish a full-time team to review the Procedures Manual. They should have a three month deadline in which to produce a new manual. Until this is complete current policy must be observed. Staff booklets should be prepared for various activities. The Advocacy Service should have access to a security manual.

3. As part of the induction process all staff should be aware of the security procedures manual and particular attention drawn to disturbance, fire, escape, hostage-taking and searching procedures.

4. All security documents should be aggregated and a copy readily available for easy reference.

5. All hospital security procedures should be clearly differentiated into those that are mandatory instructions for the entire hospital, and those which are guidelines and adaptable to the needs of the different wards/units.

6. Department managers must devise a system to ensure that all members of their staff have read and understood the security manual. The advice of the Security department must be sought for clarification if required.

7. Security Audit has been developed and included in the OSCAR audit. As a matter of urgency a security audit must be conducted in the PD Wards.

8. The present job descriptions of key staff do not place adequate emphasis on their security responsibilities within the Hospital. They should be re-written to take account of this gap.

9. The Security Department Review must be concluded, and consideration be given to the appointment of a security training officer.

10. The hospital must devise a Security Information System.

11. The structure of the management of the Security Department when concluded must be communicated to all staff.

f) SEARCHING

1. Random, routine room and general ward area searches must be mandatory in all wards, and Patient Care Teams must not be allowed to vary this policy.

2. The monitoring of this process should be the Ward Manager's responsibility and should be a part of the Security Audit reported to the general manager.

3. The PD Security Manager, when appointed, and the Clinical Nursing Manager should maintain an overview of this process, reporting any deficiencies to the Clinical Manager for action.

4. Searches of hospital property and patients' possessions must be viable.

5. An inventory of patients' possessions must be kept up to date and referred to when searching rooms.

6. Video tapes in patients' rooms should be restricted. (Video tapes which arrive in the Hospital from all sources which are not still in their cellophane wrappers should be rigorously checked, and if they contain material which does not have a rating under the Board of Censors it should be confiscated and sent to the Security Department for further investigation, including details of which patient had the video in their [his] possession and the source of it.)

In the course of the evidence, the Chairman pointed out that even this reasonably strong recommendation had its weakness. His experience from trying a case involving the importation of hardcore pornographic video tapes was that suppliers did not wrap them with explicit covers, but more often in pristine cellophane wrappers.

g) hostage-taking

Guidelines for staff must be produced and the Rampton Hospital guidance forms an excellent template. The team considering the review of the security manual may wish to consider the following points which arose from the hostage incident on the 8 June 1994:

1. Clear the lodge area of visitors (to the Visitors Centre) and staff who can't get in. The whole area can then be used by emergency services.

2. Keep police in uniform to a minimum in the campus. Transfer police C&R team in a van if possible.

3. The Estate's "Terrier" of ward plans were not accurate and hampered briefing of the police. They need urgent redrawing (with other departments) and need to be held in the Control Centre.

4. Clear establishment of facts at the incident site with the "First on Scene" staff clearly identified and in communication with the General Manager, or designated HMG member, in the Control Centre.

5. "First on Scene" must be able to describe a detailed picture and be interrogated by the control centre to confirm accuracy.

6. There should be a member of staff (HMG member) to record the events, times, personnel present, and decisions taken etc., for post incident review.

7. Police radio communications are ineffectual in our site. They require our radios.

8. Relatives of hostages. We require to give thought on how they are to be dealt with. (No relative should be allowed into the secure area where the incident is in progress.)

9. De-briefing at whatever level, and immediate support, to be given to main staff involved in the incident including hostages by a senior member of staff (HMG) before leaving the site.

h) FIRE

1. We believe that the fire in patient John O'Neill's room was a serious attempt at murder and should be investigated separately. (Despite an intensive search the investigation team was unable to obtain any record of the day report or incident form.)

i) RECOMMENDATION 39

1. The documentation produced by the Risk Management Group should be actioned.

j) INCIDENT REPORTING

1. Operational policy with guidelines must be issued immediately regarding the

incident reporting policy formulated in Brian Johnson's Report to the Authority. Staff must be trained in interpretation and recording of incidents.

2. Patient Care teams should have the previous week's day Reports and cross-reference them with recorded incidents. This must be brought to the care team's attention by Ward Managers.

3. The top copy of the incident Report should be sent to Nursing Informatics on completion and not await the signature of the RMO which can take time. This will help support the Security Information System.

4. Day Reports should be sent firstly to the Responsible Medical Officer and then passed to the Clinical Nursing Manager.

k) MAIL AND CATALOGUE FRAUD

1. There should be a policy which ties in the ordering of goods from catalogues with patients' cash. No goods should be processed into the Hospital unless proof of purchase has been obtained. (The legal position may need clarifying.)

l) TELEPHONES

1. Owen Ward's telephone should be sited on a part of the ward which facilitates monitoring of its use.

2. Owen Ward telephone policy should be reviewed and a practical policy be devised to ensure all calls can be effectively monitored. A record of approved telephone numbers should be kept for each patient having been checked by the Unit Social Workers. This should be a hospital-wide procedure. The number being dialled must be observed. (This should be hospital wide).

m) SECURITY IN STAFF AREAS

1. All internal office doors on the ward should open outwards and need strengthening. This should be undertaken throughout the Hospital.

2. The Staff Rest Room must be strictly enforced as a staff only area.

3. Consideration should be given to increasing the number of rooms available for interviewing patients, in order that the ward office and ward manager's office are not required for this purpose e.g., convert the "boot room" on each ward into two interview rooms.

4. The ward manager's offices should be on a different locking system with a uniquely suitable key system which would allow only authorised personal access.

5. Any gardening equipment should be kept to a minimum and any major horticultural undertakings should be supervised by the Rehabilitation Therapy Services Department.

6. All security items should be kept in special self locking cabinets/cupboards/drawers to avoid easy access. Consideration should also be given to the siting of these.

7. When patients are using security items such as a carving knife they should be directly supervised.

n) VISITORS

1. We recommend the team reviewing the Security Manual consider the special procedures and policies pertinent to visiting.

2. A technically robust system, similar to the Personagram, should be introduced as a matter of urgency.

3. Clinical teams in consultation with the Security Department must identify

patients' visitors who are likely to compromise the security of the Hospital. These visitors to identified patients should be thoroughly vetted by the Security Department.

4. Patients visitors who have been identified as problematic may be randomly requested to be searched at the reception area in an appropriate location.

5. Consideration of a Mental Health Act Commissioner's proposal should be given to setting up a special visiting area for such problem visitors This should eliminate direct patient/visitor contact. This would be a rarely used facility.

6. The role of reception staff, which necessitates face to face contact with visitors needs reviewing and there should be a safe area where they can retreat to in the event of an incident.

7. The closure of the South Control Centre will place additional demands on this area and consideration should be given to the redesign of the North Control Centre taking the above into consideration.

8. Ward based visiting should be a privilege earned by patients' behaviour. Until a patient has demonstrated consistent non-anti-social behaviour then certain visitors, for example direct family members, should not be allowed to visit the ward. The decision to ban visitors for a period of time needs to be taken by the clinical team in consultation with the Security Department. The patient and visitor must be informed verbally and in writing by the Clinical Manager of the ban and the reasons for the decision given.

9. Visiting areas on the wards should be restricted to a communal area i.e. Library or dining room. Special arrangements may be made for exceptions to this in consultation with the General Manager. A visitor may only be allowed to view a patient's bedroom and not enter it. Any viewing of a patient's room by a visitor will be authorised by the Nurse in Charge of the ward and accompanied at all times by a nurse. All external visits must be supervised by a nurse always being present in the room. Exceptions will be agreed by the General Manager.

10. The present policy regarding parole patients being allowed free access throughout the grounds with their visitors should be reviewed as there is currently no upper limit on patients with parole. Consideration should be given to designating specific areas i.e outside the assembly hall and ward garden areas.

o) SITE MANAGEMENT

1. There should be a clearly defined role and responsibility described for the individuals undertaking site management. (At the present time the site managers are unsure of their responsibilities.)

2. There should be assistance for the Site Manager outside normal hours in the form of at least one Ward Manager being on duty.

p) ROLE OF THE ADVOCACY SERVICE

1. The role of the Advocacy Service in times of crisis with patients should be negotiated with them.

2. The service is now in a position to offer an on-call facility and consideration should be given to supplying them with a mobile phone for their use.

2.14.23 As we have said above it is impossible to comprehend the awfulness of the events which took place on Owen Ward in June 1994 without reading the full Report and its appendices. The findings of the Report demonstrate how unmanageable and unsafe a place for staff and patients Owen Ward had become. Its numerous and sensible recommendations illustrate how the operation of Hospital, Unit and Ward needed to be

radically changed in order to provide appropriate care and treatment of patients, and to protect the staff and wider public. Even the Patients' Advocacy Service was critical of the lack of boundaries on Owen Ward.

2.14.24 The Task Force had subsumed within its task, the implementation of the Rowe Report recommendations, but the contents of the documents it produced, and the resultant SHSA policy can be searched with a fine-toothed comb without discovering any impact from that Report. By contrast the Rowe and Owen Ward Reports are very much in sympathy with the recommendations made by Miss Kinsley in 1992. The lessons from the Rowe Report were not learned and, as we will see, neither were those from the Owen Ward Report.

The External Adviser

2.14.25 As we have stated above Mrs Miles instructed an outside observer to comment on the creation of the Report. Mr Parry's Report which is dated 12 August 1994 is of considerable interest. He had been provided with the Interim (full) Report dated 16 July 1994 and the appendices attached to it. He also saw representatives of the Patients' Council, the Hospital Advisory Committee, the Patients' Advocacy Service, the psychology services and the POA.

2.14.26 Like us, Mr Parry was impressed by the Inquiry team's work:

> "I would commend the investigating team on the thoroughness with which they have carried out their work. Incidents which provoke major investigations are rarely isolated events and occur against a background of operational practice at all levels of the organisation. This is the case in this incident. The investigating team have attempted to fully address the related issues."

2.14.27 He felt the team had fully dealt with the operational matters and so he limited himself to "the wider underlying issues which have emerged from the investigation". Again we quote at length:

> **"1. Security and therapy**
>
> Following the Ashworth Inquiry Report the reforms within the Hospital have been radical and far reaching. The change of emphasis from security to therapy and greater empowerment of patients have inevitably given rise to considerable anxiety and uncertainty amongst the staff of all disciplines, particularly nurses, and this has been communicated to patients. From my discussions with various groups there is a feeling that the consequences of such radical change have not been fully thought through by the organisation as a whole. The balance of 'power' is perceived to have been passed from staff to patients, creating, in many people's view, a less safe environment in which to work. The interim Report (page 16, the first paragraph) highlights this dilemma and I would advise that, within the recommendations, the Hospital Managers enable greater dialogue between themselves and staff teams at Ward Level, in order to assess the changes in therapeutic care and provide a unity of purpose for the future. Phrases like 'the pendulum has swung too far' have been mentioned and these issues are of major concern to many staff.
>
> Interestingly, the patients themselves also express these views and understand that formal structure and clear boundaries are necessary within a high secure environment. It is clear that many of these structures and boundaries exist but, as with Owen Ward, are either ignored or diluted. To quote from the Kinsley Security Audit – 'Challenges of a modern and secure forensic psychiatry unit will need to be recognised and confronted. Security is a basic fact of life from which the therapeutic approach and all that goes with it should grow and prosper.'

2. Psychopathic disorder

Dr Coorey's paper highlights the major issues of attempting to provide treatment in a hospital setting for patients diagnosed as psychopathic disorder, who are serious offenders. The Butler Report (1975) suggested that 'the great weight of evidence supports the conclusion that psychopaths are not, in general, treatable'. Patients themselves are unclear as to the 'treatment' they are receiving within hospital. There is certainly evidence that staff find this area of work extremely stressful and worrying. The grouping of these patients together adds to the concern.

The experience of Owen Ward in attempting to provide a 'Therapeutic Community' setting with an extremely liberal regime, albeit by default, has been a lesson in how not to treat this group of patients. But there can be a positive outcome to this experience. The Reed Report on Psychopathic Disorder, recently published, invites comments from practitioners, and the Owen Ward experience could provide valuable information to the national debate on psychopathic disorder and treatability particularly with such a group of very serious offenders.

I would advise that the multi-disciplinary teams be encouraged to debate the whole issue of psychopathic disorder and its place in the high security hospital. Views should then be made known to the Department and Home Office.

This debate is all the more urgent as there is considerable concern amongst staff that other wards within the PDU, as well as Owen Ward, currently have a high potential for serious incidents, similar to that under observation.

3. Communication

The issue of communication within a hospital of this size is a complicated subject. Despite the introduction of technology, and e-mail facility throughout the Hospital, *there is a perception amongst many of the groups who spoke to me that there is a 'gulf' between senior management of the Hospital and staff on the ground floor.*

However, it appears that there were major concerns over Owen Ward for some time before the hostage incident. These concerns were either not communicated to the Hospital managers or were not given sufficient credence. Some said that concerns were expressed but received little response, and others that their views were 'blocked' and not forwarded. Whatever the truth of these comments, and hindsight is always easy, there appears to be serious concern that the reality of practice is not shared with senior managers. There is certainly a perception of isolation and lack of support amongst some staff groups.

4. Monitoring of Recommendations

A major theme throughout the investigation is the lack of action following previous Reports and recommendations, particularly the Rowe Report. There is also mention of other reviews and Reports of working groups which appear not to have been actioned or implemented. This is not surprising considering the number of incidents and investigations arising within a high security hospital.

My advice in this regard is that a designated person or persons should monitor how recommendations are actioned and provide progress Reports, so that lessons learned are implemented and maintained over a given period." [Our emphases.]

The Implementation of the Recommendations

2.14.28 As usual, after the Report was produced steps were taken, on paper at least, to bring about change, and the **"Post Owen General Recommendations For The Hospital Action Plan"** was produced in December 1994. It was compiled by Mr Tom Maxwell, the Security Manager, and makes general recommendations, because the team was aware that the problems which existed on Owen Ward also existed in other areas of the Hospital and so similar situations could have arisen elsewhere.

2.14.29 The general recommendations were made "to both reduce risk and improve the ability of staff to deliver treatment in the more stable and therapeutic environment." The Action Plan is divided into the 14 areas of the Owen Ward recommendations. The target date for implementing the recommendations varied between November 1994 and March 1995. However, as with the implementation of other recommendations in the Hospital, it is quite obvious that there was no comprehensive policy of implementing them.

2.14.30 This can readily be demonstrated. In June 1995 all the wards were checked, and we saw an audit of the PDU Wards as part of the Owen Action Plan carried out by the Security Department. Each document is stamped 23 June 1995, that is three months after all the recommendations in the Action Plan should have been actioned. This audit demonstrates that the response from the wards had been very poor. One important example concerns "patients' behavioural problems". The Owen Ward Report had recommended that such problems be dealt with on the ward. But the Security Department found on Lawrence Ward that parole ward patients had been given extra privileges which appear 'over the top' for a Special Hospital. As the Keown Report (1997), later demonstrates this remained a root cause of the Ward's problems. Another example is that five out of the six wards were not complying with the injunction that "patients should not have access to each other's rooms".

2.14.31 We also had access to the Reports on 11 SHSA Quality Review Visits carried out in 1995 and 1996. These too demonstrate a good deal of non-compliance with the Action Plan recommendations. We have already noted that Mr Kaye agreed that the Reports of those visits demonstrate there was still much to be done. Here are a few examples to illustrate the point. In the quarterly review (16–17 February 1995), it is said of Shelley Ward that the SHSA policy document was difficult to find; the policy statement regarding risk assessment was not available; the nursing plans were inadequate in dealing with seclusion and alternative management; the psychiatrists were not available to comment; few diversional activities were available and many patients wandered around aimlessly. Of Firs Ward it is said that no risk assessment policy was available and staff were unsure whether a policy was required and feared that there was a danger in making clinical practice too inflexible; staff were concerned about skill mix of the staff and the physical condition of the ward; side rooms seemed to be in a disgraceful condition, they were dirty and unhygienic and had no place in a hospital; the seclusion room was filthy; on the day of the visit a patient was in seclusion in his room but no seclusion records were being kept. In commenting in an e-mail on this review to Mrs Miles, Mr Tarbuck said, "Many members of staff have a most particular view of the operation of a therapeutic community, believing it to be, in essence, a *laissez-faire* operation."

2.14.32 In the quarterly review visit of Lawrence Ward on 28–29 February 1996, a significant year in the history of the Ward, the following comments are made about it: "patients had control over locking their own rooms, patients had full access to toilet and washing facilities; all patients able to control access to their own rooms; patients had full choice about time of going to bed; there were some house rules but they were clearly the subject of negotiation between patients and staff; at all times patients had access to all ward facilities including kitchen, TV lounge, laundry, library and bathroom; from the safety point of view there did not appear to be any anxiety from the introduction of 24-hour policy".

2.14.33 Again regarding Lawrence Ward, in an earlier Report of the quarterly review visit on 1 August 1995, it is said that the patients had full access to their rooms 24 hours a day and were given as much autonomy as possible within the confines of security requirements. Of the consultant and clinical team it noted that there was general dissatisfaction with the input of the consultant and social worker. The consultant only attended the ward for a PCT meeting, case conferences or in a crisis. One patient claimed he had not seen a consultant for five years. Twenty-five per cent of the multi-disciplinary treatment plans were examined with the following results: no interim review dates were recorded; there was no documentary evidence that reviews had taken place; PCT meetings recommended changes to patients' treatment, but treatment plans were not altered to reflect this; some treatment plans were not dated and two patients did not have treatment plans.

2.14.34 Not much it appears was happening. Mr Maxwell told us that he gave up submitting progress Reports on the Owen Ward Action Plan because it appeared pointless. Notwithstanding the audit of the PDU Wards done by the Security Department in June 1995, things ground to a halt, mainly, in his view, because Mrs Miles did not throw her weight behind the recommendations. If the Owen Ward Action Plan was to be implemented it had to be championed by the Hospital Management Group and by Mrs Miles in particular. That did not happen, with the result that people interpreted the Owen Ward recommendations as optional, rather than "must-dos".

2.14.35 Mr Maxwell admitted that the Owen Ward recommendations did sit unhappily with the Blom-Cooper recommendations. The views of staff became polarized, with many staff, including some senior nurses, the psychologists and social workers opposed to any tightening of security, which they thought was against the interests of patients. He appreciated the enormous workload Mrs Miles faced but criticized the priorities of the Hospital, whereby landscaping the grounds appeared to take precedence over improving security.

2.14.36 Mr Maxwell gave a highly pertinent example of the slow pace of change, namely the revision of the visiting policy, which Mr Backhouse in his view "sat on for 18 months or so". This was important, because the new Clinical Units were increasingly doing their own thing and visits were more and more taking place on the ward. We discuss this matter further in Part Three.

Disciplinary Action

2.14.37 Following the Owen Ward Report Mrs Miles and Dr Strickland jointly agreed that he should step down from the position of Clinical Manager. Mrs Miles then tried to launch disciplinary action against him. Given that the Hospital was still under the control of the SHSA the advice and support of Professor Taylor, the Head of Medical Services, was vital. In the event this was not forthcoming.

2.14.38 This was not the first time that Dr Strickland's performance had been under close scrutiny. Professor Taylor told us that on 25 November 1992 she, Dr Dick and Dr Higgins had written to him expressing concern about his position in the wake of the Rowe and Blom-Cooper Reports. They requested a job plan from him which reflected the urgent need to review policies on Forster Ward. They had to press him for this in a letter dated 8 February 1993. Dr Higgins was at the Hospital working on the Task Force and he took responsibility for pursuing this matter with Dr Strickland. In the event the restructuring of the Hospital meant that the original tasks set out for Dr Strickland had changed so fundamentally that he was given more time to complete his job plan.

2.14.39 Professor Taylor told us that in addition to the formal review of the work of all doctors at Ashworth she and her colleagues had intended to carry out an additional review of Dr Strickland's work, but again the restructuring led to that additional review being dropped. Dr Strickland's work was reviewed in January 1994; this review had involved Mrs Miles, who was taking over responsibility for the job planning process, following the practice of the wider NHS. No formal job plan was agreed because of the restructuring. The formal agreement of Dr Strickland's job plan was to take place in June 1994. The Owen Ward incident occurred on 8 June 1994.

2.14.40 Professor Taylor told us she had advised Mrs Miles against the appointment; she believed Dr Higgins had too. She told us that in her view Dr Strickland was not a "born leader". The Clinical Manager post was one "he probably should not have been given, and perhaps he should not have taken".

2.14.41 Given the background, why was Dr Strickland appointed to the post of Clinical Manager of the PDU? We have already criticised the failure to appoint a high quality Clinical Manager to the PDU; Mrs Miles was warned about Dr Strickland and she failed to heed those warnings.

2.14.42 Mrs Miles wrote to Dr Strickland on 1 August 1994 confirming that they had agreed he should step down from the post of Clinical Manager. Mrs Miles also said that the events on Owen Ward raised serious concerns about his clinical role on the Unit. She promised to return to this matter after discussing it with Dr Shetty.

2.14.43 On 19 September Mrs Miles wrote to Mr Kaye telling him that she believed there was a *prima facie* case for reviewing Dr Strickland's professional conduct and competence, and asking him whether he wished her to proceed with a disciplinary investigation. She set out several grounds:

(i) the failure to review the findings of the Rowe Report in any systematic way;

(ii) the failure to develop new operational procedures for the former Forster Ward despite reminders at job planning discussions in 1993 and 1994;

(iii) his admission set out in the Owen Ward Report, that he and his team had failed to observe the behaviour of patients on Owen Ward and its implications for security; and

(iv) the failure to prevent the hostage-taking incident. Specifically, Dr Strickland had failed to tell his patient, Mr Tomlinson, that his visit had been cancelled.

As we shall see there was an important error in (iv): Byron Tomlinson was not Dr Strickland's patient.

2.14.44 A memorandum dated 14 October 1994 from Mrs Miles to Mrs Nelson confirms that they had agreed to proceed under the Intermediate Procedure laid down in a 1990 Health Circular. This involved a peer review of the doctor concerned, whilst allowing a later decision to be made as to whether any further action was warranted.

2.14.45 Mrs Miles sent Professor Taylor an outline statement of the case against Dr Strickland on 26 October 1994. Professor Taylor replied on 10 November. In that letter she confirmed that she and Dr Higgins had raised concerns about Dr Strickland's failure to develop operational policies. **She did point out that Mrs Miles would have to defend her recent decision to appoint Dr Strickland to the position of Clinical Manager.**

2.14.46 Professor Taylor met Dr Strickland to discuss the outline statement of the case against him on 2 December 1994. This was a preliminary interview, after which it would be decided whether or not to proceed down the Intermediate Procedure route. On 13 December she sent a memorandum to Mrs Miles, Mrs Nelson, Mr Kaye and Dr Shetty in which she explained that she was recommending against any further disciplinary action. She gave three reasons:

(i) The outline case was "fatally flawed". The main reason for this was that Mr Tomlinson was not his patient, but Dr Crispin's. **It was not clear from Professor Taylor's evidence in what additional way, if any, the case was said to be flawed.**

(ii) Whilst accepting some failures in his overall management of the services, Dr Strickland did seem to have taken "all appropriate steps to remedy any such failure. There are systems in place for continuing to offer professional support and supervision in his current rather different role. I cannot see how pursuing the disciplinary line further would add anything at all to his future development or that of the service." She added that critical comments by other members of the team had to be weighed against the necessary disciplinary action and staff changes he had set in train, which had stirred resentment.

(iii) "Dr Strickland raised a number of important conflicts in managerial development in Ashworth Hospital, which I think do not apply just to the personality disorder unit, nor even exclusively to Ashworth. I think that for the health of the organisation we need to take the opportunity to consider these wider issues, which I think could not be done through any disciplinary procedure. Disciplinary procedure would only highlight them again . . . "

Among the examples of "conflicts" referred to by Professor Taylor were the implementation of the 24-hour opening at the same time as establishing the PDU; the caseload Dr Strickland held at the same time as he was trying to develop operational policies for the Unit; and the persistent inability to free doctors for necessary further training. She recommended finding "a method of engaging in dialogue with Dr Strickland and a medical colleague with general management at Ashworth for understanding better how these conflicts arose and could be prevented in the future."

2.14.47 Mr Kaye discussed Professor Taylor's memorandum with Mrs Miles, and then replied to her on 21 December 1994. He and Mrs Miles agreed not to proceed to the Intermediate Procedure in the light of Professor Taylor's comments.

2.14.48 The same day Professor Taylor wrote to Dr Strickland. She noted that the allegation concerning Byron Tomlinson had been dropped. The main charge that remained was the failure to develop clear policies for Forster and Owen Wards. Noting that Dr Strickland had acknowledged his failings, had relinquished the Clinical Manager post and was seeing Dr Shetty regularly for professional counselling, she stated that disciplinary action would not be pursued. That said, she indicated that Dr Strickland would need to have an additional review of his work with Dr Shetty and Mrs Miles, at which a new job plan would be agreed, reflecting any need for additional training.

2.14.49 Professor Taylor argued that although serious flaws in Dr Strickland's conduct were identified, extenuating circumstances came into play in terms of the support he was offered by the Hospital and the resentment of staff who were (quite rightly) being suspended. She did not deny that she had not pursued the validity of Dr Strickland's responses to the allegations any further, but noted that her recommendations had been discussed and agreed with Mrs Miles, Mr Kaye and Mrs Nelson. No one had voiced any opposition to her recommendation:

"My job was . . . to test the allegations and I started that process. I then came back with what I had heard and my recommendations in the context of what I had heard and my recommendations were, as you see, accepted."

2.14.50 Professor Taylor further argued that the allegation that Dr Strickland had failed to tell Mr Tomlinson that his visit was cancelled was, even if true, "hardly a case for an Immediate Procedure . . . It might have been an error of judgement, it might have been not the best thing he could have done, but that is not quite the same as an allegation of professional lack of competence."

2.14.51 Professor Taylor summarized her decision thus:

"I made a judgement that there had been failings, which I documented, and that there needed to be a formal clinical structure to minimize the chance of those failings having further impact on the service and, indeed, to improve Dr Strickland's performance generally, and that structure was, indeed, set up. And that there was nothing to be gained for the service, and certainly not for him, in pursuing a disciplinary procedure *per se* on the evidence we had, and with the balance of circumstances we had."

2.14.52 Professor Taylor noted that setting up a formal supervision arrangement as they did was very rare for a consultant. She would have preferred Dr Strickland to move from the PDU. But he wished to stay, the service had to be run and it was extremely difficult attracting anyone from within or outside Ashworth Hospital to replace him. As far as her role in the decision not to proceed was concerned, she agreed that although her position as Head of Medical Services was advisory, she was in a position to wield very considerable influence. Had the decision been taken to pursue disciplinary action she would have been responsible for initiating that action.

2.14.53 Mrs Miles said she had been very disappointed with the decision not to proceed any further along the disciplinary route. She regarded the evidence available quite sufficient to proceed against any professional, but had not felt in any position to argue with Professor Taylor over judgements of clinical competence. She pointed out that the apparent reluctance to discipline Dr Strickland sent a poor message to other staff about doctors' apparent immunity from disciplinary action.

2.14.54 We believe that Professor Taylor took the action she did because she was worried that the service might otherwise collapse. We find her reasons for not proceeding outlined in her memorandum of 13 December 1994 unconvincing. Dr Strickland had taken on a difficult post, but he had volunteered. The introduction of various "conflicts" to excuse his poor performance is inappropriate. Professor Taylor failed to grasp the nettle of poor performance when the opportunity was there. We have sympathy with Mrs Miles' disappointment with the decision. Much more could have been done to insist that Dr Strickland was more closely supervised. He probably needed a secondment outside Ashworth Hospital.

2.15.0 The Health Advisory Service Visit and *With Care In Mind Secure*

2.15.1 In 1994 the Health Advisory Service (HAS) was invited to visit Ashworth to conduct a peer review of the present functioning of the Hospital, with particular reference to the implementation of the Blom-Cooper team's recommendations. The team consisted of a number of well-respected clinicians, led by the Director of HAS, Dr Richard Williams.The fieldwork was carried out in November 1994 and the Review published in March 1995.

2.15.2 That Review, *With Care in Mind Secure*, described the management structure existing then and noted that it was based on a number of principles, the key one being devolution. In HAS' words: "All management decisions concerning patient care should, wherever practicable, be devolved to the lowest level. This should be supported by financial and management systems."

2.15.3 The HAS were in general complimentary of the changes made; we think too complimentary. However, they did also indicate some tensions. The following are particularly germane to our inquiries:

(i) the Unit General Manager had had to adopt a "top-down" approach in driving through the changes demanded in the wake of Blom-Cooper. She was now seeking to involve all staff in the business planning process. But the significant agenda of change following the implementation of the Blom-Cooper recommendations had "inevitably produced tensions, competing priorities between strategic and operational development, and occasionally confusion and lack of progress";

(ii) "the current blend of strategic and operational responsibilities has left confusion amongst some of the more junior members of staff. There is a perception of hierarchy within the Hospital Management Group in which the directors are seen as having greater seniority. The directors appear to hold a mixture of strategic developmental and operational responsibilities. Additionally, ward level nursing staff seem to share some lack of clarity about the role of the clinical manager";

(iii) the social workers and psychologists felt dispossessed with the loss of the Social Work and Psychology Departments;

(iv) "the development of the PDU has not been without incident and it would appear lessons have needed to be learned".

Many had not been learned even by 1997.

(v) the new structure depended on clinical unit managers continuing to support and involve ward managers and ward-based staff and to communicate with each other, to avoid the Units becoming isolated;

(vi) the managerial and operational responsibilities of Ward Managers were heavy, making it difficult for them to devote sufficient time from clinical leadership of the nursing team;

(vii) increased liberalization plus the introduction of 24-hour care had influenced arrangements for therapeutic programmes. This has caused a number of staff to suggest that therapy and security are at opposite ends of a spectrum of approach. However:

> "The Review team considers that this reflects a significant mis-understanding of the relationship between therapeutic ethos and the requirement of security. The Review team believes that therapy cannot be effectively instituted without clear parameters and boundaries which include those for physical safety and security."

2.15.4 The HAS team gave the SHSA and Ashworth advice on developing the Hospital's management arrangements. This advice included the creation of an Ashworth Hospital Board to take on most, if not all the functions retained by the SHSA, and the splitting-up of the Hospital Management Group into an Executive Group consisting of the Directors (as an embryo for a future autonomous Board) and a new Management Board. The former group would address major policy and strategic issues; the latter would concentrate on the operational management of the Hospital, whilst also contributing to the strategic agenda. The HAS suggested the UGM might benefit from the support of an assistant Chief Executive. The HAS also advised that the clinical units should, over time, be consolidated and become Clinical Directorates, led by clinicians. This would involve clinicians in management and improve communications between management and staff directly working with patients.

2.15.5 The HAS' Review was influential. A sub-committee of the SHSA was established in April 1995 to help the Hospital become used to a more autonomous status. The Ashworth Hospital Board was chaired by Miss Joy Young, a Non-Executive director of the SHSA, and comprised Mrs Miles, her five Executive Directors, and three Non-Executive Directors, namely the Chairman of the Hospital Advisory Committee (HAC), a member of the HAC and the SHSA's Medical Director, Dr Dilys Jones, who had succeeded Professor Taylor. The Hospital Board had no executive powers delegated to it by the SHSA. Any significant decisions still had to be made by the Authority.

2.15.6 Mrs Miles also separated the HMG into the HEG, a monthly meeting of herself and her directors focusing on big policy and strategic issues, and the HMT, the operational management group. Mr Green, the Business Development Director, was asked to chair the latter, which consisted of the four clinical unit managers and the rehabilitation and support services manager. In due course came the creation of the new Clinical Directorates.

2.15.7 We were not convinced the HAS' advice to create large new Clinical Directorates was right. In reality their creation merely reconstructed over-mighty fiefdoms rather than make the Hospital's administration more cohesive. Mr Kaye counselled against the creation of the Clinical Directorates because he feared they would be too big for a single manager to handle. He was right.

A Cover-Up?

2.15.8 The key question remains: why does the HAS Report look so very different from that produced by Mr Green and his team? Although they were produced for very different purposes, one could be forgiven for thinking that they referred to completely different hospitals. Why was this? The answer is relatively simple. Dr Williams and his team were not given access to information which would have enabled them to write a more searching Report. This requires a detailed explanation.

Negotiations

2.15.9 It seems from the correspondence we have seen that Mr Kaye was comfortable with the decision to ask the HAS to undertake the review at Ashworth. Thus a letter from him to Mr Jewesbury dated 7 February 1994 says: "Dr Williams recognises the importance of a constructive, helpful Report rather than another litany of problems." Mrs Muth, Dr Williams deputy, wrote to Mrs Miles on 22 September 1994 asking for a list of briefing documents to be made available which included "full details of incident Reports for the last 18 months". The Department of Health was also interested in the task to be undertaken by Hospital Advisory Service, and, on 3 October 1994, Mr Jewesbury wrote a letter to Mrs Muth indicating matters on which he thought the Department would like to see comment.

He wrote: "I think you are already aware of the somewhat troubled history of the management of women's services at Ashworth. This is clearly an important part of the picture and one on which we would expect to see a full appraisal in the HAS team's Report". Before he wrote that letter he and others in the department had received an e-mail from Dr John Reed dated 27 September in which he said he had:

> "never got a clear account from Pamela Taylor as to whether she is now confident that the training needs of doctors including consultants is being identified and taken up by the doctors, this would be a helpful area to look at".

He also said:

> "additionally, I think the HAS should examine how the Hospital has handled any internal enquiries including any currently under way. Changes in style and openness since the original inquiry would one hopes be apparent . . . ".

Of course, as he said in evidence, Dr Williams had not been privy to this internal correspondence. In the event he never saw the Swan and Owen Ward Reports until shortly before he gave evidence, when we asked him to read them with a view to considering how, if at all, knowledge of their contents might have affected his team's judgement.

2.15.10 In the statement he prepared following seeing those Reports but before seeing the appendices to the Owen Ward Report he said that Mr Kaye had been unwilling to release a copy of the Swan Report, but was content that Ms Hilton, the psychologist member of the HAS team who had also been a member of the Swan Report team, discuss that Report with them. Dr Williams said the negotiations concerning the release of the Swan Report took some time and he would have preferred to have seen the actual Report. That the negotiations took some time is evidenced by another letter from Mr Jewesbury dated 28 September 1994 addressed to Mr Backer-Host and others in which he wrote:

> "the management of women's services is an obvious area of concern which I am sure we need to flag up. I understand that a dialogue has already opened between the HAS and the SHSA about the release of the Swan Report on women's services."

With Care in Mind Secure Revisited

2.15.11 In his evidence Dr Williams said that although he had sometimes had to press, he had never before been refused sight of any Report he wanted to see during his time as Director of the HAS. Having since read the Report he said the Swan Report was a pretty damning Report, and that its statement that "we do consider that women should never be placed at Ashworth in the future" had never been mentioned to him by Mr Kaye. He also accepted that there was some overlap between some criticisms found in both the Swan and Owen Ward Reports.

During the course of their work the HAS team had become aware that there was a report about an incident in June 1994 of which they had not been given a copy, so they asked Mrs Miles for it and were given the nine page Report. At some stage during the course of their meetings with the executive team at Ashworth, they received a brief presentation on the Owen Ward incident which appears to have been made by Mr Tarbuck. Dr Williams said the presentation was entirely consistent with the contents of the nine page Report. It was presented as an ugly issue in respect of the hostage-taking which fortunately had not resulted in any casualty. It had been handled well by the staff themselves. One or two background problems had emerged as a result of looking into the build-up phase. It was not presented as an extraordinarily major item. Other people they spoke to at Ashworth about the incident gave them a similar story.

2.15.12 Not having seen the appendices to the Owen Ward Report prior to writing his statement, he was asked about his conclusion: "The team has come to the view that sight of the contents of the Swan Report would not necessarily have changed its opinion in respect of the major issue it saw as affecting services for women." He said he was expressing a little reserve because they were looking back with hindsight. He thought that "to write too hard a sentence . . . would be for me to be over-bold". They might have looked at some issues in more depth had they seen the Report. But the decision to create the Women's Unit with a specialist manager seemed to have focused some management attention on this area, and generally picked up the gender-specific issues. One of the Ward Managers was very impressive, and although they were only seeing embryonic changes, they had felt some degree of optimism.

However, he felt it was a short term policy to deprive his team of the fullest of pictures. The quality of the work the HAS did depended very considerably on the information they got and the openness of the way in which their hosts dealt with them. He had only read the Owen Ward Report appendices, the day before he gave evidence, and they had made a lot more impact on him than the Report itself. Had he seen the appendices before writing his statement, he said:

> "I might have been more fulsome in my comments. Looking back with hindsight, if we had had at least some of the documents in that set, and they are considerable, I think we might have done a much more rigorous job on the PDU at the time we were there."

2.15.13 Dr Williams was asked:

> Q: From a historical perspective point of view, paragraph 112 says: "The development of the PDU has not been without incident, and it would appear lessons

have needed to be learned". That, after reading the Owen Report, might be regarded as a masterly bit of understatement?

A: I think after reading the version that I had read it was about all we could substantiate with the documents.

A little later in his evidence these exchanges took place:

Professor Edwards: It is all wrapped up in rather nice elegant language though is it not. It does not jump out at you. Let me read it to you.

A: Sure.

Q: "Patient Care Teams should with their allocated security adviser, revisit the parameters of therapy and security, set protocols for ward policies which maintain both the dignity of the individual, the security of the ward and the safety of patients and staff". I have to say that is a brilliant piece of wordsmanship. But it does not force anyone to do anything does it?

A: I think the difficulty you have here is that we did not have the hard evidence that we required to actually go much further than that at the time.

The Chairman: You have now?

A: Now that I have seen the other documents I think I would have to revise – that is perhaps one area in which I would revise my view. I think we might have written in somewhat harder language.

The Chairman then invited Dr Williams to look at the last sentence of his statement. In the last paragraph he had set out a number of matters which the full version of the Report might have prompted them to consider. The last sentence reads:

"Again it is difficult to speculate but it is possible that such explorations might have resulted in the team coming to conclusions different either in degree of emphasis or scale".

The Chairman asked Dr Williams to look at the word 'possible' and invited him to say whether it would have become 'probable'. He replied, that having seen the documents over the weekend it was difficult looking back, **but he said "probable is certainly right"**.

2.15.14 Dr Williams went on to say that when his team started work they felt a little unsure about what they thought about the senior management, but, in time, as they said in their Report, they came to believe they were being treated openly and well.

The Chairman: Now you know that was not a justifiable comment?

A: I have now sadly perhaps to review that position. As you pointed out to me, sir, it is only in relatively recent times that I have realised that the Report that we were given was not the Report that we might have seen, and indeed would have made – I agree with you, sir – a significant difference if we had seen it, and that now leaves me in some considerable consternation to understand that.

Q: It is difficult to understand why?

A: I am forced to the view, and I do not think it is from our lack of inquiry, that we were not disclosed this. I think we wrote in sufficiently clear terms well before the visit to have expected disclosures.

Q: They even say in that letter, "negotiations are going on about Swan". Obviously you were going on about it for quite some time?

A: Yes. I now see this in a different light sir.

Q: It looks does it not, as though they were not coming clean?

A: That is how it looks sir.

A little later:

Mr Royce: Dr Williams your Report has to some extent in this Inquiry been paraded or waved around to suggest that most things in the garden were rosy, do you follow?
A: I am very surprised to hear that sir.

Q: We have seen, as you have now seen communications between Mr Kaye and Mr Jewesbury before you came in to the effect that you recognised the importance of a constructive, helpful Report, do you follow?
A: Mmm.

Q: We then have a picture of you not getting the Swan Report and certainly being deprived of the opportunity to see the full horror of the Owen Report, do you follow?
A: I do.

Q: And your Report coming out, as Professor Edwards has indicated wrapped in language that is soft rather than hard, constructive and helpful rather than critical do you follow?
A: Well soft rather than hard, yes. I think there are quite a lot of fairly substantial criticisms in that Report. I think having re-read it several times recently, to agree with the comment about the language used which was at the time we were attempting to be judicious. I think nonetheless we pointed out some quite significant gaps in leadership throughout the Hospital, some significant gaps in the roles of many staff; there were problems for psychologists. Clearly we remarked that there was no clear understanding of what the social work role is. I mean I could take you through a series of things which I think add up to quite an array of criticisms.

Q: There is a suggestion that to some extent you were conned. Do you think that is fair?
A: It is not the kind of language I would prefer to use, I must say.

The Chairman: Deceived?
A: Put it like this sir, I think that had we been informed otherwise, I quite agree with the remarks made earlier that we might have written in rather more robust terms.

Q: You would have done would you not?
A: We would have done.

Q: Not might?
A: We would have done, yes.

2.15.15 At this stage it is appropriate to introduce other evidence and material concerning the Swan and Owen Ward Reports.

The Evidence of Mr Kaye

2.15.16 One of the stated intentions of the SHSA was to introduce a policy of openness into what some regarded as the secret Hospitals. In paragraph **2.15.9** above we noted Dr Reed's comment about what the HAS team should check, and changes in style and openness was one such matter. In dealing with his tasks as Chief Executive of the SHSA, Mr Kaye said: "not least among those was a whole deliberate policy of openness with regard to the activities of the hospitals and with regard to relationships with the media." A little later in his evidence, Professor Edwards asked him: "these are exceptional places, and there might be exceptional circumstances, but I think you will have to work a little harder to persuade us that there really was a policy of openness with regard to the activities of the hospitals and relations with the media". In the course of his reply, Mr Kaye said there were constraints: "but you do know that if you can share your aims, if you can share the ways in which you hope to move the Hospitals, you can go a long way towards convincing many that they want to support you. It is that openness that I describe."

We pursued the point:

The Chairman: It depends on what you share with them, does it not?

A: This does not mean to say you bare your whole soul and whole heart. You would be an incredibly naive, unsophisticated manager if you adopted that tack. You do not open your front door and say what you want, but you do endeavour to be consistent and over a period of time, to demonstrate by that consistency that you mean what you are trying to do. That does not mean as the Chairman so nicely put for me that you are sharing everything. There are situations where there are difficult judgments about whether information shared is helpful to the organisation and to the purposes and directions that you are looking at or whether it is going to be counterproductive. There are Reports which are valuable, which have important information that you want to pursue and you know must be pursued, but it is questionable whether complete sharing of those, at all levels, is the best way of making progress towards the objectives they set and that you want to see achieved. I do know that the record of the SHSA . . . indicates that the hospitals were a lot more open and a lot more frank places by 1996 than they had been in 1989. I do not mean by that that everything that came across my desk I immediately put up on a big screen so that everybody could see it, because I knew there were a lot of people that would misuse the information and there are a lot of people who would use it to subvert the purposes that the Authority was trying to achieve.

2.15.17 Mr Kaye went on to say both he and his Chairman read the full Owen Ward Report and its appendices, while the other members saw the full Report but not the appendices, although they were told they were available. However, when the Chairman, Mrs Anne-Marie Nelson, gave evidence she said Mr Kaye was mistaken about this and she had only read the Report. He also said that during the life of the SHSA at least 30 Reports of a similar nature to the Owen Ward Report were received from the three hospitals. Again Mrs Nelson could not recall that number and nor could anyone else.

2.15.18 Professor Edwards then asked:

Q. "That is quite an important conclusion. Thirty Reports at least as bad as the Owen Report?"

A: Well, as serious as the Owen Report I would say.

Q: We have heard evidence that the Owen Report was absolutely awful, words like 'disastrous', and 'awful' have been used by witnesses. We have had thirty of those?

A: . . . the real difficulties that obtain in these Hospitals with these patients occasionally the sort of incidents that are serious enough that you need to investigate to understand better . . . What I am saying is that there were thirty incidents or more that were sufficiently serious to be investigated. These could comprise all sorts of things, absconsions, escapes from the Hospital, suicides, unexplained deaths of patients, a whole range of incidents that needed investigation.

Q: That is a rather different answer to the way it was first put I think.

Mr Kaye went on to say that the majority of the 30 Reports were dealt with in the same way as the Owen Ward Report. One or two Reports had special treatment, but the Owen Ward Report was dealt with and followed through in much the same way as the majority of Reports.

2.15.19 He also said: "The Department of Health would know of all of them, because we had a good communication with them, initially about incidents that would have provided the need for more investigation, and then subsequently about what the investigation produced. So the Department would be aware of all these."

We do not accept that this occurred with regard to all Reports. It certainly did not apply to

the Owen Ward Report, and we unhesitatingly accept Mr Jewesbury's evidence that he was substantially under-informed about that Report.

> Professor Edwards: All those thirty?
> A: Yes and many others besides.
>
> Professor Bluglass: So we can understand this properly, the Owen Report did not stand out against those other Reports as strikingly more serious?
> A: They were all serious.
>
> Q: It did not have any special place?
> A: It had its own seriousness, but it was not, if you like, exceptional or that important.

The Documentary Evidence

2.15.20 At this stage we need to refer to the documentary evidence. Mr Kaye's monthly Report to the Authority dated 13 June 1994 merely refers to the patient holding a female member of staff and a male patient hostage with a carving knife. He states:

> "the procedures established by the Hospital were followed and the incident was effectively resolved by the intervention of staff and the emergency services without injury. The hospital management team is currently investigating the incident and there will be a full investigation."

Mr Howlett, the Secretary to the Authority, circulated a summary of events by Mrs Miles dated 15 June 1994. This document is a reasonably accurate eleven page factual summary of the events. It was discussed at the SHSA Board meeting on 21 June. The minutes refer to the summary and record that Mrs Miles described the internal investigation team that had been set up to review the circumstances of this incident and which would report at the end of July. Moving on in time, the minutes of the Hospital Advisory Committee meeting held on 29 July record the following:

> "Mrs Miles had reviewed the interim [the full] Report of the Investigation team which had raised very serious questions regarding the leadership of the PDU, multi-disciplinary working, communications and disregard for basic security guidelines. In these circumstances she had agreed with Dr Strickland that he should stand down as Clinical Manager. She would be making temporary arrangements for three to six months. The other clinical managers had assured her that similar such problems did not occur on other wards."

Mrs Miles reported to the SHSA on 20 September 1994 on recent events at the Hospital. Authority members received the 19-page version of the Report. Mrs Miles noted that two investigations had been set up and that the first, Mr Green's investigation into the incident itself, had highlighted a number of serious problems. As a result the Clinical Manager, Dr Strickland had been asked to step down and the Ward Manager had been moved.

The final paragraph reads:

> "this final Report has been widely circulated in the Hospital. It makes a number of recommendations regarding the functioning of Owen Ward but also matters of concern for all parts of the Hospital, particularly on security related issues. Copies are available for Authority members."

It is difficult to follow this paragraph. The Report of Mr Green and his team (the interim Report) was never circulated widely. It was not circulated at all. The 19-page Report had very limited circulation indeed. Only the nine page Report (called the Final Report) was circulated in the Hospital on Friday 23 September. In evidence Mr Kaye told us he had never seen the nine page Report that was circulated and had nothing to do with its preparation. That was a matter for the General Manager.

Mr Kaye also told us by the time of the September SHSA Board meeting the members had seen the full 59-page Report, but none of them had asked to see the appendices which were in his office. He said he decided not to circulate the appendices to the members of the Authority in order to "protect them from the full deluge of documentation". He told this Inquiry he did not think the absence of the appendices diminished the Report. "I do not think it diminished from the key messages in the Report about the problems that were being encountered."

2.15.21 It is clear from her covering letter to the 19-page Report that this is the version Mrs Miles wished to circulate. However, Mr Kaye agreed with her Counsel, Mr Gilroy, that in a letter dated 19 September 1994, the day before she gave her presentation to the Authority, he was advising her to be cautious about what the published Report should contain. He said it was not an instruction, but he agreed that if Mrs Miles had not complied, she would have incurred his displeasure:

> "if she had gone ahead in a different way, and it had produced the adverse stories, then I think, displeasure, yes. It would not have been a major emotion, but yes, I would have said, 'Look you made a mistake there, did you not?'."

Mr Gilroy did not suggest to Mr Kaye that Mrs Miles had shown him the nine page document before it was published. However, in our judgment, Mr Kaye was not only an articulate Chief Executive, he expected his General Managers to take his "advice" very seriously and to act upon it. We have no doubt that not only was he the 'boss', he made sure others realised he was the 'boss'.

This is reflected in what Dr Williams told us. Having been appointed to chair the HAS review team, he wrote to the Chairman of the SHSA. This apparently incurred Mr Kaye's displeasure, because at a meeting with Dr Williams concerning the disclosure of the Swan Report, Mr Kaye apparently indicated that he should not have written to his Chairman. We also know that when he felt like giving an instruction to a General Manager he did so. Indeed, he told his counsel, Mr Hoskins, that he certainly gave Mrs Miles an instruction that Dr William's team was not to see the Swan Report.

At the end of September the Hospital Advisory Committee (HAC) met. According to the minutes Mr Dale reported that:

> "The final Report had been published the previous week and an offer had been made to the JCNC of a special meeting to discuss its contents. The Report encapsulates the core areas requiring action. He emphasised that it was not for patient information and agreed that copies would be made available to all HAC members".

This minute can only refer to the nine page Report.

The minutes of the following the HAC meeting, held on 28 October, record an interesting observation:

> "Mr Freeney (a committee member) stated his concerns as to the failure to publish a fuller Report, the problems now faced by Ruskin Ward and the delays in dealing with complaints about property."

2.15.22 The Hospital Management Group meeting held on 11 November 1994 discussed the *Report of the Investigation into Events on Owen Ward and Related Matters.* The entry reads:

> "The Report was formally received by HMG. PT (Tarbuck) reported on the implementation of the recommendations specific to the Personality Disorder Unit and CD [Dale] on those with hospital wide implications. Tom Maxwell and Ian Paterson were developing an Action Plan. The need for ownership by all members of the PCT of all ward-based security and other activities was recognised."

2.15.23 Dr, Williams and the HAS team began their work at Ashworth Hospital on 7 November and finished it on the 25th, so this meeting was actually held while the HAS team was at the Hospital. It is clear, therefore, that the Hospital was only beginning to embark on any action concerning the Owen Ward Report while the HAS team was at the Hospital. Yet the HAS team were not made aware of this activity.

In our view this failure to inform the HAS team of the details of the Owen Ward incident demonstrates that the Hospital and the SHSA were much more interested in getting praise from the HAS review rather than getting a fair and just review. The next document sets this judgment in stone.

2.15.24 It is a briefing note dated 12 December 1994 from Mr Mike Evans, a Department of Health civil servant, and addressed to his line manager, Mrs Leonard and Mr Larner, Private Secretary to the Minister with responsibility for the Special Hospitals. In addition it was copied to Ms Moriarty, the Principal Private Secretary to the Secretary of State, to the Departmental Press Office, to Mr Jewesbury, Dr Reed, and a number of other civil servants. It concerns a story in the *Sunday Express* of 11 December 1994 on the internal Report into the hostage-taking. In paragraph 3 it is said the inquiry presented a very detailed Report to the General Manager and made a number of recommendations to improve the management of both Owen Ward and the Personality Disorder Unit.

2.15.25 Paragraph 4 reads:

> "a summary of the Report, with details of staff and patients removed, was circulated within the Hospital. Following the recommendations contained within the Report a number of staff were disciplined, and some were dismissed (mainly for collaborating with patients obtaining alcohol and drugs). A number of allegations were made about other matters including those mentioned in the article concerning prostitutes, and relationships between patients and staff but these were found to be untrue."

This statement wholly misrepresents the true position. The summary referred to in all probability refers to the 19-page version and that was never circulated within the Hospital. The statement that all other allegations were found to be untrue is, itself, false.

2.15.26 In paragraph 6 the following appears:

> "the Report obtained by the newspaper was the original version and with the full details, including criticism and comments on individual staff and patients. Apparently the Report was available to Mrs Miles only. It was taken from her personal computer and an investigation is underway . . . ."

The original version was not only available to Mrs Miles. She sent a copy and the appendices to Mr Kaye. The Report was not taken from her personal computer. The hospital had a central server system with facilities for word processing. It was taken from her personal file on that system.

> *"The internal inquiry established that there were considerable management problems in the directorate and these criticisms have been met. Ashworth management acknowledges that they, like other hospitals, have a problem with illicit drug taking among patients and they are taking steps to combat this. The other allegations mentioned in the Report were found to be without foundation."*

The underlining is supplied. The first underlined passage was, to say the least, an exaggeration, and the second one was simply untrue.

2.15.27 Paragraphs 7 and 8 appear under a heading "Future Action".

> *"7. The Health Advisory Service have recently completed a three week investigation*

at the Hospital as part of action commissioned by the SHSA following the 1991 Ashworth Inquiry chaired by Sir Louis Blom-Cooper. I understand that the HAS were fully aware of the Report into Owen Ward. Their Report on the policy, procedures and management of the Hospital is not due until early 1995. Informal feed back at the end of their investigation is said to have been complementary about the changes that have taken place.

8. Ashworth management is confident that the changes made in the management and clinical structures of the Directorate and Owen Ward meet fully the problems identified in the internal Report and they believe that this will be reflected in the HAS Report. The hospital has issued a press notice with the background to the internal Report and the HAS review."

2.15.28 Again the above underlined passages were untrue.

Were the HAS Deceived?

2.15.29 During the course of his evidence, Dr Williams was introduced to the contents of Mr Evans' briefing note by the Chairman. When paragraph 7 of was read to him his comment was 'gracious'. The following ensued:

Q: When you look at that Dr Williams, someone did not want you to get to know something, did they not?

A: Well, I mean, certainly in paragraph 7, there is a gross inaccuracy there, we were not fully aware of the Report into Owen Ward.

Q: Someone concealed something from you?
A: And I have to say, not even accepting the comments made about language, would it be fair to say that we say in our Report that the problems with the PDU have been fully met and dealt with? I do not think anybody could agree that that is what we say.

Q: It has not come out at this stage. This is speculation?
A: No, but they are prophesying that we are going to say that the problems have been dealt with.

Q: They are saying there has been a leak?
A: I do not think we say that.

Q: No you do not. I agree.
A: We certainly did not say that to the Hospital when we gave an informal feed back.

Q: Nor did you get to know anything about this leakage of the Report?
A: Nothing at all.

Q: No, you were not told about it?
A: My recall is that my deputy, Mrs Muth, was approached much later. This would be February, March time, round about the time that the SHSA formally published the Report, to write a press release. I think it was written within Ashworth Hospital first, and I have to say we sent it back as being far too positive.

Q: That is the release I think I can refer you to here, it is in that file?
A: And we insisted that the press release was altered. I accept what you say, sir.

Q: What part of what I said?
A: I accept what you say, that it looks as if it was not anticipated that we would find these matters.

Q: And something was concealed from you as a result?
A: Yes sir.

Professor Edwards: Dr Williams, we know that when your Report eventually emerged it was received with a sense of relief by those who commissioned it.

Ministers would no doubt have been given reassuring messages that whilst there were still some problems things were moving well and here is the Report as evidence of it. The Hospital certainly, as Mr Royce has explained, used it to explain things were getting better. It is an important issue for us though as to how a very experienced investigating team like yours, and they were very experienced . . .
A: I think I would have to agree with that sir. There is nobody on that team who is not actually of considerable standing in the field.

Q: But something went wrong did it not. Whilst you were there, and immediately before you had been there, we have had evidence about murders, and attempted murders and drug dealing and violence and pornography and gangs of patients and suborning of staff, scams, blackmail, of young children being left with paedophiles, of low security; some of that just before you arrived, some of it whilst you were there, and also some of it still there today, according to some witnesses. So how do we make a judgment then? Either your team were very skilfully misled, or your team were frankly blind and incompetent, or the evidence that we have heard is simply exaggerated and it was not like that at all. We have simply been building a bad picture up from bits and pieces which we have picked out of evidence . . . ?

In reply, Dr Williams thought that through considerable guile and hard work they had discovered quite a lot of core issues. He did not think his team had been incompetent and therefore that left open the other two propositions – they were misled or the evidence exaggerated the position.

2.15.30 Dr Williams was then told by the Chairman that the MHAC, of which he had recently become Deputy Chairman, had been refused the full Owen Ward Report, and only received the nine page version. He said that had he been the Deputy Chairman then, he would not have liked that. He added:

"I think Professor Edwards put two other propositions other than the incompetence possibility. I think that is one of them. The other was that may be you are building up this out of proportion. Again, I am speculating Sir, and standing well outside my brief as Director of the HAS, and indeed in investigating the circumstances, but having followed the sequence through, there does seem to be some relentless connection between the various Reports that are presented. I think the same vacuum-type issues about the policy into practice if you like, the connection between the top of the organisation and the bottom where it is actually registered in action with patients, seems to have been a recurring problem."

Q: In other words, with the best will in the world, you cannot escape at the end of the day a feeling, "we were deceived"?
A: I would prefer you drew that conclusion rather than my asserting that.

Mr Royce: But just in a nutshell, we have heard a series of very similar problems over subsequent years, evidenced by subsequent Reports. Do you follow?
A: I do.

Q: It is difficult perhaps to answer this, but had you been provided with the full picture in relation to the PDU, particularly by way of the Owen Report, you might very well have been substantially more critical of what was going on there, and you might have investigated, you have indicated, in much greater depth?
A: **Yes sir, and it goes beyond that I think. I think depending on what we had found, if we had found the situation unchanged, I might have felt it necessary to take action outside the immediate brief that we had. You see it might, I suppose, have led to a situation where none of us would have been here today.**

2.15.31 We have already referred to the fact that Miss Kinsley never saw the full Owen Ward

Report or its appendices. Mr Kaye had asked her to look at an incident Report, and she looked at it from the point of view of, "did the hostage policy work?" She said, "the answer I gave him was, "Yes, it did and thank God we had it. But I do not think that I ever saw the full Report". When she was cross-examined by Mr Millar, on behalf of UNISON, he asked her to consider what she would have done as the hypothetical General Manager of Ashworth having received the full Owen Ward Report. She said the first thing was to be honest with the department who you work to about what happened. Then you have to look at the question with your staff. "You have to be prepared to bang heads when necessary, take whatever action you have to there, and I think you have to try to establish a good relationship with them."

> Q: But the essential starting point of the process is, however unattractive a proposition it may be, to put them in the picture so far as the Report is concerned and everything that has gone wrong?
> A: Yes, I think so, warts and all, and it is going to be warts for senior people as well as junior people if I may put it that way.
>
> Q: Everyone who will have a lesson to learn arising out of what has gone on?
> A: Absolutely.

Mrs. Kinsley said she could not understand why, if it happened, Mr Kaye did not make known the full picture disclosed in the Owen Ward Report, because, "from the beginning Charles made it clear, and we all agreed, that we wanted to be much more open and we wanted to get away from the secret hospital sort of label." She could not understand why the HAS team had not been allowed to see the full Report.

The Dissemination of Inquiry Reports

2.15.32 There are two significant differences between a public inquiry and an internal inquiry. The first is that while the task of a public inquiry, even one given statutory powers to obtain evidence, can be made more difficult by lack of cooperation in the production of both oral and documentary evidence, the task of an internal inquiry can be stultified. We have had powers to demand documents from the beginning, but even with those powers we were hampered, as we explained in Part One, by the late service of documents. The second difference relates to publication: whereas the SHSA had no control over the publication of a public inquiry Report, it had full control over the destiny of internal inquiry Reports, and this is clearly seen in connection with the Owen Ward and Swan Reports.

2.15.33 In connection with this, it is instructive to consider how the Blom-Cooper Inquiry was set up. After the broadcast of the television *Cutting Edge* programme, Mr Kaye told us he made an immediate statement after consulting with his then Chairman, that:

> "the Authority would have an inquiry into the information that the television programme put forward, and we started to put together the team to carry out the inquiry and discuss the terms of reference. We discussed these with our liaison at the Department of Health and rather to our surprise – and I think concern – the Department of Health's reaction was that they were not satisfied with the sort of people that we were talking about and they wanted to see the whole Inquiry placed on a different basis altogether. Despite . . . our plea for an inquiry which would be of good value, with respected persons, but could work quickly and get us results we could work with, that was turned down and the Minister decided to have the public statutory inquiry that we are familiar with which made it work on a different dimension altogether . . ."

2.15.34 We have referred to Mr Kaye's view that it is managerially naive to make frank disclosure of all Reports, but it is also naive to ignore the fact that once such a serious situation has entered the public domain it becomes a political necessity to assuage public concern. He continued, "so it was not a question that we did not want the scrutiny, the question was whether the additional publicity and depression of morale that would attend a public inquiry, whether that was beneficial. Our feeling at that stage was that it was not."

> Q: There were some pretty serious allegations that were being made?
> A: Certainly.
>
> Q: And indeed that Report from Sir Louis Blom-Cooper and his team made some pretty trenchant criticisms of the culture and the leadership and what was going on at the Hospital?
> A: Yes and those criticisms, those observations and many of the eighty odd recommendations, were very helpful to the Authority, because it carried an agenda forward – they hurried the work that we had in hand and the agenda that we had set out, and, of course much of it was based in fact on material that we supplied to the Inquiry in terms of what we were about and what our agenda was, so that it was not that the product was unwelcome, it was the damaging nature of the process . . .
>
> Q: But you welcomed the recommendations did you?
> A: Yes. They were very helpful recommendations. Very positive, very helpful and in a number of areas they helped us to move forward more quickly than I think we would have been able to do without the strength of that Inquiry and the force of its recommendations.

2.15.35 Sir Louis himself, has recently cast a shadow over the genuineness of this last observation. Some time after the Inquiry closed he wrote a memorandum dated 20 August 1998, which he sent to the Chairman of this Inquiry. In it he writes, "The [his] Committee of Inquiry's covering letter of the 6 July 1992 to the Secretary of State carries the clear inference that the Special Hospitals were unmanageable; to the extent that they were manageable, the authors of the Report did not envisage that the SHSA would achieve an appropriate level of good management. Whether that was a fair conclusion or not, it is a fact that the SHSA perceived the Report as antipathetic to its [the SHSA's] commendable efforts to effect sound management and administration at Ashworth. The failure on the part of the SHSA after it came into existence from July 1989, to put a stop to the persistent circulation of hateful literature described in Chapter XVIII of the Report, was a stark illustration of the mismanagement of Ashworth Hospital. What is not generally known is that when the SHSA was given sight of the final draft of the Report it was exceedingly displeased with its contents. So much so was its rejection of the general tenor and thrust of the Report about the future management of the Special Hospitals, that the SHSA desired to say publically that it did not accept any of the 90 recommendations. In the result the SHSA was ordered by the Secretary of State to accept the Report and all the recommendations, save for the recommendation to phase-out and ultimately end the practice of seclusion. The SHSA was ordered to deliver to the Department of Health a draft action plan in relation to the recommendations as they applied to Ashworth Hospital. It did so on 1 September 1992. At the same time the SHSA and the Department of Health set up a task force to go into Ashworth Hospital to assist management with implementation of the Action Plan."

2.15.36 This difference between Mr Kaye and Sir Louis about the reaction of the SHSA to the the recommendations was not explored in evidence. If Sir Louis is right, there are perhaps two broad explanations of the SHSA's reaction to the final draft of Blom-Cooper. One is that they were annoyed they could not control the dissemination of the Blom-Cooper Inquiry Report and thereby protect the image they wished to project of a greatly improving service with the SHSA at the helm. The other is that they knew that there was an obvious conflict between implementing Sir Louis' recommendations right across the Hospital and the implementation of Miss Kinsley's recommendations in her security audit. Mr Kaye and others have stressed the degree of political pressure they were subjected to in carrying out the across-hospital implementation of the recommendations. There is no doubt that Mr Kaye and the SHSA were well aware of the different and complex problems involved in the care and management of personality disordered offender patients, but they were given an order by their Ministerial masters.

2.15.37 We are in no doubt that the across-hospital implementation was a ministerially driven fundamental mistake. However, there was an alternative. Mr Kaye and his colleagues could have demonstrated the necessary strength and boldness to say "no". He could have pointed out, either in those early days or later, as evidence from internal inquiry Reports piled up, the difficulties of implementing the Blom-Cooper Report's recommendations across the board. He could have told Ministers that the PDU could not be administered properly, even with the best managerial system backed by wholly adequate professional services. The task at Ashworth, where both the managerial systems and clinical care were simply not good enough, was quite impossible. In 1994 wider circulation of the Owen Ward Report might have made any Minister sit up and take notice.

2.15.38 The validity of this view can be demonstrated by Mr Kaye's own evidence:

> Mr Royce: . . . are you saying that the consequences of that [difficulty of recruiting staff] you really did not have in place there people of adequate calibre to provide a service that should have been provided?
> A: Certainly we did not. We never had in the whole of the SHSA's running of Ashworth Hospital, adequate staff of the right calibre to do the job the Hospital was meant to do. And I think, incidentally, the same is true of the other two Hospitals as well, perhaps to a lesser extent for Broadmoor, but certainly absolutely true of Rampton Hospital as well.
>
> Q: Did you ever suggest that as a consequence of those problems, the Special Hospitals should be closed and some other way forward should be sought?
> A: We were in a position that we were charged with managing and improving the Special Hospitals. That was our job and that was what we set out to do . . . So the problems that we had were well known throughout Whitehall and . . . the forensic community, but we are charged with managing and improving those Hospitals. We cannot say, "What we think you ought to do is close them down",our job was to run them.
>
> Q: You might say, look these places really are impossible to manage. They are too big. Ashworth has major problems, we cannot get adequate medical staff. Really there must be a different way because you are not providing the service that should be provided?

Mr Kaye said "quite right" and went on to say they were working with the Reed Committees concerned with the shape of future services, and the joint committee of the Home Office and Department of Health looking at future services which resulted in the eventual abolition of the SHSA. He did not mention the intended limited life of the SHSA which was drawing to a close, but he said in 1995 they produced their own strategies for the future which were positive and influential. He said he understood from the Chairman of the Commissioning Board, herself, that the views they then expressed were still some of the latest thinking they were using on what the future of the service should be.

2.15.39 Then he said: "So I do not think we neglected our responsibility to say, 'Yes we will manage these services, we will do the best we can with the resources we have, but please do not think that this means that we feel that these three Special Hospitals are the answer to high security care, because the are obviously not. They are very flawed institutions'."

2.15.40 There is no evidence, so far as we can see, that the SHSA ever expressed that view, certainly not until towards the end of its existence. No doubt it should have been said and no doubt it was true. Had it been a view expressed by the SHSA, then disclosure of the full Owen Ward Report would have reinforced that judgment. Even limited disclosure to the Department of Health would have had that effect, but it was not done.

> Mr Royce: . . . apart from informing him [Mr Jewesbury] that there had been a hostage-taking incident, you may have seen from a transcript of his evidence, that he came to the conclusion in relation to Owen that he was seriously under-informed by you as to what had happened on Owen Ward, do you follow?
> A: He had the 19-page version of the Report with the SHSA papers in September.

Mr Kaye had to admit that he had no record of that, and he could not explain why there appeared to be no record of the 19-page Report, or a copy of it, in the Department's documentation.

2.15.41 Mr Kaye was referred to Mr Evans' briefing note and to Mr Jewesbury's evidence that the information on which that briefing note had been based had come from the SHSA. He agreed but added: "if I had been asked personally I would not have produced this sort of description of what had happened or the nature of the remedial action that was in process."

When he was asked if the method of disseminating information adopted with the Owen Ward Report had been adopted with other Reports, he said: "with that particular sequence? I can't think of any others with that particular sequence".

2.15.42 We have referred above to the fact that Mr Kaye said the Owen Ward Report was only one of at least 30 Reports of comparable seriousness. Eventually we received his list and have considered those which we had not already seen.

We disagree. Up to that time, from the point of view of seriousness and number of serious problems, in our judgement, the Owen Ward Report was in a class of its own.

2.15.43 Mr Kaye is an articulate, intelligent man. We have no doubt he realized that the Owen Ward Report was an outstandingly serious Report, the contents of which should have been made known if serious lessons were to be learned. What is more, despite what, in our judgment, was an intention to restrict disclosure of the full Report as much as he could, he could not but agree that its contents should have been made known on a wider basis.

> Mr Royce: . . . what was wrong with the Report . . . first of all what would have been wrong in letting people within the Hospital have a version of the 59-page Report, if necessary suitably amended so that some names were removed or encrypted, anything wrong with that?
> A: No, that is what I expected would happen with the senior managers, so that they would have the full story and the full description . . . I thought that the text of the Report was one that should have been shared with the senior managers as I shared it with authority members and senior staff at SHSA level.

2.15.44 We have no doubt that the senior staff at the Hospital did not have that full story, and we do not believe Mr Kaye intended they should or expected they would.

> Mr Royce: We were told by Mrs Miles that you were anxious that she did not distribute around the Hospital the 19-page version . . . ?
> A: Perhaps we could track it through. Would it be helpful?
>
> Q: Yes.

Mr Kaye then said the original Report was defective by reason of its bulk, but it was no different from a number of Reports that they had and which they would have wanted to share with the key people both above and below so as to bring about change and improvement.

Although previously he had said Mrs Miles produced the 19-page Report, at his request for the Authority, he said: "Janice Miles, of her own volition, prepared a shorter version for the Authority". He had been happy with that because it was "limited to the main issues within the original Report".

2.15.45 As regards the circulation of the 19-page version was concerned, he said:

> "The only reservation I ever had about the circulation of the 19-page Report was the damage that might be done to the Hospital and to the staff and to the morale of the staff by circulating the full 19-page Report across the Hospital because we know from experience that whatever was circulated through the Hospital would become public property. That was the reality. So my advice to Janice, and it was advice, it was not a command, was that when she was distributing or informing the staff at large, the whole of the Hospital, of what had happened on Owen Ward and what was being done to pursue the recommendations, she should exercise caution, because what she was saying was likely to become local news in Merseyside, and that was a note of caution that I had sounded to other managers in other situations."

2.15.46 We pursued the issue of the letter to Mrs Miles urging 'caution':

> Q: Mr Kaye, we can see from your letter of 19 September that you wrote to her and said: "With regard to distributing the synopsis in the Hospital, I would advise caution"?
> A: As far as I was concerned the 59 and the 19-page versions, they were the Report and that was the material that should have been used to talk to key staff and to others who had a legitimate interest in terms of helping them to understand what had happened and helping them to understand how we wanted to change things.
>
> Q: Let me put another scenario to you bluntly. One, you did find the Owen Ward Report, the 59-page Report, horrifying and appalling, two, that in spite of your stated policy of openness you decided to adopt a much more closed policy in relation to the dissemination of the full horror of that Owen Ward Report. Now, you would not accept that would you?
> A: No. No, that was not the case at all.
>
> Q: Right, why not let the 19-page Report be distributed that was, after all, just nine points of significant findings summarised from the main Report and the recommendations. That would have been valuable would it not, as part of the learning process from mistakes, very valuable for that to be distributed to those in the Hospital who needed to know?
> A: That is what I understood was being done.
>
> Q: Was it?
> A: That was my understanding, that the work that was going on within the PDU with the new manager of the PDU, Mr Tarbuck and other key figures were working with both the original Report and the 19-page Report.
>
> Q: There was no pressure from you at all?
> A: No.

2.15.47 It was then pointed out to Mr Kaye that Mrs Miles had said he had requested a shortened version which led to her producing the nine page final Report. He denied ever having made such a request.

In our judgment, the evidence and circumstances point to his having made that request.

2.15.48 Mr Kaye was asked about access by the MHAC to the Owen Ward Report. He agreed it was important that they should not have been deprived of all relevant information, but, inconsistently, he did not agree that the Commission should have had access to the full Report. He said he steered Mr Bingley, or more properly his local Commissioners, to meet Mrs Miles "to get a full briefing from her. My understanding is that, my assumption is that, she would use the same Report she had used with the SHSA, the 19-page version, and that she would have given that in confidence of course". We had access to a bundle of letters passing between Mr Bingley, the Chief Executive of the MHAC, and Mrs Miles. The first from Mrs Miles, dated 22 September 1992, encloses "as promised" the final Report (the nine page version). The second is Mr Bingley's reply, dated 12 October , indicating that it would be helpful to have the Reports prepared by Mr Green (the full Report) and Messers Swinerton and Gardner (concerned with staff involvement). The third, undated but stamped as received on 24 October, is Mrs Miles' response in which she refuses to release those Reports but offers to meet the Commission to discuss the outcome of the investigation.

2.15.49 There is no doubt that Mr Kaye knew that the only Report Mr Bingley was allowed to have was the nine page version. Mrs Miles had written to him on the 26 September concerning the agreed final version "which has now been circulated in the Hospital". She also said she had sent a copy to Mr Bingley. Mr Kaye also agreed that at a later meeting between the SHSA and the Commission on 2 November, access to the full Report was again refused.

> Mr Royce: Mr Kaye, surely they could be trusted, could they not? They are perfectly respectable, responsible, or was it because you thought that really the Owen Ward Report was so appalling you did not want them to see it?
> A: No, you see I have tried to demonstrate to you that I do not think the Owen Report is too appalling. It is serious but it is one of a number of Reports of the same value if you like . . .
>
> Q: . . . what I am pressing you on is this: what good reason was there for depriving them of the full picture into what had taken place on Owen in the form of the 59-page Report?
> A: Because my understanding was that they had had the full picture from Mrs Miles using the 19-page version, probably using the 19-page version at a Hospital briefing.
>
> Q: If they had had the full picture, why not let them have the Report?
> A: Precisely because it was not necessary . . .
>
> Q: But you refused to let them have the Swan Report did you not?
> A: Yes, certainly I did.
>
> Q: Why?
> A: Do you want to talk about the Swan Report?

Dissemination of the Swan Report

2.15.50 Mr Kaye then explained his reasons for withholding the Swan Report. In the fragile state of the Hospital after the Blom-Cooper Inquiry, when the Task Force was engaged in the process of reshaping the Hospital, the SHSA was beginning to get disquieting Reports about the women's service. They therefore set up the inquiry. When they received the Report they were pleased with its thoroughness but devastated "by their opening salvo when they said that they thought the only thing to do was to close the service down". The SHSA thought that was neither practicable nor sensible, and after lengthy discussion between himself, the Chairman and the Authority members, Mr Kaye continued:

> "we saw the Report as being in part helpful, in part destructive and the reason why we did not publish it to anyone, was that we did not want to broadcast in the Hospital

amongst the very staff that we were trying to remotivate and galvanise into action, a recommendation that their work should be stopped altogether".

The Chairman: Is it part of your case, part of your thesis, that the Board, your SHSA Board, were fully aware and agreed?
A: Yes certainly. As I say, Chairman, it was after considerable discussion.

Q: That is why I was asking the point.
A: Yes, very much so. So that we were in a position where we felt the only way to change things, to improve things, was not to publish or circulate beyond a very, very, limited way the full text, but to use the constructive element in it, the very detailed agenda for change and improvement, and feed that into the service, and that is what we did. And that is the reason why we did not want to share the Swan Report with anybody."

2.15.51 This argument is implausible and unconvincing when considered in the light of the refusal to let Dr Williams and his team see the Swan and Owen Ward Reports. As Dr Williams pointed out, his team was not carrying out an inquiry, they were conducting a review of the Hospital two years on from Blom-Cooper. If it was true that the Reports were concealed simply so that management and staff could bring about the essential changes and improvements needed without subjecting the Hospital to the trauma of adverse publicity and comment, why not test how far those hoped-for improvements had been made by letting Dr Williams and his team have the Swan and Owen Reports? The reality was that the SHSA could control the circulation of internal Reports; the HAS Review by contrast was going to be published and could not be controlled so easily. So the lid had to be kept firmly shut on inconvenient evidence.

2.15.52 Dr Williams, having seen the Swan Report when he gave evidence, said that he and his team had seen some sensible, albeit embryonic, changes being made. Ms Hilton, the psychologist member of his team, had no longer felt that closure was the number one option.

2.15.53 It is quite clear that Dr Williams and his team would have been fair to the Hospital in discussing the women's services. The Swan Report was an important Report. The decision about the location of women's services was one of major policy. To hide the Report was a serious misjudgment.

2.15.54 By and large Dr Williams and his team presented a fair review bearing in mind they were deprived of vital information. The only criticism we would make is that in striving to be constructive they were much too diplomatic.

2.15.55 In his evidence, Mr Kaye did not even try to defend the failure to let Dr Williams have access to the Owen Ward Report.

Mr Royce: Why not let them see the Owen Report?
A: I made no restriction at all on their seeing the Owen Report, and as far as I knew, until these proceedings they had the Owen Report. I was not aware that they had not had it.

Q: You had no idea at all?
A: No.

Q: That they were refused access to that?
A: No.

Q: This may be an area where we can agree. Do you take the view that they should have had the 57 page Owen Report?
A: And all the appendices, yes.

Q: And all the appendices. That was of fundamental importance to enable them properly to consider the situation and the history of Owen, would you agree?
A: I think it was a very significant Report that should have been in the papers that they had . . .

Q: So Mrs Miles' refusal to let them see the Owen Report you would condemn?
A: They certainly should have seen the Report, and if she had said they could not have it, I would have been surprised, and, if I had been asked, I would have said certainly they should have it.

Q: What she said in relation to this was was that she did not disclose it to them because it had been firmly pressed into her mind by you that she should not disclose it. That was her evidence. Now do you say that is wrong because, as far as you were concerned they could have it?
A: Yes.

2.15.56 We believe that Mr Kaye made a conscious decision to restrict the disclosure of the full Owen Ward Report. The decision not to release the full Report to the HAS team was Mr Kaye's responsibility. We agree that he had firmly impressed in Mrs Miles' mind that she should not disclose it.

Liaison with the Department of Health

2.15.57 Mr Jewesbury told us he did not believe he was ever sent the 59-page Owen Ward Report and its appendices, and from what he had read since about its contents, he could not possibly have forgotten receiving such a document if he had done so. Mr Royce referred him to passages in the Report: "it paints in just this brief journey through that summary a highly serious situation does it not?" He replied: "yes, I agree." His notes of the monthly meetings he had with Mr Kaye did not contain references to the Owen Ward incident. He did not believe that Mr Kaye had ever informed him that the situation on Owen Ward had been extremely serious, although he had been aware that there had been a hostage-taking incident. He was aware that there was a range of problems across the Hospital and that following the Blom-Cooper Report an action plan had been drawn up to address them. But, "as it seems to me now, there were problems in the Personality Disorder Unit which were really of a different order to the generality of things that were going on in the rest of the Hospital."

2.15.58 Concerning the HAS Review Mr Jewesbury was asked: "Do you agree that if the HAS Report was to have real validity it was very important for them to be informed of the real extent of the problems that there had been and supplied with the full and proper documentation to enable them to get beneath the surface of the problems?" He replied, "I would say that is axiomatic if you are talking about a review of this type". He considered Dr Williams ought not to have had to do battle to get material and that there should have been open disclosure of those matters from which they could and should have made a judgment.

Q: All that was allowed to happen was that he (Dr Williams) was allowed to discuss with a member of his team her recollection of Swan because she had been a member of the Swan Report team?
A: Yes.

Q: Now can you conceive as someone endeavouring to produce a policy of openness, that that could ever be considered an appropriate way ahead?
A: No, I cannot see any justification for it.

Q: No justification. Can we add this, there can be no justification for that course of action?
A: All right.

Q: Would that be fair?
A: Yes, I agree with that.

2.15.59 He went on to say that you could infer from Mr Kaye's letter to him concerning Dr Williams' appointment that it was regarded as highly desirable to have a HAS review that was generally supportive of the Hospital. He agreed that there should have been no need for a dialogue about releasing the Swan Report. It should have been released.

Q: But with hindsight, Mr Jewesbury, it must make you a little uncomfortable about what was going on, is that fair?
A: Yes. You know it is difficult to immediately think yourself back to things that were going on more than three years ago. Yes, you have raised an extremely valid question about what we were doing. I still think that I would not want to jump to the conclusion that on the basis of what I knew that I should immediately have started issuing edicts to Charles Kaye.

2.15.60 He thought he could have issued edicts because of his relationship to the Secretary of State and other Ministers, who needed to be accurately briefed. He was asked if anyone did report to the Minister on the Owen Ward Report. The internal SHSA Report which was copied to him on the day of the incident was forwarded by Mrs Leonard to the Minister's office, and after the *Sunday Express* article, Mr Evan's note was sent to the Minister's office. He said: "as far as I know, those were the only two things about the Owen Ward Report which did go to the Ministers", and he added that Mike Evans could only have got that information from the SHSA.

2.15.61 Mr Jewesbury became visibly uncomfortable when he was asked about the accuracy of the information in Mr Evan's note, which was a briefing note to the Minister. When Mr Royce asked him whether the note appeared to be a travesty of the real position, he said he thought 'travesty' did not reflect the real position. The Chairman then asked: "It is a very uncomfortable thing to live with is it not?", and he replied: "yes".

Mr Royce: The impression that it gives, or what it purports to say is: "Yes, had a few problems with illicit drug taking, but the other allegations were not well founded?
A: Yes.

Q: Even you, having had a look at the summary of the Owen Ward Report, that is a long way from being accurate is it not?
A: Yes. We knew that Ashworth was a troubled place. I think the picture that this note gives you is that these troubles include this particular bit of the Hospital but there is nothing to suggest that things are very much worse there or that there are problems of a different order.

The Chairman: The Report suggests it was very much worse?
A: Absolutely, yes, I accept that.

Q: If that had been published, it would have been terribly embarrassing would it not after Ashworth 1?
A: Embarrassing to whom?

Q: To the SHSA and the Hospital?
A: I think it clearly would have been, yes.

Q: If in fact there had been SD [Daggett] around at that time, as there was last year, who went out of the Hospital, absconded and blew the whistle, and produced 90 per cent of the material in the Owen Report, which that Report would have found to be true, as indeed in the Keown Report with regard to SD, this inquiry would have been held probably in 1994 would it not?
A: Yes, that thought has crossed my mind.

Q: In other words, that sort of activity, of failing to put this into a more public type of domain, or, if not doing that, at least acting upon it, has resulted in a delay in the investigation of very serious allegations?
A: Yes.

Q: Would you accept that. That is the picture it looks like?
A: I think it is extremely unfortunate that we were not more fully in the picture than we were.

Q: And the probability is that if you had been, and people thought it necessary to make these investigations, as opposed to having it forced upon them by publicity, they would have been made in 1994 and not 1997?
A: Yes.

Q: Do you accept that?
A: Sorry, you say, "they would have been made"

Q: These investigations would have been made in 1994, not 1997. They cover the self-same ground?
A: Yes, I agree.

Conclusions

2.15.62 We have examined the evidence surrounding the way in which the Owen Ward Report was handled in depth, partly because it became obvious to us that we would have to consider whether the then Minister was given inaccurate information. It is an important question, because it is essential that Ministers are properly and fully briefed. They are answerable to Parliament. This Inquiry was, at least, in part prompted by the fact that on the information he was given, Mr Ray Rowden, then the Director of the Commissioning Board, had produced an inaccurate briefing note for the Secretary of State which later had to be rectified.

2.15.63 It has not been possible to trace the actual source within the SHSA of the information given to Mr Evans, but we have concluded that it came from the SHSA, and as a result the then Minister was given wholly inaccurate information concerning the Owen Ward Report.

2.15.64 We have also concluded that Mr Kaye tried to belittle the relative importance of the Owen Ward Report in order to justify its non-disclosure. Mr Jewesbury was also asked about other Reports and he had certainly seen a number of them. He said: "Casting my mind back over those, a number of them, and certainly the BM (Rampton) and OB (Broadmoor) cases, those Reports revealed things which were quite seriously wrong. I would not say that what they revealed was quite of the order of what we now see to have been the Owen Report."

2.15.65 The Owen Ward incident was as we have seen the culmination of a series of incidents, all serious in themselves, on a ward that had been allowed to get out of control. We have heard already of the highly fragile state of the PDU in the summer of 1994 in the wake of the Owen Ward incident. We now look at what was being done about the situation.

2.16.0 Management Matters

2.16.1 From the setting up of the PDU onwards, there has been a continuing struggle to address the problems outlined above.

2.16.2 The main management body within the Unit was the PDU Management Team (PDUMT). All the Ward Managers were members, as were representatives of the professions. Mr Tarbuck also set up another body, the Operational Management Group (OMG) of the PDU, comprising the Ward Managers, the Senior Clinical Nurse and the Security Liaison

Officer. He introduced the post of Operations Manager and the post of Senior Clinical Nurse to give support to Ward Managers and other nurses on the clinical side.

2.16.3 Mr Tarbuck told us that local PDU ward policies and procedures would come up through the OMG to the PDUMT and, if necessary, higher up the chain. The Chair of PDUMT (the Clinical Manager) was a member of the Hospital Management Group (HMG, which became for a time the Hospital Management Team). The Chair of HMG (Mr Green) was also the Executive Director who liaised with the PDU. Mr Tarbuck felt that communications were effective. But, as is so often seen with complex managerial structures, the longer the chain is, the more links there are which might break; management problems are rarely, if ever, solved by making the organizational structures more complex.

2.16.4 Mr Tarbuck's declared aim was to get to a point where the Unit could offer a menu of therapies to patients which would provide the opportunity to move through the Hospital. He noted that this could not be done unless the system was freed up by moving on many of the patients from Lawrence Ward. No doubt it was, and still is, difficult to move personality disordered offender patients out of the high security system into medium secure units, because of the chronic shortage of long term medium secure facilities, but that was, and is, not the only problem. The wards within the PDU were never effectively structured, and Lawrence Ward itself is a good example of that failure. A number of its patients should never have been placed in its relaxed security environment.

2.16.5 Mr Tarbuck did try to "steady the ship" by, for example, establishing the new Security Liaison Role and ensuring regular searching took place (although he accepted that the quality was variable, which itself significantly over-states the quality of searching); introducing a new operational policy and the post of Operational Manager; establishing a new training programme for staff; devising core competencies for staff (some 140 out of 172 staff attended this course, despite the difficulties involved in covering their absence); reducing sickness levels and, so he said, the frequency of serious incidents; developing the Care Programme Approach and multi-disciplinary working on the Unit; and recruiting extra clinical staff. Four of the six wards had highly experienced Ward Managers. The Unit had, in Mr Tarbuck's over-optimistic view, a clearly articulated vision for the future. He considered the weaknesses of the PDU and possible methods for tackling them had been identified in the Owen Ward Report. The problem, as usual, lay in ineffectual tackling of the fundamental causes of the problems.

2.16.6 Within weeks Mr Tarbuck's successor, Mr Murphy, was identifying other weaknesses which had remained unnoticed. Mr Tarbuck's stewardship of the Unit was therefore flawed, but when basic structures and systems are wrong, it is extremely difficult to make even limited progress.

2.16.7 In March 1996 Mr Tarbuck gave a presentation to the Directors at the Hospital Management Group on the PDU. This presentation followed the usual pattern, outlining what were said to be positive achievements of the PDU but also some of the problems. He felt he had given a balanced picture although he accepted that things had become lax and it was a slow process putting security back in its rightful place. He indicated that he had flagged up, inter alia, staffing problems; pressure on beds; training needs of staff; and the problems posed by lack of storage space for patients' possessions.

One thing he did not flag up was Lawrence Ward.

2.16.8 The problems within the PDU were not limited to Owen and Lawrence Wards. The next two Reports to which we refer concern similar problems on Macaulay and Shelley Wards.

2.17.0 The Braund Report

2.17.1 The Inquiry Into Intra-Extra Hospital Activities of Patient S Braund is dated December 1995. Concerned as it is with events which took place in 1995, the last full year of the existence of the SHSA, it heralded the new year and graphically describes the state of the PDU at that time. The report team consisted of Mr Tony Moran, Ward Manager of Owen Ward, Mr Ian Paterson, Liaison Manager in the Security Department, and Mr Joe Day, the Security Lision Officer for the PDU. The Report begins with a comment which is fully justified:

> *"This Report details the activities of patient S. Braund Ruskin Ward, formerly Macaulay Ward, highlighting the way patients can with apparent ease bypass hospital rules/regulations, which if made public would draw adverse publicity to Ashworth Hospital."*

It is an incredible story.

The Embossing Machine

2.17.2 On 1 November 1995 the Ashworth mail room intercepted a parcel addressed to Muller Technologies Limited, S Braund, Macaulay, Ashworth. It was examined, and contained an embossing machine for Muller Technologies Limited, a machine typically used for embossing share certificates. Mr Braund's history already indicated the possibility of his being involved in fraudulent activities. The item was withdrawn and Mr Braund denied all knowledge of Muller Technologies Ltd. Following this, with the agreement of his consultant psychiatrist (Dr Mogallapu) the Ward invoked the Hospital's policy on inspection of mail in and out of Hospital in so far as Mr Braund was concerned.

2.17.3 Within days it became apparent that Mr Braund's nefarious activities were not confined to the embossing machine, and the Macaulay Ward PCT agreed to his computer disks being checked, in an effort to establish the depth of abuse. A total of 139 disks were removed from Mr Braund's room, eight of these contained information which indicated that a number of clinical and security concerns would require extensive investigation. Due to the serious nature of the disks' contents, it was decided to move Mr Braund to Ruskin Ward, so as to enable a complete room search to be carried out, and a re-appraisal of his clinical suitability for a parole ward.

2.17.4 The Initial search of the room and its contents revealed further information which formed the basis of the Report. The report team observed:

> **"The trail we have uncovered has led the Inquiry team to an Eldorado of security breaches, 'scams', money making ventures and breaches of the Hospital systems on a scale not encountered by the members of the team before."**

In what follows we quote from the Report and comment where appropriate.

Mail

2.17.5 Mr Braund was able to 'exploit' the Hospital's security measures on the inspection of mail. The team note:

> "The Hospital's revised mail procedure of 21 February 1994 clearly stated the role of the Patient care team is central in controlling any of their patients' access to mail items. It is the responsibility of clinical teams to decide those patients whose mail needs to be inspected – the reason for inspecting patients mail must be clearly documented in the clinical notes."

The truth was that there was no need to exploit measures which were not being enforced. Whether any mail was inspected depended on the whim of individual clinical teams and not on the existence of a hospital rule.

2.17.6 They continue:

> "Clearly in Mr Braund's case the PCTM failed to exercise the necessary controls in preventing his abuse of the system. The Inquiry team was unclear why this should be, as evidence presented to them on a number of occasions by nursing staff expressed concern at Mr Braund's activities . . ."

What the three members of the investigating team knew, or certainly ought to have known, was that it was the rule rather than the exception not to apply such controls.

It is then said that Mr Braund utilised the mail system to direct items and instruct payments to his parents' address in Muller Road, Bristol.

Information System – Computers

2.17.7 The team comment:

> "The advances in technology and the patient's access to sophisticated computer systems had led in this case to Mr Braund being able to produce documents and letters of business quality in the pursuance of fraudulent activity."
>
> "His interest in obtaining a mobile phone and modem facility further heightened our concerns in the patient's ability to access worldwide systems . . . "
>
> "Mr Braund admitted theft of a hard disk from the Patients' Day magazine (his work place), for which he was suspended for two weeks. His apparent unlimited access to high-tech equipment has led the inquiry team to believe that the patient has produced material in this department, which has aided his nefarious activities. We consider measures must be put in place to contain the misuse of computers throughout the Hospital demonstrated by Mr Braund. An effective policy and procedures for patient access requires completion."

Searching

2.17.8 A familiar story emerges:

> "Because of the volume of material Mr Braund was able to accumulate in his room, it was obvious very little checking if any, was actioned, when items were received at ward level. It also follows that room searches of any significance could not have been carried out."

This is nothing new. Nearly every Report deals with the absence of proper room searching. The full Owen Ward Report says it was impossible to search because of the amount of equipment and belongings in the patients room. Room searches were a joke, and known to be so by both patients and staff.

2.17.9 Appendix 1 to the Report is a collection of extracts from PCT Meetings from 6 April 1995 until 23 November 1995. They illustrate a lack of understanding of searching procedures and in particular the conflict seen to exist between searching and so called "patient rights". There was clearly no policy of enforcing searching.

Here are two examples. The extract for the meeting of 27 April 1995 indicates that the nursing staff were concerned about Mr Braund's general attitude and lack of compliance with ward policies. He was receiving copious amounts of wrongly addressed mail, and when questioned about it, refused to discuss it. It was said he objected to having his room searched, and the entry raises this question: "What is the position regarding the screening of his computer disks?"

In the entry for the meeting of 11 June 1995, it is said Mr Braund was asked to comply with a room/locker search as per hospital policy. He was unhappy, and believed the searching procedure was illegal and did not consent. He implied he would report it to his legal adviser. He would not prevent a search but would not be present. Because of the vast amount of expensive equipment in his room the staff were reluctant to search it in his absence in case he made spurious allegations of theft. Eventually he consented and the search was negative. "Ward manager to seek guidance from Clinical Manager (Tarbuck) regarding searches." In their defence staff argued that Macaulay was a parole ward, and therefore there had to be an element of trust between patients and staff. In addition, whilst staffing levels should have been four per shift in the day and three at night, regularly there were only three in the day which prevented room searching. The team quite rightly note that this might mitigate, but cannot excuse, meeting standards.

Illegal Substances

2.17.10 Following Mr Braund's removal to Ruskin ward, 41 Temazepam 20 mg capsules were found in a soap powder box in his room on Macaulay Ward. It had not been prescribed in the Hospital for some years and was in a decaying state. At interview with Mr Day, Mr Braund said a member of staff had given them to him when he was on Forster Ward.

This shows that searching of his rooms, in the past, on various wards, if any had taken place, did not uncover his possession of drugs.

Patient Care Team

2.17.11 The Report notes that Mr Braund had been a source of concern for a number of years regarding money-making activities. On Forster and Owen Wards he was involved in catalogue frauds using variations of his name and hospital address to obtain goods and not pay for them.

Surely he must have been an obvious candidate for regular mail checks. And why was he given parole status or why had it not been taken away from him?

2.17.12 Prior to the hostage-taking incident on Owen Ward in June 1994, Mr Braund had been moved to Macaulay Ward where he continued his catalogue activities. Security Liaison brought this to the PCT's notice in May 1995, but the PCT accepted his explanation that his father was paying all the bills. The action the PCT took was to say that all future mail was to be correctly addressed, and all transactions were to be processed by the PCT.

So this is yet another case of the PCT deciding something and then forgetting or failing to enforce it. In the light of the next part of the Report the PCT clearly ignored their responsibilities.

2.17.13 On a number of occasions staff brought their concerns about Mr Braund's activities to the notice of the PCT and minuted their concern. Yet no action was taken. The Report says perhaps this was because the medical staff required absolute proof of wrong doing before acting. This was not all:

> *"A compounding factor was the view of a senior member of the PCT who considered it was acceptable for a patient to run a company from the Hospital. From various comments made, it was obvious that the contents of the General Manager's letter dated 23 March 1995 concerning patients' activities was not known . . ."*

This refers to a letter by Mrs Miles, addressed to the Hospital in general forbidding trading by patients. We return to this much ignored directive in Part Three.

2.17.14 The team continue, with understatement:

> "The aforementioned factors would indicate the PCT not in harmony with the needs of all the ward, it lacked cohesion, direction and a sense of purpose."

They recommend:

> *"To avoid inaction at future PCTMs, we propose the Security Liaison persons have available to them the options to pursue any matter having a possible damaging aspect to it, which may reflect negatively on Ward/Hospital, and action such findings until a satisfactory outcome is known – the PCT would be kept appraised of proceedings"*

Of course this was never done. What was required was a Security Intelligence Unit with overall power to bring PCTs into line in so far as basic and essential security rules are concerned. In so far as we can see, a thread which runs through all the internal inquiry Reports is that PCTs failed in their duties and ignored their responsibilities to both staff and patients. A single security liaison person is one thing; a properly organised security intelligence unit with proper and sufficient seniority and clout is another.

Staff

2.17.15 The team record that Mr Braund wrote to a female nursing assistant suggesting a non- professional relationship. The letter concerned was a photocopy and it is not clear whether the original was ever sent. In one of his letters to a fellow patient SC dated 18–27 August 1995, he talks about showing 'her' a ring, not for the purpose of marriage, just 'simple friendship'. The Report goes on to say Mr Braund wrote that she made a commitment to him on Forster Ward. (The fellow patient gave the ring to the Inquiry team claiming to be holding it for Mr Braund because of the attention he was getting from the Security Department.) He held her cheque book for a fortnight, and she allegedly had agreed to give him all her possessions.

2.17.16 The Report noted that Mr Braund mentioned the nursing assistant many times in his correspondence. No evidence was found to suggest she returned his feelings; she did, however, admit receiving two telephone calls from Mr Braund when she was on night duty on Blake Ward during the night 24/25 December 1995. She would not elaborate. The Report said she ought to make it plain to him that no non-professional relationship existed between them. If she was unable or unwilling to do so then her position needed to be reviewed urgently.

Business

2.17.17 Matters referred to under this heading show an incredible situation which was allowed to go on.

2.17.18 Mr Braund set up 'Ventures Natrix Ltd' on 25 September 1992, to buy goods from outside – cigarettes, food, sweets and sell them to patients undercutting the patients' shop. He set up Muller Technologies Ltd on 25 September 1995. This company was apparently set up for the purpose of selling computers and computer accessories.

2.17.19 Mr Braund used a National Westminster Bank Credit Card to buy a hotel directory from 'Holiday World International' for £19.50. That was believed to be the basis of the 'Dream Breaks Holidays' scheme he set up.

Catalogue Fraud

2.17.20 The Inquiry team believed this to have been his most profitable activity "over the years". They gave "some samples"to give the flavour.

> Between 1 January 1995 and 2 April 1995, Mr Braund received 48 wrongly addressed pieces of mail.
>
> Between 30 January 1995 and 31 March 1995, he was involved in 30 inter-patient transactions.

Between 17 January 1995 and 17 March 1995, he transferred £750 from his hospital account to an outside bank. During this time his income in hospital payments was £20 per week (£180 in total) so £570 was generated by other means.

A list of demands for payment from three catalogue companies is given amounting in total to £3,267.59.

2.17.21 The team comment:

"We think this may only be a small amount of the total sum owed, as we continue to monitor his mail the true amount will eventually be known."

Inter-Patient Transfer Forms

2.17.22 The team found photocopies of Ashworth's inter-patient transfer forms, used to process financial transactions between patients. They were complete with the Ward Manager's signature and the ward stamp. No evidence was found to prove he had activated the scam, but the forms could be used to transfer money from other patients' hospital accounts to his own. We will see that a similar scam was in operation on Lawrence Ward.

Correspondence

2.17.23 The Report referred to the types of correspondence found. Some mention various business ventures, and ideas for scams; two mention escape plans; one is a copy of a letter to the nursing assistant in endearing terms. A copy of a letter dated 27 September 1995 discusses the possibility of setting up an off-shore company, obtaining a passport, then, on a day out, skipping the country (which, of course, is what Stephen Daggett was later to do).

Pornographic Contact Magazines

2.17.24 Mr Braund placed a personal advertisement in *Desire* November 1995. The Security Department, *via* the mail room, intercepted one reply. Letters to various females indicate he placed advertisements on more than one occasion. In one letter he claims to have contacted several hundred women. The Report says:

"the main theme of the letters is domination and submission of women to the extreme. He is at times quite graphic, as are the replies"

"Of great concern to us was a letter to Dawn dated 13 May 1992, in which he described the poses he wished her to be photographed in – photographs of these positions were found in his room".

"He later in his letter describes more extreme poses/positions he wishes her to be photographed in. We have no evidence that the request was fulfilled, nevertheless we *must consider the possibility he has acquired such pictures of this female and others."*

Scams

2.17.25 The Report goes on to refer to Mr Braund's description of how to set up scams of various sorts, including setting up companies and creating false identity documents.

Financial Activities

2.17.26 Apparently Mr Braund had three bank accounts; two with the National Westminster Bank – one in Maghull and the other in Liverpool – and the third with the TSB in Maghull.

2.17.27 It was recommended that since all Mr Braund's share dealings had been done via a telephone, the installation of a monitored and controlled telephone system was required, and that money being paid into outside bank accounts from a hospital account should be checked on a random basis by security and finance departments.

This is yet another Report referring to the lack of any telephone monitoring or control.

Recommendations

2.17.28 The team noted that:

> "Investigations into the contents of Mr Braund's computer disks revealed that he was in the process of attempting to upgrade his machine with a modem. The facility would allow him to access the Internet etc with a mobile phone. If successful he would have had access to world-wide information systems."

2.17.29 The Report recommended setting up a working group to review patient access and use of computer equipment. They also recommended that patients' disks should be scanned on a random basis, and, if they were password protected and permission to view them was refused, then they should be confiscated.

As will be seen from still later Reports, nothing effective was done save that a Report was compiled concerning computers. We comment on this in Part Three.

2.17.30 The team found that room searches on Macaulay were not taking place often and when they were done, they were cursory at the best. It was recommended that:

> *A dedicated team be set up to carry out the delicate process of searching patients' rooms in the PDU (and possibly hospital wide);*
>
> *Implementation as a matter of urgency of the limit to items in patient's side rooms.*

2.17.31 Interestingly the Report also recommended:

> *1. Where patient activities were drawn to the attention of PCTs and not satisfactorily dealt with, Security Liaison should be permitted to pursue such matters "without hindrance".*
>
> *2. The Security department should provide a three monthly intelligence report to the Directors of the clinical units on patient activities which may be damaging to the Hospital.*

2.17.32 The team concluded that there were still avenues which they had not explored, and because it had been so easy for Mr Braund to exploit the 'system', they did not believe his was an isolated case. They commented:

> "The conundrum this case presents is one of patients' rights versus the rights of patients in a secure environment. The concept of a patient infers compliance – cooperation – and acceptance of illness. Unfortunately within the forensic setting these elements are not accepted as a pre-requisite for care and treatment by the client group. Indeed they may be seen as a weakness to be exploited as demonstrated in this case".
>
> "The team believes the issues raised within the Report require actions which will result in a positive review of the concept of the "patient's status within a secure environment"."

That review had to wait until our Inquiry was commissioned.

2.18.0 The Finney Report: Investigation into Documents found in Patient Stephen Finney's belongings

2.18.1 This Report takes the story of Ashworth Hospital into 1996. The investigation was carried out by Carol Young, the Acting Operations Manager of the Special Needs Directorate, and Ian Paterson the Liaison Manager of the Security Department.

The Documents

2.18.2 On the 7 June 1996 a search of Stephen Finney's room on Shelley Ward was carried out following his emergency admission to Fazakerley Hospital A & E Department, due to a suspected overdose. Ten yellow tablets and two blue tablets, similar to Diazepam, were found there in a cellophane package. Following his return he attacked a member of Shelley Ward staff with a knife causing neck lacerations. He was secluded and a further search of his room was made. This time ten co-proxamol tablets, a home made lighter and two polythene wraps, each an inch square, were found Tests showed the wraps had been in contact with cannabis. Documents were also found in a brief case and two biscuit tins.

2.18.3 The documents contained information of both a clinical and security nature relating to staff and patients. They consisted of:

a) a Security Report concerning an incident on Shelley Ward on 6 September 1995 when a member of staff was attacked by a patient;

b) a Report into patient MR's complaint about nursing staff on Ruskin Ward being asleep when he was self-harming;

c) a plan of the integration of patient JS into the PDU;

d) an e-mail from Macaulay Ward regarding access of community ward patients to Shelley Ward;

e) handwritten case conference notes on Mr Finney himself;

f) copies of three extracts of Shelley Ward Day Reports; and

g) a complaint by patient MR involving loss of property.

2.18.4 On 6 June 1996, Mr Tom Catterall, Ward Manager of Shelley, had a computer floppy disk go missing from his ward office. He reported this on 7 June 1996. He wrote saying he had last seen the disk on his desk the day before. He did not think there was anything of concern on it, save one Report he had made regarding a complaint by Patient MR, which did not contain any sensitive material. However, the inquiry team thought that a), b) and g) above may have been on the disk. They also thought Mr Finney had somehow acquired the other material from some source(s) over a period of time, which pointed to his having some means of getting access to sensitive material. Mr Finney had in the past used a listening device to get information at ward level. **It will be recalled that during the Owen Ward search, a listening device was found there.**

2.18.5 The missing computer disk was never recovered. The team believed the Report about the razor incident on Shelley ward was on the floppy disk. It is not surprising the team wondered if Mr Finney had been influenced by the December 1995 razor incident Report because he had attempted to make a similar attack in Shelley Ward. Two Reports of that incident on December 6th 1995 had been found in Mr Finney's possessions. So further copies might exist.

2.18.6 The team was concerned that knowledge of the contents of the investigation of MR's allegations concerning staff being asleep on 17 December 1995, could be embarrassing if made public. They were also concerned about Mr Finney's possession of the extracts from the day Reports, because they believed a full enquiry was held in 1995 into how patients had come by the information it contained.

2.18.7 The extracts concerned included a reference to patients colluding to cause a disturbance. The first is dated 15 December 1994:

"A patient ND hinted there was going to be a major incident on Owen or Lawrence Ward which would make Owen Ward look like a tea party. The details are not

> known as yet but 5 patients are to take on staff. The patients involved are S. Finney, JT, MM, PE and ND."

The next one is dated 16 December 1994:

> "ND seen by L. Williams this AM (Friday). Divulged information re yesterday's report. Spoke further about planned incident for tomorrow (Saturday)".
>
> "Stated at least three staff would be injured or a possible hostage situation would occur. Failing this the ward would be set alight. The third alternative would be to break away from a movement and attempt to enter [and cause] damage on other wards."

The third one is dated 18 December 1994:

> "N discussed briefly events of last few days, quite evasive and guarded about his role in these events."

2.18.8 The inquiry team speculated that there could have been staff involvement in Mr Finney obtaining information, as there could have been in his obtaining the drugs. Diazepam and Co-proxamol tablets were prescribed medication at the Hospital, and while it was possible for a patient to secrete individual tablets, the 19 co-proxamol tablets were still contained in their 'blister pack'. This might indicate staff involvement in patient drug abuse.

2.18.9 *The team was concerned that the range of materials found in Mr Finney's possessions indicated availability of access to computers (patients and staff), offices and information sent to the ward or information generated at ward level.*

2.18.10 They were also concerned about "staff competency regarding awareness of boundaries and consequences relating to the receiving/giving of information to patients and staff." So many staff had access to computers that a determined patient could easily get access to computer-generated information. The team concluded that the disk was mislaid or deliberately removed from the office.

2.18.11 Mr Finney had no personal computer so he must have been assisted in printing material on the disk. A number of patients had computers and the facility to print. It was possible staff were involved and that might need further investigation, but the team believed a degree of staff collusion must have taken place.

Recommendations

2.18.12 The team made several recommendations:

(i) there should be a major review of hospital-wide communications by computer;

(ii) structural changes of Ward offices should be considered;

(iii) consideration should be given to using a room to store and access confidential material with NO patient access;

(iv) Reports of a confidential nature should not be produced at ward level;

(v) Mr Finney should be moved, as he had probably systematically managed to influence staff into colluding with him.

2.18.13 It is instructive to examine the **Report into the Razor Incident, 6 December 1995** on Shelley Ward, as it demonstrates some of the problems that particular ward laboured under from being both an assessment and high dependency ward. The incident itself was an attack by Patient DM, who was in Shelley Ward for assessment under Section 38 of the Mental Health Act 1983, on Acting Team Leader S. Messenger with a Bic razor. On 6 December DM. approached Nurse Nowell and asked if he could use his razor. After consulting Mr Messenger it was decided he could have it, and he went to his room to shave. Mr Nowell accompanied him, but stayed in the night station because no other patients were in the vicinity. DM came back along the corridor and Mr Nowell asked him for his razor. DM just walked past him. He asked him again as DM was walking towards the office. He followed him into the office, but before he could shout to Mr Messenger, DM walked behind Mr Messenger and used the razor on him. He was then restrained and placed in seclusion.

2.18.14 In his Report the Ward Manager Mr Tom Catterall, said he was concerned that at times the unhealthy mix of patients on the Ward confused staff decision making. While in possession of a razor a patient should be under continual observation. When Patient DM refused to hand the razor over, the alert was not given quickly enough, possibly because Nurse Nowell felt Patient DM was returning it to the office, which is what patients with parole status were allowed to do.

2.18.15 Mr Catterall recommended that the use of wet razors should cease; door swings should be reversed in interview rooms, offices, staff room and the clinic **(a repeat of an Owen Ward Report recommendation)**; and alarms should be installed in the main office, the staff cloak room and the kitchen. He believed the confused role of Shelley should receive immediate attention by the Hospital team; no patient should be admitted with a diagnosis of personality disorder until completion of the Wordsworth initiative.

2.18.16 In evidence, Mr Catterall expanded on the problems on Shelley Ward. Because the Ward functioned as both the admission and high dependency ward for the PDU, there was an unsafe patient mix which undermined proper assessment. The razor incident revealed the dangers of having to deal with a settled patient one minute and a highly disturbed man the next. Despite the dangers the ward was staffed as a low dependency ward, with only 21 staff for up to 18 patients. The staff had, generally, been on the Ward when its use changed, and did not want to work on the ward.

2.18.17 The fact that the PDU only had six large wards made moving disruptive patients out very difficult; thus following the incident referred to in paragraph **2.18.7** above when five patients were found to be colluding to cause a disturbance, two were moved but there was no facility to move the other three, who stayed on the ward. Mr Catterall said the staff were firefighting the whole time; unsurprisingly the Ward was not a popular one. Staff were unable to deliver the amount of care and therapy they would have liked on Shelley Ward; much hope was pinned on the Wordsworth Project, a new facility on the East Site for personality disordered patients.

2.18.18 Finally we would highlight one of the other documents found in Mr Finney's possession, namely an e-mail from T. Catterall to Macaulay Ward, 23 March 1996:

> "Shelley does not allow parole patients on the Ward. Following a request for a patient to visit we supervise contact at the entrance on occasions. This is now getting out of hand with numerous visits per day mainly from parole patients.
>
> "Staff working in the admin. have rung the ward reporting a parole patient outside the parole area and I can see this leading to a problem with senior managers in the future.
>
> "We request that patients visiting Shelley are accompanied by a base Ward staff irrespective of parole status."

In her 1992 Security Audit Miss Kinsley had criticised the practice of allowing parole patients to visit other wards because it was an easy way of distributing illicit substances and articles. As far as we can see the practice was never stopped.

2.19.0 The SHSA and the Hospitals

2.19.1 Neither the Braund nor Finney Reports ever reached the SHSA; the Braund Report was not available until just before the Authority's demise, and the Finney inquiry took place after the HSPSCB had taken over from the SHSA. Yet in both cases the abuses had been taking place it seems for years. The Owen Ward Report revealed an appalling situation on that ward. One is forced to ask, did the SHSA grasp what was going on? What mechanisms did they put in place to monitor the hospitals? Why in the case of Ashworth's PDU at least, did those mechanisms not appear to work?

2.19.2 It was and is extremely difficult to peer into the world of the Special Hospitals and discern what is really going on. (The critical television programme about Rampton which led to the Boynton Inquiry was entitled *The Secret Hospital.*) The SHSA developed a range of formal and informal instruments to help them find out what was happening and to monitor progress.

2.19.3 First, there would be reviews of progress against agreed action plans. We have described the annual Ministerial Review process above. From this would cascade a series of tasks and objectives for the hospitals which would be encapsulated in the annual "contract" signed off between the Chief Executive and UGM. This increased in sophistication through the lifetime of the Authority and set out, not only the quantity of services to be provided, but also its quality in terms of a series of quality standards. Broad statements of principle on areas such as nursing practice, security and therapy, seclusion, and staff and patients were produced, which were then translated into specific standards and placed in the annual service-level agreements.

2.19.4 Each hospital was required to report each quarter on a wide range of standards and these were used as a basis for twice-yearly reviews by the Chief Executive. Curiously, searching did not appear in any contract until the end of the SHSA's lifetime, and this was the reason given by Mr Kaye to account for the absence of any comment on searching in the Quarterly Review Reports.

2.19.5 We have seen the 1996/7 contract between the HSPSCB and Ashworth Hospital Authority, which builds on the SHSA's work. This sets out a detailed service specification and lists ten quality standards. These include standards relating to multi-disciplinary working; use of the Care Programme Approach; use of seclusion; 24-hour care; and security. The Chief Executive would report back to the Authority on the three Hospital Reviews.

2.19.6 Second, the SHSA developed a model for assessing services by way of "sampling". A sampling exercise in late 1994 developed into a programme of Quality Review Visits which were carried out towards the end of 1994/5 and throughout 1995/6. A three person team comprising one person from the SHSA, one from the Hospital and one from one of the other two hospitals would visit a selection of wards to examine specific quality standards and to report back to the UGM and to the SHSA. The aim of the visits was to provide a 'snapshot' of activity and to serve as a means of validating information supplied to the SHSA on a quarterly basis. It was intended that the visits would build on the audit activity already taking place within the Hospital. A written Report of each visit was made available to the Hospital and anonymised summaries of Quality Review Visit Reports formed part of the SHSA's quarterly Quality Reports. Details of follow-up action taken in response to Quality Review Visits were provided to the SHSA as part of the quarterly reporting cycle. This process has continued during the 96/97 and 97/98 contracting years although fewer visits have been made since the introduction of the HSPSCB.

2.19.7 Mr Kaye said in his statement these Reports were very revealing as they identified the uneven approach to issues across the Hospital and occasionally the existence of hot spots requiring attention. He described the twice-yearly Report of the Chief Executive to the Authority summarising the key features of what had been identified in each hospital as "the most significant management paper presented to the Authority".

2.19.8 We had access to the SHSA Quality Reports. The information gained is important. For example, in the first quarter of 1995/6 from a sample of 25 per cent of wards at Ashworth only 83 per cent of team meetings were minuted; notes on patients were not routinely transferred to individual patient notes; and none of the teams was able to demonstrate a system of recording completed actions or carrying forward outstanding actions. However, none of the Quality Review Reports deal with matters of security, for the reasons we outlined above.

2.19.9 None of the Quality Review Reports identified Lawrence Ward as a 'hot-spot'.

2.19.10 The SHSA and Ashworth also commissioned the Health Advisory Service to examine the Hospital two years after the Blom-Cooper Report. We have discussed this Report above.

2.19.11 We have dealt above at length with inquiries into serious incidents, most notably the Owen Ward Report. Over the lifetime of the SHSA there were a large number of Reports into serious incidents or areas of concern. The recommendations would be followed-up, and specific tasks would find their way into annual contracts, such as multi-disciplinary care planning, the absence of which was identified as a weakness on Owen Ward. They were, so Mr Kaye claimed, a deliberate attempt to help the organization learn from its mistakes.

2.19.12 We discuss the shortcomings of the system of inquiries below.

2.19.13 Further information on weaknesses of the three Hospitals could be gleaned, according to Mr Kaye, from the complaints process. The SHSA had a complaints sub-committee headed by the Vice-Chairman of the Authority and including the Chief Executive. This committee received a quarterly Report back from the hospitals of all complaints together with a brief summary of action taken. The sub-committee pursued complaints that had not been adequately dealt with.

2.19.14 The SHSA welcomed more visitors into the Hospitals and sought to develop links with outside bodies, including academic and professional links. The Mental Health Act Commission was visiting regularly in pursuance of their statutory remit. The Hospitals were undoubtedly appearing to become less secret.

2.19.15 But none of the above provided fool-proof guarantees that serious problems were being picked up, as the events on Lawrence Ward have demonstrated. The quality visits did not identify problems on that ward; the HAS review sounded warning notes about the PDU, but did not highlight those critical remarks (hampered as they were by not receiving the Owen Ward Report); the MHAC did not identify anything awry on Lawrence Ward as their commissioners were not being told of anything untoward by patients.

2.19.16 Of course there is a limit to what any visitor is likely to spot visiting the ward for an hour or two, as Mrs Nelson, Chairman of the SHSA from 1993, pointed out:

> ". . . you can only find out what is going on in a ward if someone wants you to find out. If you are in a situation where, for some reason or other, no-one is prepared to be open, it is very difficult, if not impossible, to really get to know what is happening on the ward."

2.20.0 Security Managers' Meetings

2.20.1 Was it true then that the SHSA really did not know the full picture of what was happening? Only up to a point. For there was a further source of information which was consistently providing warnings of poor and dangerous practice in all three hospitals, namely the Security Managers. If one thread of our story is the over-enthusiastic embrace of patient empowerment, another is the rearguard action fought by a number of individuals, from Miss Kinsley downwards, to keep a proper stress on security, without which therapy could not effectively take root.

2.20.2 The minutes of the Security Managers' meetings, chaired by Miss Kinsley, provide a fascinating insight into the problems facing the hospitals. We review a number of these minutes below.

5 March 1993

2.20.3 The first meeting we can trace was held on March 5th 1993, but it was not the first meeting, because it refers to previous minutes. The most important item of this meeting was item 7.6:

> "Mr Powell (Head of Nursing of the SHSA) said that any development of standards must avoid setting rigid rules. They should allow for flexibility and for discretion to be exercised as required. Mrs Simpson (Rampton) agreed with this since standards relating to the whole hospital allowed no freedom of movement to be exercised. She referred to the failure of a Security Group at Rampton to produce conclusions which the DNS (Director of Nursing Services) could accept. Accordingly, a new group had been formed which was still considering the question of audit and its link with Q/A. (Quality Assurance) The aim at Rampton was to incorporate security policies with patients' rights to ensure that the end result was not simply a numbers exercise. Mr Field (Broadmoor) added that at Broadmoor the multi-disciplinary teams were the final arbiters of security policy, short of UGMs' involvement."

2.20.4 No one from the security side queried this view, yet it was quite contrary to the view Miss Kinsley had previously expressed, that the Security Department at Ashworth seemed to be constantly trying to reconstruct itself. When one of their staff, who would have a dual responsibility to the Security Manager and to the Ward Manager, was attached to each PCT, she took that to be acceptable. She then added:

> "But I have subsequently seen, and this is recent and after my time if you like, that security seems to have been as a responsibility devolved to the clinical teams, the ward teams, and I would have seen that as totally unacceptable."

At the time of this meeting she was acting in a consultant capacity, but we have no doubt that this devolution was a fundamental mistake.

17 December 1993

2.20.5 At the next meeting the Security Managers discussed the 'Current Position of Hospital Security Departments':

> "The Broadmoor review of the Security Department had been completed. Mr Barber had been appointed as Director of Security from 1 September 1994, and would sit on the Hospital Management Team. At Rampton a similar review was being conducted. Mr Davidson was currently reporting direct to the UGM pending the outcome of the review. He wanted security to have a higher profile. He was fearful that under the Hospital reorganization, his department would be marginalised and this would not be helpful if the three clinical directorates did not follow the same course of action. The reorganization at Ashworth had meant that Mr Maxwell had had to apply for his own post. The DNS was now the Director of Professional Development responsible for Nursing Discipline, Psychology and Social Work. Mr Maxwell expressed concern about the reorganization and the difficulties he was having in getting access to wards, especially those where the clinicians were trying to keep his department away."

We return to the theme of marginalization of security below.

2.20.6 Item 8 concerns 'Recent incidents':

> "At Rampton patient TG had absconded on a shopping trip; there had been a small number of incidents involving cannabis; a nine-inch knife had been found down the side of a chair and was believed to have been left by a visitor. The security department had investigated an incident of a patient forging a letter to another patient informing her that her expected transfer would not go ahead. The patient who had forged the letter had been involved in other incidents which threatened the stability of the ward. Although this was now the responsibility of the clinical team, the security department was keeping an eye on things. Wards had been reminded of the need to follow security procedures. At Ashworth a patient had escaped from the Special Care Unit but quickly apprehended; two patients from Firs ward had attempted to escape but were caught before they reached the Hospital perimeter; a patient had attempted to abscond while on his way with three escorting nurses to a court appearance. It was discovered that it had not been necessary for him to attend court, but his clinical team had felt it would be useful to him. One patient had been involved in a roof-top incident for two hours. A knife made in the metal shop on the South site had been found on Firs ward, and one patient stabbed another patient on Elliot ward with a steak knife belonging to staff. This incident had occurred on 26 November 1993, but had not been reported to the security department..."

2.20.7 If this last entry is not a prime example of the need to ensure that there is some real co-operation between the Patient Care Teams and the Security Department, it is difficult to think of a better one.

22 February 1994

2.20.8 The position of security managers was again discussed:

> "Overall it was quite clear that all three Security Departments were going through a period of change and remained concerned, for example, about the ways some of their colleagues in the hospitals were pushing back the parameters of security."

The minutes record that Miss Kinsley told the group that its continued existence had been endorsed by the Chief Executive. She also commented that custody was a justifiable concept under the Mental Health Act and implied a special duty of care. She noted there was a vacuum in training at middle management level, and there needed to be a better emphasis on security in the ongoing training of newcomers.

26 April 1994

2.20.9 By the time of the next meeting Mr Maxwell had been appointed Security Manager at Ashworth Hospital. The control of telephones was discussed; at Rampton it was said that five or six obscene telephone calls were being made each week by patients to staff; patients were allowed unsupervised access to telephone calls, unless there were reasons for concern; some patients had devised their own telephone directory of staff. At Ashworth the minutes note that the hospital was experiencing similar problems to those at Rampton over the use of telephones by patients. Neither hospital (unlike Broadmoor) had all calls supervised as a matter of routine. Additionally, the patients had obtained access to the 999 Emergency Service and the Directory of Enquiries which should not have been possible. This situation had now been remedied. At Ashworth and Rampton the patients had discovered how to use their Mercury cards so that they were not charged for calls. (This was not a problem at Broadmoor where BT cards were used).

2.20.10 The minutes show that the Security Managers were concerned that the telephones were introduced with insufficient consideration of potential problems. There did not appear to be enough accountability by PCTs. At Ashworth and Rampton the telephones were available for 24 hours, but at Broadmoor, when 24-hour opening began, they would be unavailable after about 10 pm. The minutes say that "it was questioned whether adequate controls were being employed: the present arrangements could contribute to patients' conditions becoming worse than when they were admitted."

2.20.11 The managers continued to be concerned that security matters were being sidelined:

> "The Security Managers referred to the increasing number of difficulties caused by Patients' Councils and the Advocacy Service in their challenges to such matters as searching and the new 24-hour opening arrangements. There was a perception that WMs (Ward Managers) were losing control of their wards and patients having too great a say in what they could do. Again there was reference to the failure of care plans in that some patients were being allowed to stay in their rooms all day and only get up for meals. Others stayed up late and remained in bed until lunch time. This was a feature at all three hospitals and critical comment by the Security Departments on these practices, simply increased the resistance to the Department's advice and recommendations."

12 July 1994

2.20.12 Searching was once again an issue:

> "Ashworth and Broadmoor reported that the MHAC have said that it should not be part of hospital policy to have routine searches, since they believed this was unlawful under the Mental Health Act. Individual patients and Patients' Councils were also taking this approach and some staff were sympathetic and supported them. However, at Rampton it was considered that there was an implied right contained in the Mental Health Act to search in the absence there of statutory provisions. The meeting asked for guidance on this so they could proceed with confidence. Miss Kinsley said that she thought there was a duty of care to maintain regular but intermittent searching and not to do so would cause serious difficulties. This was to be a continuing theme in the meetings.

2.20.13 The usual item on "Recent Incidents" revealed an interesting crop. Thus at Broadmoor in May 12 litres of home made 'hooch' was found on Crowthorne/Windsor Wards; a 12 feet long nylon cord and a lighter had been found in a toilet on Shaftsbury Ward, and a male parole patient had chased a female nurse on a terrace. Incidents were increasing and the Security Department considered that the Hospital was only just keeping the lid on more serious incidents. At Rampton six lighters had been found in the possession of one patient; a patient had received a set of kitchen knives as a free gift from a catalogue company; a nurse had received a letter threatening to kill her. Two patients on trial leave had absconded but had been recovered quickly. At Ashworth on Arnold Ward a patient had set fire to his room. He was rendered unconscious but recovered. Five staff who suffered from the effect of the smoke had to attend the local hospital. A patient absconded from a toilet at Crewe railway station. He was found five hours later. A patient on Johnson Ward had set fire to his mattress. Five staff were involved in dealing with the fire and his room was extensively damaged. The Owen Ward incident was mentioned in these terms:

> "on 8 June 1994 on Owen Ward there was an incident where a patient held a female member of staff and a male patient hostage with a carving knife. The incident was effectively resolved by the intervention of staff and the emergency services without incident. The incident followed a series of other serious matters on the ward and a full investigation had been set up, which was still in operation. Seven hours after the

incident a further fire was started by a patient on Dickens Ward".

2.20.14 These Reports demonstrate yet again that serious incidents were commonplace in all three hospitals.

13 September 1994

2.20.15 By the next meeting the Owen Ward Report had been completed. Searching was again discussed:

> Item 5.2 "Miss Kinsley reported that following the last meeting of the Security Managers, she had put to Charles Kaye the concerns expressed by Ashworth and Broadmoor that the MHAC had said it should not be part of hospital policy to have routine searches, since they believed that was unlawful under the Mental Health Act. Mr Kaye had said that we needed to be able to conduct searches when we thought they were appropriate. This was part of our remit to maintain a secure environment. It did not seem to him that this infringed civil libertarian views, since we were detaining patients who were, by definition, potentially dangerous."

2.20.16 Linked to this was a discussion of the amount of patients' possessions:

> "Following concern expressed by Broadmoor over the number of videos kept by some patients, the meeting discussed what was seen as an increasing problem over the amount of patients' possessions. At Rampton the Security Department had found a marked reluctance to adopt Miss Kinsley's recommendations in her security Audit on this matter. The Department argued against the number of items kept by patients in their rooms, since this was a major fire risk, as well as making room searching a lengthy process. The hospital managers argued that to limit the number of possessions would be restricting patient's choice. However, Miss Kinsley pointed out that not applying a control actually hindered care, and she would have welcomed the Security Department advising her earlier of the problems they had been experiencing."
>
> "At Ashworth the findings of the Owen Ward inquiry were assisting the Hospital in limiting the patient's possessions".

2.20.17 As will be seen this problem at Ashworth was not solved even by 1997.

8 December 1994

2.20.18 The minutes of the following meeting record that:

> "Ashworth Hospital had introduced searching standards on the PD Unit.The quality aspect was universal, but the numerical demands varied from ward to ward. There had been some resistance to the new standards, since they were seen as breaking down good patient/staff relationships."

2.20.19 As we have seen, simply counting the number of searches (the numerical standard) is worthless without a qualitative measurement being incorporated, i.e., how well the searches were being done.

2.20.20 The minutes show that Miss Kinsley reminded the meeting about what was recorded in the minutes of the previous meeting concerning the importance of searching.

2.20.21 The recent incidents item reveals the usual sorts of incidents:

> "Rampton Hospital reported a growing number of drug-related incidents. Associated with this were suspicions of money laundering, difficulty in searching over-crowded rooms and abuse of the telephone system in making deals, intimidating weaker patients and warning of impending searches by the Police

and/or Security Department. Mr Elvins (Security Manager Rampton Hospital) reported that 60% of new admissions had a background of drug abuse. The meeting discussed the problems that were being experienced over the use and abuse of the telephone system. Only at Broadmoor and Carstairs Hospitals were all calls monitored and as a result both hospitals experienced few problems. At Ashworth Hospital there was provision for calls to be monitored, but this was rarely followed."

"At Rampton Hospital, excessive property owned by patients was still a problem. The situation was delegated to Clinical teams to decide on, but the position was abused. The hospital reported a number of incidents where patients had ganged up against staff during specific incidents. This was especially so on admission wards. All three special hospitals reported growth in intimidatory behaviour by patients and the difficulties staff were having at times in keeping control."

"At Broadmoor there had been three patient suicides in six weeks, two on an admission ward and one on the young person's ward. There was a constant problem of cannabis entering the hospital. No major cache had ever been found. Another police search was due soon in one area of the hospital."

"At Ashworth Hospital there had been several side room (meaning bed room) fires and roof-top incidents, plus an absconscion during an absence from the hospital".

2.20.22 The Security Managers' warnings did not fall on completely deaf ears. Having read the minutes of the meeting of 8 December Mr Kaye wrote a letter to Miss Kinsley dated 6 January 1995 which he copied to each of the General Managers. He pointed out that the choices and rights of patients existed within the context of a secure environment, which the staff must control. He reemphasised that searching was an essential part of their security procedures and added:

> "Management has the full right to carry our searches whenever it feels that they are appropriate. They are not to be regarded as a violation of privacy but as a necessary part of continuing to maintain a safe and secure environment for patients and staff. Any serious obstacle placed in way of proper searching of rooms and wards needs to be recorded by the security staff and brought to your attention."

2.20.23 Later on he said:

> "Individual patients' rooms must not be allowed to be cluttered with possessions to such an extent that it becomes impossible to search them. Again although patients can expect some degree of choice about possessions that they have in the room, they do not have any unlimited right to have as many things there as they can cram in. The level of possessions must be such that searching can swiftly and efficiently take place whenever it is necessary. Patients' possessions will have to be weeded out if necessary."

2.20.24 With regard to monitoring telephone calls he said:

> "I note that this is apparently carried out at Broadmoor and Carstairs, but not at our other two hospitals. Is there any good reason why it should not pertain at all hospitals to the same level? Furthermore, can we agree a date by which this will pertain?"

9 February 1995

2.20.25 At the next meeting the use of telephones was discussed again. The minutes record the following:

> "Both Carstairs and Broadmoor monitored all calls by patients. At Broadmoor Hospital the ward phones for use by the patients were kept immobilised until staff authorised the

switchboard to switch them on. All patients had validated lists of people they could telephone; some were not allowed to make telephone calls; BT telephone cards were used. All calls were monitored and no ward-to-ward calls were permitted."

"At Ashworth Hospital, there were still instances occurring of the fraudulent use of Mercury telephone cards. On some wards the telephone was locked away, but on others it was freely available. At one time the hospital policy required all calls to be monitored, but this was not being done. The switch board could not identify where the calls came from.Therapeutic policies were said to have removed restrictions on the use of the telephone."

"Rampton Hospital had set up a working party to look at telephone policy after four obscene calls were made to members of the public. For the time being all calls were being monitored until the working party reported".

"The conclusion of the meeting was that to ensure that calls were made properly and to prevent fraudulent use of 'phone-cards, all telephone calls should be monitored by staff."

2.20.26 The meeting also discussed the issue of controlling visitors. The minutes demonstrate that the various Hospitals varied in their practices. Broadmoor had introduced a new system in February 1995. It was similar to the personagram, but had the advantage of coloured photographs which provided better definition. The personagram was a system that stored photographs of approved visitors, enabling in theory the hospitals to check the identity of visitors. It never worked effectively. They expected to extend the system to cover staff. Rampton were still operating the original personagram system, but were hoping to adopt the Broadmoor system. At Ashworth the system devised by the IT department was non-operational. The Security Department had considered a new system, but the Director of Finance was currently proposing to look into an integrated system for staff and visitors. In the meantime manual records were relied on. At Carstairs all visitors would have photo- passes from April. Additionally before visitors were approved by the RMOs, a Criminal Records Office check was done on them.

2.20.27 The meeting discussed the different arrangements for receiving visitors. At Broadmoor Hospital they entered via a security arch, and all hand bags were inspected. Food and drink were not allowed in unless they were in approved containers. All goods were X-rayed. Visitors who were not on approved lists were turned away. At Rampton and Ashworth Hospitals visitors not on approved lists were referred to the clinical team or site manager for consideration. Unless their credentials could be verified they were refused admission. At Rampton food could be taken in. There was no X-ray machine and certain wrapping material could disguise the contents. Ashworth Hospital had a similar procedure but had put in a bid for an X-ray machine.

2.20.28 The perceived marginalization of security was clearly of concern:

"Concern was expressed at the meeting at the lack of cooperation sometimes by clinical staff over the accreditation of visitors, and rules requiring visitors to be approved in advance were not being observed. Security managers were also seeking to counter the lack of proper observation of visiting on wards at Ashworth and Rampton Hospitals".

2.20.29 Searching was again an important issue:

"The meeting discussed the serious concerns at all three hospitals over the amount of patients' possessions and how these hampered effective searching of their rooms. The issue was highlighted in the incident on Owen Ward, the escape from Rampton Hospital, as well as the escape from Whitemoor Prison."

> "It was agreed that it would be helpful to have guidelines on the type and quantity of items that patients were permitted to have. At present safety and security were being endangered by these items in patients' rooms, and Ashworth Hospital were considering Health and Safety guidelines on electrical items and free space to see whether these would enable the Hospital to restrict patients' possessions. It was concluded that the only way the present problem could be tackled would be by doing a thorough check of each room, identifying the items to be kept, recording those on a list, and putting the remaining items into storage. It was recognised, however, that this would be a very time consuming task."
>
> "The meeting also discussed the alterations that were sometimes made to patients' rooms by their occupants. It was considered that patients should not be allowed to modify the layout of their rooms, or to have furniture other than that supplied and fitted by the hospitals themselves."

23 March 1995

2.20.30 Under "Searching" the minutes of the next meeting show that Miss Kinsley referred to a letter sent by Mr Kaye to Mr Bingley of the MHAC setting out what he saw as the need for the Special Hospitals regularly to conduct searches. The minutes note that all three Hospitals had core standards for searching, but there was variable success over their implementation. It was accepted that there was no legal basis to permit the searching of visitors. However, if a security search or equivalent identified that the visitor was carrying an item that she/he was unwilling to disclose, the visitor could be refused admission to the Hospital.

2.20.31 We cannot understand how an issue as important as this remained so unclear for so long. A High Security Hospital is entitled to make it a condition of entry that visitors submit to searching if they want to visit.

2.20.32 Under "Patients' Possessions" the minutes noted that: "All three hospitals were experiencing difficulties in limiting patients' possessions in their rooms, and the lack of storage made it difficult to make alternative arrangements for these."

2.20.33 Under "Patients' Use of Telephones" the minutes note that: "Each hospital operated a different approach to the access and use of telephones by patients. The meeting discussed the need for a common approach and the advantages this might provide."

11 April 1995

2.20.34 Mr Kaye was present at the next meeting. "Searching" was again discussed and the problems at Ashworth explored:

> "Mr Maxwell introduced this item and described the background to the pilot study conducted at Ashworth. This led to six core standards on searching being produced which had now been introduced throughout the Hospital, involving numerical standards being negotiated with each Clinical Manager and Ward Manager. These had caused some upsets among patients and staff and accusations had been made that the standards affected therapeutic relationships and infringed the Mental Health Act and Code of Practice. Ashworth would welcome Mr Kaye's backing via a statement for the standards lest the arrangements were eroded with the passage of time. Mr Dale said that the new approach was justified by the number and nature of items found. Security items, for example, lighters, went missing regularly, so searching could be justified at any time. It had long been noted that illegal drugs were less evident than a year ago and the new searching arrangements may have contributed to this."
>
> "Mr Kaye referred to the letter he had sent to the MHAC about searching. He believed that sufficient guidance already existed, but he would consider requests to

strengthen it. Control was the key factor and we could be held to be culpable if it was not exerted. This must be discussed with staff who found it difficult to accept and he felt the agreeing of numerical standards with the clinical teams was a correct approach. Ashworth agreed to let Broadmoor and Rampton have details of the core standards so they could consider the implementation of similar arrangements at their hospitals."

2.20.35 Once again the problem of "Patients' Possessions" was discussed:

"The meeting recognised that patients' possessions should not be allowed to clutter rooms to the extent that it became impossible to search them. Mr Kaye said that possessions must be controlled and limits applied as with searching. If this meant storage areas then this should be accepted. Rampton said the question of storage should be one for the Hospital to resolve, although it could finish up as the ward's problem. Ashworth was tackling the situation from a Health and Safety aspect. A policy had been drafted and put to the UGM for consideration."

Item 8.2 "Mr Kaye said that each hospital must have a policy on possessions as well as on the number and quality of searches. The policies would vary, but they must exist. The current position at the hospitals was:-

Ashworth – Searching policy in operation, but one on possessions still to be resolved.

Rampton – Possessions policy established, and the searching policy was being revised.

Broadmoor – Searching policy was being revised. A pilot study on possessions had been conducted in several areas from a health and safety aspect.

"Mr Kaye would discuss these and other matters on this meeting's agenda when he met the UGMs tomorrow".

2.20.36 Clearly searching and the quantity of patients' possessions continued to be a major problem.

2.20.37 The meeting discussed a number of other old chestnuts. Thus under "Use of Telephones by Patients" we find:

"Mr Final introduced this item and briefly described the practice at Broadmoor Hospital . . . Ashworth explained that staffing levels prevented the monitoring of calls: some were also difficult to observe even when the telephone was in an open area of the ward. Each ward had its own practices which had derived from an earlier central policy of the Hospital. There was no real control of whom the patients telephoned and there had been abuse of the Mercury phone-cards. Although inter-ward calls were not permitted, they still occurred. A policy for the Hospital was to be drafted for consideration by HMT."

2.20.38 Under "Visiting" the minutes reveal that at Rampton all visiting was ward-based. Although these visits should be supervised, some visitors had complained about the presence of staff and there was a reluctance to enforce supervision. There were also difficulties over the authorization of visitors. At Broadmoor, the majority of visits were conducted centrally, and were supervised.

2.20.39 The situation at Ashworth was more complex. Visiting was ward-based on the South and East Sites. On the North Site, 50 per cent of the visits were conducted centrally. The supervision was inadequate on the wards and some visits were totally unsupervised. The minutes record that a draft policy to tackle this had been drafted and a Working Party was considering the issues. An additional difficulty at the Hospital was the refusal of the Social Work Department to be involved in the process of examining the suitability of visitors.

2.20.40 The meeting discussed the issue of searching staff. The minutes note:

> "Ashworth asked whether staff should be searched on a routine basis. Miss Kinsley believed that there was no right to search NHS staff, even if there was an implied right in the staff contracts. If there was a suspicion of involvement in drugs, the police should be advised, but the Hospital needed to have good grounds before the police would be prepared to proceed."

13 June 1995

2.20.41 The next meeting was held on13 June 1995. Those present welcomed the presence of Mr Kaye at the previous meeting. Searching was discussed. The minutes record the following:

> "Ashworth reported that their search standards were working well although there were variations in the number of searches conducted across different wards. The Security Liaison staff were addressing this problem and monitoring and auditing quality. The issue of searching staff was also raised as there had been, on two occasions, a suspicion that staff might be implicated in illicit drug supply."

2.20.42 We would remind the reader that at this time the events disclosed in the Braund Report were taking place (*see* 2.17.0 *et seq.* above). The authors of that Report stated that:

> **"The trail we have uncovered has led the Inquiry team to an Eldorado of security breaches, 'scams', money-making ventures and breaches of Hospital systems on a scale not encountered by the members of the team before."**

2.20.43 The minutes continue:

> "Rampton reported that they had always conducted searches of patients, their property and rooms. The search policy is currently being revisited and once it has been revised, search standards will be developed. Special search training sessions had been held in addition to the induction course in recent months. Consequently, some three hundred staff had received such training. Major headway had been made in the practice of searching by the introduction of a policy on patients' property."
>
> "Broadmoor were also in the process of updating their policy on searching. They had no search standards in operation at present. Routine searches of patients are not carried out but routine searches of rooms and property are. Special search teams have been trained for major searches."
>
> "At Carstairs, the situation was much different to the English Special Hospitals. Everything and everyone is liable to search if necessary. Visitors can be searched and must pass through a security portal. Their luggage can be checked using an X-ray machine. It is a contractual requirement for staff to be searched when necessary. Mr Finlayson reported that staff see the necessity for this and willingly participate in the procedure. Security search teams are also at Carstairs."
>
> "Mr Street (Miss Kinsley's successor) stated that in his experience, visitors were the largest potential source of contraband, especially illicit drugs. If Hospital Management Teams were to avoid the worst problems of the Prison Service, it was essential that we should make a clear statement that the presence of illicit drugs in our hospitals was unacceptable. While recognizing the differences between ourselves and prisons, we may need to reconsider the searching of visitors and staff in the future."

"In the light of recent experience (eg the smuggling of a ten inch knife into Ashworth, drugs etc) the meeting felt that searching should remain on future agendas."

2.20.44 Under 'Patients Telephones' the minutes record that:

"Rampton had ratified and implemented a policy similar to Broadmoor's. Patients had approved lists of people for both incoming and outgoing calls. Telephone calls were being treated as correspondence within the meaning of the Mental Health Act 1983. Calls to solicitors were, however, made in the sight, but out of hearing of staff. Internal calls and night calls had been eliminated. All phones could now be locked off and had been sited for easy monitoring."

"Broadmoor reported no problems with their system."

"Ashworth still had variations in procedures across wards and were debating how to rationalise their policy which was widely interpreted. There was a recognition that whilst the policy needed to be tightened up, they did not wish to be as restrictive as the other hospitals. The only internal calls allowed were on Patients' Council business."

"It was generally agreed that this issue had been resolved and no longer required to be an agenda item."

2.20.45 This last comment seems to us rather complacent, given the continuing problems over the use of telephones.

8 August 1995

2.20.46 At the next meeting searching was once again an important item on the agenda. Broadmoor had issued a new policy in June 1995, but this had still to be finalised. A formal record was kept of every search made. The searching of visitors was covered by the Hospital's Visitors' Policy. If a visitor was identified from the security canopy as carrying metal items, the source must be identified. If this could not be done and the visitor refused to be searched, then the power existed for admission to the Hospital to be refused. However, the screening only identified metal items, whereas drugs, which were a particular problem, were not picked up by this method.

2.20.47 The minutes continue:

"At Ashworth core standards on searching were being progressed. Some wards were not achieving the standards and their performance was being assessed. Draft standards on patient's possessions in side rooms had been prepared. Some WMs (Ward Managers) found them very prescriptive and they were also likely to cause storage problem."

"Rampton said that in the property policy they had now introduced, property and searching issues were inextricably linked. The criteria then is the time taken to search which reflects the amount of the patient's possessions. The effectiveness of the new arrangements was borne out by a recent search conducted by a dog-team which had been much easier to carry out than in the past. Many possessions had been put in a central store and others disposed of – a much firmer line was being taken over what would be stored and less 'rubbish' was retained."

18 October 1995

2.20.48 Unsurprisingly, searching was yet again a key theme of the next meeting. Broadmoor reported uncertainty over legal backing for searching of rooms, and a lack of enthusiasm by staff because of endangering staff/patient relationships. By contrast Rampton were experiencing no problems in the searching of rooms, and had tightened up procedures on room searches. They were now addressing searching of visitors and staff. Ashworth stressed the importance of incorporating searching as part of therapeutic care which staff found easier to accept. Lastly, Carstairs described their searching procedures which included random searches of staff and visitors as well as patients. Specially trained staff were used and all patients' rooms were searched monthly. Mr Street reminded the meeting of Mr Kaye's endorsement of searching patients' rooms.

2.20.49 The meeting went on to discuss visiting. Broadmoor expressed concern at ex-members of staff continuing to visit patients. The minutes recorded that care teams watched the position carefully, especially when relationships had formed. Rampton were reviewing their visiting procedures. At Ashworth the clinical teams needed proof to substantiate Security Department's concerns before they were willing to ban a visitor. The situation was complicated by different procedures within each Clinical Directorate.

2.20.50 The following item, on pornography, was very germane to the Lawrence Ward situation:

> "Mr Ives of the Paedophile Unit at Scotland Yard addressed the meeting on Computer Pornography, especially where children were involved. This followed concern about the ease by which patients had access to computers and how pornographic material might be obtained."
>
> "Mr Ives explained that it was now possible for computers to produce photographic-quality images, and that pornographic images of children can be created from those of adults using a scanner and other computer equipment. He set out how the law had developed in recent years over the possession of pornographic material."
>
> "It was possible to identify the material that might be used to build up photographic material, but it was also possible to disguise the possession of it by encryption and other means."

2.20.51 Sadly this timely warning of possible problems did not result in immediate action in the PDU.

6 December 1995

2.20.52 The situation as regards searching was as parlous as ever:

> Item 4 "Searching"
>
> Item 4.1 "Concern was expressed over the requirements for searching set out in the Service Specification for Security and the meeting discussed what was meant by the term. If a full search was required then this demanded a great deal of staff. Mr Street reminded the meeting that the conclusions of the Lamont Report made it clear that full searches were required. If this wasn't possible, because of shortages of staff, the General Managers would need to address the situation, since changes to the Service Specification would require the agreement of the Commissioning Board. Mr Street invited the Security Managers to let Mr Curd at Charles House know of their concerns and the different criteria that would meet their requirements."
>
> Item 4.2 "The searching of patients was not being done at present in accordance with the draft Service Specification at Ashworth and Broadmoor, nor were they conducting a search of all packages and parcels for patients."
>
> Item 4.3 "Mr Street stressed that it should be made clear that searching of visitors could be conducted. Broadmoor staff were not confident about doing this and were to receive training from British Airways. All three hospitals accepted that full searching required a big input of staffing resources and accordingly presented

particular problems. They recognised that the Service Specification would present difficult challenges for the hospitals, and particularly for the Security Departments. A further aspect referred to was the requirement for staff to monitor visits to patients. At Ashworth this meant looking in the room from time to time, whereas the Specification would require full observation."

Item 4.4 "Ashworth referred to the Specification omitting reference to telephones, and how the existing need for a telephone policy and the need to monitor it, would be incorporated in the future."

2.20.53 The next item covered visiting. The minutes record that all the Hospitals had dispensed with the personagram system and only Broadmoor had so far substituted a similar system (Equinox). Ashworth were relying on written records, but were considering installing a system being developed at HMP Whitemoor. The minutes note that:

> "The meeting discussed the arrangements at the hospitals for approving visitors and when CRO checks were made. There were particular problems over this at Ashworth, which Mr Street would discuss further on his next visit there."

13 February 1996

2.20.54 This is the final meeting for which we have seen minutes. The searching of staff was discussed. Carstairs said they conducted random searches every day on 1:6 staff entering the Hospital and also on anyone who triggered the metal detector. Occasionally 100 per cent searches were conducted and sometimes searches were carried out on staff leaving the Hospital. New X-ray equipment and metal detectors were being installed. The minutes continue:

> "The meeting accepted that before arrangements for searching staff were considered, effective policies needed to be in place in the Special Hospitals for searching visitors. However, the Security Managers accepted the importance of searching staff in order to protect them from intimidation/manipulation."

2.20.55 This was the last minute of the Security Managers bimonthly meetings since the three Hospitals became independent in April 1996. We understand that quarterly meetings have continued.

2.20.56 From 1992 when Miss Kinsley wrote her Reports on each of the Special Hospitals until the demise of the SHSA in 1996, the same problems remained unresolved. There was a total failure to get the balance of security and therapy right. Insofar as there were policies designed to exist in harmony with therapy, they were revisited on a number of occasions; there was discussion and debate between clinical and security staff but little agreement; there were never proper instructions, only policies, and certainly at Ashworth those policies could often not be found in the wards.

2.20.57 We highlight two examples of this. First, when Miss Kinsley reported on Ashworth, she said that found no policies on searching clearly set down. Three years after her Report there was still no policy on patients' possessions. She said there was a lot of controversy about that topic. Various interested lobbies maintained that patients should have more property than they should:

> "and the great defence, of course, was storage. I found it a bit difficult to accept that in large institutions there was not somewhere where things could be stored or handed out to relatives".

She clearly had in mind what our Committee had been feeling for some time. **The real problem was the lack of interest or determination to reduce the level of property held in patients' rooms particularly at ward level.**

2.20.58 Second, the same attitude was seen in the way in which ward visits were not properly supervised. Miss Kinsley said that when ward visiting was introduced, it was made quite clear that such visits should not happen unless they were properly supervised. She added:

> "But it seemed to have gone ahead without that being ensured, and Ashworth were not the only ones because I found a similar situation at Rampton when I was visiting one weekend for the purpose of an inquiry. It was very difficult to get the ward staff to accept that these visits must be properly supervised. They thought they knew their patients and it would be alright."

In so far as children visiting wards was concerned, she had no knowledge at all of that happening. As far as children visiting wards housing paedophiles was concerned, she said she was horrified, as she imagined most people were, when she read about it.

2.20.59 Ward staff could, and no doubt did imagine that supervising visits was not particularly important because according to Paragraph 26.3 of the Code of Practice, "ordinarily, inadequate staff numbers should not be a deterrent to regular visiting". As we said earlier, as applied in the high security setting this is untenable and must be changed.

2.20.60 At this point we focus in greater detail on some of the recurrent themes that emerge from the Security Managers' meetings.

2.21.0 Security and the Security Department

Crying in the Wilderness

2.21.1 A number of extracts referred to above reveal the Security Managers' feeling that they were marginalized, not only at Ashworth, but also to some extent at Broadmoor and Rampton. The marginalization of security in the years post-Blom-Cooper was a concern of many witnesses. Thus Mr Maxwell, the former Security Manager, told us that there was an insidious process by which security became essentially a matter for PCTs, and the role of security advisers became less and less important. To be against any aspect of what was perceived to be the Blom-Cooper Report's agenda was to be labelled a dinosaur. Aside from Miss Kinsley he did not believe anyone at a senior level in the SHSA or the Hospital was willing to give security a higher profile.

2.21.2 Mr Maxwell also told us that, following the creation of Clinical Units, Clinical Managers were resistant to the idea of Security Liaison Officers for each Unit. He recognized that it was difficult for the new, more autonomous units to accept central direction on procedures, directions which would lead to confrontation with patients. In any case, the most that Security Liaison Officers could say was "do this at your peril".

2.21.3 Mr Paterson, his deputy for several years, told us that security matters did not receive sufficient priority. He and his colleagues felt that they were crying in the wilderness. There was no mechanism by which Clinical Units or Directorates had to report any matters to Security, even if they had wide security implications.

2.21.4 Part of the problem was that the Security Department was always relatively small: some 50 staff in total, the vast majority of whom worked in the Control Centre. The Security Liaison Officers were over-stretched; thus although Mr Day, the Security Liaison Officer for the PDU, in theory should have attended all PCT meetings in the PDU, the PCTs on Lawrence and Macaulay Wards clashed. Given that Macaulay Ward was giving the Security Department more concerns, he rarely attended the Lawrence Ward PCT.

Community Card

2.21.5 One aspect of security which is not highlighted in the Security Managers' meetings is the community card system (formerly called parole). In their Inquiry Report Sir Louis Blom-

Cooper and his team were critical about restrictions on patient movements within the North Site and recommended that the Hospital review escorting arrangements within the Hospital confines (recommendation 34). The rationale for this was that, given the highly secure perimeter fence, the Hospital could afford to relax aspects of security somewhat inside the walls. However, the high wall gave the Hospital a false sense of security. Attention was focused on preventing patients getting out. Little thought was given to what was coming in and to what was happening inside the walls.

2.21.6 The number of patients who were allowed to hold community cards increased dramatically over the years. With it the potential for security breaches increased, as community card patients had unescorted access to various areas (including the Lawrence Ward garden, a point to which we shall return). They could visit other so-called parole wards, offering a ready route for drugs and other illicit substances. The fact that community card patients could escort their visitors within the grounds offered an easy route for such substances to be introduced into the Hospital unobserved by staff.

2.21.7 So many patients had acquired this status that Mr Paterson told us that there might be up to 100 patients walking around the site unescorted in the summer. As more and more patients on even medium dependency wards got cards then they were asking whether their wards should be parole wards too. Mr Paterson felt the Hospital needed to consider how many patients holding community card status it could safely absorb. Such status should be a privilege, not a right.

2.21.8 We agree. Community card policies must be reviewed. On a large open campus they allow different types of mentally disordered patients to mix, sharply increasing security risks. Holding a community card should be a privilege earned and a privilege which can also be lost. Furthermore, in our judgment, unless personality disordered patients are physically separated from other mentally disordered patients, allowing personality disordered patients unescorted access to an open campus creates an unacceptable security risk.

Recommendation 6

2.21.9 We recommend:
(i) The whole policy of issuing community cards should be reviewed.
(ii) The total number issued should never be such as to jeopardise fundamental security requirements.
(iii) Unless severe personality disordered individuals are physically separated from the mentally ill, those severe personality disordered individuals who hold community cards should not be allowed unescorted access to other parts of the Hospital.

Physical Security

2.21.10 Ashworth is a hospital, but it has to accommodate some individuals who would be category A in prison terms. The standards of security should reflect that fact. We were alarmed to hear that only about 65–70 per cent of the North Site is covered by security cameras and that the quality of the video pictures is not very good. Vehicles are only superficially searched entering the site; staff are not searched, nor are visitors, although their bags are searched. The personagram system for checking the identity of approved visitors never worked and has not yet so far as we are aware, been replaced by a more effective system.

2.21.11 We are aware that investment in new security measures is being planned at Ashworth. We see this investment as vital if Ashworth is to continue to hold highly dangerous patients.

2.21.12 Both Mr Paterson and Mr Gardner, the then Director of Security and Clinical Risk Management, sought to reassure us that security really had been improved. Mail was now checked centrally; independent search teams had been introduced; searching on the wards had been improved (although the quantity of patients' possessions still prevented effective searching) and there was more storage for surplus possessions; computer security had been addressed; illicit substances would always be a problem but the amount circulating in the Hospital had, they believed, been reduced; the amount of pornography available had been much reduced; children visiting had been tightened up greatly; a new telephone system was being investigated; Security now had a strong voice at Board level and there was more respect for security staff, linked to that higher status within the organization. We were pleased to hear that Mr Gardner could go to the Chief Executive to get a PCT decision challenged; he was reluctant to have a veto power lower down the organization.

2.21.13 The new Security Manual was produced during the course of our first session of hearings. This represented the first thorough revision of the Security Manual since May 1992, despite the Owen Ward recommendation for an urgent review of the manual. Mr Paterson told us that the new manual had been through an extensive process of consultation to ensure that it was right, a point supported by Mr Gardner, who told us that his Department had organized awareness sessions and training to support the introduction of the new manual. Staff were required to sign when they had read the manual and those lists would be audited. In addition, Mr Gardner told us that all Hospital policies were being put onto the Hospital's IntraNet system.

2.21.14 After so long it was time something effective was done. All these changes which had been taking place during the course of our Inquiry are still embryonic and certainly need to be revisited constantly. An example of this is the computer security policy to which we refer critically in Part Three paragraph 3.40.0 *et seq.* below. That it took so long to produce the new Security Manual is a matter which draws our most serious censure.

2.21.15 Our continuing lack of confidence in security at Ashworth Hospital even today leads us to recommend that another external review be taken of security, and that this be regularly repeated.

Recommendation 7 **2.21.16 We recommend that an independent review of all aspects of physical security at Ashworth Hospital take place and be repeated at regular intervals.**

2.22.0 Use of Telephones by Patients

2.22.1 The context for the security managers' concern about telephones was the Blom-Cooper inquiry team's recommendation on patient access to telephones:

> "76. We recommend that patients at Ashworth should have a readily accessible personal telephone system, like those generally available in general hospitals and NHS psychiatric hospitals."

2.22.2 The SHSA duly purchased the Cambridge telephone system. Responsibility for approving numbers to be telephoned and for monitoring telephone use rested with the PCT.

2.22.3 We heard a considerable amount of evidence reinforcing the concerns of the security managers quoted above. Thus it quickly emerged that the new system was open to manipulation by more able patients. The POA described the policy as "near impossible to police". Mr Dale told us that he quickly learnt of seven or eight ways of cheating the system. Patients dialled numbers which were supposedly out of bounds. The phone cards rapidly became a form of currency. Mr Tarbuck noted that when he took over the Unit, telephone calls were not being monitored. In theory, control could be exerted either by turning the telephone off, or by limiting patients' calls, or by staff members standing next to patients as calls were being made. None of these options was particularly practicable with articulate personality disordered patients who would vociferously complain if their 'rights' appeared to be infringed. Even if control had been better exerted, the PDU patients could gain access to telephones on other wards or via third parties. Without the ability to limit the numbers being called and frequency of usage, the system represented a running security breach that had to be managed.

2.22.4 Mr Green confirmed that patients quickly found ways to subvert the Cambridge system. One of the recommendations of the Owen Ward report was to review the monitoring and use of telephones, yet when in April 1995 Mr Kaye wrote to the UGMs concerning security matters he noted that there appeared to be no coherent approach to monitoring the use of telephones at Ashworth, in contrast to Broadmoor and Rampton.

2.22.5 Mr Keown and his team found evidence of telephone cards being used as currency. One patient had amassed cards worth more than £300. The father of Child A had the biggest stock of all.

2.22.6 Dr Strickland agreed with the suggestion of counsel for the RCN that monitoring telephone calls was impossible when there were limited numbers of nursing staff and a phone available 24 hours a day." **Who wants to be using a telephone at 3 am? We can see no justification for patients to be able to use the ward community telephone between midnight and 7 am, save in the most exceptional circumstances.**

Recommendation 8

2.22.7 We recommend that patients should not be allowed to use the ward telephone between the hours of midnight and 7 am save in the most exceptional circumstances.

2.22.8 Mr Gardner told us in February 1998 that a new telephone system had not yet been commissioned despite the problems with the Cambridge system, although there were several more secure systems which the Hospital was investigating.

2.22.9 Mrs Miles confirmed the problems; she agreed with Professor Edward's suggestion that to say a Blom-Cooper recommendation was unworkable was not easy.

2.22.10 The importance of this potential abuse of telephones was, as we have seen, that it enabled patients to carry out various scams and inappropriate activities. To quote the Keown Report into events on Lawrence Ward in 1996:

> "9.1. From the outset of the investigation process it was evident that the Lawrence ward community telephone . . . has been widely misused and abused by patients. The policies and procedures in place to govern the use of the community telephone proved to be inadequate at maintaining the security of the system. Patients have been able to conduct business transactions, trade in illicit goods, make unapproved telephone calls and participate in activities which can be deemed to have been fraudulent such as obtaining loans under false pretences."

2.22.11 But this is not the whole story. Mr Murphy noted that the Hospital telephone policy was well-known: the PCT was to determine whom it was appropriate for a patient to contact and to keep a list of suitable numbers It was the staff's responsibility to ensure that the right number was being called. But the Lawrence Ward policy on phones was, according to Mr Murphy: "a person can make a phone call to whoever they want whenever they want". Mr Daggett confirmed this: "patients phoned anyone they wanted 24 hours a day". Mr Murphy took action in September 1996 to insist that ward managers see the policy was enforced.

2.22.12 As it was couched this policy was very difficult to enforce and for that reason we find it difficult to criticize those staff who gave up trying to enforce an impossible set of rules. We are told that the Hospital is investigating purchasing a new system; a new system on its own, however, is not enough. It needs to be underpinned by an enforced, workable policy for telephone use.

2.23.0 Searching/Patients Possessions

2.23.1 As far as searching is concerned, there are two interlinked issues revealed by the minutes of the security managers: one, the legality of searching (of patients, visitors and staff), and two, the practicality of searching over-filled rooms. With regard to the former point, we have already discussed at length the Broadmoor judgment at **2.12.14** *et seq.* above and concur wholeheartedly with that judgment.

2.23.2 On the particular issue of searching staff we see no reason why staff should not be searched and the Carstairs practice seems an eminently sensible one. This idea was supported by Mr Paterson, notwithstanding the resource consequences. How this should be implemented should be discussed with staff representatives, but it should be implemented.

Recommendation 9 **2.23.3 We recommend that searching of staff be implemented.**

2.23.4 As far as the latter issue of patients' possessions is concerned, the Security Managers' concerns were shared by many others. Mr Tarbuck told us that when he took over the PDU four wards did not represent a problem in terms of patients' possessions. This was because they had less property in real terms (except for patients on Owen Ward) and because five beds on each ward had been taken out of commission, rooms which were used for offices, therapy rooms and for storage of patients' property. But there were problems on Lawrence and Macaulay Wards where the same strategy could not be adopted. There the Owen Ward Report recommendation on conducting searches could not be fully implemented due to the lack of storage for patients' possessions. He signalled this to the HMG and others frequently and did try to address the problem whilst taking account of the views of the patients, but in his view they had no option but to wait for the secure central storage area.

2.23.5 Mr Melia, who became Ward Manager of Macaulay Ward in August 1994, confirmed that the state of patients' rooms made searching enormously difficult. He told us that searching had ceased for some time on that ward; he reinstituted searches, much to the annoyance of patients. But the root problem remained; there was simply nowhere to put patients' property off the wards.

2.23.6 This despairing attitude appears to have been widespread. Mr Dale told us that the importance of the possessions issue was widely recognized but that no one, himself included, really gripped the problem, and in effect waited for the capital programme to sort the problem out. This was despite clear statements from Mr Kaye of staff's right and duty to search and the requirement that patients' rooms therefore not be over-cluttered. Mrs Miles told us that the amount of possessions patients had in their rooms at the time of the Owen Ward report was very much left up to PCTs. She was well aware of the problems with storage but noted that no one was beating down her door to say that it was an issue which had to be addressed as a high priority in the capital programme.

2.23.7 As far as Lawrence Ward was concerned, several witnesses told us that the quantity of possessions was considerable. Mr Moran admitted that the actual volume of possessions in patients' rooms on Lawrence Ward made searching "almost impossible". This picture was confirmed by Mr Arnold, who told us that fireproof cabinets were promised for storing excess videos, but these never materialized in his time. In their absence there was, he said, little they could do.

2.23.8 Mr Day, who became Security Liaison Officer for the PDU in January 1995, told us that patients' possessions were a continuing headache. For example, it was quite common on the PDU for patients to have more than one video recorder. When the Security Liaison Officers had first started they did draft a policy on possessions which was rejected as too draconian. It took a very long time to get a policy agreed on this issue.

2.23.9 Mr Maxwell told us that when core search standards were introduced there was negotiation with the Clinical Managers as to how many searches would be carried out on each ward. Once that was agreed the Ward Manager would be responsible for ensuring that the searches were carried out.

2.23.10 He had expected an uproar when the new searching policy was introduced, but in fact there was little complaint. This made him suspect that the returns the Security Department was receiving reporting that searching was happening were falsified. When his staff did an audit they found the quality of searching to be mixed. Those wards which had resisted the introduction of the standards were the worst, Lawrence Ward amongst them. As we have seen from the security managers' meetings, staff questioned the legality of the searches and complained that they spoiled therapeutic relationships; Mr Maxwell thought that laziness played a part, as did the fact that staff had become less skilled at saying "no" to patients.

2.23.11 Mrs Miles did ask Mr Dale to develop a policy on patients' possessions. A very lengthy policy development process followed, with much debate over the degree of freedom clinical units should have in implementing the new policy. A new policy emerged in June 1996, at which point Mrs Miles discovered the Finance Director was developing a policy on the storage of valuables. She insisted that the two be merged. The final policy had still not been finalized by the time we started hearing formal evidence, although Mr Gardner told us that a new policy was introduced in November 1997. Mr Gardner admitted that he and his colleagues had not audited the implementation of the June 1996 policy; he admitted that there had been an absence of auditing in the past to ensure that policies were properly implemented.

2.23.12 This air of pessimism, almost apathy, concerning patients' possessions was not shared by Mr Kaye and Miss Kinsley. Both thought that the problem of not having containers to store possessions was eminently soluble. Mr Kaye told us that no one ever approached him asking for extra capital for this, although he was aware of the problem. He and Miss Kinsley independently gave us the impression that the Hospital used the "lack of storage space" argument as an excuse for not tackling the, no doubt, difficult problem of challenging patients over the amount of property they had been allowed to accumulate over the years.

2.23.13 We agree with them. Storage should not be a problem as Mr Kaye said. The problem is the creation of a 'prescriptive right' over the years to keep bedrooms in an unsearchable state. And if Mr Kaye is right, Mrs Miles must bear the responsibility for not making the storage available.

Recommendation 10 **2.23.14 We recommend that, as a matter of urgency, the level of patients' possessions in bed rooms be reduced to, and thereafter maintained at, a level which permits full and thorough room searches to be carried out in a reasonable time.**

2.23.15 As far as a policy on patients' possessions was concerned, over three years after the Owen Ward incident a clear, implementable policy was not in place. This is a totally

unacceptable state of affairs as it represents a significant breach in security. It is essential that the quantity of patients' possessions should never be so great that it prevents effective searching.

2.23.16 Everyone in authority knew there was a problem. It was not seen as a high enough priority despite Owen Ward and despite the activities of patient Mr Braund. No one at senior levels got to grips with the issue, even though, as Mr Kaye confirmed, cash could have been made available. If Mr Kaye was as keen as he made out to ensure that rooms were searchable he did not call Ashworth's bluff or that of the other two Special Hospitals, because it was a common problem frequently referred to in the minutes of the Security Managers' meetings. The problem was trying to find the balance between liberalization and security. There was blameworthiness at both SHSA and hospital levels. The SHSA did not prescribe a proper system. At the Hospital level, as UGM, Mrs Miles did not seek the necessary finance to provide adequate storage space.

2.23.17 A significant problem stemmed from the very wide meaning which was being given to "therapy" and "treatment". Some RMOs and PCTs had sharply downgraded security in pursuit of illusory therapeutic gains. Mr Corrigan, for example was allowed to accumulate four VCRs on this basis, even though multiple VCRs are only required for the purpose of copying video cassette tapes. Only two VCRs are required for that purpose. To possess four is to possess a production line. It is absurd to consider possession of that number of VCRs as therapeutic or as part of treatment.

Recommendation 11 **2.23.18 We recommend that no patient should be allowed more than one video cassette recording machine in his bed room. If any copying or editing of video tapes is required this should be done under supervision within the Education Department.**

2.23.19 Fundamental requirements of security should never be compromised.

2.23.20 We discuss another aspect of controlling patients' possessions, namely controlling access to cash cards, in Part Three below.

2.24.0 Devolution and Multi-disciplinary Working

2.24.1 What had gone wrong? The Hospital had delegated as much as possible to the lowest management level in the organization, the PCTs. At the same time the creation of Clinical Units focusing on the care needs of defined groups of patients, the breaking up of the old professional hierarchies, the introduction of Ward Managers had all been designed to help create multi-disciplinary care teams with the authority to make sensible clinical decisions about their patients. The authority of the Security Department was, as we have seen, seriously eroded in the process.

2.24.2 It is important to stress that delegation in itself and the development of better multi-disciplinary working are admirable in themselves. However, to delegate successfully in that way one needs, first, a clear policy framework setting out limits to the autonomy of PCTs and Clinical Units, and their responsibility for keeping senior management informed, so that everyone knows where they stand; second, alert management at every level capable of picking up possible dangers and ready to share any concerns at a higher level, so that any necessary action can be taken; and third, strong PCTs aware of their corporate responsibilities for the security of the whole institution, not just their own patients.

2.24.3 We discuss now each of those three prerequisites in turn.

2.25.0 The Policy-Making Process

2.25.1 We mentioned above that devolution has to be accompanied by a clear framework, so that staff 'at the coalface' understand the limits of their responsibilities and powers. A number of witnesses told us that before the Blom-Cooper Inquiry policies were clearly laid down and well-understood. Whether that was wholly true or not (and the experience of the deaths of Derek Williams and Stephen Mallalieu suggests that policy at ward level was not well-developed), the events on Lawrence Ward demonstrate a clear weakness with regard to the implementation of Hospital policies. We spent much time questioning witnesses on the policy-making process to identify what went wrong. Something deeper than Lawrence Ward having a 'rogue' PCT was involved.

2.25.2 There were indications of concern in the summer of 1995 that the mechanisms for policy-making were unclear. Thus Mr Dale noted at the HEG meeting in July 1995 that there was confusion over the differing roles of the HMT, Clinical Development Group (CDG) and the Risk Management Team (RMT) in the decision-making process. Two months later there was further concern raised about the position of the RMT. Eventually in October 1995 came the "Policies Policy",dated October 1995, which sets out a number of policy statements and outlines a policy-making process. It is worth quoting extensively.

> **"POLICY STATEMENTS**
>
> "1) The General Manager will be the Policy Coordinator and will be responsible for coordinating the Policy System and determining the Key Manager for all policies.
>
> 2) The Policy Coordinator in conjunction with the Hospital Executive Group will determine which areas receive a full set of policies and which departments require policies relating to their own specific areas.
>
> The following will receive a set of appropriate policies:
>
> a) All wards.
>
> b) Day service departments.
>
> c) All members of the Hospital Executive Group, Hospital Management Team and Clinical Development Group.
>
> d) Senior Clinical Nurses.
>
> e) Senior Managers
>
> f) Chairman of the Hospital Advisory Committee.
>
> 3) Each policy will have a designated Policy Team.
>
> 4) With the approval of the General Manager/Group commissioning the policy, the appointed Key Managers will be responsible for gathering together a Policy Team; ensuring wide representation from appropriate staff within the service.
>
> 5) The Key Manager will be responsible for:
>
> a) Chairing Policy Team Meetings.
>
> b) Allocating work as required to individual members of the team.
>
> c) Gathering information.
>
> d) Ensuring consultation with appropriate parties.
>
> e) Sending out information, including copies of draft operational policies to Team Members.
>
> f) Making sure all policies under their jurisdiction are reviewed at the appropriate time in conjunction with the Policy Coordinator.
>
> g) Ensuring consistency with Special Hospital Services Authority's policies.

6) It will be the decision of each Policy Team to determine the distribution of the Policy to other departments/areas not listed in 2) above. They will base their decision on the list of areas/departments provided.

7) The Hospital Executive Group will approve and authorise the implementation of all policies.

8) All policies should be reviewed annually unless circumstances require more frequent review.

9) To aid the speed of reviews and reduce paper work, all master copies of policies should bestored electronically. The disk(s) will be kept by the P.A. to the General Manager.

10) All policies will be contained within a file which will also be accurately indexed. All new policies will be automatically included on this index.

11) Ward/Departmental Managers will be responsible for ensuring that all staff have read and had opportunity to discuss all policies issued and that they have signed accordingly on the form provided that will be attached to the policy.

12) It should be clearly stated within each ward operational policy the precise location of the policy files.

13) To ensure reviews of policies are uptodate, any new or revised policies should carry on them the date of review."

This paper was distributed to members of the Hospital Executive Group, the Hospital Management Team and the Clinical Development Group (CDG).

2.25.3 The paper set out a flowchart for the policy-making process. The need for a policy could be identified by the General Manager; by HEG, HMT or CDG, the Clinical Unit Management Team or the Ward PCT; or could arise from the Business Plan, Operational Requirements and Reviews. The Manager / Group commissioning the work would decide the membership of Policy Team and the "key manager", define the work to be done and lay down reporting mechanisms. Consultation would take place as appropriate with the HEG, HMT, CDG, Clinical Unit Ward Staff and Patients. The key manager would report to the Commissioning Group which would decide whether more needed to be done.

2.25.4 A key part of the policy-making process is ratification. All Hospital policies were to be ratified by the HEG; all clinical policies by the CDG; clinical unit operational policies by the HMT; and ward policies by the Clinical Unit Management Team. Policies would be reviewed and the consultation process restarted.

Flaws in the Policy

2.25.5 The existence of the Policies Policy is an admission that the policy process had slipped. We examine how policy-making worked in practice, both before and after this policy statement, below. But a number of points struck us about the statement itself. First, it is clear enough that there are policies which apply to different areas of the organization. Three levels are identified: Hospital wide; clinical unit; and ward level. The principle of delegation and devolving power is evident: ward-level policies are to be ratified by the Clinical Unit Management Team, but the link up to the HMT is severed.

2.25.6 However, there was no clear obligation on managers at the Clinical Unit level to report upwards what their ward policies were, and the extent to which Hospital policies were being amended. If policy making is fragmented, there must be a means of bringing policies together for monitoring and audit purposes. This was a fundamental mistake. If clause 7 of the Policies Policy means anything, then it should mean that the HEG will have approved and authorised the implementation of all policies down to Ward level. If that

approach had been used then the HEG would have known of any PCT changes or attempts to change Hospital wide policies. The truth is that the HEG did not know. The Policies Policy is too complex with too many weak links.

2.25.7 Second, monitoring and auditing are not mentioned. Reviewing policies is an annual task; monitoring should be a continuing process, and auditing involves ensuring consistency between policies. It is essential to ensure that at Clinical Unit level fundamental security requirements are nor diluted to the detriment of the Hospital.

2.25.8 Third, the whole process is too unwieldy and complex, and thus liable to break down. If such a process is necessary it reflects adversely on the problem of managing a large hospital of this type. Mrs Miles admitted to us that consultation was over-done on occasion. A hospital such as Ashworth cannot be run as a glorified 'therapeutic community'. No army could be efficiently managed without officers, non-commissioned officers and troops.

2.25.9 In considering line-management, which we deal with more fully in Part Five, it has struck us that the NHS generally has developed convoluted management structures. We have come across 'control without responsibility' and 'responsibility without control'. At every level of any organisation it is essential that people know to whom and for what they are responsible.

2.25.10 A much simpler and more understandable system is to have the top management in charge of the Hospital responsible for all the policies. Then they cannot shuffle off responsibility for them. They must have a duty to consult and heed the views of those directly affected by policies at various levels below who are directly affected by particular policies, before creating or modifying policies. Once made or modified such polices must be clearly stated and made readily available to those affected by them.

2.25.11 The top management is then responsible and accountable if policies they have put in place prove to be defective. If policies are breached below then the finger of responsibility can be accurately pointed at the person(s) responsible. In this way fault is clearly established, and the only remaining issue is the level of blameworthiness.

2.25.12 We are well aware that this could be criticized for dragging senior managers into clinical decisions and removing clinical freedom. RMOs could not make any decisions about their patients because they would be checking them with senior managers. We would make three points in reply. First, PCTs would still have clinical freedom, but within defined limits. They could not change policies willy-nilly. Second, in a unit of a sensible size (200 beds we think is the maximum) there would not be the same gulf as we have witnessed at Ashworth between senior managers and those on the 'shop-floor'. Third there are fundamental requirements of security designed to protect other patients, staff, visitors and the public which must be kept in place and which a Special Hospital is justified in keeping in place.

2.26.0 The Dissemination of Policies

2.26.1 It seems that the 'Policies Policy' was created because of the lack of a clear process for disseminating Hospital policies to wards. When asked about the dissemination of a policy in 1994, Mr Green remarked that it was left to Clinical Managers to organize dissemination within their Units. He admitted that there was no written system at that time for disseminating general Hospital policy to wards. It was a matter of sound management to ensure that the right people received the documents.

2.26.2 If Mr Green is to be believed, the dissemination of policies was sometimes lamentable. He told us that the Lawrence Ward policies, including the Hospital policies, were at the back of a filing cabinet, and needed ironing to be presentable. There appeared to be a haphazard process for communicating policies to PCTs: individual RMOs would certainly receive copies, but Mr Green did not think the PCT as a whole always received details of the policies. There was no book on each ward with all the policies in it. Clinical managers were put in place in part to plug this gap and to ensure that corporate policies were implemented and monitored, working closely with Ward Managers, who were responsible for monitoring that agreed actions took place. It did not always happen.

2.26.3 Mr Green, with his experience of the Owen Ward investigations, pointed out that sometimes the fault lay with PCTs which did not make themselves aware of Hospital policies. An example was the "red book" of security policies. It was there on the wards, but members of the PCT did not necessarily make themselves aware of the contents.

Recommendation 12 **2.26.4 We recommend that at all times an up-to-date book containing all relevant security policies and rules should be easily and readily available to all ward staff, and location and contents should be known by all ward staff.**

2.26.5 It is essential that policies should be in a clearly identified file on a ward.

2.26.6 By contrast, with a simple system such as just outlined, there would be no doubt where responsibility lies. The HEG's policy making team would have to shoulder the burden of ensuring, not only that effective policies were in place, but also their effective dissemination so that it could point the finger of responsibility towards anyone who breached a policy.

Policies in Practice

2.26.7 Such was the alleged process. Mrs Miles sought to bring a structure to the policy-making process, which she herself admitted sometimes took too long and involved too much consultation (hence it took over five years to produce a fresh version of the Security Manual). It is difficult to see how such a system could be described otherwise than as flawed.

2.26.8 The evidence we heard was that there was all too little process in the production of policies. Mr Tarbuck reported that policies and procedures appeared to arise from different groups and it was uncertain where authority to make policy official lay. Whether the Policies' Policy improved matters he did not say. The exception to this was any memo from Mrs Miles. However, this could not always have been true, having regard to how her "edicts" on patients' involvement in business and holding cash cards were received.

2.26.9 Mr Preece, the Chairman of the POA Branch at Ashworth, told us that policies could be passed on to ward-based staff *via* various routes, for example, by e-mail, or memos circulated by heads of departments and disciplines, and by senior managers. These policies might then be adapted at subsequent PCT meetings. When asked what resource nurses had available to give them a comprehensive picture, Mr Preece referred us to the "Conversation book", or daily log which gave an opportunity for nurses to note down new policies and changes. If this mode of dissemination was used, then it was an ad hoc system.

2.26.10 This, of course is no way to disseminate important information. A mere glance at any conversation book will tell you that. It contains notes made by nurses generally for the next shift. Mr Cannon, a team leader on Lawrence Ward and on occasion an Acting Ward Manager, told us he did not look at the conversation books and did not think it was for a Ward Manager to do so. Once a page was filled up and the leaf turned, it would be pure chance if anyone decided to browse through past pages for historical entries; it would be a remote prospect for new staff to get to know any policy enshrined in such a book.

2.26.11 We heard evidence that clinicians, doctors especially, felt disenfranchised from the policy process (certainly this was the evidence of Dr Strickland, Dr Crispin and Mrs Day).

They were supported at least in part by Mr Erville Millar, who agreed that professional staff had been somewhat marginalised in the production of policies. There was undoubtedly fault on both sides: the Hospital might have failed to consult effectively, but a number of clinicians paid precious little attention to the need for corporate security policies. Beyond the control of either was the sheer size of the Hospital, which made consultation and involvement of staff extremely difficult.

2.26.12 Mr Millar said he had been impressed by the quality of policy production but implementation had been faulty. He had seconded a senior manager to review all policies and to get them onto the Hospital's "Intra-net" e-mail system. However, such a system is hardly secure and it does not ensure that computerised policies will be read and implemented any more than does a hard copy system. Wherever it is necessary to have recourse to policies, an up-to -date copy should be available and known to be available.

2.26.13 Several witnesses, as we have cited above, harked back to the days pre-Blom-Cooper. Ms Young told us that in those days policies were fairly clear, known to everyone, but very tight. Mr Green told us that before the Inquiry the Hospital Management Team had kept a much firmer grip of policy making. Now each ward had its own policies relating to different functions. The number might vary considerably, depending on the patient group on the ward and their dependency level. There was no general requirement for ward policies to be passed upwards to be ratified.

2.26.14 In considering management issues and policies in respect of this patient group we come back to the importance of clarity. As Dr Hunter said when reflecting on the setting up of wards for psychopathic patients at Park Lane in the 1980s, with these sort of patients it was vital to have a clear, shared philosophy out of which derived the policies and practices of the ward, owned and shared by all staff, and developed by everyone including patients .

2.26.15 We would make a rider to that: patients might be allowed to contribute ideas, but they cannot take decisions when it comes to security. Whilst therapeutic community-type regimes work well with some less severe personality disordered individuals, it is entering dangerous territory to allow this sort of patient to become involved in negotiating security.

2.26.16 The rules adopted in the PDU paid scant regard to Hospital-wide policies (even when staff knew what they were). The challenge of moving an organization like Ashworth to embrace the new Blom-Cooper philosophy was grossly under-estimated.

2.26.17 The move towards more discriminating policies which were better attuned to the differing needs of different groups of patients would have been sound if this had been done within the framework of a context of a Hospital-wide security policy. That they did not was a fundamental error and resulted from the decision described by Mr Kaye that the Blom-Cooper recommendations were to apply on a Hospital-wide basis and no differentiation was to be made on the basis of diagnosis, such as mental illness or personality disorder.

2.26.18 We have said we would prefer to see a much more simple and accountability orientated process of policy making, but even within the existing system the appropriate principles are simple, and so simple that we can only sympathise with Miss Kinsley who found trying to get them across was like hitting her head against a wall.

Recommendation 13

2.26.19 We recommend the following principles be adopted:
(i) There must be clear hospital-wide policies which cannot be changed except at the highest management level.
(ii) Within the framework of hospital policies there will be a number of clearly defined areas where clinical units/directorates and PCTs may exercise discretion to

interpret policies to reflect the distinctive needs of a particular patient group.
(iii) Where use of such discretion is exercised the fact should be recorded.
(iv) Any changes to hospital policies should be made known to all staff by an agreed procedure such as regular team briefing. The changes should immediately be added to the Policy File, again before implementation.
(v) Policies should be clear and easily available to all staff, in a single file. Staff should be required to know the contents of policies. They should attest they have read them and re-attest regarding any changes made to them.
(vi) All staff must have read and be aware of policies before they start working on the ward.
(vii) The number of policies should be kept to a minimum so that staff are not overwhelmed by paper.

2.26.20 Simple though these principles are we can understand the difficulty in applying them in large institutions of this type, where managers are remote from the wards and where large numbers of patients of different diagnostic groups and different needs within their diagnostic groups are gathered together on a large campus in 25-bedded wards. How can one have a coherent Hospital-wide policy framework? How can managers keep in touch with what is happening on the wards?

2.26.21 We believe they cannot, at least not in a Hospital the size of Ashworth with its very particular history. The point about size is crucial. We do not believe Ashworth is manageable at its present size and with its population of different diagnostic groups. It is simply too big.

2.26.22 The same applies to the PDU because personality disordered patients vary so much in their individual requirements. Above all those personality disordered offender patients who do not want to be treated or who prove to be resistant to known therapies should not be in a hospital of this sort.

2.27.0 Formal and Informal Monitoring

2.27.1 So Ashworth Hospital had in place by October 1995 a process for developing, ratifying policy and reviewing policy. But what information were senior managers receiving as to the working of clinical and other policies, information which could identify hot spots where action was needed? As with the SHSA at national level (*see* **2.19.0** *et seq.*) there were a range of formal and informal mechanisms established.

2.27.2 A number of initiatives have been taken over the years at Ashworth to improve monitoring of activity and the quality of service provided. Thus in 1990 a Quality Assurance Department had been established at the Hospital, consisting of a small group of nursing staff who were responsible for developing a Quality Assurance Programme for nursing within the Hospital. In May 1992 an audit tool called the Observational Standards of Care and Audit Review (OSCAR), a method of ward audit originally developed and validated at Rampton Hospital, had been adopted. All wards were audited using OSCAR during the period May 1992 – August 1993 and subsequently between January 1994 and February 1995. The audit tool was reviewed and amended to incorporate Patient's Charter and other Quality Standards contained within the 1994/95 Service Level Agreement between Ashworth Hospital and the SHSA.

2.27.3 The Hospital in its submission noted that ward audits are undertaken at least annually by members of the Quality Development Department together with a representative from the ward concerned. The audits are intended to measure practice and services against the rights and standards within the Patient's Charter and other contract standards, and include assessments of patient opinions alongside patient records and where appropriate, staff opinions and ward observations. All wards receive written Reports on their performance.

Action plans are developed and progress is monitored. An anonymised summary of the results, along with a Report of performance against other contract standards is presented to the Hospital Authority Board on a quarterly basis. Results are also included in the quarterly returns to the Purchasers which are circulated to all Directorates across the Hospital.

2.27.4 A further development about which we heard a good deal was the Clinical Monitoring Report, introduced in June 1995. This was originally a collation of various separate Reports which had been available before, but it was gradually refined. It provided and provides managers with information relating to seclusion, special observations, incidents, security searches and incidents, the use of care and responsibility and serious complaints. The Report gives Care Directors and Clinical Teams an up todate picture of trends relevant to specific clinical areas and forms part of the Hospital's overall framework for the assessment and management of risk. Mrs Miles found these Reports particularly helpful in measuring trends in the Hospital. Mr Dale, who introduced them, admitted that there was perhaps an over-reliance on quantitative, as opposed to qualitative, information, but argued that they were a considerable step forward and a useful management tool.

2.27.5 We saw copies of a number of the Clinical Monitoring Reports. These are indeed useful documents. Mr Dale admitted that he and his colleagues were probably lulled into a false sense of security seeing returns stating that searching was taking place. Qualitative measures were needed as well. We agree: quality is much more important than quantity. One must remember that the problems on Lawrence Ward were not caught by this system, as Mrs Miles admitted.

2.28.0 "Visibility"

2.28.1 One very obvious informal means of monitoring what is going on is to walk the site. Mrs Miles stressed that she tried to visit two to four wards per month for several hours and did raise issues of concern with Ward Managers. She attended the Patients' Council on a quarterly basis, or more frequently if specific issues arose. Twice a year she held open meetings. She asked her directors to "adopt" a clinical unit to get them more visible in the Hospital and to give her an extra pair of eyes in each unit. Thus Mr Green "adopted" the PDU, an arrangement which, it has to be said, worked rather better when Mr Tarbuck was clinical manager than when Mr Murphy took over.

2.28.2 But one point that impressed us when we visited the Hospital was that senior managers are shut off from the secure parts of the site. The Authority Headquarters is outside the secure part of the site, in between the three parts of the old site. Whilst this made some sense when there were three different sites, it is untenable today. Although the building is only a couple of hundred yards from the secure perimeter, the physical barrier of the wall greatly increases the sense of distance.

2.28.3 Thus Mr Millar forcefully argued that Hospital management needed to be seen inside the perimeter. He told us how easy it was to become involved into other parts of the job and not to enter the secure perimeter. Mr Franey, General Manager then Chief Executive of Broadmoor between 1988 and 1997, told us that it was easy for management to seem very remote to most staff. He was very pleased that at Broadmoor everyone was inside the secure perimeter. Mrs Miles herself regretted that senior managers were outside the wall, although she pointed out that with two sites it was impossible to be inside both at once.

2.28.4 Miss Kinsley vividly expressed the same view:

> "I would not want to manage a prison from outside it, and I do not think I would have felt happy managing one of these hospitals from outside it. You do not get the feel of what goes on. You do not see things. You are not part of the scene in the same way as if you are there."

Recommendation 14 **2.28.5 We recommend that the Authority Hospital Senior Management Team is relocated within the secure perimeter of Ashworth North.**

2.29.0 Patients' Rights

2.29.1 As we have discussed, we heard a considerable amount of disquiet over the new emphasis on patients' rights post-Blom-Cooper. Things had gone "too far" and staff were afraid of saying "no" to patients, lest they become the subject of a complaint. However, quite apart from its intrinsic benefits to patients, giving patients a voice in the Hospital's affairs also offered a further semi-formal mechanism for gaining feedback on performance How well did it work in practice?

2.29.2 The importance of giving patients a voice was perhaps the central message of the Blom-Cooper Inquiry team's Report. Ashworth has taken important strides to do just that. Three innovations need to be mentioned. One, the creation of a Patients' Advocacy Service, run by a local Citizen's Advice Bureau. Two, the introduction of a rigorous complaints system. Three the establishment of a Patients' Council. In theory these present a mechanism by which important issues can be raised which otherwise might remain hidden; part of their justification is, then, that they are a means to monitor quality and address clinical and operational issues. Indeed, with the inception of the new Ashworth Hospital Authority in April 1996 a Complaints and Incidents Committee was formed, chaired by a Non-Executive Director, and given a brief which included reviewing incidents and assessing whether there was any link between complaints and incidents.

2.29.3 We heard evidence that once again personality disordered patients had gained rather more from the Blom-Cooper Report reforms than many of their colleagues. Thus Dr Strickland welcomed the development of the Patients' Advocacy Service but noted that the advocates were quickly drawn into spending a lot of time with personality disordered patients well able to speak up for themselves.

2.29.4 As far as the complaints system was concerned, Mrs Miles told us she had written to staff in September 1994 stressing that management would support them if they were carrying out agreed policies and procedures. She granted that patients were good at threatening staff with solicitors, advocates, the Mental Health Act Commission etc. Mr Franey noted that the staff at Broadmoor too felt threatened by the complaints system. Mr Murphy thought that the many of the complaints that had gone through the complaints process, leading to investigations and upset for staff and sometimes patients, might better have been dealt with at the local level. Mr Sandford of the RCN argued that there should be a screening process to differentiate between malicious and vexatious complaints and those meriting full scrutiny.

2.29.5 Finally Mr Murphy was sharply critical of the way in which the Patients' Council had been taken over by personality disordered patients and told us he was actually warned he would be assaulted if he attended one meeting.

2.29.6 This appears to be another area in which the reforms introduced in the wake of the Blom-Cooper Report have been to some extent "hijacked" by articulate personality disordered patients to the detriment of the mentally ill, women and learning disability patients.

Recommendation 15 **2.29.7 We recommend that the composition and working of the Patients' Council be reviewed to ensure that mentally ill patients are properly represented and that the Council's activities are not dominated by personality disordered patients.**

2.29.8 The Patients' Advocacy Service, the new complaints procedure and the Patients' Council are all very important and worthwhile developments. But we are struck by a remark of Professor Sines, who was commissioned by the Hospital to assess nursing on the PDU (*see* Part Four below). He commented that whilst patients had been empowered over recent years, staff had become disempowered. It is vital that a better balance be struck between the 'rights' of patients and those of managers and other staff to run the Hospital safely.

2.30.0 Patient Care Teams

2.30.1 So much for formal and informal monitoring. At the root of the clinical care and treatment offered to patients is the Patient Care Team, or PCT. As Mr Green commented in relation to the Owen Ward Report, if the PCT is dysfunctional not much will be working well either. Essential though clinical freedom is to effective care provision, it is necessary to ensure that PCTs do not trespass beyond the proper boundaries of clinical freedom if the overall safety of the Hospital is not to be undermined.

2.30.2 The problem is that whilst effective PCTs comprise a good multi-disciplinary team with sound medical leadership, the quality of the PCTs at Ashworth has always been patchy throughout the lifetime of the SHSA, as Mr Kaye admitted.

2.30.3 The introduction of Clinical Units meant that Clinical Managers were supposed to focus on the work of the PCTs, including monitoring their policies. Later still, part of the rationale for the creation of Clinical Directorates was to attract high quality medical staff who might improve the links with the PCTs. These links were not easy to forge since the RMOs did not report to those managers in a line management relationship. The RMO's statutory responsibility for the treatment of an individual patient made any such reporting arrangement difficult, if not impossible.

2.30.4 Of course, in trying to oversee the work of PCTs, the Clinical Manager or Clinical Director is in an awkward position. In seeking to monitor the work of the PCTs to ensure that wider implications of their clinical decisions are identified and addressed, then he or she is arguably interfering with the clinical responsibilities assigned to the RMO and PCT. On the other hand, failure to keep an eye on these matters risked leaving rogue PCTs to endanger the security of the whole Hospital.

2.30.5 For the system to work what is required is strong but fair local management which commands respect, and PCTs which recognized their wider responsibilities. In some parts only did this exist. The links between PCTs and more senior clinical staff were informal: individual members of PCTs might, at other meetings mention matters raised in their PCT meetings, but this was a matter left to chance in the absence of formal links upwards and downwards.

2.30.6 Mrs Miles denied that there was a serious problem with the accountability of PCTs. As bodies they were not accountable, but the individuals within them were. For his part, Mr Kaye was adamant that it was for the General Manager at the Hospital to ensure that PCTs were operating properly. There might be a degree of negotiation on issues which had a clinical component, and if need be issues would come up to the SHSA, to Mr Kaye and Dr Taylor. In theory there was a formal line right up to the Authority itself. Their view, implicitly, is that the structure was satisfactory, so long as the Clinical Manager/Director was doing his or her job.

2.30.7 But as we have said, the system is not only dependent upon Clinical Managers doing their job, it also relies on PCTs telling the Clinical Manager what was going on. There was no duty imposed on PCTs to do so. Mrs Miles noted that Hospital contracts did now, as she understood it, have a clause about having to abide by Hospital policies.

2.30.8 If PCTs are working well, then there will not be a problem. However, Mrs Miles told us that several PCTs in the PDU were not as effective as she would have liked. She was aware of some staff on the wards feeling that the PCTs were not listening to them and wanting to implement policy in their own way, rather than the way in which management wanted them to implement it. After the Owen Ward hostage-taking Report, Owen Ward made great strides. Newman was improving, but of the other four PCTs, Mrs Miles had doubts about a number of individuals. In her view some of the PCTs were reluctant to listen to the staff on the ward who were with patients day in, day out. This was a feature of the Owen and Lawrence Ward PCTs, but to some extent of Ruskin and Shelley too.

2.30.9 What role does the Medical Director have in monitoring the work of the PCT? The RMO leads the clinical team and the Medical Director is the senior doctor in the Hospital and adviser to the Board on medical matters. Dr Shetty, the then Medical Director, told us he saw his consultant colleagues regularly, providing advice, support and in some cases formal supervision. However, he did not see his role as Medical Director as being to tell his consultant colleagues what to do, to point the finger at failures to provide treatment plans and so forth. Whilst he would intervene if he saw a colleague doing anything dangerous, he did not have the power to direct his colleagues in a dictatorial way, nor did he want such a power. Dr Shetty put it bluntly: "I do not check up on my consultant colleagues".

2.30.10 We pressed Dr Shetty on this point. He admitted that he played an active part in making sure the consultants did their jobs properly. He played a key part in the consultants' job plans and so would be involved in following up performance against those plans. During the job plan discussions he would raise issues such as clinical audit, continuing professional development, performance of statutory duties, as well as more managerial issues. He was active in seeking to recruit new forensically-trained consultants.

2.30.11 However he drew a line between advice and control. He considered his task was to look at issues of quality, such as the quality of care plans, through medical audit, peer group review and job plans rather than to admonish individual RMOs. He had been unable to identify ways of monitoring the work of his colleagues. He did point out that although the RMO is responsible for the care and treatment of each patient, he or she is largely reliant on clinical colleagues to carry through the treatment plan.

2.30.12 Dr Shetty noted that where there were conflicts between therapy and security these were usually sorted out at ward level. The Security Liaison Officers were intended to bring more of a security focus to the decision-making of the PCTs. If conflict remained it could go up the security hierarchy to Mr Dale and the clinical hierarchy to Dr Shetty. That was the theory, but in practice it did not work well.

2.30.13 In discussing with Dr Shetty his role as Medical Director it struck us that Mrs Miles' view that the individuals in PCTs were accountable, albeit in an imprecise way, also reflected a general tendency at Ashworth for professionals to stay within professional boxes. Thus Dr Shetty would deal with (some) issues of medical performance, the Head of Psychology with the psychologists, the Director of Nursing with nurses, and so on. Dr Shetty, when pushed, thought that the Clinical Director or Chief Executive would have to deal with a knotty clinical or security issue, depending upon its seriousness. Likewise the Clinical Director of the PDU area would be the first port of call for clinicians worried about the lack of a particular therapy.

2.30.14 We do not think this situation is satisfactory as it stands. We discuss the role of the Medical Director in Part Four below.

2.30.15 There are steps that could be taken. Managers could seek to monitor PCT decision-making by attending meetings (of necessity an occasional occurrence) and by reading routinely minutes of PCT meetings. Mr Green told us that whilst some PCTs kept good minutes of their meetings, which found their way onto patients' notes, others did not. There was no requirement that minutes of PCT meetings be sent to senior managers. (This contrasts with Broadmoor, where Mr Franey told us that he insisted on seeing all such minutes, and attending PCT meetings when he could.) Mr Millar told us bluntly that he found no system of auditing the decision-making of the PCTs. He found some stark contradictions in terms of local policies being made. He was right.

2.30.16 From Mr Green's evidence it appears that any PCT-inspired deviation from Hospital-wide policies might be picked up – or it might not. On occasion PCTs were asked to formulate ward policies to be ratified by senior managers, but this was the exception. PCTs would only send minutes, ward policies and so forth if asked. An opportunity to monitor their work systematically was being missed.

Recommendation 16 **2.30.17 We recommend that minutes of PCT meetings within the PDU are routinely sent to and read by the Clinical Director. Relevant remarks should be entered into clinical records where they affect individual patients.**

2.30.18 The events on Lawrence Ward demonstrated that PCTs could and did act alone, oblivious to Hospital policies, a point we illustrate further below. The framework for devolving power was lacking: the route from Chief Executive downwards was clear on paper, but the route back up from the wards was not even set out on paper. Wards were given power without responsibility: the power to act as they clinically saw fit, without the responsibility to keep senior colleagues informed. The potential for this to happen will always be there: the status of the RMO ensures that, and sometimes very good clinical teams will take decisions which, although appropriate for an individual patient, have wider implications which the team do not see. Those dangers can be minimized by better multi-disciplinary co-operation in PCTs, led by RMOs who value rather than pay lip-service to multi-disciplinary input, and unobtrusive monitoring and audit of PCT decision-making. Better patient-mix after thorough assessment would also undoubtedly help.

2.31.0 An Operations Manager and Control of Policies

2.31.1 Even if Clinical Managers/Directors were keeping a watchful eye on their PCTs, that does not solve the problem of ensuring that all units/directorates are in step with broad hospital policy. Mr Green argued that what the post-Blom-Cooper management structure lacked was a Director of Operations to ensure that the four clinical unit managers (and subsequently two clinical directors) did not ignore the corporate management agenda of the Hospital. In this he was supported by Mr Dale. Mr Green chaired the Hospital Management Team (HMT), which brought together the four Clinical Managers; he told us he felt in an awkward position trying to persuade his colleagues to take on the corporate agenda without formal line management authority over them, such as a Director of Operations might have.

2.31.2 He gave an interesting example, to which we will return, of the debate over cash cards. In 1995 he had gone to the Hospital Executive Group to say that a clear direction was needed on whether patients were to be allowed to possess cash cards. The answer was "no", which Mr Green relayed back to his colleagues on the Hospital Management Team. However, Mr Tarbuck, the PDU Clinical Manager then proposed to Mrs Miles that their use should be continued. If Mr Green had the authority of a Director of Operations, in his view, the debate could have been finished there and then, provided that the ownership of decisions such as whether patients should have cash cards could not be claimed by PCTs.

2.31.3 An Operations Manager might have been the ideal person to take forward the Owen Ward action plan. Mr Maxwell clearly found it an increasingly thankless task and argued, rightly in our view, that the HMT was not the right committee to take this matter forward, as it did not have the necessary authority and Mr Green, the Chairman, was not the line manager of the four Clinical Managers.

2.31.4 Mrs Miles' view was that creating an operations director would merely draw operational issues up to the level of senior managers, as had happened in the past. She saw Mr Green's chairmanship of the HMT as a coordinating one, making the link between that group and the Executive Group. The various Clinical Managers were accountable to her.

2.31.5 Mr Dale's evidence gave further support to the need for an operations director. He was admirably candid in accepting his share of the blame in what went wrong in terms of security lapses. He pointed out that his position as Director in overall charge of security was only advisory. The Clinical Managers, then Directors, were operationally responsible for security in their units/directorates.

2.31.6 Mr Dale agreed he was responsible for hospital-wide policy but remarked that laying down mandatory policies to be applied across the board was not the ethos of the time. The devolution of responsibility down to clinical units brought with it responsibilities for devising operational policies within those units on areas such as ward visiting, access to bedrooms, use of telephones, etc. Again, there was a lacuna in the structure, a post whose remit was to address the corporate operational issues.

2.31.7 Mr Dale argued that "the failure to appoint an overall operational services manager for the Hospital left a management gap and consequently four mini 'fiefdoms' developed with the clinical units and the respective managers jealously guarding their territories from what was seen as outside direction and influence". The link between the "strategic" Hospital Executive Group and the "operational" Hospital Management Group was opaque and Mr Green's appointment as Chairman did not help particularly.

2.31.8 The combination of a flawed policy process, inadequate monitoring and over-mighty PCTs was potentially dangerous. Whether or not an Operations Manager would have been helpful, there was clearly a lack of focus on operational arrangements within the Hospital.

2.31.9 We turn now to examine the cracks in the system.

Hospital against Ward

2.31.10 Given the move towards delegating more responsibility and autonomy to Clinical Units and ward-based PCTs, it is essential that the boundaries between which policies are mandatory and which are open to local amendment by clinical teams are as clear as possible.

2.31.11 This essential task has been neglected at Ashworth despite the following recommendation emanating from the Owen Ward Report:

> **"e).. All hospital security procedures should be clearly differentiated into those which are mandatory instructions for the entire Hospital, and those which are guidelines and adaptable to the needs of the different wards/units".**

This should apply to all policies whether directly relating to security or not. We were never shown anything which clearly differentiated policies in the way suggested above; the best that could be done apparently was the list in the contract which showed which policies each Hospital had to have.

2.31.12 Professor Bluglass questioned Mrs Miles about the distinction between mandatory policies and those which could be modified locally. She replied:

> A: There would be policies that would go out as policies. There would be other things that would go out as guidelines or guidance notes.

Q:. So a policy was mandatory?
A: As far as I was concerned, yes.

Q: And a guideline was a policy which could be modified?
A: Yes."

Q: So they –
A: That is how I understood it.

Q: And so that when this was sent down to local level there would not be any doubt at all about the status of the document; it was flagged up in some way so it was very clear that this is something which has been decided at a higher level and it must be implemented and there is no question whether you like it or not?
A: I would not swear to every single document, but I am just thinking of some of the policy things that went out that were quite clear. There may have been others that were not so clear. I cannot remember every single one.

Q: It sounds to me as if the system does lay itself open to misunderstanding?
A: I think, with hindsight, you can look back and say that there were things that might have been confusing to staff.

2.31.13 Dr Coorey told us that the lack of clarity in 1994 about which policies were mandatory for the whole Hospital, and which could be modified, still obtained more than three years later. He noted that the new security manual was due out very shortly (it was produced in December 1997), and told us greater clarity appeared to be forthcoming in some areas. He was disappointed that copies of the new "Red Book" would not be sent to all key members of the PCT.

2.31.14 Mr Kaye's evidence is instructive on this point. He told us that SHSA/Hospital policies were handed down to the wards to implement. His evidence was that ward PCTs could take the decision to modify Hospital-wide policy for a given patient or patients: "the clinical team within the ward has the responsibility for the control, treatment and pathway of each patient, so they very much have those decisions". He qualified this by saying that this applied to the interpretation and applications of rules. Thus:

> "I do not think a team could say: 'That is a basic policy in the Hospital but we can disregard that'. Everybody's room had to be searched and everybody's room should be in a state where it could be searched. No team could say, 'We can disregard that'. What a team could say is, 'Well, a privilege, an access to telephones, that is more appropriate for patient X than patient Y because of his clinical condition'."

His view was that policies were clear; the difficult task was to apply the guidance and rules that existed. He would expect copies of Hospital-wide policies to be known to staff and to be available to staff on every ward. From the security point of view, however, there is a gulf between allowing X to have access to a telephone and letting him have unsupervised access to a telephone.

2.31.15 Mr Kaye was asked if he would know if a particular policy had been significantly altered by a PCT; the answer was no, unless that decision had further repercussions. Miss Kinsley's security inspections of the three Hospitals in 1992, and the shortcomings they identified, led to the SHSA laying down quality standards and the checking mechanisms we have described above.

2.31.16 Mr Kaye did point out that he had had concerns in 1995 about the way in which the Hospitals were using the information available to them, flaws which were identified by the SHSA. If senior managers were saying they did not know what was going on, then they were not following the systems laid down and not listening to the advice from the centre.

2.31.17 As we point out elsewhere, however, the SHSA cannot just shuffle off responsibility in this way: its juggling act with security and therapy amounted to a systemic failure.

2.31.18 We are well aware that the Hospital was trying to introduce more individualized care for patients. PCTs were given the power to relax rules in the interests of a particular patient. The problem was, as we have seen, there was no formal mechanism for decisions concerning an individual patient which might impinge upon the safe management of the wider Hospital to be ratified by senior managers. Particular issues affecting Hospital policies, such as excessive amounts of possessions in a patient's room, might be raised higher up the management chain, but they might not.

2.31.19 There is, of course, a grey area where clinical risk assessment, the province of the PCT, ends and general security measures begin. Difficult though this interface sometimes was, Dr Shetty told us that Hospital policy was there to be followed.

2.31.20 We pursued the issue of policy with two former Ward Managers of Lawrence Ward, Mr Arnold and Mr Moran. Mr Arnold was asked about the distinction between Hospital and ward policies in the context of room searches. His understanding was that there could be ward policies running contrary to Hospital policies. The PCT would ratify these, although some would also be ratified by the PDU Operations Group. He thought the existing Lawrence Ward policies when he took over needed to be reviewed and shortened, but Mr Tarbuck had told him that the plan was to develop unit-wide policies that could be adapted according to the dependency of the ward.

2.31.21 There were, Mr, Arnold told us, some policies which were mandatory Hospital policies. These appeared to be very broad and few in number, and did not, it seems, include room searching as far as Lawrence Ward was concerned. Others could be modified by the Clinical Unit. Then there were policies instigated by the individual Units. Lastly there were policies produced by the wards themselves. The ward policies, unit policies and unit-adapted Hospital policies did not need to be referred back upwards, so that senior managers could be completely in the dark as to what policies were in place on a given ward. He admitted the situation was confusing, although someone like him who had worked for fifteen years in the Hospital knew the ropes.

2.31.22 Mr Arnold told us that at some point in 1996 all wards were asked to provide the Hospital with copies of all localized policies. This was presumably for information, although no reason for the request was given. There was never any feedback to the ward saying that the policies were out of step with the Hospital's thinking. He admitted in response to a question from the Chairman that he had never seen any document giving PCTs carte blanche to change Hospital-wide policies.

2.31.23 Mr Moran told us that before Blom-Cooper there was a great deal of central direction; this then disappeared and it was up to PCTs to decide what to do. Sometimes it was confusing as to what policy was in force. PCTs would on occasion ignore policies if they did not seem to fit the needs of the ward. In other words, if they did not like the policy, they would change it.

2.31.24 The disputes still went on: Mr Moran gave a recent example where a patient (not on the PDU) requested a bank loan of £14,000. The PCT said no, the RMO said yes, and he had received the money, despite Mrs Miles' clear instructions concerning commercial activities. Mr Moran told us that it was only in May or June 1997 that the PDU had finally produced a policy document with all the unit policies in it.

2.31.25 Comparing Lawrence Ward to Owen Ward, Mr Moran told us that a key difference was that he and his colleagues had brought in a raft of clear, fair rules early on following the hostage-taking and insisted that patients abided by them.

2.31.26 We also pursued this point with security witnesses. Mr Paterson told us that the devolution of power to wards had been combined with a failure to define policy clearly. In his experience what then happened was that people picked which bits of which policies they wanted to follow. The lower the level of dependency on a given ward, the more likely it was that home-grown policies would emerge which failed to take into account the bigger picture.

2.31.27 Mr Maxwell told us that although Mrs Miles told staff to follow Hospital procedures in the wake of the Owen Ward Report, the majority quietly ignored her. Hence the Security Managers had asked Mr Kaye to make clear that security was central to the Hospital's running. The Clinical Managers in his view were seeking to go their own way:

> "I think they misunderstood that they were asked to formulate procedures for their own wards, and ward philosophies and so on, but it was on the understanding that they were within the parameters of the security procedures."

2.31.28 Mr Dale also admitted that there was a potential confusion between the corporate envelope of policies and the push for wards to develop their own policies. The Risk Management Team, which he chaired, recognized that a lack of clarity about what was mandatory and what was merely guidance was a risk for the organization and had done some work on this area. Whether it was yet resolved was another matter

2.31.29 Our attention was drawn to the letter covering the security "Red Book" in May 1992, which said that:

> "The security procedures are seen as a guide and must be viewed in the context of the 'relational' approach to security which aims to promote an individual approach to patient care and improve the quality of life for both patients and staff."

2.31.30 Mr Dale admitted that with hindsight this was ambiguous about the status of policies. The intention had been to get PCTs to think for themselves about these policy issues and to develop treatment regimes more attuned to individual's needs.

2.31.31 The failure to produce a comprehensive revision of the security manual between May 1992 and late 1997 probably fed the confusion and encouraged the feeling that ward-based policy was more important. Mr Dale spoke of the importance of an annual review in future. He admitted that the time taken to produce the new Security Manual was "ridiculously long". It was caused by a thorough consultation process aimed at winning the maximum ownership.

2.31.32 For a review of such an important policy document to take as long as this did is frankly incompetent.

2.31.33 Mr Tarbuck was another witness who told us that on occasion there appeared to be confusion about what was corporate policy and what was guidance. An example was the vetting of visitors. Clinical teams thought that the social workers should do it; social workers thought security should do it; security thought clinical teams should do it. He noted that sometimes policy would arrive at HMG and it was uncertain where it had come from or what its status was, although the situation improved in 1995, when Peter Green began to chair HMG/HMT. Mr Green also sat on the Executive Group, which was ultimately responsible for policy.

2.31.34 For her part Mrs Miles, when asked whether there was any formal mechanism for mediating between Hospital and ward policies over conflicts, replied that that was the job of the clinical manager and his management team. She admitted that there was no formal system of feedback from the PCTs upwards concerning the implementation of policy by PCTs. She expected clinical managers to know whether or not things were being done properly. There was an example with regard to core search standards, where Lawrence Ward objected.

On occasion she thought that policies were just not implemented by the PCT, without any decision not to do so having been made and minuted.

2.31.35 This was a muddled system. The general strategic shift towards delegating operational decisions down to the Unit/Ward level, combined with this lack of clarity was potentially dangerous.

2.32.0 Clinical Arrogance

2.32.1 This shift of power towards PCTs bred it seems a certain clinical arrogance, whereby PCTs felt they could and should override Hospital policy on occasion on clinical grounds. This may be perfectly acceptable, if the decision is well-grounded in the clinical facts of the case, if the decision is reached after a multi-disciplinary discussion and is well-documented, and if more senior managers are alerted, if only on a "for information" basis. However, as we will see at length in Part Three, staff on Lawrence Ward thought of their ward as different and special, and not bound by the ordinary rules of the Hospital and as a consequence disregarded them.

2.32.2 Mr Moran told us that the absolutely core security policy of searching was one area where the Lawrence Ward PCT felt able to ignore Hospital policy:

> "It was never raised as an issue that rooms were not being searched. Historically that had been the case. It had not posed a problem then, and it was not an issue while I was there."
>
> Q: So security procedures were not being followed on Lawrence Ward?
> A: No.
>
> Q: In contravention of procedure and policy?
> A. Yes.

Mr Moran explained that, post-Blom-Cooper, PCTs became much more independent. The Lawrence Ward PCT felt that, given the nature of the ward, its history and low staffing levels they need not search.

2.32.3 This is a very worrying admission by an experienced middle manager.

2.32.4 Another aspect of the same cavalier approach was the development of policies ad hoc, on the hoof, without any underpinning documentation. This was true, as Dr Strickland admitted, of the Lawrence Ward Shop and patient access to cash cards. In theory the system should have been, Dr Crispin explained, a regular review of policies by the PCT every six months or so.

2.32.5 Mr Millar gave us a further interesting example of this. On one occasion the Lawrence Ward PCT had reminded all staff that patients going out on LOAs should not consume alcohol. Six weeks later the policy was changed for a particular individual. He commented:

> "Now I just wonder about the messages that that gives to more junior staff about consistency and about clear rationale and understanding that governs those decisions, and of course the separate and slightly independent audit and monitoring and review of those sorts of decisions. The latter was not in place."

2.33.0 Inquiryitis

2.33.1 It is important to recognize that in an environment such as Ashworth serious incidents will happen, however good the clinical care provided, the policies and monitoring arrangements. The natural reaction to any serious incident has been to set up an inquiry, and we have discussed a number above. Could it be that the inquiries themselves have in some way hindered the process of learning?

2.33.2 It is important to point out that the inquiries we have focused upon are by no means the only serious incident reports we have received. (It is also fair to say that the PDU is not the only part of the Hospital where serious incidents occur. Far from it.) Having seen so many reports we believe we have diagnosed a disease endemic perhaps to the Special Hospital system, called "inquiryitis". The automatic response to serious problems appears to have been to set up an inquiry; and inquiry follows inquiry with breathtaking speed.

2.33.3 Mr Kaye, saw inquiries as a valuable management tool for learning within the organization. He described them as a way of monitoring progress and of learning lessons, "a management technique for finding out, for learning what is happening". Whilst this may be wholly appropriate for the most serious incidents, a quicker and more efficient managerial and professional review and response process is needed for routine incidents. We have a number of further comments to make on the experience at Ashworth, in addition to those made when dealing with the reports.

2.33.4 First, the standard of investigation often left much to be desired. Notwithstanding Mrs Miles' comment that investigation training was put in place which helped the standard of reports, we found numerous serious faults in the reports we studied in depth. For example Mr Keown and his team went far beyond their brief and failed to interview a number of key witnesses. Mr Bateson was asked to chair an investigation into events in which he had an important role. Six months after receiving the original investigation Report we received a review of the Report, distancing the Hospital from many of its conclusions. Too often, serious criticisms have been made about individuals on inadequate evidence. These inquiries should focus on discovering the facts, eschewing critical personal comments as far as possible.

Recommendation 17 **2.33.5 We recommend that internal inquiries be conducted by staff who are appropriately trained. Guidance for members of inquiry teams should emphasize that these inquiries are fact-finding.**

2.33.6 Second, if indeed the reason for holding such internal inquiries at all is to learn lessons for the future, this can only be done if Reports are shared. What is crystal-clear from our investigations is that at both the SHSA and the Hospital level Reports were not shared. Many witnesses complained about the bowdlerization of the Owen Ward Report. It was very striking that many witnesses who had or were occupying senior management positions had not seen particular Reports. Thus Mr Maxwell was put in charge of the implementation of the Owen Ward Action Plan yet was never shown the full Report. Nor did he see the full Braund Report, despite its very serious implications for the security of the Hospital. The habit of keeping Reports away from the scrutiny of others is infectious. For reasons best known to herself, Mrs Miles decided not to share the Braund Report with the SHSA.

2.33.7 A striking example of this failure to share reports came from Mr Dale, who told us that he had not seen the Braund Report of December 1995 or the Finney Report when they were produced, despite the fact that he was in charge of security and these Reports uncovered very serious breaches of security. This reflected, we were told, his advisory, as opposed to operational brief. His responsibility was to give a strategic steer and monitor what was happening; he was not operationally responsible for any security failures. Thus he was not involved in day-today operational security issues, but rather advised the UGM to ensure that Ward Mangers and Clinical Managers did not ignore legitimate corporate security concerns. By contrast Mr Franey told us that reports at Broadmoor were made available to senior colleagues, albeit the circulation might be restricted if they contained much confidential patient information.

2.33.8 We understand the reasons for being very careful with such information, especially when it affects security. However, it is extraordinary that Executive Directors, let alone the director charged with advising on security matters, did not routinely receive serious incident Reports. This must be the norm in future. Reports into serious incidents should also routinely be copied to the relevant clinical team. Too many of the Ashworth Inquiry Reports we have seen go unnecessarily beyond fact-finding. If the investigating team sticks to fact-finding this should not cause embarrassment.

Recommendation 18

2.33.9 We recommend
(i) Executive Directors and the Director in charge of Security should routinely receive and read serious incident Reports.
(ii) The relevant clinical team should also receive and read such Reports.

2.33.10 On the same theme we were struck by the fact that no one in the Hospital appeared to be coordinating serious incident reports properly and ensuring that the lessons were applied, where appropriate, across the Hospital. Such a central intelligence function would seem to be urgently required. We were struck by Mr Erville Millar's comments on this subject:

> "It appeared to me that most of the focus on risk management was centred on risks associated with individual patients and so on. I believe that there was a whole range of risk management that ought to have been addressed which was about systems and the organization itself and I believe through that process proper analysis of serious and untoward incidents would have been addressed and centrally collated . . ."

As we have said above (2.17.14) what was required was a Security Intelligence Unit to coordinate and police security matters.

Recommendation 19

2.33.11 The Risk Management Team, established in March 1995, would seem the appropriate body to develop its role, and become the intelligence unit of the Hospital drawing on the experience and expertise of the police. We so recommend.

2.33.12 External bodies with a clear interest in receiving serious incident reports did not routinely receive them. Thus the Mental Health Act Commission was not given copies of important Reports such as the Owen Ward Report and the Swan Report into Women's Services. We believe the Department of Health never received even the 19-page version of the Owen Ward Report at the time. We were also concerned that at times the Hospital did not even share with the SHSA itself. Thus Mr Kaye could not recall receiving the report of the fire in J. O'Neill's bedroom.

2.33.13 Third, Mr Millar eloquently expressed the fear that the "inquiry culture" left good, committed staff feeling that they could only be found at fault. He painted a picture of a place where complaints and incidents spawned investigations and inquiries as part of the daily routine. There was very little time to stand back and look at the bigger picture.

2.33.14 Fourth, key staff are taken out from their posts to carry out the investigations. This creates extra burdens for them and their colleagues. The number of investigations going on at any one time meant that there might be eight to ten quite senior staff doing nothing but pursuing investigations. Mrs Nelson noted that the SHSA Board members themselves found the deluge of Reports exhausting. Mr Kaye said he ensured that there were six month follow ups to Reports to reassure members that action had followed, although whether that served the purpose was another matter. Plainly it did not.

2.33.15 Fifth, once a matter has been deemed serious enough to report to the police often, no further action is taken by the Hospital. Yet given the understandable reluctance of the CPS to prosecute patients in a high security hospital this can often result in nothing concrete at all being done about a serious situation.

2.33.16 Any matter judged serious enough to be reported to the police must also merit action by Hospital management independently. Even if the police decide not to take any further action, this does not mean that no further action should be taken by management.

2.33.17 The net result appears to be an organization which, despite the best intentions, is almost paralysed when it comes to following up reports. There are various explanations for this. Partly this must be to do with inadequate reports which failed to command respect, partly with the failure to share information. It was also partly bound up with the rapidity with which another inquiry followed. To take a relatively extreme example, the implementation of the recommendations of the Rowe Report was wrapped up in the in the implementation of the recommendations of the Blom-Cooper Report, and the focus in the Rowe Report on developing medical leadership and producing clear and workable operational policies was inevitably lost in the process.

2.33.18 Mrs Nelson offered another plausible explanation for the (in her view) apparent failure to follow-up reports. She argued that reports such as the Owen Ward Hostage-Taking Report were followed-up and she made the point that Owen Ward was now regarded as being very well-run, a point made by others as well. She then said:

> "it was not that all these reports were not rigorously followed through, it is just that there was not really the capacity to do that as well as maintain the quality of the rest of the service. Where one place became a hot spot, when that was dealt with, one tended to find another hot spot came up elsewhere".

The Hospitals were never able, it seemed, to spread good practice beyond the individual practitioner and ward. If the capacity does not exist then reports cannot rigorously be followed through.

2.33.19 When we put it to Mr Kaye that inquiry followed inquiry with little let up, he attributed this to the nature of the patient population. That is not good enough. Interestingly in the book *Managing High Security Psychiatric Care* edited by Mr Kaye and Mr Franey, the editors' chapter on inquiries and inspections ends with the comment, "with hindsight we should have initiated fewer inquiries but followed them up more vigorously".

2.33.20 The answer would not be to stop holding inquiries into serious incidents. Even in the new world which we describe below serious incidents will occur, although we would hope that they would be reduced in number. However, they need to be more focused and more professional. There needs to be a presumption that reports will be appropriately circulated.

2.34.0 SHSA to SHAs

2.34.1 By 1996 we are approaching the end now of the SHSA's life. During the last two years of its life the SHSA and the Hospitals were looking forward, initially to trust status, but then to Special Health Authority status. The hospitals sought to detach themselves from the SHSA somewhat, a process Mr Kaye told us he encouraged, inasmuch as the hospitals had to stand on their own two feet eventually.

2.34.2 At the same time Mr Kaye was uncomfortable because he knew there were issues on the ground which were not right. Thus in his last Reports to the SHSA Board on his reviews of the Hospitals he identified some basic shortcomings, for example in information management, multi-disciplinary working and provision of structured activity. Thus on management information systems he reported back to the Authority in May 1995 that:

"the processes of information gathering and presentation are in their infancy in many areas. There were numerous examples from Ashworth and Rampton Hospitals, in particular, where key monitoring information specified in the Service Level Agreement and agreed to by the hospitals was poorly presented or simply not available. It was apparent that in some instances information presented had not been subject to adequate vetting.

"These shortcomings were symptomatic of the immaturity of internal systems and a general lack of coordination of reporting arrangements. They also indicate the progress yet to be made in embedding the quality control process so that it becomes accepted as an integral part of the working life of the directorates, wards and departments . . . "

2.34.3 Mr Kaye noted that on occasion UGMs had to recall Reports when errors were discovered.

2.34.4 Whilst Mr Kaye felt that each hospital had a good General Manager with reasonably good senior management teams, he told us he had misgivings about the shapes of the organizations. When asked whether they were ready for a more autonomous status Mr Kaye was commendably frank:

"No, no, they were not. That was the timetable which had been set for us and they felt they were ready. Certainly two Hospitals out of the three were, I think, straining at the leash. Broadmoor I think had a different perspective".

2.34.5 A perennial problem was attracting high quality staff, particularly doctors. The SHSA sought to make posts as attractive as possible, for example by offering research opportunities and academic links. A nursing strategy was developed to define professional standards expected of all nurses, and a parallel process was put in train for social workers, rehabilitation staff and psychologists. Clinical monitoring was introduced for nurses. The old occupations departments were refashioned into rehabilitation services feeding into the clinical work of PCTs. Yet overall at best success was mixed.

2.34.6 There remained problems over security. As stated above, the SHSA did not receive a copy of the Report into the activities of Patient Braund, a Report which, as we have said, revealed "an Eldorado of security breaches, scams, money-making ventures and breaches of the hospital system on a scale not encountered by the members of the [inquiry] team before". This Report, which Mrs Miles received in early March 1996, just weeks before the demise of the SHSA, demonstrated that the problems of poor levels of security had not disappeared. Mr Kaye accepted that this was disappointing, but not an outcome which surprised him.

2.35.0 The SHSA – A Balance Sheet

2.35.1 Over its lifetime the SHSA certainly improved its rather poor inheritance of 1989. The degrading ritual of slopping-out was eliminated and twenty-four hour opening introduced, although its rationale was ill-considered. General management was introduced and clinical audit and quality assurance programmes established. The environment of the Hospitals was greatly improved. Strategies were developed for particular patient groups, including personality disordered patients, and two major conferences on psychopathic/personality disorder were organised by the SHSA in 1991 and 1995.

2.35.2 Mr Kaye himself argued that the SHSA had made significant improvements in each of the Special Hospitals. Nonetheless he admitted that there remained weaknesses and gaps. He said bluntly:

"We never had, in the whole of the SHSA's running of Ashworth Hospital, an adequate staff of the right calibre to do the job the Hospital was meant to do, and I think, incidentally, the same is true of the other two hospitals as well, to a lesser extent at Broadmoor but certainly absolutely true for Rampton Hospital as well".

2.35.3 Mr Jewesbury confirmed that from the Department of Health's point of view things were much better in 1996 than in 1989, and that Mr Kaye had made energetic contribution to that. What criticisms we make must be seen against that background of change for the better.

2.35.4 However the improvement overall has, in our view, been overstated.

2.35.5 We spoke above about the division of responsibility for operational issues between Mr Kaye and his General Managers and said that if something was consistently going wrong, the Chief Executive of the SHSA as the chief accountable officer of the body set up to manage the High Security psychiatric system had the responsibility to do something about it. So to what extent should Mr Kaye and his colleagues be accountable for the continuing weaknesses of that system?

2.35.6 We heard that, for example, Mr Kaye exhorted his UGMs to ensure that the concerns of their security managers were addressed, but he did not do more than exhort. Despite this, on other occasions he did in effect overrule Mrs Miles. Thus we heard that, when Mr Tarbuck had advised stopping all new admissions to the PDU, Mrs Miles supported this but was checked by Mr Kaye, who did not believe that the Department of Health or the Home Office would accept such a move. Mrs Miles thought she and Mr Kaye were jointly "at fault" on this point. Mrs Miles was right, and Mr Kaye was also at fault. At that time Mr Tarbuck's advice was undoubtedly correct and he tried very hard to stop new admissions until matters had been put right in the PDU.

2.35.7 We have said above that the SHSA, and Mr Kaye in particular, knew of the problems and difficulties inherent in the management of personality disordered offender patients at the time when they set about implementing the Blom-Cooper recommendations throughout Ashworth Hospital. Whatever political pressure there may have been, we have said that the SHSA through Mr Kaye should have strongly urged the Department of Health against that course, and not having done so, they should have strongly argued for change as the dark clouds of evidence gathered in the Reports we have discussed above. This was not done, and the failure to accept Mr Tarbuck's sound advice is yet another example of not wanting to affect adversely the image the SHSA wanted those outside the Special Hospital service to see.

2.35.8 One could argue that Mr Kaye was right to try to manage the big national issues such as relation with the Departments, leaving issues such as security to the UGMs to handle. This reflects a split between the local operational issues of ensuring that security was adequate, for which the UGMs had to take responsibility, and national issues where Departments of State, Ministers and high politics entered in. So far so good. Yet there is of course a large grey area here: Mr Kaye was responsible for ensuring that the High Security psychiatric service was run as safely and effectively as possible. He does not even seem to have asked the question of the Departments, can we stop admitting? Nor does he seem to have done more than exhort in terms of security. The probable reason for this seems to us to be inherent in what we have said earlier. The result was summed-up by Miss Kinsley when, having produced her security Reports in 1992, she said she was told by the SHSA "to get on with it, but little could be delivered on the ground".

2.35.9 When pressed to say whether he accepted any share of the blame for what went wrong at Ashworth, Mr Kaye was reluctant to make a definitive response; the SHSA was a team of executives and non-executives, and to single out an individual for praise or blame was invidious.

2.35.10 We beg to differ. To err is human. To err consistently is systems failure, and the Chief Executive must take a significant share of the responsibility for the continuing weaknesses at Ashworth, which had been highlighted for years, in particular by the deficiencies in security.

2.36.0 A Special Health Authority

The New Hospital Structure

2.36.1 In April 1996 Ashworth Hospital became Ashworth Hospital Authority, with a local Board led by a Non-Executive Chairman, Mr Paul Lever, a highly experienced businessman. Mrs Miles became Chief Executive. The Board consisted of five Executive and (in theory) five Non-Executive Directors. However, one position remained vacant and another Non-Executive Director resigned in November 1996. When Mr Lever first gave evidence to us in December 1997 these vacancies remained and a further Non-Executive Director, Mr Kendrick, had become an Executive Director. This increased the load on the remaining Non-Executive Directors. Mr Lever noted that the Board had to undertake direct responsibility almost immediately for the Hospital and its services. He agreed that from April 1996 the buck effectively stopped with him and his Board.

2.36.2 At the same time the Hospital Executive Group was widened in membership to include Heads of Practice, the Director of Research and the Chairman of the Medical Advisory Committee, and retitled the Policy Board. The four clinical units were reduced to two clinical directorates, each headed by a Clinical Director. These were Mental Illness and Special Needs, which subsumed the PDU. Mr Kaye at the SHSA advised strongly against this move; he thought it unwise to make a single Clinical Director, however talented, responsible for around 200 beds containing the most difficult parts of the Hospital's population. Mr Green told us the change was influenced by the need for the Hospital to deliver savings on management costs and partly also by the advice in the HAS Report *With Care in Mind Secure*. Mr Murphy in evidence disagreed, stressing that it was designed to improve clinical practice. We have indicated above, we thought Mr Kaye's view was correct and that the recommendation to create two directorates was ill advised.

2.36.3 The Clinical Directors also assumed day to day operational control of the Hospital. One Clinical Director was appointed to chair the operational team which became the Hospital Management Group (HMG) resurrecting the previous title. It included the Head of Security and Clinical Risk Management as a full member.

2.36.4 We have mentioned before a tendency at Ashworth (though by no means confined to it) to create ever more elaborate management arrangements as an answer to deep-seated problems. In this context we found the evidence of Mr Millar on the actions he took on taking over as Acting Chief Executive, refreshing and instructive. One of his concerns when he arrived at the Hospital was to assess the overall management arrangements for the Hospital. He thought that there was a significant emphasis on professional lines of management and less emphasis on functional service management:

> "I think what I experienced was . . . an emphasis on lining up staff, as it were, in management terms, according to their professional discipline in that the doctors had a clear line of management, the nurses had a clear line of management, the social workers and psychologists separately clear lines of management; nothing critical about that in that context, but all those lines of management were like funnels that went up the organization. What I found was that there was a lack of pipework across those funnels to put effective communication and effective addressing of some of the clear management issues, and I suppose I developed my own philosophy of management as being more about managing services and people as a priority rather than the pure issues of professionalism."

2.36.5 He was concerned about this, particularly as it was unclear where lines of management accountability were at the interface between wards and patient care team. He thought that the Clinical Directors should have been general managers for the Directorate, responsible for everything in their service down to the interface with the patient. He could not see where the accountability for the work of the PCTs lay. He also thought that the Ward Managers were not always fulfilling their general management role at ward level, co-ordinating the work of the PCTs.

2.36.6 To address this matter he appointed from within two managers and gave them responsibility for the general management of all aspects of service across the Hospital. He gave Mr Gardner, the Head of Security direct access to himself. He also abolished the Hospital Management Group, seeing it as an unnecessary tier of management which got in the way of his involvement in operational issues.

The Special Needs Directorate

2.36.7 Mr James Murphy, previously Clinical Manager of the Special Needs Clinical Unit, took up post in April 1996 as Clinical Director of the Special Needs Directorate, which subsumed the PDU and the Special Needs Unit. The overall structure of the Hospital was laid down by Mrs Miles, but the Clinical Directors were given the freedom to determine the detailed structure of their Directorates.

2.36.8 We mentioned in **2.16.7** above that before he left the Hospital Mr Tarbuck gave a presentation on the PDU. Mr Murphy attended that presentation. He indicated to us that he rapidly felt, post-April 1996, that the situation on the PDU was less positive than had been presented to him.

2.36.9 Mr Murphy created a new management body for the Special Needs Directorate, the Special Needs Management Board. This comprised the Clinical Director as Chairman, two consultants (Dr Sylvester the lead consultant for the PDU, and Dr Travers for the East Site), Mr Kay the Principal Clinical Nurse, Mr Bateson the Principal Social Worker, Ms Hellin the lead psychologist and, originally, Ms Young as Acting Operations Manager. Originally there was also the Operations Group, chaired by Mr Murphy, and comprising Mr Kay, Ms Young, Mr Royal the Business Manager and a representative each from Security, Human Resources and Finance.

2.36.10 The Special Needs Directorate Board was itself a multi-disciplinary team; and Mr Murphy believed it offered a way in which PCTs could pass information upwards to the relevant lead clinician. The Operations Group tended to be coordinated by Ms Young. This was disbanded fairly soon in the lifetime of the new Directorate. Mr Murphy later dispensed with the Operations Group.

2.36.11 Mr Murphy stressed that new policies within the Directorate were put on the agenda of the Special Needs Directorate Board meetings. The various professional members of that Board would then be expected to feed back to their respective peers.

Mr Murphy and the PDU

2.36.12 We heard a good deal about the changes Mr Murphy had introduced into the management structures of the Special Needs Clinical Unit and which he wished to introduce into the PDU when the two units merged. Central to this appears to have been the replacement of the concept of Ward Manager with that of clinical leader. On each ward there were three team leader posts, one focusing on clinical aspects, one on staff development and one on operations. There was a complex "leapfrogging" arrangement for reporting upwards. This does not appear to gave been fully implemented in the PDU.

2.36.13 Mr Green, in evidence, outlined a series of changes or proposed changes to the structure of the Directorate. He portrayed a picture of Mr Murphy running an isolated empire, changing structures at whim and creating confusion. He believed that Mr Murphy had not kept Mrs Miles fully informed of what changes he was introducing. Mr Murphy firmly denied this, and this was supported by Mrs Miles.

2.36.14 We heard a good deal of evidence on the point of the disputed structures. But the precise details of the principle changes are not important. What is material is that there was considerable disquiet about the management of the Directorate amongst senior clinical nurses in particular.

2.36.15 Thus Ms Young in her evidence described the position as very unsatisfactory from April 1996: numerous changes at middle management left people upset. She eventually resigned her post. Mr Melia said he had felt progress was being made under Mr Tarbuck, but that with the arrival of Mr Murphy positive things such as core competency training for staff and group work went. He told us that from February 1977 there was no one from the PDU on the Directorate Management Team. The DMT's members were in his view avoiding the PDU and not trying to find out the true position within the Unit. Staff there felt deserted. He claimed that the Unit was now in fact very well run, as a result of being given a measure of stability and staff being given support and a clear lead. We were told (although this was disputed) that Mr Murphy rarely visited the wards. Another very experienced nurse, Mr Moran, complained that, unlike Mr Tarbuck, Mr Murphy did not meet his ward managers regularly. They did not see minutes of the Directorate Management meetings and communication suffered as a result. Mr Arnold said he was confused about the Reporting arrangements introduced by Mr Murphy.

2.36.16 It is undeniable that there was a lack of clarity over operational management within the Directorate. To some extent Mr Murphy must take some blame here. He should have been rather more proactive in communicating his new structures, rather than relying on his Directorate Board to pass on messages. This disquiet amongst more senior nurses was a problem for the Directorate which presumably caused problems for morale lower down the organization.

2.36.17 We are also mindful of the fact that the Report commissioned by the Hospital from Professor Sines into nursing on the PDU and the assessment visit commissioned by ourselves rather suggested that ward staff got on with the job and ignored the fighting over structures, etc, above them. This is a short-term solution at best and reflects inadequate leadership.

2.36.18 There was a further dispute about the cancellation of training courses for staff on the PDU by Mr Murphy. Mr Murphy claimed that he did not hold the training budget, rather it was held centrally and that he had been directed to do this by Mr Dale. He had been under pressure to reduce expenditure, and noted that he had appointed a training officer for the PDU. This caused resentment, as Mr Melia attested. Mr Dale responded that all responsibilities for training under the new arrangements were passed from him to the Clinical Managers.

2.36.19 Undoubtedly the cancellation of this training sent the wrong message to staff, for which Mr Murphy must be accountable. He ought to have explained the problem to the staff.

2.36.20 However, it is far from clear that any lack of clarity and leadership was decisive in terms of the matters we were asked to investigate. We were impressed by the measures Mr Murphy took to tighten up some of the deficiencies in security and implementation of hospital policy. By 14 May 1996, six weeks after taking up post Mr Murphy was briefing the Authority Policy Board on measures he was taking within his Directorate to combat "a tendency to ignore Hospital policy decisions at local level which was not acceptable". Very quickly he had spotted that all was not well. By the time of Mr Daggett's absconsion, Mr Murphy had sensibly shelved plans for a major restructuring of the PDU. Mr Gardner told us that Mr Murphy was instrumental in giving security a higher profile in the Hospital and worked closely with him as he sought to improve security.

2.36.21 What the disagreements over training and structures do demonstrate is that Mr Murphy was isolated from senior colleagues (apart from Mrs Miles) and from many of the staff in the PDU. To take the former point, it was very clear to us that Mr Murphy's relationship with Mr Green, who previously had adopted the PDU when it was under Mr Tarbuck's management, was not good. Mrs Miles admitted as much. Quite who was to blame in that is not clear. The fact that Mrs Miles and Mr Murphy did not alert Mr Green and other Directors to the situation on Lawrence Ward says much about the poor levels of trust at the top of the organization. We discuss this further in Part Three below.

2.36.22 As far as staff within the PDU were concerned we were told that Mr Murphy and Mrs Miles did not feel confident about tackling the problems on Lawrence Ward quickly, foreseeing objections from Dr Strickland and Dr Sylvester, the lead consultant, in particular. Mrs Miles also had concerns as time went on about some of the ward-based staff. She told us that Mr Murphy was not sure how much support he had for action amongst the care team and ward staff. It was not a case of not being able to take action, in her view, it was rather a case of going softly-softly to gather more information. With hindsight she thought she should have been more proactive and attended a PCT meeting on Lawrence Ward; she admitted that she had not read the minutes of the PCT meetings.

2.36.23 The delay in acting was fatal. Mr Daggett duly absconded.

2.36.24 The problem if anything grew worse. We were concerned to hear that Mr Murphy felt unable to visit the wards after the announcement of the Inquiry, given that he was seen as the cause of various woes.

Conclusions

2.36.25 There were clearly major personality clashes involved at a senior level in the Hospital and within the Special Needs Directorate. The organizational structures were in that sense immaterial, although we believe that Mr Murphy was wrong to get rid of the Operations Group. Be that as it may, he was unable to control the Directorate. He was isolated there and, it appears, isolated at the senior levels of the Hospital. The fact that he and Mrs Miles did not feel confident to act straightaway to address the problems identified on Lawrence Ward, combined with their obvious lack of trust of other directors, was an indictment of the senior management team of the Hospital.

2.36.26 Effective systems are important but it takes people to run them. The Clinical Director of one Directorate was isolated and unpopular; no permanent appointment had been made to the Mental Illness Directorate. Mrs Miles was fully supportive of Mr Murphy but fighting, as it were, with one hand tied behind her back due to the perceived lack of support for firm action in the PDU and concerns about the trustworthiness of other senior colleagues. This was a recipe for inaction and confusion.

2.36.27 The problem was exacerbated by an issue raised by Mr Kaye: the job of managing the Special Needs Directorate was too big. The latest structural changes had created two large directorates each effectively twice the size of the largest medium secure unit in the country. The Special Needs Directorate had some thirteen wards on two sites and represented a large organization in its own right. Each had a fair degree of autonomy. The Clinical Director could not keep an effective grip on all the wards in such a large

Directorate, nor could the Hospital keep the Clinical Directorates in step, having ceded so much power.

Recommendation 20 **2.36.28 We recommend that the PDU, if it is to survive in any form, must be managed separately as a small unit (of around 50 patients maximum), with no more than eight to 12 patients per ward**

2.36.29 Some final general thoughts. First, any system or structure is only as good as the people who work within it. Second, there is a risk of building up a larger and larger bureaucratic edifice to try to control a large institution. But paper systems alone will not guarantee that lessons from incidents are learnt, that policies are adhered to. Indeed, at times we felt that the Hospital had become almost paralysed by a huge paper chase, as committee after committee sat, pondered and deferred decisions, duly copying its minutes to other committees. The number of committees was a source of confusion to us, and presumably to many staff as well. Third, any such system can be manipulated if staff are lazy or corrupt. There is no magic answer, but the current solution cannot work effectively.

2.37.0 The High Security Psychiatric Services Commissioning Board (HSPSCB)

2.37.1 The SHSA had been set up to help the High Security Hospitals catch up with the rest of the NHS, which was fast-moving target. The introduction of the internal market following the NHS and Community Care Act 1990 left the Hospitals looking as outmoded as ever. During the latter part of its existence the SHSA was seeking to help prepare the Hospitals for trust status; in the event, due to a legal problem they had to settle for becoming Special Health Authorities. As we explained in **1.18.0** *et seq.* above in 1996 new arrangements were introduced for purchasing high security psychiatric services with the advent of a new non-statutory committee called the High Security Psychiatric Services Commissioning Board to advise the NHS Executive on the purchasing of high security services.

2.37.2 Like the SHSA, the Board is essentially a transitional body. In theory, once sufficient expertise in commissioning these low volume, high cost services is available at a more local level the HSPSCB/T in its present form can disappear. We argue in Part Seven for introducing commissioning at the regional level as soon as possible.

2.38.0 The Position of the Regional Offices (ROs)

2.38.1 We turn now to the position of the North West Regional Office (NWRO) of the NHS Executive. With the advent of the HSPSCT/B for the first time the relevant Regional Offices of the NHS Executive were brought into the picture, becoming responsible for monitoring issues relating to the financial management of the Special Hospitals. This was similar to the position with regard to trusts, except that in the case of trusts the Regional Offices also monitor purchasers who have formal contractual relationships with providers. This helps them see right across a trust's activities. In the case of the Special Hospitals the relevant Regional Offices did not monitor purchasing as the HSPSCT commissioned the service centrally.

2.38.2 The document entitled *High Security Psychiatric Services: Changes in Funding and Organization*, published in June 1995, outlined the new arrangements. It said that the new special health authorities would be accountable to Ministers through the relevant Regional Director of the NHS Executive and its Chief Executive. This is not quite how it emerged, as Mr Robert Tinston, the Regional Director of NWRO, admitted. Nor was the detailed guidance there promised for early 1996 published.

2.38.3 Mr Tinston told us that he had visited the Hospital in April 1996 to be briefed. At that time he had been told that incidents were falling and the situation was under control. With hindsight he had not been given the full picture.

2.38.4 Mr Tinston conceded that there was with hindsight some confusion over the relationships. In late 1996 he had begun to feel uneasy about some aspects of the relationship with the Hospital, because he did not feel in possession of the whole picture as far as Ashworth was concerned. As we mentioned above, many of the Regional Office's insights into trusts were gained through its rather more direct accountability relationship to health authorities.

2.38.5 When asked about the new arrangements, Mrs Nelson indicated that one difficulty was that Ministers or their officials had asked for a single point of contact for briefing purposes. Thus Mr Rowden as Director of the HSPSCT was that point of contact rather than the relevant Regional Offices. She did not feel this was a problem in the lead up to this Inquiry being set-up.

2.38.6 Mr Lever, the Chairman of Ashworth Health Authority, did not share her sanguine attitude. He strongly criticized the lack of a clear vision and strategy for the high secure psychiatric services, which in his experience of other organizations was fatal. He discerned traces of the old "command and control" attitudes of the SHSA in the supposedly "light-touch" monitoring of the HSPSCT. The communication channels were not clear. Thus, once matters started to go wrong, there was great confusion over who should tell what to whom, when. When asked bluntly whether he clearly understood the respective roles of the Regional Office and the Commissioning Board Mr Lever said no.

2.38.7 For her part Mrs Miles commented that the relationships between the Hospital, NWRO and the HSPSCB were not very clear in April 1996.

2.38.8 Events at Ashworth have forced a change. Since September 1997 the relevant Regional Offices have taken over responsibility for monitoring the breadth of each High Security Hospital's activities, including tracking the implementation of Government policy and for performance. As with health authorities this involves a formal annual accountability review. Thus the Regional Office now gets involved in a host of issues such as management of the estate, strategy, service development, etc. The formal review is followed by a management letter, in effect an agreed action plan. Since 30 September 1997 Mr Tinston confirmed that he was accountable to the Chief Executive of the NHS Executive for the overall operational performance of Ashworth Hospital Authority, although the Ashworth Board was accountable for day-to-day operational management.

2.38.9 Sir Alan Langlands stressed that neither he nor the Regional Director of the NWRO acted in a line management relationship to the Chief Executive of an Authority:

> "The Regional Director and I do act as agents of the Secretary of State. The point is that there is not a line management relationship: neither I nor the Regional Director can hire and fire the Chief Executives of a Health Authority, a Special Health Authority, or an NHS Trust. That is the job of the Chairman with the assistance of other non-executive members of the Board"

2.38.10 Sir Alan stressed that the Regional Office and the NHS Executive Headquarters had a monitoring and influencing role. Thus when he became aware of significant problems at Ashworth he took action to address them. He did so as an agent of the Secretary of State, rather than as a line manager. To act as a line manager to the Chief Executives of some 530 statutory bodies would be impossible. The only exception to this was his ability to remove a given Chief Executive's Accountable Officer status, if there was a concern about their probity. It would then be for the Chairman and Board to decide the fate of that individual.

2.38.11 Mr Tinston confirmed that he was not the dismissing officer for Chief Executives in his Region. He did of course have real influence. A hypothetical example was put to him of what he could do if he felt it was essential for Ashworth to have a Director of Security. He replied:

> "We could not force Ashworth or instruct Ashworth to appoint a director of security . . . What we would to do is, through the accountability process, draw to their attention sufficient concerns to say 'we strongly recommend that you should appoint a Director of Security'. My experience over the last five years or so that I have been involved with the region is that in 99.9 percent of cases, unless there was some overwhelming reason why not, these organizations would comply with such a request."

2.38.12 Mr Tinston noted that developments in the White Paper "The New NHS" were increasing Regional Directors' influence, given that Regional Directors would henceforth be involved in appointing Chief Executives and be advising them on personal development objectives.

2.38.13 Mr Tinston expressed the hope that the new arrangements would be more successful, although he made the important point that the nature of the external accountability arrangements superimposed on a hospital such as Ashworth were not the most important issue:

> "if there is an atmosphere of complicity and secrecy in an institution and it is possible for people to delude themselves that all is well when it is not well, then . . . it is always possible that higher authorities will not discover what is going on".

Furthermore, mutual trust and confidence were essential if accountability arrangements were to work well. He had been surprised not to have been informed earlier of the Daggett situation, not for any reason of formal accountability chains but because of his personal relationship of trust with Mrs Miles.

2.39.0 The National Picture: Conclusions

2.39.1 We are in a position to draw some conclusions about the national oversight of the services at Ashworth. Clearly in many respects the Department of Health did not know what was happening at Ashworth Hospital. In our view they should have done. Whether the fault lies with the people at Ashworth or with a defective monitoring system is a matter of judgment. It is clear though that something had gone seriously wrong, and in our judgment, as it had been in the past with the SHSA, there were problems at both ends.

2.39.2 It is important to state firmly that the direction of travel since 1989 was right: to manage the High Security Hospitals from Whitehall was a nonsense. However, delegation must necessarily be accompanied by a clear framework of who is responsible for what, and clear guidelines for when the centre was to be notified and involved. The newly-empowered management and staff have to be competent to carry out more challenging jobs while the centre must have means of ensuring that problems are promptly identified.

2.39.3 This is particularly true of high security hospitals in view of the traditional link directly to the Department of Health.

Strategy? What Strategy!

2.39.4 The overall national policy framework within which the hospitals were to work has still to emerge. Mrs Nelson noted that the bare bones of strategy for these services had been devised by the SHSA, but that the HSPSCB needed to test it further, and that this process was complex, and complicated by the General Election intervening. The most senior people at the hospitals, the Chairmen, do not seem to have been privy to developing thinking, although we think they would have something of value to contribute.

2.39.5 We see the failure to involve the hospitals more at the most senior level in the development of the strategy as a missed opportunity. The clear failures of communication between Ashworth and the HSPSCT perhaps reflects in part this failure to bring the Hospital on board. However, this would have been a difficult goal to achieve. Miss Kinsley said the relationship between the SHSA and the Special Hospitals was always somewhat tense and it became worse as independence loomed. Having gained independence there seems to have been even less interest from the Special Hospitals' point of view in building communication bridges, as evidenced by Mrs Miles' failure to pass on the Braund and Finney Reports to the HSPSCB. It still "takes two to tango".

Securing Resources

2.39.6 As far as resources are concerned we are satisfied that the Special Hospitals received a generous share of the NHS cake in the late 1980s and the 1990s, admittedly after many years of under-investment. Thus the total revenue expenditure for the three hospitals has roughly doubled between 1988–89 and 1997–98 from £63.5 million to £128.2 million; capital expenditure increased from approximately £11.9 million to just under £19 million in 1996/7. Just over £150 million has been spent on capital schemes since 1988-9 in the three Hospitals.

Monitoring the Service

2.39.7 The arrangements between the SHSA and the Department of Health appear to have worked tolerably well, but appearances can be deceptive. We have identified above a serious weakness in the relationship. The success of the arrangement depended too much on good will and too little on system, particularly since the SHSA was ultimately responsible for the Special Hospital service. Our account of the lack of sharing by Mr Kaye of the Owen Ward picture with Mr Jewesbury illustrates the point. When it came to the point of dealing with the leakage of the original Report to the *Sunday Express* neither Mr Jewesbury, nor anyone else in the Department, was in a position to judge its accuracy or otherwise. Above we have discussed what in effect was a ministerial briefing prepared by Mr Evans. No one can imagine he would have written such a note had he had, side by side, the newspaper article and the full Owen Ward Report and its appendices. In the event, from information provided to him by the SHSA, he created a ministerial blindfold. By its very nature the High Security Hospital service has a high political profile.

2.39.8 The reporting system failed badly. One consequence of this was inaccurate briefing of the Secretary of State. A further failure with regard to the situation on Lawrence Ward in 1997 led to more misbriefing of Ministers. The Department of Health failed to ensure that the communication lines were clear between Ashworth Hospital, the North West Regional Office of the NHS Executive and the HSPSCT.

2.39.9 The advent of the HSPSCT/B was marred by lack of clarity in relationships with the Special Hospitals which undermined the ability of the centre to carry out its entirely legitimate monitoring and oversight role. Yet again there was too much reliance on good will. This does not diminish the failure of Mrs Miles in particular to keep the Department of Health informed, and accurately informed. As the newly appointed Chief Executive of Ashworth Hospital, she was responsible to that hospital's board, which in turn was directly responsible to the Secretary of State, through the Chairman. Lines of communication were still too shrouded in mist. The Department of Health was not given sight of the Braund and Finney Reports.

2.39.10 There is always a danger when things go wrong of creating new bureaucratic mechanisms which create problems in their turn. We must not turn back the clock to the days of the Office Committee in London running the High Security Hospitals. But existing systems are not enough. There needs to be a mechanism for independent oversight of the services provided by the High Security Hospitals. The Mental Health Act Commission, as we have seen, is not a inspectorial body and was unaware of the problems on Lawrence Ward. The Health Advisory Service's Report in 1994 was fatally flawed by the inadequate information supplied to it. Dr Williams told us that he was given a greater level of cooperation when the HAS was pursuing a Ministerial commission.

2.39.11 Something better is needed. We are attracted by the proposals for a statutory Commission for Health Improvement at arms-length from the Government which will monitor systems and clinical quality, support local development and investigate persistent problems. The Commission will have the power to recommend the removal of management teams in cases of clear systematic failures. Mr Tinston drew our attention to this possibility when asked whether a new inspectorate was needed.

Recommendation 21 **2.39.12 We recommend that the brief of the Commission for Health Improvement should include the High Security Hospitals and that the Hospitals should be treated as a high priority for attention.**

2.40.0 The End of the Road

2.40.1 The long road to Lawrence Ward ends in Part Three where we deal with the absconsion of Stephen Daggett, his allegations and "Concerns". There we also deal with a number of other Reports which followed in the wake of their publication. Those directly relating to his absconsion, allegations and concerns are the Kendrick and Keown Reports.

2.40.2 In one area, that of computers, we saw fit to commission our own Report. Just as computers and later the internet became part of our lives, they also became part of life at Ashworth Hospital. However, very little thought was given to their security implications. We commissioned a Report from an eminent expert in information systems and security, Professor Tony Sammes from the Royal Military College of Science, because we quickly appreciated it was an area where expertise in the High Security Hospital system is lacking, although it is an area with considerable security implications. We also deal with these matters in Part Three.

PART 3 The Daggett allegations

3.1.0 Steven Daggett

His Background

3.1.1 Mr Daggett was born in 1960. During the early 1980s he was convicted of a number of offences including indecent assault on girls, indecent exposure and driving offences. Several of these offences were committed after he absconded from the Edenfield Centre at Prestwich Hospital, where he had been admitted under section 3 of the Mental Health Act. He was originally detained in Ashworth Hospital in 1984 under a hospital order with restrictions. He was given the legal classification of psychopathic disorder. In July 1989 he commenced a period of trial leave at the Edenfield Centre, Prestwich Hospital, from which he absconded in September the same year. He gave himself up to police and was returned to Ashworth. In July 1990 he was given a Conditional Discharge by a Mental Health Review Tribunal (against the advice of both the Home Office and the SHSA). In December the same year he was charged with criminal damage at Skipton Magistrates Court. Despite the opposition of the Crown Prosecution Service he was granted bail; he hired a car which he drove through a shop window in Doncaster. He was duly returned to Ashworth. In 1992 he confessed to an assault on a twelve year old girl in Worcester in November 1990, during the time he was conditionally discharged. The same year his RMO, Dr Strickland, applied to the Home Office requesting permission for Mr Daggett to have trips out of the Hospital with a single escort. At the time of his absconsion on 25 September 1996 he was a patient on Lawrence Ward. On that day he was on a shopping trip to Liverpool escorted by a single escort, namely, Enrolled Nurse, Mr James Corrigan. He returned to the Hospital on 8 October.

The Absconsion

3.1.2 Mr Daggett described the events of that day when giving evidence. He filled in a clothing form himself describing his clothes; it was not checked for accuracy. He left at 8 am for a trip which should have lasted until 2 pm. He was carrying a shoulder bag containing a change of clothing and a wallet. No one checked the bag. In the wallet was a UK Driving Licence in the name of David Brown, Mr Daggett having (perfectly legitimately) changed his name to David Brown by deed poll and informed the DVLA of the change; a ten-year passport in the name of a fellow patient on Lawrence Ward who had sold him his birth certificate; several bank cards under his new name; a Psion computer; and a pager. The bank cards, cheque book, and driving licence were all sent to an accommodation address in Essex, from whence they were sent on to the Hospital, before central control of mail was re-introduced.

3.1.3 Nurse Corrigan allowed him to enter both a bank and a building society where he withdrew large sums of money without being observed. He then visited the Marks and Spencer store in the middle of Liverpool and escaped *via* the back door. This was around 10.30 am. The Hospital was not informed until about 12.30 pm, and by this time he had been away from his escort for some time.

3.1.4 To put this incident in context, Mr Daggett's absconsion followed another incident about a month beforehand when a mentally ill patient had absconded on a trip to Blackpool.

3.1.5 During his absconsion Mr Daggett went to Holland, where he (unsuccessfully) sought work. He denied he was seeking to make his absconsion permanent; rather, he wished to stay abroad for three to six months to demonstrate the falsity of Dr Strickland's view of his progress. He kept in regular touch with the Hospital and agreed to return on condition that his concerns about the Lawrence Ward environment were investigated. On his return he was debriefed on 8 and 9 October 1996.

The Allegations

3.1.6 Mr Daggett then produced a document which he called *My Concerns.* In it he made a number of allegations about the Lawrence Ward, painting a picture of a ward where a small coterie of patients had succeeded in thoroughly undermining the Patient Care Team. He alleged that pornography, drugs and alcohol were freely available; that patients were running businesses, which was against hospital policy; that a child had been put at risk of abuse at the hands of paedophiles; that the security of the ward was severely compromised; and that a number of staff were corrupt.

3.1.7 He admitted his motives in producing the document were complex. Whilst he said he wished to protest about his care and treatment, his lack of progression through the system as promised and to expose the illicit activities taking place on Lawrence Ward, there was a less altruistic side to it, a desire to shock and to expose the whole system.

3.2.0 Evaluating the Allegations

3.2.1 In evaluating the allegations made by Mr Daggett it is as well to be aware of his background. As we indicated above, Mr Daggett is a convicted sex offender with offences against young girls. We are well aware of the propensity of some individuals with his clinical presentation to manipulate and attempt to deceive others. Nor was he innocent of some of the activities which he highlights in others. For example, he admitted that he himself had flouted the rules on Lawrence Ward, including running a computer business selling small computer parts and placing bets for patients using his Switch card.

3.2.2 It is also clear that for all his complaints about lax security Mr Daggett himself was not blameless: in November 1995 for example he complained about searching of visitors; he complained vociferously about the crack-down on cash cards in June 1996 and about mail being opened. Mr Daggett told us that the complaint about searching related to the way his parents were searched rather than the system itself, but he admitted that by June 1996 he was anxious for his absconsion plans not to be jeopardised.

3.2.3 Nor was Mr Daggett particularly forthcoming in complaining about the issues raised in *My Concerns* before his absconsion. The planning of his absconsion took several months, during which he did nothing to bring to light his concerns. However the fact that he could make the detailed preparations he did, demonstrates the lack of monitoring of patients' mail.

3.2.4 His explanation for not being more forthcoming earlier was that he had no confidence that information would not find its way back to patients and staff:

> "Any information I give [sic] anybody within those four walls would have made it back to the patients and the staff about whom I was complaining. Of that I have no doubt whatsoever. The place was like a sieve."
>
> "My safety would have been in serious jeopardy, I would have been seriously injured or possibly dead if I had made the serious revelations from within the walls of Ashworth Hospital."

As an example, Mr Daggett related one incident when he had alleged an individual was taking drugs. That patient was, Mr Daggett claimed, tipped off about the search.

3.2.5 Mr Daggett's concerns about his safety were probably well-founded. But he did not need to abscond to bring his concerns to the notice of the powers that be. We speculate that sending the *My Concerns* document to the Department of Health would have had the desired effect.

3.2.6 We do not condone or approve of Mr Daggett's absconsion. That said, the allegations made by Mr Daggett were instrumental in setting up this Inquiry. He has helped bring to light a sorry state of affairs which otherwise might never have seen the light of day, at some considerable cost to himself and his family. This deserves to be acknowledged.

3.3.0 Inquiry into the Circumstances Leading to the Absconding of SD and a Review of the Current Leave of Absence Procedure

3.3.1 After Mr Daggett's absconsion an internal inquiry was established under the chairmanship of Mr Roger Kendrick, a Non-Executive Director. The other members were Dr Coorey and Mr Gardner. The inquiry's terms of reference were to review the assessment of and management of risk in this patient's case, to inquire into the planning and organization of the trip on 25 September and to review the leave of absence procedures themselves.

3.3.2 Before discussing the Report in detail we would make several comments. First, amongst the documents we received in connection with this investigation was an e-mail from Janice Miles to Colin Dale and James Murphy dated 23 October 1996. Paragraph 5 once more has the sniff of concealment. It says "The Report, less the appendices, to be shown to the Lawrence Ward PCT, and the Mental Health and Special Needs Directorate teams. *No further copies to be made.*" Again we see a restriction placed upon the circulation of an internal Report. In the Report on the absconsion no effort seems to have been made to discover how Mr Daggett had been able to make his many preparations – changing his name by deed poll, getting a new passport, opening accounts in his new name etc. Perhaps, because he has admitted to making this preparation, it was not thought to be necessary, but his ability to do this over months raises a number of questions.

3.3.3 Second, the function of a High Security Hospital is to provide therapy for patients in conditions of security which will adequately protect the public on the one hand and hospital staff and other patients on the other. Events of two types occur in such establishments:

a. Some will be purely domestic in nature in that they do not involve a possible breakdown of the Hospital's function to protect the public or staff or other patients.

b. Others directly involve the Hospital's function to provide that protection.

Some events may be less easy to classify because they involve elements of both (a) and (b).

3.3.4 Holding Inquiries into events of either type or a mixture of both is a sensible method of ensuring that policies and practices are tested and, if necessary, are changed. An Inquiry into an (a) type event can be conducted on a wholly internal basis with little if any risk of the loyalties of the members of the Investigating Team being divided, because there will rarely, if ever, be a need to circulate their findings and recommendations to other agencies or the public. Inquiries into (b) type events and probably into mixed (a) and (b) events can, and sometimes do, place an Internal Inquiry Team in a position of embarrassment arising from a conflict of loyalties because their findings and recommendations may attract interest from other agencies, the Department of Health and the public. Inquiries into type (b) and mixed type events, should in our view have an independent Chairman to ensure the independence of the reporting team. Unless lessons are learned from analysis of what went wrong, and applied, then headings in Reports such as ***The Way Forward*** are meaningless.

3.3.5 In considering the full and shorter hostage-taking Reports we have seen a clear example of the problem. The members of that Inquiry (Mr Peter Green, Dr Placid Coorey, Mr Ian Paterson and Mr George Allan), presented an unbiased, forthright and critical Report. Having signed it they must have been prepared to stand by it. Yet they must have been aware that Janice Miles presented a substantially watered down and unsigned version in its stead but remained silent. The situation which then existed in the Personality Disorder Unit continued, it would seem, until Mr Daggett blew the whistle, and that was after the Inquiry into his absconsion had taken place. Of course, whoever read the shorter Report did not pick up that it was unsigned by the original Inquiry Team.

3.3.6 The Inquiry Team into Mr Daggett's absconsion was also an in-house team. It could be argued that because Mr Kendrick, the chairman, was a Non-Executive Director, there was an independent member of the Team, the others being Mr Gardner and Dr Coorey (a member also of the hostage-taking Inquiry Team). The object of having Non-Executive Directors, in both the public and private sectors, is to ensure that wider interests are protected. Having a Non-Executive Director involved in investigating allegations of this sort helps with objectivity. However, the circumstances in this case should have led to the Board seeking some form of external view, either as Chairman or as a member of the Inquiry Team.

3.3.7 The team's conclusions were as follows. First, they agreed with the PCT that there were few indicators to forewarn them of Mr Daggett's intention to abscond and that the assessment of his risk of absconding was properly addressed on the information available at the time.

3.3.8 We must question this statement: if the staff on the Ward had been searching properly there would have been plenty of evidence of Mr Daggett's intentions. Proper monitoring of patients' mail would also have brought much to light. In the words of Mr John Royce QC, Leading Counsel to the Inquiry, it was an escape waiting to happen. What it really comes to is that he easily deceived the ward staff.

3.3.9 But the Inquiry Team did reveal a number of worrying features of the incident. First, Mr Daggett had, unbeknownst to the PCT, changed his name by deed poll, and acquired a driving licence and opened several accounts in that name. Second, staff did not follow the proper procedures: there was no proper rub-down search of Mr Daggett on the day he absconded and his escort did not observe him closely on visits to a bank and then a building society. The Inquiry Team found that staff in general were not observing patients properly in such locations.

3.3.10 Third, the PCT did not have a consistent view on how much money patients should be allowed to take out at any one time, or on whether patients should have access to cheque and pass books. This was despite serious concern having been expressed on this issue by the Security Department in 1995. However, given the lack of supervision of patients in banks and building societies and given their access to cheque books and cash cards, the approved limit of £25 was irrelevant. Thus the Inquiry Team was concerned to discover that a patient had deposited significant amounts of money on his Leave of Absence Trips out, money which appeared not to belong to him.

3.3.11 The Report indicates that the PCT approved the carrying of cash cards in July 1995 despite a security e-mail on the 6 March 1995 which stated that a number of items should not be held by patients, namely, birth certificates, driving licences, building society/Post Office account books, bank account cheque books, cash cards/credit cards, passports and premium bonds. (It appears that the only one of these items Mr Daggett did not take out on the day he absconded was premium bonds!) We discuss the issue of patient access to cash cards at length in **3.19.0** *et seq.* below.

3.3.12 The Team concluded that the PCT had disregarded hospital policy on access to money and cash cards; because of patient pressure they had simply caved in and ignored clear policies. In his oral evidence Mr Kendrick agreed that the situation was a shambles.

3.3.13 And fourth, the Kendrick Inquiry also found that patients were able to manipulate matters so that they were given the "right" escort (as later alleged by Mr Daggett in his Dossier). The Team concluded that the Leave of Absence procedures were adequate if they were followed; clearly they had not been in this case. Mr Kendrick in evidence told us that in comparison with other wards Lawrence Ward demonstrated manifest shortcomings in its application of LOA procedures, although this was probably not of great significance in Mr Daggett's case.

It is no use saying that the leave of absence procedures are adequate if the system does not ensure they are followed.

3.3.14 Mr Kendrick accepted that it would be helpful if there was a written set of "do's and don'ts" for LOA visits for PDU patients beyond the existing LOA forms. The Inquiry Team wanted all policies surrounding LOA visits to be thoroughly reviewed.

This was often a reaction of internal reviews at Ashworth Hospital. What is required is enforcement of policies.

3.3.15 The Inquiry Team made a number of recommendations. Rub-down searches were unacceptably poor or not being carried out at all, and should be supervised by the nurse in charge of the ward. A Risk of Absconding review should be held every six months, and every three months in the case of personality disordered patients. In general, no patient should be allowed to visit a bank or building society. A further inquiry should be held into financial irregularities. The Report also, at the insistence we were told of Mr Kendrick, recommended that the RMO and significant members of the PCT should be involved in the post-incident management of events such as absconsions; the RMO had authorized the LOA trip and should carry the consequences. Mr Kendrick's understanding was that Dr Strickland had taken no interest in being involved in events following the absconsion; in his view Dr Strickland was still responsible for Mr Daggett and should have ensured he offered support and advice to the Chief Executive, and got involved in the debriefing of Mr Daggett.

3.3.16 There was a dispute on this point; Dr Strickland's counsel argued that Dr Strickland was available to help if required and that, given Mr Daggett's antipathy to him, he would not have been an appropriate person to debrief Mr Daggett on his return. **We accept this, but criticize his indifference to other matters relating to Mr Daggett's return, even though Mr Daggett was his patient.**

3.3.17 In addition to the Report itself Mr Kendrick produced a Confidential Addendum to the *Report on the Absconsion of Patient S Daggett,* (18 October 1996) and a further document *A Synopsis of the Inquiry into the Circumstances Leading to the Absconding of SD and a Review of the Current Leave of Absence Procedure.* These documents go further than the "official" Report. There are matters in both those confidential Reports which should have appeared in the actual Report. Mr Kendrick alone was involved in their composition.

3.3.18 We reproduce the synopsis below, with our comments in bold.

> **Terms of Reference and Summary Response**
>
> "1. Review the process of assessing and managing the risk associated with the patient and whether the clinical team had access to and used all available information in their decision making."
>
> "Summary Response
> The Patient Care team had identified and dealt with the three key presenting factors

> affecting the assessing and management of risk associated with this patient. There was no evidence available to change the Risk of Absconding Assessment".

What he does not say is that the risk of assessment procedures which were essentially in the hands of the PCT were ignored. It is necessary to look further into the Report for this. As we pointed out above, had proper search procedures in the ward been followed; the official rules relating to possession of passports, credit-cards, bank and building society books etc applied; had the Leave of Absence forms been kept up to date and the procedures for going out with an escort been followed, the absconsion could not, as a matter of probability, have taken place.

> "2. Inquire into the planning and organization of the trip on Wednesday 25 September, to ascertain if Leave of Absence Procedures were correctly applied."
>
> "Summary Response
> "The procedures that were followed were applied adequately. Other procedures such as rub-down searching and cash/bank book/debit cards used were not, and allowed SD to plan for his survival following his absconsion."

It is inaccurate to say that the LOA procedures were applied adequately as will be seen from an analysis of his Confidential Addendum.

> "3. Review Leave of Absence Procedures ensuring that they reflect all national guidance received in the past three years."
>
> "Summary response
> "All national guidance received in the last three years has been circulated and incorporated to the Leave of Absence Procedure."

If the words "but neglected" are added to the statement it then becomes accurate.

> "4. Prepare a Report for the Authority by 18 October 1996, detailing recommendations arising from the inquiry and commenting on whether the Leave of Absence Procedure should be equally applicable to all patient groups within the Hospital".
>
> "Summary Response
>
> "The full Report has been submitted with detailed recommendations and is attached to this synopsis. The proposal to review Personality Disorder patient's Risk of Absconding at three monthly intervals (instead of six) is included."

But the Report omits the recommendations which appear in his Confidential Addendum.

3.3.19 A summarized version of the Report then follows. On the whole it is reasonable, but in part watered-down. Nowhere in the summary or the Report is there a mention of the fact that on the day of the absconsion Mr Daggett withdrew a total of £1,400 from the bank and building society. It is necessary to go to the Report regarding Enrolled Nurse Corrigan's supervision of Mr Daggett for that.

3.3.20 The Confidential Addendum to *The Report of the Absconsion of Patient S Daggett* is dated 18 October 1996. It reads as follows:

> "1 Introduction
>
> The purpose of the confidential addendum, is to bring to your attention, matters both *personal to individual members of staff* and impressions gained during the progress of the investigation.
>
> The contents of the main Report *give a balanced view* of the areas demanded by the Terms of Reference, but necessarily has moved into peripheral areas and picked up both facts and intelligence about practices within the Hospital.

The Report does not directly criticize any individual. However, it is clear that *incompetence at least has been shown in several areas.* Further, custom and practice from years past still prevail in some of the thinking and actions of individuals.

Much of what I suggest is based on my past experience related to *confidential discussions between the Team members* were [?where] both the opinion and intuition was apparent. Consequently my comments will need further detailed investigation."
[Our emphasis].

2. Patient Care Team

"The Patient Care Team failed to follow Hospital Procedures. The issue of cash cards, bank pass books and similar documents is contrary to existing instruction. The issue continued after a request for management to give a ruling. There is culture of this nature not only on Lawrence Ward but in other parts of the Hospital. My impression is that the Patient Care Team would sooner wilt under the pressure of manipulative devious patients, than confront Senior Management with the difficulties of the situation. It is easier to make exceptions to rules without reference to the rule maker than to say "no" to the patient. To condemn the Team as a whole would be wrong, this apparent anarchy has to be looked at in terms of individuals' performances, and particularly the leader of the team."

This could and should have appeared in the main Report.

"2.1 The RMO – Dr Ian Strickland
I understand that it is not the first time that Dr Strickland has taken clinical autonomy to the verge of clinical arrogance or neglect.

It is clear that he knows that patients should not have access to financial resources, but that he has, even after checking with the management, gone ahead on the basis of his clinical autonomy.

As the leader of the Patient Care Team and the Responsible Medical Officer, under the Mental Health Act 1983, he has the prime responsibility for all aspects of patient's care and treatment. As such he seems to have the inability to relate his clinical autonomy where it is centered for [on?] one patient with the wider need for clinical equality within the Hospital. Further, he does not understand (or ignores) his duty to ensure that any actions taken in the best interest of his patients do not compromise Hospital Procedures, designed to protect the patients, staff and public safety."

"It may be that the same pressures that Personality Disorder patients exert on staff at all levels, have made it impossible for Dr Strickland to act in a responsible and accountable manner. His attitude has been to encourage the Patient Care Team to ignore or work around the standards set within the Hospital. I do not see how the Hospital can tolerate this lack of management accountability.

I have been told from many sources, of his clinical expertise, he is highly thought of, but he is clearly [not?] managerially strong enough to manage a Patient Care Team with personality disordered patients."

A responsible Inquiry Team would have made reference in the Report to the parts above which are in bold type, and it could have substantiated such comments by the annexes to the Report and the evidence it had received.

3.3.21 Mr Kendrick recommended Dr Strickland should be removed from his post pending an inquiry into "his management accountability of the Patient Care Team and its relationship with Lawrence Ward set against the standing practice and instructions within the Hospital."

This inquiry should encompass all wards. He continues:

> "3. Ward Management
>
> "Mr Arnold, Ward Manager. This is the second key area of responsibility, where, as I understand, the crossover between the Patient Care Team's plans and the clinical management line occurs. *There is evidence to show that he had attempted to challenge some of the poor practices and had tried to set a policy for Cash Cards, [but] his efforts failed."*

Mr Kendrick went on to say Mr Arnold was out of his depth and lacked the strength of character and maturity in his management post to deal with highly intelligent, manipulative and devious people such as those on his ward. *He was totally unsupported by the RMO and PCT regarding this problem.* Mr Kendrick added:

> "It also appears within the evidence that he was extremely naive in that he fell into the trap of trusting patients. He was clearly fooled by patient SD on 18 June 1996 [when he acted as his escort] and I suspect that he was also used as a "patsy" by SD during the transactions involving the finances for the patients' shop."

Mr Kendrick thought Mr Arnold did not act in a malicious or negligent way and was a young, promising nurse. He appeared caring and enthusiastic but should not be allowed to work with personality disordered patients until his management skills and personal strengths were rebuilt. He recommended he should be considered for a post in the Mental Illness ward.

3.3.22 This was a typical Ashworth Hospital reaction, of shifting problems around rather than dealing with them decisively.

3.3.23 Mr Kendrick then noted that trust was one of the themes which emerged during the Inquiry. Patients used it as a very effective weapon to manipulate and pressurize staff, in a similar way to that used by terrorists within the penal system. If staff say "no" patients immediately translate that into "not being trusted". Even when it means breaching Hospital policy the manipulation is very subtle. Developing trust may be a fundamental part of treatment, but it is a mistake to give trust actually and unconditionally.

3.3.24 In his oral evidence to us Mr Kendrick, a highly experienced prison governor by background, expanded on his comparison between personality disordered patients and terrorist prisoners. Both, he pointed out, use trust to manipulate staff and make them feel they are in the wrong if they do not extend that trust unconditionally.

3.3.25 We wonder why his sensible comments here could not have been in the main Report? It is sound advice to all those who have to deal with this group of patients.

3.3.26 Mr Kendrick then made the following recommendation:

> "a) in order to support staff within the wards and on escorts, I believe that the access to Hospital Policies should be easy and this can be done through the internal computer system. Every Hospital Policy should be available to staff. I understand there is a Policies and Procedures Project team, and I have seen their Report.
>
> "b) I would urge the Policies and Procedures Project be given top priority."

This makes good sense. It is also important that the policies should be available in hard copy on all wards. Of course a similar recommendation was made by Mr Green some years previously in the Owen Ward Report.

3.3.27 Finally Mr Kendrick addresses the topic of "management":

> "I have seen the damage done to staff confidence by poor leadership throughout this Inquiry. While we must guard the rights of the RMO to make individual clinical

judgments, there must be a method for the RMO to compare them against procedures and practices in other wards and areas of the Hospital. Where they clearly contravene any of these, there should be a consultation process through the Hospital Management Board."

This appears to recommend that the statutory duty and power of the RMO to be in complete control of the patient will need changing or there must be put in place some system of checking the effect of both the RMO's determination of a patient's therapeutic and security needs and also similar decisions of the PCT. Where they present an unacceptable conflict with usual Hospital security measures, a means of quickly bringing RMOs and PCTs back into line is needed. This should have been in the Report.

3.3.28 Mr Kendrick said that he had completed the confidential addendum at the last moment, anxious to include something on his concerns about the management of the PCT but not wishing to include anything damning on inadequate evidence in the main body of the Report. As we noted above, Dr Coorey and Mr Gardner, the other members of the Inquiry Team, were not party to this addendum, which in our view was inappropriate.

3.3.29 This Report and its Confidential Addendum paint a picture of a dysfunctional PCT which ignored Hospital rules and staff who did not obey standard procedures. They raise questions about how to enforce Hospital-wide rules, the degree of latitude to be allowed individual clinical teams and how the performance of teams should be monitored. As we have said, the fact that the most hard-hitting comments were confined to a confidential addendum is in itself disturbing.

3.3.30 However, the malaise extended beyond one dysfunctional PCT. Mr Kendrick freely granted that the PCT had done its own thing, but he did not excuse management entirely:

> "It is the skill of managers in my view, at all levels, to be perceptive of where policies and procedures are not being followed, otherwise they are not managing. So somewhere along the line it broke down."

3.3.31 Even though managers were to a great extent reliant on the reliability of information coming up to them from the ward and the good faith of those who provided that information, it should have become apparent to managers at some level that things were not going well. If you have "office-bound" management dealing with difficult patients like these things get missed. He continued:

> "I think what I am trying to get at is that the more systems and methods you put in, the more the pieces of paper to be filled in, the more you pin managers into offices. There is only one way to manage these sort of patients in my view and that is on your feet behind the staff at all levels who are having to do it. That became, I think, in Ashworth more and more difficult over the years, because more and more systems were put in like this. Nobody was trying to be dishonest. They were trying to do their best and say, 'Yes, I have had that done, I have checked that, so I am pretty sure it has been done'."

3.3.32 The responsibility for this failure to pick up on events on Lawrence Ward rested with all the senior management, Mr Kendrick told us, including the Board, who had accepted collective responsibility for the failures on Lawrence Ward when the Keown Report (see below) had been produced.

3.3.33 Finally, we note that as an RMO Dr Strickland was a leading member of the Owen Ward PCT at the time of the Owen Ward hostage-taking incident. Here again, as then, a ward under his charge had been allowed to drift into a dangerous state. We are concerned that this situation was allowed to be repeated. We discuss the working of the Lawrence Ward PCT in greater detail in **3.36.0** *et seq.* below.

3.4.0 Events Leading Up to the Inquiry

3.4.1 We were provided with ample evidence about the lead-up to the establishment of our Inquiry. These events throw light on the management of the Hospital and the degree to which the precise situation on Lawrence Ward had for years evaded the attention of senior management, and on the relationship between the Hospital and central government. Below we summarize events at the Hospital level; we discuss events on the ward itself in detail later.

3.4.2 We received evidence that the Hospital was not unaware of problems on Lawrence Ward during the summer of 1996. In May, Mr Murphy, Clinical Director of the PDU, told Mrs Miles of his concerns over the use of cash cards in the PDU and the Lawrence Ward shop. The following month inspection of mail was centralized and the Lawrence Ward shop closed. In July the PCT on Lawrence Ward discussed the visits of the child in question to the ward. But Mrs Miles for one was not aware of any concerns about Child A's visits. Mr Murphy was discussing the possibility of introducing independent search teams on to the PDU because of suspicions that searches were not being properly carried out; it seems patients were aware of this possibility, which precipitated Mr Daggett's absconsion on 25 September. The HSPSCB was advised of this absconsion, as was normal practice.

3.4.3 Inspector Marsden of Merseyside Police told us that he had investigated the absconsion of Mr Daggett. He and his Area Commander had had one of a series of regular meetings with Mrs Miles in October 1996. They had complained that the photograph they had been given of Mr Daggett was out of date and that he had been allowed out with bank books and a change of clothes, which made the information supplied to the police of little or no use. During that period the Hospital did not inform the police that Mr Daggett had made serious allegations.

3.4.4 On 28 September a search on Lawrence Ward uncovered a number of hard-core videos cassettes, including six containing child pornography and/or bestiality. The videos cassettes were found in the room previously used for the Lawrence Ward shop. An internal investigation was set up into how these videos came onto the Ward.

3.4.5 The Hospital launched an investigation into the absconsion of Mr Daggett, chaired by a Non-Executive Director, Mr Kendrick. We have discussed that Report above. He and his team reported in October 1996. The HSPSCB was sent a copy of the Kendrick Report and the Action Plan agreed by the Hospital Board on 12 November. One of the actions taken was to set up, as recommended by Mr Kendrick, a further investigation into financial and other irregularities on Lawrence Ward. This latter investigation, led by Mr Steven Keown, commenced in November 1996.

3.4.6 Mr Daggett returned to the Hospital on 8 October and was debriefed by clinical staff. He made some comments about Child A. He subsequently reported his concerns about Child A to Ms Bamber, a Patients' Advocate; this was followed by a long meeting with Mr Gardner and Mr Murphy on 29 October going through the contents of what was to become *My Concerns*. Mr Gardner's notes of that meeting indicated how shocked he was at the fact that Child A was visiting Mr Hemming. He told us that he had assumed Mr Murphy would pass on the concerns about the child to Mrs Miles. The following day Mr Daggett was moved to Rampton.

3.4.7 Mr Keown visited Mr Daggett at Rampton on 14 November. Mr Daggett was not satisfied that his allegations were being taken seriously and gave his copy of *My Concerns* to Rampton management. This was copied by Mrs Foley to Mrs Miles at Ashworth. The Express Newspaper group started to show an interest in the story and Mr Daggett's mother contacted the journalist concerned.

3.4.8 Mrs Miles was not informed of Mr Daggett's allegations and did not become aware of any concerns about Child A until she received the *My Concerns* document on 25 November.

3.4.9 Mr Ray Rowden, Director of the HSPSCT was briefed by Ashworth Hospital in late October to the effect that Mr Daggett had made a number of allegations, described as "routine". These were not described in detail. The HSPSCT was informed (incorrectly) that Mr Daggett had been in Eire during his absconsion. On 14 November, Mr James Corrigan, the Enrolled Nurse who escorted Mr Daggett at the time of his absconsion, and who was often other patients' choice as an escort because of his laxity, was dismissed by the Hospital for gross misconduct.

3.4.10 Mr Daggett's dossier was received by Mrs Miles on 25 November. On the same day the Hospital alerted Bradford Social Services Department concerning the child who had been visiting the ward. Mrs Miles read the document quickly, gave it to Mr Murphy, the Clinical Director, and Mr Dale and asked whether there was anything in it that was not being picked up by the internal investigations. Their view was that the internal inquiries were indeed picking up the main issues raised by Mr Daggett.

3.4.11 Inspector Marsden of Merseyside Police confirmed that the Police were not informed of the allegations at that point. Indeed, they only became aware of the substance of *My Concerns* when it was faxed to them by Nottinghamshire Police. At the same time a copy was sent to the Chief Constable of Merseyside Police by Mrs Mahon MP. Ashworth Hospital never gave the police a copy of the document.

3.4.12 Visits to the PDU wards by children under 14 were stopped by Mr Murphy on 29 November. An intensive search of Lawrence Ward was planned, but postponed until after Christmas; when this took place on 17 January 1997, 1,200 videos were found on the ward, 41 of which were pornographic; computers were withdrawn from personality disordered patients to check whether they contained any pornographic material and whether patients could access the Internet. Photographs of the child concerned were found, which were referred to a child protection expert, who felt that they might be paedophiliac in nature. According to Mr Rowden, the Commissioning Team was told that this was a routine search, although there was some dispute about this.

3.4.13 Inspector Marsden said that he was convinced patients had been tipped off about the search, given that one patient had reformatted his computer to make it harder to reconstruct the contents. The last time recorded on the hard disk was 00.34 on the morning of 17 January.

3.4.14 On Monday 20 January, Dr Jones, the Clinical Strategy Director of the HSPSCB, reported to Mr Rowden, following a trip to Ashworth, that Mr Daggett had in fact been in Holland, not Eire. The source was Mr Murphy. The HSPSCB senior team discussed the news.

3.4.15 We were also told that on 17 December 1996, Mr Daggett raised a number of his allegations about Ashworth with a member of the Mental Health Act Commission's Rampton Hospital Visiting Panel. He gave the Commissioner a copy of the *My Concerns* document. The Commissioner understood that these allegations were being investigated by Ashworth. She discussed the matter with her Team Leader who also discussed it with the Convenor of the Visiting Panel. The approach adopted was to write to Ashworth about Mr Daggett's concerns with the intention that, when a response was received, Mr Daggett would be visited again. The Commission wrote to Ashworth on 16 January 1997 asking for details of Mr Daggett's serious complaints and a copy of the Hospital's Report once their investigations were complete. This letter was acknowledged on 21 January but no substantive reply was received before the establishment of our Inquiry.

3.4.16 It was not until 21 February that Mr Bingley, the Chief Executive of the Commission, learned that the *My Concerns* document had in fact been received some two months previously. He immediately informed the Secretary of State's Private Office. Subsequently an internal inquiry was held which concluded that the Commission had failed to undertake fully all its responsibilities in relation to its dealings with Mr Daggett, and in particular had missed an opportunity to alert Ministers to the nature of Mr Daggett's allegations before they entered the public domain. The Commission's Visiting Policies were amended to make it clear to all Commissioners the importance of bringing any matters involving allegations of criminal activity to the notice of more senior colleagues including, if necessary, the Chief Executive. Mr Bingley accepted, when he gave evidence, that mistakes had been made and admitted that the policies setting out what Commissioners should do in such circumstances, had been insufficiently clear.

3.4.17 The *Daily Express* reported on the search of Lawrence Ward on Wednesday 22 January. The story referred to Mr Daggett, and claimed that in the search knives, a grappling hook, drugs and child pornography had been found. It also claimed that a fertilizer bomb had been discovered in the garden. The Hospital briefed the HSPSCT that there was no substance to the stories. The *Sunday Express* ran a further story on 26 January, quoting Mr Corrigan, the nurse who had been dismissed for gross misconduct. Ashworth denied the story and Mrs Miles wrote letters to the Press Complaints Commission and to Express Newspapers complaining about the stories in the Express papers.

3.4.18 At about this time a reporter contacted the Hospital, saying that he had access to the *My Concerns* document. He asked whether Child A had been abused. The evidence of Mrs Miles was that she had instructed Ms Hocking, her Communications Manager, to tell the reporter that there was no firm evidence to confirm or deny this. Ms Hocking confirmed in a written document setting out the sequence of events that she had maintained the strictly factual line that there was no decisive evidence on this point, and that the child had been supervised throughout her visits by her father. She was however, uncomfortable with the circumstantial evidence emerging to suggest the child might have been at risk. During this time she was in close contact with Ms Kate Hardy, the Communications Manager at the HSPSCT. Ms Hocking, stated that she explained to Ms Hardy the line she was taking with the media. Ms Hardy, however, maintained that Ms Hocking had given her a categorical denial that the child was abused. Mr Rowden stated that Mrs Miles had also made such a denial.

3.4.19 The HSPSCT appear to think Ashworth had given a categorical denial, and having regard to other matters which were concealed we are inclined to believe that Ashworth Hospital made that denial.

3.4.20 The Police were informed of suspicions about possible paedophile activity on the ward on 28 January. On 29 January Mrs Miles briefed Mr Tinston, the Regional Director. On Thursday 30 January Mr Rowden was told by Dr Jones that she had received a copy of the Daggett Dossier whilst on a visit at Rampton. That evening Mr Murphy contacted Mr Rowden. This call led to Mr Rowden visiting Mr Murphy, although there is a dispute over who initiated the visit. During that call Mr Murphy said that the Daggett allegations were "90 per cent true". Mrs Miles later briefed Mr Rowden that the police would be raiding the house of the ex-patient whose daughter was visiting the Hospital. It appears that the same day the Home Office had received the Daggett Dossier *via* Alice Mahon MP.

3.4.21 The following day there was a case conference in Bradford concerning the child. That evening she was taken into care. The same day police raided the house of her father in Bradford and removed some 150 videotapes and other items. It emerged that in 1992 there had been a previous case conference concerning the child; Ashworth had been asked to send Reports on the father but the then Medical Director, Dr Sylvester, had failed to answer the letter. Having read the Daggett dossier, Mr Rowden telephoned Mrs Miles and expressed concern over inadequate briefing.

3.4.22 On 3 February Mrs Miles discussed matters with Mr Tinston and Mr Rowden. Mr Rowden asked Mrs Miles why the HSPSCT were not informed of Mr Daggett's real whereabouts and why the HSPSCT had been told the child was supervised at all times. He described Mrs Miles as defensive; she had said that the father was supervising the child at all times. Mr Rowden said that this would not do. That evening, without the knowledge of Mrs Miles, Mr Rowden had dinner with Mr Murphy and several other senior staff. Mr Murphy expressed concerns about the Hospital and the Executive Directors. He said that he had received a copy of a transcript of an interview in August 1996 between a patient, Mr Finney, and his solicitor, in which Steven Finney complained about life on the PDU. This letter corroborated much of the Daggett Dossier. Mr Murphy had said that Mrs Miles had insisted that data from the January search should not be reported to the HSPSCT. He expressed his lack of confidence in the abilities of the RMOs in the PDU. Mr Rowden then briefed Mr Kerr and Mrs Nelson about his concerns. Sir Alan Langlands, the Chief Executive of the NHS Executive, was aware that Mr Rowden had met Mr Murphy.

3.4.23 On 4 February Mrs Miles and Mr Tinston agreed that there should be an independent inquiry into the management of Lawrence Ward. The Police had agreed to investigate the allegations concerning the child. Mrs Miles and senior colleagues had discussed suspending Dr Strickland but felt that this should await the result of the inquiry. Mr Rowden briefed Mr Kerr and Mrs Nelson on his return from Liverpool.

3.4.24 On 6 February officials met The Rt Hon Steven Dorrell, the then Secretary of State, to discuss the allegations. The following day Mr Dorrell announced the establishment of our Inquiry.

3.4.25 The chronology outlined above raises a number of important issues, which we deal with below.

3.5.0 The Delay in Informing the Police

3.5.1 Inspector Marsden told us that the delay in bringing in the police until February was harmful to the investigation. By that time the Lawrence Ward garden had been levelled and patients had erased their videotapes. He commented:

> "Certainly I feel if we had been called in at an earlier stage, some of the evidence that was there we would have been able to obtain and we would have been looking at a very different picture today."

3.5.2 The police should have been called in earlier, and we criticize Mrs Miles for not involving them earlier.

3.6.0 Communication

3.6.1 Whilst a number of aspects of the detailed chronology of events remain disputed, one thing is clear: Ashworth Hospital never passed Mr Daggett's document to the Department of Health. The result was that officials were always to some extent kept in the dark. Mr Rowden noted in evidence that he had been given the impression that all was under control:

> "When I realized the nature of what Mr Daggett was actually suggesting . . . which was that a child had been into this high secure environment, an eight year old child, the daughter of a known paedophile, to a ward where there were known paedophiles, that pornography caches were there in some substantial quantities, that the financial regimes in Lawrence Ward and possibly elsewhere had been severely compromised, that drugs were available, that staff collusion might have

> been on the cards, this was a rather, if I may say, more serious picture than the one I think I was being advised on up to the time I saw Steven Daggett's document myself."

3.6.2 Mr Rowden also noted that the HSPSCT had been briefed to the effect that the child had been properly supervised at all times. Ministers had been briefed to the effect that all was being properly handled; he felt that he and Ministers were thereby misled as to the true nature of events on Lawrence Ward. He thought the senior management team had been in danger of losing its grip, still confident that matters could be kept under control.

3.6.3 Mr Rowden in his evidence was surprised that a copy of *My Concerns* was not sent to the HSPSCT. For her part, Mrs Miles said that she treated the document as a patient complaint:

> ". . . Because we were already investigating, because Mr Rowden had had by this time the Report into the absconsion, I really did not see this document as being anything other than confirmation of what we were already dealing with, and it was not normal procedure to send patients' complaints to the Commissioning Board".

3.6.4 We think it was wholly unreasonable to regard this as a normal patient's complaint. It was a substantial and complex document referring to extremely serious matters within the PDU. Much of what Mr Daggett had said had been confirmed as being largely true. Mrs Miles admitted the Hospital could not be sure whether or not Child A had been abused. Mr Murphy had made it clear to her that he had grave doubts about the clinical environment of the ward.

3.6.5 Mrs Miles was quite properly briefing the police on her concerns about a possible paedophile ring and was briefing the North West Regional Office and the Commissioning Team. There was such sensitivity on the part of Mrs Miles that it coloured her judgment about how much information she should share. The briefing she was giving clearly did not give senior colleagues the information they needed effectively to assess the real situation. Quite simply, the allegation about Child A being unsupervised in the company of known paedophiles should have leapt from the page and allowed the Commissioning Team to question the Hospital about what was going on. It would have also enabled the Team to keep Ministers properly informed. Mrs Miles told us that one reason for maintaining such tight security was a worry on her part that a very senior member of staff might be involved in a paedophile ring. She disclosed the name to the Panel in strict confidence. We heard no evidence that would support such a suspicion and judge that her fears were wholly unfounded.

3.6.6 Mrs Miles expressed the view that Mr Rowden was in part to blame for the way in which events had progressed to a Public Inquiry. Leaving aside the question as to whether an Inquiry was needed (we are in no doubt that it was), Mrs Miles has only herself to blame for the failure to keep the Department of Health fully informed. Had she not been economical with the truth events might indeed have taken a different course.

3.6.7 To be fair to Mrs Miles, communication problems were not all one-way. Our attention was drawn to a letter to Mr Rowden from a patient, Mr Steven Finney, who subsequently died in February 1997. This letter alleged that nurses had given him illicit drugs, that staff brought in drugs and alcohol and that this was the tip of the iceberg. Mr Rowden took a month to forward this to the Hospital, for which he apologized.

3.6.8 Mrs Miles' failure to pass on the *My Concerns* document and Mr Rowden's failure to respond quickly to a very serious letter reflect what appears to have been a somewhat dysfunctional relationship between the Hospital and the Board. It is not within our terms of reference to attribute blame for this, and the NHS Executive has acted to clarify matters. We hope matters will have been considerably improved by the new arrangements.

3.6.9 Neither failure should have occurred if a simple two way system of communicating all matters affecting security had been established, but the failures are different in that Mrs Miles' failure involved concealing an embarrassing state of affairs. Her attempt to protect the Hospital from criticism and press censure was misjudged.

3.7.0 The Delay in Searching Lawrence Ward

3.7.1 Mr Murphy had raised his concerns about Lawrence Ward in May 1996. By August and September he and Mrs Miles were convinced that the PCT on the Ward was inadequate and that Hospital procedures had been seriously compromised. In September Mr Daggett absconded and a few days later a find of hardcore pornographic videos was made. Then Mr Daggett raised his concerns about the ward with Mr Murphy and others on 29 October. However, no major search occurred until January 1997. **We are bound to ask why the delay occurred?**

3.7.2 What is more, a two week "amnesty" was declared in the first part of October 1996 for patients to hand over illicit material. Mr Cannon, a Team Leader, told us he was not sure who declared this amnesty. Mr Arnold, the Ward Manager, told us that Mr Murphy had met the Ward Managers of the PDU as a group shortly after the videotape find and told them to make patients aware that they should hand in any illicit videotapes. However, this was not an amnesty as such, as any clinical issues raised by any videotapes handed over would be dealt with by clinical teams.

3.7.3 We asked a number of patients and staff about the delay in searching the ward. All expressed surprise. Mr Cannon accepted that a large-scale search would require bringing in extra staff, but said that his experience at Broadmoor led him to expect a large search fairly quickly. He told us that one member of staff even complained to the Security Department about the lack of action in around November that year. Mr Foster, the current Ward Manager, denied that the Ward was in any sense out of control in the weeks and months before the big search. He could not understand the delay. He confirmed that the patients had been expecting a big search for a long time.

3.7.4 We asked Mr Arnold about the delay and why he had not carried out a full search immediately. He told us that a full search of all 25 bedrooms was, in his view, beyond his authority; he would have wanted senior backing before taking such a potentially explosive step. He also did not have the staff to do it, nor was there anywhere to put the patients whilst a full search was carried out.

3.7.5 We regard these excuses as inadequate. He should have sought the necessary authority and support to do so. His rather laid back attitude in seeking assistance, if he required it, is important in this regard.

3.7.6 For her part, Mrs Miles explained that she and Mr Murphy were concentrating on managing the absconsion first and foremost before deciding how to manage the situation on the ward. The delay in searching was to allow Mr Murphy to gain more information about the precise situation and to assess what level of support he had in the PDU to do what he thought necessary. She was advised against tightening up procedures on Lawrence Ward by one of the consultants in early November 1996, but ignored that advice. (It was suggested that it was Dr Crispin who had advised against carrying out a search of Lawrence Ward in November 1996. Dr Crispin had no recollection of so doing.) Mrs Miles was, however, concerned about carrying out the search before Christmas, the Christmas period being a time of tension in a High Security Hospital, and so it was delayed until Mr Murphy was back from leave.

3.7.7 Mr Gardner told us that around this time a number of changes were being made to tighten up security, such as the reintroduction of central inspection of mail and central checking of videos. There was talk about independent search teams being introduced. There was concern that a full search at that time might have been seen as provocative. He accepted that such a search might have uncovered far more.

3.7.8 Mr Murphy, in his evidence, appeared to blame Mrs Miles for delaying a search which he was ready to carry out in December, although he noted that staff appeared to have been warned that a search was in the offing and he wished to keep an element of surprise. In the event the search on the 17th of January revealed that a large number of videotapes had been recorded over by Ceefax. Patient Q told us he had personally wiped around fifty videos in anticipation of a search. Patient H confirmed that patients were busily wiping their videotapes.

3.7.9 Mrs Miles thought that the situation needed to be approached carefully:

> ". . . in a crisis I tend to deal with things calmly, coolly and collectedly, and I think in that sort of Hospital that is the way you deal with a crisis. You do not run around like a headless chicken making a drama out of events. You have to deal with them calmly and coolly and the fact that was how I was dealing with it, I am afraid must have been interpreted by Mr Rowden – but he certainly did not ask me at the time – as me not dealing with the issues in the way that he thought I should".

Mrs Miles accepted the situation was serious, but she disputed that the Hospital was out of control.

3.7.10 We believe that Mrs Miles' delay left a potentially dangerous situation longer than necessary. We see no reason why Lawrence Ward could not have been searched very early in October at the latest. We share Inspector Marsden's view that had it taken place then much more would have been found. The totality of the evidence points to Ashworth Hospital wanting to take as much sting as possible out of a Report of the findings of the search. For this, as Chief Executive, Mrs Miles must bear the main responsibility, but others could have counselled her to act more urgently had there been a feeling that a search should have been made regardless of the consequences resulting from the findings.

3.8.0 Monitoring

3.8.1 The delay in searching so as to be sure of her ground leads one to ask why was Mrs Miles not better informed about the problems on Lawrence Ward? Mrs Miles told us that all the information she was getting back, both in terms of monitoring Reports and verbal briefings, was telling her that Lawrence Ward was stable and not a problem. It was not until Mr Murphy arrived that she realized that things were not as they should be. But this does suggest she did not have her finger on the pulse of this part of the Hospital.

3.8.2 We asked her why she had not been more visible on that particular ward. Mrs Miles admitted that she did not visit the ward, even though by September she had identified it as a potentially serious problem. She and Mr Murphy had agreed that he, as Clinical Director, should front activities within the PDU.

3.8.3 Mrs Miles can also justifiably be criticized for failing to grasp this situation more quickly. She commented to us that the procedures and processes of monitoring were in place, but that people let her down. This may be true up to a point. But it does suggest an over-readiness to accept those comforting monitoring Reports and a failure to question those in charge of the PDU more thoroughly. The record of poor performance of Dr Strickland when in charge of the Owen Ward PCT should surely have suggested the need for close monitoring by the senior management team.

3.8.4 We asked Mr Keown, author of the Report into Events on Lawrence Ward, whether Mr Murphy should have known more of what had been going on. He thought not; Lawrence

Ward was going on in its traditional way, and ward staff were familiar with the way it was run. They did not see anything out of the ordinary to report upwards.

3.8.5 But Mr Keown did think that the situation on Lawrence Ward, which we discuss at length below, should have been picked up by the PCT and members of the PDU management team. The problems posed by the garden should have been obvious; the way in which the shop was operating; the practice of allowing Mr Corrigan to run his own shop; the frequent trips to buy stock for the shop were all obvious enough. The problem was that the development of such practices on Lawrence Ward had been insidious over a number of years, so people on the ward had not seen the wood for the trees. Even so, sight must not be lost of the fact that the Lawrence Ward PCT, as had the Owen Ward PCT before it, had been instrumental in thrusting matters of security into the background.

3.8.6 The Hospital management had missed what was happening over a period of years.

3.9.0 Management Culture

3.9.1 One of the most curious aspects of this affair is the dinner at Mr Murphy's house, because it involved several senior managers of Ashworth Hospital meeting the Director of the HSPSCT in private. Mr Rowden clearly saw this as a highly unusual event, a briefing outside the management line by a senior manager who was concerned that he could not take these issues to his Chief Executive. He accordingly ensured that his Chairman and line manager were aware of, and approved, his action in going to meet Mr Murphy.

3.9.2 But Mr Murphy in his evidence presented it as a normal enough occurrence to have a meeting with a purchaser. Mrs Miles was aware of the issues; he had what he described as an open relationship with members of the HSPSCT. He saw the impetus for the meeting as coming as much from Mr Rowden as from him. However, he did not tell Mrs Miles about the meeting (contrast Mr Rowden's actions in informing his senior colleagues).

3.9.3 Mrs Miles told us she was extremely surprised that Mr Murphy had chosen to go outside the management line. He had come to her in May 1996 speaking of his concerns about Lawrence Ward and she had been working with him closely. She could not understand why he should wish to go outside the line at that point. **We believe that her procrastination in taking action played a significant part in his doing so.**

3.9.4 A further disputed point is whether Mr Murphy had stated that he and his colleagues had no confidence in Mrs Miles and her top team of directors. Mr Murphy agreed that he had expressed concerns about the management culture of the Hospital and thought the management team were not appreciating the seriousness of the position. But he denied that he and colleagues had said they had no faith in Mrs Miles. He did not feel she was well-advised.

3.9.5 Mr Michael Bateson, a Principal Social Worker, was also at the dinner. He told us that he expressed his concern to Mr Rowden that a child had been put at risk. He denied he had expressed any lack of confidence in Mrs Miles, whom he thought was taking matters seriously; his concerns were about the attitude of Mr Dale, whom he thought was underplaying the seriousness of the situation and putting the interests of Ashworth above those of the child.

3.9.6 This meeting between a senior manager of a provider hospital and one of his purchasing opposite numbers cannot be regarded as a perfectly normal meeting. Mr Rowden clearly did not understand it in this light and he was right not to do so. The action he took to brief his senior colleagues and to ensure that they understood and approved of what he was doing was, in our view, very sensible. This was a very important meeting from Mr Rowden's point of view, and whatever may have been in Mr Murphy's mind, we believe

that the impressions Mr Rowden took back with him and of which he told us were a genuine distillation of the meeting. We accept Mr Rowden's overall version of events.

3.9.7 Whatever the precise circumstances of the meeting the mere fact it took place reflects poorly on the secretive management culture of Ashworth Hospital. If Mrs Miles had been briefing Mr Rowden fully, what Mr Murphy said to him that night would not have been news.

3.9.8 If Mr Murphy had concerns about the senior managers around Mrs Miles, so too did she, judging by the fact that she did not fully brief all her senior management team about the January search before it happened. She also did not trust her head social worker enough to involve him in liaising with Bradford Social Services.

3.9.9 The impression we gained was of a beleaguered Chief Executive working very hard to control an unwieldy organization, but hampered by a senior management team riven by very serious divisions. This was compounded by a relationship with the Commissioning Team at the centre of government which was characterized by distrust and secrecy, and a new freedom for action granted by Special Health Authority status that encouraged the senior management team in their belief that they could and should do it all alone.We turn now to discuss Mr Daggett's allegations in detail.

3.10.0 The Allegations about Misuse Of Drugs And Alcohol, Financial Irregularities, Possible Paedophile Activity And The Availability Of Pornographic Material within The Personality Disorder Unit.

3.10.1 We have described how the allegations made by Mr Daggett in his 24-page document *My Concerns* came to light. We invited Mr Daggett to give evidence to the Inquiry to expand on those allegations. A number of other patients who were resident on Lawrence Ward at the relevant time also gave evidence. In addition, we called the key members of the Patient Care Team on Lawrence Ward, as well as more junior staff.

3.10.2 The allegations made by Mr Daggett are graphic and shocking.But we are well aware that personality disordered patients are quite capable of making malicious complaints and accusations. In assessing the truth or otherwise of what Mr Daggett said we have also had the benefit of the Hospital's internal inquiry into Mr Daggett's absconsion (*The Kendrick Report*), the inquiry into financial irregularities and other matters on Lawrence Ward (*The Keown Report*) and the inquiry into Child Care Issues at Ashworth Hospital Authority ("IR2"). We were also privy to the witness statements taken by Merseyside Police, and the conclusions of their investigations. The IR2 Report was later withdrawn by the Hospital on the grounds that it was deeply flawed by its lack of expertise and independence. We were told that the Hospital had withdrawn the Report in a letter from the Acting Chief Executive dated 30 September 1998. When we first saw the IR2 Report we had noted those weaknesses and placed no reliance on it except in so far as it referred to matters, for example documents, which were not so stigmatised. We deal with this matter more fully at paragraph **3.23.3** *et seq.* below.

3.10.3 Mr Keown and his team were asked to investigate financial irregularities referred to in the Kendrick Report on the absconsion of Mr Daggett, to review and comment on relevant guidelines and policies on patients' financial dealings, to consider any other matters related to the above and to make recommendations. Mr Keown and his team concentrated on events between January and October 1996. In the event, the focus of the Inquiry broadened as new issues came to light. The result is a Report which covers much, if not all, of the ground which we were asked to review.

3.10.4 Mr Keown made the point, which we echo, that the findings of his team's inquiry were very similar to that of the Owen Ward Report and the investigation into patient S.

Braund. Ashworth Hospital had failed to learn the lessons from the previous inquiries and found itself faced with the same problems of patients subverting systems for their own ends.

3.10.5 We would like to say at the outset that there were deficiencies with Mr Keown's Report. He and his team only interviewed one member of the PCT, namely Mr Arnold, and other interviewees were not given the opportunity to respond to allegations made by patients or staff. The conclusions were at times based wholly on patient reports. Several patients complained of coercion, complaints that in one case at least were partially upheld. The Report did not always amass sufficient evidence for its conclusions. In many ways it was a pity the team saw fit to range over the whole gamut of Mr Daggett's allegations. But these shortcomings do not nullify the whole investigation. The circumstances were clearly such that fuller investigations would merely have confirmed the findings.

3.10.6 Below we discuss at length the allegations made by Mr Daggett, as well as other areas of concern, such as patient access to cash cards, which emerged during our Inquiry.

3.11.0 The Allegations

3.11.1 The allegations concern the misuse of both prescribed and proscribed drugs; a trade in pornography, at least some of it involving children; poor standards of security; poor standards of clinical care, in Mr Daggett's and others' cases; financial irregularities; and possible paedophile activity.

3.11.2 By far the most serious allegations concern the possible abuse of a little girl, Child A, who over a period of years was visiting two patients on Lawrence Ward, Mr Corrigan and Mr Hemming. We feel it is important for the readers of this Report to have some impression of what sort of men these patients were. We reproduce the graphic words of Leading Counsel to the Inquiry, Mr John Royce QC, at Knutsford:

> "The first man, Mr Peter Hemming, had a very substantial history of paedophile activity with young girls. Back in 1972 he indecently assaulted a nine year old girl and then three days later he tricked a seven year old girl and a nine year old to go with him to a secluded place, where he forced the nine year old to perform oral sex. He was sent to prison. In 1975, he impersonated a police officer and in the process persuaded a 12 year old girl to allow him to search her physically, and he fondled her genitalia in the process. In 1977 he accosted a 11 year old girl in an alley. When she resisted, he banged her head against the wall. In 1978 he enticed a 11 year old boy into a building, he threatened him with a knife, forced him to strip, he committed acts of gross indecency with him, he then tied him up and kept him until the following morning, when he repeated those acts of gross indecency with that young boy. He was sentenced to six years' imprisonment, of which he served four. Five days after his release from that prison sentence, he stopped two young girls of about nine and ten. Again he pretended to be a policeman. He enticed them to an area where they were out of sight, he made them strip at knife-point, he used tape to bind and gag the younger girl. He then forced the older girl to have oral sex with him, he then started to strangle her until she lost consciousness. He then hit her head against a concrete step. When she had recovered to some extent, he bound her with tape, and stuffed a sock in her mouth. He then forced the younger girl to have oral sex with him and when the first girl managed to escape from this terrifying ordeal, he himself fled. He was convicted of indecent assault, actual bodily harm and attempted rape. It was that offence that led him to being given a hospital order unrestricted in time and that led to him coming to Ashworth Hospital.
>
> "The other man, Paul Corrigan, had a severe, serious history of abduction and buggery of young boys, and served various sentences of imprisonment. But the

offence which led him in due course to come to Ashworth is breathtaking in its awfulness. In November 1981, a 13 year old newspaper boy used to make his way across a park to deliver his newspapers. Corrigan had been released from prison early that year, but in November, he saw this lad and he hatched a plot. He plotted to kidnap him, to bind him with chains, to gag him and to cover his head with darkened goggles so that he could not see where he was going, and indeed that is what he did three weeks later with the help initially of another man. He chained him, put the goggles over his head, he forced him at knife-point back to his flat. At the flat, he was subjected, that boy, to a catalogue of torture, of sexual acts, and other activity which was so foul and degrading that it was all part of the humiliating and horrific ordeal that young man had to undergo at the hands of Paul Corrigan. Eventually he was taken out into the country, where Corrigan used the knife on that boy in a way that almost defies belief. He cut off or partially cut off his genitals; he inflicted about 100 wounds upon him, and finally he cut open his stomach and left him in a ditch to die. The body was found by three schoolboys the next day."

3.11.3 These crimes are sickening. It is against this backdrop that one must ask why this child was allowed to visit these men, frequently unsupervised, at all, let alone on any ward, but particularly on this ward housing patients with serious personality disorders, all of whom had serious criminal histories, including murder, rape and sexual assaults against children.

3.12.0 Lawrence Ward: A Ward Apart

3.12.1 Child A visited Lawrence Ward literally hundreds of times. How could such a thing happen? One needs to understand the historical background. We heard from various sources that Lawrence Ward was regarded by patients and staff alike as a bit different: a ward where patients were trusted, where there were very few incidents, a ward which largely ran itself. It had relatively low staffing levels, levels which surprised nurses like Ms Edge coming from higher dependency wards. It was the ward to which official visitors were taken, a "flagship" ward. The now notorious garden was featured in a national gardening magazine. As Mr Moran, who was Ward Manager from October 1993 to June 1994, put it in the context of searching:

> "Lawrence Ward was a highly trusted and highly privileged set of individuals. It was like no other ward in the Hospital."
>
> ". . . You aspired to go to Lawrence Ward, you earned the right to go on Lawrence Ward, because it was operated on low staffing. They have wine and cheese parties. It was a slow insidious process that the invasiveness of such things as searching ceased."

Mr Moran agreed with the suggestion of Dr Strickland and Dr Crispin's Counsel that the relaxed regime of Lawrence Ward was well-known throughout the Hospital. Both staff and patients believed Lawrence Ward was different from other wards in the Hospital.

3.12.2 And indeed in some ways it was. The Hospital provided us with a breakdown of serious incidents on the PDU between 1 July 1994 and 31 August 1997. Only 1.6% were on Lawrence Ward, compared to 41.9% on Shelley Ward and 29.3% on Ruskin. This is not to say that the ward was completely without incident: Patient E described how on his first day on Lawrence Ward in 1993 a female visitor was attacked whilst visiting a patient's room. The patient concerned was moved off the ward within half an hour. But such events were very rare. Mr Paterson the Deputy Security Manager indicated that other wards in the PDU, notably Shelley and Macaulay Wards, were of far greater concern than Lawrence Ward.

Mr Day, the first Security Liaison Officer for the PDU, missed many PCT meetings on Lawrence Ward because they clashed with the PCT meeting on Macaulay, which was far more of a "problem ward". Lawrence Ward was not a priority for the Security Department.

Ward Philosophy

3.12.3 The philosophy of the ward was enshrined in the Lawrence Ward Information Booklet, subtitled *A Fine Wind is Blowing the New Direction of Time* (a quote from D.H. Lawrence). This was revised in 1993. The Mission Statement of the ward was as follows:

> "Lawrence Ward is a democratic community of individuals brought together to improve interpersonal relationships, promote personal growth and provide insight through the use of group processes and individual therapies, the ultimate aim of which is their return to society with appropriate continued support to enable the probability of success to be maximised."

3.12.4 Dr Strickland was asked to explain the philosophy of the ward. He admitted that running a therapeutic community in a high security setting was in one sense impossible, given that the patients were detained. The paramount importance of security was also a barrier to developing such a community. But they did try to develop trust between staff and patients:

> ". . . to work in a collaborative way together, both in terms of designing their treatment programmes and carrying that forward. Also, in terms of the way that security was handled . . . if there was someone who offended against those rules they were moved off that ward."

3.12.5 This is a topic we return to later. If a patient is moved off the ward for offending against its rules, it results in the ward rules themselves never being questioned for this group of patients. The basis of the "therapeutic community" is agreement or consent, a factor usually absent, or at least fragile, in a high security setting. It follows that Dr Strickland's view that a therapeutic community was an impossible concept is almost certainly valid in this setting. As will be seen in Part Six, Dr Snowden makes the point that many of his colleagues asked to provide evidence did not fully come to terms with the problems presented by the severe end of the personality disordered group. A number of facilities which specialize in the treatment of personality disorder such as Henderson Hospital, and Grendon prison can and do funnel their intake in two ways:

> **a. they only accept those who want to co-operate and change, and**
>
> **b. they reject those who subsequently fail to co-operate fully.**

The High Security Hospitals do not have the freedom to select and reject. In dealing as they do with the very severe end of the spectrum of personality disorder, the procedures such as those at Henderson Hospital would be inappropriate. We return to this topic in Part Six.

3.12.6 Dr Strickland told us that he and his colleagues tried to look at patients' offending behaviour and their general relationships with others, to see how their behaviour could be modified, taking into account the patients' own backgrounds, which were often marked by abusive relationships. Patients would be invited into case conferences to hear what was being said about them, to try to persuade them to confront their problems. His fellow RMO on Lawrence Ward, Dr Crispin, agreed; she stressed the importance of looking at the way in which the personality disorder manifested itself, both in general behaviour and in relation to the index offences. The problem was that many patients were controlled within the confines of Ashworth but were still highly dangerous, because they had as yet not been fully assessed and their offending behaviour addressed.

3.12.7 It is an indictment of the system that patients were in Ashworth and on long-stay wards, without being fully assessed, and consequently without fully developed treatment

plans. At least two of the serious events on wards which we have considered in this Report involved such patients.

3.12.8 The espousal of a "democratic community" in a high security environment is questionable to say the least. The *A Fine Wind is Blowing . . .'* document presents a picture of the ward completely at odds with all the evidence we heard, making extravagant claims for the skills of the nursing staff and the trustworthiness of the patients.

Searching

3.12.9 The malign effect of this muddled philosophy can be demonstrated in the context of searching. The Lawrence Ward Operational Policy, dated November 1994, notes that the Ward was run along therapeutic community lines, and that all patients were carefully assessed and knew it was in their interests that the Ward ran smoothly. As a result the Lawrence Ward PCT did not conduct searches on a regular or routine basis; targeted searches were carried out when there were grounds for suspecting a particular patient. (This policy was later changed with the introduction of core search standards, but core standards concerned the number not the quality of searches.)

3.12.10 There were also practical reasons for the lack of searching, namely a shortage of staff and the quantity of possessions in some patients' rooms. Mr Moran explained that two staff were needed to carry out a search and often only two would be there on the ward. He confirmed that searching was not in fact carried out; it had gradually ceased in an insidious process. He was never led to believe that the lack of searching was leading to problems and so did not bring any problems to the attention of the PCT.

3.12.11 Mr Moran admitted that several patients had an inordinate number of possessions in their rooms. But changing anything like that was terribly difficult: that was Lawrence Ward. On the other hand, there were no serious incidents. He did not bring his concerns to the notice of senior management.

The Ward Regime

3.12.12 Mr Moran told us that when he became Ward Manager in October 1993 he found a regime with very few restrictions and very few incidents. The PCT seemed complacent about the regime, a feeling not shared by the nursing staff. The boundaries on the Ward were very loose, and he thought a better balance of therapy and security was needed. He was critical of the way in which the PCT worked, undermining, on occasion, decisions taken by nursing staff who had the responsibility of managing the Ward 24 hours a day. Mr Moran was moved to Owen Ward after the hostage-taking. Owen Ward is now regarded as a very well-run ward; the difference between Lawrence Ward and Owen Ward post-June 1994 in Mr Moran's view was that he was able to start there from scratch and run the ward as he thought fit, ignoring in fact the PCT.

3.12.13 Mr Cannon, a team leader on Lawrence Ward, confirmed the picture painted by Mr Moran. He told us that when he joined the ward in 1993 it was run in a fairly relaxed manner and was set up to be different. For the first two years he was there it was held up as an example of good practice and patient empowerment.

3.12.14 We agree with the suggestion of Counsel for Mrs Miles that whatever policy edicts were coming down from on high, the Lawrence Ward PCT would have felt entitled to ignore them. Clearly the PCT felt entitled to change policies at whim. This would have been less dangerous had such revised policies been clearly documented, together with their rationale. But Mr Moran's evidence was that they were not. This part of the Hospital was operating independently and was subtly out of control.

Ward Policies

3.12.15 Even when policies were clearly documented we found evidence that they were, on occasion, ignored on spurious grounds. The Chairman pointed out to Mr Arnold, Ward Manager between April 1995 and October 1996, that the *Fine Wind* document also lays down that patients would only be allowed one video recorder. Yet in the cases of Mr Hemming and Mr Corrigan this rule was broken by the PCT. In the case of Mr Corrigan the reason given was to enable him to copy gardening programmes, according to Mr Arnold. He could recall no reason being given for Mr Hemming having more than one video recorder.

3.12.16 The policy was a nonsense. A member of staff new to Lawrence would, we were told, be shown the Ward policies. Yet what was he or she to make of the fact that the policies were altered for a favoured few patients? And what possible use could patients have for more than one video recorder other than illicit copying?

3.12.17 Mr Arnold agreed with Professor Edwards' suggestion that the philosophy of the Hospital was to give PCTs as much discretion as possible within a framework of Hospital-wide rules. What went wrong with this goal? Mr Arnold confirmed for us that Lawrence Ward had always been regarded as different, a special ward with greater privileges. Added difficulties had been the succession of Ward Managers, which created inconsistency, and failure to monitor how policies were drifting. This was not a sudden happening, but rather a slow process over a number of years.

3.12.18 Mr Arnold gave examples of failures to ground initiatives in sound operational policies:

> "I think some of the things that occurred on Lawrence Ward, certainly things like the patients' shop, cash cards, the garden project, these schemes were at the time thought to be good initiatives . . . What they did not do was create the policies. Certainly my feeling would be before you actually set something up like that you need to create a policy."

3.12.19 With hindsight he agreed that the PCT had failed to look closely enough at things and to ask more questions. He agreed that many of the patients had succeeded in outsmarting the PCT. He admitted that the Ward was lax and policies slack, allowing patients to get up to all sorts of inappropriate activities. In his defence he said that the same had been true for some time before his arrival.

3.12.20 One should recognize here the effect of conditioning. The Report into the Escape from Whitemoor Prison drew attention to the way in which staff within special units such as the Special Security Unit at that prison get to know prisoners very well and can get "conditioned" into being less vigilant.[1] Mr Day, the first Security Liaison Officer for the PDU, drew our attention to the similar conditioning taking place on the PDU. This resulted in staff ignoring clearly laid-down policies and allowing boundaries to slip, just at Whitemoor. The attitude was "don't rock the boat".

Staffing

3.12.21 To some extent the Lawrence Ward PCT became hoist by the petard of their own rhetoric. Their policy document proclaimed the ward as a centre of excellence; the patients were said to be all worthy of trust; there were very few serious incidents. The result was that the ward was perceived outside as an easy ward to work on. Staffing levels were therefore kept low: Lawrence Ward was used almost as a "respite ward" for staff returning from long periods off work and staff would be removed from the ward to cover incidents elsewhere. The

---

1 Woodcock Sir John (1994) *Report of the Enquiry into the escape of six prisoners from the special security unit at Whitemoor Prison, Cambridgeshire, on Friday 9 September 1994*, Cmnd 2741. London: Home Office.

large number of Ward Managers, responsible for the safety and security of the ward, militated against the consistency of approach by nursing staff so important with this group.

3.12.22 The ambitious treatment model outlined in paragraph **3.12.6** required a high level of high quality staff but, for the reasons outlined above, Dr Strickland readily admitted that was not available. The deployment of nursing staff was outside the PCT's control. The original forerunner of the PDU as it were, Forster Ward, had benefited from the input of Dr Thomas-Peter, an experienced clinical psychologist (and one of our expert witnesses). But after he left the Hospital it was months before Dr Strickland could find a replacement. Dr Crispin stressed that there were many staff who wished to get involved in therapy but had to do it on their days off, or on overtime:

> "basically we might have had enough staff to contain the patients, but we certainly did not have enough staff to provide the therapy component."

Conclusions

3.12.23 We found that Lawrence Ward had been allowed to pursue its own course, untroubled by Hospital policies that conflicted with the PCT's view of life. The PCT demonstrated a dangerous belief in their own special status. The Ward policies were half-baked and poorly implemented; the staffing levels were inadequate. Yet staff were caring for a collection of highly dangerous individuals, some of whom had attained their privileged position by guile and manipulation. Thanks to the lack of overt trouble nobody reviewed the basic philosophy of the ward, what it was trying to do, and how it was trying to do it. We find it astonishing that within the context of a high security setting, a number of the patients on Lawrence Ward were considered to be of low dependency.

3.12.24 Lawrence Ward was a "low dependency ward" but by no means all of its patients were pre-discharge. Low dependency does not equal low risk. There was a crucial confusion in the minds of the PCT. Many of the initiatives we will discuss had merits for certain patient groups, but required much greater thought than the PCT was prepared to give if they were to work for this group of patients as a whole.

3.12.25 Such was Lawrence Ward. We turn now to consider Mr Daggett's complaints.

3.13.0 Clinical Care

3.13.1 Mr Daggett portrayed his absconsion as a protest against his poor clinical care. He claimed he had worked very hard on therapy, had made a large number of rehabilitation trips outside the Hospital, for example to see games at Wembley and Anfield, and had held the highest level of community card. He felt ready to move on to a medium secure unit. In May 1995 a case conference on Lawrence Ward concluded that he should be referred to a medium secure unit and a MHRT in October 1995 concurred. But by the time the referral was made the MSU concerned, Stockton Hall, had changed its admission criteria and was no longer prepared to accept him because of his background sexual offences. Mr Daggett was scathing about Dr Strickland's failure to refer him earlier.

3.13.2 The key to the referral however was that Mr Daggett would be referred when he was ready. The PCT did not feel he was ready yet. Mr Daggett admitted that he had previously absconded from a medium secure unit in 1989 and, following a conditional discharge in 1990, had re-offended by threatening a young girl with a knife. Dr Strickland commented:

> "Mr Daggett had twice been out of the Hospital, he had been transferred to an RSU where he had absconded, he had also been granted a conditional discharge by a tribunal, after which he had deteriorated fairly rapidly and actually committed a series of offences, one of which was extremely serious. It was only right I should behave in a very cautious fashion in moving him on to conditions of lesser security, with a view to him being discharged into the community."

Dr Strickland pointed out that there were problems in getting places for patients to move on to as well as resource problems in providing therapy within the Hospital.

3.13.3 Mrs Day told us that Mr Daggett definitely had more work to do in therapy and could not be considered ready for an immediate move. Mr Arnold confirmed this picture.

3.13.4 We believe that Mr Daggett's case was appropriately handled and do not criticize the PCT on that score. It is not for us to judge whether he is currently suitable for medium secure conditions, but we hope his route into medium security is not being blocked simply by the disclosures he made.

3.13.5 Mr Daggett also alleged that nursing care was poor. Handovers between shifts were inadequate, with the result that important information about the mood of the ward was not conveyed to the new shift; morale was poor; sickness rates were high; and the Ward Manager was ineffectual and commanded little respect amongst staff and, indeed, patients.

3.13.6 We heard evidence to substantiate at least some of this. Mr Cannon told us that the length of time staff spent with these difficult patients took its toll and staff were unable, himself probably included, to keep the requisite boundaries in place. We are aware from Mr Melia and Ms Edge that Lawrence Ward was used to "rehabilitate" staff returning to work after long periods off sick. The patients we heard evidence from gave mixed reports of the nursing staff on Lawrence Ward.

3.13.7 Mr Arnold told us that he had a particular interest in post-incident support of staff who had been off work. He was concerned at losing some of his most experienced staff during one of the two major staff moves that took place during his time as Ward Manager. He told us that new members of staff would be given a ward-based induction document which would be worked through. They would be encouraged to read the local policies. Both Hospital policies and ward policies were available on Lawrence Ward.

3.13.8 Mr Arnold told us that he had had no concerns about the nursing staff on Lawrence Ward. He had been very shocked to find out what Nurse Corrigan had been doing.

3.13.9 Lawrence Ward was a low dependency ward; its patients were able to look after themselves to a considerable extent. They were compliant with the regime on the whole. But they still had treatment needs, a fact which the "low dependency" label obscured.

3.13.10 We discuss the working of the Lawrence Ward PCT in greater detail below.

3.14.0 The Lawrence Ward Environment

3.14.1 Mr Daggett alleged that the Patient Care Team on Lawrence Ward was ignoring danger signals, despite warnings from his consistent complaints to the Ward Manager, Mr Arnold. He described the Ward as an "Owen Ward Mark II in the making" and alleged that a particular patient, Paul Corrigan, and his associates, intimidated other patients and to a certain extent staff whilst running a variety of scams. Four to six patients including Mr Corrigan were causing all the problems, a fact of which the PCT was well aware. The PCT, according to Mr Daggett, always protected Mr Corrigan in the face of complaints; even when in April 1994 a large number of patients on the ward voiced their concerns at a Community Meeting Mr Corrigan was able to claim he was being victimized.

3.14.2 In evidence Mr Daggett went further:

> "I am convinced that in some shape or form Mr Corrigan and his close associates held something over Dr Strickland and/or the members of the care team. I do not know what, but I am convinced there was something there."

We found no evidence to support this.

3.14.3 Mr Daggett said he had complained about aspects of the ward environment on a number of occasions to Mr Arnold, the Ward Manager. He referred to leaving a trail of information; when pressed, he said this amounted to saying to Mr Arnold and Mrs Day that they should look at Mr Corrigan and Mr Hemming's actions:

> ". . . I have never laid claim to sitting in a therapy session with Mrs Day and saying that Mr Corrigan or Mr Hemming were doing X, Y and Z. I suggested on a number of occasions that the ward regime was very, very unstable and basically those patients' behaviour was very inappropriate and she would best be served by looking towards their behaviours, not mine."

Mr Daggett argued that his safety would have been jeopardised if he had complained more overtly, for example at a case conference.

3.14.4 It would be easy to dismiss Mr Daggett's accusations as the malicious product of his own disappointments. But his concerns receive clear confirmation from a highly relevant source: the nursing staff. In 1996 the nursing staff began keeping a staff meeting book for staff to write down any concerns they might have, which Mr Arnold would then look at. This book raises a number of concerns about the ward environment:

> "ITEMS FOR DISCUSSION AT STAFF MEETING 21.7.96
>
> 1) The situation involving Peter Hemming and [Child A] is a matter of serious concern and needs addressing urgently. He has been observed on many occasions to have placed himself in situations involving [Child A] which are highly undesirable, given his history. There are a number of linked problem areas: the use of the library for the visit and its effect on other patients; the use of the garden as a visiting area and the question of its design which incorporates many hard to observe areas; the regular, unrequested extension of the visiting time; the large amounts of goods being brought to the ward for Paul Corrigan by [father of Child A] and their resale.
>
> 2) Boundaries/Guidelines/Rules. The general lack of structure to the ward is regularly raised by both staff and patients as a barrier to progress.
>
> 3) The ward environment is felt to be showing signs of heavy usage, indicated especially by the chairs in the day area and the office. The decorations are past their sell by date and are not assisted by the disregard towards communal hygiene and tidiness shown by the vast number of patients.
>
> 4) Communications are felt to be extremely poor and have not been assisted by the removal of the group structure. Matters are regularly left for the individual to apprise themselves of. Although some meetings are held on a regular basis ie PCTM, T/L, it is felt that feedback is scanty and the formal minutes are uninformative. The opportunity to raise matters for discussion at meetings is not clear.
>
> 5) Security matters:
>
> > a) Jars and bottles stored in the domestic cupboard.
> >
> > b) "Hidy hole" in the scullery.
> >
> > c) Blocking of the fire exits and corridors with items.
> >
> > d) Lack of observation in the garden area; lack of control of tools and their storage."

3.14.5 This was followed by an entry on 19 October 1996 signed by Lisa Johnson and others:

> "19.10.96
>
> 1) Why are the visits with [father of Child A and Child A] still being facilitated? (on the ward).

2) Why has no action been taken against those who had knowledge of the videos (particularly those with keys to shop ie [Patient Q, S. Booth, P. Hemming.).

3) Why are patients still not being challenged regarding their behaviour, its up to ourselves as P/NURSES [sc. primary nurses]

4) Would it not be appropriate to have staff in the night station as many 'dodgy' activities are thought to be taking place there.

5) Should the ward have lost its status as a parole ward, following this discovery (videos).

6) Should staffing levels be increased for AM, PM and night duty shifts, as the ward appears abnormally quiet given the restrictions being implemented.

7) Why does S. Booth still have keys and access to the petty cash box in w/m office.

8) Should patients . . . have keys to both kitchen and cleaners cupboard.

9) Regarding the last meeting dated 21 July 1996 Why were none of these items yet been addressed thoroughly.

10) Should the security cupboard in the office be locked, so patients can't just help themselves . . .

11) The garden shed needs to be thoroughly sorted as extra items appear to be there on top of the ones on the security check list.

12) Why was N. Bell not moved off the ward following a positive drugs test.

13) Should patients be allowed video recorders in their room – if they want to watch a video the ward has two available.

14) Patients' observation windows are often covered from the inside as well as the outside.

15) After 10 pm patients should not perhaps be allowed in each other's rooms. During other hours the doors should be left open.

16) Night staff should dispense night medication 9pm seems inappropriate for adults who stay up late on a ward like this . . ."

3.14.6 Ms Johnson took us through these comments. (We discuss the visits of Child A below.) Staff were clearly surprised that the video find had not resulted in more action, for example the loss of parole status for the ward. The fact that two patients had keys to cupboards containing potential security items and that the so-called security cupboard was not locked was very striking. Ms Johnson said the list was given to the Ward Manager and she was led to believe the points raised were discussed by the PCT.

3.14.7 Mr Daniels, a member of our Committee, made the point that this list was very similar to *My Concerns.* It is indeed.

3.14.8 A further comment, undated but presumably later, and with an illegible signature says, "Why have some patients not had room search for a few months, ie P Corrigan, S Booth. Security should come down and do thorough searches on these patients."

3.14.9 What these extracts reveal is that by 1996 a group of nurses were voicing very serious concerns about the entire ward environment.

3.14.10 This picture was further confirmed by a number of the patients we heard. Patient E, who came to the ward in 1993 after four years on Gibbon Ward, supported Mr Daggett's picture of an inner circle of patients who had a grip on the ward. He said that Mr Hemming, Mr Corrigan and Mr Bell were able to manipulate matters to their advantage and to intimidate other patients. He also confirmed the picture of laxity on the ward. When he arrived a nurse had given him a talk about the ward and told him that the regime was easy-going and if he kept himself to himself and behaved he would be left alone. That was more or less the extent of his "induction": he was not informed of any ward policy on visiting, although he was aware of a small book containing rules for the ward. He never received a copy. We were told that from 1995 onwards a three or four page document, referred to as the Lawrence Ward guidelines, was given to patients.

3.14.11 Patient E graphically illustrated the laxity of the security procedures by recounting to us how he had kept a camera in his room, which had been brought in by a visitor. This should have been kept by staff in the ward security cupboard, but on several occasions he removed it from the cupboard in the office. He had walked into the office, told a member of staff he was going to get his razor or similar item and took his camera at the same time. The member of staff took his word and signed the book accordingly.

3.14.12 Patient I arrived on Lawrence Ward in August 1996. No one had sat down with him to explain the rules of the Ward. Team Leader Mike Kenny merely told him that he would probably have to give a urine sample twice a year and have his room searched every three to four months and that he could not hit anyone. Patient I said that before he went to Lawrence Ward it had a reputation as "the nonces' mansion". It was very laid back, there were not many staff and the doors were left open; there were no checks and balances and the atmosphere was very free and easy.

3.14.13 Mr Keown's Report supports much of the picture painted by Mr Daggett. In its Executive Summary the team makes the following observations:

> "it is the view of the investigation team that a number of patients on Lawrence Ward have used and abused their privileged position on a low dependency ward. While those particular individuals may be asked to answer for their actions, the investigation team believes these patients acted in a manner which is not out of character for patients diagnosed as suffering from a personality disorder and given the apparent leeway afforded them on Lawrence Ward . . .
>
> It is the investigation team's contention that the Patient Care Team on Lawrence Ward had lost sight of the security implications and consequences of permitting patients to participate in activities based solely on trust. Consequently they were responsible, in some part, for the breaches of security that came to light as the investigation process progressed . . . .
>
> The investigation team believe that patient empowerment is essential if patients are to progress through the Special Hospital system. Empowerment, however, must be provided in an environment which is safe and secure but also balanced against the constant attempts at pushing boundaries which is expected from personality disordered patients.
>
> Checks and balances were virtually non-existent on Lawrence Ward – a recipe for disaster when one considers the patient group."

3.14.14 As we have seen, Lawrence Ward was not seen as one of the Hospital's "hot spots", and was, in fact, a place to "rehabilitate" staff after sickness leave. The relaxed regime of Lawrence Ward was well-known, but the problems there were not. Ms Edge said it was a much easier atmosphere compared to working with female personality disordered patients, who were extremely demanding. Mr Arnold was very supportive.

3.14.15 We were relieved to hear that recent security measures had made a tangible difference. Patients H, E and I admitted that things were much stricter now, rules were enforced and a structure was in place. Mr Peter Melia, a Senior Clinical Nurse on the PDU, and Mr John Foster, the current Ward Manager, confirmed this; Mr Foster pointed out that staffing had been increased from four, four and three over the three shifts to six, six and five. The number of patients had been reduced from 25 to 23. Every patient was given a rub down search, a locker check and a random search every month.

3.15.0 Drugs

3.15.1 Mr Daggett alleged that there were two drugs gangs dealing in illegal drugs within the Hospital, one of which operated within the PDU, primarily from Macaulay Ward, whilst the other gang operated within the Mental Illness Directorate. The two had clashed in the past but of late had come to an understanding that the PDU gang would give a percentage of its takings to the head of the Mental Illness gang. Drugs would come into the Hospital either via staff or patients; once agreement had been reached on the pricing of each batch several runners would distribute the drugs. He named several patients as the "runners" within the PDU. He admitted he had no proof that drugs were being brought in by staff; this claim was based on a good understanding of the way the Hospital worked.

3.15.2 Mr Daggett claimed that Lawrence Ward was ideal for distributing drugs:

> "Lawrence Ward, due to its low security and low staffing levels was an ideal place to act as a 'distribution centre' for the rest of the PDU and probably a significant part of the wider Hospital, with drugs being passed from Gibbon and Macaulay Wards, often in the Lawrence Ward garden, and sometimes through side-room windows. The garden was a favourite meeting place for the various parties to gather for a trade or a drugs drop, and there was absolutely no supervision of this area by nursing staff. It was a blind spot as far as the grounds-based cameras were concerned, and due to the overgrown nature of the garden there were many bushes, trees etc, that provided adequate cover for such drops."

3.15.3 He had seen what he believed to be drug deals taking place, although he accepted that very little evidence had come to light to prove that the Ward was a major distribution point for drugs. That said, he pointed out that the Ward's doors were open and patients were free to wander in and go into the garden without supervision, and concluded: "I am convinced to this day that a lot more drugs than perhaps the evidence points to were circulating in that area".

3.15.4 Besides traffic in illegal drugs there was also, Mr Daggett claimed, widespread abuse of prescription drugs. Several staff on Lawrence Ward were, he said, involved. They would fill in prescription cards for fictitious dosages and sell the drugs to patients, including Mr Hemming and others. Contrary to Hospital policy, one nurse, he claimed, had regular access to the dispensary; the alarm was doctored so that it would not ring when he unlocked the door. There were, Mr Daggett, claimed, few if any checks or monitoring of the use of prescription drugs. He admitted under cross-examination that he had not witnessed any nursing staff dealing in prescribed medication, although he had seen nursing staff leave patients' medication out before they went off early. These medicines might still be there the next day.

3.15.5 There is no doubt that ward practices concerning the issue of prescribed medication need to be tightened up. There is no direct evidence that nurses were involved in their illicit distribution, but there is evidence that the system would facilitate their being involved.

Recommendation 22 **3.15.6 We recommend that Ashworth Hospital should review the control and distribution of prescribed drugs so as to remove the risk of nurses becoming involved in their illegal distribution.**

3.15.7 Random testing of patients for drugs was in place but, Mr Daggett alleged, was easily evaded, since patients were unsupervised. He gave an example of one occasion when staff suspected a patient of using drugs but were afraid that he would make a complaint of harassment if they tested him alone. So they asked Mr Daggett to provide a urine sample as well, which of course proved negative. Since the main suspect was not supervised he was able to ask another patient to provide a sample and so escaped detection. This demonstrated a culture where staff were unable to do their jobs properly.

3.15.8 The evidence we heard from Lawrence Ward patients and from staff and others suggested that the Hospital had a drugs problem, but that Lawrence Ward was nothing out of the ordinary. Under cross-examination Mr Daggett admitted that he had never seen any illegal drugs on Lawrence Ward, but he had seen money changing hands for drugs on one occasion and on others he had seen money being handed over, possibly for drugs, possibly for other things.

3.15.9 Mr Keown and his team could find no evidence that Lawrence Ward was the centre of a large-scale distribution network, although they were told that a patient on Macaulay Ward was involved in the illegal supply of drugs in the Hospital and that Mr Corrigan smoked illegal drugs on the ward. The hiding places in the garden were said to have been used for hiding drugs.

3.15.10 Patient Q told us that one could get drugs on any ward in the Hospital and admitted using drugs on occasion. He speculated that drugs were brought in by visitors. He told us that there were no drug dealers to his knowledge on Lawrence Ward, nor was he aware of any abuse of prescribed medication . Patient H said it was common knowledge that there were plenty of drugs in the Hospital for those who wanted them, but that he had not personally seen them. He had heard several patients, including an individual named by Mr Daggett, did deal in drugs for cash.

3.15.11 Patient E said that he had been offered drugs by patients, but never by any patient from Lawrence Ward. Drugs were available in small amounts right across the Hospital; Lawrence Ward was nothing out of the ordinary in that respect. He had seen drug deals taking place on Gibbon Ward. Such transactions were usually done using phone cards, tobacco or some such, rather than cash. One patient told us that "sexual favours" were sometimes used in trading between patients.

3.15.12 Patient I claimed that Mr Corrigan and others used to get cannabis from a patient on Macaulay Ward. He witnessed this happening. Nursing staff knew all about this he claimed. He told us that the drugs problem was Hospital-wide and continued, despite the extra security, but was now much reduced. It was very much a soft, rather than hard, drugs problem. Patient D also told us that soft drugs were available if a patient wanted them on Lawrence Ward, but not to the extent suggested by Mr Daggett.

3.15.13 For his part Inspector Marsden was confident in asserting that drugs were coming into the Hospital undetected and being traded by patients.

3.15.14 Staff on Lawrence Ward appeared to be sanguine, even complacent about drug-taking on the ward. Nurse Edge said she was unaware of any drug dealing on Lawrence Ward, although she realized it went on in large institutions. Similarly, nursing assistant Ms Karran had seen no illegal drugs in ten years on Lawrence Ward.

3.15.15 Dr Strickland described drugs as a Hospital-wide problem, but one which if anything was worse on the Mental Illness side. Dr Crispin said she had pushed for random drug testing as she was always aware of the possibility of illegal drugs coming into the Hospital, but she had no evidence that there was a significant drug or alcohol problem on Lawrence Ward at that time.

3.15.16 Mr Arnold told us that there were yearly random drug screens. When he became aware that the procedures had become sloppy he tightened them up.

3.15.17 Lawrence Ward had a drugs problem, one which recent security measures appear to have reduced. Mr Daggett may have overstated the problem, but the generally lax security would certainly have allowed a greater drugs problem to flourish, and that needs to be vigilantly guarded against.

3.16.0 Financial Irregularities

3.16.1 Special Hospitals, as a rule, do not allow cash to be in day to day circulation. As ever, Lawrence Ward was deemed to be different. Mr Daggett made a number of allegations about the misuse of cash and of illegal trading; we supplement his themes with that of patient access to cash cards, so important to him in his absconsion.

3.16.2 Mr Daggett alleged that large amounts of cash flowed freely within the PDU; he estimated around £10,000 worth of banknotes were in circulation. He admitted this was merely an estimate, based on what was found occasionally through searching and taking into account the day-to-day transactions for items such as CDs, radios and videotapes. He frequently saw patients with £10 and £20 notes. He thought that ten to 12 patients a week were exchanging money on Lawrence Ward, and by adding the transactions together over the weeks and months arrived at this estimate.

3.16.3 Cash could be passed over by friends and family visiting, in particular by parole patients who were able to move around the grounds with considerable freedom. Supervision of ward-based visits was, Mr Daggett claimed, almost non-existent. Proper screening of visitors was essential to prevent this happening, but this was not done. No effective metal detection system was in operation.

3.16.4 Staff could easily pass cash to patients, either directly or via the cash box at the gatelodge. No checks were made as to who had left the money and why. Patients could also retain money taken out of the Hospital during a day trip; as there was no close monitoring of money taken out, it was easy to withhold some or all of one's money. Although the limit of cash was twenty-five pounds, this was not enforced as a rule. PCTs were unlikely to query amounts as large as three or four hundred pounds when a trip was requested. No one would check whether a patient had spent money on what he had said he wanted to purchase.

3.16.5 Mr Daggett admitted he had never seen visitors handing over cash to a patient, although he had seen suspicious behaviour which led him to suspect that something of the kind was going on. A member of staff had passed him cash in exchange for two speakers for a computer, which was commonplace. It was, he alleged, well known that staff would hand cash to patients to purchase things.

3.16.6 The evidence we heard suggests Mr Daggett overstated his case when he claimed that very large quantities of cash were circulating around the ward, although the laxity of ward security was such that cash could certainly be passed by the methods he mentioned. Both Patient D and Patient H told us they had never seen patients with money on Lawrence Ward. Nurse Edge told us she had never seen money changing hands on Lawrence Ward.

3.16.7 Mr Daggett's £10,000 figure was a surmise and too much weight should not be put on it. But the important fact to remember is that patients on Lawrence Ward were not supposed to hold cash at all.

3.17.0 The Lawrence Ward Shop

3.17.1 We heard much about the Lawrence Ward shop, which Mr Daggett claimed was used as a front for illicit trading, principally in pornography. He claimed that during the time the shop was open its accounts were not audited and staff had no access to the shop, its stock cupboards or its accounts.

3.17.2 The Ward shop was started when Mr Moran was Ward Manager. Patients were complaining about excessive prices in the Hospital shop. Mr Moran agreed that they could sell chocolate and lemonade to other patients and raise funds for the ward, this being in line with the high level of trust given to patients on the ward, it being a pre-discharge ward. He denied that there were any problems with the shop becoming a front for trading pornography during his time on Lawrence Ward. He told us the existence of the shop was well-known. At the time the shop opened there was no clear policy on internal business activity.

3.17.3 To describe Lawrence Ward as pre-discharge is misleading. A number of the patients on Lawrence Ward were highly dangerous and not going anywhere else for a very long time, although they were perfectly compliant with the ward regime. This is typical of the muddled thinking about the nature of the ward.

3.17.4 The shop operated from a ward utility room. Mr Greedy and Mr Hemming were the usual shopkeepers. Messrs Booth, Daggett and Bell assisted as did the visitor, the father of Child A. The accounts were kept by Mr Booth, and a fund kept in a box in the Ward Manager's office. Mr Moran said that he checked the books and stock periodically; he said there were no problems with the running of the shop in his time. Goods would be purchased on LOA trips; an order would be made and a patient would make a requisition for the cash from central finance. This money would be picked up by the nurse escorting the patient. The goods would be bought on a LOA visit and checked at the gate and then again on the ward. Mr Moran could not swear that the car bringing the staff member and patient back in was always searched. He confirmed that rub-down searches of patients leaving for, and returning from, LOA visits did take place. **There is, however, much evidence that searches were perfunctory.**

3.17.5 Any excess cash would be sent back to central finance. Mr Moran told us that the only cash kept on the ward in his time was a float of £25 in the Ward Manager's office to ensure that monies were available should the finance department have failed to get money ready at the gate for a patient's LOA visit.

3.17.6 But following Mr Moran's departure there was a succession of acting Ward Managers. No operational policies had been drawn up for the operation of the shop; Dr Strickland admitted there was no policy with regard to the shop, either with regard to the stock to be sold or the auditing of the accounts. This lack of clear boundaries for its operation, combined with a rapid turnover of Ward Managers, allowed patients to increase the shop's scope gradually without being challenged.

3.17.7 Thus the turnover of the shop soared from an original level of £50 or so a month to around £14,000 for the period January to October 1996. The records for the shop were inadequate to explain that level of turnover. Staff and parole patients from other wards were making purchases from the shop. Mr Keown agreed with Professor Edward's suggestion that virtually every ward knew about the shop on Lawrence Ward.

3.17.8 The monitoring of the shop accounts and the petty cash box in the Ward Manager's Office was inadequate at best. As we have seen, a patient, Mr Booth was the shop accountant. He kept the shop accounts on computer; Mr Arnold admitted that he did not keep copies of the monthly computer accounts. When the police tried to get access to these accounts they had been wiped off Mr Booth's computer. **It would be naive to think that had been done innocently.**

3.17.9 Mr Arnold told us that he checked the petty cash box from time to time, although day to day responsibility for the petty cash box rested again with Mr Booth. In his defence he argued that Mr Booth did not have unsupervised access to the petty cash box, and could only remove money for a planned purchase.

3.17.10 Mr Keown and his team found the financial controls over the shop completely inadequate, both at ward and Hospital level. The overseeing of the petty cash box was inadequate to ensure effective financial control:

> "This failure to provide sufficiently stringent controls and auditing trails led directly to [Mr Booth] and [Mr Corrigan] having the opportunity to misappropriate funds in a manner which has proved to be unquantifiable."

The petty cash box records (which were incomplete) show that the balance was occasionally as high as £302.30 – inflated by change from shop stocking trips. This was contrary to the well-known (but apparently undocumented rule) that all cash returned from LOA trips should be deposited in the secure box at the Control and Communications Centre from where it would be collected by the Finance and Information Directorate and credited to the appropriate Hospital budget.

3.17.11 Mr Keown and his team note that:

> "In the absence of any formal financial controls, auditing procedure and complete records of trading, the extent of trade and cash generated by the Lawrence ward shop has proven to be impossible to ascertain. The effect of cash circulating around the Hospital and the impact this had upon security in the Hospital also cannot be quantified."

3.17.12 We agree with this conclusion, which was strongly supported by the evidence we heard.

3.17.13 Mr Keown and his team also discovered that there was also a shop cash box used by the patients who acted as shopkeepers, unbeknownst to ward staff. The ubiquitous Mr Booth also looked after this box.

3.17.14 All patient transfers and bulk transactions were supposed to be processed through the patients' cash office by using inter-patient transfer (IPT) forms. They had to be signed by an approved signatory of a specified staffing grade, copies of whose signatures were held by the patients' cash office. Mr Daggett alleged that although an IPT had to be counter-signed by a Team Leader or Ward Manager and stamped with the Ward stamp these were often bulk-stamped to save time.

3.17.15 Lawrence Ward had been issued with an ink stamp in February 1993 by G. Hunjan, Deputy Director of Finance, as an added safeguard to authorising inter-patient transfers. The fear was patient forgery. This additional safeguard was not included in the inter-patient transfer procedure, but the relevant staff in the Finance Department knew of its importance. Due to the volume of inter-patient transfers the patients' cash office relied more and more and more on the approval stamp rather than the signature. So unauthorised inter-patient transfers were processed. Mr Keown and his colleagues analyzed a random sample of inter-patient transfers over three months and discovered that the proper procedure was not being followed. Mr Menkin, the Director of Finance and Information, at interview, said it was probable that every signature was not checked because of lack of time and the pressure to process requisitions, a point confirmed by two of his staff.

3.17.16 This had been corroborated by several patients in interview, who stated that it was common practice to have stacks of IPTs in their rooms to sell "bogus" goods. (It will be recalled from the Braund Report that many such transfers had been found in his room.) Ward staff apparently did not check to see whether goods actually did change hands . Mr Keown and his team believed that this lack of control allowed a trade in "ghost goods" to occur to provide apparently legitimate cover to illicit trading. A certain dot matrix printer changed hands a number of times yet appears to have been mythical, used, it seems, as a cover for other transactions.

3.17.17 This activity could have been checked if a proper system of patients' property lists had been in operation, allowing staff to check whether patients did indeed have the goods supposedly purchased. But no such system was in operation, despite this being Hospital policy. This laid the Hospital open to fraudulent claims for damage to property. Mr Moran confirmed that when he was on the ward he could not recall seeing any property lists.

3.17.18 Not surprisingly recommendation 13 of Mr Keown's Report states that transfers to patients should be observed to have taken place, and be recorded in the patient's property list.

3.17.19 The picture of the PCT's lack of grip on the situation is completed by the fact that staff did not generally have access to the shop.

3.17.20 Looking at this from the outside it seems absurd that there were any no-go areas for staff on a ward in a High Security Hospital.

3.17.21 There was also room for improvement in the Hospital oversight of the financial affairs of Lawrence Ward. First, the Finance Department apparently did not know of the existence of the Ward petty cash box, to the surprise of Mr Arnold. Second, they did not pick up the bogus use of the IPT stamp, although they should have checked all IPT forms for an authorized signature. And third, it was perfectly possible for them to have identified the increased turnover of the shop and voiced their concerns, given that most of the transactions were handled through inter-patient transfers. In the Finance Department's defence, there was an enormous number of IPT transactions to process; and Mr Keown pointed out that there was no particular reason for them to total the relevant figures up to discover the shop turnover.

The fact remains that unless these documents are audited, it is not possible to keep track of patients' trading or to maintain patients' property lists accurately.

3.17.22 In March 1995, shortly before Mr Arnold became Ward Manager of Lawrence Ward, Mrs Miles directed that "the Hospital does not consider it appropriate for patients to engage in commercial activities or deal with the public at large (which includes advertising)". The rationale for this decision was that such activity would be contrary to the Hospital's therapeutic ethos. There was also a doubt as to whether patients could enter into legally enforceable contracts. This directive had no impact on the operation of the shop.

3.17.23 The shop was actually closed in July 1995 by Mr Royal, the PDU Business Manager, because of a lack of financial controls. (Dr Strickland's Counsel pointed out quite rightly that it was not closed because it was deemed to have breached the March 1995 directive.) It reopened in December 1995, after an exchange of correspondence between Mr Arnold and Mr Menkin, Director of Finance and Information.

3.17.24 When the shop reopened there was again no effective supervision. Eventually Mr Murphy closed the shop in June 1996 following a meeting with Mr Arnold and Mr Paterson, the Deputy Security Manager, who recommended that both the Ward Shop and Mr Corrigan's shop (see below), should be closed.

3.17.25 Mr Arnold's Counsel argued that the actual sums unaccounted for in the Lawrence Ward accounts were minimal, namely £411.86, which represented under 5 per cent of the total cash drawn in the ten month period in question for shop purchases. Of this, the petty cash discrepancy was £74.39, which could be accounted for by missing cash sheets. In further mitigation, he argued that Mr Arnold did not have access to the Hospital's standard financial instructions, and that there were no financial instructions for him to follow with regard to the Lawrence Ward shop. Mr Arnold had not had training in accountancy or bookkeeping.

3.17.26 This argument assumes that no illegitimate trading took place. We quoted Mr Keown and his team above to the effect that the absence of any formal financial controls, auditing procedures and complete records of trading meant that it was impossible to discover the extent of trade and cash generated by the Lawrence Ward shop.

3.17.27 Mr Keown argued that £411 was a very significant amount in a Special Hospital. In addition, the lack of controls meant that more than this could have been in circulation, although the team found no existing evidence of this. The lack of control mechanisms meant that other significant transactions may have taken place.

3.17.28 We agree. The controls were unacceptably slack. Both Mr Arnold on the Ward and Mr Menkin and his Finance Department should have been more vigilant.

3.17.29 Where did the money go? Mr Keown and his team discovered that Mr Booth on one occasion deposited over £490 into his bank account despite the fact that he had withdrawn only £150 from his Hospital account. This demonstrated he had £340 in his possession of which his escort (who was on that occasion Mr Arnold) was unaware. This cash they speculated might have derived from illegal trading in the shop. The incident also demonstrated an inadequate rub-down search beforehand and inadequate observation. Mr Arnold told us he had deliberately chosen a small branch of Barclay's to aid observation but that had proved insufficient.

3.17.30 Mr Keown and his team believed, on the evidence of patients, that the shop had become a vehicle for illicit activity, such as pornography or other illegal or inappropriate goods. They questioned the original decision to allow the shop to start trading and criticized staff for allowing Mr Booth to maintain all trading accounts on his computer without supervision. They criticized Mr Menkin and Mr Tarbuck, the then Clinical Manager of the PDU, for allowing the shop to reopen, despite the existence of a Hospital-wide policy against patients engaging in commercial activity. Mr Tarbuck, for his part, thought the shop should not have reopened because he did not believe staff could supervise it properly, but told us that Mr Menkin, the Director of Finance, agreed to its reopening.

3.17.31 Neither Mr Moran nor Mr Arnold had any formal training in auditing or keeping accounts. The shop was set up without any clear financial instructions and no clear policy. Yet the Hospital had expertise within the Finance Department, expertise which no one seems to have thought fit to draw upon. As with other Lawrence Ward initiatives, the shop seemed like a good, therapeutic idea, but was not underpinned by clear policies.

3.17.32 We discuss the putative trade in pornography below. We broadly concur with Mr Keown's conclusions about the shop: it is totally unacceptable to have such a scheme in a High Security Hospital administered in such a slapdash way. It is highly questionable whether such a scheme should operate at all.

3.17.33 There is a further issue concerning the interpretation of policy. Mr Keown and his team interpreted the March 1995 directive on commercial activity to include all patient business activity as it was intended to do. Others had interpreted the directive in a different light and thought it irrelevant to the Lawrence Ward Shop. Mr Murphy admitted it was widely known that patients on Lawrence Ward operated a shop and that garden produce was being traded.

3.17.34 Mr Tarbuck, when asked whether he interpreted the ban on commercial activities of March 1995 as applying to the Lawrence Ward shop and the garden project, said he had understood the policy to refer to individual patients conducting private enterprises for profit from Hospital premises. The Lawrence Ward shop and garden project by contrast were contributing to ward funds and were thus essentially charitable. He did not see any difference between this and the rehabilitation therapy shop running in the Hospital; patients in both were procuring goods for sale and producing goods for sale. The only difference was that the Lawrence Ward patients received cheques under supervision, whereas in the rehabilitation shop only staff did this.

3.17.35 Mr Moran would seem to have shared this view of things. He agreed with the view put forward by Mrs Miles' Counsel that it was often very difficult to draw up policies capable of universal application. **The problem with this policy however was lack of clarity in its drafting.**

3.17.36 Seem to have been some doubt as to whether aspects of the Lawrence Ward initiative, in particular the shop and garden project, where staff bought plants from patients, came within the remit of the ban. Although the directive could have been more clearly drafted, we believe that the way in which it was interpreted in Lawrence Ward to have been rather disingenuous. There needed to be a mechanism for reviewing policies and examining any issues of interpretation. What should have happened presumably is that members of staff referred the matter to the Clinical Manager for interpretation. He could then have discussed the issue with senior colleagues. But the Lawrence Ward initiative was, as we have seen, so deep-rooted a part of the landscape that no one appears to have questioned its therapeutic value or considered whether it fell within the scope of Hospital policy.

Recommendation 23 **3.17.37 We recommend that no shop should ever be allowed on any PDU ward unless it is fully controlled by staff and regularly audited by the Finance Department.**

3.17.38 Policies need to be reviewed regularly and that is required by the "Policies Policy". Also, there needs to be a practice of staff checking local policies against Hospital policies and identifying any potential clashes. If there is any doubt there should be reference up for clarification.

3.18.0 Mr Corrigan's Shop

3.18.1 Mr Corrigan ran, with the sanction of the PCT, a shop selling items such as Christmas cards, wrapping paper, blank cassettes etc. The stock was kept in his sideroom. The profits were supposed to be ploughed back into improvements of the garden. Many of the goods offered for sale were designated as security items within the Hospital, for example brass wind chimes and glass framed pictures. Mr Corrigan's side room was so full of goods that there was insufficient room for him to lie on his bed. Security searches would have been impossible to conduct effectively.

3.18.2 Mr Daggett alleged that Child A's father would order and deliver the stock on Mr Corrigan's behalf to avoid checks by the Finance or Security departments. Staff hardly ever checked the boxes of stock from Child A's father which often contained pornographic master tapes. Blank tapes for copying the pornography were ordered as part of the shop stock. Mr Keown and his team learnt that Child A's father did indeed frequently deliver goods for Mr Corrigan and that on a number of occasions he brought his car to the Hospital to deliver stock. It is alleged that this car was not searched; certainly there is no record of any searches.

3.18.3 We consider it was irresponsible to permit an ex-patient to enter a supposedly High Security Hospital with a vehicle.

3.18.4 Mr Paterson, the Deputy Security Manager, told us that he and a colleague had estimated that Mr Corrigan was generating between £50 to £100 a month from his shop. As we have seen, he recommended to Mr Murphy in June 1996 that the potential for abuse was such that both the Ward Shop and Mr Corrigan's shop should be closed. Mr Keown and his team concluded that the PCT was unaware of the extent to which the business had expanded, particularly whilst the Lawrence Ward Shop was closed.

3.18.5 It appears that Mr .Corrigan was to be allowed to trade out his current stock; a further delivery had been arranged and this went ahead. It was not clear to us whether or not this delivery was properly searched; Mr Paterson told us it should have been searched on the ward, but there seems to have been some expectation that security staff would assist in searching. If so, this was typical of a confusion over the respective security responsibilities of gatelodge and ward staff.

3.18.6 We heard depressing evidence on this score. Mr Day, Security Liaison Officer for the PDU, told us that vehicles were inspected at the gate and any goods inside would be given a cursory glance. The ward was responsible for a detailed search. He agreed that this was not a generally agreed policy. This left plenty of room for misunderstanding and for ward staff to make assumptions about what level of searching had taken place at the gate.

3.18.7 Mr Gardner, the Head of Security and Clinical Risk Management, confirmed this picture. Proper procedures were not being followed: the gate staff thought the ward staff were conducting such vehicle searches while the ward staff thought the gate staff were conducting them.

3.18.8 In his evidence Mr Paterson told us that cars were always searched, but admitted that such was the volume of vehicle traffic coming in and out of the Hospital that a thorough search on every occasion was impossible. When a car was being driven by a member of staff (deliveries for the Lawrence Ward shop were often brought in this way) it seems any search would have been extremely cursory at best.

3.18.9 It is incredible that such a topsy-turvy situation should have been allowed to develop, and even more so to continue.

3.18.10 As with the Lawrence Ward shop, Mr Corrigan's activities were arguably not in contravention of the Hospital's policy against patients engaging in commercial activities, as set out in the March 1995 directive on commercial activities from Mrs Miles, because the policy lacked sufficient clarity. However Mr Keown could not explain what had moved the PCT to allow such a venture. The fact that it did permit it suggests that, as with the Lawrence Ward shop, the interpretation of the policy as far as Lawrence Ward was concerned was disingenuous.

3.18.11 There was a dispute as to whether the PCT actually endorsed the venture. Mr Cannon told us that the PCT was well aware of the existence of Mr Corrigan's shop. Mr Arnold claimed that the fact that Mr Corrigan's shop was making a profit was known and approved of by the PCT; Dr Strickland had no recollection of any such discussion. In contrast, Dr Strickland and Dr Crispin claimed they were unaware that Mr Corrigan was running a shop and making a profit. Mr Arnold disagreed, but said it was understood that all profits were to be ploughed back into the garden project.

3.18.12 It was put to us by Dr Strickland's Counsel that the PCT minutes for 1 August 1996 record Dr Strickland discussing with Mr Corrigan the Hospital's decision to ban commercial activity.

If the PCT was unaware of the extent of Mr Corrigan's activities before then that is equally damning.

3.18.13 Mr Corrigan also sold bedding plants and hanging baskets as part of the garden project (*see* below). Mr Daggett alleged that members of the care team were coming down to the ward and purchasing bedding plants and hanging baskets from the Lawrence Ward garden. The cash however made its way into Mr Corrigan and another patient's hands, even though it was against Hospital policy for patients to handle cash, unless it was deemed part of their rehabilitation. The sums involved were small, perhaps £15 – £30.

3.18.14 Mr Keown and his team record that Mr Corrigan and another patient were primarily responsible for the maintenance and planning of the extensive cultivation of the garden area to the rear of Lawrence Ward. The garden incorporated two garden sheds and a large greenhouse, with numerous shrubs, plants, gardening tools and sections of trellis fencing. Mr Corrigan obtained PCT approval for their purchase. The PCT fully supported this project when it was proposed by the then Ward Manager, Mr Moran, on the basis it was recreational therapy, which would also produce funds from sales to the benefit of the Initiative funds.

3.18.15 The Garden Project developed into a business selling bedding plants and hanging baskets. Mr Keown and his team found evidence that staff had been given credit by Mr Corrigan when buying shop produce. Mr Corrigan confirmed to Mr Keown he was always involved in garden sales which involved taking cash from staff and Elliot Ward patients. A fellow patient also confirmed this.

3.18.16 The search of Mr Corrigan's side room gave up garden sales records. Comparison with the petty cash records showed all recorded cash sales made by Mr Corrigan had been deposited in the petty cash box. But Mr Keown and his team noted:

> "The investigation team cannot confirm whether the records of cash sales and deposits in the ward account are accurate or whether fraud has occurred. The available records only relate to those cash sales recorded by Mr Corrigan and entered into the petty cash records by Mr Booth. Both Mr Corrigan and Mr Booth had the opportunity to misappropriate large sums of cash, the only control being their honesty."

3.18.17 We should also note the suspicions of Mr Day, who told us he had checked the payments made to visitors by patients at one point and found that around £1000 had been paid out to Child A's father, largely by Mr Corrigan, with some money coming from Mr Hemming. Mr Arnold had told him that this was because Mr Corrigan was buying stone for the garden. Mr Day was not convinced but was too hard-pressed by other priorities to pursue the matter.

3.18.18 Finally we should note that Mr Corrigan was not the only patient who was engaging in commercial activities contrary to Hospital policy and directives. Mr Keown and his team analyzed the Hospital accounts of Messrs Daggett, Booth, Adamson and Hemming; this analysis revealed that they had been or were currently engaged in commercial activities.

3.18.19 Mr Adamson admitted operating as a catalogue agent. He had three catalogue company agencies. The companies were legitimate and he met his payment liabilities. He supplied goods to other patients at the specified price. He ran a hairdressing business for patients and was paid in tobacco, stamps or other goods. He ran a tailoring repair business and his charges were reasonable. He had approval for his trading, and between April and September 1996 he received credits into his Hospital account amounting to £2,820.93.

3.18.20 A search of Mr Hemming's property disclosed that he was a catalogue agent for two companies, but the amounts involved were small and the agencies were used for personal shopping. He said he sold discount tobacco to patients at cost price. It was brought in for him by the father of Child A. The team was unable to verify these last assertions but for the period January to September 1996, his Hospital account was credited with £2,012.61 in excess of his Hospital benefits and reward payments.

3.18.21 Mr Goldwag operated a courier service when on daily leave of absence from his independent living quarters at Kent Gardens. He had brought in goods for other patients to order. He was not regularly searched when either leaving or entering the Hospital. Between January and September 1996, he received credits of £866.29 in excess of Hospital benefit and reward stages payments.

3.18.22 We discuss Mr Booth and Mr Daggett's computer ventures in **3.35.0** *et seq.* below.

3.18.23 Mr Keown and his team concluded that the PCT failed to comply with the policy statement of March 1995 by the General manager that it was "inappropriate" for patients to engage in commercial activities including advertising, in allowing the activities of these patients to continue. They note that the activities of Messrs Daggett, Corrigan, and Booth involved dealing directly with the general public. They recommended that the policy statement of 23 March 1995 be reissued to all wards, with detailed guidance to PCTs "to actively intervene and thereby prevent patients from participating in commercial activities."

3.19.0 Cash Cards

3.19.1 When he absconded Mr Daggett had cash cards in his possession which allowed him to withdraw large amounts of money to finance his absconsion. We heard a good deal of evidence about how it could happen that patients had access to these cards. **The evidence demonstrates an unfortunate lack of clarity about policy and an extremely blinkered PCT.**

3.19.2 First, the history. In September 1993 Lawrence Ward PCT allowed Messrs Daggett, Goldwag and Booth to conduct their own financial affairs including having and using personal cash cards and bank and building society pass books. They had made written requests for these facilities. There was no written evidence of PCT approval. The PCT apparently thought the requests were in keeping with the philosophy of the ward and would be beneficial for those who had demonstrated a high degree of trustworthiness and were deemed to have the skills to participate in the schemes. The PCT did not establish any policy to control the use of cash cards and the scheme went ahead without any checks in place. Senior managers were not, it seems, informed. Mr Arnold took the initiative to develop a policy much later.

3.19.3 A security e-mail on 6 March 1995 stated that a number of items should not be held by patients, namely, birth certificates, driving licences, building society/Post Office account books, bank account cheque books, cash cards/credit cards, passports and premium bonds. There was a dispute as to whether this e-mail reached the ward; it seems highly unlikely that it did not, although this was shortly before Mr Arnold joined the ward and the e-mail could conceivably have been lost in the handover.

3.19.4 We were told by Patient W that he had applied for a cash card, which was discussed on 6 July, 1995. The PCT was apparently in favour, but Mr Day, the security liaison officer for the PDU, raised concerns and discussed the matter with more senior managers. The issue was discussed at the Hospital Executive Group, which reaffirmed that cash cards should not be permitted. The HMT noted the decision the next day, 11 July 1995.

3.19.5 Dr Strickland and Dr Crispin claimed that before July 1995 they were not aware of any directive banning cash cards, but there was no directive permitting patients to have them. Patients were told that they could no longer use cash cards on LOA visits.

3.19.6 One might have thought that the directive from on high would have been enough. But no. The PCT discussed the matter on 13 July . Mr Arnold then raised the matter with Mrs Miles. In a letter to Mrs Miles of 4 August he enclosed a draft policy on the use of cash cards. The document stressed that Lawrence Ward aimed to be a therapeutic community with a strong emphasis on mutual trust between patients and staff. It argued the risks involved were at an acceptable level. The selection process involved meant that only patients who did not pose a security threat would be involved. The Lawrence Ward scheme had been in operation for 18 months with the four patients involved and there was no evidence of abuse. **But evidence of abuse had not been looked for.**

3.19.7 Mrs Miles replied to Mr Arnold on 9 August, saying that she was consulting various people. Again one might ask, why consult? Was the policy not clear enough? Mrs Miles' understanding was that the policy was clear, but that she was willing to listen to a test case. In the meantime the cards should not be used. This was also Mr Tarbuck's view. Previously he had been unaware that patients on Lawrence Ward had had cash cards. He agreed to write to Mrs Miles to see if she would accept a test case, but regarded the message as clear: these cards were not for use. Mr Tarbuck said that as far as he was aware the cash cards had been removed from patients on Lawrence Ward. He understood that a test case was submitted but did not know the outcome of that.

3.19.8 Dr Strickland wrote to Mrs Miles in October 1995 outlining the patients' views on why they should have a cash card. Of the small number of patients on Lawrence Ward who had been allowed to have them he said it had been a very beneficial thing to happen and he did not feel it posed any security risk! Mrs Miles did not believe this amounted to a proper test case.

3.19.9 The Operations Group of the PDU discussed the issue of Lawrence Ward patients being allowed cash cards on 22 November 1995. The minutes record that Mrs Miles had stated that patients should not have cash cards. Mr Tarbuck wanted the Operations Group to make a policy regarding cash cards. Mr Day (Security) pointed out that if a patient should abscond with a cash card it would enable him to obtain funds. Again: why was there any need for more discussion?

3.19.10 The "debate" appears to have dragged on and on. We saw a minute from Mr Tarbuck to Ms Young dated 2 April 1996 saying that the HMT believed patients should not hold cash cards. He then says:

> "You may care to take this proposal to the new Policy Committee for their views".

There are handwritten comments below Mr Tarbuck's signature: "Definite no from operations management team (HMT). Cards to be withdrawn and sent back, destroyed. May be able to look at in future, if policies are submitted and accepted. But no way at present".

3.19.11 This does not sound as if the message that this was firm Hospital policy was completely clear. Mrs Miles was mystified as to the reference of the "Policy Committee" referred to there.

3.19.12 Finally, Mr Murphy told us how he had had to spell out things very clearly to the PCT and patients in May 1996 that cash cards were not to be used. They were very reluctant to accept the point; eventually he asked rhetorically "which part of 'no' don't you understand"? Dr Strickland denied that he and fellow members of the PCT regarded the final instructions from management as an irritation, but rather as a helpful clear direction.

3.19.13 This is a sorry tale. Mr Keown and his team concluded that, although it was not possible in the absence of controls to say whether the cards had been inappropriately used, the lack of control allowed the patients to pursue business activities in contravention of the Hospital policy. The PCT did not even know what facilities various cards possessed. Mr Moran and Mr Arnold both said that patients were only allowed to have cards which gave access to electronic cash machines, but neither could say what facilities the relevant four patients had on their cards, and banks would not tell them on the basis it would be a breach of confidentiality. Not surprisingly, Mr Keown and his team were concerned that patients had the opportunity to obtain bank cards and credit facilities due to the PCT's inability to distinguish and thus monitor the use of commonly used and widely available bank cards.

3.19.14 The argument was put to us that removing the cash cards would probably be legally difficult.

This is immaterial. There is nothing to stop the Hospital from refusing to allow patients to have cash cards within the Hospital. Even such a policy, although a significant improvement, would not be fool-proof. Patients could possess cards held by family or friends, or give instructions by letter or telephone quoting a credit card's number and expiry date. Hence the need also to be vigilant with regard to patients' use of telephones and inspection of mail.

3.19.15 It seems that the use of the cards continued, despite PCT strictures that they should not be used, pending the resolution of the "debate". Mr Booth told Mr Keown and his team that patients handed in their cards but retained their numbers, so they could continue trading via the community phone (assuming, one supposes, they also noted the expiry dates of their cards). Lawrence Ward did not supervise outgoing calls so patients, by its use, acquired goods on external bank accounts and sold them on when they were received.

3.19.16 Mr Daggett admitted that whilst he had destroyed the cash card he held in his old name, he had not surrendered the new one he held in the name of David Brown. He commented:

> "Most patients knew they were going to be expected to cut their cash cards up. . . patients had already telephoned the bank and asked for replacement cards to be sent. Those cards were sent into the Hospital. Even though the mail was opened, those cards arrived at the ward without being stopped by security or the mail room."

3.19.17 Mr Daggett suspected that the PCT realized that patients had received replacement cards. Dr Strickland denied this.

3.19.18 Patient W told us that, although he was denied a cash card, he was given permission to open a bank account with a cheque book. He was allowed to look after this cheque book and a Post Office savings book himself and take them out on LOA visits. He was asked to hand in the books on 4 October 1996 after the absconsion of Mr Daggett. This was the only time his books had been inspected. Not everyone did so; Mr Hemming gave his cheque book to Child A's father's girlfriend and signed cheques on visits from her, supervised by nursing staff.

3.19.19 An important part of the new ward policy on the use of cash cards was that when LOA trips were being made, the patient was supposed to tell the PCT that he intended to take the card with him, and state the amount he may withdraw in cash and what it will be used for. This was to be done on the Ward LOA form. However, the team found no evidence that this was done.

3.19.20 Mr Arnold admitted that the PCT was trusting the patients to some extent not to use the cards, and of course individual escorts, who had been briefed not to allow patients to use cash machines. He admitted that the cards could be used by patients on the ward telephone. He had been reassured by the reintroduction of central searching of mail that obtaining duplicates would become more difficult, but granted that duplicate cards could have been obtained on LOA visits or before central searching of mail was reintroduced. The cards should never have been introduced without a robust written policy; but once they were in the possession of patients they could not simply be removed. He claimed that the PCT was merely awaiting a clear decision and that he himself was happy with the answer "no" when it came.

3.19.21 Mr Keown and his team note:

> "With the continued use of cash cards, the area of telephone banking and the ease by which duplicate cards can be obtained had apparently failed to be identified by the Care Team in relation to their use".

Unsurprisingly Mr Keown and his team recommended that patients should not hold personal bank cards, cheque books, or undertake telephone banking. Personal finance matters for patients would be carried out for them by the Finance and Information Directorate, and all cards, cheque books etc would be held centrally by the FID.

3.19.22 Why was this degree of manipulation allowed to happen? It came back to a question of trust: on Lawrence Ward patients were trusted not to manipulate the system.

3.19.23 Why did the situation continue? Was the PCT being wilfully obtuse? Communication is a two-way process and if people do not wish to hear then there is a limit to what can be done. Mrs Miles thought that the PCT was not inclined to listen to messages running contrary to the ethos of Lawrence Ward. The PCT claimed that the cards were not to be used on LOAs in any case during the period of the debate, a point which was confirmed by Patient W. However, their security procedures were so slack that one could not be sure that the cards were not taken out, as Mr Daggett did. The documentation supports the view that they thought a debate was taking place, rather than that a policy had been laid down which must be followed, pending the production of a clinically robust test case.

3.19.24 Mr Maxwell, Security Manager until March 1996, told us that as far as he was concerned the policy on cash cards had always been clear. Patients were not allowed to hold at ward level documents such as cash cards. Indeed in the past they had not been allowed such things at all; this policy had never officially changed, but there had been a gradual slippage in practice in the name of therapy. Although as Security Manager he could raise issues with Mr Dale and Mrs Miles his role was always advisory only. Mr Day, who first raised the issue with the PCT, was also quite clear that as far as he was concerned cash cards had never been allowed, although his e-mail to Mr Tarbuck asking him to pursue the matter with the HMT did not put it in quite those terms.

3.19.25 The context is important. Mr Tarbuck pointed out that the cash cards issue was exacerbated by the fact that patients on Eliot Ward could officially carry cash within the Hospital, yet patients on Macaulay and Lawrence Wards could not. A group of patients on these wards constantly pushed for similar "privileges". Although he was not in favour of patients in the PDU having cash, these patients constantly lobbied their case and it was not possible to justify why a group of patients on a ward for mentally ill people could carry cash whilst (non-psychotic) patients on the PDU wards could not. **This illustrates the pressure staff were under in looking after mentally ill and personality disordered patients on the same campus.**

3.19.26 Another matter to note from this episode is that Mr Tarbuck told us he had been unaware that patients on Lawrence Ward had had cash cards since September 1993. This was despite the fact that giving patients cash cards was an innovation. This was an arrangement confined, as far as the PDU was concerned, to a few patients on Lawrence Ward. It should have been clear that this was a situation not covered by existing Hospital policy; monitoring should have picked that up.

3.19.27 That the Lawrence Ward PCT pursued this initiative without reference to their superiors betrays the exercise of irresponsible clinical freedom bordering on arrogance. So firmly set were they in their idea of the "special status" of Lawrence Ward that they did not feel the need to refer such policies upwards. And again they failed to underpin a therapeutic initiative with the kind of robust policies which might have prevented abuse.

3.19.28 But the fault was not all on one side. The "debate" was allowed to go on because there was no clear mechanism for spelling out that this was Hospital policy. The tone of Mrs Miles' correspondence was not as prescriptive as it might have been; she did not spell out that "no cash cards" was Hospital policy, nor did Mr Tarbuck. Both felt presumably that they did not need to. It is certainly the case that the Lawrence Ward PCT wished to pursue their own course of action and maintain the use of cash cards. They were aided in this by the fact that there was no system for clearly defining what was and was not Hospital policy.

Recommendation 24 **3.19.29 We recommend that the Hospital develops a method for differentiating mandatory policies from guidance.**

3.20.0 Pornography

3.20.1 A number of witnesses told us that the rule of thumb at Ashworth as far as pornography was concerned was that anything that could be bought on the top shelf of a newsagent was acceptable, although there might be particular clinical issues with regard to individual patients. We do not disagree with this general approach, but we do stress the importance of controlling pornography. First, because pornographic videos in particular easily become a means of conducting illicit trading. Second, because even apparently innocuous material can have a corrupting effect on individual patients.

3.20.2 Mr Daggett alleged that the vast majority of pornographic material was brought in by Child A's father on his regular visits. He passed on obscene pornographic tapes, some of which involved children and bestiality; most were then sold on to patients on Lawrence Ward or elsewhere.

3.20.3 There were various means of distributing the tapes. One was to use patients as runners, for example Mr Bell and Mr Booth of Lawrence Ward and another patient from Ruskin Ward. Another was the Lawrence Ward garden, which offered an ideal place for trading and taking orders; Mr Daggett noted that, "during the parole hours, the daylight hours where people were allowed to wander from ward to ward, there were people coming through the front door and out the back door into the garden. Some did not even bother to do that, they came round the side of the buildings." He likened it to a car boot sale:

> "There was definitely a number of people, certainly well over 12, 15 people at a time in the garden who came in with videos and did not leave with videos; or came in without videos and left with videos, CDs, tapes . . . Basically if I wanted to sell a video recorder and I agreed a price with someone for, say, £100, if we wanted to exchange for cash, CDs or videos, tapes, whatever, or an inter-patient cash transfer, that could be done quite easily.
>
> "That was what I was trying to portray there with the notion of a car boot sale, that it could take place anytime, anywhere, and more often than not in Lawrence Ward garden, basically often under the noses of staff if staff ever went out there."

3.20.4 There were allegedly three other distribution routes. One was the Hospital library, where Mr Hemming worked part-time. This offered cover for swapping illegal videotapes. The second was the Lawrence Ward shop. Mr Daggett claimed it was a reasonable surmise that the tapes were pornographic, as otherwise why would patients be so concerned lest staff see what was going on? Patients would be spending suspiciously large amounts (£15 or more), supposedly on chocolates and crisps; because the patients were running the shop without any staff supervision there were no checks on such transfers.

3.20.5 The third route was Mr Corrigan's shop (*see* **3.18.0** *et seq.* above). When the

Lawrence Ward shop was closed down Mr Corrigan was told to close his venture down as well but instead allegedly expanded its operations, taking over the trading in video tapes.

3.20.6 Mr Daggett told us that the orders were sent by the wholesaler to Child A's father; he then brought in the stock in his own vehicle. As we have seen, the searching of goods coming into the Hospital was cursory at best, as the gate staff assumed the ward staff would do a search; when the boxes reached the ward any genuine attempt to search would be met by a display of petulance from Mr Corrigan which would dissuade that member of staff from pursuing a search. Mr Paul Boocock, a nurse on Lawrence Ward, confirmed that the boxes would be given a cursory search but that Mr Corrigan would object if anything more was done, implicitly threatening staff with the possibility of a complaint which might be upheld. He agreed with the suggestion that in effect Mr Corrigan was controlling the searching.

3.20.7 Mr Daggett alleged that on one occasion he saw Mr Corrigan take several videotapes and say to Mr Hemming and another patient 'get these done tonight, will you?". He added, "I do not think they were recording *Top of the Pops* and selling those on".

3.20.8 Mr Daggett told us that cash was often used to pay for the items, but if not an Inter Patient Transfer (IPT) form was used which could cover the cost of the legitimate goods and the videotapes. As we have seen, although an IPT had to be counter-signed by a Team Leader or Ward Manager and stamped with the Ward stamp, these were, it appears, often bulk-stamped to save time. Mr Daggett saw a nurse signing a small wad of such forms for Mr Corrigan.

3.20.9 Mr Daggett said that he himself was offered pornography but never accepted it. He saw Child A's father bringing tapes into the library, and he saw people carrying tapes.

3.20.10 That pornographic videotapes were present in abundance on Lawrence Ward was proved by the search of the boot room, previously the Lawrence Ward Shop, on 28 September 1996. This uncovered 41 pornographic videotapes.

3.20.11 Mr Keown and his team heard conflicting accounts from patients as to the ownership of the tapes, but evidence was found to support the claims made by several patients that Mr Corrigan and Mr Hemming had been copying pornographic tapes.

This is supported by their possession of more than one video recording machine each.

3.20.12 When searched, Mr Hemming's room had two video recorders in it. One was a sophisticated Super VHS recorder. A SVHS video recorder can copy at a resolution of 400 lines. In Mr Corrigan's room four VCRs were discovered and they had been linked together for copying purposes. The team were concerned that he had had four machines in his side room without being challenged by the ward staff or the PCT.

3.20.13 The only object in having two VCRs in one room is to copy or edit tapes; having four increases the copying capacity by a factor of three. It is difficult to escape the conclusion that the staff and PCT either knew what was going on and accepted it, or knew what was likely to be going on and did not want to find out. It is absurd to say that four such recorders could be justified on therapeutic grounds.

3.20.14 One patient told Mr Keown and his team that the Lawrence Ward Shop was a front for the rental and sale of pornographic tapes. Another said some tapes cost £50 for the more specialised stuff. A third said the average tape cost £10 – £15. Many sales were for cash, phone cards, and inter-patient transfers using "ghost goods". A fourth said he had seen cash change hands between patients and Mr Corrigan. The team believed the 41 tapes found in the Lawrence Ward shop were copies from tapes brought in by the father of Child A. The ownership was likely to have been shared between Mr Corrigan and Mr Hemming who was also the distributor.

3.20.15 A further, very extensive, search of Lawrence Ward on 17 January 1997 led to 831 videotapes being removed from patients' side rooms for examination. Mr Corrigan had no fewer than 225 tapes in his side room. The team were at a loss to understand how he could have amassed so many. **The answer was, simply, he was allowed to do it.**

3.20.16 Subsequent examination of the 831 tapes showed that many of these tapes had been recently wiped or re-recorded following the earlier discovery of pornographic tapes. Patients told the team that following the seizure of the 41 tapes from the shop there was, according to Ashworth folklore a "power spike" (meaning a surge caused by excessive demand) as patients wiped their own pornographic video tapes clean. Mr Hemming was asking patients to wipe tapes for him according to one patient. Another said to the Keown team that he stored ten pornographic tapes for Mr Hemming and charged him for doing so. A number of patients said that after the 41 tapes were removed from the shop, ward staff told them to get rid of any pornography they might have. The team concluded:

> "The evidence in support of the assertion that Lawrence Ward operated a sophisticated pornography ring centred around Mr Corrigan and Mr Hemming is extensive. On the balance of probability, the main supplier of all types of pornography including bestiality, sado-masochistic, child pornography and heterosexual pornography was the father of Child A."

3.20.17 They recommended banning the father of Child A from visiting the Hospital indefinitely.

3.20.18 We took a good deal of evidence on this very important matter. Unsurprisingly the father of Child A denied ever bringing pornographic material of any description into the Hospital. He claimed the videotapes were normal general release videotapes such as you would find at any video store. He confirmed bringing in material for Mr Corrigan's shop. This would be material from wholesalers delivered directly to him which he would then bring in still in their sealed boxes. He believed, but was not sure, that the material was searched at the gate and said that it was searched on the ward.

3.20.19 We did not believe his evidence, and our conclusion is strengthened by the fact that the police found pornographic videotapes when they searched his house, and by the fact that he was found to have over 1000 Ashworth telephone cards in his possession. The purpose was presumably for trading goods, as the cards rapidly acquired the status of cash within the Hospital.

3.20.20 Our patient witnesses provided ample evidence of a thriving trade in pornography on Lawrence Ward. Patient Q told us that many patients on Lawrence Ward had pornographic videotapes and he admitted exchanging some pornographic videotapes, though he denied selling them. There was a considerable amount of swapping of videotapes by patients across the Hospital; patients from other wards could come to Lawrence Ward and go to the shop, give Patient Q their videotape and he would go to his room to fetch another videotape to swap. The videotapes would be hidden in bags or down a patient's trousers; this was safe as patients were not searched going onto or coming off the ward. .

3.20.21 He recounted how Mr Hemming had brought a box of videotapes into the shop one day and asked him to store the box in the shop because a search was expected. Patient Q knew that the box contained pornographic videotapes. At around the same time he assisted Mr Hemming in wiping a dozen or so videotapes. This box of videotapes was subsequently found on 28 September 1996.

3.20.22 Patient Q told us how before Mr Daggett's absconsion videotapes could be obtained by mail order and, disguised as something like a boxing videotape, would be sent to the ward without being viewed by the Security Department. He had obtained about two dozen videotapes this way. He told us that Mr Corrigan and Mr Hemming copied videotapes. This was confirmed by Patient H, who told us that pornography of various sorts was widely available amongst patients on Lawrence Ward. Mr Corrigan and Mr Hemming were the patients to see to get a video. He told us that he had observed from the day area Child A's father handing over two videotapes on Saturdays to Mr Corrigan, who would swap these for two other videotapes. The following week new pornography would be available. Patient H himself got pornographic videotapes from Mr Corrigan and Mr Hemming. He never paid money for the videotapes and told us he had never heard rumours that videotapes were being sold from the shop. He had heard that pornographic videotapes could fetch from £10 – £15 for average tapes to £50 for specialised tapes, although he had no direct knowledge of this. He agreed that there was a trade in pornography for cash.

3.20.23 Patient E told us that Lawrence Ward had a reputation elsewhere in the Hospital as somewhere where pornography was available. He had seen some pornographic tapes, but had not bought any, nor did he see anybody else buy pornography on the ward. He did see Child A's father hand over tapes to Mr Corrigan and it was widely suspected that the former was the source of pornographic tapes. He had never received pornographic tapes from anyone on Lawrence Ward, but they were, he admitted, available from Mr Corrigan, Mr Hemming and Patient Q.

3.20.24 Patient E said he would choose to go elsewhere for videotapes, as he thought those individuals would be likely to want something in return, possibly sexual favours. Patient Q had made it very clear to him that this was a possibility.

3.20.25 Patient I told us that he was aware that pornographic videotapes were available from Lawrence Ward shop, although he had not got videotapes from there himself. The people running the shop only gave them to those they knew and trusted. He knew they were pornographic from discussions with other patients. He had visited the shop with staff before he went onto the ward and seen patients coming out with videotapes, though whether they were from the shop he could not be certain. There was no attempt to conceal them. He thought it was possible that cash was paid for videotapes. He was also aware from discussions with patients of staff bringing in videotapes for patients, probably of a normal pornographic sort rather than paedophile.

3.20.26 Patient D told us that pornographic videos were circulated, although he had never paid for one. He admitted that before the full-scale search of Lawrence Ward in January 1998 a number of individuals appeared to have amassed a large amount of pornography.

3.20.27 It is interesting to note that in October 1996 on Owen Ward patient RM, who had previously been on Lawrence Ward, was found to be holding nine hardcore pornographic videotapes in his bedroom, two of which involved children.

3.20.28 Inspector Marsden had no doubt that pornographic videotapes were available to patients at the Hospital, based on his experiences investigating Lawrence Ward and earlier incidents. He thought that it was highly plausible that videotapes had come in from visitors and from commercial suppliers.

3.20.29 We have no doubt that Mr Keown and his team were right: Child A's father, Mr Corrigan and Mr Hemming were involved in a pornographic trading operation. Whether cash changed hands for the videotapes is less certain, but probable.

3.20.30 This being so, the Lawrence Ward staff have to be severely criticized for failing to identify the weaknesses in security which allowed this situation to develop.

3.21.0 Garden Projects

3.21.1 The Lawrence Ward garden had been in existence for a number of years by the time of Mr Daggett's absconsion. Two patients (one of whom was Mr Corrigan) were largely responsible for its maintenance. The garden area incorporated two garden sheds and a large greenhouse, which were purchased from ward funds and numerous plants and tools. As we have described, as years went by the "business" side came more to the fore, with sales of bedding plants and hanging baskets.

3.21.2 Mr Keown and his team were shocked at the state of the Lawrence Ward garden. Trees had been planted and fencing erected in ways which obscured observation. The team believed this was done consciously to restrict observation by the staff. They were also concerned by the tools, equipment, chemicals, (all security items) which had been acquired without formal approval and used without supervision. The team believed the design of the garden was a long term plan initiated by Mr Corrigan to provide an area with minimal staff observation for illicit activities. In the layout, hiding places were constructed in which illicit goods could be stored..

3.21.3 This was the "show case" ward for visiting VIPs to be shown, with the garden as its centre piece. It is incredible that the security implications of the growth of trees and shrubs remained unrecognised for so long.

3.21.4 In their interviews with the Keown team, two patients said they were aware the hiding places were used to store cash, pornographic video tapes and drugs. A broken piece of a video tape was found in one hiding place, confirming that it has been used to store tapes, presumably of a hardcore pornographic nature. Patient RM told the team of a hiding place in the garden where he believed pornographic video tapes had been buried. Nothing was found there.

3.21.5 The garden tools contained a number of security items which had been acquired without formal approval and used without proper monitoring. There appeared to be no regular checking of tools and updating of the inventory of tools. Mr Keown and his team commented:

> "[the Team] believes that the design of Lawrence Ward garden was a long term plan initiated by Mr X [Corrigan] in order to provide an area which would have only minimal staff observation thereby providing Mr X and other patients with a relatively unobserved secure area in which illicit activities could have occurred."

3.21.6 This illustrates the problems inherent in this patient group who have the cunning, skill and patience to plan over an extended period to subvert control systems.

3.21.7 This corroborates the picture painted by Mr Daggett, who described the garden as ideal for "various parties to gather for a trade or a drugs drop . . . there was absolutely no supervision of this area by nursing staff. It was a blind spot as far as the grounds-based cameras were concerned, and due to the overgrown nature of the garden there were many bushes, trees etc, that provided adequate cover for such drops". He also alleged that the garden area was used for storing materials and was not searched properly.

3.21.8 We were told that the development of the garden did not go completely unchallenged. Mr Day described the development of the garden as a "security nightmare" and told us he had raised with the PCT of the difficulties posed by the trees. When he first visited the ward and garden tools were being left unattended and there was no proper inventory; Mr Arnold had tackled this, but Mr Day was not confident the level of checking had been particularly good. He told us that the PCT did note his concerns but he felt they did not wish to spoil the feature of their ward. Dr Strickland's Counsel disputed whether Mr Day had raised the security of the garden with the PCT; certainly it was not minuted. However, Dr Strickland may have missed the relevant PCT meeting, and our experience of receiving alternative versions of PCT minutes does not lead us to be over-reliant on their completeness.

3.21.9 Mr Dale admitted he did not specifically go into the garden area of Lawrence Ward. He doubted whether any of his director colleagues were aware of the garden's layout. He noted that Mr Keown and his colleagues had gone into the garden sensitized to what might have taken place there. He thought that in fairness to the PCT the problems with conifers growing up to obscure observation emerged over time, and they did not realize blind spots were being created.

3.21.10 This garden was well-known and something of a showpiece for the Hospital. Again, the "special" status of Lawrence Ward stopped people from thinking of the dangers posed by such developments.

3.22.0 Alcohol

3.22.1 Mr Daggett alleged that several members of nursing staff regularly brought in alcohol for patients, including Mr Corrigan. Mr Daggett had seen at least two members of the nursing staff doing this, including Nurse Corrigan, and heard patients commenting on which members of staff were best at getting hold of alcohol. Visitors also brought in alcohol, including the father of Child A. Alcohol could easily be brought in in soft drinks containers and stored in side rooms, as searches were virtually non-existent. Most of the patients on the ward had frequent trips out and escorting standards were lax, as indeed was security at the gate. Certain escorts were known not to monitor patients' shopping carefully. It was also common knowledge which shifts the "right staff" worked on to avoid having one's bags searched.

3.22.2 Mr Daggett made the point that patients on Lawrence Ward had tended to have worked a number of years to reach the position of trust they now held. The fact they were willing to risk their position through bringing in alcohol demonstrated their confidence in the lack of security.

3.22.3 One patient, who had unescorted leave status, was able to bring in alcohol freely, as staff rarely searched him.

3.22.4 Patient D told us that a member of staff would occasionally bring him in alcohol. Searching of staff has never been a practice at Ashworth Hospital.

3.22.5 We did not go into this area in great detail. Certainly the system was lax enough to allow the importation of alcohol. We see no reason to doubt the testimony of patients on this score.

3.23.0 Inappropriate Behaviour with a Visiting Child

3.23.1 Throughout the hearings we held we made it clear that the anonymity of Child A had to be maintained and we have continued that policy in this Report.

3.23.2 By far the most serious of Mr Daggett's allegations was that Child A regularly came to Lawrence Ward with her father and visited patients with a history of horrific offences of sex and violence. We have described the nature of those offences earlier.

3.23.3 In dealing with these allegations we have examined the Hospital's internal inquiry into Child Care Issues at Ashworth Hospital Authority, known as "IR2". This Inquiry was seriously flawed in various respects, as we have said in paragraph **3.10.2** above, not least in the initial appointment of Mr Bateson, an important figure in the recent history of these matters, as Inquiry Chairman. However, the Inquiry did yield some information not stigmatised by the Report's defects.

3.23.4 We were told of the withdrawal of the IR2 Report in a letter from the Acting Chief Executive, Mr Peter Clarke, dated 30 September 1998 which was sent following a meeting of the Ashworth Hospital Authority Board on Tuesday 29 September. That letter noted that the Board had passed the following resolution:

> "The Board noted that it had already agreed the Report's (IR2) recommendations in respect of child protection, however it concluded that the investigation process was flawed and therefore the content and recommendations regarding individuals should be set aside and no further action taken on the basis of IR2.
>
> "It was agreed that this resolution be communicated to Judge Fallon and to those named in the IR2 Report."

3.23.5 Mr Clarke's letter made no mention of the review document itself.

3.23.6 We heard nothing more until we received a copy of the Review into the IR2 Report dated 21 September 1998 addressed to Mr Paul Lever the Chairman of the Ashworth Hospital Authority Board, from an external source. The Review comprises five and a half pages. On the fifth page this appears:

> "A worry
>
> (a) If it is not too late to alert Fallon to the findings of the review, or
>
> (b) If Fallon has drawn upon the IR2 Report, and
>
> (c) If Fallon recommends action which would lead negatively to individuals recommended for further investigation by the IR2 Report."

3.23.7 The review makes three recommendations:

> "1. That all the Report's (IR2) recommendations to do with child protection issues be incorporated in the development of policies, procedures and practices for immediate implementation. To this end, we ask that the Board (at its end of September 1998 meeting) be given a full Report regarding child protection policy, procedures and practices.
>
> 2. That recommendations pertaining to individuals be dropped forthwith and the individuals in question be so advised and informed, that subject to Fallon, the matter is closed.
>
> 3. That Fallon (if not too late) is alerted to the findings of this Review."

3.23.8 We consider it surprising to say the very least that the Ashworth Authority Board, having supplied a copy of the IR2 Report to our Committee, failed to provide us with a copy of the Review as a matter of course, implicitly ignoring the third of the recommendations quoted above. The culture of secrecy does not appear to have changed.

3.23.9 Child A was born in February 1989 and first visited Lawrence Ward with her parents as a baby. Both parents have a history of mental disorder. She visited the ward with her father over a period of some years until October 1996. It is likely that she visited the ward hundreds of times in that time; between January 1994 and October 1996 computer records show that she visited on 151 occasions.

3.23.10 Mr Daggett claimed to have first been concerned when he saw Mr Hemming play with Child A in the garden unsupervised by ward staff; some of the games were, he felt, inappropriate, such as piggy-back rides and bouncing Child A on his knee. In the summer months she was in a semi-state of undress. Three or four times he saw her dressed only in her knickers.

3.23.11 Mr Daggett told us that he had seen Mr Hemming and Child A in the ward garden one Sunday and thought to himself "this cannot go on". He dated this to around May 1996.

He had been very aware of the visits since December 1993, but his concerns had grown since late 1994. In the summer of 1995 he saw Child A in a state of undress in the garden.

3.23.12 We described Mr Hemming's previous convictions for serious sexual assaults, largely with young girls, above. Mr Keown and his team were told by several patients that Mr Hemming had a continuing interest in child pornography. Having accompanied Mr Hemming on LOA visits, Mr Daggett was aware of him continuing to have a fascination for little girls. Mr Hemming had a number of photographs of Child A which, whilst not provocative in themselves, were highly unsuitable for a convicted paedophile to have in his possession. Child A's father did not, in Mr Daggett's view, object to any of Mr Hemming's activities and did not stop him taking her out into the garden unsupervised. Yet Mr Hemming was not related to her, neither was Mr Corrigan, her adopted "godfather", whose vicious and sadistic crimes we also outlined above.

3.23.13 Mr Daggett admitted under cross-examination that he never saw anything untoward sexually take place, although the behaviour he saw was inappropriate. He did bring his concerns about the visits to the attention of the Ward Manager and other nursing staff. Mr Arnold had said the visits were a matter for the care team.

3.23.14 After the search of Lawrence Ward in January 1997 it was discovered that Mr Hemming had a collection of boys' underpants and a girl's school skirt, and that Mr Corrigan had a ring binder with pictures of children in various stages of undress. Inspector Marsden also confirmed that a document detailing Mr Corrigan's index offence had been discovered at the father of Child A's house.

3.23.15 We asked a number of patients about the visits. Patient W told us that he thought Mr Hemming was getting questionable pleasure from the visits:

> ". . . in my view she was almost a toy for him to roll around with on the floor, sit astride his back naked except in her knickers, playing games out in the garden, hide and seek. To me it seemed a strange relationship, especially considering his antecedents and why he was in there. She was no relative of his and I felt for that to go on, especially in the setting it did go on, was not really right."

3.23.16 On one occasion Patient W recalled seeing Mr Hemming alone in the garden with Child A and making a sort of tent with an old blanket or bedspread and a chair:

> "I saw Hemming kneel down at the back of the chair. The chair had the bedspread or curtain over it and he knelt on the floor and then he put this bedspread or curtain over his back while he was kneeling down and the child was stood there while he did that. It looked as though they had done it before, there was not talk about 'We will do this and then we will do that', it seemed as though it was something they had done before. Then I saw her run in under the bedspread and she stood facing him underneath it, and that is all I saw."

Patient W was not aware of any other staff or patients in the garden at the time.

3.23.17 Patient Q mentioned seeing Child A riding on Mr Hemming's back or being tickled by Mr Corrigan. Patient H confirmed this. He saw her on at least two occasions dressed only in her knickers; on one of these Mr Corrigan and Mr Hemming undressed her down to her knickers and then dressed her again.

3.23.18 Patient I confirmed he had seen Child A dressed only in her underwear rolling about the floor with Mr Hemming and bouncing up and down on his knee. The play appeared normal, but once he discovered the index offences of Mr Corrigan and Mr Hemming he became concerned and spoke to staff and patients. He was aware that a number of patients had complained, to no effect. He had spoken to Mr Kenny, Mr Rogers, Ms Flaherty and Ms Karran; they agreed that it should not happen. He was not aware if they did anything about it.

3.23.19 Patient H observed what was happening in the library whilst playing snooker with a member of staff. He remarked to this particular nurse, Mr Gibbs that "Happy Hour has begun. He's getting his jollies off". By this he was referring to Mr Hemming's close physical contact with Child A. He thought the behaviour was inappropriate. Mr Gibbs replied that it was a clinical matter and not his business.

3.23.20 Patient W told us that he had mentioned the extremely physical nature of the relationship to a nurse, Steve Rogers. He had agreed the behaviour was inappropriate. Patient W told us that many patients and staff shared his concern, but that Dr Strickland approved of the visits.

3.23.21 Patient H told us he was present when Child A's father brought a little boy on to the ward as well as Child A. This happened he told us on three occasions.

3.23.22 Patient E confirmed that Child A visited more or less every weekend. The visits would start in the library then later in the afternoon she would usually be taken out into the garden. Patient E agreed that there was an unspoken rule that no one disturbed the visits in the library. He described an incident in 1993 when Mr Corrigan had told him to get out of the library. It was very much his domain. Her visits might last until 6 or 7 pm, well after the 4 pm official end of visiting. Although she was officially visiting Mr Corrigan in reality she spent most of her time with Mr Hemming. Mr Corrigan would stay in the library with Child A's father.

3.23.23 We must stress that none of our witnesses claimed to have seen anything of a sexual nature take place. Only one patient, RM, alleged that he had seen actual sexual abuse of Child A, in the form of attempted buggery by Mr Hemming. He spoke to his primary nurse, Mr Marlowe, who told us that RM had made these allegations in early 1997, not long after nine hardcore pornographic videos had been found in RM's possession on Owen Ward. (RM had previously been on Lawrence Ward.) Two of these videos involved children.

3.23.24 We are satisfied that there is no substance to this particular allegation.

3.23.25 We heard evidence that Child A visited Mr Hemming's bedroom. Patient H told us he had seen Child A in Mr Hemming's room, but that a member of staff was outside the door. This was not against the ward rules so long as the visitor was supervised. This did not always happen.

3.23.26 Patient E said that one weekend during 1995 about 3 or 3.30 pm he was returning to his room when he met a nurse, Lisa Johnson, smoking a cigarette and standing in the night station. She could see down both corridors from that point, but not of course into bedrooms. Patient E walked down the corridor to his room and, as he passed Mr Hemming's room, he saw Child A in the room with Mr Hemming . She was fully dressed and playing with a what appeared to be a colouring book. He had no idea how long they had been there. This was the only occasion that he observed Child A in Mr Hemming's room.

3.23.27 Ms Johnson started working on the ward in September 1995. She recalled the incident. Mr Hemming had asked permission from the team leader to take Child A to his bedroom and Ms Johnson had been asked to accompany them. She stood in the doorway of the room with them and they stayed there only for two to three minutes. Another member of staff accompanied her.

3.23.28 We are satisfied that Ms Johnson was with Mr Hemming and Child A whilst Child A was in Mr Hemming's room. But the child should never have been allowed to enter the room in the first place, whether or not a nurse was present.

3.23.29 Nursing staff told us about what they had seen and of their concerns. Ms Johnson saw Child A dressed only in her knickers on one occasion. She raised concerns with colleagues and Mr Arnold at that point. Mr Boocock told us he had become aware of Child A sitting on Mr Hemming's lap in the library some time in early 1996. He informed Mr Kenny, the team leader, of his concerns.

3.23.30 Ms Edge gave a vivid description of one of Child A's visits to the Ward in September 1996. She had been off work sick for a long period and had come back to the Hospital on Lawrence Ward, initially part-time, then full-time from August 1996. On Saturday 7 September she was on duty and had stayed a little late to help out. She was asked to escort Child A, her father and his girlfriend to Lawrence Ward. The atmosphere was strained and Child A very quiet. Then they came to Lawrence Ward where Mr Corrigan and Mr Hemming stood waiting:

> "I then saw what I can still see vividly in my mind every day. I saw a child open up. It was like a Christmas box being opened up in front of her, it was amazing. I could not understand how a child could be so withdrawn, so quiet, and react to people in such a way. It was such a contrast . . . She just opened up, she smiled, she was jumping up and down, she was so elated, there was such a severe change like none I have ever experienced in my own child who is about the same age.
>
> . . . She flung herself into Paul Corrigan's arms and he picked her up and she was kissing and she was just so happy, it was unbelievable, and it struck me so bizarrely. It struck me badly. I could not understand how anybody could change like that."

3.23.31 Ms Edge said it was as if they had not seen each other for years. She was concerned at the interaction between Child A and the patients and raised her concerns with Mr Arnold, who reassured her that the visits had been discussed by the PCT. She admitted to being very confused at how the PCT could have come to such a decision, attributing it at least in part to a lack of knowledge of personality disorder services. She told us that other staff she spoke to were also unsure of the PCT's decision.

3.23.32 Ms Edge approached her clinical supervisor, Mr Baker, who raised her concerns elsewhere. Mr Bateson came to see her later and reassured her the matter was in hand. Ms Edge told us that she was frightened of being seen as a whistle-blower and of patients knowing that she had raised her concerns. She said:

> "I am a female staff nurse working in a male environment. We are all aware that there are hostile and aggressive incidents occurring at all times, the probability is always there in our job and I would never like to think a year down the line that somebody did not like me very much in an incident with a patient."

3.23.33 Ms Edge's fears speak volumes about the culture of the Hospital. We applaud her action in bringing her concerns to the attention of more senior colleagues, despite her fears about possible repercussions.

3.23.34 We heard evidence from the father of Child A. He had a history of sexual offences against teenage girls and had been at Ashworth between 1982 and 1985 at which point he had got to know both Mr Corrigan and Mr Hemming. He visited the Hospital from shortly after his discharge, having got permission to do so from his then consultant Dr Hunter. Between January 1994 and October 1996 he visited on 151 occasions.

3.23.35 The father of Child A rejected any suggestion that he, Mr Corrigan and Mr Hemming had been involved in anything untoward. He confirmed that Child A was a regular weekend visitor and that she went into the library and other parts of the ward and into the garden, though never, he claimed, into patients' side rooms. He claimed that he could always observe her from the library. He described Mr Hemming's behaviour as "play, pure and simple" and told us that he had no doubts about the wisdom of introducing his daughter to Mr Corrigan and Mr Hemming. He thought Mr Corrigan was sincerely trying to address his problems and denied that Mr Hemming was still fantasizing about little girls. He pointed out that the Hospital authorities had approved the visits, although he refused to name whom he had discussed the matter with. He denied that Child A ever stripped down to her knickers. He also vehemently denied Leading Counsel John Royce QC's suggestion that he had been grooming her for paedophile purposes.

3.23.36 Child A's father also claimed that at times there were two or three other children visiting the Ward at the same time as Child A. It could get very crowded in the library. This is not the impression given by other witnesses and Inspector Marsden thought that Child A's father was mistaken in his recollection on this point.

3.23.37 Child A's father confirmed that he had brought a little boy to visit on the ward, the son of a friend of his (*see* paragraph **3.23.21**). He visited about a dozen times in 1996. He said that the Hospital authorities should have done checks on the names of his visitors before they were allowed to come in. He admitted that there was little benefit in such a visit for the boy, but said he had had no concerns about the visits.

3.23.38 We find it quite extraordinary that a little boy was brought in to visit Mr Corrigan, a man who had tortured, sexually abused and killed a teenage boy.

3.23.39 The father of Child A confirmed that Mr Hemming had visited his house once and the area on several occasions, escorted by Nurse Corrigan. A number of photographs were taken of Child A on the visit to his house by Nurse Corrigan using the ward camera. These photographs included a shot of Child A lying back on her bed and another of her sitting, fully clothed, on the lavatory. He admitted that these shots, in isolation, might appear tasteless. But he did not see any reason why Mr Hemming should not have such photos in his possession.

3.23.40 Child A's father told us that no social worker from Ashworth ever visited him before his visiting started, or indeed anybody else who had accompanied him on visits.

3.23.41 Inspector Marsden, who conducted the police investigation into events on Lawrence Ward, confirmed that Child A was interviewed twice by specially trained officers and representatives of social services. No relevant disclosures were made by her during the course of those interviews, transcripts of which we have seen. She was also examined by a doctor; this examination was inconclusive. The little boy brought in by the father of Child A had also been interviewed and no evidence was elicited from him.

3.23.42 There is no reason to doubt that Mr Hemming indulged in unsuitable play with Child A over a period of time, quite possibly years. That a child could be exposed in this manner is disgraceful. The fact that her father approved is contemptible and is not in our view an acceptable justification for the failure to act on the part of the Hospital and Lawrence Ward staff. Some nurses did indeed express their concern but they were ignored by their senior colleagues, one of whom at least believed it was in Mr Hemming's therapeutic interest for the relationship to continue. The paramountcy of the child's interests, as demanded by the Children Act 1989, was clearly not in the minds of the PCT.

3.23.43 More than anything else this episode captures the sense in which the PDU at Ashworth Hospital had degenerated and the depths to which professional standards and attitudes had dropped. What is so startling is that they did not realize how blunted their professional vision and judgement had become, and how conditioned they were to accept the unacceptable. This is a vivid example of how destructive of professional standards such

large, closed, static and complacent institutions can be.

3.23.44 We ourselves have pondered as we listened to days and days of such evidence whether we had become case-hardened to the horrors of what happened at Ashworth and the risks to which Child A was exposed. In reviewing what we have written we are not convinced that we have fully captured the awfulness of it all.

3.23.45 We found no evidence of any sexual interference including penetrative sex ever having occurred, but in our view this young child was being groomed for paedophile sexual activity. If our conclusion is correct, it is a matter of fortune that she had not already been physically abused.

Recommendation 25 **3.23.46 We recommend that no child under the age of 16 should be allowed to visit any patient on a ward.**

Recommendation 26 **3.23.47 We recommend that a child under the age of 16 should only be permitted to visit a patient who is a genuine member of his or her family, and then only if fully supervised in a place specifically prepared, designed and equipped for visiting purposes. The interests of the child must override those of any other person.**

3.23.48 We turn now to address the issue of policies, or the lack of them.

3.24.0 Visiting Policy: the Context

3.24.1 In considering the issues surrounding visiting it is helpful to outline the local and national policy context. The Blom-Cooper Report recommended that the Hospital should encourage visiting:

> "*75. We recommend that the visiting policy and procedures should be reviewed urgently to ensure maximum facilitation of visiting by family and friends, and that the SHSA promulgates a clear philosophy on visiting, which sets out the circumstances when visiting may properly be restricted."
>
> "78. We recommend that throughout their relatives' stay, families should be involved on a regular basis with their relatives' treatment."

(The asterisk indicates that this was one of the Team's central recommendations.)

The direction was thus very clear: the Hospital had to become more "visitor-friendly". The SHSA made clear in its response to the Blom-Cooper recommendations that the introduction of ward-visiting was one of the ways in which to facilitate the implementation of recommendation 78.

3.24.2 The revised Mental Health Act 1983 Code of Practice (1993) states as follows:

> "The right to be visited
>
> 26.1 All detained patients are entitled to maintain contact with and be visited by whomsoever they wish, subject only to some carefully limited exceptions. The prohibition of a visit by a person whom the patient has requested to visit or agreed to see should be regarded as a serious interference with the rights of the patient and to be taken only in exceptional circumstances (sc. clinical or security grounds) . . A decision to exclude a visitor should be taken only after other means to deal with the problem have been fully explored. Any decision to exclude a visitor should be fully documented and available for independent scrutiny by the Mental Health Act Commission."

3.24.3 It was thus clear that visiting had to be encouraged. We have adversely commented on the relevant provisions of the Code in Part 2 above.

3.25.0 Hospital Policy on Visiting

3.25.1 The development of a clear policy on visiting in the post-Blom-Cooper world seems to have been a chapter of accidents.

3.25.2 A working group was convened in 1992 under the Chairmanship of Mr Hardman, then Acting Director of Social Work Services, to draft a new policy on visiting. By April 1993 Mr Hardman's group had produced a draft policy which included the statement that "A patient may be visited every day between 2 and 4 pm as of right by whom ever they choose, irrespective of age, gender or race". **Fortunately there is no evidence that this policy was ever made operative.**

3.25.3 A further working group was convened in late 1994 or early 1995 under Mr Backhouse the Director of Social Work Services, on his initiative and after negotiation with Mr Dale. According to IR2 a draft policy was taken to the Clinical Development Group in June 1995; at that meeting Mr Tarbuck argued that this was an issue for the Hospital Management Team, and he apparently took the paper to that Group. In September Mr Tarbuck asked that HMT seek a progress Report from Mr Backhouse, who claimed he was awaiting HMT's comments. In October HMT agreed to table the Visiting Policy at HEG in December 1995. This timetable slipped. The draft policy was, it appears, ratified by HMT in January 1996 and Mr Backhouse was charged with ensuring that the "policy was operationalised by an appropriate project team and monitored". Mr Backhouse claims he was never asked by HMT to implement the Visiting Policy, although he recalled Colin Dale suggesting he reconvene the working group. He tried to do this on several occasions but was unable to do so.

3.25.4 The draft visiting policy appeared on the agenda of HEG in February 1996. The relevant extract of the minutes read as follows:

> "*Policy on Visiting*
>
> The policy had been accepted by HMT, although the absence of supporting procedures [one of which was on children visiting] had been highlighted. HMT had asked Richard Backhouse to reconvene the Visitors Group to ensure the procedures were written.
>
> The General Manager indicated that HEG could not ratify the policy document unless accompanied by procedures and CD (Mr Dale) was asked to ensure work was carried out by the next meeting."

3.25.5 Mr Dale reported that he had raised this with Mr Green and had been reassured that all was in hand. As we heard, Mr Backhouse could recall no such instruction from HMT.

3.25.6 In the reorganization of the Hospital that followed, the issue appears to have been lost. In December 1996 Mr Dale wrote to Mr Gardner, formally charging him with producing a new visitors' policy by 1 April 1997.

3.25.7 Mr Backhouse rejected any personal criticism for the delay in introducing the visiting policy. He told us that the policy was produced quickly and efficiently, the delay was at the committee stage. He also said that any shortcomings in the Report should have been picked up by the HEG. His was an expertise in adult forensic mental health; no one ever indicated to him he had a responsibility for child protection issues as well.

3.25.8 We cannot accept this. All professionals have a responsibility for the protection of children.

3.25.9 We also heard how the Hospital had received in March 1995, a draft guidance document from the Department of Health on child protection, entitled *Child Protection:*

Clarification of Arrangements Between the NHS and Other Agencies. Mrs Miles wrote to Mr Backhouse on 24 March 1995 enclosing the document and asked him whether the document had any implications for Ashworth. Mr Backhouse could not recall receiving this letter, although he could recall receiving the document, and filing it. He did not regard it as a prompt to action: "the normal time for a Department of Health guidance document to be incorporated into Hospital practice was when the ratified document was received by the Hospital".

3.25.10 This is a sorry picture. Mr Backhouse was in the prime position to develop policy on child protection at Ashworth. The March 1995 document should have prompted him to take action. He failed to do so.

3.25.11 Mr Backhouse was also challenged on recommendation 28 of the 1994 amalgamated SSI Report on the Special Hospitals, which stressed that the principles of the Children Act 1989 should be applied to all considerations of contact. He admitted that, in contrast to at least one of the other two Hospitals, the Hospital did nothing in response to this recommendation: no training was given to his social work staff on child protection, nor was a system put in place for contacting any local authority Social Services Department on a child protection issue until February 1997. The attitude of the Hospital was that the primary responsibility for the welfare of children rested with parents and the relevant agencies. Since the issue of child protection had been raised with regard to either Rampton or Broadmoor Hospitals, the attitude appears to have been that Ashworth need not worry about it. Mr Backhouse admitted that the Hospital did not bring to the SHSA's attention that no training on child protection was happening at Ashworth, which may have led the SHSA to exaggerate the degree of activity on this front across the three hospitals.

3.25.12 Again, we are not impressed by Mr Backhouse's attitude. Mr Backhouse was the obvious person to bring child protection issues to the fore. He did not do so. Nor indeed are we impressed with the SHSA, which clearly missed an opportunity to challenge Ashworth on its attitude towards child protection.

3.25.13 Counsel for the patients, Miss Irving, pointed out to Mr Backhouse that the recent IR2 investigation team had put forward recommendations which were the same as recommendations in "Working Together under the Children Act 1989", a key piece of guidance for the new Act published in 1991. Mr Backhouse could not explain why those recommendations had not been implemented between 1991 and 1998.

3.25.14 For his part, Mr Dale admitted that he should have been more proactive in ensuring that this work was taken forward, although he pointed out that the operational responsibilities shifted and he took over as Clinical Director of the Mental Illness Directorate.

3.25.15 The proposed policy produced by Mr Backhouse's group was flawed given that it was based on Paragraph 26 of the Code of Practice, which itself was ill-suited to a high security environment. Mr Backhouse agreed with Counsel for the Hospital's suggestion that, whatever its flaws, the Hospital had to take the Code of Practice as its starting point in devising a policy on visiting. Be that as it may, this does not mean that the Hospital and indeed the SHSA could not have questioned the appropriateness of parts of the Code in connection with this group of patients.

3.25.16 The failure to produce any policy at all, let alone a sensible one, was unacceptable. The implementation of the Blom-Cooper Report's recommendations forced the Hospital to become more open and accessible to visitors. If this was to be done safely a robust new policy was needed. This took literally years. Mr Backhouse and Mr Dale should both shoulder responsibility for failing to take this forward; Mr Dale at least recognized

eventually that action was needed and took steps to put things right. This does not relieve the SHSA of their responsibility higher up the chain of accountability. The SHSA espoused the Code of Practice and did nothing to highlight its fundamental weaknesses.

3.25.17 But poor as Ashworth's performance in this area was, they were not alone amongst the Social Work Departments in the Special Hospitals. The group which brought each of them together in a professional forum did not discuss child protection until February 1997.

3.25.18 We were relieved to hear that things had begun to improve by then. We heard that Ashworth did take positive steps to address child care issues inspired by an initiative at Rampton Hospital, which in April 1996 invited the National Society for the Prevention of Cruelty to Children (NSPCC) to work with that hospital on child protection procedures. Mr Backhouse from Ashworth was a guest observer at the training. In June 1997 following the problems emerging at Ashworth Mr Backhouse invited the NSPCC to work with the Hospital's Social Work Department to develop a position paper on Child Protection that could be submitted to the Inquiry and to the Hospital.

3.25.19 The paper highlights the principle that the welfare of the child should be paramount, and sets out a number of guidelines. In his evidence to us Mr Michael Taylor, the Director of Operations at the NSPCC, stressed the need for training in child protection issues. The position paper states that a child should only be allowed to visit a patient where the patient has parental responsibility and/or a significant relationship which it is in the child's interest to maintain or develop; Mr Taylor noted:

> "the purpose there is really to make it an absolute exception that is soundly tested, firstly, that the relationship is significant and, secondly, that there is a proper authoritative test that it is in the child's interest to maintain or develop that relationship, rather than as appears currently, that there is no test applied whatsoever to children visiting in those settings."

3.25.20 Mr Taylor agreed with a point put to him by Miss Irving that assessment of whether a visit by a child to a Special Hospital, or indeed a visit by a patient to a home where children were resident, was appropriate was best done by the Social Services Department where that child lived.

3.25.21 Mr Daniels put to Mr Taylor that whereas NHS Trusts are fully involved in Local Area Child Protection Committees the Special Hospitals are not. He agreed, and said that child protection issues were not part of the culture within these Hospitals. Mr Taylor thought that all social workers, even those practising in adult mental health, should have a knowledge of child protection issues. He is certainly right.

3.25.22 The paper was approved by the Hospital in October 1997 and Mr Backhouse was asked to produce an implementation and training plan. He met the NSPCC in connection with this training plan on 23 October. But on 27 October the new Chief Executive, Dr Hodge, stopped this work and the NSPCC had no further contact with the Hospital.

3.25.23 We find this deeply disappointing. Now that Dr Hodge is no longer at the Hospital we hope this contact can be revived.

Recommendation 27 **3.25.24 We recommend that contact with the NSPCC be revived, and that a training programme on child protection issues be developed in conjunction with the NSPCC.**

3.25.25 We should also note that Mr Taylor told us NSPCC's contacts with Broadmoor had proved disappointing as training sessions were poorly attended. This demonstrates the general lack of knowledge and interest in child protection in the High Security Hospitals.

3.25.26 We understand that the Social Services Inspectorate of the Department of Health, the Association of Directors of Social Services and the Heads of Social Work in the three Special Hospitals are developing protocols on children visiting the Special Hospitals. We commend this work, late though it is in coming.

3.26.0 The Lawrence Ward Policy

3.26.1 In February 1993 Mr Frank Sharp, the then Acting Ward Manager on Lawrence Ward, submitted a proposal for ward-based visiting on Lawrence Ward. We quote it in full:

> "WARD-BASED VISITING
>
> Ward-based visits have operated successfully on several wards over the years, particularly on some high and medium dependency wards where high levels of observation have been maintained but more positively staff/patient/visitor relationships have been enhanced. Potentially, I feel this would have enormous benefits to staff, patients and the visitors in the following areas:
>
> – enhanced relationships
>
> – potential problems resolved by accessibility to named nurse
>
> – forum for information exchange
>
> – potential for flexibility of visiting times
>
> The great majority of patients are in favour of visits on the ward, but perhaps naturally there are others who perceived this as an intrusion of their privacy, or that it may upset some who did not receive any visits. It was mutually agreed to limit areas for visitors (see below).
>
> CONDITIONS AND RATIONALE
>
> *1. Limited Areas*
>
> a. Visitors would be restricted to the Library (smoking permitted) and if any overspill does occur, then the dining room (no smoking area) may be used.
>
> b. Access to the ward garden area and Hospital grounds would be allowed.
>
> c. Access to view the patients' side rooms may be allowed, only under staff supervision, staff permitting.
>
> d. The toilet off the dining room to be used by visitors.
>
> *Rationale:*
> The above should help to maintain safety and reduce obtrusiveness.
>
> *2. Observations*
> Staff will maintain discreet observations in the day area.
>
> *Rationale:*
> A high level of observation was felt unnecessary because the level of trust is extended to non-observation in the Hospital grounds.
>
> *3. Escorting of Visitors to the Ward*
> In the interim period, prior to obtaining appropriate staffing levels at weekends, we propose that the patients escort their own visitors from the Assembly Hall to the Ward and return them prior to the expiry of the parole hours.
>
> Any baggage will remain in the secure area in the Assembly Hall as they would do normally when unsupervised in the grounds.
>
> This policy pertains to prescribed visiting times.
>
> *4. Duration of Visits*
> To remain within Hospital procedure, but may be altered in exceptional circumstances or by prior arrangement.

5. Refreshments

Dependent upon the average numbers of visitors per week, the Catering Manager will supply tea, milk and sugar.

ON-GOING ACTION

1. Investigate whether parcels may be brought to the ward by visitors.
2. Ascertain if we need more tables and chairs.
3. Handout to be produced to explain conditions, and "house rules" to be amended.

Review in three months' time

Frank Sharp
Acting Ward Manager
3 February 1993"

3.26.2 This proposal was referred to the Patient Care Support Team and the Risk Management Team, as well as to Mr Maxwell, the Head of Security and Mr Hardman, Acting Director of Social Work Services. The Risk Management Team approved the policy, subject to the proviso that the PCT assess each patient for suitability for receiving visits on the Ward, taking into account the suitability of the visitors in question to be on the Ward, the possible risks to family members from the patient and the likelihood of the privilege being abused.

3.26.3 The scrutiny of this proposal appears to have been minimal. No one appears to have commented on the suitability or otherwise of children visiting Lawrence Ward. Also noteworthy is the apparent discrepancy between restricting visits to the library and dining room and allowing visits to extend to the garden, and the comment that a high level of observation was felt unnecessary because these were trusted patients who were allowed to walk around the grounds unsupervised in any case.

3.26.4 Mr Arnold admitted that the policy did not specify that observation was required in the garden. So that a nurse allowing Mr Hemming to go off into the garden with Child A unobserved could not be criticized for failing to follow ward policy.

3.26.5 Dr Crispin was taken through Mr Sharp's document. She admitted that there was no written instruction that visits to the garden should be supervised and noted that with hindsight people were interpreting "observation", "monitoring" and other terms in different ways. She admitted that the PCT had failed to provide a clear statement of what they believed was in fact taking place. Another member of the PCT, psychologist Mrs Day, appeared to use "observation" and "monitoring" interchangeably.

3.26.6 As we will see, not even this minimal policy was in practice observed, given that 30 or more people might be on the ward with several visits taking place at once. Mr Cannon told us that the policy was reviewed and the areas for visiting extended, but that in essence the policy remained the same.

3.26.7 The failure to review the document thoroughly is striking given that in 1994 there was a serious allegation made concerning another child, Child B, granddaughter of a patient on Lawrence Ward. Child B claimed that on one visit her grandfather touched her breast. A social worker met the mother of the child in October 1994; the latter revealed that the patient concerned had asked her to obtain a gun catalogue. The social worker telephoned the Hospital and spoke to Dr Mark Stowell-Smith, the social worker attached to Lawrence Ward, about the request for a gun catalogue and the alleged indecent assault. Dr Stowell-Smith met the mother and the social worker. Although the patient concerned had committed manslaughter with fire arms, he also had a previous conviction for an assault on an eight year old girl.

3.26.8 Unfortunately Dr Stowell-Smith did not attend the patient's case conference in December 1994 at which the allegation might have been discussed. Dr Stowell-Smith admitted that this allegation was not reported as a child protection issue at the time. He agreed that there should have been a much more detailed analysis of visiting policies at that time.

3.26.9 Dr Crispin was also asked about this alleged incident. She told us that it was discussed in terms of the individual patient, rather than in terms of any broader policy implications. The visiting policy was not reviewed.

3.26.10 Inadequate though the policy was, its implementation was worse. Several staff witnesses were either unaware of, or unfamiliar with, the Ward policy. Thus Nurse Johnson told us that she was not aware of any policy on children visiting Lawrence Ward and she received no instructions on how she should manage such visits. She told us that visits were, in practice, not cancelled even if staffing was very low. Essentially the message was "get on with it and manage".

3.26.11 Dr Stowell-Smith told us that he was aware of the policy on visiting, although he did not recognize Mr Sharp's policy document. He had a very vague sense that the PCT would determine the suitability or otherwise of particular visitors. He told us that visitors should be observed in the garden, but could not point to where that was laid down, admitting it was a kind of assumption made by the care team. In fact the document produced by Mr Sharp does not lay down that visitors must be observed in the garden. Similarly, his belief that visits should not take place on the ward if insufficient staff were on duty to monitor the visit was not based on any documentary evidence.

3.26.12 Mrs Day told us she did not recall ever seeing Mr Sharp's document. She admitted she had taken no steps to try and find out what the visiting policy on Lawrence Ward was, although she was familiar with aspects of it. She admitted she should have known it. Her understanding was that visits should only take place if sufficient staff were available to supervise them; she told us this was raised on a number of occasions in PCT meetings.

3.26.13 Mr Foster, the current Ward Manager of Lawrence Ward, told us that the general rule on visiting on the Ward was three adults per patient, but with no restrictions on children. Nor was there any restriction on the overall numbers of visitors.

3.26.14 The Ward visiting policy was inadequate and should have been seen to be inadequate from a very early stage. The rules on observation were, as we have seen, inappropriate; there was no limit on numbers who could visit the ward; children were not even deemed worthy of mention. Yet it remained in force as far as we could tell virtually unchanged. There was no regular review. Nor were senior managers aware of the situation. It was a shambles.

3.27.0 Supervision of Visits

3.27.1 We turn now to examine a key aspect of the visits, supervision by nursing staff. Ideally, visits should have been supervised, both when Child A was on the ward and when she visited the garden. Mr Daggett told us that the view of the garden from the nursing office on Lawrence Ward was obscured by a bush. Similarly, from the library not all areas of the garden were visible. One of the nursing staff, Mr Paul Boocock, confirmed that the garden had grown extensively between 1993 and 1995/6 and that the planting had made it more and more difficult for staff to observe what was going on, deliberately or not. He also told us that the library was not a good place for visits as far as observation was concerned.

3.27.2 We have seen above that the Ward policy was vague on what level of supervision staff were expected to provide. Dr Strickland admitted that he could not point us to any instruction or document that made it clear to those supervising the visits that physical contact was not to be allowed beyond something like a pat on the head. He admitted that the policy was vague and that the lack of supervision was a "terrible state of affairs". He argued that Mr Sharp's policy document quoted above was modified in discussion at PCT meetings to the effect that visits should be supervised at all times and if there were inadequate staff the visits could not take place on the ward.

3.27.3 If such changes were minuted in PCT minutes, we have not been able to find them. There is a disagreement here between Dr Strickland and Dr Crispin on the one hand, and Mr Arnold, who said that during 1995 and 1996 any comments about the supervision of visits were made orally and not recorded. The minutes appear to support Mr Arnold.

3.27.4 Mr Arnold told us that before July 1996 the policy adopted followed Mr Sharp's original policy document and was one of discreet observation. He increased staffing to four during the day shifts, which was enough he told us to provide discreet observation, but not enough to have a one-to-one supervision of every visit.

3.27.5 He was satisfied that monitoring of the visits was taking place because he was told by Mr Cannon that ward staff had been told of the duty to monitor the visits, and ward staff confirmed to him this was taking place. He noted that PCT minutes laying down what was to be done would have been part of the handover between shifts and told us he himself observed a visit in August 1996 which was being monitored.

3.27.6 It is, however, no good to leave policy in the PCT minutes (or indeed in the patients' notes); nursing staff do not have the time to trawl through the minutes and new staff cannot be expected to look back through such records and work out how policies had been changed. If the policy was changed it should have been reissued to staff.

3.27.7 According to Mr Rowden, Mrs Miles believed that Child A's father was supervising his child. Quite apart from failing to see the Hospital's duties in this area the notion that he was supervising her is, we were told, simply wrong. Ms Johnson said bluntly that she did not observe any interaction between the father and Child A during the visits.

3.27.8 Our patient witnesses testified that there were not enough staff to provide proper supervision. Patient H told us that three staff were on duty regularly on a Saturday afternoon for 20 or so patients and their guests. He agreed that if some patients had visitors in the garden, others had visitors in their rooms and others still had visitors in the day area, then there were not enough staff to go round. He was aware of other children visiting the Ward, in this case family members of the patient concerned, and supervised to the same degree.

3.27.9 Patient W confirmed that at the weekend there would be three to four staff on duty, with perhaps three or four visits taking place at once in different rooms, including, on occasion, patients' side rooms. He told us that supervision of the visits was:

> "very sparse, I would say, very intermittent. For much of the time her visits were unobserved by the staff. There was no actual staff sitting in the room with the visit at that time, or indeed when the visit continued out in the gardens, there was no staff out there closely monitoring what went on at all."

3.27.10 Patient Q said that there would always be staff walking around seeing what was happening on the ward during visits, but they did not encroach upon patients' space. Staff did not, according to him, go with Child A and Mr Hemming into the garden. This picture was confirmed by Patient H, who told us that the visits would start off in the library and the child's father would stay there, but in warmer weather Mr Hemming would sometimes take Child A out into the garden. No member of staff would go with him.

3.27.11 Patient I agreed the visits were not supervised. He told us that there might be up to 35 or so people on the Ward at weekends, to be supervised by three staff . Parole patients could take their visitors around the grounds, visitors from other wards might be on the Ward or in the garden. He felt staff required more support.

3.27.12 We heard from a number of nursing staff on Lawrence Ward. Ms Johnson said that staff maintained discreet observation of the visits, which meant somebody glancing into the library every quarter of an hour or so. Staff did not tend to sit in on visits, but they could be observed through the door from the day area. She told us that she was less "discreet" in her observations, having come from a high dependency ward. She would go out into the garden if Child A went out there. She accepted that the visits were not properly supervised.

3.27.13 Ms Karran told us that the visits were observed, rather than supervised. By this she meant discreet observation, "not breathing down their necks". Supervision would mean having someone sitting beside the patient and visitors. But it was very hard to observe when there might be 30–35 people on the ward at a weekend. When it was possible someone would be in the day area the whole time. Ms Karran was asked whether it was true that the PCT's policy was that ward visits should be terminated if they could not be properly observed. She was not sure of that policy. She was also unaware of a directive from the PCT in June or so of 1995 that the visits should be closely monitored.

3.27.14 Ms Karran had never personally witnessed any untoward activity. She had concerns however because of the interest taken in Child A by Mr Hemming and Mr Corrigan, particularly as she grew older. She agreed that concerns were growing amongst staff in general from 1995 onwards.

3.27.15 Miss Edge stated that any nurse should know when a visitor is visiting a patient that both should be observed, but she was not sure there was a clear policy on this point. The PCT's alleged policy that if there were too few nurses to supervise properly then visits should be shifted to the central visiting area had not been clearly communicated to her. Nor had she been told of the PCT's decision that Child A should not be allowed on her own with Mr Hemming and that there should be no physical contact.

3.27.16 Mr Cannon told us that discreet observation, as required in the ward visiting policy document meant that somebody knew where they were, and was at least periodically checking up on them. He admitted that the policy allowed visitors to go into the garden and did not require a member of staff to accompany them. Staff did not sit in on the library visits or increase observation generally until the summer of 1996.

3.27.17 The Ward Managers interviewed for the IR2 investigation generally admitted that the visits were unsupervised at times. For his part, Mr Arnold told us he had thought at the time that Child A was safe. But he could not say definitely that Child A was safe throughout the time she was on the Ward when he was not there and when she was not under direct supervision. He could not have afforded to employ more staff to improve the supervision unless he had reduced the grade mix and brought in more unqualified staff.

3.27.18 Ms Johnson did not blame Mr Arnold, describing him as a very good and supportive Ward Manager, who had inherited a lot of problems on that Ward. But Mr Keown and his team did criticize Mr Arnold for failing to push harder to ensure that the concerns of nursing staff were heard.

3.27.19 The supervision of the visits was woefully inadequate, on occasion it seems non-existent. Partly the problem seems to have been insufficient staffing; partly the lack of clarity in the policy: what did "discreet observation" mean? And partly ward staff's failure to challenge the policy. Responsibility for this must rest with a succession of Ward Managers, but principally Mr Arnold.

3.28.0 The Reaction of the Patient Care Team

3.28.1 What was the PCT doing all this time? We have already seen that the ward-visiting policy was not properly reviewed. We heard a good deal of evidence on what action the PCT actually did take concerning the visits of Child A.

3.28.2 Our attention was drawn to the PCT minutes for 7 October 1993 when permission was given for Mr Corrigan to have ward-based visits, "staffing levels permitting". This rider meant, according to Dr Strickland, that someone should be observing the visits. He thought that if there were too many visitors to allow continuous observation by staff then visits should not take place on the Ward; this had been made clear by PCT minutes.

3.28.3 Had this been made clear in the PCT minutes? The evidence suggests otherwise.

3.28.4 We saw a letter dated 6 February 1997 from Mr Michael Berry, a senior clinical psychologist, to Mr Murphy admitting that back in 1992 he had encouraged a seriously disturbed young arsonist to be in contact with Child A on the grounds that it was beneficial to him in helping him to explore his emotions. This patient was at that time on Owen Ward, but had parole status and therefore had access to Lawrence Ward. Mr Berry denied he had meant to say he had "encouraged" the interaction with Child A, rather he encouraged him to discuss his interaction with Child A. They had only discussed the interaction with the child on a couple of occasions. He told us that he had been suspended then dismissed on the basis of this letter, even though the patient concerned had denied that Mr Berry had encouraged any impropriety between him and Child A.

3.28.5 It is, to say the least, a pity that this information did not suggest to Mr Berry that he should investigate the subject of the visits further.

3.28.6 Incidentally the father of Child A was convicted in November 1993 of defrauding the Hospital by submitting false mileage claims and ordered to repay £3000. However, it is by no means clear that that information was fed back to the PCT.

3.28.7 Mr Moran, who was Ward Manager between October 1993 and June 1994 told us he was aware of Child A visiting, but assumed that the visits had been approved by the PCT in the normal way.

3.28.8 The first indication of any discussion of Child A at PCT meetings was in June 1995. Mr Hemming had requested a photography book from the Hospital library. This had pictures of children in various states of undress and was deemed unsuitable. Mr Hemming claimed he was unaware of the contents. Ms Day discussed this with him. He told her that he was unaware of the content of the book, but she did not believe him; she admitted that this incident gave reason to be concerned about the visits of Child A, and told us that she did raise this issue with Mr Hemming on subsequent occasions.

3.28.9 Mrs Day agreed that, given Mr Hemming's offending history, it was very important to prevent him being alone with a child or having physical contact with a child. But she did not bring these facts to the attention of nursing staff. She told us that Mr Hemming would have been well aware that physical contact with Child A was inappropriate.

3.28.10 The resulting PCT minutes say, "To be monitored when on joint visit with [her father] when he brings his daughter in". What this meant is unclear, given that the visits should have been under observation in any case. If ward-based staff saw these notes they do not seem to have regarded them as prompting them to do anything different. For example, Ms Johnson, who joined the ward in September 1995, was unaware of the instruction. She admitted that she had not had time to read Mr Hemming's clinical notes where there were instructions about not allowing Mr Hemming to have physical contact with the child. Dr Strickland admitted there were no written instructions as to precisely what should happen and what should not. The PCT relied on the professionalism of nursing staff.

3.28.11 Again, it is no good expecting busy nurses to trawl through clinical notes to identify revisions of policy.

3.28.12 There is a dispute as to whether the PCT discussed the visits at this time, as Dr Stowell-Smith could not recall the visits of Child A to Mr Hemming being discussed on this occasion.

3.28.13 In the light of the rather unimpressive grasp Dr Stowell-Smith seemed to have on most issues we are content to accept that the PCT did discuss the visits of Child A on this occasion.

3.28.14 Mr Boocock told us that staff had had concerns dating back to late 1995. He brought up with Mr Arnold the possibility of a staff meeting to discuss a number of issues, of which the visits were just one, in December 1995. His concerns about the visits were heightened in January or February 1996 when he saw Child A astride Mr Hemming. He eventually wrote up a number of staff concerns and the meeting took place on the 21 July. This was the first staff meeting that had been held on the ward in his recollection.

3.28.15 There was a dispute between Mr Arnold and Mr Boocock as to whether the latter raised the issue of Child A visiting before July 1996; Mr Boocock noted that he was always raising issues with Mr Arnold, so the latter might not recall this particular case. Any concerns would have been couched in general terms. Mr Arnold recalled that Mr Boocock had approached him concerning the need for a full staff meeting in January or February 1996. At the time he was disciplining Mr Boocock over another matter and thought Mr Boocock might be seeking to manipulate the situation. Having discussed the request with some other staff he turned the request down. But in July a number of staff approached him with their concerns about the future of the ward, so he decided to hold a full staff meeting. We have quoted the issues raised at this meeting above. Following that meeting arrangements were put in place for full-scale staff meetings to take place every ten to 12 weeks.

3.28.16 We heard that nursing staff's concerns about the visits had grown by the summer of 1996. Ms Karran thought that the reason for the increased concern was that the child was getting older and the patients were paying her more and more attention and lavishing gifts on her. Staff had a gut feeling that things were not right. Ms Lisa Johnson told us that the most important issue raised at the staff meeting in July 1996 was the visits of Child A. The dynamics of the visits seemed to be changing and the seating in the library had been changed to make observation more difficult.

3.28.17 Team leader Mr Cannon told us that the visits of Child A were a general topic of conversation amongst staff during the summer of 1996. He raised concerns with Mrs Day which were first discussed at the PCT meeting on the 11th of July, saying that Mr Hemming had been observed having physical contact with Child A, involving her sitting on his lap and sitting on his shoulders in the garden scantily-clad. Mr Arnold's recollection was that Mr Hemming had got a foot injury on about the 8 or 9 July and staff suspected that Child A had kicked him in some form of horseplay; however, the concerns about Child A sitting on Mr Hemming's knee were voiced later. Be that as it may, the PCT minutes note that Mrs Day was to see Mr Hemming about his relationship with Child A.

3.28.18 Although the visits of Child A were a hot topic of conversation amongst the nurses, this was not true it seems of the PCT. Dr Strickland said that he was unaware of the physical contact during this period. and had never been told of the specific allegations that Child A was being given piggy-back rides and was sometimes in a state of undress. The details of the nurses' concerns were not brought to the PCT; rather, the general concerns were discussed and it was decided that Child A was not to be left alone and had to be closely observed.

3.28.19 The PCT discussed the matter again on 18 July. Mrs Day (who was not present) was to see Mr Hemming to talk about the visits. In the clinical notes the comment is made that the visits were to be closely monitored by staff. Dr Strickland told us that Mrs Day was being asked to assess whether the visits posed any risk to the child, using her knowledge of Mr Hemming. He commented that Dr Stowell-Smith as a member of the PCT could be expected to be aware of the child protection side of things.

3.28.20 Mrs Day saw Mr Hemming on 26 July 1996 and told him he was not to have any further physical contact. Mr Hemming claimed that he had never felt any sexual pleasure from the visits. They discussed strategies to prevent any problems arising, such as avoiding physical contact or being alone with the child. She reported back to the PCT on 1 August. It was agreed that the visits could continue. The PCT agreed that there should be no more physical contact between Mr Hemming and Child A and that they should not be alone together.

3.28.21 Mr Royce asked Mrs Day why the visits had not stopped forthwith, given that Mr Hemming had had physical contact with Child A, which he knew he should not have done. She agreed that with hindsight she would take a different view, but at the time she thought that with appropriate monitoring, and provided Mr Hemming and Child A were not left alone, the visits could continue. She denied that she was in any sense using Child A for therapeutic purposes, and indeed thought at the time that Child A was benefiting from the visits.

3.28.22 Mrs Day accepted that she had been over-reliant on Mr Hemming's self-reporting. She also accepted that she did not approach the issue of the visits with a view to the benefit of Child A, although she was concerned for her safety. She did point out that she had not been trained in this area and that she was unable to take advantage of as much clinical supervision as she would have liked. **This is unacceptable for a clinical psychologist. It is simply a matter of common sense.**

3.28.23 A more cogent point was her observation that searches could uncover important information, to show that a patient was not cooperating with therapy in the way he was suggesting. Because of inadequate searching she was not aware for example that Mr Hemming had children's underwear in his possession. Mr Arnold agreed that Mrs Day was reliant to some extent on the quality of information coming back from nursing staff; he noted in passing that Mr Hemming's primary nurse was Nurse Corrigan, later dismissed for gross misconduct following Mr Daggett's absconsion.

3.28.24 Reading the above one gets the impression of a PCT and a collection of nurses who were simply not communicating. The medium for communication, at least as far as the PCT was concerned, appeared to be the clinical notes. Thus Mr Arnold agreed with the suggestion of Mrs Day's Counsel that it would have been sensible for the nursing staff to put these concerns in a formal way into the clinical notes. As for the PCT communicating with ward staff, Dr Strickland told us that the clinical notes were available to staff. Therein were recorded important decisions of the PCT.

3.28.25 We have already indicated our view that using the clinical notes as the sole medium for transferring information to busy nurses was inadequate.

3.28.26 Mr Cannon said that he had handed over his notes from the PCT meeting on 1 August which noted what had been said, namely, Mr Hemming had agreed to decrease physical contact with Child A and eliminate it in the longer run; that he was not to use the garden area if no one else was there, and staff were to monitor this; staff were to observe discreetly if he did use the garden area during the visits. Mr Cannon said that this in fact meant staff should be in the garden if Mr Hemming was out there with Child A. He told us his draft minutes of the PCT meeting should have been handed on to other shifts. He admitted that discreet observation of the girl in the garden was inadequate.

3.28.27 The feedback staff understood appears to have been merely that visits should be more closely supervised. That being said, we were told by several nurse witnesses that the visits were observed more actively, and the physical contact did, it appears, cease.

3.28.28 Mr Arnold told us that in August Child A was banned from going into the garden. This follows a discussion he had had with Dr Strickland where he made clear that he could not guarantee that a member of staff would always be available to go with Mr Hemming and Child A into the garden. They had mutually agreed that the most sensible course would be to ban visits to the garden. Mr Cannon, however, told us that this decision was not passed on to him, and that Child A did visit the garden at least once in September.

3.28.29 Again the communication mechanisms within the ward on an important issue proved inadequate. If such a decision was made it should have been clearly highlighted to nurses and adhered to. It was not.

3.28.30 Mr Arnold also told us that he had spoken to Mr Melia about the visits at a Ward Managers' meeting in summer of 1996, although he did stress he was not asking Mr Melia for advice, but rather appraising him of the situation on Lawrence Ward. Mr Melia did not deny that Mr Arnold mentioned the matter to him, although he could not recall it. He thought that Mr Arnold had probably not stressed the issue particularly. He admitted that he had failed in not picking up on the importance of what Mr Arnold had said, but stressed that Mr Murphy knew as much himself in July. He also pointed out that other Ward Managers at the same meeting in July could not now recall any discussion of child visiting.

3.28.31 Mr Arnold left Lawrence Ward at the beginning of October 1996 and Mr Melia took over in an acting capacity. He told us that a patient raised concerns about the visits of Child A to the ward with him, concerns that he then discussed with some nurses, including Mr Boocock. The nurses were, in his words, "defensive", saying that they had raised this as an issue and held a meeting in July to discuss this and other issues, but that the PCT did not listen. Mr Melia felt with hindsight that the PCT genuinely believed they had good relationships with the patients and allowed the visits to go on as a result. It was, in his view, a wrong decision, but it was a considered one.

3.28.32 Mr Melia reacted to the concerns he was hearing by formally changing the visiting policy on the ward, insisting that all visits must be supervised and take place in the dining room or the central visiting hall, and that staffing levels were to be increased. He admitted that Mr Arnold had implemented similar changes the week before, but the nurses had told him that Mr Arnold's changes had not been formalized as policy. He described his action as "kneejerk". The PCT had supported the decision, but had criticized its unilateral nature; this was, in Mr Melia's view, a justifiable criticism. In mitigation he stressed the enormous pressure the Unit was under at the time.

3.28.33 Mr Melia was asked whether anyone had suggested to him that the instruction that all visits were to be supervised had already been given after the July PCT discussions. He told us that this close monitoring could not have been done in the past because staffing levels were inadequate.

3.28.34 The PCT allegedly had issued similar instructions in July, but they regarded Mr Melia's actions as amounting to a unilateral change. The PCT's reaction to Mr Melia's actions demonstrates that the instructions back in July were not clear, and that the PCT recognized a clear change in policy when they saw one.

3.28.35 We believe that Mr Melia acted properly in ensuring that swift action was taken to protect Child A at that point.

3.28.36 In October the nursing staff discussed the visits again. We have quoted the notes made by Ms Johnson at that time in full. Ms Johnson told us that these concerns were passed on to the Managers, PCT and Security, although she was relying on the nursing hierarchy to pass them on to the PCT. There is a dispute as to whether the PCT ever actually saw them. Not long afterwards staff started to sit in on Child A's visits.

3.28.37 More people, both staff and patients, started to express concerns. Thus Mr Melia was approached by Patient A.N. in October 1996, who raised concerns about Child A's visits and alleged that her father was bringing in pornographic videos. Mr Melia felt that these issues were now firmly on the PDU management agenda and did not take further action.

3.28.38 On 23 October two therapists, Ms Thorbinson and Mr Kay, met Mr Melia to discuss their concerns about the visits after patients had revealed in therapy sessions that a young girl might have been open to abuse whilst visiting the ward. Mr Melia told them the concerns were in hand. He e-mailed Mr Murphy recommending visits for children on the North Site should take place in the Central Visiting Area. On 14 November Mr Murphy replied, saying that he would recommend this change "ASAP". At the Special Needs Directorate Board meeting on 25 November this policy change was agreed.

3.28.39 Mr Melia told us that the PCT discussed the issue of the visits during the three weeks or so he was Acting Ward Manager but were content for the visits to go ahead provided that they were supervised. Mr Melia told us that although the PCT had discussed the visits of Child A at length, they did not appear to have grounded those discussions on the principle that the protection of the child should be of paramount importance.

3.28.40 Thus the PCT discussed matters again on the 24th of October with regard to Mr Corrigan and the minutes read: "Full discussion of visits by the Father of Child A and Paul's god-daughter [Child A]. Visits to continue to be observed. See clinical notes for details."

3.28.41 It is worth noting that Child A is incorrectly referred to as Mr Corrigan's god-daughter. By referring to the relationship in that way the PCT gave it a quite inappropriate status, a status which appeared to justify allowing the child to visit.

3.28.42 Mr Foster became Ward Manager on 28 October 1996. At that time the visits of Child A to the ward were still taking place, but they were confined to the library or dining hall, with two staff present. There was no physical contact allowed. He told us that he was given no particular instructions about monitoring the visits when he joined the ward.

3.28.43 Mr Foster told us that he thought it wrong for a child to be visiting a convicted sex offender in this way and had immediately raised his concerns with Mr Murphy, who told him to hang fire whilst he discussed the matter with Mrs Miles. He saw the staff meeting book shortly afterwards and passed on these concerns to Mr Murphy.

3.28.44 On 14 November the PCT discussed the issue and Mr Foster raised with Mrs Day her assessment of the visits. He was shocked to discover she had based her assessment purely on Mr Hemming's own reports of what took place. Before that meeting Mr Foster had already told Mr Murphy that he was unwilling to manage the ward so long as the visits continued; at the end of the meeting he told the PCT that Mrs Miles had decided the visits to the ward were to stop.

3.28.45 Mr Foster agreed with the Chairman's suggestion that visits could not be supervised without adequate staffing levels. He had approached Mr Murphy about staffing levels and they had been increased.

3.28.46 When we raised the issue of the PCT's actions with him Dr Strickland told us that the PCT had had many discussions about the child. Their prime concern was that Child A was safe and supervised. The PCT was always told that she was happy during the visits. He admitted that he was not aware of the visits of the young boy to Mr Corrigan; thus it was possible for a person to visit without the knowledge of the PCT.

3.28.47 Yet the PCT did not appear to have discussed the broader issue of whether it was sensible to allow such visits at all or whether the visits were benefiting Child A. Indeed Dr Stowell-Smith told us the PCT felt the contact between Mr Corrigan and Child A was a good thing for the former.

3.28.48 Dr Strickland maintained that the PCT was told the visits were supervised, as were Mr Hemming's LOA visits to Bradford. He admitted that he and the PCT failed in their responsibility to ensure that Child A's welfare was paramount in all decisions concerning her father and her visits.

3.28.49 His RMO colleague Dr Crispin surprised us somewhat by claiming she was unaware that Child A was visiting Mr Hemming at all before July 1996 and that she did not feel able to comment particularly on issues concerning Dr Strickland's patients because she did not have access to all the relevant documentation.

3.28.50 Mr Arnold agreed that the decision to allow Child A to visit was wrong. He admitted he should have been more proactive in relation to these visits and admitted that the principle that the child's interests should be paramount was not applied, although her safety was a key consideration. But the visits had prior PCT approval and he on his own could not stop the visits. He did increase staffing from three to four staff on a day shift so that supervising visits was in principle not a problem.

3.28.51 The decision to allow the visits to continue was wrong. The PCT as a whole must take responsibility for this serious error. When we look back to the introduction of the Children Act 1989, by then seven years before, and the publicity which attended it after the Cleveland Inquiry chaired by Lord Justice Butler-Sloss, we find it incredible that Doctors and Social Workers had to fall back on the lame excuse that the concept of the interests of the child being paramount was unknown to them. If that really is the case it demonstrates beyond a scintilla of doubt the depth of isolation of the Special Hospitals. It also highlights how seriously defective was the monitoring system of the SHSA.

3.29.0 Leave of Absence Trips to Bradford and the Social Worker's Role

3.29.1 Mr Hemming visited the Bradford area on seven occasion between September 1993 and April 1996, latterly escorted by Enrolled Nurse James Corrigan. On one occasion he visited Child A's father's house. The authors of IR2 note that the change of escort to Nurse Corrigan seems to have been at the request of Mr Hemming. There is evidence from photographs taken on the LOA trips that Nurse Corrigan did not adhere to the planned itinerary and visited pubs with Child A and her father. On one occasion it appears Mr Hemming picked up Child A from school. No feedback from these visits was provided to the PCT, who did not, it seems, review the visits.

3.29.2 It was the responsibility of the PCT to consider the appropriateness of such LOA trips, taking into account the risk of absconding, the safety of the public and, in particular with a Schedule 1 offender, the appropriateness of contact with children outside. The authors of IR2 could find no indication that this had been done. **Nor can we.** Dr Stowell-Smith, as a social worker, would be expected, in their view, to assess the appropriateness of such visits; he allegedly said that he no longer did that.

3.29.3 Dr Stowell-Smith told us that he did not regard that as part of his social work role and was not aware it was something other social workers in the Hospital did. The social workers had a professional responsibility to network with families and significant friends of patients, but he did not see it as a role of the social work department to vet LOA visits. He also denied it was part of his job to check that the people whose numbers patients wished to call were content to receive such calls, although PCT minutes showed that he did do this on occasion. We were told by Mr Day that Dr Stowell-Smith, did not see it as his role to vet visitors to the Hospital.

3.29.4 Mr Backhouse was asked whether Dr Stowell-Smith should have visited Child A's home and made inquiries about the people living there. He agreed that Dr Stowell-Smith should certainly have made contact with the relevant authorities.

3.29.5 Other social workers did see it as part of their duties to assess the suitability of LOA visits and indeed of potential visitors. Thus Mr Foster said that the social worker he now worked with considered the checking of individual visitors as her responsibility. However, several witnesses testified that the vetting amounted to little more than establishing the identity of the proposed visitor and that the patient wished to be visited by that person. This did not amount to a security vetting: the most a social worker could say, given that he or she would not have access to a CRO check or anything of that nature, was that they knew of no reason why that person should not visit. Mr Day, the Security Liaison Officer for the PDU, said that even this minimal vetting stopped so far as he was aware on the PDU.

3.29.6 Mr Bateson told us that when he became Principal Social Worker for the Special Needs Directorate he had raised with Dr Stowell-Smith the amount of time he was spending on therapeutic work, as opposed to core social work tasks. Dr Stowell-Smith shortly afterwards started a new post in Rehabilitation. Mr Bateson said that it was not the social worker's job to vet visitors, but as the profession which made the link with families and outside agencies they had to be party to any assessment of a visitor's suitability.

3.29.7 It became increasingly difficult for us to discern just what Dr Stowell-Smith did think was his role as social worker in the PCT.

3.29.8 Mr Daniels asked Mr Backhouse, the Head of Social Work at Ashworth, whether social work at the Hospital had lost its focus and social workers had become more interested in therapy than core social work tasks. We have seen that the SSI Inspection Report in 1994 had criticized the lack of clear laid-down policies and procedures for what services social workers would offer. Mr Backhouse replied that in response to the SSI Reports much work had been done to clarify roles and to produce a service specification for social workers. He thought the criticism was no longer valid.

3.29.9 We disagree, at least as far as Dr Stowell-Smith is concerned. He clearly was ignoring what colleagues regarded as core social work duties to continue with his therapeutic work.

Recommendation 28 **3.29.10 We recommend that the precise duties and responsibilities of social workers are clarified.**

Recommendation 29 **3.29.11 We recommend that contact with the relevant local authority social services department is always made before an LOA trip whenever there is any likelihood of a patient coming into contact with children.**

3.30.0 Liaison with Outside Bodies

3.30.1 On 1 April 1992 Bradford Social Services wrote to Dr Sylvester, the then Director of Medical Services at Ashworth, requesting information for a child protection investigation involving Child A. That letter was received in Dr Strickland's office on 3 April and records show that her father's medical records were booked out to Dr Sylvester on 24 April. Dr Sylvester told us that he could not recall receiving the letter or its contents. He accepted that it was his responsibility to reply, since Dr Hunter, the consultant to Child A's father, had left the Hospital long ago. **He accepted that by not replying he failed to do his job.**

3.30.2 Her father was given care and control of Child A.

3.30.3 There was no further contact between Bradford and Ashworth concerning Child A until November 1996, despite concerns raised in the interim and the LOA visits by Mr Hemming to the child's father's house.

3.30.4 On 14 November 1996 Dr Stowell-Smith was asked to check with Bradford whether Child A was on their "At Risk" register. He did not do this. When questioned on this point Dr Stowell-Smith said he had no recollection of that meeting or that request. He said that shortly afterwards he had moved to a different post; certainly no one subsequently checked with him whether or not he had done what he had been asked. He admitted that his failure to pursue this was an oversight.

3.30.5 Dr Stowell-Smith should be severely censured for his failure to contact Bradford as requested.

3.30.6 On 25 November Mr Bateson contacted Bradford regarding stopping ward-based visits by Child A and her father. On 20 January there was further contact regarding Child A; Bradford confirmed they had had concerns over the child in 1992, 1994 and 1995. On 28 January Mr Bateson and others met an outside expert to discuss the photographs of Child A found in patients' possession; the photographs did cause her concern. Then on 31 January a meeting involving Bradford Social Services, the Police, the Education Department and Ashworth resulted in an emergency protection order. In November 1997 it was decided by a Circuit Judge sitting in the Family Court that Child A be taken into the care of the local authority.

3.30.7 We also heard that the Home Office wrote to Dr Strickland in November 1994 regarding Mr Corrigan's proposed LOA trips, requesting information over several issues, including the visits from Child A. Almost six months later Dr Strickland replied, explaining this delay was deliberate, to give the PCT a chance to work through the list of questions posed by the Home Office. With regard to Child A, Dr Strickland said that she was Mr Corrigan's god-daughter; the visits took place on the wards and were well-supervised. The Home Office was not itself raising concerns about Child A at this point.

3.30.8 We find this delay unacceptable. It should not take six months for the PCT to agree a response to the questionnaire. The PCT also missed an opportunity to discuss the suitability of the visits. We would also point out again that Mr Corrigan was not Child A's godfather.

3.31.0 The Approach to Childcare Issues

3.31.1 We asked a number of witnesses about their knowledge of the Children Act 1989 and the principle that the benefit of the child should be paramount. The answers were deeply depressing. Dr Stowell-Smith said that the social workers in the Hospital saw childcare issues as peripheral to their work and so had not discussed the implications of the Children Act 1989. He told us that the Hospital provided no training on child protection issues and admitted his understanding of the Children Act was vague. The PCT were confident that the visits were supervised so had no concerns until July 1996: "at the time it was seen as something which had not adversely affected the visitors". He admitted that subsequently he had come to believe that children should not be visiting paedophile patients in this way.

3.31.2 Dr Stowell-Smith agreed with Dr Strickland's Counsel that the PCT was entitled to expect that he would take a lead on childcare issues.

3.31.3 The following exchange between Professor Edwards and Dr Stowell-Smith sums up the sorry picture:

> Q: I think the truth is that this [meaning child protection] was not an issue that anybody had even thought about?
> A: I would have to say yes.
>
> Q: It was not a hotly debated issue?
> A: Children were not a special issue until 1996.

3.31.4 We were amazed by Dr Stowell-Smith's lack of knowledge about the principles underlying the Children Act 1989. As Professor Bluglass pointed out to Dr Stowell-Smith, he was well-placed to be aware of the effects the presence of a young girl might have on some of the Lawrence Ward patients and to bring such issues to the attention of other members of the PCT. He should have been the first member of the PCT to raise concerns. He failed dismally.

3.31.5 Dr Strickland told us that the PCT's discussions were not concerned with whether the visits were in the interests of the child. He said:

> ". . . our discussions were founded on two things, which were the benefit to the patient, benefits to the father of bringing his child in, and the second bit was the fact that it could be done safely".

He was then asked, "Do you agree, Dr Strickland that certainly in retrospect this was a major defect in the approach of the PCT to this problem?" He replied, "The Care Team should have looked far more closely at whether there were any benefits for the child in visiting Ashworth."

3.31.6 The psychologist, Mr Berry, agreed that there was no training in child protection issues for staff. When asked whether the visits of Child A to Mr Corrigan, a paedophile, worried him he replied that "it was on a different ward, it was not my patient".

3.31.7 Mrs Day admitted that she had been completely ignorant of the demands of the Children Act 1989 when assessing Mr Hemming.

3.31.8 We have already seen in our discussion of policy-making above that important key professionals at the Special Hospitals failed to tackle child protection issues, despite the prompting of the SSI amalgamated Report in 1994 which raised it as an issue (albeit at another hospital) and the March 1995 draft guidance on child protection from the Department of Health entitled *Child Protection: Clarification of Arrangements Between the NHS and Other Agencies.*

3.31.9 With hindsight, Mr Backhouse admitted that the Special Hospitals had not adequately addressed the issue of child protection. Mr Backhouse admitted that there was probably no copy of the Area Child Protection Committee's procedures within Ashworth Hospital and no representatives from Ashworth on the Area Child Protection Committee. The unfortunate events surrounding Mr Daggett's absconsion had at least encouraged action.

3.31.10 Mr Backhouse argued that Social Work should be properly represented on the Board and that the Head of Social Work should be fully accountable for all aspects of social work practice.

3.31.11 We, however, believe that the Social Work Department must improve its organization, management, supervision and practice if it is to play its full role in the care of patients at Ashworth Hospital. We understand why social workers were deployed in the individual clinical teams, but some degree of professional oversight remains important, in our view, in order to maintain professional standards. This broke down at Ashworth.

Recommendation 30 **3.31.12 We recommend an urgent review by the SSI of the service provided by Social Workers at Ashworth Hospital, using the 1994 SSI Report as a benchmark.**

3.31.13 We asked a number of other staff about their level of knowledge of childcare issues. Mr Dale confirmed that until late 1996 the issue of children visiting the wards was just not an issue for senior managers. After the Blom-Cooper Report and the push to improve life for patients there was no attempt to look at matters from the child's point of view. The SSI visited in 1993 and their Report did not bring this issue to the Hospital's attention. Subsequently the NSPCC had been invited into the Hospital to do some work on child protection issues and had raised a number of potential problems arising from the policy of allowing children to enter the secure perimeter at all.

3.31.14 A specific criticism was made by Mr Bateson of Mr Dale's attitude towards the visits of Child A, in that he appeared to be putting the interests of the child second to those of the Hospital. Mr Dale in his evidence had argued that he was merely trying to focus people's minds on what evidence they had for their concerns. He was anxious not to leap to conclusions about an international paedophile ring being involved in Lawrence Ward.

3.31.15 We do not accept that Mr Dale was making light of the seriousness of the allegations concerning the child. But he, along with his colleagues, must be criticized for the general failure to bear in mind the paramountcy of the interests of all children including Child A.

3.31.16 Sight should not be lost of the fact that, although section 1 of the Children Act 1989 introduced the word "paramount" in relation to the interests of children, prior to that, in both private and public family law, the interests of children were always a prime consideration, albeit without that specific emphasis. Before 1989 no sensible lawyer, doctor, social worker, psychologist, hospital administrator, or responsible member of the public would have thought it appropriate to expose young children to paedophiles, particularly paedophiles with known criminal histories. Before 1989 responsible members of the public would have been horrified by the knowledge that such exposure was allowed on the basis of it being therapeutically advantageous for such criminal paedophiles, who were not even close family members. That this occurred is something for which no one involved in Ashworth Hospital can escape a degree of criticism. The SHSA did not take the matter of child protection issues seriously and had a defective monitoring system. Yet Mr Dale must take some responsibility by failing to make representations to the Hospital Board and thence on to the SHSA. Sadly there were not more like Miss Kinsley who, as mentioned in Part Two, said that had she known of children visiting paedophiles at Ashworth she would, even in retirement, have been "down to road to see Charles Kaye".

3.31.17 Despite the recent trials and tribulations, Mr Melia told us that the Hospital was still not providing training on child protection issues. Mr Foster told us that in some 20 years at Ashworth no one had talked to him about child protection until he had been on Lawrence Ward some months.

3.31.18 Finally Mrs Miles told us that although she was aware that children visited on some wards, it was never raised as a concern with her until the end of 1996, and she had no concerns given that she was assured the visits were carefully considered and supervised. She admitted that with hindsight allowing child to visit the PDU was not sensible. She was concerned that earlier worries expressed by staff in July 1996 were not passed on to her.

3.31.19 Mr Daniels pointed out to Mr Dale that every nurse in the service he manages in Nottinghamshire would know that contact with a convicted sex offender merits an automatic referral to child protection services. The ignorance of these matters at Ashworth was an example of the isolation of the hospitals from the mainstream health services. Mr Dale agreed.

3.31.20 We asked both Mrs Foley, Chief Executive of Rampton, and Mr Franey, General Manager and then Chief Executive of Broadmoor between 1988 and 1997, about child visiting. Mr Franey admitted that he would have allowed a child to visit paedophiles if the visit was properly supervised, with staff in the same room, and if the PCT had approved the visit. He admitted that staff did not have specific training on child protection. Mrs Foley told us that there was no longer child visiting on the wards at Rampton, a decision taken in reaction to events at Ashworth.

3.31.21 We were alarmed by the ignorance of child protection at all three Special Hospitals. This is a subject that High Security Services need to address.

3.32.0 Room Searching

3.32.1 Mr Daggett described room searches on Lawrence Ward as "farcical". Some patients' side rooms had not been searched for over a year, and searches were at best cursory and sometimes non-existent. Staff also warned patients of searches or retreated if a patient threatened to complain. Once a patient's room had been searched that room was "safe" for several months and could be used to store illicit materials. He claimed that on a number of occasions he and his fellow patients were tipped off about a forthcoming search. This was, he alleged, a way of helping the patients police the ward and keep its high status.

3.32.2 Mr Daggett reported how staff would, instead of actually searching his room, sit on the bed for 15 minutes watching television; then, when they thought they had been in the room for long enough leave and enter the search as 'negative'. He described this as 'common practice'. Another practice, which was naive rather than corrupt, was to say to patients "is it okay to search your room in 15 minutes?"

3.32.3 Mr Daggett told us that Mr Corrigan in particular was very adept at avoiding searching by accusing staff of victimizing him. Staff felt that patients could get them suspended by a complaint; patients felt that complaints got nowhere. In that climate people were unable to get on with their jobs.

3.32.4 Both the patients interviewed by Mr Keown and his team and our own patient witnesses agreed that the quality of searching was poor. Patient W told us that there was hardly any searching during 1995 and 1996. Patient Q said that his room was searched, although the searches did not take long. The fact that staff did not find the pornographic videotapes he told us he stored there suggests the searches were not thorough. He told us that the patient grapevine would alert people to a search in the offing.

3.32.5 Patient W reported that Mr Cannon asked some time before the large-scale search of Lawrence Ward if he had anything he ought not to have. Mr Cannon said that he had spoken to the patients to whom he was primary nurse during the time of the amnesty (i.e., October 1996) and suggested that they should hand in anything they should not have. The patient, Mr Cannon noted, would have been expecting a search in any case.

3.32.6 We also heard that Nurse Corrigan would go into a patient's room, read a pornographic magazine and then, after a few minutes, leave and record the room as having been searched.

3.32.7 Mr Day, the Security Liaison Officer for the PDU from January 1995 until March 1996, told us he had been very concerned about the quality, as opposed to the quantity, of searching. He recommended setting up special three-man search teams in each Unit to take inventories of possessions, inventories which would then be checked each time the room was searched. However, the number of possessions would have had to be reduced dramatically for that to work.

3.32.8 Why was searching so poor? It appears that a combination of rooms with too many possessions, the lack of central storage and the high level of trust shown to patients on the ward had led to a steady dilution of room searching. Thus Mr Keown and his team were very surprised by the volume of property amassed by some patients. Their rooms could not have been searched to a minimally acceptable standard because of the number of possessions. Mr Corrigan's room for example was so full that he would have had difficulty lying down on his bed. Mr Hemming had two video recorders linked together, presumably for copying videotapes. The rooms represented a security, fire and health and safety risk. Mr Cannon agreed that to search Mr Corrigan's room would have taken days. Mr Boocock said he had had concerns about the level of possessions in most patients' rooms.

3.32.9 The video taken by the team shows the extent to which patients had filled their side rooms. Staff from the IT department described Mr Booth's room as a computer.

We have seen the video. The situation was truly appalling.

3.32.10 Mr Arnold told us that when he arrived on the ward there were seven bikes being stored in various parts of the ward. He raised the issue of storage with Mr Tarbuck and Mr Melia and others; there were promises of extra storage on the way but this seemed to take forever.

3.32.11 Mr Arnold told us that he did raise the issue of Mr Corrigan's numerous video recorders with the PCT. He was told that Mr Corrigan needed two recorders to copy gardening programmes. He accepted this argument. Dr Strickland claimed that this matter was never discussed with him, but Mr Arnold was quite convinced he had raised it with him and the PCT.

3.32.12 Faced with large amounts of possessions in patients' rooms staff bowed to the inevitable and adopted a policy of partial searches. Mr Cannon, who had been a team leader on Lawrence Ward since 1993, told us that when he came to the Ward only partial searches of bedrooms were carried out as it was impractical to carry out full room searches with the number of possessions in the rooms. He was not in favour of this practice. The practice then shifted to only searching when there was specific cause, to fall in line with the Code of Practice, during the time Mr Moran was Ward Manager. We saw above that the Operational Policy of the Ward in November 1994 laid down a policy of no routine searches, with targeted searching if any strong reason emerged to suspect a patient was breaking the rules.

3.32.13 Following the Owen Ward incident core search standards were mooted and discussed at a Lawrence Ward community meeting. There was, it appears, a lot of resistance to core search standards applying to Lawrence Ward. Mr Cannon and Mr Boocock both argued for full room searches; Mr Daggett was one patient who supported them. Mr Richards, the then Ward Manager, told Mr Cannon the decision reached was that core search standards would apply, but that they would be partial searches. Neither Mr Boocock nor Mr Cannon could confirm whether this was the decision of the PCT. Mr Boocock claimed Mr Richards had put the partial searches policy in writing to him, but was unable to produce the letter, which he said was in his locker at the Hospital. (We should point out that Mr Boocock was suspended and, therefore, unable to access his locker at the Hospital. No such letter was ever produced.)

3.32.14 Mr Arnold told us he was briefed by his predecessor as Ward Manager and the three team leaders on the practice of partial searches. He was told that the practice had been authorized by the PCT. Two or three areas in a bedroom would be selected at random and searched thoroughly. Area searches of the ward would, however, be full searches. The rationale for the partial searches was the extent of patients' possessions. It was simply impossible to carry out a full room search in each case.

3.32.15 Ms Edge told us that room searches on Lawrence Ward were unlike the searches she was used to on the East Site. She was told to choose a room, choose a section of the room and search that section. She confirmed that nevertheless it would be recorded that the room had been searched, rather than just part of it.

3.32.16 This picture was confirmed by Ms Karran. She did not know whether random part-searches were consistent with ward policy guidelines, it was just a procedure they carried out, and had carried out since well before Mr Arnold became Ward Manager. She confirmed that a full room search would have taken four to five hours because of the number of possessions in the rooms.

3.32.17 So when a search of a patient's sideroom was recorded as having taken place, it was only a partial search. Yet even with partial searches Mr Keown told us that analysis of the search register for January to October 1996 suggested that the core search standards introduced in May 1995 were only met on Lawrence Ward in three months. In the ten months the shop was only searched once, on 16 March 1996. The notes read "a large amount of junk in room". On a number of occasions no rub-down search was recorded on patients going out on LOA visits. There is no record of stock for the shop ever being searched on return to the Hospital. It would appear that the van carrying the goods entered the Hospital and went to the ward without being searched. On one occasion when staff at the gate insisted on searching the car of the father of Child A, he turned around and went home.

3.32.18 Mr Keown and his team found that only one documented search was made of the garden shed for the period 1 January 1996 to 31 October 1996, on 19 June 1996. No record was found of a tool inventory or any protocol for monitoring tools. The Inquiry Team prepared an inventory of the garden shed. Chemicals stored there were in breach of the Care of Substances Hazardous to Health Regulations.

3.32.19 Unsurprisingly Mr Keown and his team recommended that the core search standards should outline the minimum *quality* of core searches.

3.32.20 Mr Arnold told us that he had identified a number of errors in the analysis of the search register and he believed that the core standards were being met, notwithstanding the conclusions of the Keown Report. He admitted that, given the partial nature of the searches, they were a deterrent at best. At the time he regarded the level of searching as adequate for the level of trust the patients were given as a whole.

3.32.21 Mr Arnold believed that the introduction of core search standards had made a difference on Lawrence Ward. That said, he admitted that nurses were not trained in searching techniques and that they were working with very out of date lists of patients' property. Although he himself did participate in searches, on the whole he was reliant on the information coming back to him that the searches had been properly carried out.

3.32.22 Despite his trust in searching on the ward, the large-scale search in January 1997 revealed things of which he and his colleagues were completely unaware, such as a stock of children's underwear. He was also unaware of the numbers of videotapes in patients' possession. Mr Keown's team pointed out that a thorough search of Mr Corrigan's room revealed a large quantity of material which was deemed clinically inappropriate, including male pornography and suggestive pictures of children. Had the PCT been aware of these pictures they might have evaluated Mr Corrigan's progress differently. The finds on the ward demonstrate that even if the standards were being met the quality of searching was very poor.

3.32.23 That searching was inadequate was undeniable. What was more open to dispute was the extent to which the PCT was aware of the policy of partial searches. Mr Arnold thought that the PCT did understand the true situation and so he never raised the issue of partial searching to their attention. He said requests for more storage were made by the Ward Manager's Group of which he was a member. He said that with hindsight he fell in with the *laissez-faire* attitude of the ward.

3.32.24 However Dr Strickland told us that he had assumed that when a search was recorded it was a full room search. He was being briefed that searches were taking place to an adequate standard. As far as he was concerned the PCT had never decided that there should be a policy of partial room searches. One is bound to ask, was he not aware of the problems with searching rooms, especially given his ultimate responsibility for all aspects of care, including security. The answer, alas, was no. He himself rarely went into patients' rooms. This was normal practice for consultants at Ashworth, though with hindsight he should have been more inquisitive. Dr Shetty told us he very rarely went into patients' side rooms.

3.32.25 Dr Crispin confirmed this general picture. She did go to patients' rooms occasionally for specific purposes, but this was not a regular occurrence. She certainly did not go with a view to monitoring whether or not the rooms could be searched. The state of some Lawrence Ward rooms was clearly unacceptable, but this had not been conveyed to the PCT. Mrs Day agreed that the PCT never authorized a policy of partial searches.

3.32.26 This was despite years of concern about the quantity of possessions in rooms. We were told that there was a policy of no searching for a time on Lawrence Ward. Doctors Strickland and Crispin should have known better and should have provided leadership in this matter.

3.32.27 At some point a decision to accept partial room searches instead of full room searches was made because the bedrooms were so full of patients' possessions. There was not even a debate within the PCT it appears before introducing such a step. The system did not require seeking approval before making a significant change in the security arrangements of the Hospital. We have no doubt that the need to seek approval should have been mandatory. It does not seem to have been passed up the management line. Security is only as strong as the weakest link; in the case of Ashworth Hospital that link was all too weak.

3.32.28 Time and again the RMOs told us that they were reliant on the nurses in particular to feed them information. This is not good enough. RMOs have the ultimate responsibility for patient care; they may not control the allocation of nurses to a ward, but they do have a responsibility to monitor what is going on. Some firm questioning of staff might have elicited enough information to give them pause for thought. The PCT with the experience of the Owen Ward hostage-taking should have been more proactive on this point. Of course, they may have been had they been privy to the Report.

3.32.29 Full room searching with cross-checking against patients' up-to-date property lists on a regular basis is essential from the point of view of security. They should be carried out by dedicated and trained teams in order to negate the manipulative ability of this group of patients.

Recommendation 31 **3.32.30 We recommend:**
(i) that on the PDU full room searches should be carried out on a regular basis by dedicated and trained teams;
(ii) the search results should be cross-checked against patients' up-to-date property lists.

3.33.0 Leave of Absence Trips

3.33.1 Mr Daggett claimed that patients commonly "shopped around" to get the right escort. Given the budget on rehabilitation trips it made sense to opt for an enrolled nurse, because he would be cheaper. Another consideration might be how conscientious a given nurse would be. Some nurses did not monitor patients closely or allowed alcohol to be drunk on trips. Mr Daggett described how he "booked" Enrolled Nurse James Corrigan to escort him on the day he planned to abscond whilst Mr Corrigan was on leave. Mr Corrigan did not supervise patients properly on LOA trips and was "up to his neck" in every bit of illicit activity going, for example, selling items such as alcohol to patients . Furthermore it was common practice he told us for patients not to be searched on leaving the Hospital.

3.33.2 Mr Daggett agreed with the proposition that Mr Corrigan, the nurse escorting him the day he absconded, was not interested in supervising him; that was why he had chosen him as his escort. Patient Q described Nurse Corrigan as "more than corrupt".

3.33.3 Patient Q told us that it was generally the case that patients took their primary nurses on LOA trips, as that was what was expected. Patient I told us that on LOAs he had been able to choose his escort, but that he had always taken his primary nurse.

3.33.4 Mr Cannon told us that he always insisted on thorough rub-down searches when a patient left the ward for a LOA visit and when he came back. He told us that on one occasion Mr Daggett had claimed Mr Cannon was victimising him by carrying out a thorough rub-down search.

3.33.5 Dr Strickland admitted that there were some problems in the use of escorts. Mr Arnold told us that the PCT's intention was that patients should be accompanied by their primary nurses on LOA visits. This could not always be guaranteed. The documentary evidence we saw indicated that it was often the case that a patient was not escorted by his primary nurse.

3.33.6 It is clear that Mr Daggett and others were able to manipulate the system to get his desired escort. This was not difficult to do as at least one member of the staff had been corrupted.

3.33.7 We heard that Mr Daggett had frequent trips out to sporting events and elsewhere. Other patients went to places like Blackpool Pleasure Beach. Mr Booth was able to surf the Internet at a shop in London. We contrast these expensive and potentially risky trips with the current policy operated at Rampton, where LOA visits are strictly limited, largely to shopping trips in local towns. We question whether LOA trips at Ashworth were tied closely enough to a programme of rehabilitation.

3.33.8 The organisation of LOA trips is far too slipshod; documentation is frequently incomplete and inaccurate. There is confusion about who should carry out rub down searches in and out of the Hospital and who should check the documentation.

Recommendation 32

3.33.9 We recommend:
(i) searches and checks of documentation on LOA trips should be carried out by the gate security staff, and complete records be kept of such searches;
(ii) escorting staff should also be searched on leaving and returning from LOA trips.

3.34.0 Use of Ward Computer

3.34.1 We heard that one patient, Mr Booth, had been allowed to access the ward computer by his primary nurse, Mr Paul Boocock. Certainly Patient Q and Patient E saw him with Mr Boocock in the staff office using a computer. According to Mr Boocock this computer belonged to a member of staff and Mr Booth was helping Mr Boocock to fix it.

3.34.2 Mr Keown told us that there was no evidence that Mr Booth had actually accessed the network, rather the concern was that he had had access to a network computer. The information that Mr Booth had worked at the ward computer with Mr Boocock came from a number of patients.

3.34.3 We asked Patient E about this matter. He said he had witnessed Mr Booth working at a computer in the Ward Manager's office on a number of occasions. A nurse, Mr Boocock, was always with him. This was unusual, as there were interview rooms available for staff to talk to patients. Mr Booth had said to Patient E once that he knew more about Patient E than the staff or Patient E himself did, which Patient E took to be a hint that Mr Booth had access to personal and clinical notes. Patient E complained to Mr Tarbuck, who asked Mr Arnold to make some preliminary investigations. Mr Arnold asked Patient E to see if any other patients were prepared to come forward to corroborate his story, which he had done, but no one was willing to do so. However, Patient E did not see Mr Booth in the Ward Manager's office with Mr Boocock again.

3.34.4 There is a dispute over the timing of this incident. Patient E said he complained in June 1995; Mr Boocock told us that he had asked Mr Booth to help him mend a computer in early 1996 and claimed that this was what was seen. Mr Arnold stated that the complaint was made before April 1996. It appears that Patient E was probably mistaken in the date of his complaint.

3.34.5 Mr Arnold admitted that he never spoke to Mr Boocock about this allegation, because he was concerned that if the matter became the subject of an official complaint it would be independently investigated and he could be open to criticism.

3.34.6 Mr Cannon agreed with the suggestion that Mr Boocock was, in general, very security-minded and unlikely to breach Hospital security in this way.

3.34.7 Mr Boocock told us that the patient, Mr Booth, had a considerable expertise in computers and that he was not the only person to consult him. He denied giving him access to the Hospital network, claiming that when he and Mr Booth were seen in the Ward Manager's office they were trying to repair the computer of one of Mr Boocock's colleagues. They had used that office so that they could disconnect the Ward Managers's systems unit from the monitor and connect the systems unit of his colleague's computer to the Ward Manager's monitor and keyboard. Working on the system's unit was a slow process because there was no computer manual. He could only do it in half hour stints spread over two weeks.

3.34.8 He said that he was not challenged when he brought in his colleague's system unit, despite the fact that he was carrying a large box into the Hospital. He admitted that he brought in software for patients on occasion.

3.34.9 One patient claimed he had seen a list of staff names and addresses on Mr Booth's computer. This would seem to support the idea that he had had access to the Hospital network. Mr Boocock noted that this would require at least two passwords. He thought that Mr Booth had not got into the network, but enjoyed pretending that he had.

3.34.10 Mr Boocock saw no reason why he and Mr Booth should not operate a computer together, given that it was a shared interest.

3.34.11 Mr Keown and his team criticized Mr Boocock for losing sight of his professional boundaries and spending many hours at computers in the company of Mr Booth.

3.34.12 We cannot substantiate the allegation that Mr Boocock allowed Mr Booth access to the network computer at Ashworth. We were concerned at Mr Boocock's cavalier attitude towards bringing in computer software for Mr Booth. To this extent he allowed their common interest in computers to impinge on his professional boundaries. But he was Mr Booth's primary nurse, and as such was expected and encouraged to develop a good relationship with him. Mr Keown and his team were too harsh in their judgment of him probably because they decided, on wholly inadequate evidence in our view, that he gave Mr Booth access to the Hospital's computer network.

3.35.0 Computers

3.35.1 We heard that patients on Lawrence Ward had easy access to personal computers. The purpose of allowing patients to have PCs was, Mr Keown told us, to provide educational and recreational facilities to patients. But he agreed that no controls were put in place and no restrictions were applied to their use. The general level of knowledge of computers of a number of the patients was far in advance of the knowledge of the staff on the ward, and patients were storing sensitive information on their computers, such as names from contact magazines, records of illicit trading and fake business references and letter-headings. Mr Booth and another patient had on their computers and disk files fake business references; letter-heads; and identity cards produced by desktop publishing and word processing software. Staff on the wards were in no position to identify what was, or was not, a possible risk.

3.35.2 Nursing staff confirmed this picture. Mr Boocock agreed that there was little control exercised over patients' use of personal computers. Mr Moran told us that the PCT had authorized computer training for two patients. Mr Arnold admitted that he personally had little knowledge of computers so would not know how to monitor potential abuses.

3.35.3 Following Mr Daggett's absconsion, it became clear that a number of Lawrence Ward patients were involved in trading in computer components and technology. Mr Daggett had been involved in trading in computer components through computer magazines. Mr Daggett said Mr Booth was doing the same. Indeed we heard that Mr Booth was running what amounted to a computer consultancy business, including writing programmes for Owen Ward, the Advocacy Service and for Aintree Hospitals Trust, and building a computer for a fellow patient. Between January and September 1996 he received into his Hospital account almost £4,000 in excess of Hospital benefit and reward stage payments. Much of Mr Booth's business operations was approved by the PCT, but it was unclear whether the extent of his business or the sums of money involved was known to the PCT. Much of his income could not be traced, since it had been deposited in an external bank to which Mr Booth would not allow access. He also acquired a password for use on the Internet, although it is unlikely he was ever able to access the Internet from within the Hospital.

3.35.4 Another concern of Mr Keown's team was that Mr Booth might have access to a mobile cellular telephone which he could use to download pornography from the Internet. No evidence was found that he did in fact possess such a telephone, although it was clear he was trying to acquire one, as a search of his property revealed correspondence from Mercury, "One 2 One" and British Telecom seeking information on their ranges of mobile telephones. Mr Daggett himself had acquired a pager on a LOA visit and claimed he had operated his computer software/hardware business with a BT pager. He advertised in computer magazines with a contact number. When contacted on his pager he would ring back on the Ward community phone.

3.35.5 Merseyside Police investigated the possibility that patients were obtaining and/or storing pornography on their personal computers. Inspector Marsden told us that they had recovered a file list from one computer (owned by Mr Booth) which strongly suggested that pornography was stored on that computer, but apparently he had notice of the search on 17 January and reformatted the hard disk at 00.34 am on 17 January. Five still pornographic images were found on his computer. No evidence was found to prove Mr Booth had accessed the Internet to obtain them, and they could have been scanned into the computer or down loaded from a diskette. Nonetheless the possibility of accessing the Internet was a concern. Inspector Marsden had also been concerned because one of the patient's computers which had been examined was equipped with a modem.

3.35.6 For their part, Mr Keown and his colleagues were satisfied that Mr Booth was the only patient who had the ability, contacts and opportunity to acquire and distribute computer generated pornographic images. Although patients commented that Mr Booth got pornographic images from the Internet, the team was unconvinced since there were so many other ways in which he could acquire pornographic material. The team also thought it highly improbable that he had used the Internet as the only means of acquiring pornographic images. It was probable that he had not got those photographs from the Internet but by scanning some photograph or document.

3.35.7 What does not appear in Mr Keown's Report is what we were told when we visited Ashworth Hospital, namely that at the time when patients wiped their tapes a number of patients actually sent their computers away from Ashworth, although goodness knows why this was permitted.

3.35.8 Indeed a number of patients on the PDU possessed powerful computers by 1996 standards. Mr Booth had made computers for fellow patients, including Mr Corrigan. Mr Corrigan's computer had (for the time) a fast 486 DX processor, and it had an image graphics card. Mr Booth's machine had a P133 processor, two floppy drives, a 800 megabyte tape streamer and its software. The drive was pass-worded. It also had a CD-ROM drive, and its hard disk was a 850 MB Seagate drive. It had a Logitech hand scanner card but no hand scanner was found in his room. The five pornographic photographs found on his hard disk drive had been scanned onto it using Coral Draw graphics software.

3.35.9 Another patient's computer had two hard disks- one a gigabyte in storage size (1,000 megabytes) and the other 90 megabytes. It had a CD-ROM drive. Yet another had a powerful computer with a 486DN266 processor, a 850 MB hard drive and a Logitech colour hand scanner plus a CD-ROM. A third had a powerful computer with a substantial hard drive. It had a sound card with integrated modem and he had various Internet software. It had a card which enabled the computer to show video and television pictures.

3.35.10 What is interesting from the Report is that a number of patients had ancillary hardware but no computers in their side rooms – hardware which was useless without a computer . For example one patient on Owen Ward had a hand scanner, a Conner Tape streamer and a 10 MB Zip backup drive. Others had computer floppy disks with computer images on them.

3.35.11 Mr Keown and his team argued that it would be unreasonable to expect staff to be *au* *fait* with all the facilities, capabilities and functions available on the wide range of computer hardware currently available:

> "the investigating team found great difficulty in understanding and evaluating the impact different types of technical devices may have had upon the integrity of the security systems at Ashworth Hospital. Computers are now available in pocket size variants, such as the Psion 3 series, which were recovered from Messrs Hemming, Booth and Braund and are complete with modem and infra red link facilities. The word computer is no longer sufficiently descriptive to cover the range of technological devices which patients can easily obtain but yet which can be used in a subversive, fraudulent and counter-therapeutic manner."

3.35.12 This is a weak criticism. You do not have to be a computer expert to know of the potentials. No doubt most nurses will have little knowledge of these things, but what of the Security and the IT departments? With a Psion 3, which is equipped with a modem all you need to access the Internet is a telephone socket!

3.35.13 The team did come to a sensible conclusion:

> "10.5 Because the risk these devices pose to Hospital security, and the lack of obvious solution, the only way to ensure no further breaches of security take place is to restrict patient access to such devices. Their use in a nefarious and subversive manner is not compatible with the Hospital's therapeutic ethos."
>
> "Recommendation 26:
> Patients should not have access to any personal technological devices which have a memory facility or can be used for the transmission of information. All access to technological devices, including computers should be in an area which is designated for the purpose and offers a controlled environment. One such area would be the education department".

3.35.14 If you consider the computer and peripheral hardware and software available on the PDU all that was lacking, if relevant components were put together, in order to access the Internet was a telephone. Mr Booth made computers. It was well within his capacity to bring such components together. He reformatted his hard drive two days before the search. Who is to know he did not remove an internal modem? In any event CD-ROM drives at that time could hold a megabyte of data. CD-ROMs take up little space and can be concealed easily. On LOA trips loaded CD-ROMs could be brought back and such was the security that it was more than probable that they would not be discovered when patients returned. They could also be brought in by visitors.

3.35.15 We were concerned about the amount of highly sophisticated equipment which patients had acquired and the apparent naivety of the Hospital's response. We were sufficiently concerned about the possibility of patients subverting systems and using computers to obtain and store pornography that we commissioned an expert, Professor Tony Sammes from the Royal Military College of Science at Shrivenham (part of Cranfield University), to inspect the IT systems at Ashworth. He and a colleague, Dr John Hunter, carried out a thorough review, for which we are very grateful. We discuss their findings in **3.39.0** *et seq.* below.

3.36.0 The Patient Care Team

3.36.1 Mr Keown and his team were very critical of the performance of the Lawrence Ward PCT, accusing it of failing to provide clinical direction and leadership in the ward, and of wilfully disobeying Hospital policy. Mr Keown and his team point to the similarity between the findings of the Owen Ward, Braund and Lawrence Ward Reports. Lessons had not been learnt, despite (or because of?) the fact that Dr Strickland for example was a member of both the Owen Ward and Lawrence Ward PCTs. More specifically, Mr Keown accused the PCT of being aware of the amount of pornographic literature in circulation and yet doing nothing. He based this on the evidence of patients who told his team they had warned staff of the amount of pornography available.

3.36.2 Mr Keown was probably being over-generous in crediting the PCT with that degree of knowledge.

3.36.3 For our part, we heard abundant evidence that in a number of areas the PCT was not abiding by Hospital policies. Thus there were core search standards in place which were not monitored; the policy on possessions was not implemented (though there is a dispute as to whether that was a realistic policy in the absence of adequate central storage facilities); the standing instructions on handling patients' financial transactions were not followed; and Hospital policy on patient access to cash cards was ignored.

3.36.4 We heard evidence on the working of the Lawrence Ward PCT. The key players did not see any real problems. Dr Strickland told us that the Lawrence Ward PCT worked as a multi-disciplinary team. He denied being the one holding all the power, and strongly denied that he ever protected any patients, in particular Mr Corrigan. Dr Crispin, Mr Arnold and Mrs Day all told us that each member of the PCT was able to make his or her voice heard, and that they were able to reach a consensus.

3.36.5 Despite the warm words, we were hard-pushed to see any obvious signs of effective multi-disciplinary working. We have already discussed the communication failures between the PCT and the ward-based staff; that lack of communication extended to within the PCT. Thus we were somewhat alarmed to hear that Mrs Day and fellow psychologists kept a separate set of notes, mainly informal notes and test results, which could, we were told, be misinterpreted by other professionals. This did not sit easily as far as we could see with a commitment to multi-disciplinary working. In answer to the questions of Counsel for the patients, Mrs Day was unable to demonstrate any clear mechanism for liaising between the psychology and social work departments to see whether checks had been made on the background of visitors.

3.36.6 Mr Daniels put it to Dr Strickland that the impression he had gained was not of a multi-disciplinary team, but a collection of individual professionals who happened to meet once a week. Dr Strickland pointed out that it was very difficult to get close multi-disciplinary working when individuals had responsibilities across several wards. One problem with PCT meetings was that they took place during ordinary working hours when a lot of staff had to be on the wards. That said, they did attempt to involve a patient's primary nurse in a discussion.

3.36.7 The PCT also struggled with irregular attendance. Some members of the PCT were irregular attenders. Dr Stowell-Smith in particular seems to have had a reputation for attending irregularly and leaving early. This was also an issue with Mr Berry, who appears to have failed to keep appointments with patients and to complete Reports when requested. Mr Berry argued he had too many patients on his workload. He did not attend the Lawrence Ward PCTs and did not work there; but he continued to have responsibility for patients there until Mrs Day took over.

3.36.8 Despite the general politeness, we were conscious of some blame-shifting between the different professions. Thus Dr Crispin told us that whilst she accepted responsibility for the care of her patients, the responsibility for the ward itself rested with the Ward Manager. She and her fellow RMOs had responsibilities but not the power to go with that responsibility: they were not in a position to control the environment in which patients were being treated.

We disagree. The RMOs had the power but did not properly apply their roles as clinical

leaders.

3.36.9 As we have seen, a previous Ward Manager, Mr Moran, was more critical of the medical leadership of the Lawrence Ward PCT. He confirmed that the Lawrence Ward PCT did on occasion feel entitled to confront Hospital policy and make representations further up the management line to prevent policies applying to Lawrence Ward patients. An example given to us dating from April 1994 was a decision to write to the Security Department asking that the opening of patients' mail should not apply to Lawrence Ward patients. He told us that the RMO would take the final decisions about certainly clinical issues, having listened to others' views. He agreed that distinguishing between clinical and non-clinical issues when the RMO's responsibilities were so all-encompassing was arbitrary.

3.36.10 The introduction of Ward Managers was never properly thought out, and the tensions in the relationship between the RMO's overarching responsibilities and the Ward Manager's day-to-day responsibility for running the ward were never resolved. The system introduced confusion as to how therapy and security could be harmonised. *See* Part four below.

3.36.11 Dr Strickland was asked whether consultants had become almost "external experts", spending all their time doing assessments, court work and writing Reports, and very little actually working on the wards. Dr Strickland described that as an exaggerated view, but pointed out that he had a large case load of patients on several wards, no senior registrar support and a heavy administrative load. In theory he could have refused to serve on some of the committees he was involved with, but would have faced considerable pressure from colleagues if he had done so.

3.36.12 Mr Arnold was candid in his self-criticism. He agreed that as Ward Manager he was responsible for leading the nursing team, maintaining standards of care and for the day-to-day security and management of the Ward. He could have taken any concerns about the regime on Lawrence Ward to the Clinical Manager. He admitted that he lacked managerial experience and that much had been happening on Lawrence Ward of which he was unaware. Mr Arnold admitted he had not worked with personality disordered patients as a group before. He agreed he would have benefited from more specialized training . He had had no formal induction on taking up the post.

3.36.13 We must balance Mr Arnold's self-criticism by noting that we heard a number of staff praising him as a good Ward Manager (for example, Ms Karran). Mr Cannon praised him, in particular with regard to his support for staff, but felt he became embroiled in non-clinical issues such as the ward shop. That said, he had inherited the situation, as had previous Ward Managers. Mr Melia told us that Mr Arnold's staff were very supportive of him and felt that the PCT had let them down, not Mr Arnold. Mr Melia was not convinced that was an accurate assessment of where the responsibility lay between Mr Arnold and the rest of the PCT, but it was firmly held.

3.36.14 We believe Mr Arnold was well-intentioned, but naive. He lacked the skills and experience to do a very difficult job.

3.36.15 Mr Daniels suggested to Mr Arnold that discussions at PCT meetings did not always get properly minuted or put into the clinical notes or care plans. This appears to have created major communication problems. Mr Arnold explained that the ward lacked proper clerical support.

3.36.16 This is not good enough. Good communication between different members of the PCT, and between the PCT and ward-based staff, was essential. It deserved more attention than it got.

3.36.17 Our discussion of the visits of Child A reveal a PCT which did not communicate effectively with ward-based nursing staff and vice versa. Instructions and changes in policy were written into the clinical notes and passed on as telegraphic comments in PCT minutes; but, as Mr Daniels pointed out, if notes in the clinical records do not get translated into formal policy documents the situation is hopeless, particularly with new staff joining the Ward, who cannot be expected to read back through clinical notes to pick up policy changes. Nursing staff were concerned, but the messages did not come through clearly.

3.36.18 Mr Arnold should have been linking the PCT and the ward staff together. He did not do this adequately. Other members of the PCT were very rarely on the ward, and when they were there did not seem to be paying adequate attention to what was going on. This did not help. If they had had closer relationships with the nursing staff the problems would have been identified earlier.

3.36.19 We felt that the Lawrence Ward PCT was reluctant to think through what it was trying to do. Much was done superficially; the attitude to record-keeping is an example, which had dangerous implications. We realize that the RMOs were very busy, but one does not get any sense of Dr Strickland in particular, and Dr Crispin, seeking to find out what was really going on; rather there is a consistent attempt to shift blame subtly onto the nurses in general, and Mr Arnold in particular. This will not do. We were left with the impression that the Lawrence Ward PCT was arrogant, with a deep sense of their own infallibility as far as the management of their patients was concerned.

3.37.0 The Investigation by Merseyside Police

3.37.1 Merseyside Police conducted a thorough investigation of events on Lawrence Ward from February 1997 onwards and passed a Report to the Crown Prosecution Service (CPS) in September. The CPS in the event decided not to prosecute any patients. An ex-member of staff was prosecuted for failing to reveal previous convictions on applying for a job at the Hospital. He was eventually given an absolute discharge.

3.37.2 The decision not to prosecute does not mean that nothing untoward was found. The CPS has to weigh up the likelihood of gaining a conviction on any given charge; and the public interest in prosecuting individuals who are already detained under conditions of high security and who, in most cases, will be subject to restriction orders. An experienced police officer after such a long and thorough inquiry cannot but come to some conclusions. We asked Inspector Marsden of Merseyside Police to share his views with us.

> The Chairman: You, in the course of this investigation, were investigating the various allegations made by Mr Daggett, the bringing in of videotapes of a pornographic nature, drugs and all the various matters which are familiar to those who have been sitting in this court.
>
> Q: Did you yourself, looking at the setup at Ashworth at that time, form a view from your experience that videotapes of that nature and drugs had or had not been brought into Ashworth?
> A: I had no doubt as a result of the experience of this investigation, but other investigations I have carried out at Ashworth prior to this, that drugs were available to patients and I have certainly no doubt that pornographic videos were certainly available as well, via the various patients within that Hospital.
>
> Q: From your general analysis, did you formulate any view as to the routes by which for instance the video tapes could be brought in?
> A: The route that has been described to this tribunal so far by various patients, together with I was present when Daggett gave evidence on Monday, the experience

that he described as being the route in, I am more than happy that that is a feasible way of getting videos into that Hospital.

Q: So coming in via visitors?
A: Yes.

Q: Via obtaining from outside commercial sources?
A: Yes.

Q: Which were undetected at the Hospital at that time by reason of their security arrangements?
A: Yes.

Q: What about drugs?
A: Yes, drugs – again from the investigation – I spent two days with Daggett obviously in an effort to try and get from him what evidence he had of what he was alleging in his document. Again Daggett explained during his interviews that it was just the culture, he knew it because he lived it, he was there and although he may not have seen silver foil being passed from one individual to another and money changing hands, apart from one incident taking place which he said took place in the Lawrence Ward garden, it is more than feasible that drugs are being passed around that Hospital. I am certainly aware through the security department, prior to this Inquiry being set up, of seizures that had been made by the security department.

Q: I suppose cannabis resin being brought in in tobacco tins mixed with tobacco and things of that sort?
A: I have also seen, again detected by the security department, within a container of talcum powder, cannabis resin being concealed within there. Some quite ingenious ways or rather not ingenious, because the security department found out about them.

Q: From your analysis of all that you collated, forgetting whether or not others may have thought it highly unlikely to have reached the necessary standard of proof beyond reasonable doubt according to a criminal trial, of the basic Daggett allegations as to what went on, what is your judgment?
A: Just with respect to the drugs?

Q: Of drugs coming in, of pornographic literature coming in?
A: Again, I am quite happy to say as a result of this Inquiry that drugs were coming into that Hospital undetected, they were being sold and supplied by patient to patient around the Hospital. I have certainly from my interviews with a number of patients where they actually describe they have actually had access to pornographic videotapes, some of which have been described containing children, and that is well documented in my Report, and I have no reason to disbelieve what I have been told. It has in a number of manners been corroborated by other witnesses.

Q: Corroborated, if you like, by uncorroborable evidence.
A: It was corroborated to my satisfaction but not to the satisfaction of the CPS.

Q: In the sense that there was so much smoke there must have been some fire?
A: Absolutely.

Q: To put it in a colloquial way.
A: Yes.

The Chairman: Thank you very much.

Mr Royce: Inspector Marsden, there were actually two matters I just wanted to ask you about in addition. In relation to property that was recovered from patients' rooms, there was a search as we know at the Hospital on 17 January, and various

items were recovered from patients' rooms which were passed on in due course to the police, to you?
A: Yes.

Q: Amongst the items in Mr Hemming's room were a collection of boys' underpants, were there not, 19 pairs of boys' underpants?
A: Yes.

Q: There was also in his room a child's school uniform skirt?
A: That is correct.

Q: In Mr Corrigan's room, there was a ring binder which contained pictures of children in various stages of undress?
A: It did, and what was more disturbing about that piece of evidence was the fact that on a number of the pages, it had actually been compiled carefully over a period of time, it would appear, but in fact you had the top halves of boys which were superimposed on top of what appeared to be adult male genitalia. To me, that had been put together over a long period of time.

Q: At Child A's father's home, you recovered a document detailing Mr Corrigan's index offence, setting out full details of that.
A: Yes.

Q: That was recovered by you as part of the investigation?
A: That is correct, and so much so that we actually contacted the Force that investigated the matter for which Corrigan was detained at Ashworth and we actually contacted them with a view to finding out whether this was in fact an accurate document, and it was. Corrigan later, when I interviewed him, actually admitted that they were the circumstances of his index offence.

The Chairman: Just finally, you heard the evidence of Child A's father this morning?
A: Yes.

Q: You heard his concession that if you take certain of the photographs of the child in isolation, he said they could be of some interest to those with paedophiliac predilections towards young girls?
A: Yes.

Q: I think in the course of your investigations, one of the things you did was to submit photographs of that nature to an expert in this subject for making that point of judgment?
A: That was actually done by the Hospital themselves, but I was aware of that fact.

Q: How consistent was Child A's father's concession with the view of that expert?
A: They were at odds to put it at the least. Certainly the –

Q: His concession, that they could be of interest to a person with paedophiliac nature?
A: Sorry, certainly they would be of interest to somebody with Hemming's background.

Q: Yes.

3.37.3 Having considered the evidence we have heard and the documents we have read we agree entirely with the Inspector's judgments.

3.37.4 He had formed another judgment as well:

Professor Edwards: When you responded to a question from the Chairman about Mr Daggett, you answered the question specifically with regard to pornography. Can I ask the question in a slightly broader sense: what is your judgment about the credibility of Mr Daggett's overall story.

A: At first I was somewhat doubtful. Having spent originally two days where we interviewed him on his original allegations, and again based on my own experience and other patients I have spoken to during the course of this Inquiry, I am quite happy that Steven Daggett is a reliable witness, and I am quite content that certain behaviour towards Child A took place and as the Chairman or Mr Royce put to her father this morning that the child was being groomed, I have no doubt about that. As I say it is amply supported by the property that was found in Hemming's room.

That is also our judgment.

3.38.0 Conclusion

3.38.1 Mr Daggett paints a picture of a ward which was out of control, where staff had lost control and where patients manipulated staff and systems more or less at will. He exaggerates in part. Nonetheless the overall picture is convincing, and confirms much of what earlier inquiries had reported.

3.39.0 Computers in the Future.

3.39.1 Finally, we noted at **3.35.15** that we were so concerned about the highly sophisticated computer equipment possessed by patients on the PDU that we commissioned an independent review of the computer systems at Ashworth Hospital. We were lucky indeed to have the services of Professor Tony Sammes, Professor of Computing and Information Systems Management at the Royal Military College of Science, Shrivenham. Professor Sammes and his colleague Dr Hunter produced a Review of Information Technology Systems at Ashworth Hospital, for us in February 1998, and Professor Sammes later gave evidence. Because of the importance of the Review to Ashworth we decided to provide the Management with the full Review as soon as possible and did so. The actual Review which we circulated to interested parties had material sensitive to the future security of the Hospital edited out and the parties were so informed. We are extremely grateful to Professor Sammes and Dr Hunter for their thorough Report.

3.39.2 Professor Sammes and Dr Hunter found that Ashworth Hospital had a relatively large and advanced computer network with almost 600 inter-connected PCs (personal computers), and 1,350 named staff users hold network accounts. "The system which is largely used for e-mail, word-processing and as an intranet, seems to be configured, using good current commercial practice, to maintain a 24-hour service."

3.39.3 Only two PCs on the Hospital network currently have access to the Internet. They are dial-up connections via modems. The one in the IT Department uses Compuserve as the ISP (Internet Service Provider), the other, in the staff library, uses AOL (America On Line) as the ISP. Apparently it is intended that two additional PCs will be set up with Internet browsing facilities for staff use only.

3.39.4 The first phase of a new software system was due for delivery in January 1998. It is called PACIS (Patient Administration and Clinical Information System), and will operate over the existing Hospital network, will hold clinical notes on patients, and will provide access to some 1,000 users.

3.39.5 The Hospital network is connected to the patient's educational network by means of a "one-way bridge". The education block is within the secure perimeter of the North site, and in it there are a number of computers for use by patients under supervision connected to a separate network with its own server. Those PCs have had their floppy disk drives disabled. Apparently the bridge link to the Hospital network was provided because the education team considered it necessary to obtain rapid on-line support from the IT Department. This view is not shared by the current Head of the Education Department who feels that a visit by IT staff could fulfil its role just as well. The "one-way bridge" itself is located in the education block, and operates by refusing to pass on packets of information from the patient's educational computers to the main Hospital network. However, it seem likely that the bridge will permit packets of information broadcast from the Hospital network to be passed to the patients' educational computers. Physical access by patients to the bridge is considered unlikely because of its proximity to the main entry control desk.

3.39.6 On 24 September 1996, the *Patients' Use of Computers Project Team Report* had been produced within the Hospital, and prior to Mr Daggett's absconsion patients had been allowed to use their own computers on the wards within the limits of that Report. Following the absconsion that facility was removed from patients.

3.39.7 The internal telephone system is controlled by an external exchange computer. A modem system with multiple pass-word protection permits access to the exchange computer and also permits re-programming should it be required. It is shortly to be replaced by a more up to date system, but currently engineers from the company can access and re-program the exchange computer remotely from their help desk and this will also apply to the new system.

3.39.8 Paragraph 4 of the Review is an assessment of the risks of the system. The first is that unauthorized access to clinical information requires a "read" access to the Hospital network which may be achieved electronically either through the direct or indirect use of an authorized working terminal or by subverting the main Hospital network in some way. The Review considers it unlikely that patients could easily gain direct use of an authorized working terminal. The possibility of patients overlooking an authorised working terminal in a ward area is minimised by suitable positioning of the computers. However, it is possible for others to gain access more readily and subsequently pass clinical information to patients, a possibility which will become more serious with the introduction of PACIS.

3.39.9 Professor Sammes noted that subversion of the Hospital network by patients is conceivable. Operational data is broadcast in packets of information throughout the entire Hospital network, and it is, theoretically, possible to read off any packets from any part of the network. Normally, terminals will only access information which matches their internal wired-in address, but software can be written so as to read all information passing over the network. Access to cabling in the wards should therefore be protected, and it is. The authors of the Review, however, suspect that the one-way bridge between the educational computers and the main Hospital network does not block incoming packets, and if that is right, then it would be possible to load software on to the educational computers that monitored all the Hospital network's information. There is also another possible way of accessing the Hospital network: the one-way bridge could be subverted by changing the internal wired-in address in a patient's educational computer. This could most easily be done by connecting the computer via a parallel port ethernet device.

3.39.10 Professor Sammes considered that there was a real risk of subverting the main Hospital network while the one-way bridge remained in place. That risk was not justified by any need for rapid on-line IT support, particularly since there was a reasonable alternative of a member of the IT staff being called in. We agree that the one-way bridge should be removed.

3.39.11 He continued: "Because of the nature and complexity of the PACIS system, it would be wise to have a full security audit carried out by an outside agency before the system is brought into use." We agree that such an audit should be done.

3.39.12 Professor Sammes also considered that the PACIS system would increase the level of risk of subverting the Hospital network by the comprehensive and sensitive information that is to be held about every patient. "For this reason a System Security Policy should be written for PACIS and software changes should be rigorously controlled through a formal Change Control Board. In addition all printed outputs from the system should carry user and session codes embedded in the documents to permit subsequent tracing of the originators." We agree this should be done.

3.39.13 In so far as access by patients to illegal and paedophile material is concerned, it is thought the most likely route is via visitors bringing in floppy disks, ZIP disks, portable hard drives or CD-ROMs which up to now the patients have been allowed to have. The authors say that the current policy of such items being taken only if passed through the IT Department for checking may be difficult to enforce without infringing the civil liberties of visitors. We agree with much of what they say in their Report but not this. If you want to travel by air, you may be required to submit to searches at Airports. If you want to visit a prisoner in prison or a patient in a High Security Hospital you should be prepared to submit to a search if requested to do so. If you refuse to be searched at an Airport then you do not fly. If you refuse to be searched at a prison or High Security Hospital then you do not visit. There is no difference.

3.39.14 No doubt someone will claim it is an infringement of civil liberty, but the security of society is of paramount importance. As a matter of general common sense, now supported by the judgments in the Judicial Review we have discussed at length above, we can see no reason why searching of visitors and their belongings should not be carried out if they want to enter the Hospital to visit a patient. Of course, they cannot be forced to be searched, but if they refuse to be searched, then, in our judgment, they can and should be refused entry.

3.39.15 As we recommended above at 2.12.32 visitors should be searched. Potential visitors should be informed that they may be asked to be searched and if they refuse then they will not be permitted to enter. Notices to this effect should be clearly displayed at the entrance to the Hospital also.

3.39.16 Although we recommend a policy of searching in any event because computer materials are not the only contraband to be considered, we also deal with the alternative approach suggested in the Review. It is to deny patients access to any devices that can use floppy disks, Zip disks [we would add also Zip drives], portable hard drives and CD-ROMs. As the Review says, "This is not to say that patients are denied access to computer equipment, just that the computer equipment with which they are provided has no means by which floppy disks, Zip disks, portable hard drives or CD-ROMs can be attached. The opportunity for copying, distributing or viewing illegal material is then much reduced."

3.39.17 How this could be achieved is set out in paragraph 4.2.3 of the Review. "This policy could be implemented by prohibiting all patients' own computers and providing, from Hospital resources, a separate network of patients' ward computers, similar to the patients' educational network. All data and software would be down loaded to the patients' ward computers from a staff controlled server. Acceptable personal material that had been approved by the IT Department could be mounted on the server. No peripheral devices (other than the keyboard and display) of any kind would be permitted on the patients' computers, and all printing would be done through a central print server. In order to help defray running costs and to inhibit demands for all patients to have ward computers, a nominal hire charge might be made."

Recommendation 33 **3.39.18 We recommend that patients should only be allowed adapted computers connected to a patients' server in their rooms.**

3.39.19 The Review deals with the Internet, which is the most accessible source of illegal material and which is used by paedophiles both to distribute material and to make contacts with children. "It is very difficult to monitor or control its use and the risk of abuse is high if it is made available to patients. The main means of access to the Internet is via a modem and an outside telephone line. To limit such access, no modem should be permitted in ward areas and access to external telephone lines should be carefully monitored by staff." The authors noted that there was a telephone point in the ward visitor's room which would normally be set for internal access only. It is conceivable that the exchange computer could be re-programmed from anywhere in the internal or external telephone network, by a telephone engineer or someone who knows the engineer's passwords, to give outside access to such a point. "This would seem to be an unnecessary risk and the policy of permitting external telephone engineers to control the exchange unchecked should be re-considered. A simple confidence check could be made regularly by instructing the exchange computer to print a list of all telephone points that have outside line access and comparing that list with an authorised list."

We agree with those views.

Recommendation 34

3.39.20 We recommend:
(i) No modems whether external or internal should be permitted in ward areas.
(ii) Patients' access to telephones should be limited to:

a. Telephone numbers on the list of the patient's list of approved numbers.
b. All telephone calls by patients should be carefully monitored, except privileged calls, such as those to legal advisers, in which cases the number should be dialled by a member of staff who, having done so ,should retire out of ear-shot, but maintain observation to ensure no other number is dialled.
c. Telephone points in ward visitors' rooms should be removed.
d. Permitting external telephone engineers to control the Hospital's telephone exchange should be reconsidered.

3.39.21 In paragraph 4.2.6 Professor Sammes and Dr Hunter note "it is also possible to access the Internet using a mobile phone and a personal organizer such as the Psion series. Mobile phones should be banned as should all electronic personal organizers, palm-top computers, hand-helds and laptops. [We also add pagers to this list as, in his evidence, Professor Sammes agreed]. In addition to providing potential access to the Internet, many of these devices can act as computer terminals on the Hospital networks and may be used as display devices for illegal material."

Recommendation 35

3.39.22 We recommend that patients are not allowed to have in the Hospital: mobile telephones, personal organisers, palm top computers, hand-helds, laptop computers and pagers.

3.39.23 The authors considered other ways of achieving unauthorised access to information. Planted listening devices is one such means, and the Report makes recommendations to combat that risk. They looked at the educational electronic workshops to assess the risk of scanners, listening devices or modern microprocessor devices being built covertly. The technology taught there and the facilities available were adequate for building simple scanners and listening devices, but it was considered unlikely that such devices could be built without the workshop staff becoming aware. Currently the technology taught and the facilities available would not support the covert development of modern microprocessor based devices.

3.39.24 The authors saw the main physical security risk to the Hospital arising from the computer systems as being through the telephone exchange computer as we have already discussed and they recommended that the policy of allowing external telephone engineers to control the exchange unchecked should be reconsidered. We agree.

3.39.25 In the Review some general observations are also made.

1. The IT team was found to be thoroughly competent, professional and well led, but by comparison with IT teams for similar levels of responsibility, particularly with the introduction of PACIS and the additional security needs of such a system, the authors considered the grade of the team leader to be on the low side. From the security point of view it was essential to retain good staff.

2. The Hospital Board should consider putting in place an over-arching Information Systems Strategy for the Hospital as a whole tied in with a comprehensive Security Strategy.

3. System Security Policies should be written for each new computer based system that has security implications. Currently this applied to the proposed gate management system.

4. The increasing importance of IT to clinical and Hospital management and the security implications of its use needed to be fully understood by all staff. Programmes for awareness training, core training and continuous professional development training should all incorporate IT and security modules. In addition, a **"Champion"** for these issues should be established at Board level.

3.39.26 In the course of his evidence Professor Sammes enlarged on some aspects of the Review.

1. The problem with the Hospital network was the intra-net. Packages of information are sent to all terminals and it is the terminal which prevents the packages from entering its actual processor. "There is nothing to prevent a packet snoop piece of software from looking at everything going on the network, and such software is not difficult to come by."

2. He was asked about the internal (October 1996) Report referred to in **3.39.6** above which said that the use of the Internet in education was something that needed thinking about for patients. He repeated his view that it was extremely difficult, almost impossible, to control. So-called "nanny software" can limit access to particular sites, but that software itself can be subverted by someone with computer knowledge. His recommended approach would be to down load educational or other approved sites to the local patients' intra-net for patients' use without them having access to the Internet itself.

3. He was concerned with the recommendation in that Report that the PCT should decide who should have computer systems. PCTs would not have the expertise to assess the risks associated with particular computer systems which was why they recommended the staff-controlled server system set out in the Report.

4. He had visited wards where patients had computers in their rooms. ". . . it would be very difficult to see whether a patient was misusing a system without having continual observation of the patient and the system for the whole time."

5. The Report's suggestion that patients should be allowed to use computers on the basis of a contract which if knowingly flouted would result in the confiscation of the

computer was not in his view wise. He very much doubted if PCTs would have the expertise to know if the contract was being flouted.

6. He disagreed with the Report's statement that "suitable peripherals and software should include CD-ROM and extra disk drives as being acceptable". They would permit access to illegal material brought in by visitors on CD-ROMs or floppy disks.

7. He did not consider the Report's statement that when a patient's computer arrived on a ward the staff should check it to be a practical solution. They would not have the expertise to check peripheral devices, particularly cards such as PCMICA cards. Encripted material might be on the hard drives. Neither did he agree with the proposal that if files on a patient's computer were password protected, or suspected to be so protected, failure to divulge the pass word would be considered a breach of the policy. "I think it would be possible to hide information even from the IT department, and I did not see any particular tools in the IT department which would enable information to be found if it had been hidden in what is known as the master boot record."

3.39.27 Junior Counsel to the Inquiry, Mr Blair, pursued the practical issues involved in simply checking computer disks:

Mr Blair: In terms of disks themselves, can I simply put some examples and ask for your observations? Mr Paterson who was a security man at the Hospital wrote a memo in July 1996, worried about a patient having more than 500 computer disks. Another example . . . SB [Booth] had 139 and complained if any staff wanted to look at them, and Patient Q, when Lawrence Ward was searched in January 1997, on my calculation, had 1,321 floppy disks in his room. What sort of time would be involved in checking that sort of volume of material for illicit . . . ?
A: I would suggest to check a single floppy disk adequately might take as much as half an hour, to do a single disk, to do it adequately . . . If one is trying to ensure that there is no illegal material, it is not enough just to note the name of the file and the type of the file . . . It is necessary therefore to examine every file on the disk.

8. One of the consequences of the system suggested in the Report was that printing would have to be done centrally rather than by connecting a printer to an individual's parallel port which would not be a device available to patients. It concerns private correspondence which a patient might not want to print in such a way. There was no way round this. Such letters or other confidential documents would have to be hand-written or typed on a typewriter. **In our judgment this is a necessary price to pay for the degree of security which the suggested system provides.**

9. He saw no problem in so far as games were concerned, and one can well understand patients having an interest in playing games on their computers. A cassette holder of CD-ROMs could be loaded on the central server for particular games and down loaded to patients' computers.

10. Later in his evidence he recommended that pagers should not be permitted either.

11. He was asked about the need of an IT champion and what he meant by that:

A: In order to implement an effective information and security policy, the process needs to come from Board level and there should be an information system strategy which is fully endorsed and supported by the Board. At the same time, in order to ensure that IT and . . . the problems associated with IT and security are properly recognized and treated throughout the Hospital, it is strongly recommended that there is a member of the Board whose special concern is that of IT, and therefore acts as the IT champion for the Hospital.

Q: What are the dangers if there is not someone doing that?
A: It is that IT can become marginalised and it is also possible then that the IT department becomes disillusioned, perhaps, and perhaps not as effective as it should be, and then there is a risk of losing the quality of staff that is essential for an organisation which is putting so much dependency on its IT systems.

12. On behalf of the Hospital Mr Thorold asked Professor Sammes what led him to a recommendation that would remove all of these facilities from every patient.

A: I would claim, sir, that the proposal does not remove the facilities from the patient but it permits the access to the information via a central server. It does not deny access to the information or to the software. If that software is approved by the IT department, it can be loaded onto the central server as can any of the personal files.

13. We have referred above to the drawback so far as personal and private correspondence is concerned, and Mr Thorold re-visited that topic. The Professor was less concerned about a printer provided that all the rest of the system was put in place. He said that each ward could have a print server to which patients' computers could down load hard copy but they would not be able to keep a copy in a file on the hard disk. He also agreed that "given the control over the illegal material I do not see that there would be a problem in letting patients have a printer."

Recommendation 36 **3.39.28 We recommend that before patients are allowed to have personal computer printers, it is demonstrated that the parallel port to which such a printer must be connected could not also be used for unacceptable devices.**

3.39.29 This completes our review of evidence and documents for the purpose of reporting on Part 1 of our Terms of reference which we do in Part Five.

PART 4 The professions

4.1.0 Introduction

4.1.1 Having recounted the litany of failures of the PDU at Ashworth Hospital very serious questions must be asked about each of the professions. We have made a number of highly critical comments about individual professionals working on the Unit. In this part of our Report we discuss each of the main professions operating within the PDU and make a number of general comments. We also comment on multi-disciplinary working on the Unit.

4.1.2 In doing so we are aware that it is easy to criticize with hindsight and also to focus on the negative. As part of our work we thought it important to get an independent view on the PDU, to give us a sense of how the Unit was functioning some time after the events on Lawrence Ward. We heard much about the problems of the Unit in the past; but what were its strengths and weaknesses now? Was it capable of doing the job it had set out to do?

4.1.3 We therefore asked a team of three independent clinicians to review the current patient care and staffing arrangements of the PDU. Dr Adrian Grounds, University Lecturer in Forensic Psychiatry at Cambridge University, led the team, assisted by Mr Tony Hillis, Director of Nursing Services at Reaside Clinic and Ms Lyn Suddards, Clinical Nurse Manager at the Henderson Hospital. Both Dr Grounds and Ms Suddards later gave oral evidence to us. We discuss their findings below. We are most grateful to Dr Grounds, Mr Hillis and Ms Suddards for their careful work.

4.1.4 We also had the advantage of a second independent assessment Report, this time commissioned by Ashworth Hospital itself, entitled *Independent Evaluation and Review of the Quality of Nursing Care Provision in the Personality Disorder Unit.* This was undertaken by Professor David Sines from the University of Ulster. Professor Sines had in fact given evidence to the Blom-Cooper Inquiry in 1992, so he was able to benchmark changes over the last five years. He carried out his assessment not long before our own assessment team visited the PDU.

4.1.5 We then turn to the individual professions, focusing on the doctors first and foremost. We make no apologies for this. The legal status of the RMOs and the resulting leadership position they hold within the PCT inevitably puts doctors to the fore, even when dealing with patients whose care calls for predominantly psychological methods. The weakness of a number of the PCTs in the PDU forces us to question whether the deficit in medical leadership identified by Sir Louis and his team in 1992 has been addressed. We also reflect on whether the existing RMO framework is right, examining whether an appropriately trained and experienced psychologist would be a better person to take on the "Responsible Officer" position.

4.1.6 We also discuss the nurses at Ashworth. The only profession in 24-hour contact with patients, they are uniquely placed to provide therapy in a secure environment. They are also the most vulnerable to the manipulative and disruptive behaviour exhibited by many severely personality disordered patients. Several issues were raised by the RCN and by UNISON as being of particular concern to nurses at Ashworth, notably the position of bank nurses and 24-hour care. We comment on these and other issues below.

4.1.7 More briefly we also comment on two other groups of professionals, namely social workers and psychologists.

4.1.8 Multi-disciplinary working, or the lack of it, has been a prominent theme of inquiry reports and we make some comments on this.

4.1.9 To complete the picture we offer a few thoughts on "social therapists" and what role they might play in the future care and management of severely personality disordered individuals.

4.2.0 The Assessment Visit

Terms of Reference

4.2.1 The team's remit was to carry-out a fact-finding visit to the PDU, concentrating on the following areas:

(i) the philosophy of care in the Personality Disorder Unit and its clinical leadership;

(ii) staffing levels, selection, gender mix and training;

(iii) the role of different professional groups in clinical teams; and

(iv) the regimes, activities, treatments and care plans for patients.

4.2.2 The team spent a week in the Hospital in December 1997, visiting the wards both during the day and at night, attending clinical meetings, reviewing records and interviewing staff and patients using a semi-structured questionnaire. 45 of the 99 patients residing on the Unit at the time of the visit agreed to be interviewed. Dr Grounds told us it was difficult to explain why some patients had agreed to be interviewed and others had not; he and his colleagues had not detected any systematic bias in the sample. 52 out of 149 ward-based staff were interviewed, seven consultants, the Acting Clinical Manager of the Unit, the Chief Executive and others.

The Patients

4.2.3 A substantial proportion of patients had committed serious sexual offences and primarily had psychosexual disorders. Some patients had previously been in other Special Hospitals before their admission to Ashworth. Dr Grounds described the patient group as very heterogeneous; many had profoundly abnormal personalities where psychosexual pathology was prominent. He said they were a distinctive group:

> "Yes, the Ashworth group are rather distinctive. They are a surprisingly old group with many years of Special Hospital experience, many of them, and with a high proportion of serious sexual offenders among them."

4.2.4 These patients required sophisticated programmes to address their disorders of personality so as to reduce the risk of them reoffending. For many the likelihood was that they would remain most of their remaining years in a secure environment, though Dr Grounds told us that in some cases once active treatment was offered it was surprising what progress a patient might make. He also stressed that even in the most apparently hopeless cases it was very important to hold out the possibility of progress, otherwise life became very difficult for patients and staff. The main impression from the team's visit was that in many cases not enough had been tried in a coherent, systematic way, and that resources limited what could be done.

4.2.5 Dr Grounds stressed that, for all their faults Special Hospitals offered an environment within which individual psychological work could be carried out, where research could be taken forward and where people with very fragile personalities could cope. Prison by contrast was ill-equipped to cope in all three of these areas. Similarly in many cases individuals were far more likely to reveal aspects of their offending behaviour in a hospital rather than a prison setting.

4.2.6 Professor Edwards put it to Dr Grounds that the mix of patients on the ward should be improved so that patients with little hope of further progress might not undermine the treatment prospects of other patients who might have just been admitted. Dr Grounds was sceptical; the things that concerned patients about their fellow-patients were not radically different views of treatment but other aspects, eg how intimidating they were, how disturbed, and so forth.

Functional Organisation of the Wards

4.2.7 Dr Grounds told us that the Unit was supposed to work according to a three stage model in which individual wards were allocated different broad functions. Within this model, Ruskin and Newman Wards were seen as focusing on promoting "structured living". This would include the control of disruptive behaviour and the fostering of consistent programmes of activity and work. The second stage (Owen and Macaulay Wards) focused on social learning, and would include offence orientated work and group and therapeutic community approaches. The third stage concentrated on resocialisation. The primary location for the resocialisation work was planned to be a new facility, the Wordsworth Project, a 16-bedded unit on the East Site of the Hospital which would use a social therapy model.

4.2.8 In practice, however, the work and regimes of the wards did not perfectly reflect this tripartite model for a number of reasons. The wards had different histories, cultures, and mixed patient groups; at the time of the visit, Lawrence Ward had been designated as a "reassessment ward" for patients identified as requiring a new, thorough, multi-disciplinary reassessment for the Home Office; the Wordsworth Unit was still being planned and Macaulay Ward was effectively operating as "parole ward"; and lastly, in the summer of 1997 the PDU wards had been reduced from six to five when Shelley Ward was removed from the Unit to become a Decant Ward to facilitate refurbishment elsewhere in the Hospital. Shelley Ward had acted as an admission and a high dependency ward for the PDU and its closure effectively left the PDU without an admission facility and closed to new admissions for an indefinite period. Dr Grounds told us that this decision had been demoralizing to staff. In our view, it is vitally important to have a separate assessment facility.

4.2.9 Dr Grounds and his team noted that most staff appeared to know how their ward related to other wards on the Unit, although this was not the case on Lawrence Ward, where there was continuing uncertainty as to the future purpose of the ward. There were also clear differences between the wards in their culture and atmosphere. For example, Ruskin Ward was felt to be relatively lacking in a therapeutic atmosphere, whereas Owen Ward was a more pleasant environment and there was a collaborative atmosphere with more interaction between staff and patients.

Ward Management

4.2.10 Each ward on the PDU had a Ward Manager. Nursing staff were split into three teams, each with its own team leader responsible for the delivery of nursing care and treatment within the care plan which reflected the agreed ward philosophy and function. The possible development of three separate and distinct team approaches within a ward was largely, but not wholly, avoided through strong leadership at Ward Management level and interteam communication through staff working within other shifts from time to time. Generally ward staff did not consider that there were significant differences of approach between the three teams that covered the ward on different shifts. Patients, however, were more aware of differences of atmosphere and approach, but had found ways of accommodating to this; for example, if they wished to talk about a difficulty they would wait until the shift they felt most comfortable with came on duty. Dr Grounds and his colleagues had felt there was scope for better communication and closer liaison between the three shifts.

4.2.11 Morale was reasonable in light of the events of the recent past. The staff were resilient and were resigned to constantly changing senior managerial arrangements. Dr Grounds noted that the Unit was on its fourth clinical manager in three years; changes at that level were expected and seen as remote from the life on the ward and delivery of care to patients. Many of the senior managers were rarely seen on the wards. Support from more senior managers was regarded as a pleasant surprise. Dr Grounds agreed with Mr Daniels' suggestion that this meant the main source of support was the PCT, a dangerous situation if the PCT was a dysfunctional one. He also noted that the feeling that senior managers were remote reflected the size of the Hospital and the physical remoteness of the administrative headquarters outside the wall. The team could not comment directly on the adequacy or otherwise of management at the Hospital, but that was the clear feeling on the wards.

4.2.12 Dr Grounds and his colleagues noted the moves to reassert central control over policy; whilst the need to do this was almost universally accepted by staff and patients alike, there was a concern about policies becoming too inflexible and thereby hindering therapeutic activities. For example, the new rules required that the night stations near the patients bedrooms were to be manned by two staff at all times, thereby reducing the availability of staff for therapeutic activity. Dr Grounds noted that there was a recognition that greater flexibility might be needed in the light of experience.

Staff Recruitment and Training

4.2.13 It was generally the case that the Ward Managers and Team Leaders had been specifically recruited to work on the PDU, together with a minority of other nursing staff. Most nurses, however, had been allocated to the PDU from within Ashworth, either through transfers or because their ward became designated as belonging to the PDU. Their enthusiasm for working on the Unit varied.

4.2.14 Most nursing staff referred to the Core Competencies Course designed by the Senior Clinical Nurse as the only specific training they had received in relation to managing patients with personality disorder. Dr Grounds noted that staff had commented frequently on the lack of preparation and training for work on the Unit. The sense that the Unit had been set up too quickly came across strongly from many staff.

Clinical Leadership and the Contribution of Different Professional Groups

4.2.15 There was a strong sense on the wards that clinical leadership emanated from the Ward Manager and Team Leaders. This was the team's impression too. The ward staff generally did not see clinical leadership as emanating from the RMOs, and many expressed a desire for a greater degree of medical input. Dr Grounds noted that whilst the Clinical Nurse Manager had put much effort into trying to formulate a model of practice for the Unit and train people in core competencies, the RMOs had been little involved in taking this work forward. He added that the RMOs' administrative workload, in any case, made it difficult for them to be very involved. There were only two RMOs devoted to the PDU at the time, where five or six were needed. Relatively little time was spent by the RMOs in trying to understand the psychological lives of patients. The new consultants who had been attracted to the Hospital worked on the Mental Illness side; relatively speaking it was the older consultants who had been in the Hospital for a long time who gravitated towards the PDU. At the time of the visit very good work by nurses and psychologists was compensating for the lack of equivalently good medical input.

4.2.16 Dr Grounds stressed the importance of psychiatrists being more involved in the patients' care and treatment. The good work being done by the nurses and psychologists needed to be put in the context of a thorough psychiatric assessment of the patient's disorder and its relation to the offending:

> "It is the psychiatrists who must take the lead in developing that understanding, developing that clinical assessment. It sets the framework within which others work."

4.2.17 The clinical psychology contributions to assessment and treatment were highly valued by ward staff, but recognised to be overstretched and insufficient. Overall the therapeutic culture of the wards appeared to be shaped by the senior nursing staff, supplemented by systematic contributions from clinical psychologists.

Staff perceptions of Treatability and Therapeutic Work

4.2.18 There was a widespread view among staff and patients that there were therapeutic needs that were not being met, notwithstanding the fact that more patients were attending treatment groups than in previous years.

4.2.19 The experience of clinical supervision was highly variable amongst ward nursing staff. Some had arrangements for supervision that they valued, but it was our impression that supervision was arranged on a personal, *ad hoc* basis, rather than systematically organised. Ward staff commonly thought that the stress of working with a highly disturbed patient group, untrained, and with little formal supervision, was largely unrecognised.

4.2.20 In relation to the Committee of Inquiry, the pervasive message from ward staff was that they were involved in a worthwhile and beneficial enterprise on the Personality Disorder Unit. They wanted support and time. The concept of the PDU had taken time to be understood and implemented; the Unit needed an opportunity to consolidate and develop a stable tradition.

4.2.21 There was a widely held view that the reforms that had followed the Inquiry chaired by Sir Louis Blom-Cooper QC, had been correct in principle, but implemented too quickly and in a way that led to disempowerment and intimidation of staff. There had now been a degree of recovery of confidence and control. In the light of this, the view was expressed that, if a future agenda of change was recommended by the Committee of Inquiry, ward staff would need to be given time and the process of change would need to be carefully managed.

Patient Timetables, Activities and Treatment

4.2.22 The great majority of patients had daily timetables of structured activities including work, education, and sports. A small number of patients were fully employed on the wards with domestic and cleaning duties. Most patients could attend social events off the ward in the evenings. A minority did not receive outside visits.

4.2.23 The patients' views of the Hospital as a place to live varied from being positive to vehemently negative. In some cases the negative views were attributed to the recently tightened security measures. Information was systematically collected on the extent to which patients were engaged in specific forms of treatment on all five PDU wards. A considerable number were awaiting forms of group therapy. Dr Grounds noted that the standard of clinical assessment was good, but shortages of clinical psychologists in particular meant frustrating delays in treatment.

4.2.24 There was a discrepancy between the positive philosophies of treatment espoused by the nursing staff, and the patients' descriptions of how they experienced their Patient Care Teams. The majority of patients had predominantly negative views about their experience of care and treatment, describing a sense of mistrust, decisions being made without consultation, and staff being unavailable or lacking time. Patients also expressed concern about delays to their progress when they had changes of RMO. But there was a desire for an opportunity to continue with treatment, and they also agreed that the reforming agendas of the past had been too quick and destabilising. Some patients, however, were wholly negative about the Hospital.

Conclusions

4.2.25 Dr Grounds and his team stressed that the psychiatric care and management of the patients on the PDU at Ashworth Hospital was an exceptionally challenging task, given the particular characteristics of the patient group. Despite the serious incidents of recent years, the rapid changes of management and organisation, and our own Inquiry, the quality and morale of staff on the PDU was high. The nurses were committed, enthusiastic and realistic; clearly much had been learnt through the traumatic events of recent years, resulting in high quality ward-based nursing leadership. There appeared to be a sound balance between therapy and control. The criticisms made in the 1995 HAS Report *With Care in Mind Secure* of staff insecurity and the lack of a coherent treatment model on the PDU no longer applied. Dr Grounds commented:

> "One thing we do know about the treatment of patients of this kind in Special Hospitals is that the cornerstone of the therapeutic endeavour is the quality of your nursing staff and the support they give to the therapeutic endeavours, and if that is not in place you can do very little. In Ashworth it is in place."

4.2.26 In relation to treatment, the contributions to assessment and to individual and group treatment by clinical psychologists were clearly excellent and highly valued. This input ideally needed to be increased.

4.2.27 Three matters concerned the team however. First, the treatment and management of individual patients did not seem to be underpinned by thorough, comprehensive psychiatric assessment of the nature and origins of their psychopathology. The focus of clinical discussion and decision-making was predominantly on social behaviour and administrative and risk issues, rather than on seeking a psychological understanding of the patient. Dr Grounds agreed that the psychiatric input was clearly inadequate, although other clinicians were compensating for this lack. Whilst the assessment was good, there were shortcomings in the application of those assessments to help understand the offending behaviour and to design an appropriate treatment programme:

> ". . . what is needed is to focus on a clear and shared understanding of the patients' psychopathology, the reasons for their offending, psychologically, and to keep those in mind as targets of treatment and to monitor how treatment progresses."

4.2.28 Second, arrangements for the clinical supervision of ward-based staff did not appear to be sufficiently systematic and well organised. Such supervision is particularly important in the context of work with personality disordered patients.

4.2.29 Third, the Unit lacked highly experienced psychodynamic contributions to the assessment and treatment of its patients. This would compliment the other approaches to assessment and would help a vigilant awareness of the depth of patients' psychopathology.

4.2.30 Dr Grounds recognized major shortcomings in terms of a patient mix that was still unsatisfactory, a shortage of psychiatric input, a shortage of clinical psychology input, long delays in providing treatments and long-standing problems in recruiting doctors.Yet overall the team argued that the work of the PDU at Ashworth Hospital should be supported. This conclusion was reached not only for the pragmatic reason that there was a substantial population of patients who would have to remain on the Unit. More positively, it was because of the substantial expertise, commitment and good judgement that had developed amongst existing staff.

4.2.31 If the Hospital were to continue to provide a specialist service for patients with psychopathic disorder, such a service might have to be justified by demonstrating that it was providing benefits that other services could not deliver. For example, therapeutic community approaches and sex offender treatment programmes could be replicated in the Prison Service. Two distinctive features that Ashworth Hospital could further develop, and which would not be provided in the Prison Service, would be programmes of individual psychotherapeutic work, and a substantive academic research base in relation to psychopathic disorder.

4.2.32 Finally, the team stressed that if the Committee of Inquiry in due course recommended substantive changes to the life of the Hospital, the experience of recent years indicated that any agenda of change should be carefully paced and managed so as not to be destabilising or counterproductive in its effects.

4.2.33 We take the comments of Dr Grounds and colleagues extremely seriously. We are gratified that the nurses on the PDU in particular have developed in expertise and are providing a better service. In the short term the Unit is functioning. However, we remain convinced that in the longer term the situation of the PDU is unsustainable. It has too many patients, the wards are too big, the patient mix is wrong and there is still no credible medical leadership. In Part Seven we call for the closure of Ashworth; we recognize the dangers in such a step but are convinced the Hospital itself is too corrupted ever to provide a satisfactory quality of service. That said, it is essential that the skills and hard-won experience of the staff working on the PDU at Ashworth are preserved in new services.

4.3.0 Professor Sines' Assessment Visit

4.3.1 Professor Sines told us that over the five or so years since his work for the Blom-Cooper Inquiry the culture of nursing had definitely changed from a custodial one to one of client-focused care. He was generally complimentary about the nursing staff and described the overall standard of care on the Unit as commendable. There was particular praise for Mr Moran and his staff on Owen Ward.

4.3.2 Professor Sines praised nurses for the strides they had made. But he identified a number of problems in implementing a radical post-inquiry action plan in a relatively short period of time. The priority status given to patient empowerment had given rise to a major source of conflict for nurses and was an often quoted reason for the loss of control experienced by staff during the Owen and Lawrence Ward incidents. Staff appeared to be confused about the balance between their security and therapeutic roles.

4.3.3 The empowerment of patients was seen as a sharp contrast to the lack of empowerment of nurses. Staff reported to Professor Sines they had been discouraged from engaging in therapeutic practices during the past two years. There was a feeling of low status amongst Ward Managers and the nursing work force.

4.3.4 This was borne out by evidence given by Patient A:

> "Basically they [nurses] need a greater voice. They need people to take them seriously and to listen to what they have to say. After all, the nursing staff are the people that are with us 24 hours of the day, so it would seem logical that they have a larger or greater say than, say the social worker for instance who only sees you perhaps once a year."

4.3.5 Professor Sines identified serious problems with the management of the Unit. The relatively frequent changes in Clinical Director had left staff confused. There was a lack of face-to-face communication and an over-reliance on e-mail. He was told that managers were rarely to be seen on the wards. Whilst there were lots of good ideas in evidence, no one person appeared to be in charge of a coherent implementation strategy. Staff were filling the leadership void with their own definitions of policy.

4.3.6 Unsurprisingly therefore the quality and standards of care within the PDU were variable. Some wards were working well but there was very little apparent sharing of good practice. No one was pulling the work of the wards all together. Although there were patches of clinical excellence, they were taking place in a management vacuum. Professor Sines argued that Ward Managers were not close enough to decision-making: there were too many layers between them and the Chief Executive.

4.3.7 Under the heading "Management and Leadership", Professor Sines described "the provisions of a dysfunctional vertical management system that had effectively placed three levels of accountability between the Ward Manager and the Ashworth Hospital Authority". He described Ward Managers as being confused with regard to the changes in the management structure of the Hospital. Professor Sines broadened this issue when he gave evidence:

> ". . . another complex issue here was the actual allocation of responsibility to some of those senior managers. Their own tasks were not clearly defined in my view, or they were too broad to be able to discharge the functions I would expect, for example, of an Executive Nurse or others; so the separation of managerial accountability, which can work in a very well-calibrated system, but on this occasion I think there was a definite systems failure."

4.3.8 Under the heading Clinical Practice, Professor Sines felt a positive development had been the appointment of Senior Clinical Nurse Managers within the PDU. He felt that they had, alongside advanced Nurse Practitioners, made a significant impact on the provision of skilled nursing care to PDU patients.

4.3.9 These two assessment Reports demonstrate that the nurses on the PDU have made real progress in caring for and managing this very difficult group. However, care standards are still very patchy; the RMOs are conspicuous by their absence; the Unit is not configured properly to deliver high quality care; and the nurses are proceeding in a management vacuum, unsupported by those above them. It is an untenable situation.

4.4.0 The Doctors

4.4.1 We heard a good deal of evidence about the competence and performance of the doctors at Ashworth Hospital. The patients we heard had very mixed views. Whilst some were positive about the treatment they had received at Ashworth, there were complaints that RMOs were 'never there', that they changed frequently, that they resisted recommending a discharge to MHRTs even when they admitted they could do nothing positive in hospital. We were struck by the evidence of one patient, Patient C, who told us that his RMOs had made it quite clear that they did not know what to do with him.

4.4.2 We heard from Dr John Reed, former Senior Principal Medical Officer within the Department of Health and Chairman of the Reed Committee on Mentally Disordered Offenders. Dr Reed talked frankly about the problems of recruiting good doctors into the High Security Hospitals. In this setting consultants were "much constrained in making independent decisions about their patients including decisions about admission."

4.4.3 Dr Reed explained that forensic psychiatry was a specialty in which demand exceeded supply and the best doctors found their way into the regional forensic services which were a more attractive place to work. There had developed what Dr Reed described as a:

> "self-reinforcing circle of unattractive posts leading to less able candidates being appointed, leading to the hospitals being even less attractive places to work."

Mrs Nelson, the Chairman of the SHSA from 1993, referred to the Special Hospitals as a "clinical backwater".

4.4.4 The problem of medical leadership was a key weakness identified by Sir Louis Blom-Cooper and his recommendation 44 called on the SHSA to tackle the problem. We saw a minute dating from July 1992 written by Dr Dilys Jones, then a Senior Medical Officer of the Department of Health in which she commented that:

> **"the 'villains of the piece' do not come out as primarily the POA, but the weak management (in general/medical and nursing terms). There is no effectual management support, the professional disciplines are fragmented and there is no leadership. No sense of purpose (certainly not therapeutic purpose) comes through at all. There is no staff structure".**

Later in the same minute she wrote that medical leadership was:

> **"really non-existent at the Ashworth site. Many consultants had negative and anti-therapeutic attitudes and a tendency to collude with the prevailing culture, probably as a means of survival."**

4.4.5 Some of these doctors are still in post.

4.4.6 Perhaps the most compelling evidence of the inadequacy of the doctors came in a note made by Dr Reed of a telephone conversation he had had with Professor Pamela Taylor, at that time Head of Medical Services at the SHSA, about the various doctors at Ashworth. We should say that Professor Taylor in her evidence told us that she had never seen the note, far less agreed with it, and said "it fits in part only with what I believe to have been my views at the time, but certainly would be my views now". That said, we accept Dr Reed's note as an accurate record of the conversation.

4.4.7 In this conversation Professor Taylor commented on the Ashworth consultants as follows:

> Doctor 1: moderately capable but with a serious alcohol problem which they were keeping an eye on.
>
> Doctor 2: moderately capable but feeble.
>
> Doctor 3: appalling. Action would have to be taken.
>
> Doctor 4: never there and had an appalling record of not meeting deadlines; a decent man out of his depth.
>
> Doctor 5: weak. Lacking in leadership and inclining as the wind blows.
>
> Doctor 6: made very poor provision for patients on the ward. Did not appear to recognize many of their needs.
>
> Doctor 7: lazy.
>
> Doctor 8: unstable and not clinically good.

There were three competent doctors.

4.4.8 We thought hard about taking this evidence in public (and repeating it here) as some of these clinicians are still treating patients at Ashworth. We are aware that many of the patients followed our hearings very closely. On balance we concluded that the situation was so bad that it had to be exposed.

4.4.9 Having heard Professor Taylor's then views on the doctors Dr Reed told us he thought she intended to conduct a rigorous review of the doctors' working patterns and the need for additional training and support for the consultants at Ashworth. Professor Taylor certainly saw a number of the consultants, and having done so wrote letters to two of them, which she copied to other people including Dr Reed. He than wrote a minute to Mr Jewesbury with copies of the two letters she had sent. In the minute he said:

> "I enclose copies of letters from Dr Taylor to [two of the doctors concerned]. I must admit I find it hard to see consistency between these summaries and the picture painted by the enquiry and by Dr Taylor herself in her regular meetings with me."

4.4.10 Dr Reed said he was sure he discussed the apparent change of view with Professor Taylor when they next met. He was asked whether she had said she had changed her mind about these doctors, or whether she had decided nothing could be done. He replied:

> "I think more the first, although a combination of the two, because there certainly is a limited amount that could be done, because where do you get replacement doctors from if you wanted to make a change? But rather more of the first, that having thought about it in more detail and having interviewed the individual doctors she had changed her mind."

4.4.11 Professor Taylor did indeed offer a different opinion of the same colleagues when invited to do so by the Committee of Inquiry. She argued that Dr Reed's minute over-stated the problems. However, although she was more charitable in her view of the same doctors she still offered an essentially critical opinion. She admitted that the quality of doctors at Ashworth was mixed at every level and that the SHSA was to some extent struggling to change the situation, since, for several years, no one had wanted to go there. Once the Blom-Cooper Inquiry was announced, it was only by the skin of the teeth that the training programme had been saved. Meanwhile pressure was applied at the other Special Hospitals to appoint doctors even though they might have bare minimum qualifications.

4.4.12 Professor Taylor's arguments aside, this appalling account of the competence and performance of these doctors at Ashworth fits in with the general evidence we received from a number of witnesses. Mr Bingley from the MHAC told us that the Commission "had concerns about one or two professional groups at the Hospital and I have to say that includes the doctors but not all of them by any means."

4.4.13 Mr Jewesbury said that during the whole of his time monitoring the SHSA, the problem of the inadequacy of the medical leadership at Ashworth was never satisfactorily resolved. Mr Murphy told us of his "grave concern about the quality of the doctors".

4.4.14 What could be done about this situation? Dr Reed regarded it as the principal duty of Professor Taylor as Head of Medical Services to do something about the poor performers and attract new doctors into the Special Hospitals. Mrs Miles told us that insofar as clinical competency was concerned the only person who could address that and take it forward was Professor Taylor. Mr Lever took the same view.

4.4.15 Professor Taylor herself accepted that the "buck" stopped with her as far as medical ethos was concerned. She argued that it was impossible to be fully accountable for the clinical ethos of the Hospital, given the poor inheritance. The SHSA faced an enormous task in trying to bring Ashworth into the NHS mainstream.

4.4.16 Professor Taylor argued that she did take steps to improve the situation. Thus she had reviewed the work of each of the Ashworth consultants with Dr Higgins and Dr Dick, both members of the SHSA. Gradually, trained forensic consultant psychiatrists were recruited. Training was organized for the weaker doctors but it was often very difficult to release doctors for this training. Academic links were established with Liverpool University. Professor Taylor stressed that the doctors had been told of the importance of attending case conferences and in a couple of cases their attendance had been monitored. She thought that Ashworth perhaps had a particular problem with doctors suffering from poor health.

4.4.17 The root problem was trying to provide a service with almost 600 patients who had nowhere else to go. The SHSA was forced to try to sustain doctors so long as no clear professional or other misconduct case was being made against them, as otherwise the surviving doctors would be left with caseloads of 90-100. She did not think that the SHSA retained truly incompetent doctors, as they would be eased out in one way or another. She claimed that what the Authority was often unable to do was release doctors to undertake training, as otherwise the service would collapse.

4.4.18 We are not convinced that everything possible was done to release doctors at Ashworth for training, by for instance encouraging temporary transfers from Broadmoor or elsewhere.

4.4.19 Professor Taylor regarded her task as being to build up steadily the core of good quality doctors. The Headquarters SHSA staff were in London, not the three hospitals, so with the best will in the world the job of changing the culture could only be done by getting the right people in place. She claimed that this was beginning to happen. That said, she told us that even with a dozen superb forensic psychiatrists Ashworth would have struggled if the other members of the PCTs were poor. It was very difficult to make progress with that group of RMOs, but progress had been made.

4.4.20 Mr Kaye was, if anything, blunter than Professor Taylor about the situation:

> "we faced an almost impossible dilemma, in that the only way we could keep the Hospital going and provide a just-acceptable work load for consultants, and the work load was far too high at that stage for individual consultants, was to retain doctors that we felt were really not worthy of the job that we asked them to do, and we knew that."

In his view this problem had been endemic in the Special Hospitals for years and it is still a problem. It is one of the insolubles of the whole business.

> The Chairman: Are you really saying that the apparent change of heart of Dr Taylor from Dr Reed's expressed view in his note is for the pragmatic reason that you just could not get rid of the doctors. They had to be kept otherwise the whole process would have fallen to bits. As simple as that?
> A: As simple as that.

We reject entirely that nothing could be done because otherwise the Hospital would close. If these levels of incompetency and poor performance had occurred in another specialty, such as general surgery, immediate and decisive action would have had to be taken. The same should have happened in this case.

4.4.21 Despite Professor Taylor's optimism about improvements in the standard of doctors at Ashworth, we are not so sure as major problems remain and we understand that one or two of those offered the chance of improvement have left. We are aware that during Dr Shetty's time as Medical Director new consultants were recruited. But the PDU remained the poor relation. Whatever improvements had taken place in the Hospital as a whole they had not reached the PDU.

4.4.22 We have already criticized Professor Taylor's handling of the attempted disciplining of Dr Strickland over the Owen Ward incident in 1994. Professor Taylor frankly failed to make significant progress at Ashworth as far as the PDU was concerned. She did not do

enough to motivate the doctors to improve, or to provide opportunities for further training. Our criticism is tempered by the recognition that the problems she was facing were deep-rooted and fraught with difficulty.

4.4.23 Dr Obholzer, who gave evidence to us on behalf of the Royal College of Psychiatrists, accepted that there were staffing and professional problems at Ashworth. He invited us to pay regard to what he regarded as the "toxic emotional processes" in Special Hospitals:

> "we are dealing with the most disturbed individuals in society, incarcerated with each other for a very long period of time, working with staff groups who are also there for a very long period of time and there is a corrosive effect on the staff group unless in fact management is aware of this, unless all the staff groups are in touch with this."

4.4.24 The College also strongly supported the idea of joint appointments with other parts of the psychiatric services to minimize the professional isolation.

4.4.25 In our view much more needs to be done to improve the quality of psychiatry at Ashworth. The professional isolation must end. Consultants in the high security end of forensic psychiatry must be part of mainstream professional education and development. Our proposals in Part Seven to create clinical networks should enable this to happen. As a young and developing specialty forensic psychiatry needs encouragement and investment. The standards for appointing consultants were clearly breached at Ashworth on the grounds of expediency. The ability to provide professional leadership, a key component of the consultant's role, was rare at Ashworth. This was a serious error by all concerned at Ashworth.

4.4.26 Of course the problem is not confined to Ashworth. A number of witnesses emphasized the importance of improved psychiatric training in the diagnosis and management of personality disorder. The failure to develop this thus far was linked in part to the lack of a consensus over which system of classification (DSM-IV, ICD-10, etc) should be used. Other witnesses referred to the need for improved training for all staff groups. Dr Snowden said that the "elitist view" that regarded assessment as far more important than treatment had been an ill-conceived approach.

4.4.27 At the present time teaching in the diagnosis and treatment of personality disorder at undergraduate, postgraduate and professional levels in all professions is very limited and, taking into account the prevalence of personality disorder in society, its importance in general practice, in general psychiatric practice, in prisons and hospital, we believe that urgent steps should be taken to achieve a radical improvement. This is very important in seeking to improve the status of work in this field.

4.5.0 The Role of the RMO

4.5.1 In relation to a patient liable to be detained under an application for assessment (section 2 or section 4) or for treatment (section 3) or under Part III of the Mental Health Act 1983, the Responsible Medical Officer (RMO) is the registered practitioner in charge of the treatment of the patient (sections 34(1), 55(1)). This is usually the patient's consultant. Responsible Medical Officer has the same meaning in respect of consent to treatment provisions. In practice the RMO is the term used for the medical practitioner responsible for a detained patient or a patient who is liable to be detained.

4.5.2 In relation to a patient who is subject to guardianship the RMO is the medical officer authorised by the Social Services Authority to act as the RMO (section 34(1)). He can be authorised to act as RMO generally, or in any particular case, or for any particular purpose, but the Act does not state that he is in charge of the treatment of a guardianship patient.

4.5.3 The RMO has specific powers and duties under Parts II and III of the Act which include the power to grant leave of absence, to make statutory reports for the renewal of the authority for detention, or guardianship, to bar the discharge of certain patients by the nearest relative and to discharge certain patients (such as those non-restricted patients liable to detention or guardianship).

4.5.4 The RMO is the doctor "in charge of the patient's treatment" and "medical treatment" includes care, habilitation and rehabilitation "under medical supervision" (section 145(1)). The term has no meaning outside the specific functions given to the RMO in the Act and the term has no meaning in respect of informal patients. The Act does not specify that the RMO must be a consultant, so that he could be any registered practitioner "in charge of the treatment of the patient". He is usually a consultant but occasionally is an associate specialist or other doctor who is not a consultant.

4.5.5 It is commonly the case that a consultant who has responsibility for patients and for whom he is the RMO if they are detained (as they usually are in a Special Hospital), also has other responsibilities of an administrative kind, such as Medical Director or Clinical Director. It is good practice for doctors in administrative roles to retain some clinical responsibility for patients. Dr Strickland had such responsibility when he was clinical manager. There is no apparent conflict in this, bearing in mind the defined statutory responsibilities of the RMO.

4.5.6 While the statutory responsibilities of the RMO are as described above it would not be possible for a member of any other profession than the medical profession to undertake this role. However, it has been suggested and supported by some (eg Dr Thomas-Peter, a forensic psychologist) that if the principal provider of therapy for those with a personality disorder is a psychologist, then the legislation could be amended with respect to patients who only have a personality disorder, without co-morbidity, to permit him to be the *psychologist in charge of the patient's treatment* instead of a registered medical practitioner.

4.5.7 However, in practice many patients have co-morbidity, or move between diagnostic categories as we have heard in evidence. Further, patients with personality disorder sometimes require medication which a psychologist is not authorised to prescribe. By training, a psychologist is unable to make medical assessments and a patient's treatment would have to be managed by an RMO at different stages. The care and management of these patients is more than simple "general practitioner" supervision.

4.5.8 The consultant in charge of the patient's care should be the leader of the clinical team, even though he delegates the chair at meetings from time to time to another member of the team. As a consultant and as RMO, he has the responsibility for the patient.

4.5.9 We recognize that RMOs exercise very considerable power over patients' lives. Some psychiatrists exercise their powers and duties in a very personal manner. Others effectively share with colleagues in their multi-disciplinary team, although they retain the personal accountability for treatment. The principle that one person is in ultimate clinical charge of an individual patient, even if care is provided by a multi-disciplinary team, is well-rooted in the NHS, and is sound. Whenever the service is being provided within the NHS the RMO role should continue, in our view, to be exercised by an appropriately qualified doctors. There should, however, be a means of peer review of the competencies of doctors who are given this power to exercise.

Recommendation 37 **4.5.10 We recommend that the position of RMO should be an accredited post which is reviewed at no more than five-yearly intervals.**

4.5.11 This may cause operational problems on occasion but if Trusts are attempting to provide services without competent doctors that represents a crisis that needs to be addressed. Some quality standards should never be compromised.

4.6.0 The Medical Director

4.6.1 The Medical Director at Ashworth is the principal clinical adviser to the Authority and a member of the Board. He does not have a line management relationship with his consultant colleagues. We discussed above in connection with the Patient Care Team the role of the Medical Director in overseeing the work of PCTs. Dr Shetty was for the most part "hands-off" in his approach, telling us that he did not see it as his role to interfere with consultant colleagues, unless he became aware of something positively dangerous.

4.6.2 The position of the consultant is of course a rather special one. The following quotes from *The Responsibilities of Consultant Psychiatrists,* a Revised Statement produced by the Royal College of Psychiatrists (Council Report CR51, July 1996). demonstrate the point:

> 7. Referrals
> "Consultants have the ultimate responsibility and authority to diagnose illness and prescribe treatment. This authority may be delegated to other professionals, but the responsibility cannot be abrogated . . ."
>
> 8. Responsibility for Care
> "Consultants have a responsibility towards the community they serve through the GPs, who must be kept fully informed about matters relating to their patients' care. *Consultant psychiatrists retain the ultimate responsibility for all aspects of medical care of an in-patient under their care, including discharge . . .*" [our emphasis.].
>
> 10. Accountability
> "Consultants are accountable for their decisions and actions in four ways:
>
> > (i) they are answerable to their patients;
> >
> > (ii) in professional judgments, they are answerable to the courts or the Medical Councils and are not ultimately responsible to the employer or management;
> >
> > (iii) consultants are accountable to the their employer and management in matters of general conduct in ordinary employment and non-professional issues, and can be held responsible for executing decisions of management as these properly apply to them;
> >
> > (iv) where the health or competence of a colleague is in question, or a colleague's actions may jeopardise patient safety, it is the responsibility of consultants to seek help through the appropriate channels . . ."
>
> Annex 1. The Consultant's Role
> "Consultants are first and foremost responsible to their patients for the establishment of a medically effective, trustworthy and confidential relationship within the limits of the law . . ."
>
> [From] Annex 2. Multi-disciplinary functioning
> ". . . By virtue of the length, breadth and content of the consultant's training the consultant psychiatrist occupies a crucial role in the leadership of the multi-disciplinary team, responsible for the care of people with mental disorders."

4.6.3 The clinical freedom of a consultant is non-negotiable. Dr Shetty had good reason for not wishing to second-guess his consultant colleagues on clinical judgments. But the quoted passages show that clinical freedom is not an absolute. If that clinical freedom is exercised dangerously medical colleagues have a duty to speak out. And doctors are not released from the obligation to obey the rules of the organization, for example to turn up for appointments, to abide by Hospital policies, to lead the multi-disciplinary team in a way that allows all members to contribute. Here there is space for the Medical Director to play a larger role.

4.6.4 We debated whether the position of the Medical Director should be changed. One option in NHS organizations with relatively few consultant staff such as a Special Hospital would be to make the Medical Director accountable for the performance management of all the doctors, including personal conduct, job plans, the organization of their work and their training and development. Had such a system been in place the problems at Ashworth might have been tackled sooner.

4.6.5 An alternative would be to vest responsibility for developing Clinical Governance in the position of Medical Director. Given the sorry recent history of the medical staff at Ashworth we believe this could be an important step towards improving medical leadership within the Hospital.

Recommendation 38

4.6.6 We recommend that the new policies relating to clinical governance spell out as clearly as possible the powers and authority of a Medical Director in such a way as to strengthen the role in an acceptable manner.

4.7.0 The Nurses

4.7.1 Nurses are by far the largest numerically of the professions involved in delivering services in High Security Hospitals. They are the only care staff group that offer a 24-hour service. As a profession nursing has suffered heavy criticism in previous inquiries into Special Hospitals. The Blom-Cooper Inquiry was particularly critical.

4.7.2 It is therefore of some relief that the picture on the PDU at Ashworth is less bleak. We know that some staff were corrupt, the most notable example being Enrolled Nurse James Corrigan, Mr Daggett's escort on the day he absconded. We heard much about the failings of individual nurses. But we also heard praise for the job nurses were doing.

4.7.3 Thus as we have seen in **4.2.0** *et seq.* above our assessment team praised the job nurses were currently doing on the PDU. The team spent a considerable amount of their time with nurses, interviewing 35 per cent of the PDU nurses (52). The team observed that the therapeutic culture of the wards appeared to be predominantly shaped by the senior nursing staff. The team concluded that the nursing approach on the wards was characterised by commitment, enthusiasm and realism. That said, the team also noted a lack of understanding of the development of the psychopathology of patients with personality disorder and a corresponding lack of empathy of some staff.

4.7.4 Ward-based nursing staff are to be commended for maintaining their enthusiasm and commitment. We note the criticism of some nurses' lack of knowledge of personality disorder but believe that this reflects the paucity of relevant training and the lack of medical leadership.

4.7.5 It is clear that the PDU now has a cadre of experienced committed staff. Weaknesses remain. We discuss some of these weakness below, as well as other issues which were highlighted during the course of our hearings.

Balancing Security and Therapy

4.7.6 The role of the nurse in High Security Services has always been fraught with the tension of being seen as the person who "polices" the Hospital and as the enforcer of the rules and discipline. Some staff believe that this can conflict with the nurse's therapeutic role.

4.7.7 Miss Kinsley recalled that during her Security Audit of Ashworth in 1992 she met staff who took this view:

> "two [Ward Managers] were of the view that searching was not an appropriate nursing task. And one of those actually thought it conflicted with the Code of Practice."

4.7.8 We heard much evidence concerning the weaknesses of security practices on the wards. Ashworth Hospital has now introduced Independent Search Teams to ensure that searching is carried out to a sufficiently high standard.

4.7.9 The introduction of independent teams is controversial. Whilst the quality of searching should improve, and ward-based staff escape the opprobrium attached to carrying out searching, there is a danger that nurses on the ward cease to think that security is their business. One patient told us that he preferred staff known to him to be doing the searching.

4.7.10 In some other countries security is provided by security staff, therapy by therapeutic staff. This is the situation for example in the Holland TBS system. Experience around the world is mixed. In Canada and New South Wales, Australia, for example, we are aware that security staff and nursing staff have worked together in the management of mentally disordered patients. This has resulted in tensions between the two, with the security staff tending to develop a cynical and patronizing attitude towards the caring role of nursing staff, and the nurses resenting the lack of involvement of security staff in the care of patients.

4.7.11 We support the introduction of independent search teams but note that security in a high security setting remains everyone's responsibility, nurses included. Management must ensure that the independent teams do not lead to complacency on the wards.

Training, Education and Supervision

4.7.12 Working with severely personality disordered individuals is difficult and stressful. It is emotionally draining and can be physically dangerous. Staff need to feel that they are well-trained and that they have support available, not least to talk through issues and to give a different perspective on a problem. This is a key way of preventing emotional manipulation by personality disordered patients who are adept at undermining staff and systems.

4.7.13 However, many witnesses called attention to the fact that there was very little training for nurses working on the PDU. There was considerable praise for Mr Tarbuck's initiative in this area and criticism of Mr Murphy's decision to cut that training short. We also heard that nursing supervision was piecemeal and that there was little monitoring of its value and effectiveness. Adequate support for individual nurses, in terms of training education and clinical supervision, was, and is, lacking.

4.7.14 It is unfortunately the case that nurses have no specific recognised programme of post-basic education for working with patients who are diagnosed as primarily personality disordered. This reflects in large part the lack of a knowledge base on which to build training programmes. In his evidence to us Professor Kevin Gournay, Professor of Psychiatric Nursing at the Institute of Psychiatry, reported on a literature search he had carried out. He found that despite the large number of papers identified, the nursing literature itself contained no outcome data regarding nursing interventions.

4.7.15 Yet as nurses have 24-hour care of patients, Professor Gournay concluded that how nurses discharge their responsibilities is likely to have more effect than anything else that occurs, in treatment terms. Professor Gournay suggested the implementation of a training package similar to the Thorn Programme,[1] to underpin working with this group of patients. **There is a need to develop an evidence-based treatment and management model for staff**

---

1 The Thorn Programme is a training/education initiative designed for mental health professionals working with severely mentally ill patients and their immediate families and carers. The programme focuses on patient and carer education and the development of skills-based interventions.

working with personality disordered patients, building on the work of the many talented staff currently working in this challenging speciality.

Recommendation 39 **4.7.16 We recommend the development of training for nurses in the treatment and management of personality disorder with appropriate certification.**

4.7.17 We also call attention to the need for a structured system of clinical supervision to support the practice and personal needs of staff.

Nursing and 24-hour opening

4.7.18 One of the points UNISON made to us during the course of the Inquiry was that the SHSA commitment to 24-hour opening was (to quote their written evidence) a "well-intentioned initiative which was introduced too hastily and went too far – to the extent that basic therapeutic principles were lost sight of". The normal structure of the day was ignored and patients ceased to adhere to their care plans.

4.7.19 We have some sympathy with that view. It is undoubtedly true that implementing 24-hour opening represented a significant cost in both financial and organisation terms. It is reported to have cost some £3.6 million pounds in additional nursing resources. (Ms Young, one-time Acting Operations Manager for the PDU, told us that they were struggling to staff the PDU wards during the day yet were opening at night.) Like many initiatives post Blom-Cooper it suffered from speedy implementation and subsequent abuse. We heard of patients spending the night time awake and the day time asleep. This appeared to go unrectified and was perceived as an unresolvable issue.

4.7.20 Acting Chief Executive Erville Millar stated:

> "I think broadly amongst staff there was an acceptance that 24-hour opening was here to stay and was right and proper and was a humane regime. It was the fact that they felt helpless and powerless and unsupported in challenging those individual patients who would choose to stay up all night and then sleep all day, and that clearly they saw those individuals as abusing the system by not engaging in any meaningful or therapeutic programme and just being there."

4.7.21 We do not recommend a return to the old practice of locking patients up. Hospitals are not prisons, and in a mental health care setting patients should not be routinely locked in their rooms. But there does need to be a clear expectation on all patients that they keep to a certain structure of day. (We have already recommended that patients should not have access to the telephone during the night.) Staying up all night without good cause must be seen as a clinical issue to be dealt with. Staff do not need keys to ensure that patients keep to a sensible pattern of day; they need clear expectations understood by all and enforced fairly.

4.7.22 When we visited Holland we observed that patients were confined to their rooms for an hour when shifts changed so that staff could have a meeting. Again we do not wish to see patients locked up, but we do see value in ward staff having a regular handover meeting, during which time patients are expected to stay in their rooms.

4.7.23 In addition, we believe that considerably more attention must be given to 24-hour opening in High Security Hospitals. Where the intention is that for the majority of the night patients are expected to be asleep, it is both an expensive and inappropriate use of scarce trained nursing staff. Professor Sines argued that the move to 24-hour care was not managed very well and that poor use was made of expensive trained staff. We agree.

4.7.24 There is a clear difference between a distressed patient needing a skilled nurse and the need to provide security for patients and staff at night time.

Recommendation 40 **4.7.25 We recommend that a thorough review takes place of night staffing at Ashworth Hospital.**

Dealing with the Difficult

4.7.26 In any organisation there will be "bad apples". The hope is that a culture will exist where such "bad apples" will be exposed and dealt with as appropriate. In Ashworth, it is clear from our independent review team, the external reviewers and our own experience that there is a wealth of talented and committed nurses. However, the absconsion of Mr Daggett was assisted by a nurse who was considered by many to be corrupt. Nobody blew the whistle. That the Ward Manager had no anxieties about any of his nursing staff, and this nurse in particular, raises concerns.

4.7.27 We also heard evidence from a nurse, Mr Paul Boocock, who on his own admission was a disgruntled member of staff who had been subject to disciplinary proceedings on about three occasions. He was unhappy on the ward; the Ward Manager thought he was unsuitable for the ward; yet there was no effective mechanism either for addressing his performance and attitude or for moving him to a ward where he might fit in rather better.

4.7.28 We heard evidence of poor staff induction procedures, non-existent performance review and staff being placed on wards such as Lawrence Ward for health reasons.

4.7.29 This gives an impression of an organisation with poor personnel control and inadequate attention to critical human resource management issues. Issues such as these are normal requirements of any large organisation employing significant numbers of staff. Staff need and deserve good managers and management practices.

The Use of Bank Staff

4.7.30 On a number of occasions concerns were raised about the employment of bank nursing staff. The Nurse Bank started in 1992. UNISON told us that at first such staff received a very short induction period of two days, later increased to four. They had to have been employed within the NHS for at least a year. Ashworth staff were not allowed to be in the nursing bank. UNISON argued that recruiting and retaining permanent staff who understood the peculiar demands of high security forensic nursing was a more appropriate means of staffing the Hospital.

4.7.31 In his evidence to us Mr Ryan of UNISON also made the point that if bank staff were to be used they should be allocated to one ward, or even Unit, so that they at least built up some experience in a given area and became known to staff there, instead of being allocated anywhere in the Hospital as the occasion demanded. Professor Sines supported this approach.

4.7.32 Several witnesses testified to the potential dangers of the bank nurse system. Ms Young admitted that putting inexperienced bank staff in the PDU was problematic. Mr Day told us that on one occasion on Ruskin Ward he had found one staff nurse very new to the Hospital, one regular care assistant and four bank staff. Four of the six staff were female. This situation was, in Mr Day's words, "dangerous". Miss Kinsley told us that she was unhappy with the use of bank staff, although she recognized the financial constraints. She had counselled that such staff should be put in less sensitive places.

4.7.33 Mrs Miles pointed out that there was considerable pressure on her and senior managers before her to reduce the amounts paid in overtime. She admitted that at times the number of bank staff on wards in the PDU was too high, because of the need to cover for absent permanent staff.

4.7.34 We accept the need for some flexibility of staffing arrangements. But to place inexperienced staff on wards full of personality disordered individuals is simply dangerous.

Recommendation 41 **4.7.35 We recommend that as far as possible bank staff be allocated to particular areas of the Hospital, and that induction for bank staff opting to work within the PDU includes some additional instruction on working with personality disordered patients.**

The Role of the Ward Manager

4.7.36 The introduction of Ward Managers in 1992 was designed to bring a cohesion to the running of wards which had been lacking before. Up to then a charge nurse had run each of the three shifts. This had led to a lack of consistency in the running of the ward, something remarked upon in the Reports on the deaths of both Stephen Mallalieu and Derek Williams. The Ward Manager was responsible for the day-to-day operation of the ward, including security, and for recruiting staff and managing a budget for the ward.

4.7.37 UNISON argued that the position of Ward Manager was ill-defined, as it introduced ambiguity over who was running the ward, the RMO or the Ward Manager. Whereas previously charge nurses had been empowered to take decisions, now there was a Court of Appeal in the shape of the Ward Manager. Much of his or her time became taken up by dealing with issues which should have been resolved by more junior staff. This view was given some support by Ms Young's comment that when she first became a Ward Manager on Ruskin Ward she felt like putting a big sign saying "No" on her door, because of the constant demands from patients.

4.7.38 UNISON also argued that by recruiting a number of Ward Managers from outside the Hospital a number of disenchanted former charge nurses were left, albeit on protected pay. One of our witnesses, Mr Boocock, fell into that category.

4.7.39 The position of Ward Manager is a vital position that ought to combine professional leadership with the management of the nursing staff and the ward environment. But its introduction was not thought through sufficiently. We found evidence of a lack of clarity in various parts of the PDU over which aspects of the running of the ward were properly the RMO's responsibility, and which were the Ward Manager's. This lack of clarity was never resolved. The situation on Lawrence Ward was made worse by the long series of acting Ward Managers, which led to inconsistent practices.

4.7.40 A better role definition between the Ward Manager and professional colleagues such as the RMO is an important first step. Fundamentally however there need to be good professional relationships between doctors, nurses and other disciplines. When these relationship go wrong, as they will from time to time, senior clinicians in the Hospital should intervene.

4.8.0 The Social Workers

4.8.1 In Part Three of our Report we have been extremely critical of the ignorance of basic child protection arrangements shown by social workers at Ashworth, including the Head of Social Work Practice. We also criticized the management of the service, inadequate supervision and a lack of clarity over what precisely social workers were expected to do. The reorganization of the Hospital, leaving the Head of Social Work Practice as a "general without an army", made the situation even worse. It is depressing to recognize in our analysis many of the faults which the Social Services Inspectorate (SSI) found when it visited the Hospital in 1993.

4.8.2 We have recommended that the SSI repeat their inspection. We also criticize the leadership of the Department; strong new leadership is urgently needed.

4.8.3 The regional networks we recommend in Part Seven should provide an enhanced role for social workers in working with local social work departments. This should benefit both social workers and patients.

4.8.4 Finally we would urge whoever is in charge of the Department to redouble efforts to reduce its professional isolation.

4.9.0 The Psychologists

4.9.1 Our assessment team were complimentary about the current contribution of psychologists to the PDU. Whilst we have been critical of Mrs Day, it is clear that she is held in high regard by many patients.

4.9.2 As with the Head of Social Work Practice, the reorganization of the Hospital left the Head of Psychology with no real function. Morale and performance suffered as a result.

4.9.3 Psychologists will continue to make a vital contribution to caring for this group, although the effectiveness of much of what they do is still under-researched. We were concerned that the management and supervision of Mrs Day left something to be desired and note, that as with nursing staff, systematic clinical supervision should be put in place as soon as possible.

4.9.4 We heard an alarming story from one patient about two psychologists having a fight in the car park whilst at the same time providing anger management to the patients. Such behaviour does little for the professional standing of psychologists.

4.9.5 We heard from the majority of our expert witnesses that psychological therapies were crucially important in the treatment of personality disordered patients, yet we noticed that there were too few psychologists in the PDU and that they were not helping to shape the services on the PDU.

Recommendation 42 **4.9.6 We recommend that input of clinical psychology to the PDU should be sharply increased.**

4.10.0 Multi-disciplinary Working

4.10.1 It is clear to us that the multi-disciplinary teams on Owen Ward in 1994 and Lawrence Ward in 1996 (not to mention the PCT on Macaulay Ward in 1995) were not functioning as robust multi-disciplinary teams. It is also clear to us that without a strong multi-disciplinary team caring for severely personality disordered patients becomes even more fraught with difficulty.

4.10.2 To work well in such an environment, teams have to have above all strong leadership. By this we do not mean an autocratic RMO, but someone who can give the team a consistent sense of direction, who will stick by agreed policies and confront unacceptable behaviour by patients (and indeed by staff). Second, clarity of philosophy, roles and policies is vital. Third, good communication is essential, in particular between the PCT itself and the ward-based staff who will rarely attend PCT meetings. And fourth, realism: forensic patients in high security are there because of their potential danger. Staff must avoid both therapeutic pessimism, which turns staff into glorified jailers, and over-optimism, which encourages staff to take their eyes off the ball.

4.10.3 On Lawrence Ward there was not strong, consistent leadership, a clear direction, good communication or realism. The PCT became complacent, convinced that they alone had the answers.

4.10.4 How can this be prevented? There is no magic cure. PCTs must take time to work – and train – together. They must work out clear policies and abide by them, and they must try to avoid complacency.

4.11.0 Social Therapy – Time for a New Profession?

4.11.1 When we visited the TBS system in Holland we found that the staff on the wards were not on the whole nurses but social therapists. Personality disordered individuals cannot fit into society and abide by its norms; social therapists are trained to try to "resocialize" them. Social therapists in Holland tend to be quite mature individuals who have pursued some other career before undertaking their training in social therapy. Pay and status is, we were told, quite high.

4.11.2 It is an intriguing model. To their credit Ashworth Hospital had discussed with a local university the possibility of running a course on social therapy and, we understand, will in due course staff the new Wordsworth Project with social therapists.

4.11.3 We believe that this model is worth considering for severely personality disordered individuals both in hospital and the penal system who do not have attendant psychoses.

Recommendation 42 **4.11.4 We recommend the HSPSCB funds work in the area of social therapy.**

PART 5 Accountability and Responsibilities

5.1.0 Accountability

5.1.1 Our Report is critical about the conduct and performance of a number of individuals. We deal with each later in this section.

5.1.2 We have tried hard to distinguish between criticizing individuals for specific blameworthy conduct and poor performance on the one hand, and systemic failures on the other. Our most important criticisms are about the system itself which we regard as wholly outdated and ineffective. Who, we asked ourselves, is accountable when a whole system is flawed and to whom. We also searched for some principles that might assist us in judging fairly those individuals who were working within such a system. We did not find any. Instead we found confusion and ambiguity.

5.1.3 The ambiguity starts at the top. The NHS Executive led by Sir Alan Langlands is not in charge of the NHS in the accepted sense of that expression. The NHS Executive is part of the Department of Health. The Chief Executive and his staff are civil servants. They have no direct line of accountability for the actions and conduct of NHS field authorities. They are advisers to Ministers and secure the implementation of national policy on behalf of Ministers. They monitor the day-to-day performance of Health Authorities on behalf of the Minister and in some cases make delegated decisions on his behalf.

5.1.4 The monitoring of the performance of NHS Trusts is carried out by the NHS Executive who approve or otherwise their annual business plans. Trusts are answerable for their performance to Regional Offices, the Chief Executive and ultimately to the Secretary of State. Their accountability, however, is said to be direct to the Secretary of State.

5.1.5 We accept the evidence we received on this point, but point out that this is not the way the Department of Health sometimes describes its own role or acts. The seminal paper on this matter *Department of Health: Statement of Responsibilities and Accountabilities 1995* describes the role of the Chief Executive as being "responsible for and directly accountable to the Secretary of State for the management and performance of the NHS in England".

5.1.6 A number of witnesses including civil servants made it plain that officials can, and sometimes do, intervene directly in the affairs of NHS field authorities. No doubt they do so in the name of the Secretary of State. Mr Tinston, the Regional Director for the NHS Executive in the North West, regarded himself as being responsible for the overall performance of Ashworth Hospital although, strictly speaking, of course he was not. As a member of Sir Alan Langlands' NHS Executive Board he is a civil servant and an adviser to Ministers. In practice he wielded significant power once it became clear that things were going seriously wrong at Ashworth, including a direct involvement with the Chairman Mr Lever in making decisions about Chief Executives following the suspension of Mrs Miles. Yet in theory Regional Directors do not have any powers to hire and fire Health Authority or NHS Trust Chief Executives or any other of their employees. This is a matter for the Boards who appoint them.

5.1.7 In the world of the NHS even the most straightforward proposition has to be qualified. Each Chief Executive is an Accountable Officer in so far as the Public Accounts Committee is concerned and Sir Alan Langlands can remove this status and effectively sack the individual concerned.

5.1.8 Mr Rowden, as Director of the HSPSCB, in his day was also a civil servant who did not hesitate to exercise substantial power when he judged it necessary.

5.1.9 To complicate matters the Chair of the Ashworth Board, like all chairs in the NHS, is appointed by, and reports directly to, the Secretary of State. There is another Chair at each Regional Office working with the Regional Director but they have no committee to chair. They are regarded as being the eyes and ears of Ministers. They too wield significant power over chairs in their regions as they pass on Ministerial messages and report on performance. It is an extraordinarily complex network of relationships, power and influence at the top of a very large public service. Mr Lever said in his statement to us that the Ashworth Board soon became aware of the confusing nature of external accountability arrangements, and that subsequent events illustrated a fundamental structural weakness of what was a dual accountability to the Regional Office and the HSPSCB.

5.1.10 We have concluded that the polite fiction that Regional chairs and officials are merely advisers and agents of the Secretary of State is just that: a fiction. It is an increasingly unconvincing fiction to boot, as Regional Directors are due to gain yet more influence behind the scenes. Thus Mr Tinston told us that the proposals in the White Paper "The New NHS", if implemented, would increase his powers:

> "The White Paper give us slightly more 'ins' around [power over] Chief Executives. It does not give us any more line management responsibility, but it makes us very clearly involved in the appointment process for Chief Executives, much more clearly than has been the case hitherto, and secondly it gives us a role in what is called 'Chief Executive personal development arrangements'."

5.1.11 The reality is that no sensible Chief Executive would treat their Regional Director as anything other than as line manager in all but name. The existing accountability arrangements do not make sense and should be sorted out, as lack of clarity at the top of any organisation is usually a recipe for disaster.

5.1.12 We see no grounds for criticising individual officials at either the NHS Executive or the wider Department of Health for the events we have been inquiring into, except perhaps for an unthinking insistence that the whole of the Blom-Cooper recommendations be applied across the board. But somebody has to be accountable.

5.1.13 At one level it is clear that those charged with the operational management of the service should be accountable for putting things right and for resigning should matters be deemed sufficiently serious. Thus for shortcomings in matters such as operational security and the personal conduct of individual staff the buck stops at the Ashworth Board (or the SHSA prior to April 1996). Many of the failings at Ashworth were preventable. The body charged with managing the system must accept accountability for those failings.

5.1.14 There is, we believe, a longstanding tradition in the public service that when things go really seriously wrong the person at the top of the organisation should stand down. In effect they accept public accountability, whether or not they are directly personally blameworthy for what has gone wrong. There can have been few worse examples of NHS failure than the scandalous events at Ashworth Hospital. Given the seriousness of events at Ashworth we believe this accountability amounts to the need for resignations at the most senior level.

5.1.15 However, this is not the end of the matter. The reason the issue of accountability is important to this Inquiry is our determination not to savage individuals who may have simply been doing their best in a system that was flawed. Given our earlier conclusion that the principal villain of the piece at Ashworth was 'the System' we have little choice but to trace the accountability chain further up, to Ministers. They are in charge . . . or are they? Aneurin Bevan thought Ministers of Health had to be accountable to Parliament for everything that happened in the NHS he had created.

5.1.16 In more recent times it seems to us that the doctrine of Ministerial accountability in its pure Bevanite form has shifted to the point where Ministers are accountable for policy but not for the actions of the officials who implement it. Many Health Authority Chairs and Chief Executives have either resigned or been sacked in recent years when things have gone wrong. We can recall no example of a Minister resigning as a consequence of a failure in the NHS in all of its 50-year history.

5.1.17 We reach three conclusions on this matter:

First, that the chain of accountability between the Department of Health and NHS Authorities needs to be looked at again. We see no reason why Health Authorities should not be accountable to the NHS Executive, who in their turn account to Ministers. Whatever Ministers finally decide should be crystal clear.

Second, that those managing the system at the operational level must be held accountable for many of the failings we have identified, whether or not they are personally blameworthy.

Third, that as things stand today, Ministers must accept accountability for the overall system failure and take steps to put it right.

5.1.18 The Secretary of State at the time things started to go seriously wrong was the Rt Hon Virginia Bottomley. She and her Ministerial colleagues did indeed react strongly to see that the recommendations of the Blom-Cooper Report were implemented. They, like everybody else, it seems, failed to pay regard to the different types of patient inside the special hospitals. The pressure for change backfired. A more thoughtful and carefully prepared programme of change would have been more appropriate. In saying this we understand and sympathise with Ministers' impatience to improve services. We observe an important mistake from which lessons should be learnt rather than make a serious criticism or attribute blame.

5.1.19 If, however, similar events occur after our Report, the latest in a long series, we doubt that another inquiry would be so forgiving. Not to act now to reform the High Security Hospitals would be irresponsible. We have been reassured by the present Secretary of State and his officials that they do intend to act. However, in this publicly unpopular and unattractive territory, policy objectives have not always been turned into action, as our Report illustrates graphically.

5.1.20 The accountability chain at Ashworth Hospital level was also full of confusion and ambiguity:

(i) the Chair accounts to both the Secretary of State and his Board;

(ii) the Chief Executive is accountable both to the Board, and to Sir Alan Langlands with regard to the Accountable Officer function;

(iii) the Medical Director is an adviser only and has no authority over his medical colleagues or accountability for their professional work;

(iv) the Director of Nursing doubled-up at Ashworth as Head of Security and is managerially, but not professionally, accountable for the work of the other professions, including psychology and social work;

(v) much authority has been devolved to ward and Patient Care Team levels but without a clear overall framework of rules.

5.1.21 Complex interprofessional relationships are inevitable in a service like the NHS. It is possible to distinguish between professional accountability to a senior colleague and managerial accountability to a manager in another discipline. However, when arrangements like this are in play clarity is crucial. We heard a lot of evidence about overly complicated, unclear and very bureaucratic management and committee structures at Ashworth. The management systems did not facilitate or support good patient care

5.1.22 This is particularly true where doctors are concerned. In the case of Ashworth the Medical Director's role was neutered. The Medical Director of today is required to play a key role in monitoring and developing the competencies of all doctors working in the Trust so as to ensure that robust clinical standards are maintained and clinical governance policies are adhered to. He must be in a position to deal decisively with inadequate performance. We discussed this in **4.6.0** *et seq.*

Recommendation 44 **5.1.23 We recommend that Ministers reflect on our comments and consider whether the chains of accountability in the NHS, at all levels, should be reviewed and clarified.**

5.2.0 Comments on individuals and organisations

5.2.1 We have made a number of observations about the conduct of individuals and organisations in the preceding pages of this Report. In what follows we briefly summarize our views on each of the major ones involved.

5.3.0 Department of Health Ministers

5.3.1 We are clear that the principal villain of the piece at Ashworth was the system, rather than any particular individual or individuals. The system, to use our own words from earlier in the Report, was, and is, rotten. It needs radical change. The ultimate responsibility for this does indeed lie with Ministers. Ministers of the day did react strongly to the Blom-Cooper Report and they, like everybody else, failed to pay regard to the management of the different types of patient inside the Special Hospitals. The pressure for change backfired. A more mature, thoughtful and carefully prepared programme of change would have been more appropriate.

5.4.0 Mrs Anne-Marie Nelson – Formerly Chairman of the SHSA

5.4.1 Mrs. Nelson was Chairman of the SHSA from July 1993. We acknowledge that under her tenure the SHSA made substantial progress in certain areas.

5.4.2 We are concerned only with Mrs Nelson in her capacity as Chairman of the Special Hospitals Service Authority. We make no criticism of any of her personal actions. The question we pose is simple: does she and her Board carry any degree of collective and corporate responsibility for the operational failures we describe at Ashworth Hospital, the management of which was their responsibility? We state below that a member of that Board, namely the Chief Executive Mr Kaye, would in our view have been expected to resign had he still been in post. The handling of both the Swan Report and the Owen Ward Report was discussed and agreed by the Board. Should then the Chairman accept responsibility for the decisions of her Board and for the overall problems at Ashworth?

5.4.3 We did not find it easy to reach a judgement. After much reflection we do conclude that if public accountability is to have any meaning then the most appropriate response remains that of resignation when events as serious as those we describe above occur. This may seem harsh but chairing a public body is an onerous task. In accordance with the principles we have set out above, had the SHSA still been in existence she would have been expected to step down.

5.5.0 Mr Charles Kaye – Formerly Chief Executive of the SHSA

5.5.1 We have heard a number of witnesses praise Mr Kaye for his achievements. Thus Mr Jewesbury commented on his energy and commitment to pursuing the goals of the SHSA. Mrs Nelson similarly was impressed by his energy and the way in which he tackled an extraordinarily difficult job. The SHSA under his stewardship made substantial progress in certain areas.

5.5.2 However, we have a number of serious criticisms to make of Mr Kaye. To take the PDU first, he knew that the creation of a large unit comprising over 100 personality disordered patients was a high risk venture. He knew that he had in place a relatively inexperienced General Manager. He knew that the Unit had a weak Clinical Manager. This was not just a reasonable risk that went wrong despite the best efforts of all those involved. It was a high risk that was sharply increased by incompetence.

5.5.3 Second, Mr Kaye must also have realised that applying the Blom-Cooper recommendations across the board without distinguishing the special needs of personality disordered patients was bound to lead to trouble. He should have intervened either initially, or, if not at that stage because it was politically impossible to do so, at a later stage when things started to go wrong.

5.5.4 Third, Mr Kaye's actions were at odds with his fine rhetoric about the SHSA's policy of openness. Far from increasing openness, he encouraged a climate of secrecy and suppressed two very important Reports. In doing so he prevented the organization from learning lessons over the longer term in pursuit of the short term goal of avoiding poor publicity.

5.5.5 Fourth, and linked to the above, Mr Kaye failed to keep the Department of Health adequately informed, resulting in Ministers being misled.

5.5.6 Fifth, as Chief Executive he bears the predominant responsibility for the performance of his Authority and for events at Ashworth during his tenure of office. On the basis of the Owen Ward Report itself (and there are many more) the Authority presided over a scandalous and corrupt Hospital.

5.5.7 We acknowledge that Mr Kaye was pursuing a national policy of devolution of authority down to units. However, we do not accept that this removes his final accountability.

5.5.8 When events such as we have described happen in the public sector resignation is usually regarded as the only appropriate response. Were the SHSA still extant, and Mr Kaye still its Chief Executive, we believe his position would be untenable.

5.6.0 Professor Pamela Taylor – Formerly Head of Medical Services with the SHSA

5.6.1 Professor Pamela Taylor was a helpful and authoritative expert witness. We were less impressed by her performance as Head of Medical Services of the SHSA. She was well aware of the inadequacies of her clinical colleagues at Ashworth Hospital and failed to take rigorous enough action to remedy matters. We understand the difficulties of recruiting and retaining high quality forensic psychiatrists. But we do not accept the argument that nothing could be done in the short to medium term on the grounds that it was better to have some inadequate doctors in charge of patients than to have none at all. She did not do enough to tackle the problems of poor doctors at the Hospital. She could have made more effort to arrange for closer supervision, further training, or the secondment of doctors who would benefit from this.

5.6.2 Given that Professor Taylor was eminently well-placed to understand the risks posed by the creation of the PDU, she must take some criticism for her part in the SHSA's decision to approve the creation of the Unit and for failing to act more urgently to address the poor standard of medical services when things began to go wrong. We repeat what we said about the SHSA Chief Executive: this was not just a reasonable risk that went wrong despite the best efforts of all those involved. It was a high risk that was sharply increased by incompetence.

5.6.3 She must also have realised that applying the Blom-Cooper recommendations across the board without distinguishing the special needs of personality disordered patients was bound to lead to trouble. She should have intervened either initially, or if not at that stage because it was politically impossible to do so, at a later stage when things started to go wrong.

5.6.4 These omissions on her part played no small part in the continuing problems at Ashworth and for this she must attract our severe criticism. As Head of Medical Services she was expected to provide clinical leadership and to tackle difficult problems. She did neither with sufficient rigour or effort.

5.7.0 Mr Paul Lever – Chairman of Ashworth Special Health Authority

5.7.1 Mr Lever has now been in post for over two and a half years. During that time the Hospital has had no fewer than four substantive or acting Chief Executives. Mr Daggett absconded and the appalling state of affairs on Lawrence Ward was revealed. When he gave evidence for a second time Mr Lever was very candid in admitting that the Hospital was not in its present form recoverable.

5.7.2 He was frank in accepting his Board's responsibility and accountability for events at Ashworth. He worked hard to deal with the problems but in our view he still has to be accountable as Chairman of the Board for what happened during his period of office. This accords with the principles above and, if he had not already indicated an intention to step down early in 1999 we would have recommended that he do so.

5.8.0 Mrs Janice Miles – Formerly Ashworth's General Manager, and then its Chief Executive

5.8.1 We acknowledge that Ashworth Hospital made genuine progress in certain areas during Mrs Miles' tenure. We are also well aware that the Hospital is an extremely difficult unit to manage.

5.8.2 However we believe that she did not have the experience to cope with a Hospital as complex and challenging as Ashworth. She failed to provide effective leadership herself and indeed failed to develop an effective senior management team. Although she was the Chief Executive she did not have her finger on the pulse of the Hospital. Security was marginalized in the pursuit of the post-Blom-Cooper "liberalization" of the Hospital regime.

5.8.3 We believe that Mrs Miles was over-influenced by Mr Kaye. As a result she handled the dissemination of the Owen Ward Report badly.

5.8.4 We seriously censure Mrs Miles for her handling of the aftermath of Mr Daggett's absconsion, and in particular for concealing details of the absconsion of Mr Daggett from the Department of Health.

5.8.5 We also criticize her for failing to order a search of Lawrence Ward immediately after the find of hardcore pornographic videos in September 1996.

5.8.6 Frankly she was out of her depth in managing such a complex place as Ashworth Hospital. In our judgement she was rightly suspended for mishandling the Daggett absconsion and if she were still in post we would have expected her to resign.

5.9.0 Mr Peter Green – Formerly Ashworth's Executive Director of Business Development

5.9.1 Mr Green wrote an excellent Report on the Owen Ward Hostage-Taking Incident and was assiduous in his service of this Committee. We were surprised at the timing of his enforced departure from Ashworth in the middle of the Inquiry which he had been assisting for some time. He was, however, a member of a dysfunctional senior management team and must therefore share some accountability for that.

5.10.0 Mr Colin Dale – Formerly Executive Nurse Director, Ashworth Hospital

5.10.1 In addition to his role as the most senior professional nurse in the organisation and the Executive Nurse Director on the Board, Mr Dale was directly accountable for the control centre, gate, and perimeter security, and he carried the policy lead for security on the Board. As a consequence he must accept the principle burden of our criticisms about the poor security and the security policy at Ashworth Hospital.

5.10.2 We acknowledge that Mr Dale's post was overloaded and that he was given too many key roles in the organization. He was also ill-equipped for his role as the Executive Director with responsibility for Security. We acknowledge that he was candid in accepting responsibility for the failure to maintain a proper balance between security and therapy. In particular, he admitted that the revision of the security manual took an unacceptably long time, as did the production of a new policy on visiting.

5.10.3 He was accused of making light of the allegations concerning Child A. In fairness to Mr Dale, we should point out that we do not accept that he did underplay the seriousness of the allegations.

5.10.4 Mr Dale failed to give proper priority to security. He was a member of a dysfunctional senior management team and must take his share of accountability for that. He was not the right man for such a multi-faceted job. He would have been better focused on providing nursing leadership and developing nursing practice.

5.11.0 Mr Thomas Maxwell – Formerly Security Manager at Ashworth

5.11.1 Mr Maxwell was a poor head of security, even given the organisational weaknesses within which he was expected to operate.

5.11.2 We acknowledge that Mr Maxwell did his level best to maintain the security of the Hospital. He found himself in a difficult position as security was reduced to an irrelevance as the Hospital pursued the Blom-Cooper changes. He had no formal training in security, as was the tradition at Ashworth Hospital. We think the principal accountability rests not with him but with the most senior people in the organisation responsible for security policy, *ie* Mr Charles Kaye, Mrs Janice Miles and Mr Colin Dale.

5.11.3 Mr Maxwell was charged with implementing the Owen Ward Action Plan. He failed in this task, although much of the blame for this must rest with Mr Dale and Mrs Miles who failed to give him proper support. He was not even given the full Owen Ward Report.

5.12.0 Mr James Gardner – Formerly Director of Security and Clinical Risk Management (currently suspended)

5.12.1 Mr Gardner took over as Head of Security and Clinical Risk Management in April 1996 and continued in post until he was suspended early in 1998. We accept that he was making vigorous efforts to improve security but serious weaknesses remained well into 1997. He was unable to overcome the same systemic problems which faced his predecessor Mr Maxwell, despite, in our view, being a more able and motivated man. He impressed us and it came to us as a surprise when he was suspended.

5.13.0 Mr Paul Tarbuck – Formerly Clinical Manager of the Personality Disorder Unit

5.13.1 Mr Tarbuck took over the PDU in August 1994 at a time when the Unit was in a very dangerous state. By the time he left in March 1996 he had given the Unit some stability. He made a number of improvements, including the development of a vision for the Unit; the introduction of core competency training for staff; and the development of operational policies.

5.13.2 Mr Tarbuck must be praised for the work he did in keeping the PDU afloat. That said, the events revealed in the Braund Report, demonstrating that all was not well, took place during his tenure. In addition, Mr Tarbuck was unaware of the true situation on Lawrence Ward. In consequence we must criticize him for overstating the improvements in the Unit. His successor, Mr Murphy, rapidly found that serious problems existed when he took over in April 1996.

5.13.3 We also believe that Mr Tarbuck must share some of the responsibility for failing to tackle long-standing problems such as the excessive amount of possessions in some patients' bedrooms.

5.14.0 Mr James Murphy – Clinical Director of the Special Needs Directorate

5.14.1 We praise Mr Murphy for his speed in identifying problems in the PDU. He took a number of steps to improve security, including stopping children visiting wards and closing the Lawrence Ward Shop. It was as a result of his interventions that Mr Rowden was able to correct previously misleading briefing to Ministers.

5.14.2 However he was unable to build an effective management team for the PDU, failed to get the support and respect of his colleagues within the unit, and was isolated within the senior management team of the Hospital. We believe the latter point is largely a reflection of the dysfunctional nature of that senior team.

5.14.3 We do criticize him for the failure to launch a full-scale search of Lawrence Ward in September or early October 1996.

5.14.4 He never got to grips with his role as leader of his team. We understand he is now on long term sick leave.

5.15.0 Dr Joseph Sylvester – Formerly Director of Medical Services, Ashworth Hospital

5.15.1 Bradford Social Services wrote to Dr Sylvester in April 1992 asking for access to the medical records of the father of Child A for a child protection hearing. The father of Child A had consented to their application. Dr Sylvester admitted that he failed to respond to the letter, despite being reminded by his secretary. Child A remained in the care of her father.

5.15.2 We criticize Dr Sylvester for this serious oversight which deprived Bradford Social Services of important information and which, Dr Sylvester admitted, might have been a contributory factor in Child A remaining in the care of her father.

5.16.0 Dr Girish Shetty – Formerly Medical Director, Ashworth Hospital

5.16.1 We heard a considerable amount of praise for Dr Shetty's qualities as a clinician. We have high regard for his clinical standing.

5.16.2 We do have concerns about his performance as Medical Director. We are well aware that he was reluctant to take on the job in the first place and recognize that he did succeed in attracting consultants to Ashworth. However, we judge that he was not robust enough to tackle the poor performance of many of his colleagues.

5.17.0 Dr Ian Strickland – Formerly Clinical Manager of the PDU, and Consultant Forensic Psychiatrist on Lawrence Ward

5.17.1 We believe that Dr Strickland failed to show proper clinical leadership over a number of years, resulting in a series of very serious incidents.

5.17.2 He was, by his own admission, an inadequate Clinical Manager of the PDU.

5.17.3 Owen Ward, under his leadership, degenerated to a point at which patients and staff were put at risk.

5.17.4 The regime of Lawrence Ward, under his leadership, was such that Child A was put at serious risk.

5.17.5 Over a period of years he wilfully disregarded Hospital policies and modified them as he saw fit. He had little idea of what was happening on the wards.

5.17.6 He failed to balance security and therapy. In our judgement his professional competence falls well below what we consider to be the minimum required of a hospital consultant. He attracts our severe criticism and censure.

5.17.7 The Hospital needs to proceed with disciplinary action in order to consider his continued employment as a consultant psychiatrist. A reference to the GMC in this case would seem appropriate.

5.18.0 Dr Zona Crispin – Formerly Consultant Forensic Psychiatrist on Lawrence Ward

5.18.1 Dr Crispin must take some part of the responsibility for the events on Lawrence Ward. She revealed considerable ignorance of the state of the ward and of the proper balance of security and therapy.

5.18.2 We recognize she was proactive in seeking to tackle problems in Owen Ward in 1994 and was a conscientious doctor.

5.18.3 We do not recommend any further action. We do, however, think she was naive and that her loyalty to her medical colleague clouded her judgement.

5.19.0 Mr Richard Backhouse – Head of Social Work Practice

5.19.1 We believe that Mr Backhouse, as Head of Social Work Practice, should have ensured that the principles of the Children Act 1989 were understood and implemented throughout the Hospital. They were not. This was despite the fact that in March 1995 the Department of Health circulated draft guidance entitled *Child Protection: Clarification of Arrangements between the NHS and Other Agencies*. Mrs Miles specifically asked Mr Backhouse whether there was anything that the Hospital should do in response; he failed to reply. He admitted that he had not taken on board the importance of child protection. This was a very serious omission.

5.19.2 Mr Backhouse also accepted a share of the responsibility for Child A's continued visits. He was right to do so.

5.19.3 Mr Backhouse was asked to produce a Visiting Policy. This was held up by various committees, but he must take a share of the blame for the long delay in producing a workable policy.

5.19.4 We believe that Mr Backhouse's conduct should be reviewed in a disciplinary setting to establish whether he is still a suitable person to be Head of Social Work Practice at Ashworth.

5.20.0 Mr Michael Bateson – Principal Social Worker

5.20.1 Mr Bateson took appropriate action to protect Child A. As a Senior Social Worker in a department which has attracted our severe criticism he is partly responsible for the failure to address adequately child protection issues. We found the *IR2 Investigation into Child Care Issues at Ashworth Hospital Authority* flawed, and he should never have been asked to chair this investigation.

5.21.0 Dr Mark Stowell-Smith – Formerly Social Worker on Lawrence Ward

5.21.1 We found that Dr Stowell-Smith ignored core social work activities in favour of pursuing his therapeutic work. We were amazed at his lack of knowledge of the Children Act 1989 and at his failure to provide social work expertise to discussions on Child A's visits. He failed to contact Bradford Social Services as requested in connection with Child A.

5.21.2 He attracts our serious criticism, and were he still at Ashworth Hospital, we would recommend that a disciplinary investigation be held into his professional performance.

5.22.0 Mrs Pamela Day – Clinical Psychologist on Lawrence Ward

5.22.1 Mrs Day admitted she was over-reliant on the self-reports of Mr Hemming and did not approach the visits of Child A with a view to the benefit of the child.

5.22.2 She admitted complete ignorance of child protection issues and the Children Act 1989 at the time.

5.22.3 Her judgement was seriously at fault as she herself admitted. We believe she has learnt from this experience and we recommend no further action.

5.23.0 Mr Michael Berry – Formerly Clinical Psychologist, Ashworth Hospital

5.23.1 We heard evidence that Mr Berry was a poor member of the multi-disciplinary team, that he failed to co-operate readily with inquiries and that he was extremely defensive with regard to criticism. We heard mixed reports of his clinical performance and critical reports about his personal behaviour.

5.23.2 We do not regard behaviour of this sort as acceptable in a professional. His conduct and performance did little to enhance the reputation of psychology in the minds of either patients or colleagues in other disciplines.

5.24.0 Mr Alan Arnold – Formerly Ward Manager of Lawrence Ward

5.24.1 We acknowledge that most of the nursing staff on Lawrence Ward praised Mr Arnold. We are aware that he was very inexperienced in caring for and managing this patient group and that he did not receive proper training and induction. We know that he inherited a very difficult situation. He also acknowledged a number of weaknesses in his management of the ward. He was one of a succession of Ward Managers on Lawrence Ward who operated outside Hospital policies.

5.24.2 Mr Arnold struck us as a naive but well-intentioned Ward Manager. He is to be commended for his candour in his evidence before us. However, he was not aware that security had become totally compromised or that at least one nurse was highly corrupt. He had little conception of the potential for mischief of 20 or so severely personality disordered patients. He needs a considerable amount of further training.

5.24.3 We understand that Mr Arnold has been disciplined for his part in the events on Lawrence Ward. We have nothing further to add in view of that.

5.25.0 Nurse Paul Boocock – Nurse on Lawrence Ward

5.25.1 Mr Boocock was alleged to have allowed a patient access to the Hospital computer network. We found no evidence to substantiate this allegation. We are not convinced that he overstepped professional boundaries with that patient.

5.25.2 His career at Ashworth Hospital has been somewhat chequered and he would have benefitted from stronger management direction.

5.26.0 Enrolled Nurse James Corrigan – Nurse on Lawrence Ward

5.26.1 We heard evidence that Mr Corrigan was highly corrupt. He was quite rightly dismissed for gross misconduct.

5.26.2 The details of his gross misconduct were forwarded to the UKCC for consideration and the case is currently under investigation. We urge early action.

5.27.0 Father of Child A

5.27.1 The father of Child A must attract the strongest possible censure for exposing his daughter to serious risk on Lawrence Ward. We believe he was permitting her to be groomed for paedophile purposes. The decision to remove Child A from his care, given the evidence we have heard, was right, proper and long overdue.

5.27.2 We are also satisfied that the father of Child A was importing pornographic videos into Ashworth Hospital in order to trade them with patients.

5.27.3 We regard his behaviour with contempt.

PART 6 Personality disorder

6.1.0 Personality Disorder – A Short History

The Early History

6.1.1 A discussion of personality disorder must begin with the concept of psychopathic disorder or psychopathy, which has caused so much difficulty for doctors, administrators, legal draftsmen and the courts for at least half a century. Walker and McCabe[1] observed in 1973 that "the history of 'psychopathy' begins with the formation of a concept in the minds of philosophers and mad-doctors. Thereafter, the concept becomes linked with a succession of ill-defined terms of art, until one of these is seized on by legislators and bundled into the statute book. The resulting trouble takes half a century to recognise and remedy, and today it remains uncertain whether the remedy is entirely successful".

6.1.2 According to the distinguished historians of psychiatry, Hunter and Macalpine[2] the term psychopathy was first introduced by Ernst von Feuchtersleben, a Viennese physician in 1845, meaning then mental disease as distinguished from neurosis or functional disease of nerves. But Lewis (see below) said that Koch first used the word psychopathic.

6.1.3 The modern use of the term "psychopathic" has French, German and Anglo-American origins[3] but it is Prichard, an English psychiatrist, who is credited with defining a new group of disorders which he called "moral insanity"[4] and "moral imbecility" endorsing an earlier concept of the French psychiatrist Pinel (1801)[5] of "mania without delirium" (*manie sans délire)* characterised by emotional instability and social drift, that is to say, psychological factors. This is generally agreed to be the meaning of moral in Prichard's moral insanity (rather than sinful, anti-social or asocial) as his definition makes clear. It is . . . "a morbid perversion of the feelings, affections, and active powers, without any illusion or erroneous conviction impressed upon the understanding: it sometimes co-exists with an apparently unimpaired state of the intellectual faculties".

6.1.4 Although Prichard (1835) is often said to be the first British psychiatrist to recognise psychopathy there is considerable doubt as to whether the disorder he described has more than a passing resemblance to the meaning associated with the word today. Henry Maudsley,[6] a great English psychiatrist, said that many people regarded moral insanity as an "unfounded medical invention", as a "most dangerous medical doctrine" but that he, himself,

1 Walker N and McCabe S (1973) *Crime and insanity in England.* Vol II, Edinburgh University Press, Edinburgh

2 Hunter R and Macalpine I (1963) *Three hundred years of psychiatry 1535–1860.* Oxford University Press, Oxford

3 Sass H and Herpertz S (1995) in *A history of clinical psychiatry* by Berrios G E and Porter R, Athlone Press, London

4 Prichard J C (1835) *A treatise on insanity and other disorders affecting the mind.* Sherwood, London

5 Pinel P (1801) *Traité médico-philosophique sur l'alienation mentale, où la manie.* Paris

6 Maudsley H (1874) *Responsibility and mental disease.* 1st ed, Appleton, New York

was convinced that such a condition really existed and was an indication that the affective life of the individual was profoundly deranged. "Such a person has no capacity for true moral feeling, his impulses and desires are egoistic, his conduct is governed by immoral motives." (Maudsley 1874)

6.1.5 Moral insanity gradually fell into disuse, but moral imbecility was defined further and incorporated in the Mental Deficiency Act of 1913, subsequently changed to "moral defective" in the Act of 1917. Its contemporary meaning, which is closer to anti-social personality, has evolved from the influence of French, German and American psychiatrists during the hundred years and more following Prichard when defects of "the moral sense" continued to persist, virtually until the Mental Health Act of 1959; indeed its current usage still has moral and pejorative resonance.

6.1.6 Thus, Morel (1857)[7] introduced the notion of "degenerative (and pathological) deviations from normality of which mental disorder was a consequence; an idea which influenced the Italian criminologist Lombroso (1876)[8] who developed the concept of the "born criminal" whose behaviour resulted from an atavistic reversion of development.

6.1.7 Kraepelin (1896)[9] formulated the concept of "psychopathic states", influenced by the French theory of biological degeneration. It forms the basis of the typology of his pupil Schneider, and Henderson (1939) warmly acknowledges his ideas.

6.1.8 Koch (1889)[10] and (1891–93)[11] applied the term "psychopathic inferiority" meaning something similar to the current term "psychopathy" and divided this group into genetic and acquired groupings with further sub-divisions.

6.1.9 Kurt Schneider (1923)[12] published a monograph that differentiated ten forms of psychopathic personality and he defined psychopathic personalities as "those abnormal personalities who suffer from their abnormality or whose abnormality cause society to suffer".

6.1.10 In 1941, Cleckley[13] graphically coined the phrase of a "convincing mask of sanity" to characterize individuals exhibiting abnormal characteristics who are neither mentally defective nor psychotic. He delineated 16 criteria for the diagnosis of psychopathy, originating an understanding of the condition in terms of personality traits.

Sir David Henderson

6.1.11 But it was Sir David Henderson[14] who influenced the British concept of psychopathy as we have it today with his emphasis on an abnormality of constitution, shaped by heredity and environment, rather than the earlier idea of degeneration. He said (p18) "I prefer to use the term psychopathic state because it does not stress unduly either innate or acquired characteristics, and does not imply total mental unsoundness, defect or delinquency, but yet allows for modifications of all of them."

6.1.12 He went on to say (p.18) that psychopathic state "is the name we apply to those

---

7 Morel B A (1857) *Traité des dégénérescences physiques, intellectuelles et morales de l'espèce humaine et des causes qui produisent ces varietés maladives.* Ballière, Paris

8 Lombroso C (1976) L'uomo deliquente. Milan

9 Kraeplin E (1896) *Psychiatrie, ein lehrbuch für studierende und aerzte.* Reprinted 1976. Classics in psychiatry, Arno Press, New York

10 Koch J L A (1889) *Kurzgefaßter leitfaden der psychiatrie,* 2nd ed. Dom'schen Buchhandlung, Ravensburg

11 Koch J L A (1891–1893) *Die psychopathischen minderwertigkeiten.* Maier, Ravensburg.

12 Schneider K (1923) *Die psychopathischen personlichkeiten.* Thieme, Leipzig

13 Cleckley H (1941) *The mask of sanity, an attempt to clarify some issues about the so-called psychopathic personality.* C V Mosby Co, St Louis

14 Henderson Sir D K (1939) *Psychopathic states,* Chapman and Hall. New York

individuals who conform to a certain intellectual standard, sometimes high, sometimes approaching the realm of defect but yet not amounting to it, who throughout their lives, or from a comparatively early age, have exhibited disorders of conduct of an anti-social or asocial nature, usually of a recurrent or episodic type, which, in many instances, have proved difficult to influence by methods of social, penal and medical care and treatment and for whom we have no adequate provision of a preventive or curative nature. The inadequacy or deviation or failure to adjust to ordinary social life is not a mere wilfulness or badness which can be threatened or thrashed out of the individual so involved, but constitutes a true illness for which we have no specific explanation".

6.1.13 Henderson's contribution was his linkage of aggressive and anti-social personality characteristics with psychopathy which also encompasses individuals with other characteristics; indeed each group merges into one another (p.43). He introduced his ideas in his Salmon Lectures to the New York Academy of Medicine in 1939 and his classification included three forms of psychopathy; the predominantly aggressive, the predominantly inadequate and the predominantly creative.

6.1.14 However, the Butler Report was later to comment (para 5.10) that these sub-divisions were brought together in one category on a highly complex psychological theory and were not based on descriptions of observed behaviour.

6.1.15 Henderson's classification was widely used in the period following the Second World War and continued to be recommended in the 1969 edition of his textbook[15] where a helpful description of "psychopathic states" is given in simple terms:

> "They constitute a rebellious, individualistic group who fail to fit in to their social milieu, and whose emotional instability is largely determined by a state of psychological immaturity which prevents them from adapting to reality and profiting from experience. They may be adult in years, but emotionally they are so slow and backward and uncontrolled that they behave like dangerous children. They lack judgement, foresight and ordinary prudence. It is the sheer stupidity of their conduct which is so apalling. The judicial, deciding, selecting processes described as intelligence, and the energizing, emotivating, driving powers called character do not work in harmony. They are the misfits of society, the despair of parents, doctors, ministers, lawyers and social workers."

6.1.16 Sir David Henderson had considerable influence upon the Royal Commission on Capital Punishment (1949–53)[16] which commented however, (para. 393), that it had heard much evidence on psychopathy but found that "there is no generally accepted definition of this term, and no consensus of opinion about the scope or nature of the mental condition which it is intended to describe" . . . The Commission was convinced that the concept of psychopathic disorder was a legitimate one, but that it is much easier to recognise than to define; "no two psychiatrists were likely to give the same definition.

The Percy Commission 1954–57 and the Mental Health Act 1959

6.1.17 The Royal Commission on the Law Relating to Mental Illness and Mental Deficiency 1954–57[17] reviewed the existing law which had evolved in a wide variety of statutes during previous decades. The Commission received expert evidence (although not from Sir David Henderson) on "the feeble-minded, moral defectives and psychopaths" (para. 169) and noted

---

15 Batchelor IRC (1969) *Henderson and Gillespie's textbook of psychiatry*, 10th ed. OUP, Oxford

16 Royal Commission on Capital Punishment 1949–1953 *Report* (1953). Cmnd 8932. HMSO London (Chairman: Sir Arthur Gowers)

17 Royal Commission on the Law Relating to Mental Illness and Mental Deficiency 1954-1957. *Report.* Cmnd 169. HMSO (Chairman: Lord Percy of Newcastle)

that the term "psychopath" is used by psychiatrists and sociologists in different ways, each giving a different emphasis to the importance of aggression in their definition. They reviewed the evidence for the efficacy of treatment. Various methods had been applied, from training under conditions of strict security, to physical treatment, psychotherapy, and group therapy. Some psychopaths responded to each of the treatment methods, others did not. Penal powers seemed to work well with certain psychopaths. The Commission thought that whilst often it would not be possible in the present state of knowledge to cure the underlying condition, treatment and training might enable the patient to regulate his behaviour so that he could live a normal life.

6.1.18 The Royal Commission argued that such training was likely to work best when the patient's disorder was recognised early in life and he was given treatment or training before the anti-social behaviours became ingrained (para. 345). They therefore argued there was a strong case for compulsory powers to ensure training or treatment in Hospital for psychopathic patients in adolescence or early adult life (para. 354). They did not argue, however, for compulsory powers to detain adult psychopaths for treatment except when their conduct was serious enough to bring them into conflict with the law, and when such treatment appeared to be the most appropriate means of disposal (para. 517). There would need to be safeguards for controlling the release of psychopathic patients who were regarded as dangerous to other people (paras. 518–9).

6.1.19 The Commission also recommended identifying three main groups of patients for "administrative purposes", (presumably meaning for legislative purposes), the mentally ill, the severely subnormal, and psychopathic patients who would include those previously regarded as feebleminded persons or moral defectives. In the event most of the Commissions' recommendations passed into law and became the basis of the Mental Health Act 1959. But **non-offending psychopaths aged 21 or over were excluded from compulsory treatment (section 21 (2)), and the Home Secretary was given powers to control the discharge of dangerous patients (section 65)**. But the psychopathic group was divided in the Act into "psychopathic disorder" and "subnormality".

6.1.20 The Commission could not agree on a specific definition of psychopathy for a new Mental Health Act (see Walker and McCabe referred to above) and it was left to the then Ministry of Health to propose that it should be defined as

> a "persistent disorder of personality (whether or not including subnormality of intelligence) which results in abnormally aggressive or seriously irresponsible conduct on the part of the patient and requires or is susceptible to medical treatment".

6.1.21 Baroness Wootton considered that for the purposes of detention on the grounds of disordered personality the aggressive or irresponsible conduct should be dangerous and she vigorously attacked this definition in the Bill's passage through the House of Lords. The final form of the definition introduced "psychopathic disorder" into English law for the first time as a generic classification which might lead to detention under the Act of 1959:

> Section 4 (4) In this Act "psychopathic disorder" means a persistent disorder or disability of mind (whether or not including subnormality of intelligence) which results in abnormally aggressive or seriously irresponsible conduct on the part of the patient, and requires or is susceptible to medical treatment.

6.1.22 The inadequacies of this classification were recognised from the outset, notably by Lady Wootton (*see*, for instance her book, *Crime and Penal Policy 1978*, p. 230ff)[18] who famously drew attention to the absurdity of the circular process whereby mental abnormality

18 Wootton of Abinger, Baroness (1978) *Crime and Penal Policy.* George Allen and Unwin, London

is inferred from anti-social behaviour, while anti-social behaviour is explained by the presence of the "persistent disorder" (the nature of which is not described). The classification of *mental illness* in the Act on the other hand relies not on an association with an abnormality of behaviour but on the psychiatrists' recognition of clinical symptoms. According to Dr Graham Robertson in his evidence to us the promise that it would soon be possible to make the diagnosis and treatment of personality disorders a scientific matter influenced the deliberations of the Royal Commission, but Dr Robertson commented "that promise remains unfulfilled (and) the concept remains enshrined in law."

6.1.23 The endorsement of psychopathy as a form of mental disorder recognised by law gave encouragement to its legitimacy as a clinical diagnostic category even though soon after the creation of this legal category of mental disorder the Working Party on the Special Hospitals expressed its anxiety about the consequences.

The Working Party on the Special Hospitals

6.1.24 The Working Party on the Special Hospitals[19] was appointed in 1959 by the then Minister of Health, The Rt Hon Enoch Powell, to consider the role of the Special Hospitals and the classes of patients to be treated in them, having regard to the new mental health law (the Mental Health Act 1959) and to the provision to be made by the hospital service generally.

6.1.25 The Report was very concerned about the impact of introducing the new category of psychopathic disorder into the law, the way that it might be used, the numbers of new patients that might emerge and the effect on secure bed requirements since:

> "medical knowledge about it is still at an early stage and there is little agreement as to what medical treatment is appropriate or possible."

And section 31 continued:

> "this disagreement . . . incidentally, is likely to be of importance as regards the number of people who will be admitted to hospital for compulsory treatment for psychopathic disorder, since part of the statutory definition of psychopathic disorder is that it should require or be susceptible to medical treatment. There is therefore inevitably much uncertainty about what will, or indeed should, be done in the National Health Service to provide treatment for psychopathic disorder. But the element of uncertainty must not be overstated. A considerable number of patients, a main constituent in whose condition is psychopathic disorder, are now being treated in the Special Hospitals. The same is true for National Health Service Hospitals that have units for the more difficult types of patient or solely for psychopaths. But many, probably the great majority, of these patients are either not severely psychopathic or else suffer also from other types of mental disorder, in particular subnormality. A special problem is likely to be set by patients who are classified as suffering from no other form of mental disorder than psychopathy, who maybe referred to the health service in increasing numbers".

6.1.26 The Report also recommended that the different categories of patient specified in the 1959 Act should be treated in separate units:

> "the main departure from present practice would be the provision of a separate hospital or unit for . . . patients whose predominant feature is psychopathic behaviour. Such a hospital or unit, as well as making an intensive therapeutic effort, should provide ample facilities for investigation and research. It would need

19 Special Hospitals. *Report of a Working Party* (1961) Ministry of Health. HMSO, London (Chairman: Mr D Emery)

enthusiastic direction, and there would have to be strong medical, nursing and occupational staff. Full occupational and recreational facilities would have to be provided." (para. 54).

6.1.27 The Working Party recommended in its Report of 1961 that "diagnostic centres" should be set up to provide investigatory and diagnostic services for psychopaths and other very difficult patients, which would be allied to facilities for research and the treatment of long-stay psychopathic patients. It also recommended that psychiatric services in the regions of the NHS should have a range of services of different levels of security (p.11):

> "we recommend that security arrangements short of those provided at Special Hospitals, should continue to be provided in the National Health Service, and that, with this in mind, Regional Hospital Boards should arrange their psychiatric services so as to ensure that there is a variety of types of hospital unit, including some secure units, and that transfers can be made between them as necessary."

6.1.28 However the Estimates Committee of the House of Commons[20] noted in its Report on the Special Hospitals and The State Hospital in 1968 that (para. 97) few of the Working Party's recommendations had so far been implemented, although it was said that one small diagnostic centre was due to be opened shortly (we believe this was in North London), and there were also plans for a long-stay treatment unit for psychopaths in the same region. The Estimates Committee continued:

> "The Ministry . . . wishes to proceed slowly in this matter in the light of the experience to be gained in the initial developments." The Committee was persuaded (para.97) that caution is the proper policy to pursue, particularly as a considerable variety of medical opinion was offered on the most appropriate type of treatment for the psychopathic offender. Much of the evidence given to the Committee (para. 106) favoured a greater flexibility in the allocation of psychopaths within the prison – Special Hospital nexus since "there will never be a sharp dividing line between offenders and sick people."

6.1.29 Sir Aubrey Lewis[21], the most distinguished psychiatrist of his day, in 1974 called psychopathic personality "a most elusive category", one of a cluster of terms which have been used more or less interchangeably or successively in the last 150 years to denote a lifelong propensity to behaviour which falls mid-way between normality and psychosis. "*Mania sine delirio,* moral insanity, moral imbecility, psychopathy, degenerate constitution, congenital delinquency, constitutional inferiority – these and other semantic variations on a dubious theme have been bandied around by psychiatrists and lawyers in a prodigious output of repetitious articles" (p133).

The Butler Report and the Aarvold Report

6.1.30 The Committee on Mentally Abnormal Offenders was established in September 1972 in the aftermath of the trial on two charges of murder and two of attempted murder of Graham Young, (*see* Bowden 1996) a notorious poisoner who had been released after eight years in Broadmoor, with little or no arrangements for community supervision. Although diagnosed as suffering from psychopathic disorder he was not recommended for a hospital order and he was sentenced to life imprisonment. According to Bowden,[22] within an hour of the verdict the then Home Secretary, the Rt Hon Reginald Maudling, announced in the House of

---

20 Second Report from the Estimates Committee. Session 1967–1968. *The Special Hospitals and the State Hospital* -31-vii HMSO, London

21 Lewis A (1974) Psychopathic Personality: a most elusive category. *Psychological Medicine.* 4. 133–144

22 Bowden P (1996) Graham Young (1947–90) The St Albans Poisoner: his life and times. *Criminal Behaviour and Mental Health* 17. 24 Supplement

Commons that he was setting up two inquiries; one to be chaired by Sir Carl Aarvold, the Recorder of London, was to advise "whether the procedures, as now improved, for the discharge and supervision of patients subject to special restrictions under section 65 of the Mental Health Act 1959, are satisfactory or whether there are further changes within the existing law, which should be made". The Aarvold Report[23] (1973) was published in January 1973 and made important recommendations about the discharge of restricted patients and its advice resulted in the creation of the Advisory Board for Restricted Patients

6.1.31 The second inquiry was to be chaired by Lord Butler of Saffron Walden.

The Advisory Board on Restricted Patients

6.1.32 The Board was set up on the recommendation of Sir Carl Aarvold's committee to give independent advice to the Minister of State in the Home Office who has responsibility for criminal policy and who has to take decisions about "restricted patients" on behalf of the Home Secretary. Advice is needed where it is difficult to predict the likelihood of serious re-offending. The cases to be considered are brought to the Board's attention by the Health Division (previously C3) of the Home Office but the formal decision to refer cases rests with the Minister.

The Committee on Mentally Abnormal Offenders

6.1.33 The Committee on Mentally Abnormal Offenders was set up on 21 September 1972, published an Interim Report on 20 April 1974, and published a final Report in October 1975.[24] The remit of the Butler Committee was:

> (a) to consider to what extent and on what criteria the law should recognise mental disorder or abnormality in a person accused of a criminal offence as a factor affecting his liability to be tried and convicted, and his disposal;
>
> (b) to consider what, if any, changes are necessary in the powers, procedure and facilities relating to appropriate treatment, in prison, hospital or the community, for offenders suffering from mental disorder or abnormality, and to their discharge and aftercare; and to make recommendations.

6.1.34 We concentrate below on the elements of the Report most relevant to our own Inquiry. Butler himself notes how much evidence heard by the Committee was concerned with the nature, treatability and management of psychopathic disorder (para. 1.18).

6.1.35 Chapter 5 of the Report is devoted to psychopaths (paras. 5.1–5.57, pp77–100). The Report outlines a brief history of psychopathic disorder and concluded that the concept of psychopathic disorder has given rise to serious confusion:

> "in essence it was originally a causal theory about hypothetical brain disorder to explain and to bring into one category all those persons who were not "insane" yet not mentally normal. This theory is no longer held. Later the term was used to describe clinical types but the definitions themselves and the types included in them varied from author to author" (para. 5.15).

6.1.36 The Committee heard much evidence suggesting that the term "psychopathic disorder" should be removed from the Mental Health Act 1959. Witnesses argued that the term was interpreted in very different ways by individual psychiatrists and was liable to abuse; that the concept of psychopathy was circular in that it inferred mental disorder from anti-social disorder; that there was no clear distinction between offenders regarded as

23 Aarvold, Sir C, Hill, Sir D, and Newton G P (1973) *Report on the Review of Procedures for the Discharge and Supervision of Psychiatric Patients Subject to Special Restrictions.* Cmnd. 5191 HMSO. London

24 Committee on Mentally Abnormal Offenders (1975) *Report* Home Office, Department of Health and Social Security. Cmnd 6244. HMSO London (Chairman: Lord Butler of Saffron Walden KG)

psychopaths and other offenders; that the term was harmful and stigmatising; and that the definition of mental disorder in section 4(1) (any other disorder or disability of mind) without reference to psychopathy, was sufficient to allow treatable psychopaths to be admitted to hospital. Witnesses also noted that in Scotland (despite the influence of the Scottish psychiatrist, Sir David Henderson), and in Northern Ireland, it had not been found necessary to make use of the term in legislation.

6.1.37 Lord Butler and his colleagues wanted to leave the door open for those psychiatrists who felt able to treat this group and so they were against removing psychopathic disorder from the Act, which would prevent compulsory detention. But they agreed that the term was unhelpful and stigmatising and recognised that "the class of persons to whom the term psychopathic disorder relates is not a single category identifiable by any medical, biological, or psychological criteria" (para. 5.23).

6.1.38 They continued:

> "... there is no clear trend of expert opinion about what the preferable solution may be, nor even any general agreement about the nature of the disorder..."

(a comment which the Reed Report considered in 1992 "is still valid today".

6.1.39 The proposed solution was to replace "psychopathic disorder" with "personality disorder" in section 4(1), and to repeal section 4(4), which defined psychopathic disorder. This change would accord more with clinical usage and allow for compulsory detention where the interests of the public and the patient demanded it.

6.1.40 Lord Butler also considered the question of treatability in detail and stated that:

> "the great weight of evidence presented to us tends to support the conclusion that psychopaths are not, in general, treatable, at least in medical terms" (para. 5.34).

6.1.41 Lord Butler's pessimism about the medical treatment of psychopaths led him to recommend clarifying section 60(1) of the Mental Health Act 1959 to make it absolutely clear **that prisons were required to cater for offenders with dangerous anti-social tendencies unless a court was fully satisfied that a hospital order would be therapeutically beneficial** (para. 5.40, cf 13.8) The Committee recognised that reducing the number of indeterminate hospital orders in this way potentially increased the number of mentally disordered individuals who were regarded as dangerous, but who would have to be released at the end of their determinate sentences, despite the potential risk to the public. Lord Butler recommended the introduction of **reviewable sentences** for such men who were regarded as still dangerous, but who were not acceptable for treatment in hospital, either because their disorder was not sufficiently severe, or because no hospital would receive them, or for other reasons, for example, because an individual was a psychopath with dangerous anti-social tendencies. Such sentences would be subject to statutory review at regular intervals (paras. 4.39-4.45).

6.1.42 Despite his Committee's pessimistic conclusion on treatability, Lord Butler did believe that, properly used, the penal system offered an environment that could benefit dangerous psychopaths. His Committee was attracted to the idea of **"training units" in prisons** for dangerous anti-social psychopaths which would aim to encourage the natural process of maturation. These would use workshop, recreational and educational facilities within a prison unit to offer a highly structured environment for such offenders. They would be different from Grendon, which took a highly selected group of relatively intelligent prisoners into a therapeutic community, rather:

> "it is our intention that training units should cater for psychopaths with dangerous anti-social tendencies aged between 17 or 18 and 35, for whom special psychiatric

treatment is not available, who are willing to undertake the training offered, and are likely to benefit from it and will have a chance of employment on release, but who in the meantime require secure containment."

6.1.43 Lord Butler estimated that around 750 places might be needed. He recommended setting up two units at first, to be evaluated by a carefully designed research programme. He recognised the potential problem of putting a large number of psychopaths together in one institution but noted that the Committee thought that peer pressure would make such individuals less of a risk than when they had the opportunity of manipulating other prisoners. Lord Butler also noted the importance of having high quality staff supported by disciplines outside the institution and linked to academic departments.

Lord Butler and his team did not stop there. They recommended introducing powers for courts to "remand" patients to hospital under an "interim hospital order" for a maximum of six months so that their suitability for treatment could be assessed (paras. 12.5–6). His Committee discussed but rejected the idea of some kind of hybrid order combining a section 60 hospital order and a sentence of imprisonment to be served should the offender be unresponsive, arguing that "it seems to us undesirable that the court should not clearly decide in so important a matter as the loss of a man's liberty, between a punitive sentence and an order for medical treatment" (para. 14.10). And they recommended tightening up the criteria for restriction orders, making it clear that such orders were for the safety of the public. In view of the difficulty in determining how long such a restriction order should be in force the Committee recommended removing the facility for making a restriction order of limited duration (para. 14.24–5).

6.1.44 Twenty or more years later the Butler Report can be seen to have marked a turning point in the history of forensic psychiatry. It remains a key reference and it repays careful study. Yet, in the event, little of the Butler Report was implemented with the very important exception of the network of Regional (Medium) Secure Units which has much improved the range of services for mentally abnormal offenders, and some of the legislative recommendations which were incorporated in the Mental Health Act of 1983.

6.1.45 The Butler Report placed considerable emphasis upon the importance of establishing secure hospital units in each Health Region, so much so that an interim Report was published to recommend their implementation as a matter of urgency. The units were for those mentally disordered persons, offenders and non-offenders alike, who do not require the degree of security offered by the Special Hospitals. An internal Working Party of the Department of Health (Chairman: Dr James Glancy) had also been considering the need for secure accommodation of this kind and agreed that the need for these units was established. Lord Butler considered that 40 beds per million of the population were required (2,000 beds) while Dr Glancy estimated a need for 20 beds per million (1,000 beds). The Secretary of State of the day, the Rt Hon Barbara Castle accepted Glancy's estimate in the first instance and said that the situation would be reviewed when the first 1,000 beds were in place. In fact, implementation was a painfully difficult matter and by the time of the Reed Review, 17 years after the Butler Report, only 600 beds were in place. There are now 1,600. Most of the beds have been used for adult mentally ill patients and a few for those with psychopathic disorder. We have been told by the Department of Health that there are approximately 100 patients in medium secure units detained under the classification of psychopathic disorder. Athough the Regional Medium Secure Units have been under constant pressure, they have been a success story, attracting generally high quality staff and providing much improved conditions for treatment and management. They have also provided a focus for the development of academic teaching and research facilities as Lord Butler intended. Yet the current provision is still insufficient to cope with the demand for beds, which adds to the reluctance of psychiatrists to accept patients with a classification of psychopathic disorder.

6.1.46 Dr John Reed commented in evidence that he felt that the Butler Report still had continued validity and he was still broadly in agreement with its recommendations. This was also the strongly held view of psychiatrists according to Chiswick, McIsaac and McClintock (1984) when they reported on their research on the prosecution process in Scotland.[25]

Better Services for the Mentally Ill

6.1.47 In 1975 the White Paper, *Better Services for the Mentally Ill*,[26] was also published which also recognised that the term "psychopath" had come to carry considerable stigma (para. 1.11) and that there had been a reaction against it in favour of "personality disorder with anti-social trends". There was also considerable uncertainty about the extent to which people with personality disorders can be helped by the mental health services and further research was needed. "It is generally accepted that such people do not readily respond to traditional psychiatric treatment and indeed there are difficulties of principle in determining those cases in which it is proper to regard a behaviour pattern as a 'disorder'."

A Review of the Mental Health Act 1959

6.1.48 In 1976 the Government published a consultation paper[27] which reviewed the Mental Health Act 1959 and the Butler Report's proposals but was reluctant to remove the possibility of treatment from those who could benefit from it by taking psychopathy out of the Act altogether. This sentiment echoed the view of the 1961 Working Party on the Special Hospitals (see above) which also did not wish to discourage treatment and emphasised the need for more research. It recommended the establishment of diagnostic and treatment centres with three main functions: to provide an investigatory and diagnostic service for the patients referred to them and to give advice on subsequent disposal and treatment; to provide treatment where necessary on a long-term basis; and to provide facilities for research. The object was to provide services for patients who present special difficulty because of their aggressive, anti-social or criminal tendencies and who also present special problems of diagnosis, treatment and management.

6.1.49 When the time came to amend the 1959 Act despite doubts and uncertainties about psychopathic disorder there was surprisingly little pressure from reformists, the professional, charitable and voluntary bodies to make any radical changes to the Act on this topic (see for instance the proposals from MIND (Gostin 1977[28]) who simply drew attention to the Butler Report's proposals). There was one exception, however.

6.1.50 Over the years concern had been growing about the assumption of treatability in the 1959 definition of psychopathic disorder; that (section 4. (4)) psychopathic disorder means a persistent disorder . . . (which) . . . requires or is susceptible to medical treatment. In order to recognise that some persons suffering from this disorder may be treatable and others not, the definition in the new Act removed the words referring to treatability and moved them to a qualifying subsection which indicated that one of the grounds for detaining an individual suffering from psychopathic disorder is that such treatment is *likely to alleviate or prevent a deterioration of his condition.* This change meant that although the category of "psychopathic disorder" continued to be recognised in the new Act, compulsory detention was dependent on a number of factors of which one was the treatability of the patient. The

25 Chiswick D, McIsaac M W, McClintock FH (1984) *Prosecution of the mentally disturbed.* Aberdeen University Press, Aberdeen

26 *Better Services for the Mentally Ill* (1975) Department of Health and Social Security. Cmnd 6233. HMSO London

27 *A Review of the Mental Health Act 1959* (1976) Department of Health and Social Security. HMSO London

28 Gostin L (1977) *A Human Condition.* MIND. London

intention was to allow clinicians to discriminate between those who were and were not treatable and to protect patients from inappropriate detention in a hospital.

6.1.51 "Medical treatment" under the 1959 Act included (section 147) nursing, and also "care and training under medical supervision". As defined by the 1983 Act (section 145) medical treatment includes nursing, and also includes "care, habilitation and rehabilitation under medical supervision".

The Mental Health Act 1983

6.1.52 The Mental Health Act 1983 retains psychopathic disorder as a category of mental disorder:

> "Section 1(2) In this Act –
>
> mental disorder" means mental illness, arrested or incomplete development of mind, psychopathic disorder and any other disorder or disability of mind and "mentally disordered" shall be construed accordingly;
>
> "severe mental impairment" means a state of arrested or incomplete development of mind which includes severe impairment of intelligence and social functioning and is associated with abnormally aggressive or seriously irresponsible conduct on the part of the person concerned and "severely mentally impaired" shall be construed accordingly;
>
> "mental impairment" means a state of arrested or incomplete development of mind (not amounting to severe mental impairment) which includes significant impairment of intelligence and social functioning and is associated with abnormally aggressive or seriously irresponsible conduct on the part of the person concerned and "mentally impaired" shall be construed accordingly;
>
> "psychopathic disorder" means a persistent disorder or disability of mind (whether or not including significant impairment of intelligence) which results in abnormally aggressive or seriously irresponsible conduct on the part of the person concerned."

6.1.53 More than one of the conditions set out in this definition may affect the patient at any one time. For many of the purposes of the Act a general classification of "mental disorder" is not sufficient and one of the four specific categories of mental disorder is required; mental illness, severe mental impairment, mental impairment or psychopathic disorder. A specific classification must be made for an admission for treatment (section 3), a reception into guardianship (section 7), a hospital order or guardianship order made by a court (section 37), an interim hospital order (section 38) and a transfer of a sentenced prisoner from prison to hospital (section 47).

6.1.54 Jones (1996)[29] gives an analysis of the meaning of the terms in Section 1:

> "Any other disorder or disability of mind" could, according to Gostin and Fennell (1992)[30], include "personality disorders". A person who suffers from a disorder which comes within this category is eligible for detention under sections 2 ,4, 5, 135 and 136 of the Act, that is to say sections authorising short term detention."
>
> "Significant impairment of intelligence" in the definition of psychopathic disorder means mental impairment."
>
> "The definition of psychopathic disorder does not refer to treatability. The effect of sections 3, 37 and 47 is that psychopathic and mentally impaired persons cannot be

---

29 Jones R J (1996) *Mental Health Act Manual* 5th ed. Sweet and Maxwell, London

30 Gostin L and Fennell P (1992) *Mental Health Tribunal Procedure,* 2nd ed. Oyez, Longman, London

compulsorily admitted to hospital for treatment unless it can be shown that the medical treatment (definition above) is likely to alleviate or prevent deterioration of their condition."

In **R v Canons Park Mental Health Review Tribunal, ex p. A**. [1994] 2 All E.R. 659, (C.A) , Roch L J suggested the following principles that should be applied to a treatability test:

> First, if a tribunal were to be satisfied that the patient's detention in hospital was simply an attempt to coerce the patient into participating in group therapy, then the tribunal would be under a duty to direct discharge. Second, treatment in hospital will satisfy the treatability test although it is unlikely to alleviate the patient's condition, provided that it is likely to prevent deterioration. Third, treatment in hospital will satisfy the treatability test although it will not immediately alleviate or prevent deterioration of the patient's condition, provided that alleviation or stabilisation is likely in due course. Fourth, the treatability test can still be met although initially there may be some deterioration in the patient's condition, due for example to the patient's initial anger at being detained. Fifth, it must be remembered that medical treatment in hospital covers nursing and also includes care, habilitation and rehabilitation under medical supervision. Sixth, the treatability test is satisfied if nursing care etc. are likely to lead to an alleviation of the patient's condition in that the patient is likely to gain an insight into his problem or cease to be uncooperative in his attitude towards treatment which would potentially have lasting benefit".

6.1.55 The implications of this decision for the discharge of psychopathic patients are considered by Estella Baker and John Crichton in "Ex parte A: Psychopathy, treatability and the law", *Journal of Forensic Psychiatry*, Vol 6, No 1, 101–119.

6.1.56 Renewal of detention orders also includes these principles and is discussed in detail in Jones, R, *Mental Health Act Manual*, 5th Ed, 1996.

6.1.57 The phrase "abnormally aggressive or seriously irresponsible" appears in three categories and it has caused concern that this can cause confusion and mis-classification. Jones comments that what is "abnormally aggressive" or "seriously irresponsible" must, to a certain extent, depend upon the cultural and social context within which the behaviour occurs (p.21). The Mental Health Commission has defined the terms "abnormally aggressive" and "seriously irresponsible" as follows: " 'abnormally aggressive conduct' is behaviour which is mostly unpredictable and severe, causing damage or distress and occurring either recently or persistently or with excessive severity. 'Seriously irresponsible conduct' is behaviour which frequently constitutes a serious or potentially serious danger, where the person concerned does not show appropriate regard for the consequences."

Other Jurisdictions

6.1.58 The Mental Health (Scotland) Act 1984 defines mental disorder as "mental illness or mental handicap however caused or manifested" (section 1 (2)). Psychopathic disorder or personality disorder are not mentioned but the term mental disorder appears to encompass those who would be classified as suffering from psychopathic disorder in England and Wales as it includes mental disorders which are persistent and manifested only by abnormally aggressive or seriously irresponsible conduct.

6.1.59 In the Mental Health (Northern Ireland) Order 1986, mental illness is defined for the first time in United Kingdom mental health legislation. Mental illness is a "state of mind which affects a person's thinking, perceiving, emotion or judgement to the extent that he requires care or medical treatment in his own interests or in the interests of other people". But, "no person shall be treated under this Order as suffering from mental disorder, or from any form of mental disorder by reason only of personality disorder . . ."

Psychopathic Disorder: The need for Reform, DHSS and Home Office Consultation Paper 1986

6.1.60 In 1986, increased concern for public safety and the release or possible release from Special Hospitals of psychopathic offender patients who might re-offend led the Government to issue a consultation document.[31]

6.1.61 This partly resulted from changes which had been brought about following the case of X v UK (1981) 4 E.H.R.R. 181 which held that the position in which the Home Secretary had sole responsibility for the discharge of restricted patients (with tribunals acting in an advisory capacity only) was not in conformity with Article 5(4) of the European Convention on Human Rights which entitles those detained on grounds of unsoundness of mind to a review of the lawfulness of their detention at periodic intervals before a court which must be empowered to order their discharge. The law was altered so that MHRTs had the authority to make decisions on the absolute, or conditional, discharge of patients subject to a restriction order imposed by a court, even to the extent of over-ruling the Home Secretary's objections.

6.1.62 It was felt that there were now three principal problems:

(i) uncertainties regarding the concept of personality disorder, its diagnosis, treatability and relationship with offending;

(ii) the practical difficulties, particularly in an artificial environment, in assessing improvement and predicting future behaviour in the community if a patient were discharged;

(iii) anxiety about a small number of cases where tribunals, applying the statutory criteria, had discharged patients appropriately, the public was nevertheless felt to be at risk.

6.1.63 The Working Group which produced the afore-mentioned consultation document felt that it was beyond their remit to consider excluding psychopathic disorder from the Act or to change its definition but they considered other changes:

(i) for this group of offenders, a new provision which would enable the court to sentence the offender to a term of imprisonment and to direct that he be admitted to hospital from court;

(ii) the deletion from section 37 of any reference to psychopathic disorder (with the possibility of transfer from prison to hospital under sections 47 and 49 of the Act);

(iii) amendment of section 37 so that a hospital order could be made in the case of a psychopathic offender only when a restriction order (section 41) would not be appropriate.

In the event no changes resulted from this consultation but advice was given to improve practice within the existing statutory provisions.

Report of the Working Group on Psychopathic Disorder 1993

6.1.64 One of the recommendations of the joint Department of Health and Home Office Review of Services for Mentally Disordered Offenders and Others Requiring Similar Services,

---

31 Health Notice (1986). *Health service organisation: offenders suffering from psychopathic disorder.* HN(86)28. Department of Health and Social Security

which completed its work in July 1992 was that a separate working group should be established to examine psychopathic (personality) disorder.

6.1.65 This joint Department of Health/Home Office Working Group on Psychopathic Disorder[32] was set up in September 1992 under the chairmanship of Dr John Reed CB with the following terms of reference:

> "to consider the services needed for those people who present special problems of violent behaviour or repeat offending because of their personality, whether or not they are otherwise mentally disordered, taking account of both the interests of the individuals concerned and the protection of other people. In particular:
>
> > "to consider, in the light of present knowledge, what methods of management, or treatment, are likely to be most effective in reducing violent or offending behaviour;
> >
> > to consider whether these require the provision of any new services in addition to, or in place of, those available at present;
> >
> > to advise how the services, whether within the Prison Service, the health services, or elsewhere, may most effectively be made available to those in need;
> >
> > to consider whether any changes are needed in the present legal provisions relating to psychopathic disorder in the interests of more effective provision of services;
> >
> > to advise on any research which might facilitate the better understanding of the definition, management, or treatment, of this group of offenders;
> >
> > to consider the resource implications of any proposals, including their cost effectiveness."

6.1.66 The Group identified three main issues: **diagnosis and treatment** – what is psychopathic disorder; **service development** – what services are needed, and who should deliver them; and **legislation** – is the present framework right? The Group commissioned a literature review by Dr Bridget Dolan and Dr (now Professor) Jeremy Coid and reviewed the current pattern of services.

6.1.67 The Working Group's initial conclusion is a melancholy one: from the evidence gathered, the group reached an initial conclusion that there was insufficient information available to answer in full the questions posed in the terms of reference. No firm conclusions could be reached about what methods of management, or treatment, were likely to be most effective in improving health and reducing violent or offending behaviour. Instead a pragmatic approach was needed in which a wide range of services in many settings (including the community) was provided (para. 4.8).

6.1.68 In the face of this lack of knowledge the Group duly recommended a variety of research programmes, on treatment interventions (using the multi-method criteria for categorising severe personality disorder recommended by Dolan and Coid) (paras. 6.12–14), on risk assessment (8.14) and on aetiology (9.2). The Group argued that specialised settings in prison and hospital should be developed, with greater flexibility for individuals to move from one to another. Research into the outcomes of the different services with particular sub-groups of patients was needed to illuminate effectiveness (paras. 9.13–15). They also proposed a service research and development project on the assessment of need for services for personality disordered individuals (paras. 9.23–25).

---

32 Department of Health, Home Office. Working Group on Psychopathic Disorder (1994). *Report.* Department of Health/Home Office (Chairman: Dr John Reed CB)

6.1.69 The Group was able to come to firmer recommendations in the legislative arena. First, they discussed the statutory definition of "psychopathic disorder". Three options were considered:

(i) to retain the existing statutory definition;

(ii) to adopt the Scottish definition; or

(iii) to replace the term "psychopathic disorder" with "personality disorder".

6.1.70 In favour of (i) there were two lines of argument. One was negative; there was no satisfactory alternative, however flawed the current situation might be. The other was more positive; the current term was comprehensible to lawyers and Ministers, was reasonably flexible and there was a fair measure of agreement amongst clinicians on the common traits of the condition.

6.1.71 The Scottish legislation does not mention psychopathic or personality disorder, but it does refer to "abnormally aggressive and seriously irresponsible conduct". (section 17 (1)(a)(i)). One might replace the legal categories in the Mental Health Act 1983 with a single category of mental disorder, leaving it to clinicians to interpret this. But the Working Group felt this might cause considerable confusion and even more inconsistency of practice.

6.1.72 The Working Group, like the Butler Committee before them, were attracted by (iii), the idea of replacing the inaccurate, stigmatising and unhelpful term "psychopathic disorder" with "personality disorder", but without seeking to define personality disorder in the statute and, like "mental illness" leaving it to clinical interpretation.

6.1.73 The Group then discussed the working of sections 37 and 41 of the Act and this aspect, of their deliberations is referred to again later in this Report where we address this topic.

6.1.74 With reference to treatability, the Dolan and Coid review, influenced the Group's opinion that "the term psychopathic disorder does not represent a single clinical disorder but is a legal category describing a number of personality disorders which contribute to the person carrying out anti-social acts, usually of an episodic type" (para. 2.2). No change in the treatability criterion in the Act was recommended despite evidence of widely differing applications of the criteria, because they saw no viable alternatives, but recommended that section 48 of the Act (transfer from prison to hospital of remand prisoners), be extended to include psychopathic disorder.

6.1.75 This Working Group was the first since the Butler Report to make a serious attempt to address the problem of psychopathy and personality disorder. Dr Reed told us in evidence that from his considerable and lengthy experience this was by far the most difficult topic that he had taken on to review and in retrospect the Working Group had the wrong structure, with too many representatives from an extensive range of interests. It had proved extremely difficult to get agreement on a wide range of issues and, he said that is why the Report comes down insofar as its principal recommendations are concerned by simply saying "we need to know more".

> "It is an extraordinarily difficult subject to produce very positive conclusions, it is very hard to reach agreement on its definition, we do not know what it is caused by, we do not know how to measure it, we do not know what interventions are effective and we do not know very well how to measure the consequences of intervention".

He felt, looking back, that a more effective Group would have had fewer members and would have taken expert evidence.

6.2.0 Psychopathic Disorder and Personality Disorder

6.2.1 Psychopathic disorder now has three meanings. It is a legal classification as one of the four categories of mental disorder in the Mental Health Act 1983; it is a clinical diagnostic construct or category in some classifications and it is used as a term of abuse in the vernacular. It has also acquired a pejorative connotation in clinical work (Higgins 1995)[33], particularly when a patient is identified as "a psychopath" or as "psychopathic," with the implication that the patient is untreatable, has no proper place in a hospital and is disliked by clinical staff. The term has survived increasingly widespread criticism as recorded in many official Reports (see above) and professional publications and has attracted cogent arguments for its replacement.

Legal category of psychopathic disorder

6.2.2 The Mental Health Act 1983 defines psychopathic disorder as follows:

> Section 1(2) "psychopathic disorder is a persistent disorder or disability of mind (whether or not including significant impairment of intelligence) which results in abnormally aggressive or severely irresponsible conduct."

The Royal Commission on the Law relating to Mental Illness and Mental Deficiency made clear in its Chapters 2 and 3 that groups of patients are defined in the law only in connection with compulsory powers of detention. With the development of clinical diagnostic classifications that do not have a direct correlation with the single legal classification there is clearly scope for increasing confusion.

Clinical Classifications of Personality Disorder

6.2.3 Gelder, Gath and Mayou (1989),[34] authors of the leading textbook of psychiatry, begin their discussion of this topic with the observation that each category in any classification scheme represents an ideal type that few patients fit exactly. They quote Schneider (1950)[35]:

> "Any clinician would be greatly embarrassed if asked to classify into appropriate types the psychopaths (that is abnormal personalities) encountered in any one year. There are only a few cases in which one of the characteristic types of description or combinations can be applied without further qualification. Human beings resist precise measurement and, unlike the phenomena of disease, abnormal individuals cannot be classified neatly in the manner of clinical diagnosis".

The International Classification of Disease-10 *(ICD-10) (World Health Organization 1992)*

6.2.4 The ICD-10 classification of personality disorders includes a variety of clinically significant conditions and behaviours each of which is classified according to clusters of traits that correspond to the most frequent or conspicuous behaviour manifestations. General diagnostic guidelines are given for **specific personality disorders** as follows:

> "Conditions not directly attributable to gross brain damage or disease or to another psychiatric disorder, meeting the following criteria:
>
> > (a) markedly disharmonious attitudes and behaviour, involving usually several areas of functioning, e.g. affectivity, arousal, impulse control, ways of perceiving and thinking, and style of relating to others;
> >
> > (b) the abnormal behaviour pattern is enduring, of long standing, and not limited to episodes of mental illness;
> >
> > (c) the abnormal behaviour pattern is pervasive and clearly maladaptive to a broad range of personal and social situations;

33 Higgins J (1995) Crime and mental disorder II, Forensic aspects of psychiatric disorder. In Chiswick D and Cope R eds. *Seminars in Practical Forensic Psychiatry.* Gaskell Press, London

34 Gelder M, Gath D and Mayou R (1989) *Oxford Textbook of Psychiatry*, 2nd ed. Oxford University Press, Oxford

35 Schneider K (1963) *Psychopathic Personalities* (translation of 9th ed. By M W Hamilton). Cassell, London

(d) the above manifestations always appear during childhood or adolescence and continue into adulthood;

(e) the disorder leads to considerable personal distress but this may only become apparent late in its course;

(f) the disorder is usually, but not invariably, associated with significant problems in occupational and social performance.

6.2.5 There are ten categories of specific personality disorder in this grouping (the category F60) as follows:

"F60.0 Paranoid personality disorder
F60.1 Schizoid personality disorder
F60.2 Dissocial personality disorder
F60.3 Emotionally unstable personality disorder
.30 Impulsive type
.31 Borderline type
F60.4 Histrionic personality disorder
F60.5 Anankastic personality disorder
F60.6 Anxious (avoidant) personality disorder
F60.7 Dependent personality disorder
F60.8 Other specific personality disorders
F.60.9 Personality disorder, unspecified."

F60.2 *dissocial personality disorder* equates with the limited descriptive elements of psychopathy in the legal definition. Indeed, a footnote indicates that dissocial personality disorder includes: amoral, anti-social, psychopathic, and sociopathic personality disorder. It has the following characteristics:

"A personality disorder, usually coming to attention because of a gross disparity between behaviour and the prevailing social norms, and is characterised by:

(a) callous unconcern for the feelings of others;

(b) gross and persistent attitude of irresponsibility and disregard for social norms, rules and obligations;

(c) incapacity to maintain enduring relationships, though having no difficulty in establishing them;

(d) very low tolerance to frustration and a low threshold for discharge of aggression, including violence;

(e) incapacity to experience guilt or to profit from experience, particularly punishment;

(f) marked proneness to blame others, or to offer plausible rationalisations, for the behaviour that has brought the patient into conflict with society."

The Diagnostic and Statistical Manual *(DSM-IV; American Psychiatric Association)*

6.2.6 The American Psychiatric Association has developed a multi-axial system to assist clinicians to plan treatment and predict outcome. There are five axes included in the DSM-IV multi-axial classification:

Axis I Clinical Disorders

Other Conditions That May Be a Focus of Clinical Attention.

Axis II Personality Disorders; Mental Retardation.

Axis III General Medical Conditions.

Axis IV Psychosocial and Environmental Problems.

Axis V Global Assessment of Functioning.

6.2.7 A multi-axial evaluation will describe the patient in terms of the presence of disorders on one or more Axes, or the principal, secondary and other diagnoses are simply listed as are relevant to the care and treatment of the patient. Personality Disorders in this classification are coded on Axis II. The diagnosis of Personality Disorders according to the Manual (p630) requires an evaluation of the individual's long-term patterns of functioning, and the particular personality features must be evident by early adulthood. The personality traits that define these disorders must also be distinguished from characteristics that emerge in response to specific situational stressors or more transient mental states.

The clinician should assess the stability of the personality traits over time and across different situations. Although a single interview with the person is sometimes sufficient for making the diagnosis, it is often necessary to conduct more than one interview and to space these over time. Assessment may also be complicated by the fact that the individual may not consider the characteristics that define a Personality Disorder problematic. To help overcome this difficulty, supplementary information from other informants may be helpful.

6.2.8 DSM-IV describes 10 specific personality disorders grouped into three clusters based on descriptive similarities:

"*Cluster A Personality Disorders*
301.0 Paranoid Personality Disorder
301.20 Schizoid Personality Disorder
301.22 Schizotypal Personality Disorder

"*Cluster B Personality Disorders*
301.7 Anti-social Personality Disorders
301.83 Borderline Personality Disorder
301.50 Histrionic Personality Disorder
301.81 Narcissistic Personality Disorder

"*Cluster C Personality Disorders*
301.82 Avoidant Personality Disorder
301.6 Dependent Personality Disorder
301.83 Obsessive-Compulsive Personality Disorder
301.9 Personality Disorder Not Other wise Specified

6.2.9 Of the above, 301.7 Anti-social Personality Disorder correlates most closely with psychopathy, the diagnostic criteria for which is as follows:

A: there is a pervasive pattern of disregard for and violation of the rights of others occurring since age 15 years, as indicated by three (or more) of the following:

(1) failure to conform to social norms with respect to lawful behaviours as indicated by repeatedly performing acts that are grounds for arrest;

(2) deceitfulness, as indicated by repeated lying, use of aliases, or conning others for profit or for pleasure;

(3) impulsivity or failure to plan ahead;

(4) irritability and aggressiveness, as indicated by repeated physical fights or assaults;

(5) reckless disregard for safety of self or others;

(6) consistent irresponsibility, as indicated by repeated failure to sustain consistent work behaviour or honour financial obligations;

(7) lack of remorse as indicated by being different to or rationalizing having hurt, mistreated, or stolen from another,

B: The individual is at least age 18 years.

C: There is evidence of conduct disorder with onset before the age of 15 years.

D: The occurrence of anti-social behaviour is not exclusively during the course of a schizophrenic or a manic episode.

Dimensional Models for Personality Disorders

6.2.10 An alternative to the categorical approach to classification is the dimensional perspective described in the DSM-IV Manual which is based upon the hypothesis that Personality Disorders represent maladaptive variants of personality traits that merge imperceptibly into normality and into one another.

Hare's Psychopathy Checklist *(PCL- Revised)*

6.2.11 Hare (1991)[36] took 16 criteria delineated by Cleckley (referred to above) as characteristic in the diagnosis of psychopathy and, with further refinement, developed a 20-item check-list consisting of characteristic traits found typically in psychopathy and which can be used in making a diagnosis according to Hare's scheme. This classification is particularly useful for research purposes and for determining severity. The items are a compromise between what the patient self-reports and what the clinician observes about his behaviour. There are other classifications and typologies of importance and they are discussed in detail in the book by Dolan and Coid (referred to above).

6.2.12 The evidence of the British Psychological Society advised us that the reliability of diagnosis using the DSM and ICD classifications is poor, the high levels of co-morbidity of personality disorders make discrimination difficult and that diagnosis has little predictive validity in terms of providing information about likely treatment outcome or in terms of indicating the appropriate treatment type.

Diagnosis of Personality Disorder

6.2.13 In their paper Marlowe and Sugarman (1997[37]) note that it is generally agreed that the diagnosis of personality disorder of any type should not be made unless certain conditions are met. Based upon the "clusters" described above in DSM-IV:

Cluster A – Patients often seem odd or eccentric (such as paranoid or schizoid). Schizotypal disorder is often included in this cluster.

Cluster B – Patients may seem dramatic, emotional, or erratic (such as dissocial, histrionic, or borderline type of emotionally unstable personality).

Cluster C – Patients present as anxious or fearful (such as dependent, anxious, anankastic.

6.2.14 The DSM-IV Manual lists general diagnostic criteria for a Personality Disorder:

"A. An enduring pattern of inner experience and behaviour that deviates markedly from the expectations of the individuals culture. This pattern is manifested in two (or more) of the following areas:

(1) cognition (ie, ways of perceiving and interpreting self, other people and events);

(2) affectivity (ie, the range, intensity, liability, and appropriateness of emotional response);

(3) inter-personal functioning;

(4) impulse control.

36 Hare RD (1991) *The Hare Psychopathy Checklist.* Revised. Multi Health Systems, Toronto

37 Marlowe M and Sugarman P (1997) Disorders of Personality. *British Medical Journal,* **131**, 176–179

B. The enduring pattern is inflexible and pervasive across a broad range of personal and social situations.

C. The enduring pattern leads to clinically significant distress or impairment in social, occupational, or other important areas of functioning.

D. The pattern is stable and of long duration and its onset can be traced back at least to adolescence or early adulthood.

E. The enduring pattern is not better accounted for as a manifestation or consequence of another mental disorder.

F. The enduring pattern is not due to the direct physiological effects of a substance (e.g. a drug of abuse, a medication) or a general medical condition (e.g. head trauma)."

6.3.0 The "Lottery"

6.3.1 Whether or not a convicted offender is diagnosed as suffering from psychopathic disorder and becomes the subject of a hospital order is, to a considerable extent, a matter of chance. If it is thought that an accused person may be suffering from a mental disorder a psychiatric assessment is requested by the prosecution or defence, or both, prior to the hearing for the purpose, usually, of giving advice with reference to criminal responsibility and disposal in the event of conviction. There are not uncommonly two assessments, one for each side.

6.3.2 After conviction the Judge will consider any recommendations including any evidence justifying consideration of a hospital order (section 37, Mental Health Act 1983) made by two doctors, one of whom must be approved for the purposes of section 12, Mental Health Act 1983. Medical recommendations must specify the class of mental disorder present and the doctors must agree. After he has considered all the facts and if he has it in mind, the Judge may make an order. A bed must be available in an appropriate hospital. (At the High Security Hospitals, their Admissions Board must accept the recommendation for admission). After hearing oral evidence from one of the doctors, the Judge may, if he considers it appropriate, make a hospital order under section 37 of the Act. He may also add to the hospital order a restriction order under section 41. The consequences of a restriction order are that the patient can not be discharged, be given leave of absence or be transferred to another hospital without the agreement of the Home Secretary.

6.3.3 Psychiatric assessments are frequently given following one interview, they are not always carried out by psychiatrists trained in forensic psychiatry, the doctors do not always have access to all the previous documentation relating to the history of the patient. In addition, it is believed that psychiatrists have widely differing views and degrees of optimism or pessimism about the diagnosis and treatability of psychopathic disorder (see for instance Cope (1996)[38] who carried out a survey of the opinions of forensic psychiatrists on this subject).

6.3.4 So that for the convicted man the outcome depends upon:

(i) his presentation being recognised as possibly related to psychopathic disorder;

(ii) the views of the assessing medical practitioners, their experience and training, (and, we heard in evidence, an important factor can be the interest of a particular patient to the doctor);

(iii) the availability of an appropriately secure bed;

(iv) the decision of the judge, taking all the circumstances into account.

---

38 Cope R (1992) A survey of forensic psychiatrists'views on psychopathic disorder. *Journal of Forensic Psychiatry*; 4: 2

6.3.5 The grounds for the clinician's diagnosis are rarely challenged. As Dr Chiswick (1992)[39] has said, of the Mental Health Act classification of psychopathic disorder: "There has been little legal exploration of its meaning and no authoritative testing of terms such as 'abnormally aggressive' or 'seriously irresponsible'. Its legal interpretation is whatever a particular court decides at a particular time."

6.3.6 Dr Chiswick, in the same paper, refers to the 'very elasticity' of the personality disorder category. Because its definition is legal, not clinical, and is unlikely to be the subject of scrutiny, it is possible for almost any violent offender to slip into this category. He continues:

> "What is special about those classified and accepted for admission by a special hospital psychiatrist? Tens of thousands of men are convicted of violent crimes every year; a handful find their way into Special Hospitals – how do they get selected? Do the 400 psychopaths detained in Special Hospitals share common clinical features that are absent in the thousands of violent men who are processed through the penal system?"

6.3.7 Bearing in mind the indeterminate nature of such an order with respect to psychopathic disorder (which we will discuss further) it may not always be perceived as the most desirable outcome by the individual offender himself. Indeed, as Hoggett (1990)[40] points out (p. 52), far from amounting to an excuse, the label 'psychopath' is likely to do an offender more harm than good. If a hospital order is not recommended or a hospital place cannot be found, the court may be tempted to impose a prison sentence at the top of the range because, by definition, he is more than usually dangerous.

6.3.8 The uncertainties in this process have been called a "lottery" and many witnesses were in agreement that there are substantial and important steps that can be taken to minimise the element of chance which presently determines the placement of some offenders. (We address this in our recommendations).

6.4.0 Terminology and Diagnosis of Personality Disorder

Expert Evidence to this Inquiry

6.4.1 It was crystal-clear from an early stage of this Inquiry that opinion on these topics was not likely to be straightforward or unanimous. As is evident from the history of this subject as outlined above there is an extensive record of differing views and disagreement and a lack of definition and scientific objectivity about personality disorder. It is also evident from the difficulties that the Royal College of Psychiatrists encountered in preparing evidence for this Inquiry. The College was unable to give us any guidance in our endeavour to elucidate the definition and treatment of personality disorder:

> "There has been a wide spectrum of opinion within the College and particularly within the Forensic Psychiatry Section about this . . ." (Dr Anton Obholzer.)

6.4.2 The College, as the body which represents psychiatry and psychiatrists in the United Kingdom might have been expected to provide us with a clear and contemporaneous view about the diagnosis and treatment of severe personality disorder. We understand and sympathise with the problems they faced in trying to do so. Instead they urged "caution against coming to hard and fast conclusions about matters which are of considerable professional debate throughout the world and where research evidence to date is lacking in many areas".

6.4.3 It has been our objective to attempt to clear the water and to make our eventual

39 Chiswick D (1992) Compulsory treatment of patients with psychopathic disorder: an abnormally aggressive or seriously irresponsible exercise? *Criminal Behaviour and Mental Health*; **2**: 2.106–113

40 Hoggett B (1990) *Mental Health Law* 3rd ed. Sweet and Maxwell, London

recommendations with as much understanding as possible of the opinion and experience of British practitioners and researchers today.

6.4.4 There is no doubt that more research is needed, a great deal more, to improve the validity and reliability of clinical diagnosis and classification, treatability, and types of treatment, the assessment of need for this patient group, to define the services that are required and to redefine this field of social policy. That is all true; but in the meantime, we believe the time has come to grasp the nettle and recommend the way forward in the light of our understanding at the present time, bearing in mind the need to provide a framework that is capable of change in the light of developments in the future.

6.4.5 We decided to invite statements from a range of expert opinion and to set aside two weeks of our public hearings to allow questioning and cross-examination of many of them. We also received statements from many other witnesses relevant to this subject. We particularly canvassed opinion about the validity of the diagnosis of severe personality disorder, the value of treatment, the services needed to meet the needs of individuals suffering from severe personality disorder and the relevance of the legal category of "psychopathic disorder". We discussed many other issues with those who were good enough to respond to our invitation to appear before us in person, and we are most grateful to them for their assistance.

Definition

6.4.6 There is no simple and generally accepted definition of severe personality disorder, as Professor John Gunn explained, and a number of witnesses noted, it is not a term that appears in any of the existing classifications.

6.4.7 The terms used to define psychopathy have moral and political overtones and "psychopath" is now in disrepute. T*he Hare Checklist* is a long string of pejorative adjectives derived from Cleckley's description of psychopathy and although this diagnostic system is increasingly used there was criticism of it from a number of witnesses. Professor Pamela Taylor, for instance, felt that although there is evidence for reliability, the nature of the terms used might be reflecting the personal prejudices of the interviewers and therapists. Others, however, considered it a valuable tool in the assessment of risk of causing serious harm to others.

6.4.8 "Psychopath" is stigmatising and to be avoided, but because of its association with anti-social behaviour it is seen in a moral as well as a medical context.

6.4.9 Is personality disorder "a disease"? Applying one model, the justification for this interpretation depends upon the use of criteria given by Scadding (1990)[41] who described diseases as conditions which place an individual at biological disadvantage. Professor Gunn, who drew our attention to this concept, also referred us to his and Professor Taylor's edited textbook[42] where concepts of disease (and its differentiation from "illness", "disorder" and other terms) are discussed in detail. They argue for and adopt the term "disease" in preference to the term "disorder" in their book, but confess that "not all our authors share the editors' enthusiasm for this perspective and some . . . have refused to call personality disorders diseases". In their oral evidence it was common ground among the psychiatrists who gave evidence that some personality disordered individuals proved to be treatment resistant.

6.4.10 The morbidity and mortality, suicide rates and response to ameliorative measures (rather than cure) justify regarding personality disorder as a disease and properly as a medical

41 Scadding JG (1990) The semantic problems of psychiatry. *Psychological Medicine,* **20** 243–8

42 Gunn J and Taylor P (eds) (1993) *Forensic Psychiatry. Clinical, legal and ethical issues.* Butterworth-Heinemann, Oxford

problem of management in the opinion of Professors Gunn and Taylor. We are aware from evidence from a variety of sources that personality disorder presents a serious and costly public health problem in terms of its consequences such as alcoholism, drug abuse, criminality, child abuse or neglect, HIV transmission, violence and high level of medical consultations. Others drew attention to established evidence from long-term follow-up studies that demonstrate that conduct disorders in childhood have high predictive value for the development of psychopathic and related personality disorders in later life (e.g. Robins 1966,[43] West 1969,[44] Scott 1977[45]).

6.4.11 Another recent approach, said Professor Blackburn in evidence, is that the common feature of illnesses is that they are disabilities or dysfunctions that are harmful to the individual, or others, and within those terms, personality disorders can be regarded as illnesses to be dealt with as mental health problems.

6.4.12 The problem is not so much the validity of diagnostic systems, which are established, but the poor quality of training in diagnosis in the United Kingdom, and a lack of consensus about which system should be used (according to Professor Coid). It is notable, as Professors Coid and Blackburn have both said, that those classified as "psychopathic disorder" under the Act often in fact have more than one personality disorder in terms of diagnosis and are a heterogeneous group.

6.4.13 Questions about the treatability of "legal psychopaths" have to be distinguished from questions about "clinical psychopaths". No single clinical category of personality disorder predominates and only some "legal psychopaths" meet the criteria for anti-social personality disorder. Indeed, Professor Coid told us that in 1992 he found that only 23 per cent of males and 31 per cent of females detained as suffering from psychopathic disorder under the Act met the PCLR (Hare) criteria. Many legal psychopaths have suffered from mental illnesses in the past and many patients within the legal category of mental illness meet the diagnostic criteria for personality disorder. In short, the legal categories are often arbitrary, the reliability (that is to say the consistency or agreement between clinicians) of diagnosis is poor, with the exception of anti-social personality disorder, and diagnosis has little predictive reliability with respect to treatment outcome (according to the evidence of Professor Coid, Professor Blackburn, and Dr Thomas-Peter among others). Dr Snowden considered that the replacement of "psychopathic disorder" with "personality disorder" would achieve a closer correspondence between the legal classification and the clinical diagnostic category increasingly now described in terms of ICD-10 and DSM-IVR.

What is a personality disorder?

6.4.14 Dr Chiswick, in his evidence to us made clear that personality disorder exists as a clinical entity and he quoted a summary of its key features given by Marlowe and Sugarman (1997)[46] in a paper in the British Medical Journal which is likely to command broad professional agreement and which seem to us simple and useful:

> The patient: *displays a pattern of* behaviour, emotional response, perception of self
>
> *which is*: evident in early life, persistent into adulthood, pervasive, inflexible, a deviation from the patient's cultural norm
>
> *and leads to* distress to self, others or society

---

43 Robins L (1966) *Deviant children grown up; a sociological and psychiatric study of sociopathic personality.* Williams and Wilkins, Baltimore

44 West DJ (1969) *Present conduct and future delinquency.* Heinemann Educational books, London

45 Scott PD (1977) Assessing dangerousness in criminals. *British Journal of Psychiatry*, **131**, 127–142

46 Marlowe M and Sugarman P (1997) *cited above*

but is not attributable to: other psychiatric disorder (e.g. schizophrenia or drug misuse, or to other physical disorder (e.g. intoxication or brain disease)).

6.4.15 Dr Chiswick made the point that the term personality disorder is a recognised type of psychiatric disorder and that it is appropriate and useful to distinguish severe forms from others that are less severe just as in medicine clinicians refer to "severe coronary artery disease" or "severe respiratory disease". One may therefore distinguish "severe personality disorder", even though some of our witnesses claimed that it was not a recognisable term. The terms "dissocial" and "anti-social personality disorder" are, he said, terms of art used in the two major classifications and the preface to those volumes indicates that these have developed as research based diagnoses with research-based diagnostic criteria.

6.4.16 Dr Snowden, and Professor Gunn in evidence, drew our attention to the use of the term "severe personality disorder" by Tyrer and Johnson (1996)[47] who suggests that severity of personality disorder ranges from personality difficulty (a tendency for enduring patterns of behaviour to interfere with social functioning at times of stress), simple personality disorder (particularly personality disorders) and the most severe – diffuse personality disorder characterised by widespread personality abnormalities covering more than one type of personality disorder.

6.4.17 Dr Dolan in evidence said "if you accept the notion that people have personalities then you accept that there will be variations among the personalities that people have; you move then to talk of "normal" and "abnormal. There are some people who interact with others in a way that society is unable to accept and they are disordered personalities. The core of personality disorder is the way that people interact with others." Dr Dolan considered that the adjective "severe" when it is applied referred to the behaviour and its dangerousness, rather than the underlying personality disorder itself.

6.4.18 Dr Snowden agreed that no method of classification is entirely satisfactory and any study is complicated by the imprecise use of the term "personality disorder" by clinicians.

6.4.19 Dr Graham Robertson told us that when he was carrying out his research on offenders in Broadmoor, he and his collaborator, Mrs Suzanne Dell,[48] concluded that they could not understand what the term "psychopathy" meant and it was easier to define this population by what it was not "and they were not, after spending years in Broadmoor, obviously suffering from mental illness."

6.4.20 Professor Taylor considered that ICD-10 gives a good and practical working definition with its emphasis on early onset, persistence, inflexibility and considerable potential for personal distress. Professor West, in evidence agreed and added that it is very much a matter of degree in distinguishing between those who will not be regarded as disordered and those who are. In answer to a question from one of us, Professor Bluglass, he said that it can be understood both as an extreme variant at one end of the spectrum of personality characteristics; on the other hand it seems to be more linked with a gradual development of personality as a result of disordered upbringing. A serious practical and theoretical complication is the frequency of co-morbidity.

6.4.21 Dr Ian Keitch put it simply; there are a significant number whose personality characteristics/traits are sufficiently different from the norm to characterise them as disordered. Such individuals often show extreme violence of a physical and/or sexual nature

---

47 Tyrer P and Johnson T (1996) Establishing the severity of personality disorder. *American Journal of Psychiatry*. **153**. 12. 1593–1597

48 Dell S and Robertson G (1988) *Sentenced to Hospital*. (Maudsley Monograph No 32), Oxford University Press, Oxford

which brings them into contact with the Criminal Justice System. Such individuals are clearly seen as abnormal by the majority of the population.

6.4.22 Professor Taylor emphasised the importance of describing the personality in terms of personal characteristics and history, independently from behaviour that is socially defined, particularly anti-social behaviour. She pointed out that in the mental health legislation mental illness is not defined by its expression in terms of offending, but psychopathic disorder is, and there seems to her to be no justification for that distinction (the circular definition identified by Baroness Wootton). It is worth noting here that the Percy Commission commented (para. 339) that:

> "It is clear that in so far as it may be right to treat anti-social behaviour as a medical problem and to subject the patient to special compulsory powers on the ground that he is mentally abnormal, the treatment and the use of compulsion must be based on a medical diagnosis of the individual patient's condition, not merely on evidence of his behaviour".

6.4.23 Professor Taylor also drew attention to the need to recognise that just as more than one physical disorder may co-exist with another, so, in her view, there is no good reason to insist that all features of mental ill-health should be forced into one diagnostic category. She agreed with Professor West that co-morbidity is common. Professor Blackburn observed that recent research, including his own, indicates that pure disorders are very rare and co-morbidity is common. Many people with personality disorders have other mental disorders as well, and similarly many of those in the mental illness category have concurring personality disorders so that contrary to the popular assumption that it is their psychosis that makes them dangerous, it may actually be the personality disorder in many cases. In his view the argument may therefore be supported that the separation of mentally ill and psychopathic disorder is not really very prudent and may not be clinically very meaningful. Coid (1992)[49] by way of example, found that 80 per cent of legal psychopaths had suffered from some form of psychiatric disorder during their lives. Mbatia and Tyrer (1988)[50] found that 56 per cent of a sample of mentally ill patients at Rampton met the criteria for personality disorder.

6.4.24 Dr Clive Meux also drew attention to the co-morbidity of personality disorder and mental illness in many patients, to the extent that their legal label may be inappropriate over time as the characteristics of their prevailing condition changes. He found the categorical approach was not particularly useful in personality disorder and he favoured a "dimensional approach" as more pragmatic and relevant to treatment; establishing a hierarchy and constellation of problems to be addressed in an individual patient.

6.4.25 Professor Coid advised us that it is important to decide which system to use in practice and that he uses DSM-IV. If one is going to study those at the severe end of the spectrum, those actually in forensic populations, then he considered it advisable also to use an additional instrument such as Hare's psychopathy rating scale.

6.4.26 In his submission to us, Professor Coid outlined, with reference to his chapter in Tyrer and Stein (1993)[51], how a diagnostic approach should be taken with severe personality disorder. It should be divided into:

> (i) a measure of Axis II psychopathology – ideally involving a system such as DSM-IV categories together with Hare's Psychopathology Checklist;

---

49 Coid J (1992) DSMIII Diagnosis of criminal psychopaths: a way forward. *Criminal Behaviour and Mental Health*. **2**. 78–94

50 Mbatia J and Tyrer P (1988) *Personality status of dangerous patients in a special hospital.* In Tyrer P, ed, Personality disorders: diagnosis, management and course. Pp 105–111. Wright, London

51 Tyrer P. Stein G, (1993) *Personality Disorder Reviewed.* Gaskell Press, London.

(ii) an assessment of the patient for additional Axis I psychopathology (major mental disorder);

(iii) a systematic description of the patient's problem behaviour, including criminal behaviour;

(iv) all three areas should be examined taking a longitudinal approach, i.e. examining the presence of the psychopathology over the lifetime.

Those patients who score towards the top end of the PCLR can be described as the "true clinical psychopath" and they may be suffering from multiple types of personality disorder.

6.4.27 Dr Thomas-Peter made the point that the kind of therapeutic intervention you are capable of providing tends to drive the nature of the assessment that is undertaken.

Epidemiology of Personality Disorder

6.4.28 About 10per cent of the general population suffer from a personality disorder (Professor Gunn's statement; Dr Chiswick quoting Casey and Tyrer 1986[52]; and de Girolamo and Reich 1993[53]) and over half of those in (psychiatrically) treated populations (Merikangas and Weissman 1986[54]) may be expected to suffer from one of them. Yet, psychiatric hospital admission for people with a primary diagnosis of personality disorder is very low, probably less than 2 per cent of the 200,000 annual psychiatric admissions of all kinds (Dr Chiswick's statement).

6.4.29 Although the Mental Health Act makes provision for a Court to make a hospital order (Section 37) with a restriction order (Section 41), of the thousands of violent offenders who appeared before the courts in 1995 only 12 were detained under these provisions (Department of Health 1996)[55].

6.4.30 The community prevalence rate of anti-social personality disorder (ASPD) is found to be two to three per cent with fair consistency (15 studies gathered by Moran and Jenkins (1997)[56]) and this is reflected by a similar finding in general psychiatric patients (one to three per cent). There are numerous prison studies up to 1983 (quoted by Coid 1993) and since 1983, but they concentrate on the prevalence of "personality disorder" rather than looking at the prevalence of the sub-categories. Professor Gunn and his colleagues from the Institute of Psychiatry in London carried out the most quoted survey (Gunn J, Maden A, Swinton M 1991[57]. This was a population survey based upon a five per cent sample of men serving a prison sentence and they found that 37 per cent of this sample (652) had a psychiatric disorder of which 10 per cent had a personality disorder (177). They represented "the more severe end of the spectrum of personality disorder", and three-quarters of them were judged in need of psychiatric treatment (but not necessarily in hospital).

6.4.31 Approximately 25 per cent of the population of the Special Hospitals have been

---

52 Casey P R and Tyrer P J (1986) Personality, functioning and symptomatology. *Journal of Psychiatric Research*. **20**, 363–374

53 de Giromalo G and Reich J H (1993) *Personality disorders.* WHO, Geneva

54 Merikangas K R and Weissman M H (1986) *Epidemiology of DSMIII Axis II personality disorders.* In: *APA Annual Review,* ed A J Frances and R E Hales (vol 5, Psychiatric Update, pp258–278), American Psychiatric Press. Washington DC. Quoted in Dowson J H and Grounds A T (*op cit)*

55 Department of Health (1996) Statistical Bulletin 1996/10 *In-patients formally detained in hospitals under the Mental Health Act 1993 and other legislation. England 1989–1990 to 1994–1995.* Government Statistical Service, London

56 Moran P and Jenkins R (1997) *Review of epidemiology and needs assessment of psychopathy.* HSPSCB Research and Development Conference. 15 October 1997

57 Gunn J, Maden A and Swinton M (1991) Treatment needs of prisoners with psychiatric disorders. *British Medical Journal.* 303. 338–341

classified as 'psychopathic disorder' uncomplicated by psychosis for a long period. If we also include those with mental impairment and severe mental impairment, who could be said also to be in the psychopathic group (abnormally aggressive and seriously irresponsible, but with impairment of intelligence), then 33 per cent of the total number of patients accepted for a special hospital bed have been psychopaths, but the numbers have been declining over the past few years.

6.4.32 However, the most recent Report from the Office for National Statistics[58] on a survey of prisoners carried out in 1997 (reported 26 June 1998) found that among those who had a clinical interview over three quarters of men on remand and two-thirds of those who were sentenced had a personality disorder. Half of the women were also rated as having a personality disorder. The most common type of personality disorder was anti-social, found in 63 per cent of the male remand, 49 per cent of male sentenced and 31 per cent of female prisoners.

6.4.33 Paranoid and borderline personality disorders were the next most common – 29 per cent of male remand, 20 per cent of male sentenced and 16 per cent of female prisoners were assessed as having a paranoid personality disorder. The equivalent figures for borderline personality disorder were 23, 14 and 20 per cent respectively. Paranoid personality disorder is often found combined with Anti-social Personality Disorder (ASPD) in criminal populations. Mental disorder is common.

6.4.34 Between 1986 and 1994 the male patient population with a classification of psychopathic disorder in the Special Hospitals was stable at approximately 330 (310 – 341) and the female population ranged between 116 and 86.

6.4.35 In 1994 all patients from the North-West NHS Region currently detained in Special Hospitals were assessed and of 119 patients, 34 were classified as psychopathic (Shaw J, McKenna J, Snowden P, Boyd C, McMahon D and Kilshaw J 1994[59]).

6.4.36 Fifty per cent of all discharged special hospital patients commit a subsequent offence and 10 per cent or more carry out a serious violent or sexual crime (Chiswick 1995 in Chiswick D and Cope R, referred to above). Patients in the category psychopathic disorder are re-convicted at twice the rate of mentally ill patients.

6.5.0 Conclusions

6.5.1 From the evidence we have heard and from the statements and publications we have read we conclude that:

> (i) official Reports, many publications, statements from a majority of our witnesses and the replies of our expert witnesses in evidence confirm that there continues to be much scepticism, uncertainty and lack of agreement about the nature, diagnosis and the validity and reliability of existing classifications of personality disorder, although a minority expressed greater confidence.

But there is considerable agreement as follows:

> (ii) personality disorder is a recognized mental disorder;
>
> (iii) it incorporates a wide range of conditions with different characteristics;
>
> (iv) it presents with varying degrees of severity;

---

58 Singleton N, Meltzer H and Gatward R, with Coid J and Deasy D (1998). *Psychiatric morbidity among prisoners.* Office of National Statistics. The Stationery Office, London

59 Shaw J, McKenna J, Snowden P, Boyd C, McMahon D and Kilshaw J (1994) The North-West Region. I: Clinical features and Placement needs of Patients detained in Special Hospitals. *Journal of Forensic Psychiatry* **5**. 1. 93–105

(v) severe personality disorder is a useful descriptive term to refer to a sub-group of patients with severe degrees of personality disorder (just as the term severe is used in other medical conditions);

(vi) it is associated with a significant level of morbidity and mortality and it is an important public health and economic problem associated with a wide variety of medical consultations;

(vii) about 10 per cent of the general population have a personality disorder; about two to three per cent per cent have an anti-social personality disorder and a very high proportion of male and female remand and sentenced prisoners have been assessed as having an anti-social personality disorder;

(viii) co-morbidity with other mental disorders is common. For some, the principal classification can change over time;

(ix) personality disorder is classified in a variety of ways, all of which have advantages and limitations. The categorical approach is criticized and some see value in the dimensional approach as more relevant to treatment;

(x) anti-social/dissocial personality disorder is not the only variety of personality disorder which may justify compulsory detention under the Mental Health Act;

(xi) "psychopathic disorder" is a redundant term.

6.6.0 Treatment and Management

6.6.1 It appears evident from these conclusions about the nature of personality disorder that it is a heterogeneous group. We have shown from the evidence given to us that about 10 per cent of the population have a personality disorder and that two to three per cent have an anti-social personality disorder.[60] However, that does not mean that in a population of, say, 50 million people, one million are psychopaths. Nor does it mean that the NHS needs to provide ongoing psychiatric care for more than a fraction of this group, although their general demands for healthcare will exceed those of the rest of the population.

6.6.2 We also know that while risk of danger is associated more with the anti-social or dissocial sub-group of personality disorder, it is by no means limited to that sub-group. Nor is a personality disordered offender's risk of danger to the public simply proportional to the current severity of his personality disorder. That was made clear by Dr Snowden in both his written and oral evidence. As will be seen from the evidence we subsequently quote, improvement in personality in mental health terms does not necessarily mean there is also a reduction in the individual's risk of causing serious harm to others.

6.6.3 The relatively small group we refer to as severe personality disordered offenders have two co-existing characteristics: one is a personality disorder or disorders, one of which is often anti-social personality disorder, and the other is a serious risk of causing serious harm to others. See also paragraph **6.6.7** below.

6.6.4 In 1992 Dr Rosemarie Cope surveyed all British consultant forensic psychiatrists for their views on psychopathic disorder.[61] Ninety per cent responded. As far as treatability was concerned she found that:

> "... there are firmly held and widely differing views on treatability. Only a minority of respondents, about ten per cent. were totally dismissive of psychopaths and their treatability. There was a similar proportion of enthusiasts who stated equally vehemently that psychiatrists had a duty to treat this group of patients who caused

---

60 Moran P and Jenkins R (1997) *cited above*

61 Cope R (1992) *Op. Cit.*

suffering to themselves and society. Most respondents were somewhere in between, with a range of views, according to the type of case, about where treatment should take place, under what legislation and by whom."

6.6.5 During the course of hearing the evidence we discovered no forensic psychiatrist optimistic about treatability who did not concede that some severe personality disorders proved to be totally resistant to all known treatment methods and approaches. In order to demonstrate this to the reader we feel it would be helpful to quote more extensively from two of our witnesses who reflect in their evidence the two ends of the spectrum of views on treatability. Dr Snowden is a good example of those who believe that success may be achieved with those individuals who are not severely personality disordered, but currently not with those who are severely personality disordered. Professor Taylor is a good example of those who deem it right never to give up, and never to stop trying. We deal with Dr Snowden's evidence first. Both are distinguished consultant forensic psychiatrists,

6.6.6 As we mentioned above we have adopted the term "severe personality disorder" to describe personality disordered offenders whose disorder was such that it was associated with their presenting in addition an unacceptable risk of danger to others. This enables us to avoid using the legal classification of "psychopathic disorder" which so many now find to be a stigmatic and unacceptable term. In his statement, Dr Snowden as did others queried our use of this phrase, and when he gave evidence, the Chairman explained our reasoning and indicated the type of personality disordered offender we were considering.

> Q: The ones that require this rather special treatment and cause so much manipulative and difficult trouble whether in hospital or in prison.
> A: Yes.
>
> Q: That is our idea of using this term. Perhaps you would like to comment on that as an idea.
> A: Well, I think as you see I actually come round to that idea as I progress through my written evidence.
>
> Q: You analyze our minds actually.
> A: Right, I struggled with it and, in fact, I found it quite helpful being asked to appear because it has actually made me read around the subject more than I had done, and I think quite an important paper by a very eminent clinician is . . . the paper by Tyrer . . . who is I think one of the most eminent psychiatrists working in the field of personality disorder in this country, describes three gradations which he believes can stand side by side with the classifications that doctors are happier using at present, ICD-10 and DSM, and he describes personality difficulty, a simple personality disorder and diffuse personality disorder, which is, I think the same as your severe personality disorder, and what it is and what he describes it as is a diffuse personality disorder characterised by widespread personality abnormalities, covering more than one type of personality disorder.
>
> So it is a heterogeneous group in clinical terms but it is at the severe end and I think if you look at all the patients who currently find themselves in the Special Hospitals, they are very difficult to categorise as one single personality disorder or the other, or having one particular problem or the other. They are the harder end.
>
> So after going round the houses I have come to the conclusion that it is a satisfactory way of describing the group, and then I went on to further describe the group that I think we are focusing on which are those that are detained in hospital with a psychopathic classification, who are also on a restriction order, because I think they are at the furthest end of the severe end.

6.6.7 As we gathered evidence surrounding this problem, it became clear that we were not so much concerned with personality disorder or personality disorders, but with the degree of risk of danger to others possessed by offenders who have personality disorders. Setting aside self-harm which, of course, is not unimportant, it is this factor which determines the need for compulsory segregation from society whether in hospital or prison. It is a factor to which Dr Snowden, in particular, has given much thought. It is also the factor which appears to influence strongly the current thinking within the Dutch TBS clinics. The Dutch espouse the concept of the "therapeutic community" with perhaps more realism than has been the case in this country. They have faced the inevitable fact that some personality disordered offenders cannot be changed to a point where they cease to pose an unacceptable danger to society. So they are building a number of small special units dedicated to the purpose of humane containment.

6.6.8 Considering this problem of risk, Dr Snowden did not like the word "dangerousness" which he thought was too subjective, and preferred to think about "risk of danger", and we agree with that approach. He added that he hoped he had been able to encourage the Home Office Advisory Board on Restricted Prisoners to think about risk because there are all sorts of risks. At the moment there were no check lists, or dangerousness or risk tools. Aware as he was, for instance, that the Parole Board had a very useful sort of measure to help to guide their discussions, and although such a measure helped in large populations it was less helpful in individual cases. He said:

> "I am a great believer in the view that clinical risk assessment is actually a core skill, which is not necessarily a clinical skill I think others can do it and it is very much based on adequate information and very clear thinking."

He also thought it should be multi-disciplinary,

> "because you need a number of approaches and I think the views of nursing staff in particular who are working with patients 24 hours a day, unlike the psychiatrist who is just visiting, are exceedingly important".

A little later he said,

> "I think, to think clearly and perhaps to be able to stand back, I think to distance oneself from the problem and to be able to look at it objectively, is a trick that we do not always share, and I think that I have it, but I do not have it all the time either."

6.6.9 Dr Snowden was also concerned that the importance of risk was being missed. He said in answer to Professor Bluglass:

> "I think that a lot of what I have heard so far from colleagues both in the pro and anti camp about the treatability issue I think misses the point and I think this is perhaps what you are focusing on when one is dealing with a very seriously worrying, very seriously dangerous mentally ill individual who has offended. Perhaps in the setting of mental illness, you improve their mental health. You hope that that will reduce the risk of re-offending but it is very rare that the whole explanation for the offending is entirely bound up in that illness. There are often other factors, but usually it is possible to deal with those as best one can and move the patient forward. I think the same is true in personality disorders, but I think people have been missing the point when they have been discussing this area because improvement of personality, improvement of mental health does not necessarily mean reduction of risk, because in these particularly difficult, very severely worrying individuals, the connection between their personality and their phenomenology and the offence is quite complex and it may be that the contribution from personality may not be the major factor. It might be alcohol, it might be drugs, it might be the environment that the person is moving in . . . So assessment of treatment and whether or not they would

benefit from therapeutic intervention is I think one sort of section of thought and activity, but that does not necessarily mean that the patient or person is going to be less risky, that risk is still tolerable for the community. And that is a position that one is often in on the Advisory Board."

A little later:

> "It is quite complicated and it may be that personality disorder is one of the important variables that one needs to consider in the offending behaviour, but I think one must not – just as one must not with someone with schizophrenia,- think that if there is an offence and they have schizophrenia, that the offence is driven by the schizophrenia.
>
> I am certainly suggesting that in this group their personality disorder probably contributed to their offending but it does not necessarily mean that wellness in terms of their personality disorder significantly reduces risk, or that it will significantly reduce risk enough to make them tolerable in the community."

6.6.10 In his statement, Dr Snowden said:

> "For these patients treatment is only of value if internal distress is reduced, and for society if the risk of harm to others can be reduced and managed. However, there is no evidence that such patients benefit from a pure treatment approach in a secure hospital setting."

He was asked by Mr Royce to expand on that and also on his view of the invalidity of comparing the Special Hospitals with a therapeutic environment such as at the Henderson Hospital. He said:

> "Well there is not research evidence, unless you have heard it from anyone else or you are likely to hear it, that would convince myself and others who think like me that the treatment as it is currently structured is valid. There has not been research on this particular group. The outcome research is not really available. There is no measure of the comparison of different models.
>
> What is being suggested is that the research that is being done at the Henderson Hospital, their outcome research, suggests that this is the sort of model that would benefit patients in a special hospital. The only research that I have found . . . is a meta- analysis on treatment effectiveness in psychopathy . . . and what it shows is from the studies that have been culled in the English and Spanish literature that if you compare psychopaths before treatment with how they are after treatment, there is evidence of improvement, but not if they are very severe psychopaths, so it is at the low end, and not if it is on an in-patient basis"[62].
>
> The Chairman: The moderate type can be improved but not the severe type?
>
> Professor Bluglass: The sort that go to the Henderson might?
> A: Yes, the sort that go to the Henderson, which is a very valuable institution but it has very strict criteria for admission. If patients are unable to cope with the environment that they are in, or, if others think that they are not, then they get excluded from the institution and it is a very sort of refined group who – some of them may have an offending history but we are not talking about the severe end. I think we are talking about those that Tyrer referred to as the simple personality disorders rather than the diffuse personality disorders . . . The paper also suggests that when you compare psychopaths as against other personality disordered individuals they do

---

62 Garrido V, Esteban C and Molero C (1996). *The effectiveness in the treatment of psychopathy: a meta-analysis.* International Perspectives on Psychopathy. Division of Criminological and Legal Psychology. 24. Eds Cooke D, Forth AE, Newman J and Hare RD. Summary of papers presented at the NATO ASI on Psychopathy. November 1996. Alvor, Portugal

particularly badly, particularly if you are comparing therapeutic community treatments, particularly if they are criminals. So, I think there is no research base that really underpins practice as it is, but that does not mean that that cannot be developed and I do not think anyone can say that the way patients are managed in a special hospital is completely wrong because there is no evidence to prove that from the research evidence. There may be other reasons why people think it is an unwise way of managing these patients, but the research evidence really does not prove it one way or the other, sadly.

Q: You could take from that, from what you have said, the view that treatment is not proved to be of value, so what are we doing medicalising this group and trying to provide treatment? On the other hand you could take the view expressed by others that with other conditions which are long-standing for which we do not have a very clear therapeutic approach like established carcinoma or chronic renal disease, we would not say that we should not do anything, we should do our best?
A: No.

Q: What view would you take?
A: My view is that it is wrong and futile for psychiatrists to avoid dealing with this clinical group in the broad sense, because they will impact and they do impact in every aspect of psychiatry. They amount to, I think I am correct in saying, 11 per cent of the population. They may present with dual diagnosis, they have greater physical morbidity and I think the evidence at the moment is that we cannot say that they are untreatable, and I think the evidence in fact is that on certain variables you can show that there is some improvement. These studies here that I am quoting suggest that if you look at a group of psychopaths before and after treatment they do improve, but I think one would generalise from this paper that the likelihood of improvement becomes less and less the more severe the personality [disorder] is. That has certain face validity. You would accept that.

6.6.11 We have quoted in paragraph **2.0.0** the introduction which Professor Pamela Taylor wrote to the collection of papers read at the SHSA conference on Psychopathic Disorder held in August 1991. There she said that if the Special Hospitals only had to deal with the mentally ill and not those with personality disorder they would have a glowing record, but they were required to deal also with such patients. The Chairman asked her about this view.

Q: There is almost a hint in that, is there not, that you are saying, "If we could deal with the mentally ill as an entity away from the psychopaths or what ever they are, we could do a better job for them, and perhaps we could do, if not as good a job, a better job for the personality disordered if they are not mixed together?"
A: No I think the nearer parallel would be to say if we could treat people in the health service only with acute infections and forget about the people who have cancer, we would have a much better record in terms of success with treatment.

Q: I wonder if we are a bit at cross-purposes. I do not think anyone would suggest that if a person has a mixed diagnosis, clearly with treatable aspects, it is quite wrong to treat them outside a hospital because they can respond to proper treatment which you know to be responsive. But if you have your pure, simple psychopath, just the one diagnosis, these odd people you agree turn out to be quite resistant to treatment. At the end of the day, it does not matter where they are, whether they are in prison, or hospital, they are contained. As you know in Holland there are one or two units for those people specially. Would you like to see those few of the whole taken outside the area where the other people are being treated and managed?
A: First of all I do not think that I have ever said that I regard personality disorder that

is uncomplicated by psychosis as resistant to treatment. I would be fairly sure that there are some of those people who are resistant to the treatments we have at the moment . . .

Q: I am not suggesting the multi problem. I am just suggesting to you, I am asking you what you think about the person who is just, if you like a bad person, to use the old context. The person who turns out to be totally resistant to treatment, but is still a danger to the public. How would you like to see those people dealt with who are at the moment in the special hospital system?
A: I think the whole point is that somebody who has a personality disorder is not simply a bad person. I think there has been a tendency to describe them that way in some quarters, because it can make life easier if somebody is healthy but bad then it is clearly purely a problem for the criminal justice system and the health services can wash their hands of them, but as soon as you start to say that somebody has a personality disorder, even though that personality disorder may, in some cases, be uncomplicated by any other disorder, you are nevertheless saying that they have a disorder of health.

Q: But if you agree, as I think you were saying, that it turns out that such a person additionally proves to be totally resistant to treatment, what do you want to do with them?
A: Personally, I think it would depend on the presentation, but I would not be unwilling to keep them in the hospital system. We would not automatically remove from the hospital system other people with serious disorders which are presently untreatable, although I regret to say that in certain areas like neurology there has been a tendency to do that. People with multiple sclerosis or whatever, for which until comparatively recently there was very little specific treatment to be offered, they were very often rejected from services, even though it was patently obvious they had a disorder of health. I do not think that is right and I do not think it is right in relation to personality disorder either.

I think the task is then to define better what that resistance is and work towards however long it may take and acknowledging for that particular individual the development might be too late, but work towards finding the appropriate measure of treatment.

Q: I was not concerned about the differences of philosophy of approach. I was just wondering where you would like to see that sort of person placed irrespective of your philosophy?
A: I do accept personality disorder as a health problem and therefore, I think that the Health Service has a responsibility. I am aware that not everyone would agree with me, but I think that position can be justified.

Professor Edwards: The secret is the definition of "disorder of health", and that is where the disagreement is, about whether the whole range of personality variation makes a health problem?
A: That is why we agreed we were talking about the serious end of the spectrum, where there was unequivocal disorder, rather than the fringes . . .

Professor Bluglass: We also recognise that prison studies and other studies show that a very substantial proportion of the population in prisons has a health problem of one sort or another, alcohol, tobacco, neurosis, personality disorder, degrees of mental illness, but you are not proposing that because they have a health problem they should all be in hospital. You accept that many of those people have to take responsibility for whatever they have done, they go to prison, but you are saying some should go to hospital. It is a question of what proportion of that large number

of offenders, go to hospital rather than prison?
A: Indeed. It is back to the point that not everyone with a health problem, whatever it is, would end up in hospital. You have to try and make the judgment as to when hospital is actually going to be constructive.

Q: It is not in opposition to your thesis to say that people with personality disorder should be dealt with in prison?
A: That some health service could be provided within the prison setting, but where nobody would benefit from in-patient hospital treatment, I am arguing that that is inappropriate in prisons. It may not be impossible to set up a hospital service within a prison and some American prisons have gone down that road. It is something that personally I do not find attractive, but I think in this country is extremely unlikely to happen effectively in practice.

Q: Generally speaking in countries that have done that it has been poor quality and unsuccessful has it not?
A: Or in areas where the country is extremely rich and the prison has become a very special kind of industry within a rich community.

Professor Edwards: We have heard, for the last how many weeks, that the Health Service is not very good at it either, have we not? Caring is not exclusively the province of the health professionals. Caring is a philosophy which can be embraced by other professions, is it not?
A: I think the problem in relation to personality disorder is we are not really just talking about caring. We are talking about treatments as well and once you move from a position of –

Q: We are not. Not for the people the Chairman was talking about, because for the most part they are resistant to treatment, they do not want it and we do not have any treatment that we know has any value?
A: We may need to unpack the concept of resistance, because there is a problem, there is a question as to whether people who are not motivated for treatment can be treated or not and again I think in relation to personality disorder, we simply have insufficient knowledge of the role of motivation in treatment and the role of treatment in stimulating motivation, if you will. One of the articles that I appended to my notes goes through that in relation to substance misuse work, where there are very considerable parallels. There is the same kind of moral attitude to substance abuse, that it is bad rather than mad, and it is a criminal justice problem since it is a moral problem and not a health problem, but in fact to the health services the health problems that are associated are immense. By the same token, the beginnings of recognition of that have started to review the question as to whether motivation in treatment is really necessary to success in the drug and addiction field and the suggestion is that it is not. There is evidence to show that actually people who start off at least in a coerced contract do better than those who do not and there may well be parallels for us in the personality disorder area.

Q: It is late on a Friday afternoon to be having a long, philosophical discussion.
A: It is more than philosophy though, because there is evidence in that case.

Q: If you take that view, every sex offender currently in the Prison Service probably in your view ought to be across in the health sector?
A: No, not necessarily.

Q: Surely a sex offence – again I am using the offence to make the diagnosis – suggests in the majority of cases some deviation of personality, does it not?
A: The offence *per se* does not and that is the distinction I am seeking to make in trying to separate out an anti-social act *per se* from other orders or disorders in

personality. The act, of course, is an unpleasant, anti-social maybe even disordered act, but an act does not necessarily make a wholly disordered person.

The Chairman: Is there not a dichotomy there, which I suggest may appear in your paper, between the philosophy that you never abandon treatment, no matter how resistant the person is, and the practice of those, such as yourself, who promote that philosophy this way? You take Henderson, you take Woodstock; it is part of the contract at Woodstock that you want the treatment. It is part of the entrance terms at Henderson, you want the treatment. You cannot get into Grendon unless you want the treatment, yet you argue in your paper, and there are examples that you quote, where in some situations, some conditions, those who have started by being resistant to treatment have proved in the long run to have produced better results, as you said. But why is it that all those who promote the concept of treatability to the point when you say, yes, I wholly accept at the moment there is no apparent solution, but down the road there may well be and therefore we must go on. Why do people who promote that philosophy not actually put it in practice in the way they go about operating their units?
A: I think partly because there is a difference between the ideal and what one can do in practice. In an ideal world, there would be no rationing of any kind in a Health Service. Everyone would receive according to their needs. In practice, that is not true in any part of the Health Service and it is certainly not true in the part of the Health Service which offers services to people with personality disorder. There are very small numbers of units that do that, and their potential clientele is large and one starts with the promising cases.

Q: Assuming it is partially an economic argument, which I fully accept, why do you not then take it to my last suggestion? If you have your dangerous personality disordered person who has committed a serious offence, and who has proved to be totally resistant to treatment, you accept that some are bound to be in prison. Why not put those relatively few people in a prison setting? There does not have to be a separate unit for a prison setting, but put them in a prison setting and release the hospital for those with more potential?
A: In practice, that is what we think we are doing at the moment.

Q: You cannot under section 37/41. You can only do it on a 47/49 basis, prison sentence first.
A: Yes, we can move prison sentence people across, we have that capacity. Although in practice we are taking people that we think will do well in the unit in the sense that most of them are reasonably well motivated, even though that motivation may fluctuate somewhat, and they have characteristics which are well definable that we think we have ways of modifying, there is no inherent resistance to taking others. I think that we should do more of that, the question is simply how we achieve it.

Q: You cannot get rid of those who are in your system back to the prison?
A: We cannot move them on quickly enough, the ones we take.

Q: Suppose you could?
A: Supposing I could, what I would then want to do is to take over a number of research beds to resolve the question better as to whether we are simply living in a state of delusion that those people who are motivated do better, or whether indeed your men back in prison who at the moment are being rather truculent about anything that is offered could be persuaded to engage and actually do very well given the opportunity.

Professor Bluglass: At the moment you have got about 100 people in the rest of Broadmoor who are classified as PD, have you not?

A: Something of that order.

Q: You have to make provision for them first, have you not? They are not getting any specialised approach.
A: They are getting in many cases, this is something else we are checking at the moment, but we believe, and certainly clinical impression would suggest. that they are getting treatment, but they are not getting a particular cluster of treatment delivery.

The Chairman: They are not getting the same treatment they are getting at Woodstock.
A: They are not getting the particular cluster we give in Woodstock. It may turn out they do better after all.

6.6.12 Both Professor Taylor and Dr Snowden accept that, at present, in our group of "severe personality disordered offenders" there are a number who appear to be totally resistant to known therapeutic approaches. We use the word "totally resistant" because it is Professor Taylor's term, although we see no difference between that term and "untreatable". Dr Snowden would take them out of the Special Hospital system as it is currently structured; Professor Taylor would keep them within it on the basis that they still present a "health problem".

6.7.0 The Size of the Problem

6.7.1 We now consider the potential number of personality disordered offenders at the severe end of the spectrum with whom we are particularly concerned.

6.7.2 It has proved very difficult to obtain figures and at present no overall statistics appear to be kept and maintained. There a number of reasons for this:

(i) at present the Home Office does not collect information on the mental health of prisoners on a routine basis. There have been several studies in the past thirty years which have been concerned with the mental health of prisoners and more recently the studies by Gunn and Maden[63, 64, 65] (1991, 1995, 1996) have been the principal sources of information. These studies used psychiatrists to carry out interviews in a sample of prisons. More recently, in 1997, the Department of Health commissioned the Office of National Statistics (ONS) to carry out a survey among prisoners in England and Wales.[66] This was published as we were completing this Report in November 1998. It involved a sample of inmates in all locations in all 131 prisons in England and Wales using experienced lay and clinical interviewers;

(ii) a result of the "lottery" is that many severe personality disordered offenders go to prison where their psychopathy may remain undetected even though some of them might benefit from therapeutic management;

(iii) the patient group classified as suffering from psychopathic disorder does not equate precisely to the small group with which we are concerned.

6.7.3 We have made some broadly-based estimates of the "size of the problem" from all the information available to us with a particular emphasis on the group of offenders who are

63 Gunn J, Maden A and Swinton M (1991) *Mentally Disordered Prisoners,* Department of Forensic Psychiatry, Institute of Psychiatry, London.

64 Maden A, Taylor CJA, Brooke D, Gunn J (1995) *Mental Disorder in Remand Prisoners,* Department of Psychiatry, Institute of Psychiatry, London.

65 Maden A (1996) Women, Prisons and Psychiatry: Mental Disorder behind bars, Butterworth-Heinemann Ltd, Oxford

66 Singleton N.Meltzer H,Gatward R (1998) *Op. Cit*

diagnosed as suffering from anti-social personality disorder and who, in addition, are at risk of causing serious harm to others. We stress, however, that certainty in this area, given the paucity of hard information, is impossible to achieve at present.

6.7.4 We have been given statistics for in-patients at the three Special Hospitals by ward, gender and legal classification as at 27 November.

Total patients in Ashworth, Broadmoor and Rampton – 27 November

Hospital	(a) Total: M	F	(b) PD	(c) PD+Other	(d) Other+PD	(e) Other
Ashworth	400	48	128	8	30	282
Broadmoor	385	56	103	10	41	287
Rampton	381	65	117	30	29	270
Totals	*1,335*		*348*	*48*	*100*	*839*
	M: 1,166	F: 169	M: 290 F: 54	Combined totals (c) and (d) M: 113 F35		

6.7.5 These statistics indicate that about 25 per cent of the Special Hospital population have a legal classification of psychopathic disorder alone, and 11 per cent psychopathic disorder with another classification. Of this 11 per cent approximately two thirds have mental illness as the primary diagnosis and personality disorder as a secondary diagnosis while one third have a primary diagnosis of personality disorder and a secondary diagnosis of a mental illness.

6.7.6 Dr Tony Maden and his collaborators[67] surveyed a 20 per cent sample of the 1700 patients then in Special Hospitals to estimate their treatment and security needs. They found there were 63 patients in their sample (48 men and 15 women) with a primary diagnosis of personality disorder. The primary diagnosis of personality disorder was associated with the following other diagnoses (not legal classifications): mental handicap (15 cases), sexual disorder (13 cases), alcohol dependence (12), epilepsy (2) and neurosis (1). The research team estimated that 52 per cent of the 63 patients could immediately benefit from transfer to medium security, but an independent team of clinicians considered that only 27 per cent could benefit from transfer to medium security. The researchers estimated that in five years 48 per cent could be in the community and the clinicians estimated 65 per cent.

6.7.7 If Maden and his collaborators are correct then on the more conservative estimate approximately 25 per cent of those with personality disorder in high security could be moved to medium security. Of the 348 with a classification of psychopathic disorder, 86 could move if beds were available and medium secure units could take them and 258 would remain. However, these vacated beds would then be taken up by transferred prisoners who could benefit from therapeutic management.

6.7.8 Of our expert witnesses Professor John Gunn, who was closely involved in several of the studies cited, was best placed to give us some assistance on treatment and security needs in different settings. He kindly gave us two statements. His estimates for bed requirements at different levels of security are based on his three surveys cited above, on sentenced prisoners, on remanded prisoners and on Special Hospital patients. Each of these provided an estimate of beds needed in hospital for each sample group, with a national estimate of bed need extrapolated from his findings for the sample in each group. The samples in the sentenced and remand groups, it should be stressed, included young men and women, as well as adult men.

67 Maden T, Curle C, Meux C, Burrow S, Gunn J (1995) *Treatment and Security Needs of Special Hospital Patients.* Whurr Publishers. London

6.7.9 His findings were as follows collated from the three studies:

Total National Need for Security Beds (Professor John Gunn)

Source of Estimate	High Security	Medium Security	Low Security
Sentenced Prisoners	309	363	472
Remanded Prisoners	15	342	373
Special Hospital	632	786	290
Total	*956*	*1,491*	*1,135*
Current	1,700	1,491	Unknown
Change Needed	–700	+1,500	+1,200

6.7.10 These figures, for all categories of mental disorder, indicate that about half the patients in high security at the time of the studies were estimated by Professor Gunn and his colleagues as requiring a lower level of security, but he has explained that this does not mean that only half the present number of beds in high security is needed because it is necessary to take into account those who, on his estimates, are inappropriately placed in prisons. He believes that the number of beds in high security should not be reduced much below 1,000 beds. At the time of the preparation of this Report there were a total of approximately 1,330 patients in Special Hospitals.

6.7.11 We are concerned with the diagnostic category of personality disorder. Professor Gunn's group did not place emphasis on diagnostic distinctions as they considered that the important matter is the level of security required. He grouped together all the non-psychotic diagnostic groups, which included difficult patients such as those with organic disorders and sexual deviations. About a third of the requirement for high security beds is from this broad group.

6.7.12 In their original Report on the study of treatment needs of prisoners with psychiatric disorders,[68] a prevalence study based upon a five per cent sample of men serving prison sentences, they diagnosed personality disorder in 177 (per cent) of 1,769 prisoners. The cases they identified represented the more severe end of the spectrum of personality disorder and 74 per cent of men in this category were assessed for treatment or management needs,that is eight per cent of the total sample (145 prisoners). Of these, 31 required treatment in prison, 31 required further assessment, 39 could benefit from a therapeutic community and six patients were considered suitable for transfer to hospital, mostly requiring medium security facilities. Thirty eight prisoners with a primary diagnosis of personality disorder were not recommended for specified treatment. So finally, six per cent were recommended for more specialized management.

6.7.13 At the time of this study (April 1988 to June 1989) the sentenced male prison population was 28,602 men and 8,141 young offenders, and by the end of July 1997, when the ONS study took place, the sentenced population was 47,983.

6.7.14 A rough calculation will show that taking Professor Gunn's estimates ten per cent of the present prison population may have severe personality disorder (approximately 5,000), of which three quarters may benefit from management and treatment in prison, further assessment, therapeutic community or hospital (in very rough figures 3,000). From his figures a very small proportion of this group will require hospital, but as he defined them as severely personality disordered we assume they would require high security. If we extrapolate further from Professor Gunn's findings about 30 per cent of this group would not be recommended

68 Gunn J, Maden A, Swinton M (1991) Treatment needs of prisoners with psychiatric disorders, *British Medical Journal* **303**. 338–340

for specialized management and about two-thirds are a potential problem group for treatment and/or management; in round figures **2,000**.

6.7.15 It is estimated (Department of Health) that there are about 100 individuals with psychopathic disorder in medium security accommodation.

6.7.16 We can then arrive at a rough estimate of the number of severely personality disordered men in prison and high and medium security hospital accommodation as follows: 290 men in High Security Hospitals classified as psychopathically disordered alone;113 men with personality disorder with another disorder; 2,000 prisoners with severe personality disorder in the male sentenced prison population; and 100 men in the medium security hospitals. This amounts to **2,503**, or in round figures **2,500** who have treatment or management needs in a variety of settings.

Men with Specialized Management Needs – Personality Disorder (Round Figures)

PD Only (Special Hospital)	300
PD+ Other Disorder (Special Hospital)	100
Male Sentenced Prison Population	2,000
Medium Security	100
Total	*2,500*

6.7.17 Professor Gunn stressed that while estimates like these are better than nothing they should be seen for what they are, rough estimates:

> "Supply and demand always interact and it is possible to notice quite big shifts in institutional populations as social attitudes change; note for example the way in which the prison population is rising. Secondly these figures were a snapshot of a dynamic service with a considerable flow through it. The figures here assume that input and output will always be in balance. This may or may not be the case."

We agree. An estimate of treatment need is a complex and difficult matter and we have spent much time trying to understand the statistics.

6.7.18 We have said we received towards the end of our Inquiry the important survey published by the Office of National Statistics[69] reporting the results of a prevalence study of psychiatric morbidity amongst prisoners in England and Wales. We had been given limited information from this survey earlier. We referred to this survey in **6.4.32** above.

6.7.19 We have not in the time available been able to evaluate this Report fully. But the results are, on the face of it, alarming. The prevalence rate for any functional psychosis in the past year for instance was 7 per cent for male sentenced prisoners compared with a finding of 2.4 per cent by Professor Gunn and his colleagues.[70] The prevalence of personality disorder was 78 per cent for male remand prisoners, 64 per cent male sentenced prisoners (compared to 10 per cent in Gunn et al) and 50 per cent for female prisoners. Anti-social personality disorder had the highest prevalence of any category of personality disorder. Among the sub-sample who had a clinical interview, 63 per cent of the male remand prisoners, 49 per cent of the male sentenced prisoners and 31 per cent of the female prisoners were assessed as having anti-social personality disorder. The findings in this survey are for a much higher prevalence of anti-social disorder in particular than any previous British survey. The Report will require careful critical analysis.

6.7.20 Although the ONS survey is without doubt important it was based upon different

69 Singleton N, Meltzer H and Gatward R with Coid J and Deasy D (1998). *Psychiatric morbidity among prisoners*. Office of National Statistics. The Stationery Office, London

70 Gunn J, Maden A, Swinton M (1991) *Op. Cit.*

criteria to those used by Professor Gunn and his colleagues and does not, as they do, address treatment needs. We have therefore continued to base our broad estimates of treatment need on Professor Gunn's statistics, as these are the only surveys available and his figures cannot be further refined from the ONS study.

6.7.21 Professor Gunn also provided us with his estimate of the total high security in-patient requirements for non-psychotic patients (including organic disorders and sexual deviations). He thought that 284 beds were required. His estimate is based upon three surveys carried out at different times and with different methodologies, and at a time when the prison population was much lower. We believe that this figure of around **300** represents the minimum high security in-patients beds required for severely personality disordered individuals. The need for special provision in prisons will be require further detailed study but will not be less than **100** and probably much more.

6.7.22 We emphasize the importance of establishing new high security services along the lines we propose in Part Seven commencing with an initial provision as we describe above. Further refinements of our estimates should continue at the same time, but new service developments should not be held back by the need for "more research". It is evident that change is needed now. In our judgement there is a minimum level, which is well founded, of 400 places between prison and hospital for which immediate investment must be made as a matter of urgency.

Recommendation 45

6.7.23 The numbers, as Professor Gunn described them, are a rough estimate. We recommend:
(i) that 300 places in hospital and 100 places in prison be provided for the severely personality disordered group as soon as possible.
(ii) that before any longer term investment is made the Government sets up an expert group with resources to commission research to establish a sound base for future service development.

6.8.0 The Treatment and Management of Personality Disorder

6.8.1 We set aside two weeks in order to hear evidence from forensic psychiatrists, forensic psychologists, forensic nurses and others, many of whom had provided us with submissions. Later we held a seminar at which to test out our preliminary views.

6.8.2 In their book, Professor Coid and Dr Dolan[71] listed some previous statements about the treatment and management of psychopathy; they make depressing reading and we have taken the liberty of reproducing them in full. The authors state that:

> "It is impossible to review the research literature on the treatment of psychopathy without being impressed by two major features; firstly, that research investigations of treatment outcome of psychopathy are few and of poor quality; secondly, and more worryingly, that despite several decades of reviewers commenting to that effect, no obvious improvement has come to date".

6.8.3 The following are some of the statements that have been made:

> "No satisfactory means of dealing with them [psychopaths] was presented by any psychiatric authority, and meanwhile their status in the eyes of the law made it impossible to treat them at all". (Cleckley 1941)[72]

---

71 Dolan B and Coid J (i993) *Psychopathic and anti-social personality disorders: treatment and research issues.* Gaskell, London

72 Cleckley H (1941) *The mask of sanity; an attempt to clarify some issues about the so-called psychopathic personality.* CV Mosby Co, New York

"Until research can be undertaken the problem of treatment and management of these patients is likely to continue to be far more costly and far more difficult than is at present generally understood". (Stafford-Clark 1951)[73]

"All forms of treatment of psychopaths are as yet inadequately, or not at all, assessed, and furthermore, it would seem that a variety of methods are being applied without adequate assessment of the individuals to be treated." (Scott 1963)[74]

"There is, of course, no evidence to demonstrate or to indicate that psychiatry has yet found a therapy that cures or profoundly changes the psychopath". (Cleckley 1964)[75]

"At this point no one knows what the best approach is, and many programmes are still in their initial and experimental stages". (Carney 1976)[76]

"In answering the question of whether personality disorder can be treated by psychological methods, the answer must be 'possibly'since more investigation and longterm followups are needed before an affirmative answer can be given". (Blackburn 1983)[77]

"One can not review the literature on treatment of personality disorder without being impressed with how little we know about these conditions". (Frosch 1983)[78]

"The state of the treatment literature on anti-social personality disorder is inadequate" (Quality Assurance Project 1991)[79]

6.8.4 Professor Coid, in his submission, told us that, having reviewed the published work, he and Dr Dolan concluded that there was no evidence that the treatments they reviewed were effective; at the same time they found no evidence that they were not. Some patients do appear to respond to treatment whilst others do not; but it is not known why they do not, although there is considerable evidence that the more severe the abnormality of personality, the less likely to effect any change. In evidence, he told us that the *Hare Psychopathy Checklist*, Revised, gives a very good measure of treatability in this way. But that does not mean that attempts should not be made to give treatment. Some cases may respond, and in their book they urge caution in accepting too readily that these patients are "untreatable" noting that the "untreatability" of psychopaths may in part result from the professionals'inadequate assessment in the first place, followed by an inability to develop, describe, research and adequately demonstrate the efficacy of treatment strategies.

6.8.5 In Part One we have referred to the evidence of Dr Reed in connection with the difficulty he had in reaching consensus amongst the members of the Working Group on Psychopathic Disorder. He said that the Report was a compromise, hence the Report's principal recommendation was "we need to know more". We wonder if Coid and Dolan's conclusion that it could not be said whether or not treatment was effective does not fall into the same category of compromise.

73 Stafford-Clark D, Pond D and Doust JWL (1951) The psychopath in prison: a preliminary report of a co-operative research. *British Journal of Delinquency*, 117–129

74 Scott PD (1963) Psychopathy. *Postgraduate Medical Journal*, **39**, 1–7

75 Cleckley H (1964) *The mask of sanity*, 4th ed. St Louis. CV Mosby Co

76 Carney FL (1976) Treatment of aggressive patients. *Rage, Hate, Assault and Other Forms of Violence.* Spectrum Publications, New York

77 Blackburn R (1983) Are personality disorders treatable? *Issues in Criminology and Legal Psychology*, **4**, 23–26

78 Frosch JP (1983) The treatment of borderline and anti-social personality disorders. *Hospital and Community Psychiatry*, **34**, 243–248

79 Quality Assurance Project (1991) Treatment outlines for anti-social personality disorder. *Australia and New Zealand Journal of Psychiatry*, 25, 541–547

6.8.6 Whether it was or not Professor Coid together with Professor Tyrer has added to this collection of observations. Recently in a letter published in *The Times* newspaper (31 October 1998) in answer to a letter written by the Home Secretary, the Rt Hon Jack Straw MP they say:

> "As Dr Robert Kendell (letter 29 October) has pointed out, we do not have any proven effective treatment for those with anti-social personality disorder; yet psychiatrists are being asked to provide healthcare of an unspecified nature for this group in the hope that tragedies such as the Michael Stone case can be prevented."

6.8.7 It is a significant problem, said Professor Coid, that psychotic patients, who are given priority, are increasingly occupying secure beds. With the change in the pattern of provision of services, the closure of long stay wards, and the move of resources to the community, fewer patients with personality disorder can be treated in hospital. The admission rate of male psychopaths to high security hospitals and medium secure units has fallen although the numbers of people detained under the Mental Health Act generally has increased.

6.8.8 Dr Dolan conceded that some patients are untreatable, or rather some that we have failed to treat successfully. This is partly because our research knowledge is not good enough and partly because our services are not good enough. She agreed that there would always be some who will be treatment resistant or for whom no appropriate management can be devised. She believed that therapeutic units in prison could be created for this group. But in answer to questions from Miss Irving, Counsel for the patients, Dr Dolan would not go so far as to say that psychopaths can not be treated:

> Q: When you wrote in your document *Understanding the Enigma* in 1995, you were very clear to say that as far as you were concerned there was no evidence to support the claim that psychopaths can not be treated?
> A: Mmm
>
> Q: You say: "There was no literature to justify this statement and until we are satisfied that all possible treatment interventions have been tried, adequately evaluated and then shown to fail, we cannot claim that the psychopath is untreatable." Does that remain your view today?
> A: Indeed it does, yes.

6.8.9 Dr Dolan was an enthusiastic advocate of the therapeutic community approach and she thought many of its principles could be applied in many other services irrespective of the need for security:

> Dr Dolan: I do not say that that is the only way to treat people with personality disorder, but I think aspects of that can be lifted from it and applied to all services, and I see that what I have heard of difficulties with services have been where some of the important things about structure and culture of services have been ignored, and where there has not been a coherent model of treatment, a philosophy which everybody working in the service is signed up to and is therefore furthering, it just allows personality disorder people to manipulate staff, to split staff, to kind of capitalise on disagreements within the team about, say, what they are working towards, what their view of the disorder is, what their view of the treatment approach should be. . .
>
> Professor Bluglass: I was really asking you whether you see a different approach, perhaps a psychologically led approach, with psychologists leading therapy, perhaps, with medical services in the background to assist; or whether you see just an improved service based upon what already exists and enhancing it? A. I have difficulties in answering that. When you say "different approach", I am not convinced that I know or anybody knows what the approach is at the moment, that

we are looking for something different from. My reading of the literature is that the approach is very piecemeal you put people in a unit, you grab a piece of this, a piece of that, like from a menu. You know we have a bit of group therapy this year, we will have drugs next year, we might do some cognitive therapy at the same time; but it is a very unplanned approach.

6.8.10 Dr Dolan agreed that there are a range of hospitals and clinics which treat and manage persons with a personality disorder but only three places which claim to have a special expertise, in developing treatment services, in carrying out research and publishing.

She went on to say in reply to a question from Professor Edwards that she would regard the problems of this group as a disorder, but not a disease:

> Professor Edwards: So it may not have anything to do with the medical system?
> A: Arguably not, but the medical system has colonised it, taken it into its empire and it is stuck there now. I do not think it is too big a task to unpick it.
>
> Q: So it has colonised it?
> A: Because nobody else wanted to.
>
> Q: I guess for the most part there is a very caring objective of saying there are people here in trouble who we feel an obligation to try and help, so in order to do that they have had to put the medical label on them?
> A: One of the defining criteria for personality disorder is that through their actions not only they cause others to suffer but they suffer and it is that phrase about them suffering which is often forgotten I think, and that is what brings them right within the realm of mental health.
>
> Q: If somebody else were to colonise this group of people an interesting word this, "colonise", we have not had that used before, who would they be, do you think? Would it be psychologists, prison officers, probation officers, community nurses?
> A: I think I probably said psychiatrists and I probably should have said mental health workers as a whole. It is not just the medics, it is mental health workers who have colonised it. I do not think anybody else would want it.
>
> Q: Do you think anybody else could cope and I use the word "cope", not "treat" could cope with these people better than the mental health systems?
> A: No, I think other people are asked to. I mean, social workers are asked to and probation officers. Mainly they are probably the people who deal with more personality disorder than the rest of the health professionals put together."

6.8.11 Dr Snowden told us with candour that in his opinion the lack of evidence on treatment efficacy had encouraged the development of treatment facilities in the Special Hospitals and some medium secure units by enthusiasts, who by virtue of the fact that they have found themselves working with these patients become "experts" by default. Because the Act allows the detention of patients with the classification of psychopathic disorder they have therefore been referred to these hospitals. The value of such treatment has not been considered in depth:

> "although many of those involved in the assessment and treatment of severe personality disorders are convinced of the value of treatment, they are enthusiasts, who arguably have the easier task in terms of risk."

There is, he said, less optimism amongst those in the Regional Secure Units who often are those who have to make decisions on discharge and those clinicians who are asked to take responsibility for patients who are "better" and supposedly ready for less security and/or community living. Generally those who take discharge decisions are not those who admitted the patient or who were responsible for them in Special Hospitals.

6.8.12 Dr Chiswick told us that Special Hospitals (in normal circumstances, we add) take no risks with their patients. They are rarely allowed unescorted access to the community, whereas those who rehabilitate through the medium secure system must bear the responsibility of controlled introduction to the outside world with its attendant risks.

It is not surprising to have heard that the consultants and others in the medium secure unit system often lack confidence in the care that has been given in Special Hospitals. and knowing that they will be held accountable if things go wrong, they take a cautious approach to the assumption of responsibility for a very difficult group of patients.

6.8.13 Dr Chiswick, however, in his evidence before us illustrated the way in which a claim to be able to treat personality disorder is not uncommonly accepted by courts without challenge and is seized as a pragmatic solution for the disposal of a difficult case:

> The Chairman: What you are really saying is this, is it not, that people who have personality disorder have it, full stop. It does not seem to trouble society unless they have committed an offence and then, because they have committed an offence, having regard to their personality disorder there is then a risk of further offending and so, in order to try to do something about that, their disorder is looked at. It may result either in their going to prison, if it is not considered appropriately, or it may result in their going to a hospital, but the raison d'etre for the entrance into either system is the offence which has been committed and the rationale for keeping them there is future danger?
>
> A: Yes, I think that basically that is the case. The rationale is, if a psychiatrist gave evidence and said a person who perhaps had committed manslaughter, and personality disorder was deemed to be the grounds for a plea of diminished responsibility, if the psychiatrist said: "I have a treatment for this condition and the treatment takes 24 hours and then the person will be cured of the personality disorder". I do not believe any judge in the world would agree to that as the disposal and allow the person to have some sort of instant treatment. The judges are persuaded to accept it in my opinion, with all due humility, because also...
>
> Q: I think you are right.
>
> A: It also combines protection for the public and it provides an indeterminate sentence, which will be very acceptable to the judge for obvious reasons. So if someone said something vaguely positive about treatment that makes everybody feel they are doing a good job, protecting society, perhaps providing some treatment for the person all in one. And the point is that in court nobody will argue the opposite case. I mean, there will not be a discussion. There will not be an adversarial discussion of the opposite view because that does not happen under our, system.

6.8.14 In his statement to us, Professor Blackburn provides a detailed discussion about current approaches to treatment. The notion of "cure" is not appropriate and total personality change is not a realistic aim. The goal is to produce more adaptive and constructive ways of dealing with situations and relationships that have been problematic in the person's life. Psychological treatment needs to be based on an established theory of personality. Current treatment approaches build on the psychodynamic, behavioural and cognitive methods which were developed by the 1970s and several psychotherapeutic methods recently developed.

6.8.15 Professor Gunn, addressing "treatability", also pointed out that very few medical conditions are totally curable and medical treatment on the whole is not about "curing". And that is certainly so in longstanding disorders. Ameliorative interventions are common in general medicine, but are often not regarded seriously in psychiatry with respect to personality disorders. He referred to the "bizarre notion" that because they are seen in moral as well as medical terms they can be dealt with as "bad people" and punished and then as "sick people" and healed.

6.8.16 Dr Bob Johnson, who had considerable experience developing a unique model of therapy in Parkhurst Prison C Wing, enthusiastically claimed that all severe personality disorder is treatable. His hypothesis is that severe personality disordered patients are suffering from "toxic rage" and hidden fears frozen from infancy, which account for their grossly destructive and anti-social acts. These emotions are very difficult to access due to paralysed emotional development, resulting from previous abuse. Nevertheless, it is possible to effect change through a process of intensive structured psychotherapy employing a cognitive emotional method. Although other witnesses referred to psycho-therapeutic approaches, none referred to his formulation which seemed to us to be singularly eccentric.

6.8.17 A number of witnesses told us that after many years of inaction there was now an increasing interest in the problem of personality disorder. Professor Gunn referred us to the texts by Dowson and Grounds (1995)[80], Tyrer (1988)[81], Tyrer and Stein (1993)[82] and Dolan and Coid (1993)[83] and told us of the sharp rise in published research papers on this topic. Most of these papers are not about those at the severe end of the spectrum, but rather those patients with personality disorders who can be managed in outpatient and standard inpatient settings. Now he argued is a good time to capitalise on this interest and extend it to the management of the "severe" end of the spectrum.

6.8.18 Professor Gunn emphasised among the current available treatment approaches the importance of the multi-disciplinary approach, involving doctor, nurse, psychologist, occupational therapist and social worker, who should be integrated by management in a coherent way. The important evidence from the literature is the remarkable lack of controlled trials of treatment.

6.8.19 It can be said that pharmacological treatments have a definite place in the treatment for instance of anxiety, depressive symptoms, paranoid symptoms and in the treatment of drug dependency. Few psychotherapeutic treatments have been subject to properly controlled trials, although individual case reports indicate that cognitive behaviour therapy can be useful. Group therapies of all kinds are useful, but again there is a paucity of controlled trials. The treatment that is particularly helpful, and advocated in Britain, is group therapy which has become established in hospitals such as the Woodstock Unit at Broadmoor and prison settings such as Grendon Underwood (*see* below).

6.8.20 Dr Ian Keitch expressing a view on behalf of Rampton Hospital, drew attention to the technique known as dialectic behaviour therapy as developed by Marsha Linehan, and told us that there is evidence to suggest that it is of value in treating those with severe personality disorder that is manifest by serious self injurious/para-suicidal behaviour.

6.8.21 In the opinion of Professor West, the therapeutic community approach is the one that has accumulated the most evidence in its favour and he quoted the experience at the Henderson Hospital where this method of treatment has been used for many years with measurable improvement. Although the patients are not detained and do not have such serious problems as those in high security care it is argued that the essentials of the method

80 Dowson JH and Grounds A (1995) *Personality Disorders: Recognition and Clinical Management.* Cambridge University Press, Cambridge

81 Tyrer P (1988) *Personality Disorders: Diagnosis, Treatment and Course.* Wright, London

82 Tyrer P and Stein G (1993) *op. cit.*

83 Dolan B and Coid J (1993) *op. cit.*

can be applied in high security (Norton 1992)[84] and a good example of its use for violent and recalcitrant prisoners was the Barlinnie experiment which achieved a striking reduction in anti-social behaviour that persisted even after the men were returned to the stressful conditions of an ordinary prison (Cooke1989[85], Whatmore 1990[86]). The members of this Inquiry visited a special unit in a prison in Geneva, La Pâquerette Sociotherapeutic Centre at Champ-Dollon Prison, which operated successfully on a similar model (de Montmollin, Zimmerman, Bernheim and Harding 1986[87]; Bernheim and de Montmollin 1990[88]; Bernheim 1991[89]). (This service is described in Appendix Eight.)

6.8.22 Professor West agreed with Mr Royce, that there is sometimes a grey area between management and treatment:

> A: Yes if methods of control, which of course include secure provisions, are thought of as being something apart from treatment. But what I am trying to suggest I think is that there is not the conflict between these two things necessarily, as is sometimes thought. I mean, it is sometimes complained that the security arrangements are antitherapeutic and that may indeed be so, but I think there is an absolute necessity to preserve the safety of the patient and those around him or her in the patient's interests, so that is all part, as it were, of trying to help the patient to a more normal form of living. To allow them free rein is not helpful."

6.8.23 Professor West emphasised that the social environment (or milieu)in psychiatric treatment has for long been regarded as an important element in therapy and Dowson (1995)[90] tells us that Main (1946)[91] first introduced the term "therapeutic community", which has come to imply frequent group meetings, an emphasis on problems involving social relationships, good interpersonal communication, flattening of the pyramid of institutional authority, free emotional expression and examination of institutional roles.

6.8.24 Dr Dowson adds that this type of organization "produces its own problems" and this is perhaps evident from this Inquiry. It is, however, an approach about which we heard a great deal from a number of our witnesses with particular mention of the success of the Henderson Hospital, a hospital which has long experience in treating selected volunteer patients with personality disorders (but not patients with severe disorders with whom we are particularly concerned.)

6.8.25 The therapeutic community has also developed in other settings including the prison system where the regime at Grendon Prison is of particular note. Some of us visited this prison. It took 25 years to establish following the East Hubert Report (1939)[92] on the Psychological Treatment of Crime, and it is now a therapeutic centre for the treatment of prisoners, many of whom have personality disorders, in the prison system. We also

---

84 Norton K (1992) In the prison of severe personality disorder. *Journal of Forensic Psychiatry*, **8**, 285–298

85 Cooke DJ (1989) Containing violent prisoners: an analysis of the Barlinnie special unit. *British Journal of Criminology*, **129**, 129-143

86 Whatmore P (1990) The special unit at Barlinnie Prison, in Bluglass R and Bowden P (eds) *Principles and Practice of Forensic Psychiatry.* Churchill Livingstone, London and Edinburgh

87 De Montmollin M-J, Zimmerman E, Bernheim J and Harding TW (1986) Sociotherapeutic treatment of delinquents in prison. International Journal of Offender *Therapy and Comparative Criminology*, **30**, 1, 25-34

88 Bernheim J and de Montmollin M-J (1990) A special unit in Geneva, in Bluglass R and Bowden P (eds) *Principles and Practice of Forensic Psychiatry.* Churchill Livingstone, London and Edinburgh

89 Bernheim J (1991) *Sociothérapie institutionelle de détenus presentant un desordre grave du charactère: l'expérience de "La Pâquerette" a Champ-Dollon Prison* (Genève), in Justice et Psychiatrie, École Nationale de la Magistrature

90 Dowson JH (1995) Group psychotherapies, in Dowson JH and Grounds A (eds) *Personality Disorders: Recognition and Clinical Management.* Cambridge University Press, Cambridge

91 Main TF (1946) *The hospital as a therapeutic institution.* Bulletin of the Menninger Clinic, 10, 66–71

understand that after many years of procrastination, a second prison to be run on the same principles is to be established in Staffordshire.

6.8.26 The Max Glatt Unit at Wormwood Scrubs Prison, which we visited, is an attempt to replicate the Grendon approach. We were impressed by the enthusiasm of the staff, but we understood that the work of this Unit is constrained by insufficient resources, lack of training and lack of professional input. The staff can be withdrawn at times of staff shortages and the Unit is dependent on the goodwill of the officers and their ingenuity to keep going. Professor Gunn commented that:

> "it is a remarkable testament to the resilience of this treatment, and to its effectiveness that the two units (Henderson and Grendon) which have both been under constant attack for their lack of scientific foundation and their supposed expensiveness, have survived and to this day are flourishing".

6.8.27 Professor West reminded us of the once prevalent assumption that for psychopaths the passage of time is the key to improvement; that they ultimately mature and grow up but that this view discourages the development of active treatment programmes. This was a point also made by Dr Meux in his statement in which he said that treatment interventions may speed maturity or actually produce improvement in a way that maturity alone can not. Professor West went on to say that for an improved service the particular needs of psychopaths should be recognised. Behaviour modification and attitudinal change are the essential goals. Whatever techniques are used a number of basic provisions are needed:

1. A secure and controlled environment.
2. Explicit institutional policies with clear rules on infractions which are not regarded as, or exploited as, retributive punishment.
3. Thorough assessment of the needs of each patient in order to devise an individualised treatment programme of care and treatment, taking into account social situation as well as personality deficits and setting realistic, measurable goals. Clinical psychologists should have a lead role in the formulation and implementation of behavioural treatments.
4. The establishment of a personalised therapeutic relationship.
5. The maintenance of a forward-looking ethos that emphasises the therapeutic purpose of regulations and interventions. The manipulation of rewards and the graded relaxation of restrictions is a necessary element in the process of behaviour modification and the control of anti-social conduct. It should be promoted as a legally acceptable and positive component of therapy.
6. Continuing and realistic registration of progress towards agreed goals.
7. A flexible system of transfers through the system as security requirements change, with eventual discharge into the community under continuing active supervision for as long as necessary. Continuity of care and aftercare is essential.
8. Attention to the special needs of sex offenders, with psychophysiological testing of sexual responses in relevant cases, the use and monitoring of libido-suppressing drugs when necessary and attention to attitudinal changes well as the acquisition of sociosexual skills.
9. Recognition and attention to personality disorders among the mentally ill.

6.8.28 In his statement Dr Chiswick asked the rhetorical question "what is the object of treatment?" Certainly prevention of offending is a crucial aim for all offender patients detained in hospital for treatment. The common treatment approaches to personality disorder

---

92 East WN and Hubert WH de B (1939) *The psychological treatment of crime.* HMSO, London

(with an emphasis on psychological and social methods) may have little impact on the likelihood of reoffending. Improved social skills, interpersonal functioning, victim awareness, anger management and sex education, all acquired in the setting of a secure hospital, may be of little relevance to a discharged patient facing the stresses of life, relationships and survival in the community. Approximately 50 per cent of all discharged special hospital patients commit a subsequent offence and ten per cent carry out a serious violent or sexual crime. Patients in the category psychopathic disorder are convicted at twice the rate of mentally ill patients. It should be pointed out however that as a group discharged patients re-offend at far lower levels than do released prisoners. (Kershaw, Dowdeswell and Goodman 1997)[93].

6.8.29 Dr Christopher Hunter, in his statement, quoted a range of surveys of psychiatric opinion in the UK and overseas to conclude that some psychiatrists consider that psychopathy is a treatable condition some of the time (Tennent, Tennent, Prins and Bedford (1993)[94]; Gray and Hutchinson (1964)[95]; Cope (1992)[96]). Psychologists, who were also surveyed by Tennent *et al* (1993), showed that they had a more positive view but he showed from his quoted evidence that there are still considerable differences of opinion.

6.8.30 The British Psychological Society was more restrained than some of our witnesses, observing that there was little doubt that the value of treatment remains a very contentious issue and this is exacerbated by the paucity of appropriate outcome evaluation. They acknowledged that in the past there has been a tendency towards pessimism regarding the treatment of personality disorders, but currently there was cause for cautious optimism. Cognitivebehavioural interventions offer considerable scope, focusing upon specific problem behaviours, a technique that has flourished with a number of other problem behaviours in other settings.

6.8.31 A similar view was given by Professor Blackburn in his statement, that:

1. A few studies suggest that clinical psychopaths do not respond very favourably to traditional therapeutic interventions (e.g. individual psychotherapy, therapeutic communities), but there is insufficient evidence to support the opinion of some clinicians that "nothing works" with this group;

2. There is at least preliminary evidence that some offenders with personality disorders (mainly those who are not clinical psychopaths, and this would include most legal psychopaths in Special Hospitals) do change with psychological treatment (e.g. cognitivebehavioural methods, eclectic psychotherapy, therapeutic community).

6.8.32 Professor Taylor emphasised the morbidity in personality disorder and the justification for seeing this as an important health issue. She speculated that the resistance among professional clinicians to accepting people with personality disorder was most often to do with dislike, countertransference or fear of failure with its risk of having to take or share responsibility for any associated violence when things go wrong. She also challenged the notion that for personality disorder, unlike other mental disorders, change can only be achieved if the subject wants to change and is motivated to do so. Even though there may be a lack of insight, she maintained that it is a reasonable intermediate goal in treatment to

93 Kershaw C, Dowdeswell P and Goodman J (1997) Restricted patients – reconvictions and recalls by the end of 1995: England and Wales. *Home Office Statistical Bulletin 1/97.* Home Office, London

94 Tennent G, Tennent D, Prins H and Bedford A (1993) Is psychopathic disorder a treatable condition? *Medicine, Science and the Law*, 33(1), 63–66

95 Gray KG and Hutchinson HC (1964) The psychopathic personality: a survey of Canadian psychiatrists'opinions. *Canadian Psychiatric Association Journal*, 9, 452–461

96 Cope R (1992) *cited above*

enable the individual to recognise a state of disorder and to accept the therapeutic consequences that follow. She illustrated her point with the example of work in the USA on the treatment of substance abuse disorders which shows that the reasons for engaging in treatment may not be of primary importance; that many people who have been forced into treatment do as well as, and in some cases, better than those seeking voluntary help. Changes in the law that permits this approach could leave personality disorder in the unique position of being the only serious disorder for which there is a requirement that the individual sufferer should have made major progress towards health before qualifying for treatment.

6.8.33 We noted, however, that this approach is not a universal one and at Grendon, the Henderson Hospital, and Geneva, to mention three examples, subjects must volunteer for a treatment programme.

6.8.34 Dr Grounds felt that there are three contributions that a special hospital environment can provide that can not be provided in prison. First, it is easier in principle to carry out individual psychological work, and it is very difficult in prison where there are insufficient resources to do so. Second, they can provide a research base for clinical work and the development of new treatment approaches which the prison is not well structured to provide. Third, he was sure that some people with severe forms of personality disorder, particularly those with fragile personality structures, can cope much better and be much more stable in a special hospital environment rather than a prison environment.

6.9.0 Personality Disorder and Dangerousness

6.9.1 In **6.6.5** *et seq.* we refer to Dr Snowden's evidence that the relationship between personality disorder and dangerousness is a complex one. The two may not have a direct relationship and many other factors related to the personality disorder may be of greater importance, for example, alcohol, drugs or a particular person or situation. Dr Snowden invited us to think in terms of "risk" and "risk assessment" rather than dangerousness which is too subjective. Clinical risk assessment is a core skill and it is very much based on good information about the individual patient and it requires a multidisciplinary input from a range of professionals who know the patient, who are well experienced and have an empathy for this sort of work.

6.9.2 The views given above by Professor Taylor and Dr Snowden take us back to the crucial question of the object of treatment. This was addressed by many of our expert witnesses. Dr Chiswick said in his statement that :

> "Prevention of offending is a crucial aim for all offender patients. In mentally ill patients the successful treatment of the illness normally reduces the likelihood of offending. Offending by personality disordered patients is less clearly understood; motivation for offending is a speculative science".

Mr Royce pursued this point in his crossexamination:

> Q: How much confidence can we have in the beneficial effects of treatment in the Special Hospitals provided to those with severe personality disorders?
> A: Well not enough confidence to make confident decisions about their discharge.
>
> Q: Right.
> A: Patients receiving these treatments might appear to function better within a special hospital setting. I do not think that tells you very much about the likelihood of reoffending in the community. I think one has to contrast it with the situation with mental illness. In a mentally disordered offender who offends, one is looking at a relationship between the offending and the psychiatric disorder, and in its most simplistic terms one might say treat the disorder and the risk of further offending is reduced. That does depend on how close is the relationship between the offence

and the disorder, and even in people with a mental illness that relationship might not always be as close as you would imagine. Sometimes there is a very direct relationship, a person acts on delusions or in response to hallucinations or because they perceive they have a paranoid perception of their environment and believe things are happening to them and they commit a crime, often a very violent crime, in response to those very abnormal symptoms, and those symptoms can be treated and you might assume therefore that the risk of offending is reduced.

In relation to offending by people with a personality disorder, what is one treating? If a person gets into relationship problems with someone else, male or female; acts violently perhaps in a sexual setting, perhaps not, or commits some other violent crime, in the absence of a mental illness what is it exactly that one can be confident about treating that is going to reduce the risk of reoffending? It is very likely that the person has a troubled background. So what? It is very likely that they might have abnormal sexual fantasies. So what? It is very likely that they might abuse substances. So what? What do any of these things tell you about that particular offence? You are dependent on an account of that offence from that person, perhaps supplemented by other information. You are dependent on that person for an account of improvement, whatever that might mean, and you are trying to make decisions about their discharge to an environment which you cannot control. You cannot control the people they meet, the substances they take, or the lifestyle they lead, and that can make prediction virtually impossible.

So the things that you might want to do in hospital which sound on a common sense basis worthwhile; to explore their sexual pathology, psychopathology, to look at anger management, to discuss victim awareness, improve their social skills, we think all these things are good things to do. They are probably a good use of time. Whether they actually reduce the likelihood of that particular person offending, nobody knows.

6.10.0 General Conclusions

6.10.1 It is evident from all the evidence that we have heard and read that there continues to be a wide diversity of opinion among experts from all the professions about the treatment and management of personality disorder and particularly severe personality disorder. There have always been dedicated enthusiasts convinced that they have the answer within their grasp, but there are also the sceptics, probably the majority, who point to the lack of credible evidence that treatment works. The picture has changed little over the decades and the comments of those who have considered this question in Royal Commissions or Reports, such as that of Lord Butler, seem as relevant today as they were when they were written.

6.10.2 We are impressed by the compassion of those who continue to strive to develop improved methods of management and treatment, but we were less impressed by those who have urged us to proceed cautiously and by dubious claims about the success of much that has been attempted so far.

6.10.3 There is no disagreement that there are a wide variety of personality disorders of varying degrees of severity and we have received substantial support for the simple and practical step that we have taken by referring particularly to a group of "severe personality disorders". We include here anti-social personality disorder/dissocial personality disorder which present special problems because of their association with violence and dangerousness. But the aetiology of personality disorder is still unknown.

6.10.4 It is clear that there are very few specialist services dedicated to the treatment and management of personality disorder, a paucity of welltrained staff with an enthusiasm and interest in this group and little or no training in the education of psychiatrists, psychologists or nurses. Indeed there is no consistent body of opinion about what such training should be.

6.10.5 A few generalisations can be made with which there is general agreement:

1. Some personality disorders are more treatable than others and they are the conditions which are less severe and which have a low association with violence.
2. Some personality disorders are sometimes treatable.
3. Some, particularly severe personality disorders, are resistant to treatment or frankly untreatable, although they may benefit from management and humane containment.

6.10.6 The appropriate setting for the management and/or treatment of personality disorder depends upon many factors and must take into account public safety as well as the needs of the individual. Management must be within services providing an appropriate level of security.

6.10.7 There is substantial agreement that psychological methods of treatment are more effective than anything else and that pharmacological treatments are generally inappropriate for this group. Therapeutic community approaches are helpful for some patients, especially those who are not detained in hospital, but they also can make worthwhile contributions in other settings. We found Professor West's principles of management very helpful (*see* **6.8.27** above).

6.10.8 Hospital management and treatment is appropriate for compliant patients and those who do not suffer from anti-social personality disorders. But we cannot accept that all persons with personality disorders are necessarily suffering from 'disease,'equivalent to physical disease or that they should always be primarily a matter of concern for health services. This conclusion represents the opinion of the majority of our witnesses and most of those who have expressed views about this elsewhere. Certainly some individuals will benefit from health service care; it is a matter of careful assessment in each case. But in any event there is no satisfactory way of assessing outcome and future risk, even though sound treatment programmes have been implemented. There is no doubt that much research is needed and funding for it provided. But changes cannot wait for the outcome of such research that may take many years to complete. We are convinced that the future organisation of management and treatment services for severe personality disorder must be planned on the basis of experience of professionals at the present time, and mental health legislation and service planning must reflect that approach.

6.10.9 After we analyzed the views expressed to us in the two weeks we devoted to evidence on "management and treatability" and tested our analysis in a seminar on this topic, we are of the view that the changes we propose later in management and the law, need to be grounded in realism and not idealism. We believe, however, they nonetheless embrace the need for further and better research and we feel, will provide a better framework for both management and research.

6.10.10 As we have said before, and we are heartened in our view by the weight of evidence we have heard, the time has come for change by facing the persisting problem of treatability head on. It may be, for example, that at some time in the future, perhaps through the developing understanding of genetics, a different approach may become realistic, but society just cannot go on waiting in hope.

6.10.11 We can see no rational justification for keeping this very manipulative and troublesome sub-group in expensive therapeutic units providing management and treatment techniques from which they gain no benefit. We also believe that our proposals in Part Seven of our Report will go a long way towards ensuring the safety of others in society, including other patients who are mentally ill.

PART 7 Time for change

7.1.0 The Problems

7.1.1 We heard much evidence on the problems facing the Special Hospitals. By common consent these hospitals are still very isolated from the rest of the forensic system, both geographically and culturally. As a result they have failed to attract sufficient numbers of high quality staff. Many Special Hospital patients do not need high security but cannot be moved on for lack of facilities elsewhere, a situation which contributes to a feeling of apathy on the part of staff and patients. Whilst improvements have been made in recent years, the quality of clinical care is still unacceptably patchy.

7.1.2 These problems, albeit very real and very serious, would be all the more manageable were it not for the presence of severely personality disordered patients. As we have seen, such individuals are difficult to care for and manage both in prison and in hospital. We have talked about the lottery which leaves some men languishing in hospitals for many years, whilst others with similar offending histories and psychopathology go to jail and are eventually released much sooner, whether or not they remain dangerous. In hospital those who are resistant to treatment can easily undermine the treatment of others, corrupt staff and damage the mentally ill. In prison they require a highly structured regime with some therapeutic input. They rarely get it.

7.1.3 The system which cares for and manages severely personality disordered individuals who offend is a mess. It would be tempting to dismiss the severe end of personality disorder as not a medical problem, leaving the penal system to pick up the pieces. But the NHS and health professionals cannot completely wash their hands of severe personality disorder; some individuals are willing to be helped in the right environment and the existence of dual diagnosis means that mentally ill people will present with disordered personalities, even if their mental illness can be readily addressed. What is needed is a radical reappraisal of how the forensic psychiatric services and the Criminal Justice System deal with severely personality disordered individuals. The model we outline below would, we believe, improve matters for severely personality disordered individuals, the staff who care for and manage them, the mentally ill who would be cared for in a different environment and, by extension, the public.

7.2.0 A New Model

7.2.1 There are several key principles that any new system must embody:

(i) **flexibility**. There must be clear pathways between different levels of security within the NHS and private forensic services, and between the NHS and the penal system;

(ii) a **regional focus** for all forensic care. High, medium and low security must be managed as a network of local services;

(iii) **specialist services** for personality disorder within the penal and hospital systems with easy access between the two;

(iv) a **separation** of personality disordered patients from mentally ill patients;

(v) an **end to the lottery**. A national system for assessing personality disordered individuals is needed, incorporating national standards for assessment;

(vi) **hospitals are not prisons.** Only those who are willing and able to benefit should be transferred to and remain in hospitals. There should be no more hospital orders for personality disordered individuals.

7.2.2. Below we sketch out a new model embodying these principles.

7.3.0 A Regional Network

7.3.1 With an argument which appears to be based largely on Broadmoor, the Special Hospital system has its champions.[1] However, we believe the only way to end the isolation of the Special Hospitals is to make them fully part and parcel of regional forensic psychiatric services. There needs to be a network of forensic services embracing all levels of security from high security to the community. Only then, we believe, would there be a mechanism for ensuring that patients can be moved flexibly around according to need. High security would become truly part of the NHS system. Staff could move around the system to gain wider experience, prevent burn-out and professional isolation.

7.3.2 This policy goal is simple to state, but the implications are profound. The national purchasing role would have to be devolved to regional level. New management arrangements would be needed at the regional level for these services. Capital development would be needed. A large number of patients currently in the High Security Hospital system would need to be moved as the alternative facilities become available. Many staff would also have to move. The relationship of the Prison Service to such a network would have to be close and effective. We discuss these points below.

Providing and Managing a Regional Service: Alternative Models

7.3.3 There a number of ways in which regional forensic networks could be developed. We do not wish to recommend a single model but instead suggest alternatives. If different models emerge across the country it will be important that they easily link with each other whenever this becomes necessary to resolve the problems of individual patients.

7.3.4 The boundaries of the eight English Regional Offices of the Department of Health seem to be as good a starting point as any for these networks as they will fit with any networks developed in other clinical specialities and simplify co-ordination enormously. There might be variations in London and the South. What matters is that they are clear and manageable and have a sensible link to the Prison Service. We assume there will be no more than ten forensic networks in England.

Recommendation 46 **7.3.5 We recommend that all purchasing for forensic services is managed on a region-wide basis.**

7.3.6 In respect of the above recommendation we would very much like the proposed Local Commissioning Groups to be connected to the process and represented on any Health Authority Purchasing Consortia. We assume each of these consortia will be shaping their investment within the framework of a national strategic policy framework. Such a framework would be the responsibility of the HSPSCB, which would of course lose its purchasing role once purchasing was devolved to rgional level.

---

1 Gunn J. Maden A (1998) Should the English Special Hospitals be closed? Maudsley Discussion Paper No 6 Institute of Psychiatry. London

7.3.7 We envisage that each Region would appoint a Regional Forensic Network Co-ordinator. He or she would negotiate annual agreements with the forensic providers in the Regional Network (NHS and Independent) and monitor performance and delivery of services. The agreements and contract would enable the Co-ordinator to intervene when patients became stuck or blocked. The Co-ordinator would act as the final arbiter (perhaps when necessary with independent expert advice) when provider units did not agree about the placement of particular patients. If a provider unit wished to limit the range of cases it could be expected to admit then this would be specified in advance in the agreement or contract.

7.3.8 The Regional Co-ordinator could be based either in a Regional Office or with a lead Health Authority. He would have to be a figure of real authority and respected by clinicians and managers alike. The individual components of the network on the ground would continue to be managed by each NHS Trust or Independent Provider who would be accountable for quality standards.

7.3.9 There are essentially two alternatives for the management of the provider networks. One is to create a specialist forensic NHS Trust which manages all the assets in the region where they are located. It would employ all the staff but need not manage all the buildings and support services. Mental Health Trusts that have their acute units in the middle of Acute General Hospitals will be familiar with this model. The Chief Executive and his senior colleagues would thus manage the forensic network. They might also handle detailed investment decisions and patient placement within an overall budget agreed in advance with the Health Authority purchasing consortium. We would envisage such a Trust providing a full spectrum of care from high security to community supervision (although the latter might be done by another local Trust by arrangement for patients with uncomplicated problems).

7.3.10 An alternative to a Specialist Trust would be simply to extend the role of an existing Mental Health Trust and give it a region-wide lead role. This would have the benefit of further integrating forensic services with mainstream mental health care. Any NHS Trust with a lead role would have to develop an effective partnership with any independent providers and take care that a conflict of interest did not arise.

7.3.11 In any model the network would adopt nationally agreed assessment criteria and protocols for assessment and treatment. Each network would also contribute to professional training and development as well as research.

7.3.12 We would stress that restructuring of the system is dependent upon the provision of more medium secure, and long term medium secure beds. This will allow the movement to an appropriate level of secure care of those mentally disordered patients who continue unnecessarily in high security care.

7.3.13 When we debated this subject at our management seminar there were proponents for both the models we have discussed or variations on them. We are all agreed it would be sensible to leave the detailed design to regions provided this led to an effective and responsive network that worked and had mechanisms for resolving disagreements quickly and decisively.

7.3.14 Our proposed regional health networks would work closely with the Prison Service. The prisons would have within them many prisoners with personality disorder. Those at the severe end of the spectrum will need managing in a specialist environment within the Prison Service, with appropriate therapeutic backup. We think they may value particularly the support of psychologists.

7.3.15 It is also essential that once a person with severe personality disorder is returned to the community he is supported and supervised by those who have a detailed knowledge of him.

That is to say the multi-disciplinary team that has provided care prior to his release.

Recommendation 47 **7.3.16 We recommend :**
(i) the establishment of regional networks of forensic services embracing all levels of security from high security to the community;
(ii) the transfer of high security facilities to regional networks;
(iii) the urgent provision of more medium secure and long-term medium secure accommodation within the regional networks;
(iv) the development of increased functional integration between prison services for persons with severe personality disorder and the regional forensic services;
(v) the continuing care of those with severe personality disorder should always be provided by a multi-disciplinary team with a detailed knowledge of the individual.

New Services

7.3.17 It is not for us to say how many high security units would be needed across the country. Four to six units, each with a maximum of 200 beds, strikes us as a sensible estimate. The sites of the current Special Hospitals should not be regarded as sacrosanct; what is vital is that the high security units have close links with medium security units and the rest of the forensic network, including prisons. We discuss our ideas for new units for personality disordered patients below.

The Prison Service

7.3.18 When we discussed the relationship of the Prison Service to our proposed network there was general support for the view that the NHS should take over responsibility for commissioning and providing healthcare within prisons. Only thus would there be an opportunity to provide a truly integrated high quality service across the whole range of forensic services. We wholeheartedly concur with this view.

Recommendation 48 **7.3.19 We recommend that the NHS takes over responsibility for healthcare within prisons.**

7.3.20 The point at which the Prison Service links to these NHS networks would need to be agreed in advance, with a mechanism for resolving any disagreements that may arise.

Future of the Special Hospitals

7.3.21 We heard a lot of evidence about the future of the Special Hospitals. One view is that they could and should be phased out once the new regional networks are in place. Others would wish to retain them as part of these networks. We favour their long term replacement. Our remit restricts us to Ashworth about which we make recommendations. The Hospital is unmanageable in anything approaching its present form (and indeed the present Chairman admitted as much to us in evidence). Early change is both inevitable and urgent. We would support any moves to merge it into another Trust.

However, after much reflection we have reached a more fundamental conclusion. Ashworth Hospital's reputation is so badly damaged (and our Report will make it worse) that we see no realistic prospect of it ever recruiting and retaining sufficient numbers of high quality staff who can be proud of the place at which they work. The Hospital's negative, defensive and blame ridden culture is so deeply ingrained that we doubt that even the most talented management team would find it possible to turn it around. The scars and tensions left behind by the events of recent years will poison the therapeutic environment and hinder the development of sensitive multi-disciplinary working that is so crucial in the care of these patients.

It is time for a decisive change. Ashworth Hospital should close in its entirety at the earliest opportunity. No doubt an alternative non-NHS use could be found for the buildings and estate and thus preserve employment opportunities for those who wish them. It may be useful as a prison.

7.3.22 This can only happen once the appropriate regional networks and new services are in place. We therefore believe that the priority for developing a forensic network is in Ashworth Hospital's catchment area. Mr Tinston, the Regional Director of the North West Regional Office of the NHS Executive, told us that much work has already been done on developing an integrated regional forensic service in the North West. The development of such a network of forensic services in the North West, West Midlands and other parts of Ashworth's catchment area, including the development of alternative high secure facilities, would make Ashworth Hospital redundant.

Recommendation 49 **7.3.23 We recommend that Ashworth Hospital should close in its entirety at the earliest opportunity.**

7.3.24 Any changes on the scale we are suggesting would mean disrupting the lives of many patients, not to mention staff. We do not do this lightly, but we are convinced that the system in its present form is rotten and unsustainable, and trying to sustain it will only make matters worse.

7.4.0 The Management of Personality Disorder within the Forensic Network

7.4.1 We turn now to the management of personality disordered individuals within this system. As we said above, forensic psychiatry cannot wash its hands of personality disorder, even if it wished to. But a more realistic approach must be taken as to the likely benefits of treatment. It is important to leave the way open for admitting failure when treatment is demonstrably failing.

7.4.2 We are well aware that people suffering from severe personality disorder are likely to prove very difficult to manage in whatever setting they find themselves in. At present there is a large concentration in Special Hospitals, where they are adept at manipulating vulnerable mentally ill patients (and also on occasion staff). Many individuals, with more or less the same psychopathology, can be found in prisons, particularly in Grendon, but also in other special units set up to deal with difficult, disturbed and otherwise troublesome inmates. Our best guess is that there are around **400** individuals of the severely personality disordered group we have identified in High Security Hospitals or prison. There will be a further unquantified number of such people in the community. We have discussed how we decided to use the term "severe personality disordered offender" in paragraph **6.6.3** *et seq.* above.

7.4.3 We are also well aware that working with severely personality disordered individuals is not popular; nobody is offering to take on their care. There is also a considerable shortage of knowledge and expertise in this field.

7.4.4 That said, we do not believe that doing nothing is an acceptable policy. However unfortunate the starting point we have no other. We do believe there is a better alternative.

7.4.5 First, we are convinced that courts should no longer have the option of passing a hospital order on a personality disordered offender. This would prevent severely personality disordered individuals on such orders becoming stuck in the system. The Prison Service would therefore take responsibility for offenders suffering from severe personality disorder (but not mental illness) who were assessed as being unwilling or unable to benefit from hospital care. This might increase the prison population slightly over time. It should be pointed out that removing the power to pass a hospital order in these cases would formalize what is a very strong trend amongst psychiatrists against recommending hospital orders for legal psychopaths.

7.4.6 Second, transfer to the NHS should only take place after a careful assessment has suggested that an individual was motivated and might benefit from care within the NHS. This assessment would be carried out according to agreed national protocols. Personality disordered offenders who were assessed as being suitable for treatment would go to hospital on a transfer direction.

7.4.7 Severely personality disordered individuals do need specialist care. Both the NHS and the Prison Service should develop specialist units for individuals with severe personality disorder. **We do not wish to be prescriptive, but we think that such units in both prisons and hospitals should house no more than 50 patients or prisoners. Similarly, no more than 10 patients should be housed in a sub-unit or on a ward.**

7.4.8 We are convinced that personality disordered patients should be kept physically separate from mentally ill patients. This should help avoid many of the control problems evident at Ashworth. In prisons, prisoners with severe personality disorder (but no significant mental health problems) should also be kept clearly distinct from fellow prisoners.

7.4.9 The primary clinical input to both the prison and hospital units should be from psychologists and nurses, with a continuing input from forensic psychiatrists. We discuss the role of the RMO, and whether the current arrangements should change, in Part Four.

7.4.10 Finally, in order to protect society against dangerous personality disordered offenders whose offences have not attracted an indefinite sentence, we recommend the introduction of reviewable sentences for dangerous offenders for offences where the punishment for the offence is not fixed by law. This would allow a tariff sentence to be passed which would be reviewed and, if appropriate, renewed, for periods of up to two years.

7.4.11 We discuss now in detail the arguments for, and ramifications of, changing the law in this fashion. We then outline how severely personality disordered offenders would be managed in the new system. And we say a little more about the assessment process and the new specialist units.

7.5.0 The New Legal Framework

The Current Framework

7.5.1 Our proposals will need a certain amount of primary legislation, because if our recommendations are adopted changes to the Mental Health Act 1983 will be required. In addition it will be necessary to introduce a new type of sentence – a **'reviewable sentence'**. New though this sentence would be, it is not a new concept. Its origin is enshrined in the Butler Committee Report to which we have referred.

7.5.2 As we heard the expert evidence concerning 'psychopathy', it became clear that although so much has been written about the inappropriateness of the legal term 'psychopathic disorder', the real issue is how offenders in this legal category who represent a substantial risk of causing serious harm to others should be managed and cared for. This is the factor which determines the need for their compulsory segregation from society whether in hospital or prison (*see* paragraph **6.6.7**). As we say in paragraph **6.6.8**, "dangerousness" is too subjective a concept; it is far better to think in terms of "risk of danger" or "risk of causing serious harm" whether that risk is a risk of causing physical or psychological harm. We also mention in paragraph **6.6.9**, Dr Snowden's concern that many of his colleagues missed the point that we were not so much concerned with precise medical terminology, but were focusing on "very seriously worrying and very seriously dangerous" people who have offended. It is worth repeating the following extract from his evidence:

> "... I think people have been missing the point when they have been discussing this area, because improvement of personality, improvement of mental health does not necessarily mean reduction of risk, because on these particularly difficult, very worrying individuals, the connection between their personality and their phenomenology and the offence is quite complex and it may be that the contribution from personality may not be the major factor. It might be alcohol, it might be drugs, it might be the environment that the person is moving in . . . So assessment of treatment and whether or not they would benefit from therapeutic intervention is I think one sort of section of thought and activity, but it does not necessarily mean that the patient or person is going to be less risky, that risk is still tolerable for the community . . . I am certainly suggesting that in this group their personality disorder probably contributed to their offending but it does not necessarily mean that wellness in terms of their personality disorder significantly reduces risk, or that it will significantly reduce risk enough to make them tolerable in the community."

7.5.3 The risk of causing harm to others which personality disordered offenders frequently present is the real problem from the point of view of the public, and it is wholly understandable that the public do not want to see serious offenders, who still present an unacceptable level of risk of causing harm to others, released into the community even when their date of release has arrived.

7.5.4 In the past this problem has been tackled in a piecemeal way. Over the years, and particularly in recent years, maximum sentences for certain offences have been increased; the number of offences for which a discretionary life sentence is the maximum sentence has been increased. Section 2 (2)(b) of the Criminal Justice Act 1991 introduced the longer than commensurate prison sentence for violent and sexual offences to "protect the public from serious harm". Sections 2, 3 and 4 of The Crime (Sentences) Act 1997 introduced mandatory life sentences for certain second offences and mandatory fixed sentences for other offences. That Act also amended the Mental Health Act 1983 by adding to it sections 45 A and 45 B which introduced the so called 'hybrid' sentence (*see* below).

7.5.5 Most of this piecemeal legislation has been directed towards assuaging public fear of further serious offences being committed by prisoners after their release, but in reality all that is achieved is to put rather crude sentencing tools in the hands of judges. At the time of sentencing no judge is in a position to assess when the risk of causing serious harm to others, which he judges an offender to possess, will be sufficiently reduced to a tolerable level. A longer than commensurate sentence may prove to be too long or not long enough. The hybrid sentence is only available for a determinate sentence. Instead of either passing a determinate sentence or making a hospital order with or without restriction it allows a judge both to pass a prison sentence and to send an offender to hospital (from which he can be remitted back to prison should treatment not be successful). It was thought this should go some way to prevent the Special Hospitals having to manage personality disordered offenders indeterminately when in reality they are being used as custodial units. But it still means that at their release date, prisoners have to be released even though they may still present a serious risk of causing harm to others.

A Reviewable Sentence

7.5.6 The new hybrid sentence is not enough. Something more radical is needed, something which will enable the Criminal Justice System to monitor and control more effectively the risk severely personality disordered offenders may pose of causing harm to others if released. We propose introducing a reviewable sentence for personality disordered offenders for whose offence(s) a mandatory life sentence is not available. (It is not required when a life sentence is passed because an offender subject to a life sentence can only be released on the authority of the Home Secretary. If he is released he is released on licence and is subject to recall.) The effect of the reviewable sentence would be that the offender is sentenced to a term of imprisonment justified by the usual tariff principles. At the time of his earliest date of release his case would be reviewed by a new judicially-led body, which we have called the Reviewable Sentence Board (RSB). The offender would be able to be represented and call evidence. The Board would have the offender's criminal and medical history before it as well as multi-disciplinary reports directed to the state of his personality disorder and his current level of risk of harming others. Where appropriate the RSB could renew the sentence for up to two years at a time; it could also conditionally discharge the offender for a period up to two years. If satisfied that the offender no longer presents a substantial risk of causing serious harm to others, the Board could discharge him. Such proposals as we make, if adopted, could be effected by amendments to the Mental Health Act 1983, or by being incorporated in a new Mental Health Act, or by introducing a few clauses into a Criminal Justice Bill. The detail of our proposals is set out below at paragraph **7.8.0**.

7.5.7 Here we restrict ourselves within our terms of reference to personality disordered offenders. However, such a measure would have some similarities with legislation passed in other countries to cope with the problem of dangerous offenders. For example, Canada and Australia have passed "Dangerous Offender" legislation. Given that offenders other than personality disordered offenders also present a substantial risk of causing harm to others after release from prison, the Government may wish to consider introducing legislation based on the reviewable sentence principle for other types of offender as well. Certainly there is grave public concern when prisoners still considered to possess a substantial risk of causing harm to others have to be released. It is an understandable concern which we believe justifies consideration of a wider application of the "reviewable" sentence than our terms of reference permit.

Recommendation 50

7.5.8 We recommend the creation of:
(i) a new sentence called a 'Reviewable Sentence';
(ii) a 'Reviewable Sentence Board'.

Witnesses' Views

7.5.9 No witness we heard was satisfied with the current legislation. There was a unanimous view that "psychopathic disorder" should be removed from Mental Health legislation. There was a general consensus that offenders with a primary diagnosis of personality disorder should not be subjected to hospital orders, and that insofar as any were managed in hospital units they should be so managed pursuant to transfer directions from prison. There was also a general consensus that the "reviewable" sentence is the appropriate sentencing provision for those personality disordered offenders who presented a substantial risk of causing serious harm to others. While accepting the need for a "reviewable sentence", one or two at our legal seminar expressed the view that the "reviewable sentence" should be without a time limit- in effect a potential life sentence to reflect what in theory it can be. The majority, however, shared our view that it should be for a fixed term but renewable for periods of up to two years.

7.5.10 The forensic medical fraternity disliked the term "psychopathic disorder" from the start and there is general agreement that the term is pejorative and stigmatizing. Other observers, however, make the point that if "personality disorder" replaces it then, in time, that phrase will become equally stigmatizing.

7.5.11 There are other and better reasons for finally abandoning the use of "psychopathic disorder". It is a legal not a medical term. It only approximately equates with the classifications now used, and although it is those who are in the anti-social or dissocial sub-group who tend to be so described, as we have discussed in Part Six, other personality disorders may from time to time justify detention under the Mental Health Act in its present form, or the passing of a reviewable sentence.

7.6.0 The Rationale for Change

7.6.1 In his submission to us Dr Chiswick made some helpful proposals about the principles to consider in reforming mental health legislation with reference to personality disorder. He succinctly stated important issues.

Mental health legislation:

> (i) should reflect the reality of contemporary clinical practice – the indefinite detention of serious offenders with personality disorder who thereby become a lifetime responsibility of psychiatric services is not sustainable;
>
> (ii) is not the appropriate legal vehicle if the primary purpose is the control of antisocial behaviour– indefinite detention should not be delivered through the "backdoor" of psychiatry;
>
> (iii) should continue to be enabling and not directive – the discretion of clinicians and of courts should continue. Neither clinicians nor courts should be required to take mandatory action according to the necessarily fragile categories of mental health law;
>
> (iv) should have different standards for compulsion in personality disorder compared with mental illness – at present the only difference is the treatability test. A more stringent range of reviews and interpretation of the criteria for detention is necessary;
>
> (v) requires a new approach in respect of patients with personality disorder.

7.6.2 In neither the Mental Health Act of 1959 nor that of 1983 was "mental illness" defined. Lack of definition does not seem to have caused problems, at least for some people. We note that the Royal Commission on the Law Relating to Mental Illness and Mental Deficiency felt that the term "mental illness" would be used "in the same sense as at present" (paragraph 17 (a)) if undefined in the Act.

7.6.3 In his usual trenchant way Lawton L.J., in **W. v. L. [1974] Q.B. 711, C.A.** gave the only authoritative statement in English law on the meaning of mental illness in the case of a man who was found by the Court of Appeal to be both psychopathic and mentally ill. The case concerned a man who exhibited cruelty to animals and other violent behaviour that could easily be classified as psychopathic, but (as it occurred during the period of the 1959 Act and he was over the age of 21), he could not be detained for longer than 28 days unless he was also mentally ill. The doctors could not agree, but one described him as suffering from an "episodic epileptoid psychosis" which raised the question as to whether or not he was also mentally ill. Lord Justice Lawton said

> ". . . the words 'mental illness' are "ordinary words of the English language. They have no particular medical significance. They have no particular legal significance. How should the court construe them? The answer . . . is . . . that the ordinary words of the English language should be construed in the way that ordinary sensible people would construe them. That being my judgement the right test, then I ask myself, what would the ordinary sensible person have said about the patient's condition in this case if he had been informed of his behaviour . . ? In my judgement such a person would have said: "well, the fellow is obviously mentally ill".

7.6.4 Brenda Hoggett (now The Hon. Mrs Justice Hale) criticized this approach (1990):

> "It is impossible not to think of this as the 'man-must-be-mad' test. It simply adds fuel to the fire of those who accuse the mental hygiene laws of being a sophisticated machine for the suppression of the unusual, eccentric or inconvenient behaviour (and in this country without due process of law). It pays scant regard to the painstaking efforts of psychiatrists to distinguish mental health from mental illness by means of carefully described deficiencies, not in behaviour, but in mental functioning. It tells us nothing about why some people who are cruel to animals should be regarded as responsible for their actions and some should not."[2]

7.6.5 Of course there are many definable mental illnesses, but doctors manage quite well without being told what they are in legislation.

7.6.6 The term "personality" refers to those enduring qualities of an individual shown in his ways of behaving in a wide variety of circumstances; personality traits are enduring patterns of perceiving, relating to, and thinking about the environment and oneself that are exhibited in a wide range of social and personal contexts. (DSM-IV p.630). It is not possible to define "personality disorder" in such a way that a range of personality disorders could successfully be encompassed within it. The term 'personality disorder' is easily understood as is the term "mental illness". As with mental illness its interpretation can be left to the clinicians who, we believe should be required to justify a diagnosis by reference to agreed standards (which we will return to). The element of "risk" or danger that may be associated with personality disorder we consider should be for judicial appraisal with appropriate advice.

7.6.7 We have given careful consideration to all the evidence and have reviewed the arguments for and against the changes we propose and believe that it is appropriate, fair, and will permit other important improvements in the management of patients with a personality disorder to remove psychopathic disorder from legislation.

Recommendation 51

7.6.8 We recommend:
(i) removing 'psychopathic disorder' from the Mental Health Act 1983;
(ii) replacing it with 'personality disorder', save in the specific instances set out below; and
(iii) not defining 'personality disorder' in the Act.
(See Appendix 9 for all suggested amendments to the 1983 Act.)

7.6.9 Section 1 (2) of the Mental Health Act 1983 would then read:

> "In this Act –
>
> > 'mental disorder' means mental illness, arrested or incomplete development of mind, personality disorder and any other disorder or disability of mind."

7.6.10 One consequence of this change is that the defining terms 'abnormally aggressive and seriously irresponsible' would remain in the definition of 'severe mental impairment' and 'mental impairment'. We have not received any evidence on the implications of this; indeed it is outside our terms of reference. We consider that it should be examined further.

Recommendation 52

7.6.11 We recommend that those currently undertaking the review of the Mental Health Act should be asked to consider the definitions of severe mental impairment and mental impairment in the light of our recommendations.

2 Hoggett B (1990) *Mental Health Law* 3rd. ed. Sweet and Maxwell. London

Hospital Orders

7.6.12 It was the Percy Commission[3] that recommended the inclusion of psychopathic disorder in the categories that could be subject to a hospital order. The Commission considered that the use of special compulsory powers on grounds of the patient's mental disorder is justifiable when:

(a) there is reasonable certainty that the patient is suffering from a pathological mental disorder and requires hospital or community care; and

(b) suitable care cannot be provided without the use of compulsory powers; and

(c) if the patient himself is unwilling to receive the form of care which is considered necessary, there is at least a strong likelihood that his unwillingness is due to a lack of appreciation of his own condition deriving from the mental disorder itself; and

(d) there is also either

(i) a good prospect of benefit to the patient from the treatment proposed – an expectation that it will either cure or alleviate his mental disorder or strengthen his ability to regulate his social behaviour in spite of the underlying disorder, or bring him substantial benefit in the form of protection from neglect or exploitation from others; or

(ii) a strong need to protect others from anti-social behaviour by the patient.

7.6.13 The Commission was clear that the treatment and use of compulsion must be based on a medical diagnosis of the individual patient's condition, not merely on evidence of his behaviour. They went on to say

"The patient's pattern of behaviour over a period of time may be a perfectly valid basis for a medical diagnosis of mental disorder, and may distinguish him from other people who may have performed similar antisocial acts but who are not considered to be suffering from a pathological mental disorder. But if such patients are to be subject to the same sort of compulsory powers as apply to the mentally ill and severely subnormal patients, it would mean to put the case against such powers in the baldest form that people who have not broken the criminal law might be subject to compulsory detention in hospital as the result of a diagnosis which is largely based on a record of behaviour which is not criminal and which in other individuals might not be held to indicate psychopathic personality either, and that on the basis of a similar diagnosis a person who has broken the criminal law might be detained in hospital for a period which in some cases might exceed even the maximum possible term of imprisonment for the offence which has been the occasion for the application of these compulsory powers".

7.6.14 There is extensive discussion and some uncertainty expressed in Lord Percy's report about the extent to which psychopathic disorder should be introduced into mental health legislation. Ultimately, and partly as a result of the recommendations of the Commission in the Mental Health Act 1959:

(i) psychopathic disorder was included within the general category mental disorder for compulsory admission to hospital for treatment for twenty-eight days;

(ii) admission to hospital for treatment or placement under guardianship was only applicable to a patient suffering from psychopathic disorder under the age of twenty-one years;

(iii) the order for treatment or guardianship was for a period not exceeding one year

---

3 Royal Commission on the Law Relating to Mental Illness and Mental Deficiency 1954–1957. *Report.* Cmnd. 169 HMSO (Chairman: Lord Percy of Newcastle)

and was renewable for two years at a time, but in the case of psychopathic disorder only, guardianship could not be renewed after the age of twenty-five;

(iv) a hospital order was applicable to psychopathic disorder as for other mental disorders.

The principle resulting from the deliberations of the Percy Commission and the Mental Health Act 1959 was that a convicted offender was either "bad" and received the appropriate penal disposal or he was "mad" and he was ordered to hospital for as long as it was necessary. A "therapeutic" disposal was to be, as far as it was possible, similar to a civil commitment unless special safeguards were necessary to protect the public and were applied by the court (restriction orders).

7.6.15 The Butler Committee recognised the problems associated with a Hospital Order:

(i) if it subsequently turns out that the Order is inappropriate it cannot be reversed except for reasons justifying an appeal. The case cannot otherwise return to Court for an alternative disposal.

(ii) the patient on a hospital order without a restriction order can be discharged on the decision of the Responsible Medical Officer or by a Mental Health Review Tribunal (to which he has a right of application after six months detention). This is entirely right if he is "cured", or improved sufficiently to manage in the community. It presents obvious problems and risks if the patient has been wrongly diagnosed, or if he has simply refused to cooperate with treatment or if he has been deemed untreatable.

(iii) a patient on a Hospital Order with a Restriction Order is detained indefinitely. The Restriction Order remains in force unless the Home Secretary removes the restrictions (a rare occurrence) or until he is absolutely discharged. For as long as the restrictions last, there is no need for his detention to be renewed periodically under section 20 (s. 41 (3) (a)). This means that no one is under any statutory obligation to consider whether the grounds for detaining him still apply. But, the Act provides that the RMO must examine the patient and report to the Home Secretary at such intervals as the latter may require but not exceeding a year (section 1 (6)). The Home Secretary does not have to agree to the patient's discharge even though he no longer meets the criteria for detention. His duty is to protect the public.

(iv) the Mental Health Review Tribunal may discharge a patient even if the Home Secretary disagrees, thus his concern that psychopaths may be discharged even though they may be dangerous and a risk.

These arrangements mean that a psychopathic patient can be detained for much longer than is justified by his mental condition and for a longer, or much longer, period than he would have spent in prison for the offence he committed.

7.6.16 The arrangements mean that if the patient turns out to be treatment resistant or refuses to cooperate in treatment, there is nothing that the clinical team can do about it. He cannot be sent to prison and cannot be discharged. In effect detention in hospital is preventive detention (and the result of the "lottery" (*see* above)).

7.6.17 The socalled "hybrid order" to which we have referred above was introduced in part to diminish the problems outlined above, but it is too early to say whether or not it will prove successful. Insofar as we understand it has not yet been used by the Courts.

7.6.18 We agree with those who have criticised the present system that results, in effect, in hospital being used as a form of imprisonment for some patients. For patients with personality disorder it would be more honest and just for the patient and for the clinical team to provide that an offender with personality disorder should receive an appropriate sentence and then be transferred from prison to appropriate therapeutic facilities, (assuming that he is considered to be suitable for treatment and is willing to undergo such treatment) following a thorough and skilled assessment using nationally agreed assessment protocols.

7.6.19 The effect of the recommendations we are making would be that personality disordered offenders would no longer be eligible to be made the subject of hospital orders. Nor would they be able to be transferred to hospital from prison under section 47. However personality disordered offenders whose post-sentence clinical management assessment deems that they are likely to benefit from therapeutic care and management should be transferable to a secure hospital unit, provided that they are willing to undergo such treatment. These would be the bases upon which our new form of transfer order for personality disordered offenders would be made.

Recommendation 53

7.6.20 We recommend:-
(i) abolishing hospital orders (with or without restriction), and of the present form of transfer orders, for individuals suffering from personality disorder by not replacing "psychopathic disorder" with "personality disorder" in sections 37(2)(a)(i) and 47(1)(a) and (b) of the 1983 Act;
(ii) that a new transfer direction be enacted to facilitate such transfers on those bases. This would facilitate transfer of personality disordered offenders when appropriate, and also their transfer back under section 50 of the Act if appropriate.

7.7.0 Other Consequential Amendments

7.7.1 Section 38 of the Mental Health Act 1983 provides for the making of interim hospital orders after conviction for up to twelve months. If our proposals are adopted then it will be necessary to remove "psychopathic disorder" from section 38(1)(a). This is because the section is concerned with assessment in cases where a hospital order may be appropriate which would no longer be the case for personality disordered offenders. Given that we recommend below a new assessment regime, provision will have to be made for transferring personality disordered offenders for assessment.

Recommendation 54

7.7.2 We recommend that Section 38(1)(a) be amended by removing "psychopathic disorder", and that a provision for an interim transfer direction for assessment for up to twelve months be enacted to provide such transfers for personality disordered offenders from prison.

Non-offenders Suffering from a Personality Disorder (Civil Sections)

7.7.3 We recognise that it may be necessary to admit to hospital compulsorily a patient suffering from one of the categories of personality disorder who is not an offender, when his personality disorder is of a nature or degree which makes it appropriate for him to receive medical treatment in a hospital, and when he is likely to respond to such treatment.

7.7.4 Although we have heard conflicting evidence about treatability, we accept that some patients may benefit from treatment and the door should be left open for them to be admitted for treatment. This could be achieved under section 3 of the Act. For minor offenders the Court Diversion scheme seems an appropriate vehicle to develop.

Recommendation 55 **7.7.5 We recommend:**
(i) that "personality disorder" should replace "psychopathic disorder" in Part II of the Mental Health Act 1983 and the deletion of "psychopathic disorder" altogether from section 3(2)(b);
(ii) for minor offenders we recommend further development of the Court Diversion scheme to facilitate admission and treatment under Part II of the Act.

7.7.6 Insofar as Part II is concerned, this would necessitate amendments to ss.3(2)(a) and (b), 7(2), 11(6), 16(2), 20(4)(a), 20(7)(a), 25A(4)(a), 25C(1), and 25G(4)(a).

7.7.7 These changes would also preserve the making of Guardianship Applications in civil cases.

7.7.8 If the reviewable sentence is adopted, then in our judgment there will be no place for the hybrid sentence introduced by the Crime Sentences Act 1997. The amendments that Act made to the Mental Health Act 1983, in particular, sections 45A and 45B, should then be repealed.

7.7.9 Because, under our proposals, all personality disordered offenders would be subject to a prison sentence, the Mental Health Review Tribunal would not be concerned with personality disordered offenders, since they would no longer be sent to hospital on hospital orders. Nevertheless there would be some personality disordered individuals in hospital pursuant to transfer directions. Should the Tribunal's role regarding such transferred prisoners change, since, as reviewable sentenced offenders, their cases will be under review by the Reviewable Sentence Board? Two views may be taken. The first is to leave the review tribunal in place. If this is decided then, for example, if a MHRT took the view, as at present it can, that a transferred patient was no longer suffering from personality disorder all it could do would be to send the patient back to prison where he would be kept until the RSB decided that he no longer presented a risk of causing serious harm to others. The other view is that it is unnecessary to have two judicially led bodies dealing with the same problem. We have debated this point but do not feel that the existence of these two bodies would cause difficulty, and we assume the MHRT will continue to review the cases of personality disordered offenders who have been transferred to a secure hospital unit.

7.7.10 Finally in Part X (Interpretation), "psychopathic disorder" should be removed from section 145(1).

7.7.11 For convenience, in Appendix 9 we set out the changes in the context of the current provisions of the Mental Health Act 1983.

7.8.0 The Reviewable Sentence – the Process

7.8.1 We set out at the end of this Part a flow chart of how our recommended reviewable sentence would work in practice. The only significant way in which it appears our concept differs from Lord Butler's proposal is that, in our view, the reviewable sentence should not be, in effect, a life sentence but one which is renewable every two years after the offender's earliest date of release. We have already referred to this potential sentence as being vital to dealing with personality disordered offenders with a risk of causing serious harm to others. The flow chart will assist in following the text

7.8.2 The sentencing Judge will become aware, as is presently the case, of concerns about the psychiatric condition of the Defendant. These arise either from his own observations, from counsel in the case, the Probation Service, or from psychiatric reports obtained during the course of the proceedings. He will also be aware of the offender's antecedent history. The

Judge will, in the first instance, wish to know if the Defendant has a "Mental Disorder" falling within the 1983 Act, and will adjourn sentence in order to obtain psychiatric reports (if they have not already been obtained). This will be done either during a remand in custody, by a remand to a hospital under section 35 or whilst on bail.

7.8.3 If the reports conclude that the Defendant is not suffering from a mental disorder he will fall to be sentenced in the ordinary way with the usual range of sentences. If the Defendant is found to be suffering principally from a mental illness, or from mental impairment (severe or otherwise), the Judge will have available (as at present) the option of imposing a "hospital order" (section 37), with or without restriction (under section 41). If, however, the Defendant is identified as principally having a personality disorder the judge will commission, on behalf of the Court, a **"Pre-Sentence Assessment"** report from an "Assessment Team", led by a Consultant Psychiatrist who has had forensic training. This Assessment will be undertaken using a nationally agreed framework of criteria for identifying Personality Disorders. Non co-operation in this assessment may permit the Judge to draw appropriate inferences if sufficient existing background material is available to him.

7.8.4 It is quite possible (perhaps probable) that at this stage the Defence team may themselves also seek to obtain a further psychiatric report to address the questions which the judge will have to consider at the next Court appearance (see below).

7.8.5 The Assessment Team might report that the Defendant is not suffering from a Mental Disorder after all, or that he is principally suffering from a mental illness, or from mental impairment (severe or otherwise). The Judge would then have the options mentioned above. However, if the Assessment Team conclude that he is suffering principally from a Personality Disorder the Judge must first consider and determine any dispute there may be about that diagnosis, as raised by the Defence and supported by any contrary psychiatric opinion.

7.8.6 If the Judge concludes on the expert evidence that:

(a) the Defendant does have a Personality Disorder, then he must go on to ask himself, on the basis of all the information before him, whether:

(b) the Defendant "presently poses a substantial risk of causing serious harm to others".

7.8.7 If his conclusion to (a) is "Yes", but to (b) is "No", then he will pass a tariff prison sentence. If, however, the Judge's conclusion both as to (a) and (b) is "Yes", then he will be obliged to pass a **"Reviewable Sentence"** of X years, where X is the normal tariff length of sentence. The offender will then enter the prison system.

Compliance with the European Convention on Human Rights.

7.8.8 In our view the proposals we make comply with the ECHR. The "Reviewable Sentence" may only be imposed by a Crown Court (a competent Court) after fulfilling a rigorous set of conditions precedent under a procedure prescribed by law. The Court must have available to it independent psychiatric opinions and will hear representations and expert evidence by or on behalf of a Defendant. It will only be available in the light of findings by the Judge that the Defendant has a Personality Disorder and that he poses a substantial risk of causing serious harm to others (which will be based upon such matters as the circumstances of his latest offence(s), his antecedents, previous convictions and any opinions expressed by Psychiatrists and Probation Officers).

The element of indeterminacy which will exist – inasmuch as the RSB may continue detention for up to two years at a time after the tariff period of the sentence expires – is a lawful detention based upon the original conviction and sentence (**Guzzardi v. Italy** (6/11/80 Series A No.39) 3 EHRR 333, para.100; **X v. United Kingdom** (24/10/81 Series A No.46) 4 EHRR 55, para.39;

Van Droogenbroeck v. Belgium (24/6/82 Series A No. 50) 4 EHRR 443, paras.35 & 39; **Weeks v. United Kingdom** (2/3/87 Series A No.1114) 10 EHRR 293, paras. 41–53; and **Eriksen v. Norway** (27/5/97 102/1995/608/696) paras.76–78).

Further, the availability of Mental Health Review Tribunals for those transferred to hospital whilst serving a Reviewable Sentence, and the procedures and powers of the RSB are ones which in our opinion comply with Article 5(4). (We consider that there will need to be a statutory right of appeal from a decision of an RSB to detain a "reviewable sentence" prisoner further, which will probably be most appropriate to a Divisional Court of the Queen's Bench Division of the High Court.)

7.9.0 The Management of Sentenced Offenders with Personality Disorder

7.9.1 This is illustrated in a second flow chart found below.

7.9.2 If a "Reviewable Sentence" is passed (or an Assessment Team has identified personality disorder in someone given either a determinate sentence (or Life Imprisonment)) then we recommend that there be a compulsory, detailed, multi-disciplinary "Clinical Management Assessment" to identify the appropriate location, therapy (if any), and Care Plan for the Defendant.

7.9.3 This is an imperative requirement of our proposals, for it is essential that the opportunity of full health care provision is available to this category of person. We consider that only in this fashion will this part of the "lottery" be corrected, namely the existing inconsistent and often inaccurate selection of a few to benefit from an erratic and inadequate system of therapy, which many offenders subsequently reject, but who nevertheless remain inappropriately trapped in expensive High Security Hospital places.

7.9.4 The Management Assessment will be carried out by a multi-disciplinary team, applying nationally agreed criteria, either within a **"Prison Special Unit"** or in a **"High Security Hospital Unit"** on an interim transfer for assessment. This may well take up to a year and will determine, what therapy would be best for him, what therapy he is willing to undergo, what his detailed Care Plan is to be, where he should be located, and when his care and management are next to be reviewed.

7.9.5 In Part Two we have referred to the problems and dangers of placing individuals in residential wards while they are being assessed. We are in no doubt that all assessments should be made in separate assessment facilities whether in prisons or high security hospitals.

Recommendation 56 **7.9.6 We recommend that all Clinical Management Assessments are carried out in separate assessment facilities.**

7.9.7 If he is found to be likely to respond to therapy, and is willing to undergo what is planned, he will be transferred to a High Security Hospital Unit.

7.9.8 If it is found that he is unwilling to undergo therapy, or that he will not respond to what therapeutic regimes are available, he will be kept in a "Special Unit" in prison for the care and management of those with personality disorders.

7.9.9 This set of facilities will be subject to flexible arrangements for transfer between hospitals and special prison units as appropriate from time to time. It is essential that blockages in the various parts of the new system do not diminish the availability and effectiveness of healthcare provision for those who will respond and are willing to co-operate. Even the assessment system proposed may not always prove successful and it is essential to provide flexible movement from prison to hospital and from hospital to prison. In addition there must be flexibility of movement between the prison special unit and the general part of the prison.

7.9.10 With the approach of the offender's earliest date of release, preparations will be made for a "review" of his sentence by the Reviewable Sentence Board. We think it should be of a similar, but not necessarily identical, structure to that of the Parole Board and be chaired by a Circuit Judge. We also believe that the Crown should be legally represented unless counsel is appointed to the Board. At the hearing the offender will be represented by lawyers and will be able to call evidence. The Board will have before it the offender's dossier of personal and offending history, the records kept on him during his stay in prison and/or hospital and a multi-disciplinary report directed to his present and potential state of personality disorder and, where possible, the level of his current risk of causing serious harm to others. The RSB will then either renew the sentence for up to no more than two years at a time, or order his discharge which could either be absolute, or conditional for a period of no more than two years. A further offence or breach of conditions would result in a recall. It is also possible to consider a provision of release on licence. A conditional discharge or a licence provision would be reconsidered towards the expiration of its time. If the RSB renews a sentence, the review process would be repeated at two yearly intervals.

7.9.11 We considered at some length whether we should recommend defining risk of causing serious harm to others. We decided, however that this was a judicial function. As Lord Justice Swinton Thomas said at our legal seminar, Judges routinely have to bear in mind the "dangerousness" of an offender as part of the sentencing process. We also gained the impression from the consultants we heard, that they would feel freer to make appropriate recommendations if the burden of determining risk in any particular case was placed on the Judge in the first instance and then on the RSB.

7.9.12 We believe that such a regime would offer distinct advantages over current arrangements. We believe that the public would be better defended thereby against violent offenders such as Mr Stone, convicted of a horrific double murder shortly before our report was published. From what we have read in the press reports of Mr Stone's antecedent criminal and medical history, he would have been a classic candidate for assessment for a reviewable sentence at the time of his previous sentence.

7.10.0 Assessment

7.10.1 We have discussed at various points in our report the problem of the so-called lottery, the uncertain process by which a small number of (usually) serious offenders become classified as psychopathically disordered and end up in Special Hospital, whereas the majority with similar clinical features serve out their time in prison. Much comes down to the vagaries of assessment. The new assessment regime we have proposed is an attempt to reduce, if we cannot eliminate, the lack of clarity and unfairness of the current system.

7.10.2 This is not a straightforward task. As we described in Part Six above, there are two major international classifications of psychiatric disorders, ICD-10 and DSM-IV. Different clinicians favour different classifications, and other approaches such as Hare's Check list. We have also identified a group which we have called severely personality disordered offenders. This group does not precisely align with either antisocial or dissocial personality disorder, or the legal classification of psychopathic disorder, although the usefulness of defining this group was accepted in discussion by many of those who gave expert evidence. We have not been convinced so far that it is useful to divide this group into further sub-categories.

7.10.3 We believe the best way forward is to devise a consistent and standardized assessment protocol which would be operated by an approved multi-disciplinary assessment team, led by a forensically trained psychiatrist, along the lines described above. That team might have input from a number of different disciplines, including psychiatry, psychology, nursing, social work, probation and so on. The team would focus on the presence or otherwise of severe personality disorder, but might also offer views on the dangerousness or otherwise of the individual.

7.10.4 We are aware that producing such a protocol is fraught with difficulties. Drs Dolan and Coid in their review of the literature on the treatment of psychopathic and anti-social personality disorders examine each of the five diagnostic approaches available to researchers and diagnosticians and note:

> "... each has a different developmental origin and requires some degree of specific training in its use. Each one takes a different perspective of the same individual and is ultimately based on a quite different intellectual framework. It is probable that the approaches also show considerable overlap with one another, but researchers have gone little way in examining this possibility. Thus, although some diagnostic categories show a degree of reliability and internal validity, diagnostic approaches to personality disorder continue to lag behind developments in the major clinical syndromes." [page 11].

7.10.5 Dr Dolan and Professor Coid argue that no one diagnostic approach is sufficient to capture all the features of a patient's psychopathology. In an appendix to their book (page 277 *et. seq.*) they outline a possible standardised assessment of psychopathic disorder. This would involve three elements. The first element would be an assessment of personality disorder, using one or more of the main diagnostic approaches, for example, DSM-IV, ICD-10 or PCL-R. The second would be a detailed psychiatric history to cover all major mental disorders. The third element would be a detailed behavioural history, including any criminal history.

7.10.6 They offer a useful starting point. When we discussed this issue at our seminar on the management of personality disorder there was a consensus that a broad assessment protocol for severe personality disorder could be developed.

Recommendation 57 **7.10.7 We recommend that the Department of Health and the Home Office convene a working group to develop a standardised assessment protocol for severe personality disorder, involving all the appropriate representative bodies.**

7.11.0 Specialist Units

7.11.1 Given the control problems and difficulty in creating a proper patient mix in a unit of 100 or more patients, with wards housing more than 20 men, and bearing in mind the risks posed by this group towards mentally ill patients, we believe that the best way forward would be to develop a number of small units for severely personality disordered individuals within the High Security Hospital and prison system. These would be physically separate from accommodation for mentally ill patients or other prisoners. Our suggested size is units of 50 places divided up into wards or sub-units of ten beds.

7.11.2 Our suggestions for the size of units and sub-units/wards reflect our experience of visiting other services both in England and abroad. Thus we were impressed by the new Personality Disorder service at Rampton, which comprises three wards accommodating up to 42 patients. Staff there told us that they believed that was more or less the optimum size for their service, because good communication between staff was so important.

7.11.3 Similarly, services we visited overseas generally had eight to ten patients per ward or sub-unit. This appeared to provide a sense of community without offering serious control problems for staff. We visited a very impressive prison unit, the Sociotherapeutic Unit at Champ-Dollon Prison in Geneva, which houses 11 severely personality disordered men in a therapeutic community, which appeared to us to be a model of how a prison could provide a specialist service for this group.

7.11.4 We have stressed above that the NHS should be responsible for the clinical input into the prison specialist units.

Recommendation 58 **7.11.5 We recommend that the Department of Health and the Home Office develop special units for severely personality disordered offenders, housing no more than 50 men, in sub-units of eight to 12.**

7.12.0 A Third Way?

7.12.1 In propounding the above model we are aware that there are alternatives. Another response to the weaknesses of provision for severely personality disordered offenders in prisons and hospitals would be to create a new third service, what one might call a "Third Way".

7.12.2 A new service might be created, closely linked to secure hospitals and prisons, but with a separate management. Severely personality disordered individuals who are presently disruptive in hospitals and prisons could be placed in small units focused on their needs. Prison rules would be in force to maintain security, but be combined with an enhanced therapeutic input. The close links with the NHS and the Prison Service would facilitate movement of patients and prisoners as clinically appropriate.

7.12.3 Developing such a service would not necessarily mean a massive building programme; it could be developed in a number of existing locations, tested out and rolled out across the country. Legislation would be needed, but there is a review of the Mental Health Act underway.

7.12.4 We can see a number of potential advantages to such a development. One is simply that it would signal a decisive break from the past, and the chance to make a new beginning. We have seen at length the difficulties Ashworth Hospital has had in managing these individuals; for its part, the Prison Service has developed a number of special units over the years but, Grendon apart, has struggled to maintain them. What tends to happen is that the units lack autonomy and so are very vulnerable when the Prison Service or the host prison is under particular pressure. A third service would, by contrast, be autonomous. It would also be free of much of the weight of history and accumulated failures.

7.12.5 Second, the concentration of individuals with severe personality disorder would give a clarity of purpose to the new units, would foster the development of new skills such as social therapy and facilitate well-focused research.

7.12.6 Third, the Prison Service would benefit from the removal of these individuals from the general system, and the hospitals and mentally ill patients would benefit from severely personality disordered patients being placed elsewhere.

7.12.7 Fourth, costs would be lower than in the Special Hospitals (although higher than in prisons).

7.12.8 Despite these potential advantages we remain unconvinced. We perceive a number of powerful objections. First, why create a new bureaucracy? It seems likely that the Department of Health and the Home Office would be fighting over who really owned the new units.

7.12.9 Second, we suspect that the new service would be neither one thing nor the other, neither a true healthcare service nor a proper penal one.

7.12.10 Third, how would the service attract good staff? It seems all too likely that the units would be isolated from the therapeutic mainstream.

7.12.11 Fourth, despite the review of the Mental Health Act, new legislation may be years in the future. Whilst our model is dependent in part on legislative changes, much can be achieved without a great deal of primary legislation.

7.12.12 On either model concentrating the most problematic people in the system could be a recipe for disaster, as it was in the PDU at Ashworth. We believe that most, if not all of the proposed benefits of the Third Service could be achieved by developing a forensic network in the NHS with good links across to the Prison Service, where staff are themselves knitted into a network.

7.12.13 We shall leave the final cautionary word to one of the founding fathers of forensic psychiatry, the late Dr Peter Scott CBE. He was sceptical about the decision to develop Regional (Medium) Secure Units. In his Denis Carroll Lecture in 1975 he maintained that psychiatry had failed (a) the dangerous offender and (b) the unrewarding, degenerate, "not nice" offender.[4] He defined the two groups as follows: a dangerous offender is one who risks or brings about destruction which is severe, irreversible, unpredictable and untreatable. No matter how destructive a person has been in the past, he is not dangerous if he is treatable. The unrewarding patient is essentially one who does not 'pay' for his treatment, either by (i) dependence, or (ii) by getting better, or (iii) in either process by showing gratitude to his carers, cheerfully if possible. The 'not nice' patients are the ones who habitually appear to be well able to look after themselves but do not, who break institutional rules, get drunk, upset other patients, or even quietly go to the devil in their own way quite heedless of nurse or doctor.

7.12.14 Detaining, custodial institutions have two aims, one therapeutic, the other custodial. These can and should be complementary, but there is a tendency for these functions to polarize out and eventually split like a living cell into two separate institutions. Dr Scott warned that the solution to the Special Hospital problem in the 1970s was not to build new institutions (secure units) but to put the funds into improving care in prisons. The medium secure units would, he predicted, be selective, excluding the most difficult patients such as psychopaths and those requiring high security or long-term care. In due course new problems would arise and the tendency to divide would return.

7.12.15 The present story of failure appears to have confirmed Dr Scott's predictions. Both we and those proposing the "Third Way" need to heed his warning.

4 Scott PD (1975) *Has psychiatry failed in the treatment of offenders?* The Fifth Denis Carroll Lecture. Institute for the Study and Treatment of Delinquency.

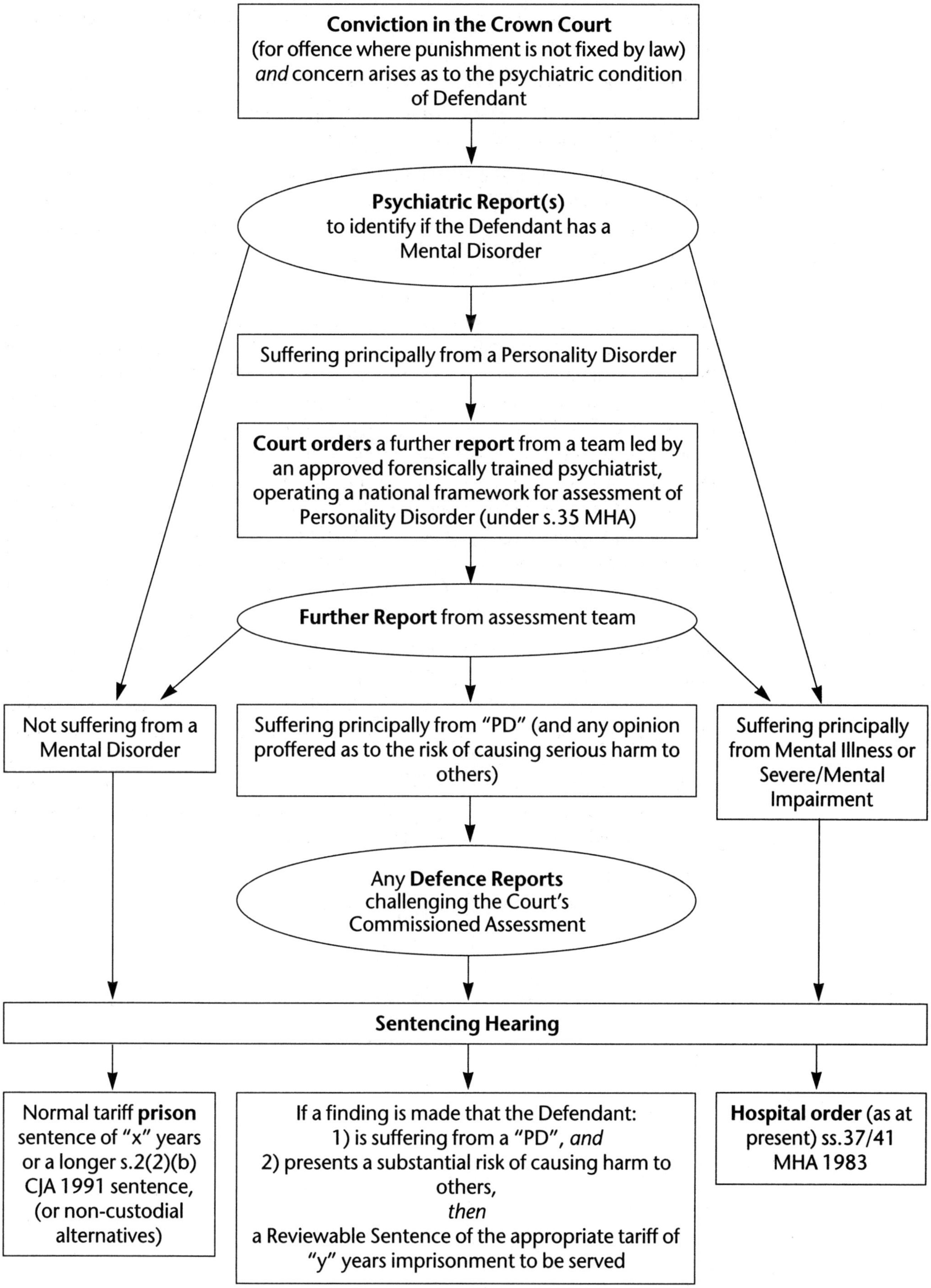
Conviction in the Crown Court
(for offence where punishment is not fixed by law)
and concern arises as to the psychiatric condition of Defendant
Psychiatric Report(s)
to identify if the Defendant has a Mental Disorder
Suffering principally from a Personality Disorder
Court orders a further report from a team led by an approved forensically trained psychiatrist, operating a national framework for assessment of Personality Disorder (under s.35 MHA)
Further Report from assessment team
Not suffering from a Mental Disorder
Suffering principally from "PD" (and any opinion proffered as to the risk of causing serious harm to others)
Suffering principally from Mental Illness or Severe/Mental Impairment
Any Defence Reports challenging the Court's Commissioned Assessment
Sentencing Hearing
Normal tariff prison sentence of "x" years or a longer s.2(2)(b) CJA 1991 sentence, (or non-custodial alternatives)
If a finding is made that the Defendant:
1) is suffering from a "PD", and
2) presents a substantial risk of causing harm to others,
then
a Reviewable Sentence of the appropriate tariff of "y" years imprisonment to be served
Hospital order (as at present) ss.37/41 MHA 1983

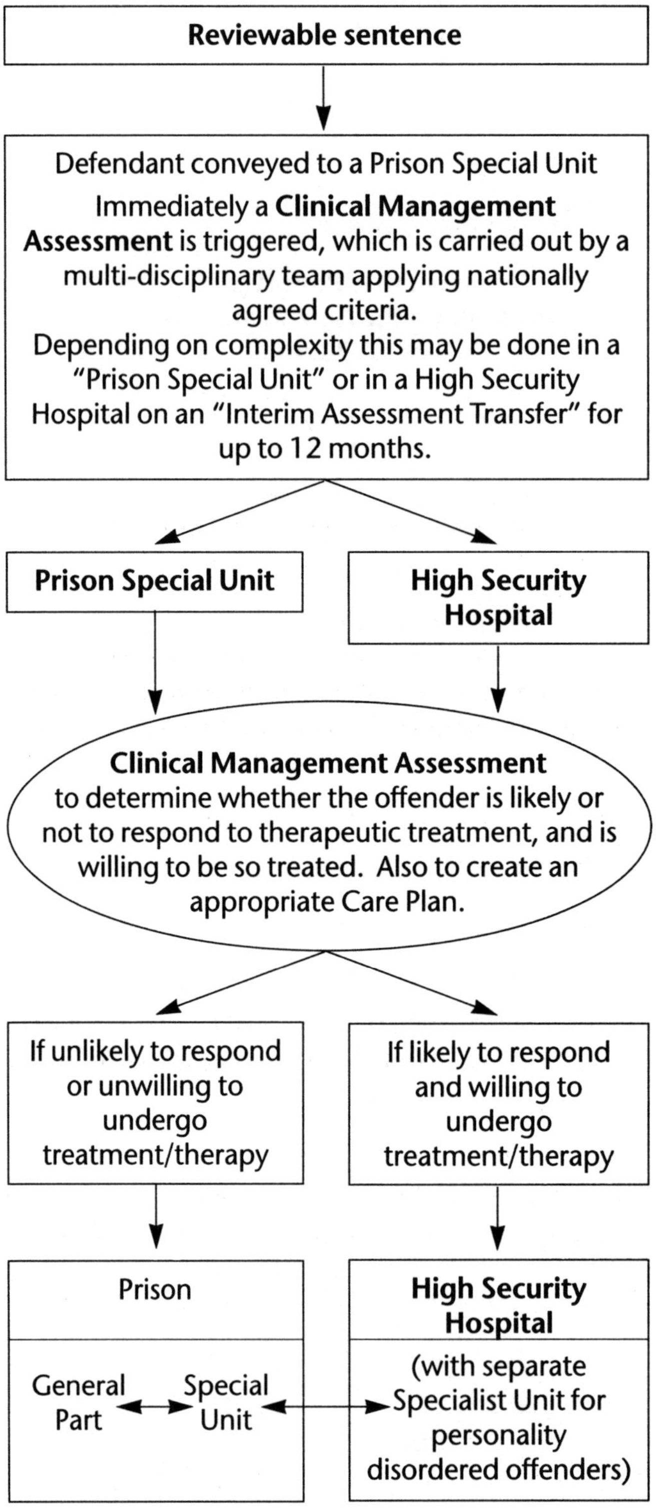
Reviewable sentence
Defendant conveyed to a Prison Special Unit
Immediately a Clinical Management Assessment is triggered, which is carried out by a multi-disciplinary team applying nationally agreed criteria.
Depending on complexity this may be done in a "Prison Special Unit" or in a High Security Hospital on an "Interim Assessment Transfer" for up to 12 months.
Prison Special Unit
High Security Hospital
Clinical Management Assessment
to determine whether the offender is likely or not to respond to therapeutic treatment, and is willing to be so treated. Also to create an appropriate Care Plan.
If unlikely to respond or unwilling to undergo treatment/therapy
If likely to respond and willing to undergo treatment/therapy
Prison
General Part
Special Unit
High Security Hospital
(with separate Specialist Unit for personality disordered offenders)

PART 8 Recommendations

Ashworth Hospital

Recommendation 14

2.28.5 We recommend that the Authority Hospital Senior Management Team is relocated within the secure perimeter of Ashworth North.

Recommendation 15

2.29.7 We recommend that the composition and working of the Patients' Council be reviewed to ensure that mentally ill patients are properly represented and that the Council's activities are not dominated by personality disordered patients.

Recommendation 49

7.3.23 We recommend that Ashworth Hospital should close in its entirety at the earliest opportunity.

The Personality Disorder Unit

Recommendation 16

2.30.17 We recommend that minutes of PCT meetings within the PDU are routinely sent to and read by the Clinical Director. Relevant remarks should be entered into clinical records where they affect individual patients

Recommendation 20

2.36.28 We recommend that the PDU, if it is to survive in any form, must be managed separately as a small unit (of around 50 patients maximum), with no more than 8 to 12 patients per ward.

Recommendation 23

3.17.37 We recommend that no shop should ever be allowed on any PDU ward unless it is fully controlled by staff and regularly audited by the Finance Department

Future Services

Recommendation 45

6.7.23 The numbers [of severely personality disordered offenders], as Professor Gunn described them, are a rough estimate. We recommend:

> (i) that 300 places in hospital and 100 places in prison be provided for this severely personality disordered group as soon as possible;
>
> (ii) that before any longer-term investment is made the Government sets up an expert group with resources to commission research so as to establish a sound base for future service development.

Recommendation 46

7.3.5 We recommend that all purchasing for forensic services is managed on a region-wide basis.

Recommendation 47

7.3.16 We recommend:

(i) the establishment of regional networks of forensic services embracing all levels of security from high security to the community;

(ii) the transfer of high security facilities to regional networks;

(iii) the urgent provision of more medium secure and long-term medium secure accommodation within the regional networks;

(iv) the development of increased functional integration between prison services for persons with severe personality disorder and the regional forensic services;

(v) the continuing care of those with severe personality disorder should always be provided by a multi-disciplinary team with a detailed knowledge of the individual.

Recommendation 56

7.9.6 We recommend that all Clinical Management Assessments are carried out in separate assessment facilities.

Recommendation 57

7.10.7 We recommend that the Department of Health and the Home Office convene a working group to develop a standardised assessment protocol for severe personality disorder, involving all the appropriate representative bodies.

Recommendation 58

7.11.5 We recommend that the Department of Health and the Home Office develop special units for severely personality disordered offenders, housing no more than 50 men, in sub-units of 8 to 12.

Prison Service

Recommendation 48

7.3.19 We recommend that the NHS takes over responsibility for healthcare within prisons.

Monitoring and Inspection

Recommendation 21

2.39.12 We recommend that the brief of the Commission for Health Improvement should include the High Security Hospitals and that the Hospitals should be treated as a high priority for attention.

Accountability in the NHS

Recommendation 44

5.1.23 We recommend that Ministers reflect on our comments and consider whether the chains of accountability in the NHS, at all levels, should be reviewed and clarified.

Mental Health Legislation

Recommendation 50

7.5.8 We recommend the creation of:

(i) a new sentence called a "Reviewable Sentence";

(ii) a "Reviewable Sentence Board".

Recommendation 51

7.6.8 We recommend:

(i) removing "psychopathic disorder" from the Mental Health Act 1983;

(ii) replacing it with "personality disorder", save in the specific instances set out below; and

(iii) not defining "personality disorder" in the Act.

(See Appendix 9 for all suggested amendments to the 1983 Act.)

Recommendation 52

7.6.11 We recommend that those currently undertaking the review of the Mental Health Act should be asked to consider the definitions of severe mental impairment and mental impairment in the light of our recommendations.

Recommendation 53

7.6.20 We recommend:

(i) abolishing hospital orders (with or without restriction), and of the present form of transfer orders, for individuals suffering from personality disorder by not replacing "psychopathic disorder" with "personality disorder" in sections 37(2)(a)(i) and 47(1)(a) and (b) of the 1983 Act;

(ii) that a new transfer direction be enacted to facilitate such transfers on those bases. This would facilitate transfer of personality disordered offenders when appropriate, and also their transfer back under section 50 of the Act if appropriate.

Recommendation 54

7.7.2 We recommend that section 38 (1)(a) be amended by removing "psychopathic disorder", and that a provision for an interim transfer direction for assessment for up to 12 months be enacted to provide such transfers for personality disordered offenders from prison.

Recommendation 55

7.7.5 We recommend:

(i) that "personality disorder" should replace "psychopathic disorder" in Part II of the Mental Health Act 1983 and the deletion of "psychopathic disorder" altogether from section 3(2)(b);

(ii) for minor offenders we recommend further development of the Court Diversion scheme to facilitate admission and treatment under Part II of the Act.

Policies

Recommendation 12

2.26.4 We recommend that at all times an up to date book containing all relevant security policies and rules should be easily and readily available to all ward staff, and its location and contents should be known by all ward staff.

Recommendation 13

2.26.19 We recommend the following principles be adopted:

(i) there must be clear hospital-wide policies which cannot be changed except at the highest management level;

(ii) within the framework of hospital policies there will be a number of clearly defined areas where clinical units/directorates and PCTs may exercise discretion to interpret policies to reflect the distinctive needs of a particular patient group;

(iii) where use of such discretion is exercised the fact should be recorded;

(iv) any changes to hospital policies should be made known to all staff by an agreed procedure such as regular team briefing. The changes should immediately be added the Policy File, again before implementation;

(v) policies should be clear and easily available to all staff, in a single file. Staff should be required to know the contents of policies. They should attest they have read them and re-attest regarding any changes made to them;

(vi) all staff must have read and be aware of policies before they start working on the ward;

(vii) the number of policies should be kept to a minimum so that staff are not overwhelmed by paper.

Recommendation 24

3.19.29 We recommend that the Hospital develops a method for differentiating mandatory policies from guidance.

Child Protection

Recommendation 25

3.23.46 We recommend that no child under the age of 16 should be allowed to visit any patient on a ward.

Recommendation 26

3.23.47 We recommend that a child under the age of 16 should only be permitted to visit a patient who is a genuine member of his or her family, and then only if fully supervised in a place specifically prepared, designed and equipped for visiting purposes. The interests of the child must override those of any other person.

Recommendation 27

3.25.24 We recommend that contact with the NSPCC be revived, and that a training programme on child protection issues be developed in conjunction with the NSPCC.

Social Work Department

Recommendation 28

3.29.10 We recommend that the precise duties and responsibilities of social workers are clarified.

Recommendation 29

3.29.11 We recommend that contact with the relevant local authority social services department is always made before an LOA trip whenever there is any likelihood of a patient coming into contact with children.

Recommendation 30

3.31.12 We recommend an urgent review by the SSI of the service provided by Social Workers at Ashworth Hospital, using the 1994 SSI Report as a benchmark.

Physical Security

Recommendation 7

2.21.16 We recommend that an independent review of all aspects of physical security at Ashworth Hospital take place and be repeated at regular intervals.

Searching

Recommendation 2

2.12.13 We recommend that paragraph 25 of the Code of Practice be rewritten to reflect the special circumstances of any high security setting.

Recommendation 3

2.12.32 We recommend that Ashworth Hospital introduces searches of visitors and that paragraph 26 of the Code of Practice be amended to make it crystal clear that in a high security setting visitors who refuse to be searched will not be admitted.

Recommendation 9

2.23.3 We recommend that searching of staff be implemented.

Recommendation 10

2.23.14 We recommend that, as a matter of urgency, the level of patients' possessions in bedrooms be reduced to, and thereafter maintained at, a level which permits full and thorough room searches to be carried out in a reasonable time.

Recommendation 31

3.32.30 We recommend:

(i) that on the PDU full room searches should be carried out on a regular basis by dedicated and trained teams;

(ii) the search results should be cross-checked against patients' up to date property lists.

Recommendation 32

3.33.9 We recommend:

(i) searches and checks of documentation on LOA trips should be carried out by the gate security staff, and complete records be kept of such searches;

(ii) escorting staff should also be searched on leaving and returning from LOA trips.

Patients' Mail

Recommendation 5

2.12.39 We recommend that policies which allow staff effectively to control and monitor patients' mail are agreed and consistently implemented.

Security Intelligence Unit

Recommendation 19

2.33.11 The Risk Management Team, established in March 1995, would seem the appropriate body to develop its role, and become the intelligence unit of the Hospital drawing on the experience and expertise of the police. We so recommend.

Community Card/Parole

Recommendation 6

2.21.9 We recommend:

(i) the whole policy of issuing community cards should be reviewed;

(ii) the total number issued should never be such as to jeopardise fundamental security requirements;

(iii) unless severe personality disordered individuals are physically separated from the mentally ill, those severe personality disordered individuals who hold community cards should not be allowed unescorted access to other parts of the Hospital.

Recommendation 4

2.12.37 We recommend that it is essential to control and monitor the use of ward-based telephones carefully in order to prevent abuse, control fraud and prevent the introduction into the Hospital of prohibited substances and articles.

Recommendation 8

2.22.7 We recommend that patients should not be allowed to use the ward telephone between the hours of midnight and 7am save in the most exceptional circumstances.

Video Cassette Recorders

Recommendation 11

2.23.18 We recommend that no patient should be allowed more than one video cassette recording machine in his bedroom. If any copying or editing of videotapes is required this should be done under supervision within the Education department.

Internal Inquiries

Recommendation 17

2.33.5 We recommend that internal inquiries be conducted by staff who are appropriately trained. Guidance for members of inquiry teams should emphasize that these inquiries are fact-finding.

Recommendation 18

2.33.9 We recommend:

(i) Executive Directors and the Director in charge of Security should routinely receive and read serious incident reports;

(ii) the relevant clinical team should also receive and read such reports.

The Professions

Recommendation 22

3.15.6 We recommend that Ashworth Hospital should review the control and distribution of prescribed drugs so as to remove the risk of nurses becoming involved in their illegal distribution.

Recommendation 37

4.5.10 We recommend that the position of RMO should be an accredited post which is reviewed at no more than five-yearly intervals.

Recommendation 38

4.6.6 We recommend that the new policies relating to clinical governance spell out as clearly as possible the powers and authority of a Medical Director in such a way as to strengthen the role in an acceptable manner.

Recommendation 39

4.7.16 We recommend the development of training for nurses in the treatment and management of personality disorder with appropriate certification.

Recommendation 40

4.7.25 We recommend that a thorough review takes place of night staffing at Ashworth Hospital.

Recommendation 41

4.7.35 We recommend that as far as possible bank staff be allocated to particular areas of the Hospital, and that induction for bank staff opting to work within the PDU includes some additional instruction on working with personality disordered patients.

Recommendation 42

4.9.6 We recommend that input of clinical psychology to the PDU should be sharply increased.

Recommendation 43

4.11.4 We recommend the HSPSCB funds work in the area of social therapy.

Computers and IT Security

Recommendation 33

3.39.18 We recommend that patients should only be allowed adapted computers connected to a patients' server in their rooms.

Recommendation 34

3.39.20 We recommend:

(a) no modems whether external or internal should be permitted in ward areas;

(b) patients' access to telephones should be limited to:

(i) telephone numbers on the list of the patient's list of approved numbers;

(ii) all telephone calls by patients should be carefully monitored, except privileged calls, such as those to legal advisers, in which cases the number should be dialled by a member of staff who, having done so, should retire out of ear-shot, but maintain observation to ensure no other number is dialled;

(iii) telephone points in ward visitors' rooms should be removed;

(iv) permitting external telephone engineers to control the Hospital's telephone exchange should be reconsidered.

Recommendation 35

3.39.22 We recommend that patients are not allowed to have in the Hospital:

mobile telephones; personal organizers; palm top computers; hand-helds; laptop computers; and pagers.

Recommendation 36

3.39.28 We recommend that before patients are allowed to have personal computer printers, it is demonstrated that the parallel port to which such a printer must be connected could not also be used for unacceptable devices.

Ethnic Minorities

Recommendation 1

1.24.10 We recommend that the service needs of individuals from minority ethnic groups who suffer from severe personality disorder should be the subject of further study.

APPENDIX 1 The establishment of the Inquiry

House of Commons – 10 February 1997

Ashworth Hospital

3.30 pm

The Secretary of State for Health (Mr Stephen Dorrell): With permission, I should like to make a statement about action being taken to address the allegations involving the Personality Disorder Unit at Ashworth Hospital in Merseyside. The unit comprises six wards, with 115 patients, within the total population of Ashworth Hospital of 473 patients.

Hon members will be aware that last Friday I instituted urgent action to address the very serious situation that had been brought to my attention in the preceding few days. In October last year, Steven Daggett, a patient at Ashworth Hospital, made a number of allegations, including the misuse of drugs and alcohol, financial irregularities, the availability of pornographic material, and possible paedophile activity involving a child visitor within the Personality Disorder Unit.

I am advised that the Hospital began investigations at that time and that a subsequent ward search on 17 January found a large amount of pornographic material. Despite the availability of this evidence and of Mr Daggett's allegations, the Hospital continued to maintain that press reports of unacceptable and possibly unlawful activity within the Personality Disorder Unit were unfounded.

On 28 January, the Home Office received a letter from the Hon Member for Halifax (Mrs Mahon) enclosing a 60-page dossier setting out the detail of Mr Daggett's allegations. The dossier was passed by the Home Office to my Department.

On 31 January, police visited the home of a former Ashworth patient who had continued to be a frequent visitor to the Hospital. Following that action, a child has been taken into the care of the local authority under an emergency protection order.

In light of the allegations made by Mr Daggett and of other evidence that has recently become available, I made three announcements on Friday of last week. First, the Hospital has suspended three members of staff, including the Chief Executive. An acting Chief Executive was appointed with immediate effect. He is Mr Erville Millar, Chief Executive of Lambeth Health Care NHS Trust, who has a strong background in mental health services. I can further inform the House this afternoon that the Hospital has today suspended a member of its medical staff.

Secondly, I established on Friday a statutory inquiry under section 84 of the National Health Service Act 1977 to review the clinical policies and the management of the Personality Disorder Unit at Ashworth Hospital. The inquiry will be led by His Honour Judge Peter Fallon QC a recently retired senior circuit judge. A section 84 inquiry has the power to summon witnesses and to take evidence on oath. The inquiry will determine how and on what terms it takes evidence. It will also be for the inquiry to ensure that its work does not compromise continuing police investigations or possible criminal proceedings, but I would expect it to report within a year. That report will be published.

The terms of reference for the inquiry will be published as soon as possible. They will make it clear that, as it is activities within the Hospital's Personality Disorder Unit that have caused recent concern, the inquiry should focus on the policies, management and clinical care provided by that unit. The inquiry will, however, also wish to follow up any wider questions that are necessary to the proper consideration of the issues.

The third announcement I made on Friday was on the alleged involvement of a child. The Chief Inspector of Social Services, Sir Herbert Laming, has asked the local authority concerned for a full report on the handling of the case by its social services department. I will decide, in the light of that report, whether further action needs to be taken.

The allegations that have been made about Ashworth Hospital are extremely serious, and the public are entitled to reassurance on two counts. First, Ashworth Hospital must be properly managed and must provide a high level of security for the benefit both of patients and of the public at large. Secondly, the Hospital must also ensure that its patients receive a high standard of clinical care. The action that I announced on Friday is directed at the achievement of both those objectives.

APPENDIX 2 The Inquiry Process

The Inquiry Process

1. Every Public Inquiry is likely to raise a number of challenges for its Chairman (together with his/her Legal Team and Secretariat) in formulating the most appropriate procedures to adopt.

2. Some of the factors which will affect the way an Inquiry proceeds include the fields within which it is commissioned to undertake its investigations; the breadth of its terms of reference (for example, whether it is simply required to make findings of fact as to what went wrong in a given situation, or whether broader questions of public policy are to be considered); and the degree of likelihood that serious and damaging criticisms of individuals may be made.

3. Whilst the procedures adopted for one Inquiry may not be appropriate in every case, those responsible for setting up and running one such as this may well derive some assistance from our experiences.

4. We have therefore invited Counsel appointed to this Inquiry to set out some of the elements of the process which were found to be important, or helpful, or challenging.

Setting up the Inquiry

Chairman and Panel

5. The success of an Inquiry of this nature, the making of definitive recommendations which will stand the test of time, and the persuasiveness of its conclusions will crucially depend upon the quality of those appointed.

6. A feature of Inquiries is the absence of a body of formal precedent laying down strict procedural rules. Accordingly, if the margins of the Inquiry are not made sufficiently clear at the outset, and the authority of the Chairman is not stamped upon the process at a very early stage, there is ample opportunity for it to become bogged-down with the submission of a mass of material of marginal relevance, and for parties and witnesses to seek to divert the attention of the Panel onto their own preferred agendas. Consequently it is essential that a Chairman has the ability to keep a firm hand on the proceedings and to enforce the rules adopted to govern its conduct.

7. It is also essential that the Chairman is involved from the outset in identifying the sources of information to be tapped and the lines to be pursued. He will then be best able to have a clear oversight of the early stages of the process, and to give a clear lead to his Secretariat and Legal Team in order properly to prepare for the task of addressing the Terms of Reference.

8. A successful inquiry depends very largely upon good teamwork between members of the Panel, and between the Panel, its legal team and the secretariat. At times it can be a stressful experience spending long periods together in the context of a job which carries with it heavy obligations - marshalling vast volumes of evidence; the assessment of witnesses who are variously vulnerable, nervous or highly expert; understanding and considering how to improve complex human management systems; and challenging those who simply wish to maintain the status quo rather than look for a better way.

Secretariat

9. The preparation for and smooth running of an Inquiry depends upon a Secretariat who have excellent organizational and administrative abilities, together with a confident grasp of all the issues. Intelligent advice to the Panel and a knowledgable approach to the subject in hand is invaluable, as is a high level of interpersonal skills.

The Legal Team

10. It is important for Counsel and Solicitor to be involved at an early stage.

11. A huge amount of preparatory work will be necessary. Counsel must therefore be fully committed to the process. A close liaison with the Chairman and Secretariat is important from the very beginning since independent advice on the shape and direction of the Inquiry may be helpful, and it is at this stage that the Inquiry procedure must be drawn up, "Salmon letters" and representation considered, and the scheduling of the hearings and witnesses arranged.

12. The Solicitor must also have the ability to grasp the issues as quickly as possible; he must be skilled and efficient in taking statements from potential witnesses and in organizing and marshalling material so that it is collated and presented clearly for use later on. This will avoid embarrassment later.

Preparing the way for the Oral Hearings

Terms of Reference

13. These will have been drafted and will form the basis of the Panel's remit. However, there is a preliminary question that may arise as to how widely or narrowly they should be interpreted. This is important to decide, because it will determine how extensive the trawl for evidence should be and identify the range of witnesses who should be called.

14. In the case of this Inquiry the Terms of Reference covered not only an investigation of the problems that had arisen at Ashworth on the Personality Disorder Unit but also questions of the appropriate clinical care and security provision for this group of patients. The Panel recognised that this raised important and far-reaching questions that which had not been adequately addressed in the past, still less satisfactorily resolved, and that there was a need for an authoritative conclusion about the appropriate provision of services for the future. They were exceptionally well-qualified to examine this, and therefore the Terms of Reference were interpreted widely in order to confront the problems comprehensively.

Powers

15. The authority upon which the Inquiry is established is an important factor to bear in mind. This Inquiry was a statutory Inquiry giving it considerable powers.

16. Thus under Section 84 of the National Health Service Act 1977 there was a power to require persons to attend to give evidence and produce documents, and a power of imprisonment for refusal to do so.

17. On one occasion we found that it was necessary for us to draft a *Subpoena Duces Tecum* with a view to issuing it in the Crown Office, but the notification of this to the witness in question proved a sufficient incentive to persuade that witness to produce documents which had until then been withheld on the basis that they had been private and confidential.

18. The other areas in which the extent of our powers came into question involved the handling of press reporting, and the disclosure of documents, names of witnesses, and of transcripts of witnesses' testimony. Each is dealt with below.

Gathering the Material

19. The principal source of material here was Ashworth Hospital itself. It was necessary to set up a team there to gather the vast bulk of documentary material, and the Hospital obliged in that task.

20. Some difficulties arose because it appeared that not everyone in the Hospital was prepared to comply with the requests for disclosure of all documentation concerning the PDU. It is important that all potentially relevant material is gathered. The price to be paid for this, however, is that the decision on the actual relevance must be for the Panel, albeit that much of this can be delegated to the Legal Team.

21. A mammoth task ensues in numbering, cataloguing, indexing, copying, distributing, and filing the material. In our case the images were also scanned and put on CD-ROM, with character recognition undertaken as well for future wordprocessing.

Parties and Representation

22. It is necessary to try to identify as soon as possible who has an interest in appearing as a party at the Inquiry, with the opportunity where appropriate to cross-examine witnesses. Some will be obvious. Others only emerge on consideration of the material as it emerges.

23. Ashworth Hospital itself, in addition to being a party, arranged for its Counsel to represent the interests of various employees. It also funded separate representation for the former Chief Executive, Mrs Janice Miles.

24. The Unions had an important part to play. The Royal College of Nursing and UNISON were represented. The Prison Officers Association chose on this occasion not to be represented but did appear through their officers. The interests of two individual nurses were represented by Counsel on behalf of the RCN.

25. The representation of two Consultants was arranged by their medical defence organisation.

26. We also took the view that it was important for the patients as a group to be represented by one firm of Solicitors and Counsel. This was not in response to any application but as Counsel to the Inquiry we were concerned that their interests would not otherwise be adequately protected.

27. It may be necessary for a party to be represented for part only of the Inquiry hearings. In a number of instances representation was granted on a limited basis.

28. In a few cases a scheduled witness who was not a party asked for a legal representative to be allowed to assist and support them. In these instances their representative was not given a right of audience but was permitted to advise the witness as necessary. Their representative also had access to Counsel to the Inquiry in case there was a need to raise any important matters which had been omitted.

Funding

29. Where there was no organisation or body providing funding for legal representation it was proper for legal costs to be met from the public purse. These applications were considered on paper by the Chairman on a case by case basis on their merits.

30. Some applications were granted before the first preliminary hearing. Others were only made at that stage.

Analysing the Material

31. The problem with thousands upon thousands of pages of material is that you can become blinded by the storm. The only way this can be managed is by a process of methodical reading and analysis, which takes a considerable amount of time on the part of those involved in the preparation of documents to be used and disclosed to parties.

The Criminal Investigations

32. The Merseyside Police were carrying out an investigation into various aspects of what had allegedly taken place on Lawrence Ward. In particular they were concerned with possible child abuse. This meant that various witnesses and potential witnesses were concerned as to whether they might be subject to prosecution. There was accordingly some reluctance to give statements to us.

33. It also meant that if those witnesses were called before any decision had been made about prosecution we might be faced with witnesses refusing to answer questions on the ground that they might incriminate themselves.

34. This was one of the reasons which led to a decision to deal with the second, general part of our "Terms of Reference" first.

35. Unfortunately the submission of the Police File to the Crown Prosecution Service took longer than expected and then there was a substantial delay in the CPS making a decision about whether there should be any prosecutions. However, when we could wait no longer and a decision by the Crown Prosecution Service was still awaited the Police co-operated with us by showing us the witness statements they had taken. This was at a time when our first hearing was well under way.

36. Out of an abundance of caution those Police Statements were initially read only by Counsel to the Inquiry who advised upon the additional witnesses who should be approached to give evidence. When those witnesses raised no legal objections to appearing and answering questions their Police Statements were disclosed.

Procedures

37. Our main proposed procedure was published prior to the first preliminary hearing. A further set of procedures was produced before the hearings commenced. Both are attached below.

38. We were concerned to achieve expedition and fairness. We bore in mind however that the inquisitorial process is quite different from the adversarial.

39. Statements would in the main stand as a witness' evidence. There could be clarification or amplification.

40. Cross-examination by a party would only be allowed if it was demonstrable that the party was adversely effected by the evidence.

41. We took the view that all evidence was to be given on oath or affirmation rather than having to try to distinguish between various categories of witness. No-one expressed any objection to this.

42. We included a provision enabling the Committee to alter its procedures in the light of experience should that prove necessary. This (a) enables sensible modification to be made and (b) avoids anyone trying to seek Judicial Review on the basis that the Committee is not following its own procedures.

"Salmon" Letters

43. These are, and will continue to be, a source of difficulty. Sir Louis Blom-Cooper pointed out in his report into Ashworth Hospital the many problems that can arise with them. They should only be issued where there is a strong case for potential criticism.

44. They may cause heightened anxiety in recipients which may endure for a long time until the report is published.

45. Again, as Sir Louis concluded a Committee may feel it right having considered all the evidence to criticize someone who has not received a Salmon letter, and the Committee should not refrain from doing so.

46. We tried to restrict the sending of such letters to the central figures and tried so to frame them as to make it clear there had been no prejudging of the issues. Thus they consisted of a series of questions on the subjects which particularly affected that witness. An example appears at the end of this Appendix.

47. It is also important to emphasise that these letters should not be regarded too technically or precisely. They are not pleadings. The letters were not disclosed to other parties since they had no significance in themselves as Inquiry documents.

Distribution of Documentary Material and Statements to Parties

48. Many of the documents contained sensitive material. While it was in the main desirable for parties to have access to this material, there were sound reasons for restricting its further publication. We required written undertakings from parties to use the material and statements solely for the purposes of the Inquiry; not to disclose these to anyone else and to return them at the conclusion of the Inquiry. In certain cases a request was made to disclose particular documents to a Third Party who was preparing a potential witness statement for submission to the Inquiry on behalf of one of the parties. In such cases the Third Party was asked first to sign the Undertaking themselves. A copy of the Undertaking appears at the end of this Appendix.

49. A further complication arose in relation to providing access to the confidential clinical notes of certain patients to professionals whose clinical judgements were in question. The Hospital was properly anxious to ensure that any sight of those clinical notes was correctly authorized. (Those notes had been provided for Professor Bluglass (the psychiatrist on the Panel) to view.) The matter was resolved by the Chairman making an Order that the Hospital give access to those notes to the clinicians in question and their legal representatives for the sole purpose of use in the Inquiry in order to deal with clinical decisions which they had made concerning those patients.

50. We sought to obtain, or invited submission of, statements from all potentially relevant witnesses. These were kept confidential until decisions had been taken on which should be called.

51. Similarly a party would not be provided with other parties statements until he or she had submitted a statement. This was because there were obvious potential conflicts between certain parties.

LiveNote

52. The LiveNote computer-aided transcription system was of immense value. Skilled stenographers produced a very accurate real-time transcript which saved a huge amount of time and energy. The corrected transcript was available each evening in paper and "ASCII" format on disc.

53. This was a necessity for a Inquiry such as this. It enabled searchable annotations to be made instantaneously, and text could be highlighted in relation to identified categories of issues which would have to be revisited later with other witnesses. Excerpts, and reports of all the evidence on highlighted issues, could be printed out later at will and incorporated into draft documents.

54. One matter of interest which arose was the public availability of the transcript. Leaving aside questions of copyright which we did not enter into, there was concern that some parts of the evidence would be seen by patients at the hospital involving contested testimony about the professional standards of individuals who were still working with them. In one instance it was felt essential that individual clinicians' names should be replaced by code letters, but otherwise the transcripts reflected the real identities.

Document Scanning

55. Disclosed documents and statements were scanned into CD-ROM format. This was accessed through the "Concordance" and "Opticon" Programs.

56. Relatively speedy display of these images on large computer screens for witnesses and the Panel during the hearings was enormously helpful since it saved searching for and manhandling the hard copy by each of the Panel members and witnesses from amongst the huge numbers of files of documents.

The Hearings

Preliminary hearings

57 We held two preliminary hearings on 7 August and 10 October 1997. These were essential to deal with the host of preliminary matters including procedures, timetabling and any unresolved matters of representation. They also concentrated the minds of parties on the task ahead.

Venue of Hearings

58. It is important to have a good spacious room with temperature control and satisfactory acoustics; numerous power points for computers; decent conference and storage rooms; facilities for the media; proper refreshment facilities; and good security. Ideally these hearings should be held in a dedicated room to reduce the necessity to move documents and equipment frequently.

Sitting Arrangements

59. We decided to sit for four days a week rather than five. This proved to be an excellent decision. It enabled participants to manage other professional commitments which would otherwise have been impossible during a long hearing. A good deal of valuable preparatory work was also done on the "spare day".

60. We also sat in three sessions of up to seven weeks each. Some panel members would not have been able to serve but for these breaks due to their other commitments. It was also found to have the advantage that each session could be approached with renewed energy and enthusiasm.

Keeping to the timetable

61. It is very important to prevent the hearings gathering a momentum of their own and thereby upsetting the predetermined timetable. This is always a potential problem in the courts and can be prevented by firm control of proceedings. It therefore helps if the Chairman has judicial experience.

62. One modification we did make proved to be of great benefit. In order to ensure we kept reasonably to our timetable we introduced a system of allocation of time for parties to cross-examine.

63. Each representative put in a "bid time" for each witness. These were considered by Junior Counsel to the Inquiry who gave a provisional allotted time, subject to the Chairman's discretion. The Chairman also occasionally used his discretion to increase time allocations, according to the circumstances.

64. Although initially this system was not greeted with a warm embrace, after a while everyone appreciated its value and it undoubtedly concentrated the mind and improved cross-examination techniques.

Press Reporting Restrictions

65. An Order was made by the Chairman prohibiting publication of any material leading to the identification of Child A – the child who visited Lawrence Ward. Some may argue there was no power under section 39 of the Children and Young Persons Act 1933 to do so as the Inquiry was not "a Court". Nonetheless the press respected this and it is arguable there was an inherent common law power to make such order in any event. The child's identity was obviously protected in relation to the allied care proceedings that had been determined against her father. It may also be arguable that under the amended Schedule of offences covered by the Sexual Offences (Amendment) Act 1992 the Press were in any event prevented from such reporting, whether or not an Order was made.

66. A further Order was made later on in the Inquiry by the Chairman when it transpired that patient witnesses who were still at Ashworth and whose testimony we were anxious to hear stated that they would decline to participate voluntarily in the proceedings if their names were released and published in the Press. The reason they gave was that their index offences were notorious and they had been unfairly pilloried in the past by certain sections of the Press on the basis of inaccurate leaked "stories" which had caused their families and themselves considerable suffering. They had no faith in sections of the Press fairly reporting complaints that they might have of the system or their treatment in the light of their index offences. In order to secure their evidence, an Order restricting the publication of their true identities was therefore made by the Chairman under what was considered to be an inferred and inherent common law jurisdiction to regulate the procedure of the Inquiry. This fell into a similar category to the anonymity provided to the victims of blackmail who give evidence in criminal trials. Some of the Press informally but vigorously queried this Order, but no formal challenge was mounted, and it was respected.

Final Submissions

67. We firmly concluded that it is wholly inappropriate for a public Judicial Inquiry, where the parties are properly represented by Counsel, and where "Salmon" type letters are served in good time, to distribute sections of its Draft Report and Conclusions to the persons affected by them for their comments and observations. A number of other recent Inquiries where this has been done have come to our notice in which Chairmen have felt constrained to re-open or re-convene their Inquiries in order to revisit their conclusions and hear complaints from parties about them. This has in some cases led to enormous delay in producing the final report. The purpose of a public Judicial Inquiry is to hear evidence, to test it critically, and to reach conclusions upon it.

68. The procedure which we considered most appropriate was to provide for succinct final submissions, those to be in writing and supplemented orally. We limited the number of words in the written submissions (which varied from party to party) in order to keep these to the principal points. A copy of our notice appears at the end of this Appendix. This was not welcomed by several parties, but it is a practice adopted increasingly often in the case of appeals in the court system. In fact it proved itself to be an admirable tool to obtain the parties' main points, and concentrated minds well.

Seminars

69. Seminars have become a fashionable adjunct to judicial inquiries. We held three in all. We found them valuable in that they allowed the Panel to test their preliminary thinking. Seminars also have the advantage of allowing the Panel to hear the views of a much larger group of people than could possibly be called to give evidence.

R. JOHN ROYCE Q.C.

PETER BLAIR

PRESS NOTICE

from the

COMMITTEE OF INQUIRY INTO THE PERSONALITY DISORDER UNIT, ASHWORTH SPECIAL HOSPITAL

CHAIRMAN:	His Honour Peter Fallon QC	SECRETARY:	Tim Baxter, Room 649,
MEMBERS:	Professor Robert Bluglass CBE		Wellington House,
	Professor Brian Edwards CBE		133-155 Waterloo Road,
	Mr Granville Daniels		London SE1 8UG

No. 2 Tuesday 28 July
1997

COMMITTEE OF INQUIRY ANNOUNCES ITS INTENDED PROCEDURE

The Committee of Inquiry would like to make a number of preliminary remarks about the legal aspects of the forthcoming Inquiry hearings.

First, this is an Inquiry and not an adversarial trial. It is for the Committee of Inquiry to determine how it will proceed. Any person who considers that he or she has relevant information should write to the Secretariat at the above address. It will be for the Committee to decide whom to ask to give evidence.

Any party may apply to the Committee to call a witness. Any application should be in writing to the Secretariat giving the name and address of the potential witness, together with a statement setting out the evidence.

The Committee of Inquiry hopes that everyone will regard it as important to assist their work. The Committee will ensure that witnesses are given proper consideration and **will only allow such examination as in its view is of help in ascertaining the truth of the matters under investigation**. Questions simply directed to the issue of credibility will not normally be permitted.

The Committee will grant patients within the Personality Disorder Unit representation at public expense. However, the Committee intends to limit this representation to a single firm, save where there is pressing reason to grant a particular patient individual representation.

Procedure at the Hearings

Statements of proposed witnesses will be supplied to legal representatives in advance. The Committee may decide that such statements shall stand as the witnesses' evidence, with Counsel to the Inquiry merely asking questions to amplify or clarify certain areas. In relation to some witnesses, however, it may be desirable for their evidence to be given in response to questions by Counsel to the Inquiry.

Those parties granted legal representation may then be given an opportunity to examine the witnesses further. This will be subject to constraints already outlined and must be confined to matters affecting those whom they legally represent.

Counsel to the Inquiry may re-examine witnesses. This may not be limited to matters arising out of further examination, but the Committee may give leave to other parties to ask further questions on fresh matters raised if it considers it necessary.

Where a witness is legally represented his or her Counsel will examine first. The Committee may decide that a witness' statement shall stand as his or her evidence. Other legal representatives may then examine the witness provided that they restrict their questions to matters affecting those whom they legally represent.

Questioning of witnesses should be conducted with reasonable brevity. The Committee will ensure that matters proceed at a proper pace.

All evidence will be taken on oath or affirmation.

The Committee will determine what it regards as relevant. Hearsay evidence will, if relevant, be admissible, but of course will generally be of less weight than direct evidence.

There will be no closing address by Counsel to the Inquiry, but legal representatives are invited at the conclusion of the evidence to put in written submissions. The Committee may invite short oral submissions in addition if it considers it desirable.

The Committee proposes that the hearings will be held in public unless reasonable grounds are advanced for any particular part of the evidence to be given in private.

There will be facilities available for the media at the preliminary and full hearings.

The Committee will make further statements concerning the procedures to be adopted at the Inquiry hearings in due course.

The Committee reserves the right to alter its procedures in the light of experience, should this prove to be necessary.

17 October 1997

FURTHER DIRECTIONS ON PROCEDURE

1. UNREPRESENTED PARTIES

If having received a statement from an unrepresented party, the Tribunal decides to call such a witness, he/she will be examined by junior counsel for the Inquiry. Any necessary cross-examination of such a witness will be conducted by leading counsel for the Inquiry.

2. REPRESENTED PARTIES

If having received a statement from a party represented by a solicitor and/or counsel, the Tribunal decides to call such a witness, his solicitor or counsel will be permitted to examine him/her in chief.

3. CROSS-EXAMINATION

Cross-examination of other parties will only be permitted if their evidence demonstrably adversely affects the evidence contained in the written statement of parties who seek leave to cross-examine. This principle will be used by the Inquiry in exercising its discretion to allow counsel/solicitors representing other interested parties to cross-examine.

Counsel for the Inquiry may cross-examine represented parties.

4. RE-EXAMINATION

If it is necessary witnesses may be re-examined by their counsel/solicitor.

5. WITNESSES ON BEHALF OF A PARTY

If a party wishes a witness or witnesses to be heard, then a statement of such a witness's evidence must be produced, or that witness's statement will be taken by the Solicitor for the Inquiry. If, in its discretion, the Committee decides that such a statement contains evidence which may be material, then if the party is unrepresented, such evidence will be called in chief by junior counsel for the Inquiry, or by the solicitor or counsel for a represented party.

6. HEARSAY EVIDENCE

The rule against hearsay evidence will not apply, but in practice the Committee will give very limited weight to hearsay evidence for the purpose of arriving at any adverse finding against anyone appearing before it.

7. OPENING STATEMENTS

After counsel for the Inquiry has made an opening statement, the solicitor or counsel for represented parties may, if it is deemed necessary, make a statement, limited in duration to 10 minutes, referring to a particular point or a document so as to put the case in an entirely different light, and go far to mitigate the effect on the public of any criticism made in opening by counsel for the Inquiry.

Peter Fallon
Chairman,
Committee of Inquiry into the Personality Disorder Unit, Ashworth Special Hospital

SAMPLE "SALMON" LETTER

The Committee of Inquiry has identified the following particular areas which it is interested in examining from the point of view of your role as.......at Ashworth Special Hospital.

It wishes to hear evidence from you on......

Other matters may emerge, but we wish to provide you with an indication of the following issues in advance of your giving evidence so that you may be the better prepared to help us with them.

Was there a policy about child visits on PDU wards?

What was your involvement in relation to decisions concerning the visits of the child of a former patient who was visiting the PDU?

What part did you play in relation to permitting such visits?

When that child was still visiting the PDU, which patients were you aware had contact with that child?

Did you speak with any of your colleagues, nurses or other clinical staff, about your knowledge of contact between patients and the child?

What part did you play in relation to the continuation of such visits?

What supervision was being provided for such visits?

Was it conscionable for this child to be able regularly to visit Lawrence Ward amongst paedophile patients, and to visit without proper supervision?

Was the matter ever considered/reported as a "child protection" issue?

Did you have any contact with the Bradford Social Services Department who were concerned with the child? If so, what was the nature of your contact? If not, why not?

Were the child's interests in visiting the PDU regarded as the paramount consideration, or were other factors involved? If so, what were the other factors?

Did you read, or hear of, the concerns expressed in the Lawrence Ward Staff Meeting Book (Inquiry document - **C44**)? What actions did you take to respond to them?

Are there alleged incident(s) and/or concerns which have been expressed about any other child visitors to the PDU of which you have been aware? If so, what are the nature of these and what has been your involvement?

UNDERTAKING

WE UNDERTAKE not to disclose or pass on, to any third party the material supplied to us by the Inquiry Secretariat or any of the information contained within that material.

WE FURTHER UNDERTAKE to ensure that the material and information supplied to us is used solely for the purposes of this Inquiry, and at the conclusion of the Inquiry to return all the material and any copies of it to the Secretariat.

Signed :- ....

For and on behalf of :- ....

Dated :- ....

FINAL SUBMISSIONS TO THE FALLON INQUIRY

In writing:

Each represented party will be entitled to provide any final written submissions to the inquiry subject to the conditions set out below. If parties do not fulfil these conditions they will not be accepted and will not be read.

(1) The submissions shall be limited to the numbers of words indicated separately to each party.

(2) 8 (eight) copies shall be delivered to the Secretariat's Office by Wednesday 24 June 1998 at the very latest, and will not be read if received later.

(It would also assist if a copy could be provided in a version of "Wordperfect" on floppy disc).

(3) They shall be printed on A4 paper, already hole punched, double spaced, and in a font of at least 12pts.

Oral:

Principal parties' legal representatives may also be invited to appear before the Inquiry Panel to make a 10 (ten) minute, strictly time limited, oral persuasive presentation of their case. Junior counsel to the Inquiry will notify those who are so invited.

The provisional date for this will be the morning (only) of 6th July 1998 in London, and will be a public session.

APPENDIX 3 Parties and their Representatives before the Inquiry

Counsel to the Inquiry

Mr John Royce QC, and Mr Peter Blair

Solicitor to the Inquiry

Mr. Huw James

Parties (listed in alphabetical order)	*Representatives*
Mr Alan Arnold and Mr James Murphy	Mr Philip Engelman, instructed by the Royal College of Nursing Legal Department
Ashworth Hospital Authority	Mr Oliver Thorold, instructed by Messrs Reid Minty, London
Mr Michael Berry	Mr Roy Lewis, instructed by Messrs Irwin Mitchell, London
Mr Paul Boocock and Dr Mark Stowell-Smith	Mr John Benson, instructed by Messrs John A Behn Twyford & Co
Dr Zona Crispin and Dr Ian Strickland	Mr John Russell, instructed by Messrs Le Brasseur J Tickle, Leeds
Mr Steven Daggett	Mr Kris Gledhill, instructed by Messrs J P Mewies & Co, Skipton
Mrs Pamela Day	Mr Declan O'Dempsey, instructed by Messrs Rowley Ashworth, Wimbledon
Mr Charles Kaye and other members of the former SHSA	Mr William Hoskins, instructed by Messrs Reid Minty, London
Mental Health Act Commission	Ms Alice Robinson, instructed by the MHAC
Mrs Janice Miles	Mr Paul Gilroy, instructed by Messrs Hammond Suddards, Manchester
Patients of Ashworth Hospital	Ms Gillian Irving, instructed by Messrs Pannone & Partners, Manchester
Prison Officers' Association	Were party to the Inquiry but were not legally represented throughout the proceedings
Royal College of Nursing	Mr Philip Engelman, instructed by the Royal College of Nursing Legal Department
Dr Joseph Sylvester	Mr Richard Bradley, instructed by Messrs Berrymans Lace Mawer, Liverpool
UNISON	Mr Gavin Millar, instructed by Messrs Thompsons, London

Most of the above were only represented for part of the hearings

APPENDIX 4 Oral Witnesses

Mr Peter Green	Executive Director, Service Development, Ashworth Hospital
Dr John Reed	Former Senior Principal Medical Officer, Department of Health; Medical Inspector on HM Inspectorate of Prisons
Dr James Higgins	Consultant Forensic Psychiatrist, the Scott Clinic
Mr Ian Paterson	Security Liaison Manager, Ashworth Hospital
Dr Girish Shetty	Medical Director, Ashworth Hospital
Dr Placid Coorey	Consultant Forensic Psychiatrist, Ashworth Hospital
Mr John Parry	Clinical Services Manager, the Scott Clinic
Mr Thomas Maxwell	Former Security Manager (1994-96), Ashworth Hospital
Mr William Scully	Operations Manager in the Mental Health Directorate, Ashworth Hospital
Mr Anthony Moran	Ward Manager, Owen Ward, Ashworth Hospital
Mr Kevin Barron	Associate Director of Ashworth Hospital
Ms Carol Young	Former Acting Operations Manager, PDU, Ashworth Hospital
Mr Thomas Catterall	Former Ward Manager of Shelley Ward, later Site Manager, Ashworth Hospital
Mr Roger Kendrick	Associate Director, former Non-Executive Director, Ashworth Hospital Authority
Mr Stephen Keown	Rehabilitation Services Manager, Acting Clinical Director for Special Needs, Ashworth Hospital
Sir Alan Langlands	Chief Executive of the NHS Executive, Department of Health
Mr Charles Kaye	Former Chief Executive of the SHSA
Mr Paul Lever	Chairman, Ashworth Hospital Authority
Professsor Pamela Taylor	Former Head of Medical Services, SHSA; Professor of Special Hospital Psychiatry, The Maudsley Institute of Psychiatry
Mrs Anne-Marie Nelson	Former Chairman of the SHSA; Chairman of the HSPSCB
Dr Dilys Jones	Clinical Strategy Director to the HSPSCB and Senior Policy Adviser in Forensic Mental Health within the Health Services Directorate, NHS Executive, Department of Health
Mr James Murphy	Clinical Director, Special Needs Directorate, Ashworth Hospital
Mr Paul Tarbuck	Former Clinical Manager of the PDU, Ashworth Hospital
Mr Ray Rowden	Former Director of the HSPSCB
Patients A, B, C, D, E, F, G, H	Patients from the PDU, Ashworth Hospital
Patient M	Chairman of the Patients' Council, Ashworth Hospital
Mr Anthony Robertson	Councillor, Maghull Town Council
Mr David Bamber	Councillor, Maghull Town Council
Mrs Janice Miles	Former Chief Executive of Ashworth Hospital Authority

Mr Colin Dale	Executive Nurse Director, Ashworth Hospital Authority
Mr Robert Tinston	Regional Director, North West Regional Office of the NHS Executive, Department of Health
Mr James Gardner	Director of Security & Clinical Risk Management, Ashworth Hospital
Mr Joseph Day	Former Security Liaison Officer, PDU, Ashworth Hospital
Dr Richard Williams	Former Director of the former NHS Health Advisory Service
Mr Erville Millar	Acting Chief Executive of Ashworth Hospital Authority 1997
Professor Anthony Sammes	Professor of Computing Science, Royal Military College of Science, Cranfield University
Mr Ian Jewesbury	Former Department of Health official
Dr Bridget Dolan	Honorary Senior Lecturer in Forensic Psychology, St George's Medical School, London
Dr Michael Longfield	Director of Healthcare, HM Prison Service
Mr Michael Boyle	Head of the Mental Health & Criminal Cases Unit, Home Office
Dr Adrian Grounds	University Lecturer in Forensic Psychiatry, Institute of Criminology, University of Cambridge
Ms Lyn Suddards	Clinical Nurse Manager, Henderson Hospital, Sutton
Mr William Bingley	Chief Executive of the Mental Health Act Commission
Ms Sarah Breach	MHAC Convenor of the Panel of Commissioners for Ashworth Hospital
Dr David Thomas QC	Reader in Criminal Justice at the Institute of Criminology, University of Cambridge
Professor Donald West	Emeritus Professor of Clinical Criminology, Institute of Criminology, University of Cambridge
Dr Graham Robertson	Senior Clinical Psychologist, The Maudsley Hospital
Dr Derek Chiswick	Consultant Forensic Psychiatrist with the Edinburgh Healthcare NHS Trust, and Honorary Senior Lecturer, University of Edinburgh
Miss Joy Kinsley	Former Director of Security, SHSA
Dr Ian Keitch	Consultant Forensic Psychiatrist, Rampton Hospital
Mr Todd Hogue	Consultant Forensic Psychologist, Rampton Hospital
Mr John Hodge	Head of Professional Practice and Head of Psychology, Rampton Hospital
Dr Peter Snowden	Consultant Forensic Psychiatrist at the Edenfield Centre, Prestwich, and a member of the Home Office Advisory Board on Restricted Patients
Professor Jeremy Coid	Professor of Forensic Psychiatry, Head of the Department of Psychological Medicine at St Bartholomew's & the Royal London School of Medicine & Dentistry
Professor David Sines	Head of School of Health Sciences, University of Ulster
Dr Robert Johnson	Acting Head of Therapy, Ashworth Hospital
Professor Ronald Blackburn	Professor of Clinical and Forensic Psychological Studies, University of Liverpool
Professor John Gunn	Professor of Forensic Psychiatry, The Maudsley Institute of Psychiatry
Dr Brian Thomas-Peter	Head of Psychology, Reaside Clinic, Birmingham
Dr Clive Meux	Consultant Forensic Psychiatrist, Broadmoor Hospital; Senior Lecturer in Forensic Psychiatry, The Maudsley Institute of Psychiatry
Mr Stephen Daggett	Former Ashworth Hospital patient
Patients W, Q, H, E and I (Patients H and E are not the same as denoted earlier)	Patients from the PDU, Ashworth Hospital
Mr Damien Marlow	Staff Nurse, Owen Ward, Ashworth Hospital
Ms Lisa Johnson	Nurse, Lawrence Ward, Ashworth Hospital
Mr AA	Father of Child A
Inspector Robert Marsden	Inspector in the Merseyside Police Force

Ms Juliet Edge	Staff Nurse, Lawrence Ward, Ashworth Hospital
Ms Brenda Karran	Nursing Assistant, Lawrence Ward, Ashworth Hospital
Mr Peter Melia	Senior Clinical Nurse, PDU, Ashworth Hospital
Mr John Foster	Ward Manager, Lawrence Ward, Ashworth Hospital
Dr Ian Strickland	Consultant Forensic Psychiatrist, Ashworth Hospital
Dr Zona Crispin	Consultant Forensic Psychiatrist, Ashworth Hospital
Mrs Pamela Day	Consultant Clinical Psychologist, Ashworth Hospital
Mr Richard Backhouse	Head of Social Work Practice, Ashworth Hospital
Mr Michael Berry	Former Clinical Psychologist, Owen Ward, Ashworth Hospital
Mr Michael Bateson	Principal Social Worker, Acting Head of Social Work Practice, Ashworth Hospital
Mr David Preece	Chairman of the Ashworth Hospital Branch of the POA
Mr Alan Arnold	Former Ward Manager, Lawrence Ward, Ashworth Hospital
Dr Mark Stowell-Smith	Former Senior Social Worker, Lawrence Ward, Ashworth Hospital
Mr Thomas Sandford	South Thames Regional Office for the RCN, former RCN Advisor on Mental Health
Professor Kevin Gournay	Professor of Psychiatric Nursing, The Maudsley Institute of Psychiatry
Dr Christopher Hunter	Consultant Forensic Psychiatrist, Clinical Director of the Caswell Clinic, South Wales Forensic Psychiatric Service
Mr Michael Taylor	Director of Operations, NSPCC
Dr Joseph Sylvester	Consultant Psychiatrist, Ashworth Hospital
Mr Harry Ryan	Assistant Secretary, UNISON Health Care Branch, Ashworth Hospital
Mr William Berry	Associate Regional Secretary, UNISON North West Region
Mr Alan Franey	Former Chief Executive of Broadmoor Hospital Authority
Mr William Cannon	Team Leader, Lawrence Ward, Ashworth Hospital
Dr Anton Obholzer	Consultant Psychiatrist, Tavistock & Portman NHS Trust; Chairman of the Royal College of Psychiatrists' Working Group into the Definition and Treatment of Personality Disorder
Mr Paul Boocock	Staff Nurse, Lawrence Ward, Ashworth Hospital
Dr Hilary Hodge	Chief Executive, Ashworth Hospital Authority
Mrs Sheila Foley	Chief Executive, Rampton Hospital Authority

APPENDIX 5 Statements and submissions disclosed to all parties

Dr Robert Johnson
Prison Officers' Association
Maghull Town Council
Professor Ronald Blackburn
Professor Pamela Taylor
Patients' Council, Ashworth Hospital
Mr Richard Backhouse
Mr Paul Lever
Dr John Reed
NSPCC
Sir Alan Langlands
Mr Paul Tarbuck
Dr Adrian Grounds
Ashworth Hospital Authority
UNISON
Mrs Anne-Marie Nelson
Dr Joseph Sylvester
Dr Ian Strickland
Dr Hirallal Mogallapu
Mental Health Act Commission
Mr Charles Kaye
Mrs Janice Miles
Mrs Pamela Day
Mr Ray Rowden
Ms Joy Kinsley
Ms Carol Young
Mr Paul Warren
Mr Ian Paterson
Royal College of Nursing
Mr Alan Franey
Mr John Parry
Mr Colin Dale
Mr Peter Green
Mr Anthony Moran
Mr Peter Melia
Mr Joseph Day
Mr Alan Cooke
Dr James Higgins
Mr Thomas Maxwell
Dr Girish Shetty
Dr Placid Coorey
Mr Ian Jewesbury
Mr Thomas Catterall
Mr William Scully
Mr Kevin Barron
Mr Martin Royal
Mr Roger Kendrick
Mr James Gardner
Mr James Murphy
Mr Stephen Keown
Dr Zona Crispin
Mr John Foster
Dr Dilys Jones
Mr N J Earwaker
Patients A, B, C, D, E, F, G, H and M
Professor Donald West
Dr Clive Meux
Dr Graham Robertson
Mr Robert Tinston
Mr Michael Bateson
Professor John Gunn
Professor Anthony Sammes
Dr Richard Williams
Mr John Hodge
Mr Erville Millar
Professor Jeremy Coid
Dr Peter Snowden
Dr Bridget Dolan
Mr Michael Boyle
Dr Michael Longfield
Dr Adrian Grounds, Ms Lyn Suddards & Mr Tony Hill's (assessment team)
Professor David Sines
Mrs Sheila Foley
Rampton Hospital Authority
Dr Ian Keitch
Dr Derek Chiswick
Dr David Thomas
British Psychological Society
Mr Alan Arnold
Mr Steven Daggett
Patients E(2), H(2), I, Q, W
Mr Damien Marlow
Ms Lisa Johnson
Ms Brenda Karran
Mr William Cannon
Mr Paul Boocock
Mr Michael Berry
Inspector Robert Marsden
Ms Juliet Edge
Mr Paul Corrigan
Patient BP
Mr AA (father of Child A)
Royal College of Psychiatrists
Dr Mark Stowell-Smith
Dr Hilary Hodge

APPENDIX 6 Bibliography

Aarvold C., Hill D. and Newton G. P. (1973) *Report on the Review of Procedures for the Discharge and Supervision of Psychiatric Patients Subject to Special Restrictions,* Cmnd 5191. London: HMSO.

Anon (1991) 'Treatment outlines for anti-social personality disorder: the Quality Assurance Project', *Australia and New Zealand Journal of Psychiatry* **25**, 541–7.

Batchelor I. R. C. (1969) *Henderson and Gillespies textbook of psychiatry,* 10th edition. Oxford: Oxford University Press.

Bernheim J. and de Montmollin M.-J. (1990) 'A special unit in Geneva' in Bluglass R. and Bowden P. (eds) *Principles and Practice of Forensic Psychiatry.* London: Churchill Livingstone.

Bernheim J. (1991) 'Sociothérapie institutionelle de détenus présentant un désordre grave du charactère: l'expérience de "La Pâquerette" a Champ-Dollon (Genève)' in *Justice et Psychiatrie.* Paris: École Nationale de la Magistrature.

Department of Health and Social Security (1975) *Better services for the mentally ill,* Cmnd 6233. London: HMSO.

Blackburn R. (1983) 'Are personality orders treatable?', *Issues in Criminological and Legal Psychology* **4**, 23–6.

Blom-Cooper Sir L., Brown M., Dolan R. and Murphy E. (1992) *Report of the Committee of Inquiry into Complaints about Ashworth Hospital,* Cmnd 2028, vols 1 and 2 (Chairman: Sir Louis Blom-Cooper). London: HMSO.

Bluglass R. (1988) 'Mentally disordered prisoners: reports but no improvements', *British Medical Journal* **296**, 1757–8.

Bluglass R. (1992) 'The special hospitals', *British Medical Journal* **305**, 323–4.

Bowden P. (1996) 'Graham Young (1947–90), the St Albans poisoner: his life and times', *Criminal Behaviour and Mental Health* **17** (suppl), 24.

Boynton Sir J., Department of Health and Social Security (1980) *Report of the Review of Rampton Hospital,* Cmnd 8073 (Chairman: Sir John Boynton). London: HMSO.

Carney F. L. (1976) *Treatment of aggressive patients. Rage, Hate, Assault and other Forms of Violence.* New York: Spectrum Publications.

Casey P. R. and Tyrer P. J. (1986) 'Personality, functioning and symptomatology', *Journal of Psychiatric Research* **20**, 363–74.

Chiswick D., McIsaac M. W. and McClintock F. H. (1984) *Prosecution of the mentally disturbed.* Aberdeen: Aberdeen University Press.

Chiswick D. (1992) 'Compulsory treatment of patients with psychopathic disorder: an abnormally aggressive or seriously irresponsible exercise?', *Psychopathic Disorder, Criminal Behaviour and Mental Health* **2** (suppl), 106–13.

Cleckley H. (1941) *The mask of sanity: an attempt to clarify some issues about the so-called psychopathic personality.* St Louis: C. V. Mosby.

Coid J. (1992) 'DSM-III diagnosis in criminal psychopaths: a way forward', *Criminal Behaviour and Mental Health* **2**, 78–94.

Cooke D. J. (1989) 'Containing violent prisoners: an analysis of the Barlinnie Special Unit', *British Journal of Criminology* **29**, 129–43.

Cope R. (1992) 'A survey of forensic psychiatrists' views on psychopathic disorder', *Journal of Forensic Psychiatry* **4**(2), 215–35.

De Giromalo G. and Reich J. H. (1993) *Personality disorders.* Geneva: World Health Organization.

Dell S. and Robertson G. (1988) *Sentenced to hospital: offenders in Broadmoor* (Maudsley Monograph no. 32). Oxford: Oxford University Press.

de Montmollin M.-J., Zimmerman E., Bernheim J. and Harding T. W. (1986) 'Sociotherapeutic treatment of delinquents in prison', *International Journal of Offender Therapy and Comparative Criminology* **30**, 25-34.

Department of Health and Social Security (1976) *A Review of the Mental Health Act 1959.* London: HMSO.

Department of Health and Social Security (1986) *Offenders suffering from psychopathic disorder* (Health notice: HN(86)28). London: Department of Health and Social Security.

Department of Health (1996) *In-patients formally detained in hospitals under the Mental Health Act 1983 and other legislation. England 1989–90 to 1994–95* (Statistical bulletin: 1996/10). London: Government Statistical Service.

Dolan B. and Coid J. (1993) *Psychopathic and anti-social personality disorders: treatment and research issues.* London: Gaskell.

Dowson J. H. (1995) 'Group psychotherapies' in Dowson J. H. and Grounds A. (eds) *Personality disorders: recognition and clinical management.* Cambridge: Cambridge University Press.

East W. N. and Hubert W. H. de B. (1939) *The psychological treatment of crime.* London: HMSO.

Frosch J. P. (1983) 'The treatment of anti-social and borderline personality disorders', *Hospital and Community Psychiatry* **34**, 243–8.

Garrido V., Esteban C. and Molero C. (1996) 'The effectiveness in the treatment of psychopathy: a meta-analysis', *International Perspectives on Psychopathy. Division of Criminological and Legal Psychology* **24**. Summary of papers, edited by Cooke D., Forth A. E., Newman J. and Hare R. D., presented at the NATO ASI on Psychopathy held in Alvor, Portugal.

Gelder M., Gath D. and Mayou R. (1989) *Oxford textbook of psychiatry,* 2nd edition. Oxford: Oxford University Press.

Gostin L. (1977) *A Human Condition.* London: MIND.

Gostin L. and Fennell P. (1992) *Mental health tribunal procedure*, 2nd edition. London: Oyez, Longman.

Gray K. G. and Hutchinson H. C. (1964) 'The psychopathic personality: a survey of Canadian psychiatrists' opinions', *Canadian Psychiatric Association Journal* **9**, 452–61.

Gunn J., Maden A. and Swinton M. (1991) *Mentally disordered prisoners*. London: Department of Forensic Psychiatry, Institute of Psychiatry.

Gunn J., Maden A. and Swinton M. (1991) 'Treatment needs of prisoners with psychiatric disorders', *British Medical Journal* **303**, 338–41.

Gunn J. and Taylor P. (eds) (1993) *Forensic psychiatry: clinical, legal and ethical issues*. Oxford: Butterworth- Heinemann.

Hare R. D. (1991) *The Hare psychopathy checklist*, revised edition. Toronto: Multi Health Systems.

Henderson D. K. (1939) *Psychopathic states*. New York: Chapman and Hall.

Higgins J. (1995) 'Crime and mental disorder II: forensic aspects of psychiatric disorder' in Chiswick D. and Cope R. (eds) *Seminars in practical forensic psychiatry*. London: Gaskell Press.

HM Chief Inspector of Prisons for England and Wales (1997) *HM Prisons Grendon and Springhill: report of a full inspection, 1-12 September*. London: Home Office.

Hoggett B. (1990) *Mental health law*, 3rd edition. London: Sweet and Maxwell.

Hunter R. and Macalpine I. (1963) *Three hundred years of psychiatry 1535–1860*. Oxford: Oxford University Press.

House of Commons, Estimates Committee (1968) *The special hospitals and the state hospital: second report from the Estimates Committee. Session 1967–68* (HC 31; vol vii). London: HMSO.

Jones R. M. (1996) *Mental Health Act Manual*, 5th edition. London: Sweet and Maxwell.

Kershaw C., Dowdeswell P. and Goodman J. (1997) *Restricted patients: reconvictions and recalls by the end of 1995; England and Wales* (Statistical Bulletin: 1/97). London: Home Office.

Koch J. L. A. (1889) *Kurzgefaßter leitfaden der psychiatrie*, 2nd edition. Ravensburg: Dom'schen Buchhandlung.

Koch J. L. A. (1891–1893) *Die psychopathischen minderwertigkeiten*. Ravensburg: Maier.

Kraepelin E. (1896) *Psychiatrie, ein lehrbruch für studierende und aerzte*. Reprinted 1976 (*Classics in Psychiatry*). New York: Arno Press.

Lewis A. (1974) 'Psychopathic personality: a most elusive category', *Psychological Medicine* **4**, 133–40.

Lombroso C. (1976) *L'uomo deliquente*. Milan.

Maden A., Taylor C. J. A., Brooke D., and Gunn J. (1995) *Mental disorder in remand prisoners*. London: Department of Psychiatry, Institute of Psychiatry.

Maden A. (1996) *Women, prisons and psychiatry: mental disorder behind bars*. Oxford: Butterworth-Heinemann.

Maden T., Curle C., Meux C., Burrow S. and Gunn J. (1995) *The treatment and security needs of special hospital patients.* London: Whurr Publishers.

Main T. F. (1946) 'The hospital as a therapeutic institution', *Bulletin of the Menninger Clinic* **10**, 66–71.

Marlowe M. and Sugarman P. (1997) 'ABC of mental health: disorders of personality', *British Medical Journal,* **315**, 176–9.

Marshall P. (1997) *A reconviction study of HMP Grendon therapeutic community* (Home Office Research and Statistics Directorate Research Findings no. 53). London: Home Office.

Maudsley H. (1874) *Responsibility and mental disease.* New York: Appleton

Mbatia J. and Tyrer P. (1988) 'Personality status of dangerous patients in a special hospital' in Tyrer P. (ed.) *Personality disorders: diagnosis, management and course.* London: Wright.

Mentally abnormal offenders: report of the Committee (1975), Cmnd 6244 (Chairman: Lord Butler of Saffron Walden). London: HMSO.

Merikangas K. R., Weissman M. H. (1986) 'Epidemiology of DSMIII Axis II personality disorders' in Frances A. J. and Hales R. E. (eds) *APA Annual Review* (Psychiatric Update: vol 5, 258–78). Washington DC.: American Psychiatric Press.

Ministry of Health (1961) *Special hospitals: report of the Working Party* (Chairman: Mr D. Emery). London: HMSO.

Moran P. and Jenkins R. (1997) 'Review of epidemiology and needs assessment of psychopathy. Paper read at HSPSCB Research and Development Conference (15 October).

Morel B. A. (1857) *Traité des dégénérescences physiques, intellectuelles et morales de l'espèce humaine et des causes qui produisent ces variétés maladive.* Paris: Baillière.

Murphy E. (1997) 'The future of Britain's high security hospitals', *British Medical Journal* **314**, 1292–3.

NHS Health Advisory Service/DHSS Social Services Inspectorate (1988) *Report on the services provided by Broadmoor Hospital.* London: HAS/SSI.

Norton K. (1997) 'In the prison of severe personality disorder', *Journal of Forensic Psychiatry* **8**, 285–98.

Pinel P. (1801) *Traité médico-philosophique sur l'aliénation mentale, ou'la manie.* Paris.

Prichard J. C. (1835) *A treatise on insanity and other disorders affecting the mind.* London: Sherwood.

Reed J., Department of Health and Home Office (1992) *Review of health and social services for mentally disordered offenders and others requiring similar services. Services for people from black and ethnic minority groups: issues of race and culture. A discussion paper* (Chairman: Dr John Reed). London: Department of Health.

Reed J. and Department of Health (1994) *Report of the Working Group on High Security and Related Psychiatric Provision* (Chairman: Dr John Reed). London: Department of Health.

Reed J., Department of Health and Home Office (1994) *Working Group on Psychopathic Disorder. Report* (Chairman: Dr John Reed). London: Department of Health.

Report of the Royal Commission on Capital Punishment (1952), Cmnd 8932 (Chairman: Sir Arthur Gowers). London: HMSO.

Report of the Royal Commission on the Law Relating to Mental Illness and Mental Deficiency (1957), Cmnd 169 (Chairman: Lord Percy of Newcastle). London: HMSO.

Robins L. (1966) *Deviant children grown up: a sociological and psychiatric study of sociopathic personality.* Baltimore: Williams & Wilkins.

Royal Commission on Tribunals of Inquiry (1966), Cmnd 3121 (Chairman: Rt Hon Lord Justice Salmon). London: HMSO.

Sass H. and Herpertz S. (1995) in Berrios G. E. and Porter R. *A history of clinical psychiatry.* London: Athlone Press.

Scadding J. G. (1990) 'The semantic problems of psychiatry', *Psychological Medicine* **20**, 243–8.

Schneider K. (1923) *Die psychopathischen personlichkeiten.* Leipzig: Thieme.

Schneider K. (1950) *Psychopathic Personalities.* London: Cassell.

Scott P. D. (1963) 'Psychopathy', *Postgraduate Medical Journal* **39**, 1–7.

Scott P. D. (1977) 'Assessing dangerousness in criminals', *British Journal of Psychiatry* **131**, 127–42.

Scott Sir R. (1996) *Report of the Inquiry into the Export of Defence Equipment and Dual-Use Goods to Iraq and Related Prosecutions* (HC 115: vols I–VI). London: HMSO.

Shaw J., McKenna J., Snowden P., Boyd C., McMahon D. and Kilshaw J. (1994) 'The north west region. I: clinical features and placement needs of patients detained in Special Hospitals', *Journal of Forensic Psychiatry* **5**, 93–105.

Singleton N., Meltzer H., Gatward R., Coid J. and Deasy D. (1998) *Psychiatric morbidity among prisoners.* London: The Stationery Office.

Stafford-Clark D., Pond D. and Doust J. W. L. (1951) 'The psychopath in prison: a preliminary report of a co-operative research', *British Journal of Delinquency,* 117–29.

Taylor P. (1992) 'Introductory note to the 1991 SHSA seminar on psychopathic disorder', *Criminal Behaviour and Mental Health* **2**, 2.

Tennent G., Tennent D., Prins H. and Bedford A. (1993) 'Is psychopathic disorder a treatable condition?', *Medicine, Science and the Law* **33**, 63–6.

Tyrer P. (1988) *Personality disorders: diagnosis, management and course.* London: Wright.

Tyrer P. and Stein G. (eds) (1993) *Personality disorder reviewed.* London: Gaskell.

Tyrer P. and Johnson T. (1996) 'Establishing the severity of personality disorder', *American Journal of Psychiatry* **153**, 1593–7.

Walker N. and McCabe S. (1973) *Crime and insanity in England,* Vol II. Edinburgh: Edinburgh University Press.

West D. J. (1969) *Present conduct and future delinquency.* London: Heinemann Educational Books.

Whatmore P. (1990) 'The special unit at Barlinnie Prison' in Bluglass R. and Bowden P. (eds) *Principles and Practice of Forensic Psychiatry*. London: Churchill Livingstone.

Woodcock Sir J. (1994) *Report of the enquiry into the escape of six prisoners from the special security unit at Whitemoor Prison, Cambridgeshire, on Friday 9 September 1994: the Woodcock Enquiry*, Cmnd 2741 (Chairman: Sir John Woodcock). London: HMSO.

Wootton of Abinger, Baroness (1978) *Crime and penal policy*. London: George Allen and Unwin.

APPENDIX 7 Forensic Psychiatry – Secure Units

High Security Hospitals

Ashworth Special Hospital, Liverpool
Broadmoor Special Hospital, Crowthorne
Rampton Special Hospital, Retford
The State Hospital, Carstairs, Lanarkshire

Medium Secure Units

Anglia and Oxford

Marlborough House RSU, Milton Keynes
Norvic Clinic, Norwich
Wallingford Clinic, Fairmile Hospital

North Thames

Camlet Lodge, Chase Farm Hospital, Enfield
John Howard Centre, Hackney
Runwell Hospital, Wickford
Three Bridges RSU, Southall

North West Region

Edenfield Centre, Prestwich
Langdale Unit, Preston
Scott Clinic, St Helens

Northen and Yorkshire

The Bamburgh Clinic, St Nicholas Hospital, Newcastle upon Tyne
The Humber Centre for Forensic Psychiatry, Hull
Hutton Centre, St Luke's Hospital, Middlesbrough
Newton Lodge RSU, Wakefield

South Thames

Ashen Hill, Hellingly, Halesham
Bracton Centre, Bexley Hospital
Cane Hill Forensic Mental Health Unit, Coulsdon
Denis Hill Unit, Bethlem Royal Hospital, Beckenham
Kent Forensic Psychiatric Service, Trevor Gibbens Unit, Maidstone
Shaftesbury Clinic, Springfield Hospital, Tooting

South and West

Butler Clinic, Langdon Hospital, Dawlish
Fromeside Clinic, Stapleton, Bristol
Ravenswood House, Knowle, Fareham

Trent

Arnold Lodge, Leicester
Wathwood Hospital RSU, Rotherham

West Midlands

Hatherton Centre, Stafford
Reaside Clinic, Birmingham

Wales

North Wales Forensic Psychiatric Service Bryn-Y-Neuadd Hospital, Conwy
South Wales Forensic Psychiatric Service, Caswell Clinic, Glanrhyd Hospital, Bridgend

Independent Sector

Chadwick Lodge (formerly Blenheim House), Milton Keynes
Kneesworth House Hospital, Royston, Herts
Llanarth Court Hospital, Gwent
Redford Lodge, Edmonton, London
St Andrew's Hospital, Chandos Pole
Lowther Division, Northampton
Stockton Hall Psychiatric Hospital, York

Prison Service

HMYOI Aylesbury, Bucks
HYYOI and Remand Centre Feltham
HM Prison Gartree, Market Harborough
HMYOI & Remand Centre Glen Parva, Wigston, Leicestershire
HM Prison Grendon/Spring Hill, Aylesbury
HM Prison Wormwood Scrubs, London

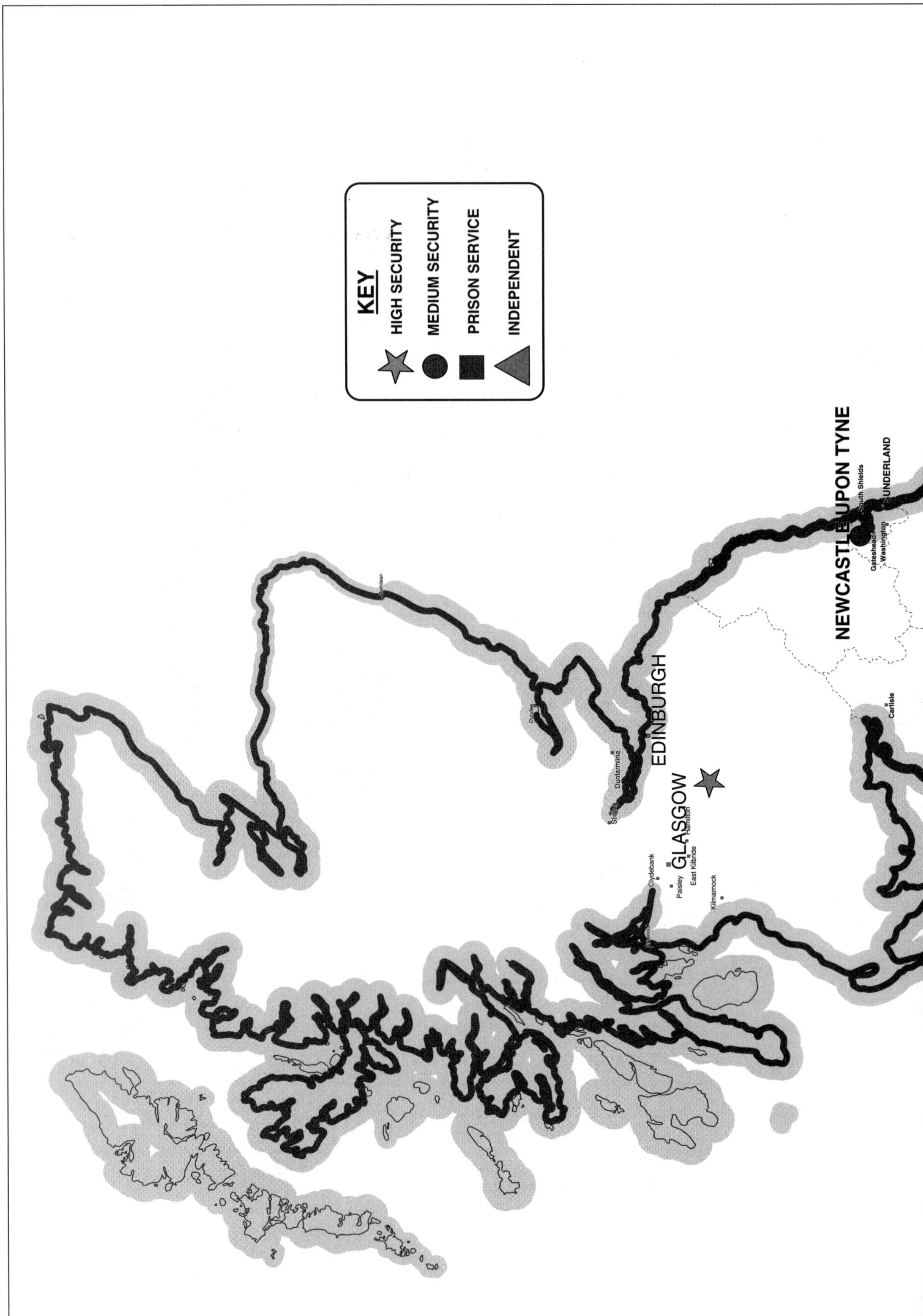
KEY
HIGH SECURITY
MEDIUM SECURITY
PRISON SERVICE
INDEPENDENT
NEWCASTLE UPON TYNE
South Shields
SUNDERLAND
Gateshead
Washington
Carlisle
EDINBURGH
GLASGOW
Dunfermline
Hamilton
East Kilbride
Clydebank
Paisley
Kilmarnock

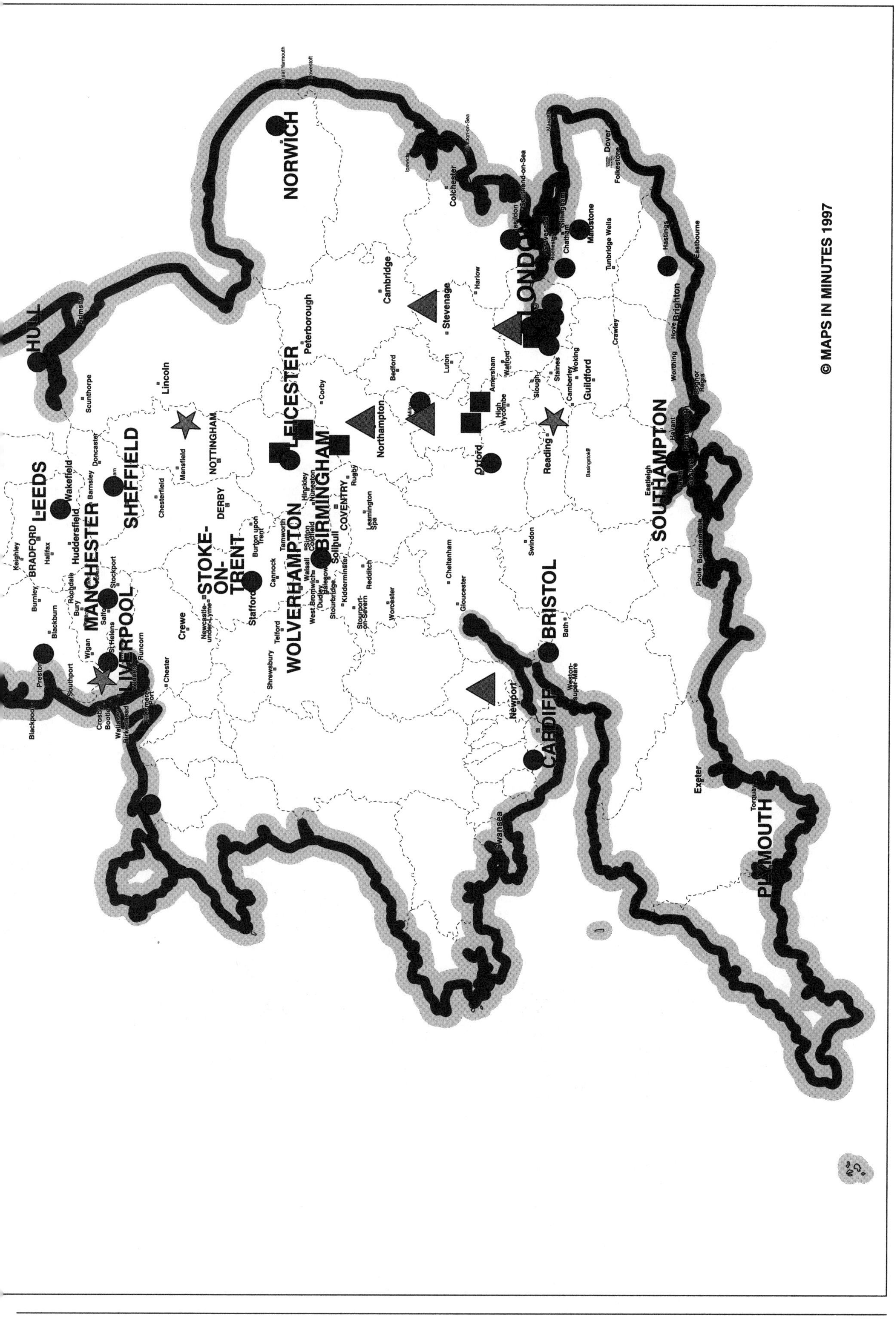
HULL
LEEDS
BRADFORD
Wakefield
Huddersfield
MANCHESTER
LIVERPOOL
SHEFFIELD
NORWICH
NOTTINGHAM
DERBY
LEICESTER
BIRMINGHAM
WOLVERHAMPTON
COVENTRY
STOKE-ON-TRENT
Peterborough
Cambridge
Stevenage
Northampton
Oxford
Reading
LONDON
Colchester
Maidstone
Dover
Brighton
SOUTHAMPTON
BRISTOL
CARDIFF
Newport
Swansea
Gloucester
Cheltenham
Exeter
PLYMOUTH
Lincoln
Chester
Crewe
Preston
Blackpool
© MAPS IN MINUTES 1997

APPENDIX 8 Visits

1. Members of the Committee of Inquiry, individually and as a group, visited a number of hospitals and prisons which care for and manage personality disordered individuals, both in England and abroad. We describe each service briefly below. It should be stressed that we have in no way sought to assess the quality of service provided by any of these institutions.

2. We are most grateful for the generous way in which staff at these units gave freely of their time and expertise. They have greatly stimulated our thinking.

Great Britain

(i) High Security Hospitals

3. We visited **Ashworth Hospital** and viewed Lawrence Ward and a number of other wards, both on the North and East Sites. We also heard evidence for two days in early February 1997 within the North Site of the Hospital.

4. In January 1998 we visited Woodstock Ward at **Broadmoor Hospital**. This ward is a 25-bedded unit which specializes in the psychotherapeutic treatment of young men, most of whom suffer from personality disorder. We also met a number of senior managers and clinicians.

5. The same month we visited the Personality Disorder Service at **Rarnpton Hospital**. This service comprises three wards, an assessment ward (Connaught Ward), a treatment ward (Evans) and a rehabilitation and continuing care ward (Hawthorns Villa). The planned capacity of the service is 42. Again we met a number of senior managers and clinicians.

6. Mr Daniels visited the State Hospital at **Carstairs**, Lanarkshire. Carstairs is the provider of high and medium security beds for Scotland and Northern Ireland. It accommodates on average 225 patients. Although psychopathic disorder is not mentioned in Scottish Mental Health legislation many of the patients at Carstairs suffer from disordered personalities.

(ii) Medium Security Hospitals

7. The Committee visited the **Reaside Clinic**, Birmingham, in April 1998. Reaside has 90 beds and is the largest NHS medium secure unit in the country.

8. Members of the Committee also visited **Chadwick Lodge** in Milton Keynes, a recently-opened independent sector medium secure unit. The hospital will have 40 beds. The intention is to offer long-term medium secure accommodation there.

9. We visited **Kneesworth House** near Royston, Hertfordshire. This is an independent sector medium secure unit with 145 beds, including a 15-bedded ward for personality disorded patients.

(iii) Prisons

10. Mr Daniels visited **Grendon Underwood Prison**. Grendon, established in 1962,is a therapeutic prison catering for around 225 prisoners. Prisoners can be referred to Grendon from any part of the prison system, although it only caters for men who are serving long enough sentences to allow them to receive at least 18 months in therapy. Potential inmates must be motivated to change and be willing to comply with the regime. Thus they must not take drugs or drink alcohol, or use violence. The prison does not accept prisoners on psychotropic medication. Breaking the rules or non-compliance leads to transfer back to the mainstream prison population.

11. Members of the Committee visited the **Max Glatt Centre** at Wormwood Scrub Prison, West London. This therapeutic wing caters for 35 men, focusing particularly on drug abuse and sexual offending.

12. We also visited the Close Supervision Unit at **Woodhill Prison**, Milton Keynes. This was recently set up as part of a new approach to managing the very small group of men within the prison system subject to the Continuous Assessment Scheme (CAS), the last resort for managing disruptive prisoners. These men are so disruptive within the system that they tend to be moved from prison to prison. Many are held in segregation units. Under the CAS their cases are reviewed every six weeks; if they continue to be disruptive they may be moved every six weeks from segregation unit to segregation unit. A number of these men suffer from severe personality disorders and some have been in Special Hospitals in the past (the Prison Service told us that 12 of the 40 prisoners on the Continuous Assessment Scheme as of March 1998 had been in a Special Hospital at some point in their sentence, although they were unable to give us any information on diagnoses).

13. Since February 1998 the Prison service has adopted a new approach, based on a system of five Close Supervision Centres (CSCs), each holding a small number of prisoners, with varying regimes ranging from highly restricted to more open regimes. Prisoners have the opportunity for graduated progression through the system and back into the mainstream prison estate through sustained good behaviour.

14. The CSC estate is based at Woodhill Prison in Milton Keynes (which operates three of the five centres), Hull and Durham. Prisoner entering the system go to the Structure Regime Centre at Woodhill for assessment; prisoners who continue to be disruptive or dangerous move to the Restricted Regime Centre at Woodhill with a strict, no association regime. Compliance earns a move to the Intervention Centre at Woodhill offering structured therapy and full association. There are further Intervention Centres at Hull and Durham.

The Netherlands

15. In January 1998 we visited a number of services in the **TBS** ("Terbeschikkingstelling") system in the Netherlands. The Dutch system for managing personality disordered offenders has been widely studied. It is interestingly different from the UK model, as it is concerned above all with the reduction of risk to society posed by mentally disturbed offenders who are assessed as being not fully responsible for their actions. There is no treatability test; rather, the stress is on reducing the potential dangerousness of such people. The system has traditionally dealt with personality disordered offenders, although there are now increasing numbers of psychotic individuals with TBS orders.

16. The system operates roughly as follows. When a person accused of a serious offence is thought to have been suffering from some form of defective development and/or pathological disturbance of mind at the time of the alleged crime such that he cannot be regarded as wholly responsible for that crime, if proved, a judge can request an assessment of his mental condition to be carried out. The purpose of this assessment is, first, to assess whether the person has a disorder, and to what extent he can be held responsible for his actions; and, second, if a disorder is present, how strongly that disorder is linked to the offence. This leads to a recommendation as to the degree of responsibility the defendand should bear for the crime, if proved, on a sliding scale from "fully responsible" to "not responsible", and a judgement as to whether this person would be likely to commit another crime on the basis of diminished responsibility.

17. When a person is found to have diminished responsibility **and** to be dangerous a TBS order (roughly equivalent to a "hospital order") may be ordered. Assuming the defendant is found guilty he is sentenced to a particular term, depending on the nature of the offence and the degree to which he is regarded as responsible, and to a TBS order. After serving his sentence he is then sent to be assessed at the **Meijers Institute** in Utrecht, which determines which of the TBS clinics he should be treated at. He then goes on to a clinic. The staff in TBS Clinics are predominantly social therapists rather than trained psychiatric nurses, reflecting the emphasis on "resocializing" the TBS patient.

18. The TBS order is reviewed every two years, if possible by the same judge who originally imposed the TBS order. The judge can order release from the order against the hospital's advice. In principle a TBS order can last for life, although the average is around five or six years.

19. The Committee visited the **Pieter Baan Centre** and **F.S. Meijers Institute** in Utrecht; the **Dr S. van Mesdag Clinic** in Groningen and the **Van der Hoeven Clinic** in Utrecht. The **Pieter Baan Centre** is the main assessment centre for remand prisoners. Prisoners referred to the Centre spend seven weeks there being assessed by a multi-disciplinary team, led by a lawyer, and consisting of a psychiatrist, psychologist, social worker and a social therapist. The team has access to criminal records and, if the individual under observation agrees, to any clinical notes. The Centre has 32 beds, divided up into four wards. At the end of the seven weeks a report is produced advising the court on the degree of responsibility the prisoner bears for the offence (the assessment team work on the assumption that each person under observation is guilty) and the likelihood of recidivism, and make a recommendation as to whether or not that person should be made subject to a TBS order, if found guilty.

20. The **F.S. Meijers Institute** is located next door to the Pieter Baan Centre. Its main function, as mentioned above, is to assess which TBS clinic is most suitable for a given individual. It has 32 beds in four wards.

21. The **Dr S. van Mesdag Clinic** is possibly the nearest equivalent to a high security hospital in Holland. It has 145 beds, soon to increase to 180. The patient population is roughly equally divided between psychotic and personality disordered men.

22. The **Dr Henri Van der Hoeven Clinic** in Utrecht is very similar to an English medium secure unit (the Reaside Clinic was closely modelled on it). It has 85 beds within the Clinic and 15 based outside. It operates very broadly on a therapeutic community model.

Germany

23. We visited two hospitals in North Rhine-Westfalia, Düren and Eickelborn. North Rhine-Westfalia is the largest Land (state) in Germany, with 18 million inhabitants out of a total population of 80 million. German law allows for the compulsory detention in a psychiatric hospital of mentally disturbed offenders, drug addicts and alcoholics. The issue in law is whether a individual is not responsible or in part not responsible for the criminal act in question **and** whether in view of his or her condition he or she is likely to reoffend seriously in the future.

24. Düren was built in the mid-1980s as a so-called "forensic village", designed to provide a complete therapeutic milieu. All the buildings, including the wards, are laid out along a main street; there are also extensive grounds, all within the secure perimeter. Some 120 patients, all men, are housed there; approximately half suffer from personality disorders, half from psychoses. The perimeter wall itself is invisible from outside the hospital.

25. The **Westfalian Centre for Forensic Psychiatry at Eickelborn** is the largest forensic facility in Germany with over 300 beds. It is located within a larger hospital; the forensic wards are surrounded by individual fences. The wards themselves have something of the feel of Rampton, being located in two or three-storied houses. The Centre caters for patients with personality disorders, mental illness and learning disability, and for drug addicts.

Switzerland

26. We visited the Sociotherapeutic Centre at **Champ-Dollon Prison** in Geneva. This centre houses 11 severely personality disordered prisoners in a wing of a remand prison; the Centre itself is run by the University Institute of Legal Medicine, although a number of prison guards work on the wing. The prisoners are usually young men who have repeatedly demonstrated violent behaviour or sexual misconduct, and who have feelings of anxiety and depression. None are psychotic. The wing is run as a highly-structured community.

APPENDIX 9 Amendments to the Mental Health Act 1983

Part I

Application of Act: "mental disorder"

1. – (1) The provisions of this Act shall have effect with respect to the reception, care and treatment of mentally disordered patients, the management of their property and other related matters.

(2) In this Act –

"mental disorder" means mental illness, arrested or incomplete development of mind, personality ~~psychopathic~~ disorder and any other disorder or disability of mind and "mentally disordered" shall be construed accordingly;

"severe mental impairment" means a state of arrested or incomplete development of mind which includes severe impairment of intelligence and social functioning and is associated with abnormally aggressive or seriously irresponsible conduct on the part of the person concerned and "severely mentally impaired" shall be construed accordingly;

"mental impairment" means a state of arrested or incomplete development of mind (not amounting to severe mental impairment) which includes significant impairment of intelligence and social functioning and is associated with abnormally aggressive or seriously irresponsible conduct on the part of the person concerned and "mentally impaired" shall be construed accordingly;

~~"psychopathic disorder" means a persistent disorder or disability of mind (whether or not including significant impairment of intelligence) which results in abnormally aggressive or seriously irresponsible conduct on the part of the person concerned~~;

and other expressions shall have the meanings assigned to them in section 145 below.

(3) Nothing in subsection (2) above shall be construed as implying that a person may be dealt with under this Act as suffering from mental disorder, or from any form of mental disorder described in this section, by reason only of promiscuity or other immoral conduct, sexual deviancy or dependence on alcohol or drugs.

Part II

["~~Psychopathic disorder~~" replaced by "personality disorder" in ss.3(2)(a), 7(2)(a), 11(6), 16(2), 20(4)(a), 20(7)(a), 25A(4)(a), 25C(1), 25G(4)(a). "Psychopathic disorder" deleted from s.3(2)(b)]

Part III

Remand to hospital for report on accused's mental condition

35. – (1) Subject to the provisions of this section, the Crown Court or a magistrates' court may remand an accused person to a hospital specified by the court for a report on his mental condition.

(2) For the purposes of this section an accused person is -

(a) in relation to the Crown Court, any person who is awaiting trial before the court for an offence punishable with imprisonment or who has been arraigned before the court for such an offence and has not yet been sentenced or otherwise dealt with for the offence on which he has been arraigned;

(b) in relation to a magistrates' court, any person who has been convicted by the court of an offence punishable on summary conviction with imprisonment and any person charged with such an offence if the court is satisfied that he did the act or made the omission charged or he has consented to the exercise by the court of the powers conferred by this section.

(3) Subject to subsection (4) below, the powers conferred by this section may be exercised if –

(a) the court is satisfied, on the written or oral evidence of a registered medical practitioner that there is reason to suspect that the accused person is suffering from mental illness, ~~psychopathic~~ personality disorder, severe mental impairment or mental impairment; and

(b) the court is of the opinion that it would be impracticable for a report on his mental condition to be made if he were remanded on bail; but those powers shall not be exercised by the Crown Court in respect of a person who has been convicted before the court if the sentence for the offence of which he has been convicted is fixed by law.

(4) The court shall not remand an accused person to a hospital under this section unless satisfied, on the written or oral evidence of the registered medical practitioner who would be responsible for making the report or of some other person representing the managers of the hospital, that arrangements have been made for his admission to that hospital and for his admission to it within the period of seven days beginning with the date of the remand; and if the court is so satisfied it may, pending his admission, give directions for his conveyance to and detention in a place of safety.

(5) Where a court has remanded an accused person under this section it may further remand him if it appears to the court, on the written or oral evidence of the registered medical practitioner responsible for making the report, that a further remand is necessary for completing the assessment of the accused person's mental condition.

(6) The power of further remanding an accused person under this section may be exercised by the court without his being brought before the court if he is represented by counsel or a solicitor and his counsel or solicitor is given an opportunity of being heard.

(7) An accused person shall not be remanded or further remanded under this section for more than 28 days at a time or for more than 12 weeks in all; and the court may at any time terminate the remand if it appears to the court that it is appropriate to do so.

(8) . . . (9) . . . (10) . . .

Powers of courts to order hospital admission or guardianship

37. – (1) Where a person is convicted before the Crown Court of an offence punishable with imprisonment other than an offence the sentence for which is fixed by law, or is convicted by a magistrates' court of an offence punishable on summary conviction with imprisonment, and the conditions mentioned in subsection (2) below are satisfied, the court may by order authorise his admission to and detention in such hospital as may be specified in the order or, as the case may be, place him under the guardianship of a local social services authority or of such other person approved by a local social services authority as may be so specified.

(2) The conditions referred to in subsection (1) above are that –

(a) the court is satisfied, on the written or oral evidence of two registered medical practitioners, that the offender is suffering from mental illness, ~~psychopathic disorder~~, severe mental impairment or mental impairment and that either –

(i) ~~the~~ that mental disorder from which the offender is suffering is of a nature or degree which makes it appropriate for him to be detained in a hospital for medical treatment and, in the case of ~~psychopathic disorder or~~ mental impairment, that such treatment is likely to alleviate or prevent a deterioration of his condition; or

(ii) in the case of an offender who has attained the age of 16 years, ~~the~~ that mental disorder is of a nature or degree which warrants his reception into guardianship under this Act; and

(b) the court is of the opinion, having regard to all the circumstances including the nature of the offence and the character and antecedents of the offender, and to the other available methods of dealing with him, that the most suitable method of disposing of the case is by means of an order under this section.

(3) . . . (4) . . . (5) . . . (6) . . .

(7) A hospital order or guardianship order shall specify the form or forms of mental disorder referred to in subsection (2)(a) above from which, upon the evidence taken into account under that subsection, the offender is found by the court to be suffering; and no such order shall be made unless the offender is described by each of the practitioners whose evidence is taken into account under that subsection as suffering from the same one of those forms of mental disorder, whether or not he is also described by either of them as suffering from another of them.

(8) . . .

Interim hospital orders

38. – (1) Where a person is convicted before the Crown Court of an offence punishable with imprisonment (other than an offence the sentence for which is fixed by law) or is convicted by a magistrates' court of an offence punishable on summary conviction with imprisonment and the court before or by which he is convicted is satisfied, on the written or oral evidence of two registered medical practitioners –

(a) that the offender is suffering from mental illness, ~~psychopathic disorder~~, severe mental impairment or mental impairment; and

(b) that there is reason to suppose that the mental disorder from which the offender is suffering is such that it may be appropriate for a hospital order to be made in his case; the court may, before making a hospital order or dealing with him in some other way, make an order (in this Act referred to as "an interim hospital order") authorising his admission to such hospital as may be specified in the order and his detention there in accordance with this section.

(2) . . . (3) . . . (4) . . .

(5) An interim hospital order –

(a) shall be in force for such period, not exceeding 12 weeks, as the court may specify when making the order; but

(b) may be renewed for further periods of not more than 28 days at a time if it appears to the court, on the written or oral evidence of the responsible medical officer, that the continuation of the order is warranted;

but no such order shall continue in force for more than twelve months in all and the court shall terminate the order if it makes a hospital order in respect of the offender or decides after considering the written or oral evidence of the responsible medical officer to deal with the offender in some other way.

(6) . . . (7) . . .

Power of higher courts to restrict discharge from hospital

41. –(1) Where a hospital order is made in respect of an offender by the Crown Court, and it appears to the court, having regard to the nature of the offence, the antecedents of the offender and the risk of his committing further offences if set at large, that it is necessary for the protection of the public from serious harm so to do, the court may, subject to the provisions of this section, further order that the offender shall be subject to the special restrictions set out in this section, either without limit of time or during such period as may be specified in the order; and an order under this section shall be known as "a restriction order".

(2) A restriction order shall not be made in the case of any person unless at least one of the registered medical practitioners whose evidence is taken into account by the court under section 37(2)(a) above has given evidence orally before the court.

(3) The special restrictions applicable to a patient in respect of whom a restriction order is in force are as follows:

(a) none of the provisions of Part II of this Act relating to the duration, renewal and expiration of authority for the detention of patients shall apply, and the patient shall continue to be liable to be detained by virtue of the relevant hospital order until he is duly discharged under the said Part II or absolutely discharged under sections 42, 73, 74 or 75 below;

(b) no application shall be made to a Mental Health Review Tribunal in respect of a patient under sections 66 or 69(1) below;

(c) the following powers shall be exercisable only with the consent of the Secretary of State, namely –

(i) power to grant leave of absence to the patient under section 17 above;

(ii) power to transfer the patient in pursuance of regulations under section 19 above; and

(iii) power to order the discharge of the patient under section 23 above;

and if leave of absence is granted under the said section 17 power to recall the patient under that section shall vest in the Secretary of State as well as the responsible medical officer; and

(d) the power of the Secretary of State to recall the patient under the said section 18 above may be exercised at any time;

and in relation to any such patient section 40(4) above shall have effect as if it referred to Part II of Schedule 1 to this Act instead of Part I of that Schedule.

(4) . . . (5) . . .

(6) While a person is subject to a restriction order the responsible medical officer shall at such intervals (not exceeding one year) as the Secretary of State may direct examine and report to the Secretary of State on that person; and every report shall contain such particulars as the Secretary of State may require.

Hospital and limitation directions
Power of higher courts to direct hospital admission

45A. 1) This section applies where, in the case of a person convicted before the Crown Court of an offence the sentence for which is not fixed by law -

(a) the conditions mentioned in subsection (2) below are fulfilled; and

(b) except where the offence is one the sentence for which falls to be imposed under section 2 of the Crime (Sentences) Act 1997, the court considers making a hospital order in respect of him before deciding to impose a sentence of imprisonment ("the relevant sentence") in respect of the offence.

(2) The conditions referred to in subsection (1) above are that the court is satisfied, on the written or oral evidence of two registered medical practitioners -

(a) that the offender is suffering from psychopathic disorder;

(b) that the mental disorder from which the offender is suffering is of a nature or degree which makes it appropriate for him to be detained in a hospital for medical treatment; and

(c) that such treatment is likely to alleviate or prevent a deterioration of his condition.

(3) The court may give both of the following directions, namely -

(a) a direction that, instead of being removed to and detained in a prison, the offender be removed to and detained in such hospital as may be specified in the direction (in this Act referred to as a "hospital direction"); and

(b) a direction that the offender be subject to the special restrictions set out in section 41 above (in this Act referred to as a "limitation direction").

(4) . . . (9) . . .

(10) The Secretary of State may by order provide that this section shall have effect as if the reference in subsection (2) above to psychopathic disorder included a reference to a mental disorder of such other description as may be specified in the order.

(11) An order made under this section may -

(a) apply generally, or in relation to such classes of offenders or offences as may be specified in the order;

(b) provide that any reference in this section to a sentence of imprisonment, or to a prison, shall include a reference to a custodial sentence, or to an institution, of such description as may be so specified; and

(c) include such supplementary, incidental or consequential provisions as appear to the Secretary of State to be necessary or expedient.

Effect of hospital and limitation directions

45B. (1) . . . (3) . . .

Transfer to Hospital of prisoners, etc.
Removal to hospital of persons serving sentences of imprisonment, etc.

47. – (1) If in the case of a person serving a sentence of imprisonment the Secretary of State is satisfied, by reports from at least two registered medical practitioners-

(a) that the said person is a suffering from mental illness, psychopathic disorder, severe mental impairment or mental impairment; and

(b) that the mental disorder from which that person is suffering is of a nature or degree which makes it appropriate for him to be detained in a hospital for medical treatment and, in the case of ~~psychopathic disorder or~~ mental impairment, that such treatment is likely to alleviate or prevent the deterioration of his condition; the Secretary of State may, if he is of the opinion having regard to the public interest and all the circumstances that it is expedient so to do, by warrant direct that that person be removed to and detained in such hospital (not being a mental nursing home) as may be specified in the direction; and a direction under this section shall be known as "a transfer direction".

(2) A transfer direction shall cease to have effect at the expiration of the period of 14 days beginning with the date on which it is given unless within that period the person with respect to whom it was given has been received into the hospital specified in the direction.

(3) A transfer direction with respect to any person shall have the same effect as a hospital order made in his case.

(4) A transfer direction shall specify the form or forms of mental disorder referred to in paragraph (a) of subsection (1) above from which, upon the reports taken into account under that subsection, the patient is found by the Secretary of State to be suffering: and no such direction shall be given unless the patient is described in each of those reports as suffering from the same form of disorder, whether or not he is also described in either of them as suffering from another form.

(5) References in this part of this Act to a person serving a sentence of imprisonment include references –

(a) to a person detained in pursuance of any sentence or order for detention made by a court in criminal proceedings (other than an order under any enactment to which section 46 above applies);

(b) to a person committed to custody under section 115 (3) of the Magistrates Courts Act 1980 (which relates to persons who fail to comply with an order to enter into recognisances to keep the peace or be of good behaviour); and

(c) to a person committed by a court to a prison or other institution to which the Prison Act 1952 applies in default of payment of any sum adjudged to be paid on his conviction.

Restrictions on discharge of prisoners removed to hospital

49. – (1) Where a transfer direction is given in respect of any person, the Secretary of State, if he thinks fit, may by warrant further direct that that person shall be subject to the special restrictions set out in section 41 above; and where the Secretary of State gives a transfer direction in respect of any such person as is described in paragraph (a) or (b) of section 48(2) above, he shall also give a direction under this section applying those restrictions to him.

(2) A direction under this section shall have the same effect as a restriction order made under section 41 above and shall be known as "a restriction direction."

(3) While a person is subject to a restriction direction the responsible medical officer shall at such intervals (not exceeding one year) as the Secretary of State may direct examine and report to the Secretary of State on the person; and every report shall contain such particulars as the Secretary of State may require.

50. – (1) Where a transfer direction and a restriction direction have been given in respect of a person serving a sentence of imprisonment and before the expiration of that person's sentence the Secretary of State is notified by the responsible medical officer, any other registered medical practitioner or a Mental Health Review Tribunal that that person no longer requires treatment in hospital for mental disorder or that no effective treatment for his disorder can be given in the hospital to which he has been removed, the Secretary of State may –

(a) by warrant direct that he be remitted to any prison or other institution in which he might have been detained if he had not been removed to hospital, there to be dealt with as if he had not been so removed; or

(b) exercise any power of releasing him on licence or discharging him . . . the transfer direction and the restriction direction shall cease to have effect.

(2) A restriction direction in the case of a person serving a sentence of imprisonment shall cease to have effect on the expiration of the sentence.

(3) . . . (4) . . .

Part V

Discharge of patients
Powers of tribunals

72. – (1) Where application is made to a Mental Health Review Tribunal by or in respect of a patient who is liable to be detained under this Act, the Tribunal may in any case direct that the patient be discharged, and –

(a) ..

(b) the Tribunal shall direct the discharge of a patient liable to be detained otherwise than under section 2 above if they are satisfied –

(i) that he is not then suffering from mental illness, ~~psychopathic~~ personality disorder, severe mental impairment or mental impairment or from any of those forms of disorder of a nature or degree which makes it appropriate for him to be liable to be detained in a hospital for medical treatment; or . . .

(4) Where application is made to a Mental Health Review Tribunal by or in respect of a patient who is subject to Guardianship under this Act, the Tribunal may in any case direct that the patient be discharged, and shall so direct if they are satisfied –

(a) that he is not then suffering from mental illness, ~~psychopathic~~ personality disorder, severe mental impairment or mental impairment; or

(b) that it is not necessary in the interests of the welfare of the patient, or for the protection of other persons, that the patient should remain under such Guardianship.

Part X

Interpretation

145. – (1) In this Act, unless the context otherwise requires –

. . . "Mental disorder," "severe mental impairment," and "mental impairment", and "psychopathic disorder" have the meanings given in section 1 above; . . .

Index

References are to paragraph numbers or to Appendices

Paragraph numbers ending in 0, eg 2.4.0, refer to the whole of the following section, eg up to but not including 2.5.0

Single letters in paretheses eg 2.14.22 (p) refer to subparagraphs where they are identified by letters.

Numbers after colons in references to Appendices refer to paragraphs within the Appendices.

A

G

H

M

Q

R

T

U

V

Index compiled by JR Sampson

Printed in the UK by The Stationery Office Limited on behalf of the Controller of Her Majesty's Stationery Office
Dd 5068285 1/99 19585 403353 J70296